MASSACHUSETTS

PRENTICE HALL
LITERATURE

PENGUIN  EDITION

PEARSON

Prentice
Hall

Upper Saddle River, New Jersey

Boston, Massachusetts

ISBN: 0-13-165277-X

2 3 4 5 6 7 8 9 10   10 09 08 07 06

Cover: *Hand With Flowers*, Pablo Picasso, Art Resource, NY, © 2005 Estate of Pablo Picasso/Artists Rights Society (ARS), New York

ACKNOWLEDGMENTS

Grateful acknowledgment is made to the following for copyrighted material:

Airmont Publishing Company, Inc. "Water" from *The Story of My Life* by Helen Keller. Copyright © 1965 by Airmont Publishing Company, Inc. Reprinted by permission of Airmont Publishing Company, Inc.

Dr. Ricardo E. Alegría "The Three Wishes" from *The Three Wishes: A Collection of Puerto Rican Folktales*, selected and adapted by Ricardo E. Alegría. Copyright © 1969 by Ricardo E. Alegría. Reprinted by permission of the author.

The American Society for the Prevention of Cruelty to Animals (ASPCA) "Website: Animaland" by Staff from *www.animaland.org*. Copyright © 2005 The American Society for the Prevention of Cruelty to Animals. Reprinted with permission of the ASPCA. All Rights Reserved.

Atheneum Books for Young Readers, an imprint of Simon & Schuster Childen's Publishing Division "Stray" reprinted with the permission of Atheneum Books for Young Readers, an imprint of Simon & Schuster Childen's Publishing Division from *Every Living Thing* by Cynthia Rylant. Copyright © 1985 by Cynthia Rylant.

Ballantine Books "The Lady and the Spider" from *All I Really Need to Know I Learned in Kindergarten* by Robert Fulghum. Copyright © 1986, 1988 by Robert L. Fulghum. All rights reserved under International and Pan-American Copyright Conventions.

The Bancroft Library, Administration Offices "Letter from a Concentration Camp" by Yoshiko Uchida from *The Big Book For Peace*. Text copyright © 1990 by Yoshiko Uchida. Courtesy of the Bancroft Library, University of California, Berkeley.

Susan Bergholz Literary Services "Names/Nombres," copyright © 1985 by Julia Alvarez. First published in Nuestro. March, 1985. From *"Something To Declare"* by Julia Alvarez. Copyright © 1998 by Julia Alvarez, published by Plume, an imprint of Penguin Group (USA), Inc, in 1999. "Eleven" from *Woman Hollering Creek* by Sandra Cisneros. Copyright © 1991 by Sandra Cisneros. Published by Vintage Books, a division of Random House, Inc., and originally in hardcover by Random House, Inc. Reprinted by permission of Susan Bergholz Literary Services, New York. All rights reserved.

BOA Editions Limited "Alphabet" from *Fuel* by Naomi Shihab Nye. Copyright © 1998 by Naomi Shihab Nye. All rights reserved. Reprinted by permission of BOA Editions Ltd. c/o The Permissions Company.

Georges Borchardt, Inc., for the Estate of John Gardner "Dragon, Dragon" from *Dragon, Dragon and Other Tales*, by John Gardner. Copyright © 1975 by Boskydell Artists Ltd. Reprinted by permission of Georges Borchardt, Inc., for the Estate of John Gardner.

(Continued on page R61, which is hereby considered an extension of this copyright page.)

CONTRIBUTING AUTHORS

The contributing authors guided the direction and philosophy of *Prentice Hall Literature: Penguin Edition*. Working with the development team, they helped to build the pedagogical integrity of the program and to ensure its relevance for today's teachers and students.

Kevin Feldman

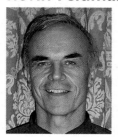

Kevin Feldman, Ed.D., is the Director of Reading and Intervention for the Sonoma County Office of Education and an independent educational consultant. He publishes and provides consultancy and training nationally, focusing upon improving school-wide literacy skills as well as targeted interventions for struggling readers, special needs students, and second language learners. Dr. Feldman is the co-author of the California Special Education Reading Task Force report and the lead program author for the 2002 Prentice Hall secondary language arts program *Timeless Voices, Timeless Themes*. He serves as technical consultant to the California Reading and Literature Project and the CalSTAT State Special Education Improvement Project. Dr. Feldman has taught for nineteen years at the university level in Special Education and Masters' level programs for the University of California, Riverside, and Sonoma State University.

Dr. Feldman earned his undergraduate degree in Psychology from Washington State University and has a Master's Degree from UC Riverside in Special Education, Learning Disabilities, and Instructional Design. He has an Ed.D. from the University of San Francisco in Curriculum and Instruction.

Sharon Vaughan

Sharon Vaughn, Ph.D., is the H.E. Hartfelder/The Southland Corporation Regents Professor at the University of Texas and also director of the Vaughn Gross Center for Reading and Language Arts at the University of Texas (VGCRLA). As director of the VGCRLA, she leads more than five major initiatives, including The Central Regional Reading First Technical Assistance Center; the Three-Tier Reading Research Project; a bilingual-biliteracy (English/Spanish) intervention research study; the first through fourth grade Teacher Reading Academies that have been used for teacher education throughout Texas and the nation; and the creation of online professional development in reading for teachers and other interested professionals.

Dr. Vaughn has published more than ten books and over one hundred research articles. She is Editor in Chief of the *Journal of Learning Disabilities* and serves on the editorial board of more than ten research journals, including the *Journal of Educational Psychology,* the *American Educational Research Journal,* and the *Journal of Special Education.*

Kate Kinsella

Kate Kinsella, Ed.D., is a teacher educator in the Department of Secondary Education at San Francisco State University. She teaches coursework addressing academic language and literacy development in linguistically and culturally diverse classrooms. She maintains secondary classroom involvement by teaching an academic literacy class for adolescent English learners through the University's Step to College Program. She publishes and provides consultancy and training nationally, focusing upon responsible instructional practices that provide second language learners and less proficient readers in grades 4–12 with the language and literacy skills vital to educational mobility.

Dr. Kinsella is the program author for *Reading in the Content Areas: Strategies for Reading Success*, published by Pearson Learning, and the lead program author for the 2002 Prentice Hall secondary language arts program *Timeless Voices, Timeless Themes*. She is the co-editor of the CATESOL Journal (CA Assn. of Teachers of ESL) and serves on the editorial board for the California Reader. A former Fulbright scholar, Dr. Kinsella has received numerous awards, including the prestigious Marcus Foster Memorial Reading Award, offered by the California Reading Association in 2002 to a California educator who has made a significant statewide impact on both policy and pedagogy in the area of literacy.

Differentiated Instruction Advisor
Don Deshler

Don Deshler, Ph.D., is the Director of the Center for Research on Learning (CRL) at the University of Kansas. Dr. Deshler's expertise centers on adolescent literacy, learning strategic instruction, and instructional strategies for teaching content area classes to academically diverse classes. He is the author of *Teaching Content to All: Evidence-Based Inclusive Practices in Middle and Secondary Schools,* a text which presents the instructional practices that have been tested and validated through his research at CRL.

UNIT AUTHORS

An award-winning contemporary author hosts each unit in each level of Prentice Hall Literature. Serving as a guide for your students, these authors introduce literary concepts, answer questions about their work, and discuss their own writing processes, using their works as models. Following are the featured unit authors for Grade 6.

Jane **Yolen** (b. 1939)

Unit 1: Fiction and Nonfiction Called America's Hans Christian Andersen, Jane Yolen is well suited to serve as a guide for this unit. Her more than 200 books include works of fiction such as the *Young Merlin Trilogy* and nonfiction volumes such as *The Perfect Wizard*, a picture-book biography of Andersen himself. Her numerous awards include the Caldecott Medal, two Nebula Awards, two Christopher Medals, and a National Book Award nomination.

Jean Craighead **George** (b. 1919)

Unit 2: The Short Story As a master storyteller with more than one hundred books to her credit, Jean Craighead George is the perfect author to explain the short story. Among her books are *Julie of the Wolves*, winner of the Newbery Medal, and *My Side of the Mountain*, a Newbery Honor Book. Like these classic titles, more recent books such as *Tree Castle Island* and *Blue Sky* demonstrate Ms. George's love of nature and the outdoors.

Zlata **Filipović** (b. 1980)

Unit 3: Types of Nonfiction Zlata Filipović has written various types of nonfiction. She achieved international fame with *Zlata's Diary: A Child's Life in Sarajevo*, a book she wrote when she was still a girl. Since that time, Ms. Filipović has given numerous speeches promoting the cause of peace. She has also written prefaces for other writers' works of nonfiction, including *The Freedom Writers Diary* and *Milosevic: The People's Tyrant*.

Gary **Soto** (b. 1952)

Unit 4: Poetry Raised in Fresno, California, Gary Soto has written poetry for both young readers and adults. His volume *Neighborhood Odes*, for readers aged 8 to 14, received a starred review in *The Horn Book*, and his *New and Selected Poems* was a finalist for the National Book Award. Mr. Soto was one of the youngest poets to appear in the prestigious *Norton Anthology of Modern Poetry*.

Joseph **Bruchac** (b. 1942)

Unit 5: Drama Joseph Bruchac is the ideal guide for the unit on drama and performance. He has written more than seventy books for adults and children, including *Pushing Up the Sky: Seven Native American Plays for Children*. In addition, he is a renowned storyteller and performs Native American tales for a wide variety of audiences. He received the Storyteller of the Year Award from the Wordcraft Circle of Native Writers and Storytellers.

Julius **Lester** (b. 1939)

Unit 6: Themes in Folk Literature Julius Lester is well qualified as a guide to folk literature because he often draws on folk tales, legends, and true stories from the past in his own work. He gives old tales the freshness of today's "street-talk language," and his books help readers appreciate the rich heritage of African Americans. Among the many awards he has received for his children's books are the John Newbery Medal and the Coretta Scott King Honor Medal.

State of Massachusetts
Program Advisors

David Bernstein
English Department Chairman
Minnechaug Regional High School
Wilbraham, Massachusetts

Joseph Calabrese
English/Reading Department Head
East Longmeadow High School
East Longmeadow, Massachusetts

Lois Hedberg
English Teacher
Springfield High School
Springfield, Massachusetts

Martin J. McEvoy, Jr.
English/Language Arts Teacher
Putnam High School
Springfield, Massachusetts

Massachusetts

Academic Achievement Handbook

Unit 1 — Fiction and Nonfiction

MA
All selections and workshops in this unit support your Massachusetts standards.

Part Two
Reading Skills Focus: Fact and Opinion

Unit 2 Short Stories

From the Author's Desk

Jean Craighead George

Part One
Reading Skills Focus: Make Inferences

All selections and workshops in this unit support your Massachusetts standards.

Part Two
Reading Skills Focus: Draw Conclusions

Unit 3

Types of Nonfiction
Narrative, Expository, and Reflective

Part One
Reading Skills Focus: Author's Purpose

***All selections and workshops in this unit support your
Massachusetts standards.***

Part Two
Reading Skills Focus: Main Idea

Part One
Reading Skills Focus: Context Clues

All selections and workshops in this unit support your Massachusetts standards.

Unit 5 Drama

All selections and workshops in this unit support your Massachusetts standards.

Part Two
Reading Skills Focus: Compare and Contrast

MA *All selections and workshops in this unit support your
Massachusetts standards.*

SELECTIONS BY READING SKILL

Unit 1

Part One: Make Predictions

Part Two: Fact and Opinion

Unit Two

Part One: Make Inferences

Part Two: Draw Conclusions

■ Unit Three

Part One: Author's Purpose

Recognize Details That Indicate Author's Purpose

Ask Questions to Understand Author's Purpose

Part Two: Main Idea

Using Key Details to Determine the Main Idea

Distinguish Between Important and Unimportant Details

■ Unit Four

Part One: Context Clues

Preview to Identify Unfamiliar Words

Read Ahead to Find Context Clues

(Continued on next page)

Part Two: Paraphrase

Read Aloud According to Punctuation

■ Unit Five

Part One: Summarize

Reread to Identify Main Events

Part Two: Compare and Contrast

Picture the Action to Compare and Contrast

■ Unit Six

Part One: Cause and Effect

Identify Clue Words

Ask Questions to Analyze Cause-and-Effect Relationships

Part Two: Purpose for Reading

Preview the Text to Set a Purpose for Reading

Make Connections

SELECTIONS BY THEME

■ Growing and Changing

■ Reaching Out

■ Proving Yourself

■ Seeing It Through

Mysterious Worlds

Sense and Nonsense

INFORMATIONAL TEXTS AND OTHER NONFICTION

■ Reading Informational Materials—Instructional Workshops

■ Additional Nonfiction—Selections by Type

■ Literature in Context

**A wealth of expository nonfiction is found throughout this program.
Nonfiction texts are highlighted in red in the Index.**

COMPARING LITERARY WORKS

WORKSHOPS

■ Writing Workshops

■ Spelling Workshops

■ Communications Workshops

Your Guide to Massachusetts Standards and Testing

What is the Massachusetts Curriculum Framework?

The **English Language Arts Curriculum Framework** was established by educators and specialists who are committed to advancing the achievement and success of students in Massachusetts. Your Language Arts or English teachers are responsible for helping you master all of the learning standards that are part of the framework. The standards are divided into four Strands or content areas: Language, Reading and Literature, Composition and Media. Here is a learning standard for sixth grade as well as a question that assesses your understanding of the standard.

Learning Strand Groupings

To help you better understand the Curriculum Framework, each Strand has been assigned a name and abbreviation that relates to what it covers. The Strand and associated standards that cover Reading and Literature, for example, have been given the abbreviation RL.

As a student in Massachusetts, your English Language Arts skills are tested in grades 3 through 8 and 10. The test is called the **Massachusetts Comprehensive Assessment System (MCAS) English Language Arts Test.** This test includes two parts: The Reading and Literature Test, which you will take at each of the above grade levels; and the Composition Test, which you take in grades 7 and 10 only.

SAMPLE STANDARD

RL.12.3
Identify and analyze the elements of setting, characterization, and plot (including conflict).

SAMPLE QUESTION

❶ According to the excerpt, what causes Mistress Mary to stop and look at the young boy?
A. He is playing on his pipe.
B. The animals lead her to him.
C. He calls for her.
D. He is blocking her path.
(RL.12.3)

Sankaty Head Lighthouse, Nantucket, Massachusetts

Massachusetts Curriculum Framework

Grade 6

The following pages list the Massachusetts English Language Arts Curriculum Framework and individual Learning Standards, which specify what you will learn this year.

General Standard 1: Discussion: Students will use agreed-upon rules for informal and formal discussions in small and large groups.

LA.1.3	Apply understanding of agreed-upon rules and individual roles in order to make decisions.

General Standard 2: Questioning, Listening, and Contributing: Students will pose questions, listen to the ideas of others, and contribute their own information or ideas in group discussions or interviews in order to acquire knowledge.

LA.2.3	Gather relevant information for a research project or composition through interviews.

General Standard 3: Oral Presentation: Students will make oral presentations that demonstrate appropriate consideration of audience, purpose, and the information to be conveyed.

LA.3.8	Give oral presentations for various purposes, showing appropriate changes in delivery (gestures, vocabulary, pace, visuals) and using language for dramatic effect.
LA.3.9	Use teacher-developed assessment criteria to prepare their presentations.

General Standard 4: Vocabulary and Concept Development: Students will understand and acquire new vocabulary and use it correctly in reading and writing.

LA.4.17	Determine the meaning of unfamiliar words using context clues.
LA.4.18	Determine the meaning of unfamiliar words using knowledge of common Greek and Latin roots, suffixes, and prefixes.
LA.4.19	Determine pronunciations, meanings, alternate word choices, and parts of speech of words using dictionaries and thesauruses.

General Standard 5: Structure and Origins of Modern English: Students will analyze standard English grammar and usage and recognize how its vocabulary has developed and been influenced by other languages.

LA.5.9	Identify the eight basic parts of speech (noun, pronoun, verb, adverb, adjective, conjunction, preposition, interjection).
LA.5.10	Expand or reduce sentences (adding or deleting modifiers, combining or decombining sentences).

Key to Standard Codes

LA	Language
RL	Reading and Literature
CO	Composition
ME	Media

MASSACHUSETTS

LA.5.11	Identify verb phrases and verb tenses.
LA.5.12	Recognize that a word performs different functions according to its position in the sentence.
LA.5.13	Identify simple and compound sentences.
LA.5.14	Identify correct mechanics and correct sentence structure.

General Standard 6: Formal and Informal English: Students will describe, analyze, and use appropriately formal and informal English.

LA.6.4	Demonstrate through role-playing appropriate use of formal and informal language.
LA.6.5	Write stories using a mix of formal and informal language.
LA.6.6	Identify differences between oral and written language patterns.

General Standard 8: Understanding a Text: Students will identify the basic facts and main ideas in a text and use them as the basis for interpretation.

For imaginative/literary texts:

RL.8.19	Identify and analyze sensory details and figurative language.
RL.8.20	Identify and analyze the author's use of dialogue and description.

For informational/expository texts:

RL.8.21	Recognize organizational structures (chronological order, logical order, cause and effect, classification schemes).
RL.8.22	Identify and analyze main ideas, supporting ideas, and supporting details.

General Standard 9: Making Connections: Students will deepen their understanding of a literary or non-literary work by relating it to its contemporary context or historical background.

RL.9.4	Relate a literary work to information about its setting.

General Standard 10: Genre: Students will identify, analyze, and apply knowledge of the characteristics of different genres.

RL.10.3	Identify and analyze the characteristics of various genres (poetry, fiction, nonfiction, short story, dramatic literature) as forms with distinct characteristics and purposes.

General Standard 11: Theme: Students will identify, analyze, and apply knowledge of theme in a literary work and provide evidence from the text to support their understanding.

RL.11.3	Apply knowledge of the concept that theme refers to the main idea and meaning of a selection, whether it is implied or stated.

General Standard 12: Fiction: Students will identify, analyze, and apply knowledge of the structure and elements of fiction and provide evidence from the text to support their understanding.

RL.12.3	Identify and analyze the elements of setting, characterization, and plot.

General Standard 13: Nonfiction: Students will identify, analyze, and apply knowledge of the purpose, structure, and elements of nonfiction or informational materials and provide evidence from the text to support their understanding.

RL Reading and Literature

RL.13.13	Identify and use knowledge of common textual features (paragraphs, topic sentences, concluding sentences, glossary, index).
RL.13.14	Identify and use knowledge of common graphic features (charts, maps, diagrams, captions, illustrations).
RL.13.15	Identify and use knowledge of common organizational structures (chronological order, logical order, cause and effect, classification schemes).
RL.13.17	Identify and analyze main ideas, supporting ideas, and supporting details.

General Standard 14: Poetry: Students will identify, analyze, and apply knowledge of the theme, structure, and elements of poetry and provide evidence from the text to support their understanding.

RL.14.3	Respond to and analyze the effects of sound, figurative language, and graphics in order to uncover meaning in poetry: • sound (alliteration, onomatopoeia, rhyme scheme); • figurative language (personification, metaphor, simile, hyperbole); and • graphics (capital letters, line length).

General Standard 15: Style and Language: Students will identify and analyze how an author's words appeal to the senses, create imagery, suggest mood, set tone and provide evidence from the text to support their understanding.

RL.15.3	Identify imagery, figurative language, rhythm, or flow when responding to literature.
RL.15.4	Identify and analyze the importance of shades of meaning in determining word choice in a piece of literature.

General Standard 16: Myth, Traditional Narrative, and Classical Literature: Students will identify, analyze, and apply knowledge of the themes, structure, and elements of myths, traditional narratives, and classical literature and provide evidence from the text to support their understanding.

RL.16.7	Compare traditional literature from different cultures.
RL.16.8	Identify common structures (magic helper, rule of three, transformation) and stylistic elements (hyperbole, refrain, simile) in traditional literature.

General Standard 17: Dramatic Literature: Students will identify, analyze, and apply knowledge of the themes, structure, and elements of drama and provide evidence from the text to support their understanding.

RL.17.3	Identify and analyze structural elements particular to dramatic literature (scenes, acts, cast of characters, stage directions) in the plays they read, view, write, and perform.
RL.17.4	Identify and analyze the similarities and differences between a narrative text and its film or play version.

MASSACHUSETTS

General Standard 18: Dramatic Reading and Performance: Students will plan and present dramatic readings, recitations, and performances that demonstrate appropriate consideration of audience and purpose.

RL.18.3 Develop characters through the use of basic acting skills (memorization, sensory recall, concentration, diction, body alignment, expressive detail) and self-assess using teacher-developed criteria before performing.

General Standard 19: Writing: Students will write with a clear focus, coherence, organization, and sufficient detail.

CO   Composition

For imaginative/literary writing:

CO.19.14 Write stories or scripts containing the basic elements of fiction (characters, dialogue, setting, plot with a clear resolution).

CO.19.15 Write poems using poetic techniques (alliteration, onomatopoeia), figurative language (simile, metaphor), and graphic elements (capital letters, line length).

For informational/expository writing:

CO.19.16 Write brief research reports with clear focus and supporting detail.

CO.19.17 Write a short explanation of a process that includes a topic statement, supporting details, and a conclusion.

CO.19.18 Write formal letters to correspondents such as authors, newspapers, businesses, or government officials.

General Standard 20: Consideration of Audience and Purpose: Students will write for different audiences and purposes.

CO.20.3 Make distinctions among fiction, nonfiction, dramatic literature, and poetry, and use these genres selectively when writing for different purposes.

General Standard 21: Revising: Students will demonstrate improvement in organization, content, paragraph development, level of detail, style, tone, and word choice (diction) in their compositions after revising them.

CO.21.4 Revise writing to improve level of detail and precision of language after determining where to add images and sensory detail, combine sentences, vary sentences, and rearrange text.

General Standard 22: Standard English Conventions: Students will use knowledge of standard English conventions in their writing, revising, and editing.

CO.22.7 Use additional knowledge of correct mechanics, correct sentence structure, and correct standard English spelling when writing, revising, and editing.

General Standard 23: Organize Ideas in Writing: Students will organize ideas in writing in a way that makes sense for their program.

CO.23.6 Decide on the placement of descriptive details about setting, characters, and events in stories.

CO.23.7	Group related ideas and place them in logical order when writing summaries or reports.
CO.23.8	Organize information about a topic into a coherent paragraph with a topic sentence, sufficient supporting detail, and a concluding sentence.

General Standard 24: Research: Students will gather information from a variety of sources, analyze and evaluate the quality of the information they obtain, and use it to answer their own questions.

CO.24.3	Apply steps for obtaining information from a variety of sources, organizing information, documenting sources, and presenting research in individual and group projects:

- use an expanded range of print and non-print sources (atlases, databases, electronic, on-line resources);
- follow established criteria for evaluating information;
- locate specific information within resources by using indexes, tables of contents, electronic search key words;
- organize and present research using the grades 5–6 Learning Standards in the Composition Strand as a guide for writing; and
- provide appropriate documentation in a consistent format.

General Standard 25: Evaluating Writing and Presentations: Students will develop and use appropriate rhetorical, logical, and stylistic criteria for assessing final versions of their compositions or research projects before presenting them to varied audiences.

CO.25.3	Use prescribed criteria from a scoring rubric to evaluate compositions, recitations, or performances before presenting them to an audience.

ME   Media

General Standard 26: Analysis of Media: Students will identify, analyze, and apply knowledge of the conventions, elements, and techniques of film, radio, video, television, multimedia productions, the Internet, and emerging technologies, and provide evidence from the works to support their understanding.

ME.26.3	Identify techniques used in educational reference software and web sites and describe how these techniques are the same as or different from the techniques used by authors and illustrators of print materials.

General Standard 27: Media Production: Students will design and create coherent media productions with a clear controlling idea, adequate detail, and appropriate consideration of audience, purpose, and medium.

ME.27.3	Create a media production using effective images, text, music, sound effects, or graphics.

MA ■ 35

MCAS ELA Test
Scoring Guides

The MCAS ELA Test assesses student writing in two ways. The Language and Literature Test includes Open-Response questions that assess your reading comprehension skills by requiring you to explain your understanding of a reading selection in writing. The 4-point Scoring Guide below is used to assess this response. The Composition Test requires you to respond in detail to an independent writing prompt. The Scoring Guides on the next page are used to assess this response; they address the areas of Topic/Idea Development and Standard English Conventions.

Use these Scoring Guides to evaluate and improve your writing. This will make you a stronger reader, writer, and test taker.

Language and Literature

4 *Points*	Response is a complete, clear, and accurate explanation. Relevant and specific textual evidence, presented through direct quotation, paraphrase, or a combination of both methods, is included in the response.
3 *Points*	Response is a fairly complete, clear, and accurate explanation. Relevant but often general textual evidence, presented through direct quotation, paraphrase, or a combination of both methods, is included in the response.
2 *Points*	Response is a partial, possibly unclear, explanation that offers either a mix of accurate and inaccurate evidence or simply a piece or two of accurate evidence by itself. Some relevant but general and vague textual evidence, presented through direct quotation or paraphrase, is included in the response.
1 *Point*	Exhibiting varying degrees of clarity, response is a minimal explanation that consists of largely inaccurate evidence, a general statement, or a few snippets of detail. Little, if any, relevant textual evidence (either through direct quotation or paraphrase) is included in the response.
0 *Points*	Response is incorrect, irrelevant, or contains insufficient evidence to show any understanding of the selection.

Topic/Idea Development

6 **Points**	• Rich topic/idea development • Careful and/or subtle organization • Effective/rich use of language
5 **Points**	• Full topic/idea development • Logical organization • Strong details • Appropriate use of language
4 **Points**	• Moderate topic/idea development and organization • Adequate, relevant details • Some variety in language
3 **Points**	• Rudimentary topic/idea development and/or organization • Basic supporting details • Simplistic language
2 **Points**	• Limited or weak topic/idea development, organization, and/or details • Limited awareness of audience and/or task
1 **Point**	• Limited topic/idea development, organization, and/or details • Little or no awareness of audience and/or task

Standard English Conventions

4 **Points**	• Control of sentence structure, grammar and usage, and mechanics (length and complexity of essay provide opportunity for student to show control of standard English conventions)
3 **Points**	• Errors do not interfere with communication and/or • Few errors relative to length of essay or complexity of sentence structure, grammar and usage, and mechanics
2 **Points**	• Errors interfere somewhat with communication and/or • Too many errors relative to the length of the essay or complexity of sentence structure, grammar and usage, and mechanics
1 **Point**	• Errors seriously interfere with communication AND • Little control of sentence structure, grammar and usage, and mechanics

MCAS Composition Test Practice

In grades 7 and 10, students are required to take the MCAS Composition Test. This test requires you to write a composition in response to a prompt. Below are two sample prompts. Use the prompts to practice writing in the test format. Then use the MCAS ELA Test Scoring Guide on the previous page to evaluate how well you did.

Sample Writing Prompt 1

Most people could benefit from improving at least one thing about themselves. It may be a personality trait, an area of study, or an overall approach to life.

Think about one thing that you would like to improve about yourself. In a well-developed composition, describe what you will improve and how you plan to make the change. Explain how the change will make you a better person.

As you write your composition, be sure to:

- Consider the topic carefully.
- Organize your composition so that your ideas flow logically.
- Use correct grammar.
- Choose language that is well suited to the purpose, audience, and context of your composition.

Sample Writing Prompt 2

Everyone has experienced disappointment in life. Think about a time when things did not turn out as you had hoped. How did you react to this situation? Did you learn anything valuable as a result?

In a well-developed composition, describe a time when you were disappointed. Explain what happened and what you gained from the experience.

 **MCAS Skills Review**

Skills Practice for the MCAS ELA Language and Literature Test Grade 6

Are You Ready?

Your mastery of the Massachusetts Curriculum Framework is measured by the MCAS Language and Literature Test. To do well on this test, you need to practice the skills assessed.

MCAS Skills Review provides six short tests with questions that assess skills tested on the MCAS. Your teacher will set the pace for the review. As you work through the material, note the Skill Focus for each test and the types of questions that pose a struggle for you.

For a full length practice test, use the one in the *MCAS Preparation Workbook.*

MCAS Skills Review

Test	Use After Unit	Skill Focus	Skill Review
1	1	Make Predictions	19–86
		Fact and Opinion	87–154
2	2	Make Inferences	173–250
		Draw Conclusions	251–343
3	3	Author's Purpose	363–428
		Main Idea	429–503
4	4	Context Clues	517–570
		Paraphrase	571–633
5	5	Summarize	649–700
		Compare and Contrast	701–757
6	6	Cause and Effect	775–840
		Purpose for Reading	841–931

A Note to Parents

The Massachusetts English Language Arts Curriculum Framework outlines the knowledge that your child needs to succeed on the MCAS. Using the chart to the left, you can help your child review the skills covered in the textbook and monitor your child's progress toward mastering these concepts.

MCAS Skills Review

The Secret Garden

by Frances Hodgson Burnett

*I*t was a very strange thing indeed. She quite caught her breath as she stopped to look at it. A boy was sitting under a tree, with his back against it, playing on a rough wooden pipe. He was a funny looking boy about twelve. He looked very clean and his nose turned up and his cheeks were as red as poppies and never had Mistress Mary seen such round and such blue eyes in any boy's face. And on the trunk of the tree he leaned against, a brown squirrel was clinging and watching him, and from behind a bush nearby a cock pheasant was delicately stretching his neck to peep out, and quite near him were two rabbits sitting up and sniffing with tremulous noses—and actually it appeared as if they were all drawing near to watch him and listen to the strange low little call his pipe seemed to make.

When he saw Mary he held up his hand and spoke to her in a voice almost as low as and rather like his piping.

"Don't tha move," he said. "It'd flight 'em."

❶ Based on the excerpt, Mary will **most likely**

A. listen to the boy.

B. scold the boy.

C. chase the rabbits.

D. run away.

❷ What is Mary's attitude toward the young boy?

A. interested   C. confident

B. jealous   D. doubtful

❸ Which of the following **best** expresses an opinion?

A. Animals drew near to him.

B. He was sitting under a tree.

C. He spoke with a low voice.

D. He played on his pipe.

❹ Which of the following **best** expresses Mary's mood throughout the excerpt?

A. relaxed   C. embarrassed

B. frightened   D. excited

❺ According to the excerpt, what causes Mistress Mary to stop and look at the young boy?

A. He is playing on his pipe.

B. The animals lead her to him.

C. He calls for her.

D. He is blocking her path.

Write your answer to open-response question 6 on a blank sheet of paper.

❻ Describe the relationship between the boy and the animals watching him. Use relevant and specific information from the excerpt to support your answer.

Corresponding Learning Standards

Question 1: RL.8.22	Question 4: RL.12.3
Question 2: RL.8.20	Question 5: RL.12.3
Question 3: RL.8.20	

MCAS Skills Review

The Wonderful Wizard of Oz

by L. Frank Baum

Three were men and one a woman, and all were oddly dressed. They wore round hats that rose to a small point a foot above their heads, with little bells around the brims that tinkled sweetly as they moved. The hats of the men were blue; the little woman's hat was white, and she wore a white gown that hung in pleats from her shoulders. Over it were sprinkled little stars that glistened in the sun like diamonds. The men were dressed in blue, of the same shade as their hats, and wore well-polished boots with a deep roll of blue at the tops. The men, Dorothy thought, were about as old as Uncle Henry, for two of them had beards. But the little woman was doubtless much older. Her face was covered with wrinkles, her hair was nearly white, and she walked rather stiffly.

❶ What does Dorothy's reaction to the new people suggest?

A. Dorothy is observant.

B. Dorothy is critical.

C. Dorothy is embarrassed.

D. Dorothy is courageous.

❷ Which of the following **best** describes the new people?

A. They are unfriendly.

B. They all look the same.

C. They wear strange clothes.

D. They appear to be old.

❸ Read the sentence from the excerpt in the box below.

> Her face was covered with wrinkles, her hair was nearly white, and she walked rather stiffly.

What part of speech is the word *stiffly* as it is used in this sentence?

A. adverb   C. noun

B. adjective   D. verb

❹ Which of the following **best** describes the setting of this excerpt?

A. lonely   C. dangerous

B. ordinary   D. unusual

❺ This excerpt is **best** summarized by which statement?

A. Dorothy comes across strange and interesting people.

B. Dorothy comes across three men and a woman.

C. The little woman appears older than the men.

D. The men wear hats with bells around the brims.

Corresponding Learning Standards

Question 1: RL.12.3   Question 4: RL.12.3
Question 2: RL.12.3   Question 5: RL.12.3
Question 3: LA.5.9

MCAS Skills Review

Up From Slavery: An Autobiography
by Booker T. Washington

After the coming of freedom there were two points upon which practically all the people on our place were agreed, and I find that this was generally true throughout the South: that they must change their names, and that they must leave the old plantation for at least a few days or weeks in order that they might really feel sure that they were free.

In some way a feeling got among the colored people that it was far from proper for them to bear the surname of their former owners, and a great many of them took other surnames. This was one of the first signs of freedom. When they were slaves, a colored person was simply called "John" or "Susan." There was seldom occasion for more than the use of the one name.

❶ The author wrote this selection primarily to
A. debate.
B. compare.
C. critique.
D. inform.

❷ Reread paragraph 2. What causes the author to note the arrival of freedom?
A. Former slaves took names like "John" and "Susan."
B. Owners called former slaves by name.
C. Former slaves took on new surnames.
D. Owners gave their surnames to former slaves.

❸ Which of these **best** expresses the main idea of this article?
A. It is easy to take freedom for granted.
B. Changing one's name is the best part about freedom.
C. One has to live in the South to appreciate freedom.
D. One must experience freedom to believe it.

❹ Which of the following **best** expresses the narrator's mood throughout the excerpt?
A. confidence about newfound freedom
B. doubt in one's ability to appreciate freedom
C. anxiety that freedom may soon come
D. sadness over a lack of freedom

❺ How is the information in this excerpt organized?
A. in order of events as they happened
B. by providing a series of examples
C. by alternating between past and present
D. in order of importance, from most to least

Write your answer to open-response question 6 on a blank sheet of paper.

❻ Why do you think it was so important to slaves that they change their names? Use relevant and specific information from the excerpt to support your answer.

Corresponding Learning Standards

Question 1: RL.10.3	Question 4: RL.15.4
Question 2: RL.13.13	Question 5: RL.13.15
Question 3: RL.13.17	Question 6: CO.19.17

MCAS Skills Review

A Narrow Fellow in the Grass

by Emily Dickinson

A narrow fellow in the grass
Occasionally rides;
You may have met him,—did you not?
His notice sudden is.

The grass divides as with a comb,
A spotted shaft is seen;
And then it closes at your feet
And opens further on.

He likes a boggy acre,
A floor too cool for corn.
Yet when a child, and barefoot,
I more than once, at morn,

Have passed, I thought, a whip-lash
Unbraiding in the sun,—
When, stooping to secure it,
It wrinkled, and was gone.

❶ What is the main purpose of stanzas 3 and 4?

A. to show that the narrator prefers to walk barefoot

B. to explain the appearance of the narrow fellow

C. to describe the time of day

D. to retell a childhood experience

❷ In stanza 4, the word *secure* means

A. capture.   C. avoid.

B. believe.   D. mistake.

❸ The speaker in the poem is likely to

A. be afraid of strange things.

B. always be in a hurry.

C. find pleasure in small things.

D. spend little time outdoors.

❹ Seeing the narrow fellow reminds the speaker of which of the following?

A. childhood

B. combing her hair

C. playing in a cornfield

D. old friends

❺ Read the line from stanza 2 in the box below.

> The grass divides as with a comb,

This line contains an example of which of the following?

A. hyperbole   C. a metaphor

B. a simile   D. paradox

❻ What does the phrase "his notice sudden is" suggest?

A. The poet cannot see the narrow fellow.

B. The narrow fellow comes and goes quickly.

C. The poet looks away from the narrow fellow.

D. The narrow fellow is in constant view.

Corresponding Learning Standards

Question 1: RL.8.20	Question 4: RL.8.20
Question 2: LA.4.17	Question 5: RL.14.3
Question 3: RL.8.20	Question 6: RL.15.4

MASSACHUSETTS

The Cherry Orchard
by Anton Chekhov

LOPAKHIN: The only remarkable thing about the orchard is that it's very large. It only bears fruit every other year, and even then you don't know what to do with them; nobody buys any.

GAEV: This orchard is mentioned in the "Encyclopaedic Dictionary."

LOPAKHIN: [*Looks at his watch*] If we can't think of anything and don't make up our minds to anything, then on August 22, both the cherry orchard and the whole estate will be up for auction. Make up your mind! I swear there's no other way out, I'll swear it again.

FIERS: In the old days, forty or fifty years back, they dried the cherries, soaked them and pickled them, and made jam of them, and it used to happen that . . .

GAEV: Be quiet, Fiers.

FIERS: And then we'd send the dried cherries off in carts to Moscow and Kharkov. And money! And the dried cherries were soft, juicy, sweet, and nicely scented . . . They knew the way . . .

LUBOV: What was the way?

FIERS: They've forgotten. Nobody remembers.

❶ What does Lopakhin want the other characters in the excerpt to do?

A. learn how to preserve cherries

B. protect the cherry orchard

C. sell the whole estate

D. share stories

❷ According to the excerpt, what will happen on August 22?

A. Cherries will be shipped to Moscow and Khartov.

B. The cherry season will begin.

C. The cherry orchard will go up for auction.

D. Gaev will buy the estate.

❸ How does the playwright indicate stage directions in this play?

A. He uses capital letters followed by a period.

B. He uses ellipses.

C. He alternates between speakers.

D. He uses italics within brackets.

❹ What is the purpose of the ellipses (. . .) in lines 13 and 14?

A. to show the speaker's excitement

B. to indicate pauses in the speaker's thoughts

C. to show that the speaker is being interrupted

D. to show that the speaker has difficulty with the English language

❺ Which of the following best summarizes the theme of this excerpt?

A. Some things are most important because of the memories attached to them.

B. Some things are not worth preserving, regardless of their importance.

C. People should avoid living in the past.

D. People often forget things on purpose.

Corresponding Learning Standards

Question 1: RL.12.3	Question 4: LA.5.14
Question 2: RL.12.3	Question 5: RL.11.3
Question 3: RL.17.3	

The Miser

by Aesop

A Miser sold all that he had and bought a lump of gold, which he buried in a hole in the ground by the side of an old wall and went to look at it daily. One of his workmen observed his frequent visits to the spot and decided to watch his movements. He soon discovered the secret of his hidden treasure, and digging down, came to the lump of gold, and stole it. The Miser, on his next visit, found the hole empty and began to tear his hair and to make loud <u>lamentations</u>. A neighbor, seeing him overcome with grief and learning the cause, said, "Pray do not grieve so; but go and take a stone, and place it in the hole, and fancy that the gold is still lying there. It will do you quite the same service; for when the gold was there, you had it not, as you did not make the slightest use of it."

❶ How does the Miser lose his gold?

A. It is stolen.

B. He spends it all.

C. He gives it away.

D. It is misplaced.

❷ Why is the main character called "the Miser"?

A. He likes to bury his valuables.

B. He becomes upset easily.

C. He only cares about saving money.

D. He doesn't care about his belongings.

❸ Based on the excerpt, the Miser will **most likely**

A. place a stone in the empty hole.

B. steal somebody else's gold.

C. ignore his neighbor's advice.

D. forget about the gold.

❹ Reread the excerpt. What does the word *lamentations* mean?

A. cries

B. praises

C. discoveries

D. visitations

❺ How is the workman able to find the gold?

A. The Miser's neighbor leads him to it.

B. The Miser tells him where it is buried.

C. He finds it by accident.

D. He follows the Miser to the burial location.

Write your answer to open-response question 6 on a blank sheet of paper.

❻ Describe the main lesson of this fable. Use relevant and specific information from the excerpt to support your answer.

Corresponding Learning Standards	
Question 1: RL.12.3	Question 4: LA.4.17
Question 2: RL.16.8	Question 5: RL.12.3
Question 3: RL.8.20	

Unit 1

Fiction and Nonfiction

Unit 1 Overview

Introduction
Exploring Fiction
and Nonfiction

Part 1: Make
Predictions

Part 2: Fact and
Opinion

Introduction:
Fiction and Nonfiction

Jane Yolen

From the Author's Desk

Jane Yolen
Talks About the Forms

Nonfiction is prose writing that presents ideas or tells about real people, places, or events. When I was young, I thought writing nonfiction meant writing about real-life happenings for newspapers and magazines, which was what my father did. My father had been a foreign correspondent in World War II. I thought I was going to grow up and be a reporter, too.

Unlike my father, though, whose reading passion was nonfiction, I loved **fiction**: made-up tales like mysteries, historical novels, fantasy novels, fairy tales.

▲ Jane Yolen, recognized as one of America's greatest storytellers, has charmed children and adults with her many books.

The Storyteller's Nose for Good Gossip

I knew I could write nonfiction. After all, I'd been born to it. But somehow I was convinced that writing fiction was something that I lacked the genes for—as if a fiction writer needs to have ancestors who were solid liars.

Now I know better. The best fiction is written by people who have both the reporter's eye for place and

◄ Critical Viewing How does this picture reflect a love of reading, which Jane Yolen says she developed as a child? **[Interpret]**

the storyteller's nose for good gossip. And the finest nonfiction has to have well-drawn **characters** and a story arc. Only the nonfiction writer is not supposed to make anything up.

How can fiction and nonfiction be so closely related? Because good writing is good writing.

Fairy Stories Belonged to Everyone

My first love of reading fiction was sparked by fairy stories. Though every tale told of a specific place, the themes of the tales belonged to everyone: Be true to your word, honor your parents, be kind to old ladies in the woods, don't talk to wolves. Like my friend Terri Windling, who edits fairy tales, I believed those tales spoke to all of us at some point in our lives.

> Why do we continue to be enspelled by fairy tales, after all these centuries? . . . Because we all have encountered wicked wolves, faced trial by fire, found fairy godmothers. We have all set off into unknown woods at one point in life or another.
>
> **from "Women and Fairy Tales"**
> —Terri Windling

Folk tales often begin and end with a familiar phrase: "Once upon a time . . ." and "They lived happily ever after." One day I realized that the ending phrase meant that though the story was over, the lives of those heroes were not. It was that realization that started me on my own journey into writing fiction.

More About the Author

Jane **Yolen** (b. 1939)

Jane Yolen has said, "It seems like I've been writing since birth!" She had her earliest success as a writer in first grade. She wrote the class musical about vegetables getting together to make a salad. Since then, she has written more than two hundred books. Yolen often bases her stories on folklore. The selchie—or silkie—in "Greyling" is a character from the folklore of Scotland and Ireland.

Fast Facts
▶ Yolen has composed songs for rock groups.
▶ In college, Yolen wrote her American Intellectual History final in rhyme and received an A+.

Learning About Fiction and Nonfiction

Elements of Fiction

Fiction is writing that tells about imaginary characters and events. All works of fiction share certain basic elements.

- They include made-up people or animals called **characters** and a made-up series of events called the **plot.**
- Fictional works take place in a time and location, or **setting,** which may or may not be real.
- They are told by a speaker called the **narrator.**
- Fiction is told from a certain perspective, or **point of view. First-person point of view** is the perspective of a character in the story. **Third-person point of view** is the perspective of a narrator outside the story.
- Fiction often includes a **theme,** or message about life.

Types of Fiction

Novels are long works of fiction. A novel has a plot in which characters face a problem in a specific time and place. In addition to its main plot, a novel may introduce **subplots,** or minor stories within the larger story.

Novellas are works of fiction that are longer than short stories but shorter than novels.

Short stories are brief works of fiction. Like a novel, a short story has characters, a setting, and a plot. Unlike a novel, it has a single conflict and is meant to be read in one sitting.

Cow Writers Block

Characteristics of Nonfiction

Nonfiction works differ from fiction in a few important ways.

- Nonfiction writings deal only with real people, events, or ideas.
- They are **narrated,** or told, from the **author's perspective,** or point of view. Nonfiction works have a specific **tone** that reflects the writer's attitude toward a subject.
- Nonfiction reflects a **writer's purpose,** or reason for writing. This might be to explain, persuade, inform, or entertain.

Types of Nonfiction

Biographies tell the story of someone's life. A biography is usually told from the third-person point of view.

Autobiographies tell the story of the author's life. An autobiography is told from the first-person point of view.

Letters are written forms of communication from one person to another. A letter might share information, thoughts, or feelings.

Journals and diaries are records of daily events and the writer's thoughts and feelings about them.

Essays are brief written works based on a particular subject.

Informational texts are the documents we come across in everyday life, including instructions and newspaper articles.

Speeches are works that are delivered orally to an audience.

▼ **Critical Viewing**
What questions about this image could nonfiction writing answer? **[Synthesize]**

Check Your Understanding

Indicate whether each literary work is an example of fiction or nonfiction.

1. a letter from a famous author to his son

2. an essay about global warming

3. a first-person account of what it is like to live on Pluto

From the Author's Desk
Jane Yolen Introduces "Greyling"

Everyone in my family sang. My mother had been a gifted contralto—a female singer with a low voice—though her voice had hoarsened and changed. My father played guitar as if it were a ukulele, and performed cowboy songs. My brother and I were both musicians and singers.

Songs, Stories, and Settings

I loved long, sad English and Scottish ballads, songs or song-like poems that tell a story. Among my favorites was "The Great Selchie of Sule Skerry." The **setting** is the beautiful and dangerous cold sea around Scotland, on the skerries (the rocks) that jut out of the sea where the seals sun themselves, and on the spare, bare islands near the coast.

The fisher folk of Shetland and Orkney still tell many strange tales of characters called selchies—or silkies—seals who can take on human form, usually by shrugging out of their skins. There is **conflict** in those stories—human against nature, human against magical creature, human against himself or herself.

A Story Born With My First Child

Long before my husband and I bought a house in Scotland near the North Sea, I had learned the selchie song. But I never thought about using the tale as the basis for a story until I had my first child, my daughter Heidi.

Sitting in a darkened room and rocking her to sleep, I started to sing "The Great Selchie of Sule Skerry," and the idea for the beginning of a **plot** simply popped into my head: a childless couple who rescue an abandoned seal pup on the shore.

As soon as Heidi fell asleep, I went to my typewriter (this was long before personal computers) and began the tale. It took about four months of revising and rewriting to get it right as I struggled to set the story, to make the characters come alive, to make their tensions real.

Greyling

Jane Yolen

Once on a time when wishes were aplenty, a fisherman and his wife lived by the side of the sea. All that they ate came out of the sea. Their hut was covered with the finest mosses that kept them cool in the summer and warm in the winter. And there was nothing they needed or wanted except a child.

Each morning, when the moon touched down behind the water and the sun rose up behind the plains, the wife would say to the fisherman, "You have your boat and your nets and your lines. But I have no baby to hold in my arms." And again, in the evening, it was the same. She would weep and wail and rock the cradle that stood by the hearth. But year in and year out the cradle stayed empty.

Now the fisherman was also sad that they had no child. But he kept his sorrow to himself so that his wife would not know his <u>grief</u> and thus double her own. Indeed, he would leave the hut each morning with a breath of song and return each night with a whistle on his lips. His nets were full but his heart was empty, yet he never told his wife.

One sunny day, when the beach was a tan thread spun between sea and plain, the fisherman as usual went down to his boat. But this day he found a small grey seal stranded on the sandbar, crying for its own.

The fisherman looked up the beach and down. He looked in front of him and behind. And he looked to the town on the

Jane Yolen
Author's Insight
I took the familiar "once upon a time" opening and changed it around to make it my own.

Vocabulary Builder
grief (grēf) *n.* deep sadness

great grey cliffs that <u>sheared</u> off into the sea. But there were no other seals in sight.

So he shrugged his shoulders and took off his shirt. Then he dipped it into the water and wrapped the seal pup carefully in its folds.

"You have no father and you have no mother," he said. "And I have no child. So you shall come home with me."

And the fisherman did no fishing that day but brought the seal pup, wrapped in his shirt, straight home to his wife.

When she saw him coming home early with no shirt on, the fisherman's wife ran out of the hut, fear riding in her heart. Then she looked wonderingly at the bundle which he held in his arms.

"It's nothing," he said, "but a seal pup I found stranded in the shallows and longing for its own. I thought we could give it love and care until it is old enough to seek its kin."

The fisherman's wife nodded and took the bundle. Then she uncovered the wrapping and gave a loud cry. "Nothing!" she said. "You call this nothing?"

The fisherman looked. Instead of a seal lying in the folds, there was a strange child with great grey eyes and silvery grey hair, smiling up at him.

The fisherman wrung his hands. "It is a selchie," he cried. "I have heard of them. They are men upon the land and seals in the sea. I thought it was but a tale."

"Then he shall remain a man upon the land," said the fisherman's wife, clasping the child in her arms, "for I shall never let him return to the sea."

"Never," agreed the fisherman, for he knew how his wife had wanted a child. And in his secret heart, he wanted one, too. Yet he felt, somehow, it was wrong.

"We shall call him Greyling," said the fisherman's wife, "for his eyes and hair are the color of a storm-coming sky. Greyling, though he has brought sunlight into our home."

And though they still lived by the side of the water in a hut covered with mosses that kept them warm in the winter and cool in the summer, the boy Greyling was never allowed into the sea.

He grew from a child to a lad. He grew from a lad to a young man. He gathered driftwood for his mother's hearth and searched the tide pools for shells for her mantel. He

Vocabulary Builder
sheared (shird) *v.* cut off sharply

Fiction
Characters Yolen invented the fisherman, his wife, and their child for this fictional story.

**Reading Check**

What has changed suddenly for the fisherman and his wife?

mended his father's nets and tended his father's boat. But though he often stood by the shore or high in the town on the great grey cliffs, looking and longing and grieving in his heart for what he did not really know, he never went into the sea.

Then one wind-wailing morning just fifteen years from the day that Greyling had been found, a great storm blew up suddenly in the North. It was such a storm as had never been seen before: the sky turned nearly black and even the fish had trouble swimming. The wind pushed huge waves onto the shore. The waters gobbled up the little hut on the beach. And Greyling and the fisherman's wife were forced to flee to the town high on the great grey cliffs. There they looked down at the roiling, boiling, sea. Far from shore they spied the fisherman's boat, its sails flapping like the wings of a wounded gull. And clinging to the broken mast was the fisherman himself, sinking deeper with every wave.

The fisherman's wife gave a terrible cry. "Will no one save him?" she called to the people of the town who had gathered on the edge of the cliff. "Will no one save my own dear husband who is all of life to me?"

But the townsmen looked away. There was no man there who dared risk his life in that sea, even to save a drowning soul.

"Will no one at all save him?" she cried out again.

"Let the boy go," said one old man, pointing at Greyling with his stick. "He looks strong enough."

But the fisherman's wife clasped Greyling in her arms and held his ears with her hands. She did not want him to go into the sea. She was afraid he would never return.

"Will no one save my own dear heart?" cried the fisherman's wife for a third and last time.

But shaking their heads, the people of the town edged to their houses and shut their doors and locked their windows and set their backs to the ocean and their faces to the fires that glowed in every hearth.

"I will save him, Mother," cried Greyling, "or die as I try."

And before she could tell him no, he broke from her grasp and dived from the top of the great cliffs, down, down, down into the tumbling sea.

"He will surely sink," whispered the women as they ran from their warm fires to watch.

"He will certainly drown," called the men as they took down their spyglasses from the shelves.

They gathered on the cliffs and watched the boy dive down into the sea.

As Greyling disappeared beneath the waves, little fingers of foam tore at his clothes. They snatched his shirt and his

Jane Yolen
Author's Insight
The number three is very prominent in folk tales, though no one has ever adequately (to my satisfaction) explained why.

Reading Check

Why doesn't the fisherman's wife want Greyling to go in the sea?

pants and his shoes and sent them bubbling away to the shore. And as Greyling went deeper beneath the waves, even his skin seemed to <u>slough</u> off till he swam, free at last, in the sleek grey coat of a great grey seal.

The selchie had returned to the sea.

But the people of the town did not see this. All they saw was the diving boy disappearing under the waves and then, farther out, a large seal swimming toward the boat that <u>wallowed</u> in the sea. The sleek grey seal, with no effort at all, eased the fisherman to the shore though the waves were wild and bright with foam. And then, with a final salute, it turned its back on the land and headed joyously out to sea.

The fisherman's wife hurried down to the sand. And behind her followed the people of the town. They searched up the beach and down, but they did not find the boy.

"A brave son," said the men when they found his shirt, for they thought he was certainly drowned.

"A very brave son," said the women when they found his shoes, for they thought him lost for sure.

"Has he really gone?" asked the fisherman's wife of her husband when at last they were alone.

"Yes, quite gone," the fisherman said to her. "Gone where his heart calls, gone to the great wide sea. And though my heart grieves at his leaving, it tells me this way is best."

The fisherman's wife sighed. And then she cried. But at last she agreed that, perhaps, it was best. "For he is both man and seal," she said. "And though we cared for him for a while, now he must care for himself." And she never cried again. So once more they lived alone by the side of the sea in a new little hut which was covered with mosses to keep them warm in the winter and cool in the summer.

Yet, once a year, a great grey seal is seen at night near the fisherman's home. And the people in town talk of it, and wonder. But seals do come to the shore and men do go to the sea; and so the townfolk do not dwell upon it very long.

But it is no ordinary seal. It is Greyling himself come home—come to tell his parents tales of the lands that lie far beyond the waters, and to sing them songs of the wonders that lie far beneath the sea.

Vocabulary Builder
slough (sluf) *v.* be cast off; be gotten rid of

Vocabulary Builder
wallowed (wäl´ ōd) *v.* rolled and tilted

Fiction
Plot The conversation between the fisherman and his wife reveals that they both understand what has happened to their son.

Q. Did you ever write a story about the adventures of Greyling after he left home?

A. No, but it would make a lovely novel, wouldn't it? I can see it now—Greyling's adventures in the great wide sea. Finding a lovely selchie girl, fighting off sharks, maybe a wicked magician who catches him in a fishing net . . .

Q. Does this story teach a lesson?

A. I don't like to think that lessons—morals—should be taught in a story. It makes the tale feel like a pill that needs to be swallowed. "Here, this will be good for you. Take at least one story before bedtime." But of course a story is *about* something. It has a meaning, a theme. That is different, though, from teaching a lesson, for it grows organically from the story. For example, reading about the March girls in *Little Women* made me look at my own family in a different way.

StudentCorner

Q. Why did you choose not to give your characters names?
—Emily Hickox, Boonton Township, New Jersey

A. Many folk tales do not have named characters. So Greyling has a name, but his parents do not. Think of Snow White: her stepmother, mother, and father do not have names. Think of Hansel and Gretel—their father, stepmother, and the wicked witch do not have names. What does this tell you about them? Probably that they are not the center of the tale.

 Writing Workshop: *Work in Progress*

Descriptive Essay

For a descriptive essay you may write, list the places that are most important to you. Next to each item on your list, imagine a good photograph of the place and describe what you see. Then, write a sentence describing how you feel about the place. Save your Place List in your writing portfolio.

From the Author's Desk
Jane Yolen Introduces "My Heart Is in the Highlands"

As a children's book writer, I am often asked to give **speeches** at conferences, or professional meetings. But giving speeches for over forty years means that I am constantly looking for new things to talk about.

Word Choice: The Day Is *Dreech* and Here's a *Haar*

When we bought our house in Scotland, I found a *lot* of new things to put into my speeches. First of all, though Americans and Scots presumably speak the same language, we don't. American cars have hoods, trunks, and run on gas. Scottish cars have bonnets, boots, and run on petrol. We wear undershirts; they wear vests. Our babies have diapers; theirs have nappies. When it rains a lot and is miserable outside, the Scots say that the day is *dreech* (drēkh). There is a sea mist that often crosses our garden in Scotland, and it is called a *haar* (har).

Borrowing the Stuff of Fiction

All this means that when I am talking directly to an **audience,** I have to find new ways to think about the ordinary, everyday things, which is an excellent exercise for a writer. I find that I borrow the stuff of fiction to write my talks or nonfiction.

Making Description Come Alive

For example, in this speech I use a central idea—explaining one thing by using another. In this instance, I explain how memory works by describing the building of Scottish houses. To make my **description** come alive, I also use lyrical language and create a sense of place through accounts of things seen, heard, tasted, and touched.

Good writing is good writing, whether in fiction or nonfiction. *That* is the bottom line.

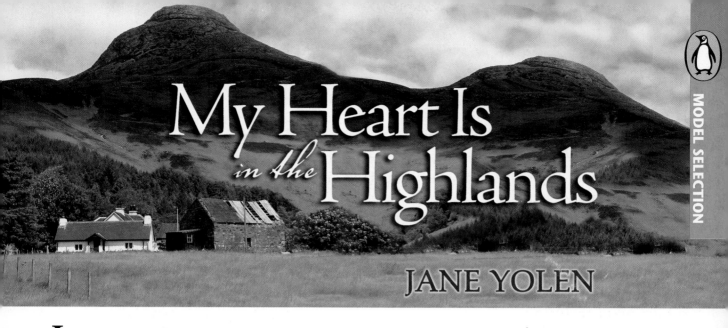

My Heart Is in the Highlands

JANE YOLEN

I first set foot on Scottish soil in the mid '80s, when my husband and I—between conferences (science fiction for me, computer science for him)—took a trip north from Brighton.

We drove, being used to long road trips and camping vacations with our children, and were predictably stunned by Edinburgh and its looming castle on the hill. None of America, and blessed little of Brighton, had prepared us for such a sight.

But it was when we began our ascent through the Highlands that it became clear to us that here was the home of the heart. . . .

I love the white-washed stone cottages here in Scotland, small cozy homes that seem to have grown rough hewn right up from the land. I love the gray stone mansions and the tall stone tower houses, too.

If you search the histories of any individual town here, or a particular street, you will find that these homes and walled gardens have often been built upon older, vanished buildings. Where a kirk or a tollbooth or a great hall once stood, now a townsman's seven-room house with mod cons squats.[1]

But it is not just the site that has been cannibalized. The very stones have been reused. So in Scotland history lies upon history. As a wonderful little book on the royal burgh

---

1. kirk (kʉrk) **. . . mod cons squats** Where churches or other structures were, now there are houses with modern conveniences.

Nonfiction
Author's Perspective
This paragraph explains the author's point of view about the place she was visiting and justifies the speech's title.

Reading Check

What does the author like about the Scottish landscape?

of Falkland in the Kingdom of Fife[2] puts it: "Absorbing stones from an old building into the fabric of the later one is . . . a way of holding on to the past."

After the stones have been pulled together and balanced and mortared into place, the walls are harled, or roughcast[3] so as to protect the soft stone and mortar from the winter winds and heavy gales.

Stones, harling, a way of holding on to the past. It's all a perfect metaphor for writing a book, especially books set here in Scotland.

Writers use stones from the past, reshaping and rebuilding with them. And then they protect the soft memories with a harling of technique.

How can it be otherwise? All fiction uses memory. Or re-memory for those of us whose grasp of the past is exceeded by the need to embellish, decorate, deepen, widen and otherwise change what was actual.

As a writer, I am made up of the little building blocks of my own private history, and what I know of the world that has already been rebuilt upon. My infancy told to me so often by my parents in delicious anecdote, my childhood captured in photos and catchlines, my adolescence in letters and journals, my young adulthood in poetry and prose.

I simply take those story-stones and use them again in any new building. Or I thieve from my closest friends and relatives, from my husband's life and my children. They don't just endure such thievery—they expect it. A warning— get to know me well and you will most certainly find yourself enshrined in one of my books.

But even those closest to me sometimes have trouble identifying themselves when next they meet themselves in fiction. For they will have been metamorphosed[4] into a toad or a selchie or a wind blowing in over the wall. Even I don't always know whose bones lie beneath a particular character's skin.

That's because fiction (to mix this metaphor hopelessly) is a magic mirror that gives back a changed self.

Jane Yolen
Author's Insight
I have been building up to this line from the beginning of the speech. Indeed, when I was thinking about writing it, this was my original thought.

Nonfiction
Tone Yolen's attitude toward her writing and her family is both serious and humorous at the same time.

---

2. **royal burgh** (bʉrg) . . . **Fife** Falkland, once the home of the Earls of Fife, is a Scottish town created by royal charter.
3. **roughcast** (ruf′ kast′) *adj.* coarse stucco for covering outside walls.
4. **metamorphosed** (met′ ə môr′ fōzd′) *v.* changed in form or shape.

Q. **Why do the Scottish have different names for things than we do?**

A. The Scots language is a combination of British English, Norwegian, Gaelic, and Scots Gaelic. They have taken words from different languages. American English has taken words from British English, Spanish, African, Yiddish, French, Italian—and lots of other languages besides. Each country has a rich tongue. They differ because many of their sources differ, though the main part of the rich stew of language is British English.

StudentCorner

Q. **What do you mean when you say at the end of the speech, "That's because fiction (to mix this metaphor hopelessly) is a magic mirror that gives back a changed self"?**
          —Katie Bliss, Pleasant View, Tennessee

A. I mean that we recognize ourselves in the fiction we read (that's the mirror part) but that the act of reading changes us (that's the magic part)—it makes us think and grow.

   All fiction does that to some extent, but great fiction changes us the most. I remember reading about King Arthur the first time, which set for the rest of my days how I felt about loyalty and honor. All the fairy tales taught me that magic has consequences. So what I read—what I chose to read—helped me grow into the human being I am today. I looked into the magic mirror of fiction and became a better person because of it.

 Writing Workshop: *Work in Progress*

Descriptive Essay

Review the place list from your writing portfolio, and choose one place to use as the focus of a descriptive essay. Add to the sentence by discussing why you like this place, what memories you have about it, and why the place is so special to you. Put this work in your writing portfolio.

Apply the Skills

Fiction and Nonfiction

Thinking About the Selections

1. **Respond:** Do you agree that Greyling belongs in the sea? Why or why not?
2. **(a) Evaluate:** Should the fisherman and his wife have kept Greyling from the sea? Why or why not?
   (b) Draw Conclusions: What main idea about parents and children does this tale present?
3. **(a) Compare:** According to "My Heart Is in the Highlands," how is writing a book like reusing old stones?
   (b) Interpret: How do old memories change into new works of fiction?

Fiction and Nonfiction Review

4. **(a)** Using a chart like the one shown, find details that show "Greyling" is **fiction. (b)** Share your answers with a partner. How has sharing changed your answers?

Fictional Details	Importance to the Story

5. **(a)** What do you think is the **purpose** of "My Heart Is in the Highlands"? Explain. **(b)** Based on the speech, where does the idea for "Greyling" come from? Support your answer with details from the speech and the story.

Research the Author

Using Internet and library resources, create a **bulletin board display** to show Jane Yolen's life and work. Follow these steps:
- Locate a Web page or home page for the writer on the Internet. Download information about her family, education, and literary works.
- Find photographs of the author or book jackets to use.
- Select several of the author's books you think will appeal to classmates. Using information from the Internet or book jackets, write a short summary of each to motivate students to read her books.

QuickReview

Selections at a Glance

Greyling is the story of a selchie, a creature that takes the form of a human on land and a seal in the sea.
My Heart Is in the Highlands explains how the author uses past experiences to construct new works of fiction.

Go **Online**
—Assessment
For: Self-test
Visit: www.PHSchool.com
Web Code: ela-6101

Fiction: literary works that describe made-up people and events

Nonfiction: literary works that describe real people and events or ideas

Purpose: a writer's reason for writing

Unit 1 Part 1

Make Predictions

Skills You Will Learn

Reading Skill: *Use Prior Knowledge to Make Predictions*
Literary Analysis: *Plot*

Reading Skill: *Read Ahead to Verify Predictions*
Literary Analysis: *Narrator and Point of View*

Reading Skill: *Analyze Text Structure*

Literary Analysis: *Comparing Fiction and Nonfiction*

Literature You Will Read

Reading and Vocabulary Skills Preview

Reading: Predicting

▶ **Predicting** is making a logical assumption about what will happen next.

Skills and Strategies You Will Learn in Part 1

In Part 1, you will learn

- to **use your prior knowledge,** or what you already know, to help you **make predictions** (p. 22)
- to **identify and use clues** in a narrative that help you make and **support predictions** (p. 22)
- to **read ahead to confirm or verify predictions** (p. 42)
- to **revise predictions** based on new information (p. 42)
- to **use text structure** to make **predictions** about content of informational materials (p. 62)

Using the Skills and Strategies in Part 1

Making and checking predictions helps you organize and remember information and details. Having logical expectations as you read, and then keeping track of how well a work follows those expectations, keeps you actively involved in noticing and evaluating details and information.

Dad and I started through the woods, looking for firewood. As we rounded a bend, we heard a frantic rustling in the leaves. Dad said, "Look, Jenny!" When I looked in the direction of the noise, I couldn't believe my eyes.

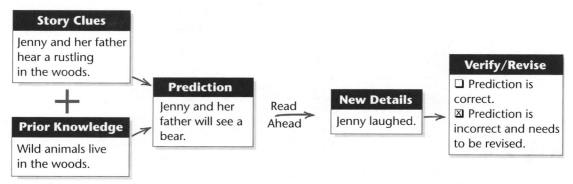

Story Clues
Jenny and her father hear a rustling in the woods.

+

Prior Knowledge
Wild animals live in the woods.

Prediction
Jenny and her father will see a bear.

Read Ahead →

New Details
Jenny laughed.

Verify/Revise
☐ Prediction is correct.
☒ Prediction is incorrect and needs to be revised.

As you read the literature in this part, you will practice making predictions and checking their accuracy.

Academic Vocabulary: Words for Discussing Predictions

The following words will help you write and talk about predictions as you read the selections in this unit.

Word	Definition	Example Sentence
predict *v.*	make a logical assumption about what will happen next	I **predict** that the characters will be trapped by the storm.
verify *v.*	prove to be true	I can **verify** my prediction with the details in the next paragraph.
support *v.*	uphold; offer proof	I **support** my prediction with my knowledge about storms.
revise *v.*	think about something again in order to make improvements	I had to **revise** my prediction based on the new details.
prior *adj.*	happening before the present time	I lived in the mountains **prior** to moving to the city.

Vocabulary Skill: Word Roots

▶ The **root** of a word is the part of the word that contains its basic meaning.

In Part 1, you will learn
- Latin root *-dict-* (p. 40)
- Latin root *-ver-* (p. 40)
- Latin root *-port-* (p. 60)

Roots have come into the English language from many other languages, including ancient Greek and Latin. Many dictionary entries tell you the root or roots of a word.

The original word comes from Latin   *The prefix means "back"*

re•vise (ri vīz′) *vt.* [Fr *reviser* < L *revisere* <*re-*, "back" + *visere*, "to see"] to read over or reflect on something carefully to correct, improve, or strengthen as necessary

The root means "to see"

Activity Look up each word in the chart and identify its root. Then, explain how knowing the meaning of the roots helps you to understand and remember the meaning of each word.

These skills will help you become a better reader. Practice them with either "Stray" (p. 24) or "The Homecoming" (p. 31).

Reading Skill

A **prediction** is a logical guess about what will happen next in a story. You can **use your prior knowledge** to help you make predictions. To do this, relate what you already know to details in a story. For example, if you have ever moved to a new neighborhood, you know that making new friends can be difficult. If the story tells you that a character is shy, you can combine what you know with the information in the story to predict that the character will not make friends easily.

Literary Analysis

Plot is the arrangement of events in a story. The plot includes the following elements:

- **Exposition:** introduction of the setting, characters, and basic situation
- **Conflict:** the story's central problem
- **Rising Action:** events that increase tension
- **Climax:** high point of the story, when the story's outcome becomes clear
- **Falling Action:** events that follow the climax
- **Resolution:** the final outcome

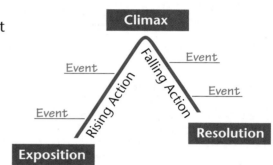

Vocabulary Builder

Stray

- **timidly** (tim´ id lē) *adv.* in a way that shows fear or shyness (p. 24) *Frightened, Rosa <u>timidly</u> asked a question.*

- **grudgingly** (gruj´ iŋ lē) *adv.* in an unwilling or resentful way (p. 25) *Max <u>grudgingly</u> admitted his mistake.*

- **ignore** (ig nôr´) *v.* pay no attention to (p. 26) *Anna tried to <u>ignore</u> the car alarm.*

The Homecoming

- **escorting** (es kôrt´ iŋ) *v.* going with as a companion (p. 32) *Kyla helped by <u>escorting</u> the children to school.*

- **distracted** (di strakt´ id) *adj.* unable to concentrate (p. 33) *The students were <u>distracted</u> by the storm.*

- **recognize** (rek´ əg nīz´) *v.* know and remember (p. 37) *Tran did not <u>recognize</u> his aunt at first.*

Build Understanding • *Stray*

Background

Animal Shelters Animal shelters take in stray and unwanted animals like the dog in "Stray." Although they can seem crowded, noisy, and smelly, most shelters have the best interests of the animals at heart. In addition to caring for animals, many shelters provide education on the responsibilities of having a pet.

Connecting to the Literature

Reading/Writing Connection In "Stray," a girl tries to persuade her parents to let her keep an abandoned puppy. Make two lists: one that presents several benefits of owning a dog and another that presents several problems associated with owning a dog. Use at least three of the following words: *consume, enrich, purchase, require.*

Meet the Author

Cynthia **Rylant** (b. 1954)

As a child, Cynthia Rylant never imagined that she would be a writer. "I always felt my life was too limited," she says. "Nothing to write about." At age twenty-four, however, she found that her life did in fact contain the seeds of many stories. Her first book, *When I Was Young in the Mountains,* describes her childhood in the hills of West Virginia. Cynthia lived with her grandparents for four years in a tiny house without plumbing. The hardships she experienced are reflected in "Stray."

Fast Facts

▶ Unlike many writers, Rylant does not use a computer to write her stories. Instead, she writes by hand on yellow legal pads.

▶ Since the publication of her first book, Rylant has written more than sixty children's books.

▶ Rylant has two dogs and two cats of her own.

Go **O**nline
Author Link

For: More about the author
Visit: www.PHSchool.com
Web Code: ele-9102

Stray

CYNTHIA RYLANT

In January, a puppy wandered onto the property of Mr. Amos Lacey and his wife, Mamie, and their daughter, Doris. Icicles hung three feet or more from the eaves of houses, snowdrifts swallowed up automobiles and the birds were so fluffed up they looked comic.

The puppy had been abandoned, and it made its way down the road toward the Laceys' small house, its ears tucked, its tail between its legs, shivering.

Doris, whose school had been called off because of the snow, was out shoveling the cinderblock front steps when she spotted the pup on the road. She set down the shovel.

"Hey! Come on!" she called.

The puppy stopped in the road, wagging its tail <u>timidly</u>, trembling with shyness and cold.

Doris trudged[1] through the yard, went up the shoveled drive and met the dog.

"Come on, Pooch."

"Where did *that* come from?" Mrs. Lacey asked as soon as Doris put the dog down in the kitchen.

Mr. Lacey was at the table, cleaning his fingernails with his pocketknife. The snow was keeping him home from his job at the warehouse.

"I don't know where it came from," he said mildly, "but I know for sure where it's going."

Doris hugged the puppy hard against her. She said nothing.

Because the roads would be too bad for travel for many days, Mr. Lacey couldn't get out to take the puppy to the pound[2] in the city right away. He agreed to let it sleep in the basement while Mrs. Lacey grudgingly let Doris feed it table scraps. The woman was sensitive about throwing out food.

By the looks of it, Doris figured the puppy was about six months old, and on its way to being a big dog. She thought it might have some shepherd in it.

Four days passed and the puppy did not complain. It never cried in the night or howled at the wind. It didn't tear up everything in the basement. It wouldn't even follow Doris up the basement steps unless it was invited.

It was a good dog.

Several times Doris had opened the door in the kitchen that led to the basement and the puppy had been there, all stretched out, on the top step. Doris knew it had wanted some company and that it had lain against the door, listening to the talk in the kitchen, smelling the food, being a part of things. It always wagged its tail, eyes all sleepy, when she found it there.

Even after a week had gone by, Doris didn't name the dog. She knew her parents wouldn't let her keep it, that her father made so little money any pets were out of the question, and that the pup would definitely go to the pound when the weather cleared.

Still, she tried talking to them about the dog at dinner one night.

---

1. **trudged** (trujd) *v.* walked as if tired or with effort.
2. **pound** (pound) *n.* animal shelter.

Vocabulary Builder
grudgingly (gruj´ iŋ lē) *adv.* in an unwilling or resentful way

Reading Skill
Make Predictions
Based on what you know about big dogs, do you predict that Mr. Lacey will change his mind?

Literary Analysis
Plot What action up until this point in the story suggests a conflict? Explain.

Reading Check

How do Doris's parents feel about the puppy?

"She's a good dog, isn't she?" Doris said, hoping one of them would agree with her.

Her parents glanced at each other and went on eating.

"She's not much trouble," Doris added. "I like her." She smiled at them, but they continued to <u>ignore</u> her.

"I figure she's real smart," Doris said to her mother. "I could teach her things."

Mrs. Lacey just shook her head and stuffed a forkful of sweet potato in her mouth. Doris fell silent, praying the weather would never clear.

But on Saturday, nine days after the dog had arrived, the sun was shining and the roads were plowed. Mr. Lacey opened up the trunk of his car and came into the house.

Doris was sitting alone in the living room, hugging a pillow and rocking back and forth on the edge of a chair. She was trying not to cry but she was not strong enough. Her face was wet and red, her eyes full of distress.

Mrs. Lacey looked into the room from the doorway.

"Mama," Doris said in a small voice. "Please."

Mrs. Lacey shook her head.

"You know we can't afford a dog, Doris. You try to act more grown-up about this."

Doris pressed her face into the pillow.

Outside, she heard the trunk of the car slam shut, one of the doors open and close, the old engine cough and choke and finally start up.

"Daddy," she whispered. "Please."

She heard the car travel down the road, and, though it was early afternoon, she could do nothing but go to her bed. She cried herself to sleep, and her dreams were full of searching and searching for things lost.

It was nearly night when she finally woke up. Lying there, like stone, still exhausted, she wondered if she would ever in her life have anything. She stared at the wall for a while.

Literature in Context

Health Connection

Pet Projects Whether you love dogs, cats, or even iguanas, your pet affects your mood and your health. Studies have shown that owning and cuddling a pet can relieve stress. Pets also help lower heart rates and blood pressure and lift spirits. Some hospitals and nursing homes have pet therapy programs to provide these benefits to their patients. Pets in these programs—mostly specially trained dogs—make friends easily, listen attentively, and give love without judging.

Connect to the Literature

Why do you think Doris wants to keep the puppy?

Vocabulary Builder
ignore (ig nôr′) *v.*
pay no attention to

But she started feeling hungry, and she knew she'd have to make herself get out of bed and eat some dinner. She wanted not to go into the kitchen, past the basement door. She wanted not to face her parents.

But she rose up heavily.

Her parents were sitting at the table, dinner over, drinking coffee. They looked at her when she came in, but she kept her head down. No one spoke.

Doris made herself a glass of powdered milk and drank it all down. Then she picked up a cold biscuit and started out of the room.

"You'd better feed that mutt before it dies of starvation," Mr. Lacey said.

Doris turned around.

"What?"

"I said, you'd better feed your dog. I figure it's looking for you."

Doris put her hand to her mouth.

"You didn't take her?" she asked.

◀ Critical Viewing
Why might a girl like Doris become attached to a dog like this one? [Analyze]

"Oh, I took her all right," her father answered. "Worst looking place I've ever seen. Ten dogs to a cage. Smell was enough to knock you down. And they give an animal six days to live. Then they kill it with some kind of a shot."

Doris stared at her father.

"I wouldn't leave an *ant* in that place," he said. "So I brought the dog back."

Mrs. Lacey was smiling at him and shaking her head as if she would never, ever, understand him.

Mr. Lacey sipped his coffee.

"Well," he said, "are you going to feed it or not?"

Literary Analysis
Plot What is surprising about the resolution of the conflict?

Apply the Skills

Stray

Thinking About the Selection

1. **(a) Respond:** Do you think the Laceys care about Doris's feelings? Explain. **(b) Discuss:** In a group, discuss your responses. Choose one to share with the class.
2. **(a) Recall:** Why do the Laceys wait before taking the dog to the pound? **(b) Evaluate:** How easy or difficult is it to keep the dog during this time? **(c) Analyze:** Why does Doris have difficulty giving the dog away?
3. **(a) Recall:** What does Doris do when her father first tells her that she cannot keep the dog? **(b) Analyze:** Explain why Doris reacts this way.
4. **(a) Recall:** In your own words, restate Mr. Lacey's description of the pound. **(b) Analyze:** Why does Mr. Lacey change his mind about keeping the dog?
5. **(a) Take a Position:** Do you think that Doris should have made a stronger case for keeping the dog? Why or why not? **(b) Speculate:** What can Doris do in the future to show her father that he was right about keeping the dog?

Reading Skill

6. Copy and complete the chart to show how you used prior knowledge and story clues to **predict** the answer to each of these questions. One question has been done for you: What will Doris do with the puppy she finds?
   (a) What will her parents say about the puppy?
   (b) What will her father do when the weather finally clears?

Prior Knowledge	Details From Story	Prediction
Puppies are cute.	The puppy is abandoned.	Doris will want to keep it.
(a)		
(b)		

Literary Analysis

7. What is the *conflict* in the **plot** of this story?
8. What is the *climax,* or high point, in the story? Explain.

QuickReview

Story at a Glance
A girl rescues an abandoned puppy, but her parents insist that the family cannot keep the dog.

Go Online
Assessment
For: Self-test
Visit: www.PHSchool.com
Web Code: ela-6103

Prediction: logical guess about what will happen next

Plot: arrangement of events in a story, including *exposition, conflict, rising action, climax, falling action, resolution*

Vocabulary Builder

Practice Rewrite each sentence. Your new sentence should include a vocabulary word from the list on page 22 and express nearly the same meaning as the original sentence.

1. The boys pay no attention to the No Swimming sign.
2. Kay forces herself to congratulate the winner.
3. Juan blushes as he greets the new teacher.

Writing

Doris's father uses strong words to describe the local animal shelter. Write a **news report** about Doris's rescue of the dog and her family's decision to keep it.

- Use details from the story.
- Use an effective lead sentence that contains a statistic, a quotation, or another detail to capture the reader's attention. Follow with short, clear sentences that sum up the basic facts. Include examples and details that support your main point.

For *Grammar, Vocabulary,* and *Assessment,* see **Build Language Skills,** pages 40–41.

Extend Your Learning

Listening and Speaking Prepare a **speech** about ways to improve conditions at the animal shelter in Doris's hometown. Begin by describing the original conditions at the shelter. Then, suggest ways to correct the problems. When you are finished, present your speech to the class.

Research and Technology With a group, search the Internet and library resources to find information on caring for puppies and dogs. Use the information to create a **brochure** for new pet owners. Present information in these categories:

- general feeding instructions for puppies and dogs
- tips about training puppies
- keeping dogs happy and healthy

Short Story

Background

Chess In "The Homecoming," the main character loses track of time as he watches two men play chess. Chess is a board game that dates back to the sixth century. The object is to *checkmate,* or trap, the opponent's main chess piece, called a *king.* This ancient game of skill can take several hours to complete. The game in the story takes even longer than that!

Connecting to the Literature

Reading/Writing Connection The main character in this story returns to his village after a long absence to find that much has changed. Imagine that you left your town and returned many years later. Write several sentences about the changes that you might expect to see. Use at least three of the following words: *expand, transform, diminish, modify.*

Review

For **Reading Skill, Literary Analysis,** and **Vocabulary Builder,** see page 22.

Meet the Author

Laurence **Yep** (b. 1948)

Laurence Yep was born and raised in San Francisco, California. A third-generation Chinese American, he began writing in high school and sold his first story when he was just eighteen years old. Since then, he has written many books for young people and has won numerous awards. Much of Yep's subject matter reflects his interest in other worlds. His books of science fiction and fantasy tell of strange events in mysterious lands.

Belonging to Two Cultures In his early years, Yep says, he "wanted to be as American as possible." In his early twenties, he became interested in his Chinese roots. He began researching and writing novels about Chinese immigrants and their descendants. During this time, Yep wrote a book based on Chinese folk tales, which included "The Homecoming."

Go **O**nline
Author Link

For: More about the author
Visit: www.PHSchool.com
Web Code: ele-9103

The Homecoming
Laurence Yep

Once there was a woodcutter who minded everyone's business but his own. If you were digging a hole, he knew a better way to grip the shovel. If you were cooking a fish, he knew a better recipe. As his village said, he knew a little of everything and most of nothing.

If his wife and children hadn't made palm leaf fans, the family would have starved. Finally his wife got tired of everyone laughing at them. "You're supposed to be a wood-cutter. Go up to the hill and cut some firewood."

"Any fool can do that." The woodcutter picked up his hatchet.[1] "In the mountains there's plenty of tall oak. That's what burns best."

His wife pointed out the window. "But there's a stand of pine just over the ridgetop."

Her husband looked pained. "Pine won't sell as well. I'll take my load into town, where folk are too busy to cut their own.

---

1. **hatchet** (hach´ it) *n.* a short-handled ax.

Literary Analysis
Plot What information about the characters and the situation is revealed in the exposition?

✓ **Reading Check**

Why does the woodcutter refuse to do what his wife suggests?

Then I'll come back with loads of cash." With a laugh, he shouldered his long pole. After he cut the wood, he would tie it into two big bundles and place each at the end of the pole. Then he would balance the load on his shoulder.

Waving good-bye to his children, he left their house; but his wife walked right with him. "What are you doing?" he asked.

His wife folded her arms as they walked along. "<u>Escorting</u> you."

He slowed down by a boy who was making a kite out of paper and rice paste. "That thing will never fly. You should—"

His wife caught his arm and pulled him along. "Don't be such a busybody."[2]

---

2. **busybody** (biz´ ē bäd´ ē) *n.* a person who is unusually interested in other people's business.

Vocabulary Builder
escorting (es kort´ iŋ) *v.* going with as a companion

◄ Critical Viewing
What advice might the woodcutter have for the different people in this picture? [Speculate]

"If a neighbor's doing something wrong, it's the charitable thing to set that person straight." He tried to stop by a man who was feeding his ducks. "Say, friend. Those ducks'll get fatter if—"

His wife yanked him away and gave him a good shake. "Do I have to blindfold you? We have two children to feed."

"I'm not lazy," he grumbled.

She kept dragging him out of the village. "I never said you were. You can do the work of two people when no one else is around. You're just too easily <u>distracted</u>."

She went with him to the very edge of the fields and sent him on his way. "Remember," she called after him. "Don't talk to anyone."

He walked with long, steady strides through the wooded hills. "I'll show her. It isn't how often you do something, it's how you do it. I'll cut twice the wood and sell it for double the price and come back in half the time."

Complaining loudly to himself, he moved deep into the mountains. I want just the right sort of oak, he thought to himself. As he walked along, he kept an eye out for a likely tree.

He didn't see the funny old man until he bumped into him. "Oof, watch where you're going," the old man said.

The old man had a head that bulged as big as a melon. He was dressed in a yellow robe embroidered with storks and pine trees.

Playing chess with the old man was another man so fat he could not close his robe. In his hand he had a large fan painted with drinking scenes.

The fat man wagged a finger at the old man. "Don't try to change the subject. I've got you. It's checkmate in two moves."

The funny old man looked back at the chessboard. The lines were a bright red on yellow paper, and the chess pieces were flat disks with words painted in gold on their tops.

"Is it now, is it now?" the funny old man mused.

The woodcutter remembered his wife's warning. But he said to himself, "I'm not actually talking to them. I'm advising them." So he put down his hatchet and pole.

Vocabulary Builder
distracted (di strakt′ id) *adj.* unable to concentrate

Reading Skill
Make Predictions
Do you think the woodcutter will stop to talk to anyone on his way? On what do you base your prediction?

Reading Check

What warning is the woodcutter remembering?

"Actually, if you moved that piece"—he jabbed at a disk—"and moved it there"—he pointed at a spot on the board—"you'd have him."

But the old man moved a different disk.

The fat man scratched the top of his bald head. "Now how'd you think of that?"

The woodcutter rubbed his chin. "Yes, how did you think of that?" But then he nodded his head and pointed to one of the fat man's disks. "Still, if you shifted that one, you'd win."

However, the fat man ignored him as he made another move.

"Well," the woodcutter said to the old man, "you've got him now."

But the old man paid him no more mind than the fat man. "Hmmm," he murmured, and set his chin on his fist as he studied the board.

The woodcutter became so caught up in the game that he squatted down. "I know what you have to do. I'll be right here just in case you need to ask."

Neither man said anything to the woodcutter. They just went on playing, and as they played, the woodcutter became more and more fascinated. He forgot about chopping wood. He even forgot about going home.

When it was night, the funny old man opened a big basket and lifted out a lantern covered with stars. He hung it from a tree and the game went on. Night passed on into day, but the woodcutter was as involved in the game now as the two men.

"Let's take a break." The old man slipped a peach from one big sleeve. The peach was big as the woodcutter's fist, and it filled the woods with a sweet aroma.

"You're just stalling for time," the fat man said. "Move."

"I'm hungry," the old man complained, and took a big bite. However, he shoved a piece along the board. When he held the peach out to the fat man, the fat man bit into it hungrily.

Alternating moves and bites, they went on until there was nothing left of the peach except the peach stone. "I feel much better now," the old man said, and threw the stone over his shoulder.

Literary Analysis
Plot How do the woodcutter's actions increase the story's tension?

Reading Skill
Make Predictions How does your prior knowledge of other stories help you predict that something unusual will happen?

As the two men had eaten the peach, the woodcutter had discovered that he was famished,[3] but the only thing was the peach stone. "Maybe I can suck on this stone and forget about being hungry. But I wish one of them would ask me for help. We could finish this game a lot quicker."

He tucked the stone into his mouth and tasted some of the peach juices. Instantly, he felt himself filled with energy. Goodness, he thought, I feel like there were lightning bolts zipping around inside me. And he went on watching the game with new energy.

After seven days, the old man stopped and stretched. "I think we're going to have to call this game a draw."

The fat man sighed. "I agree." He began to pick up the pieces.

The woodcutter spat out the stone. "But you could win easily."

The old man finally noticed him. "Are you still here?"

The woodcutter thought that this was his chance now to do a good deed.[4] "It's been a most interesting game. However, if you—"

But the old man made shooing motions with his hands. "You should've gone home long ago."

"But I—" began the woodcutter.

The fat man rose. "Go home. It may already be too late."

That's a funny thing to say, the woodcutter thought. He turned around to get his things. But big, fat mushrooms

---

3. famished (fam´ isht) *adj.* very hungry.
4. deed (dēd) *n.* something that is done; an act.

had sprouted among the roots of the trees. A brown carpet surrounded him. He brushed the mushrooms aside until he found a rusty hatchet blade. He couldn't find a trace of the hatchet shaft or of his carrying pole.

Puzzled, he picked up the hatchet blade. "This can't be mine. My hatchet was practically new. Have you two gentlemen seen it?" He turned around again, but the two men had disappeared along with the chessboard and chess pieces.

"That's gratitude for you." Picking up the rusty hatchet blade, the woodcutter tried to make his way back through the woods; but he could not find the way he had come up. "It's like someone rearranged all the trees."

Somehow he made his way out of the mountains. However, fields and villages now stood where there had once been wooded hills. "What are you doing here?" he asked a farmer.

"What are you?" the farmer snorted, and went back to working in his field.

The woodcutter thought about telling him that he was swinging his hoe wrong, but he remembered what the two men had said. So he hurried home instead.

The woodcutter followed the river until he reached his own

village, but as he walked through the fields, he didn't <u>recognize</u> one person. There was even a pond before the village gates. It had never been there before. He broke into a run, but there was a different house in the spot where his home had been. Even so, he burst into the place.

Two strange children looked up from the table, and a strange woman picked up a broom. "Out!"

The woodcutter raised his arms protectively. "Wait, I live here."

But the woman beat the woodcutter with a broom until he retreated into the street. By now, a crowd had gathered. The woodcutter looked around desperately "What's happened to my village? Doesn't anyone know me?"

The village schoolteacher had come out of the school. He asked the woodcutter his name, and when the woodcutter told him, the school-teacher pulled at his whiskers. "That name sounds familiar, but it can't be."

With the crowd following them, he led the woodcutter to the clan temple. "I collect odd, interesting stories." The schoolteacher got out a thick book. "There's a strange incident in the clan book." He leafed through the book toward the beginning and pointed to a name. "A wood-cutter left the village and never came back." He added quietly, "But that was several thousand years ago."

"That's impossible," the woodcutter insisted. "I just stayed away to watch two men play a game of chess."

The schoolteacher sighed. "The two men must have been saints. Time doesn't pass for them as it does for us."

And at that moment, the woodcutter remembered his wife's warning.

But it was too late now.

◀ **Critical Viewing** What details in this picture show how the returning woodcutter might have felt? **[Speculate]**

Vocabulary Builder
recognize (rek´əg nīz´)
v. know and remember

Reading Skill
Make Predictions
What prior knowledge helps you use the ax, the trees, the pond, and the house as clues to predict the outcome of the story?

Literary Analysis
Plot Why is the schoolteacher important to the resolution of the story?

Apply the Skills

The Homecoming

Thinking About the Selection

1. **Respond:** What questions do you have after reading the story? Write them in the first column of a three-column chart. Exchange charts with a partner. In the second column of your partner's chart, write answers to his or her questions. Discuss your work. In the third column, explain how your understanding of the story has or has not changed.

2. **(a) Interpret:** What do the villagers mean by saying the woodcutter "knew a little of everything and most of nothing"? **(b) Connect:** How do the woodcutter's actions support this statement? **(c) Evaluate:** Why is this description important to the story?

3. **(a) Recall:** How do the chess players react to the woodcutter? **(b) Infer:** Why do they treat him this way?

4. **(a) Analyze:** What lesson is expressed in this story? **(b) Take a Position:** Do you agree or disagree with the lesson being taught? Explain.

Reading Skill

5. Copy and complete the chart to show how you made a prediction to answer each question. One question has been done for you: What will the woodcutter do in the forest? **(a)** What will the woodcutter do when he sees the two men playing chess? **(b)** What will happen when the woodcutter leaves the forest?

Prior Knowledge	Details From Story	Prediction
Busybodies like talking to people.	The woodcutter is a busybody.	The woodcutter will stop to talk.
(a)		
(b)		

Literary Analysis

6. What is the *conflict* in the **plot** of this story?
7. What is the *climax,* or high point, in the story? Explain.

QuickReview

Story at a Glance
A woodcutter becomes distracted from his work and loses everything.

Go Online
Assessment
For: Self-test
Visit: www.PHSchool.com
Web Code: ela-6104

Prediction: logical guess about what will happen next in a story

Plot: arrangement of events in a story, including *exposition, conflict, rising action, climax, falling action, resolution*

Vocabulary Builder

Practice Rewrite each sentence. Your new sentence should include a vocabulary word from the list on page 22 and express nearly the same meaning as the original sentence.

1. I was unable to concentrate because of the loud music.
2. Tony will be taking visitors on a tour of the school.
3. At first, Serena did not know the man with the fake beard was her uncle.

Writing

Write a **news report** about the woodcutter's return to his village. In your report, describe the woodcutter, tell his story, and explain the villagers' reactions to him.

- Use an effective lead sentence that captures the reader's attention. For example, you might use a quote from the woman with the broom.
- Follow the lead sentence with short, clear sentences that sum up the basic facts.
- Continue with facts and quotations from villagers.

For *Grammar, Vocabulary,* and *Assessment,* see **Build Language Skills,** pages 40–41.

Extend Your Learning

Listening and Speaking Imagine that you are the woodcutter, and prepare and present a **speech** explaining why you like being a busybody. Find details in the text that support your position. Then, present your speech to the class.

Research and Technology With a group, search the Internet and library resources to find information on Chinese immortals. Use the information to create a **brochure.** Present information in these categories:

- common characteristics of Chinese immortals
- folk tales about Chinese immortals

Build Language Skills

Stray • The Homecoming

Vocabulary Skill

Roots The word *predict* contains the prefix ***pre-,*** meaning "before," and the root ***-dict-,*** which comes from the Latin word for "to say or tell." Knowing the meanings of the prefix and root helps you to understand that *predict* means "to say or tell what might happen before it happens."

➤ **Example:** The black clouds helped us to *predict* the rainstorm.

The word *verify* contains the **Latin root -ver-,** which means "truth." Knowing the meaning of the root helps you to understand that *verify* means "make sure it is true."

➤ **Example:** He checked her driver's license to *verify* her age.

Practice Use a dictionary to find the definition for each of the following words. Then, explain the meaning of each one based on the meanings of the Latin roots *-dict-* and *-ver-*.

1. diction   **3.** edict   **5.** verdict

2. dictation   **4.** verify

Grammar Lesson

Common and Proper Nouns All nouns are considered either *common* or *proper*. A **common noun** names any one of a group of people, places, or things. A **proper noun** names a particular person, place, or thing. Proper nouns are always capitalized. Common nouns are not capitalized unless they are at the beginning of a sentence or in a title.

MorePractice

For more practice with nouns, see the Grammar Handbook, p. R31.

Practice Copy the sentences. Circle the common nouns and underline the proper nouns. Then, choose two of the sentences to rewrite. Replace the common nouns with proper nouns. Replace the proper nouns with common nouns.

1. Did Coach Nuñez win the award?

2. Two rabbits hopped across State Street.

3. Carla is president of the science club.

4. The movie is about a famous athlete.

5. Lee School now has a vegetable garden.

*W*G *Prentice Hall Writing and Grammar Connection: Chapter 14, Section 1.*

Reading: Make Predictions

Directions: *Read the selection. Then, answer the questions.*

Glenn wanted to surprise his mother by making her a cake. He searched the kitchen for ingredients. There were no eggs or baking powder, but Glenn decided to make the cake anyway. Glenn mixed the ingredients and poured the mixture into a pan. He set the pan in a heated oven, but he forgot to set the timer.

1. Based on the first sentence, which of the following is most likely to happen?
   A Glenn will not finish the cake.
   B Glenn will enjoy the cake.
   C Glenn will bake a cake.
   D Glenn's mother will come home early.

2. Which prediction is probably incorrect?
   A The cake will turn out beautifully.
   B The cake will burn.
   C Glenn's family will not have cake for dessert.
   D Glenn will follow the recipe more carefully next time.

3. What is the most logical prediction?
   A The cake will be delicious.
   B The cake will not taste good.
   C The cake will be better than the one in the recipe.
   D The cake will be ready in time.

4. How will Glenn feel when his mother comes home?
   A He will feel proud that he tried to bake a cake.
   B He will feel excited about making such a delicious cake.
   C He will feel embarrassed that the cake did not turn out well.
   D He will feel hurt that his mother did not like the cake.

Timed Writing: Description

Review either "Stray" or "The Homecoming." Describe how the events in either plot changed the main character's life.
(20 minutes)

 ## Writing Workshop: *Work in Progress*

Descriptive Essay
Choose one place from your list of places. Add why you like it, what memories you have about the place, and why it is special to you. Put this work in your writing portfolio.

These skills will help you become a better reader. Practice them with either "The Drive-In Movies" (p. 44) or "The Market Square Dog" (p. 51).

Reading Skill

Predictions are reasonable guesses about what is most likely to happen next. Base your predictions on details in the literature and on your own experience. Keep track of your predictions using a diagram like the one shown. Then, **read ahead to check your prediction.** When you find details that show your original prediction may be wrong, **revise your prediction.** Use these new details to correct and change your ideas.

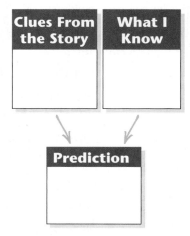

Literary Analysis

The **narrator** is the voice that tells a true or imagined story. **Point of view** is the perspective from which the story is told. The following two points of view are the most common:

- **first-person point of view:** The narrator participates in the action of the story and refers to himself or herself as "I." Readers know only what the narrator sees, thinks, and feels.
- **third-person point of view:** The narrator does not participate in the action of the story. As an outside observer, a third-person narrator can share information that the characters do not know.

Most true stories about a writer's life are told in the first person.

Vocabulary Builder

The Drive-In Movies

- **prelude** (prā´ lōōd) *n.* introduction to a main event (p. 45) *We sang the school song as a prelude to the big game.*
- **evident** (ev´ə dənt) *adj.* easy to see; very clear (p. 46) *Her happiness was evident in her cheery smile.*
- **winced** (winst) *v.* drew back slightly, as if in pain; cringed (p. 47) *The boy winced as the nurse gave him a shot.*

The Market Square Dog

- **trotted** (trät´təd) *v.* ran in a graceful, light way (p. 51) *The new pony trotted across the field.*
- **anxiously** (aŋk´shəs lē) *adv.* in a worried or uneasy way (p. 54) *I watched anxiously as my little brother swam in the river.*
- **custody** (kus´tə dē) *n.* protection or supervision (p. 57) *The stolen jewels remained in the custody of the police.*

Background

Drive-In Theaters A drive-in is an outdoor movie theater in which people watch the movie from their cars. The first drive-in movie theater opened in Camden, New Jersey, in 1933. In the late 1950s, when their popularity was at its peak, there were 5,000 drive-ins.

Connecting to the Literature

Reading/Writing Connection In "The Drive-In Movies," a boy works hard to earn a special privilege—a family outing to the drive-in. Make a list of ways that you earn privileges. Use at least three of the following words: *accomplish, assist, cooperate, demonstrate, respond.*

Meet the Author

Gary **Soto** (b. 1952)

As a child, Gary Soto loved the bustle and energy of his Fresno, California, neighborhood. When Soto was six years old, however, a government program changed his neighborhood by replacing many rundown buildings with new ones. "It didn't work in our area," Soto declares today. "The houses were bulldozed, and in their place grew weeds." As he grew older, Soto continued to feel a sense of loss over his old neighborhood. Today, he believes that his pain and sadness led him to become a writer. Writing helped him to get his feelings down on paper, where he could see them and think about them.

Fast Facts

▶ Soto was once a farm worker in California's San Joaquin Valley.

▶ Today, he is an award-winning author of fiction, short stories, poems, and children's picture books.

▶ Much of Soto's work is based on his own experiences and the settings of his childhood.

Go **Online**
Author Link

For: More about the author
Visit: www.PHSchool.com
Web Code: ele-9104

The Drive-In Movies

GARY SOTO

For our family, moviegoing was rare. But if our mom, tired from a week of candling eggs,[1] woke up happy on a Saturday morning, there was a chance we might later scramble to our blue Chevy and beat nightfall to the Starlight Drive-In. My brother and sister knew this. I knew this. So on Saturday we tried to be good. We sat in the cool shadows of the TV with the volume low and watched cartoons, a <u>prelude</u> of what was to come.

One Saturday I decided to be extra good. When she came out of the bedroom tying her robe, she yawned a hat-sized yawn and blinked red eyes at the weak brew of coffee I had fixed for her. I made her toast with strawberry jam spread to all the corners and set the three boxes of cereal in front of her. If she didn't care to eat cereal, she could always look at the back of the boxes as she drank her coffee.

I went outside. The lawn was tall but too wet with dew to mow. I picked up a trowel[2] and began to weed the flower bed. The weeds were really bermuda grass, long stringers that ran finger-deep in the ground. I got to work quickly and in no time crescents of earth began rising under my fingernails. I was sweaty hot. My knees hurt from kneeling, and my brain was dull from making the trowel go up and down, dribbling crumbs of earth. I dug for half an hour,

Literary Analysis
Narrator and Point of View What clues here indicate the narrator is telling the story from the first-person point of view?

Vocabulary Builder
prelude (prā′ lo͞od′) *n.* introduction to a main event

✓**Reading Check**

Why is the narrator being extra good?

---

1. candling eggs examining uncooked eggs for freshness by placing them in front of a burning candle.
2. trowel (trou′ əl) *n.* a small hand tool used by gardeners to weed or dig.

◄ **Critical Viewing** How is seeing a movie at a drive-in like this one different from seeing it in a regular theater? **[Speculate]**

then stopped to play with the neighbor's dog and pop ticks from his poor snout.

I then mowed the lawn, which was still beaded with dew and noisy with bees hovering over clover. This job was less dull because as I pushed the mower over the shaggy lawn, I could see it looked tidier. My brother and sister watched from the window. Their faces were fat with cereal, a third helping. I made a face at them when they asked how come I was working. Rick pointed to part of the lawn. "You missed some over there." I ignored him and kept my attention on the windmill of grassy blades.

While I was emptying the catcher, a bee stung the bottom of my foot. I danced on one leg and was ready to cry when Mother showed her face at the window. I sat down on the grass and examined my foot: the stinger was pulsating. I pulled it out quickly, ran water over the sting and packed it with mud, Grandmother's remedy.

Hobbling, I returned to the flower bed where I pulled more stringers and again played with the dog. More ticks had migrated to his snout. I swept the front steps, took out the garbage, cleaned the lint filter to the dryer (easy), plucked hair from the industrial wash basin in the garage (also easy), hosed off the patio, smashed three snails sucking paint from the house (disgusting but fun), tied a bundle of newspapers, put away toys, and, finally, seeing that almost everything was done and the sun was not too high, started waxing the car.

My brother joined me with an old gym sock, and our sister watched us while sucking on a cherry Kool-Aid ice cube. The liquid wax drooled onto the sock, and we began to swirl the white slop on the chrome. My arms ached from buffing, which though less boring than weeding, was harder. But the beauty was <u>evident</u>. The shine, hurting our eyes and glinting like an armful of dimes, brought Mother out. She

Literature in Context

Social Studies Connection

Drive-In Movies The first drive-in movie theater had three speakers near the screen to project sound, like a kind of loudspeaker system. If you parked near the screen, you could hear every word perfectly. If you lived nearby, you heard every word, too. A later system of individual speakers, placed on the car door when the window was rolled down, satisfied angry neighbors. Unfortunately, drivers sometimes drove away with the speaker still attached to the door.

Connect to the Literature

Why might a trip to the drive-in movies be a reward for the narrator?

Vocabulary Builder
evident (ev´ə dənt) *adj.* easy to see; very clear

looked around the yard and said, "Pretty good." She <u>winced</u> at the grille and returned inside the house.

We began to wax the paint. My brother applied the liquid and I followed him rubbing hard in wide circles as we moved around the car. I began to hurry because my arms were hurting and my stung foot looked like a water balloon. We were working around the trunk when Rick pounded on the bottle of wax. He squeezed the bottle and it sneezed a few more white drops.

We looked at each other. "There's some on the sock," I said. "Let's keep going."

We polished and buffed, sweat weeping on our brows. We got scared when we noticed that the gym sock was now blue. The paint was coming off. Our sister fit ice cubes into our mouths and we worked harder, more intently, more dedicated to the car and our mother. We ran the sock over the chrome, trying to pick up extra wax. But there wasn't enough to cover the entire car. Only half got waxed, but we thought it was better than nothing and went inside for lunch. After lunch, we returned outside with tasty sandwiches.

Rick and I nearly jumped. The waxed side of the car was foggy white. We took a rag and began to polish vigorously and nearly in tears, but the fog wouldn't come off. I blamed Rick and he blamed me. Debra stood at the window, not wanting to get involved. Now, not only would we not go to the movies, but Mom would surely snap a branch from the plum tree and chase us around the yard.

Mom came out and looked at us with hands on her aproned hips. Finally, she said, "You boys worked so hard." She turned on the garden hose and washed the car. That night we did go to the drive-in. The first feature was about nothing, and the second feature, starring Jerry Lewis, was *Cinderfella*. I tried to stay awake. I kept a wad of homemade popcorn in my cheek and laughed when Jerry Lewis fit golf tees in his nose. I rubbed my watery eyes. I laughed and looked at my mom. I promised myself I would remember that scene with the golf tees and promised myself not to work so hard the coming Saturday. Twenty minutes into the movie, I fell asleep with one hand in the popcorn.

Apply the Skills

The Drive-In Movies

Thinking About the Selection

1. **Respond:** How would you have felt if you had worked so hard and then fallen asleep at the movies?
2. **(a) Recall:** How does Soto persuade his mother to take the family to the drive-in movies? **(b) Draw Conclusions:** Why do you think Soto's mother does not get angry with the children for making a mess with the car wax?
3. **(a) Recall:** What two things does Soto promise himself to remember? **(b) Assess:** Do you think he still has fond memories of that day and night? Why or why not?
4. **(a) Take a Position:** Do you think children should have to work hard on chores before their parents allow them to do something enjoyable? Why or why not? **(b) Discuss:** In a small group, share your responses. Then, as a group, choose one response to share with the class.

Reading Skill

5. **(a)** Did you **predict** that Soto's mother would take the family to the drive-in movies? **(b)** On what details did you base your prediction?
6. As you read, did you change any predictions? Explain.

Literary Analysis

7. Make a chart like the one shown to note how Soto's **point of view** affects what readers know about some events in the story.

Event	Details Provided by Narrator
The narrator is stung by a bee.	The sting hurts.

8. What details would you expect to find if the **narrator** were Soto's mother?

QuickReview

Story at a Glance
A young Gary Soto tells about a childhood experience in which he may have worked too hard to gain a reward.

Go **O**nline
Assessment
For: Self-test
Visit: www.PHSchool.com
Web Code: ela-6105

Prediction: a reasonable guess about what will happen next in a story

Narrator: the voice that tells a story

Point of view: the perspective from which the narrative is told. A story will usually be told from either the *first-person* or the *third-person point of view.*

Vocabulary Builder

Practice Synonyms are words with similar meanings. For each item, choose a synonym from the vocabulary list on page 42.

1. clear, obvious, _____
2. beginning, introduction, _____
3. shrank back, cringed, _____

Writing

Gary Soto's **autobiographical narrative** is packed with details about an event in his own life. Write an autobiographical narrative about an event, a person, or a period in your life.

- First, brainstorm for ideas from your life experience. Then, narrow your topic to a single event or experience.
- List the details. Then, number them in the order in which they occurred. Use your ordered list to write your autobiographical narrative.

For *Grammar, Vocabulary,* and *Assessment,* see **Build Language Skills,** pages 60–61.

Extend Your Learning

Listening and Speaking With a partner, act out a **conversation** that Soto and his mother might have had the morning after their trip to the drive-in. Use details from the story, as well as your own creative ideas, to invent an interesting dialogue.

Research and Technology With a group of classmates, use the Internet and other reference materials to find more information on Gary Soto. Then, working independently, use your research to write a **response** to the following statement: *Writers should write about what they know—people, events, details, and lessons from their own lives.*

Autobiography

Background

Veterinary Medicine Veterinarians are doctors who are trained to prevent, diagnose, and treat illnesses in animals. Like doctors who treat humans, veterinarians must attend medical school. Most veterinarians in urban and suburban locations treat household pets. Some veterinarians, like the author of this story, work in the country. They treat cows, horses, and other farm animals in addition to pets.

Connecting to the Literature

Reading/Writing Connection In this story, a country veterinarian and a police officer show compassion for a stray dog. Write about a time when you saw someone demonstrate compassion. Use at least three of the following words: *assist, contribute, involve, respond.*

Review

For **Reading Skill, Literary Analysis,** and **Vocabulary Builder,** see page 42.

Meet the Author

James **Herriot** (1916–1995)

James Herriot is a pen name for the real-life veterinarian James Alfred Wight, who was born in Scotland and received his veterinary training at Glasgow Veterinary College. After graduating in 1939, Herriot moved to the rural area of Yorkshire, England, and was a veterinarian there for fifty years. As a country doctor, he traveled from farm to farm and village to village, treating animals that needed his care. At age fifty, he began writing, sharing stories based on his experiences as a veterinarian. Despite his fame as a writer, he remained a quiet, modest country doctor throughout his life.

Fast Facts

▶ Herriot treated dogs, cats, sheep, cows, horses, and even a troubled "talking" parakeet that refused to talk.

▶ His first book, *All Creatures Great and Small,* was the basis for a television series.

▶ In all, he wrote fifteen books, which became so popular that they sold 50 million copies in twenty countries.

Go Online
Author Link

For: More about the author
Visit: www.PHSchool.com
Web Code: ele-9105

THE MARKET SQUARE DOG

James Herriot

On market days when the farmers around Darrowby brought their goods to the little town to sell, I used to take a walk across the cobbled square to meet the farmers who gathered there to chat. One of the farmers was telling me about his sick cow when we saw the little dog among the market stalls. The thing that made us notice the dog was that he was sitting up, begging, in front of the stall selling cakes and biscuits.

"Look at that little chap,"[1] the farmer said. "I wonder where he's come from?"

As he spoke, the stallholder threw him a bun which the dog devoured eagerly, but when the man came round and stretched out a hand the little animal <u>trotted</u> away. He stopped, however, at another stall which sold eggs, butter, cheese and scones. Without hesitation, he sat up again in the begging position, rock steady, paws dangling, head pointing expectantly.

**Literary Analysis
Narrator and Point of View** How do you know that this story is told from the first-person point of view?

**Vocabulary Builder
trotted** (trät´ təd) *v.* ran in a graceful, light way

---

1. chap (chap) *n.* a fellow or boy.

I nudged my companion. "There he goes again. I always think a dog looks very appealing sitting up like that."

The farmer nodded. "Yes, he's a bonny[2] little thing, isn't he? What breed would you call him?"

"A cross, I'd say. He's like a small sheepdog, but there's a touch of something else—maybe terrier."

It wasn't long before the dog was munching a biscuit, and this time I walked over to him, and as I drew near I spoke gently. "Here, boy," I said, squatting down in front of him. "Come on, let's have a look at you."

He turned to face me, and for a moment two friendly brown eyes gazed at me from a wonderfully attractive face. The fringed tail waved in response to my words, but as I moved nearer he turned and trotted away among the market-day crowd until he was lost to sight.

I was standing there, trying to see where he had gone, when a young policeman came up to me.

"I've been watching that wee[3] dog begging among the stalls all morning," he said, "but, like you, I haven't been able to get near him."

"Yes, it's strange. You can see he's friendly, but he's also afraid. I wonder who owns him."

"I reckon he's a stray, Mr. Herriot. I'm interested in dogs myself and fancy I know just about all of them around here. But this one is a stranger to me."

I nodded. "I'm sure you're right. Anything could have happened to him. He could have been ill-treated by somebody and run away, or he could have been dumped from a car."

▲ **Critical Viewing** Why is a market like the one shown here a good place for a hungry dog to look for food? **[Analyze]**

---

2. bonny (bän´ ē) *adj.* attractive, pretty, or handsome.
3. wee (wē) *adj.* small, tiny.

"Yes," the policeman replied, "there are some cruel people about. I don't know how anybody can leave a helpless animal to fend for itself like that. I've had a few tries at catching him, but it's no good."

The memory stayed with me for the rest of the day. It is our duty to look after the animals who depend on us and it worried me to think of the little creature wandering about in a strange place, sitting up and asking for help in the only way he knew.

Market day is on a Monday and on the Friday of that week my wife Helen and I had a treat planned for ourselves; we were going to the races in Brawton. Helen was making up a picnic basket with home-made ham-and-egg-pie, chicken sandwiches and a chocolate cake. I was wearing my best suit and I couldn't help feeling very smart[4] because country vets have to work mostly in the fields and cowsheds and I hardly ever got dressed up. Helen, too, had put on her best dress and a fancy hat I had never seen before. As a vet's wife, she too had to work very hard and we weren't able to go out together very often.

We were just about to leave the house when the doorbell rang. It was the young policeman I had been talking to on market day.

"I've got that dog, Mr. Herriot," he said. "You know—the one that was begging in the market square."

"Oh good," I replied, "so you managed to catch him at last."

The policeman paused. "No, not really. One of our men found him lying by the roadside about a mile out of town and brought him in. I'm afraid he's been knocked down. We've got him here in the car."

I went out and looked into the car. The little dog was lying very still on the back seat, but when I stroked the dark coat his tail stirred briefly.

"He can still manage a wag, anyway," I said.

The policeman nodded. "Yes, there's no doubt he's a good-natured wee thing."

I tried to examine him as much as possible without touching because I didn't want to hurt him, but I could see that he had cuts all over his body and one hind leg lay in

---

4. **smart** (smärt) *adj.* stylish, well-dressed.

Reading Skill
Make Predictions
What do you think might happen to the dog? Read ahead to verify your prediction.

Literary Analysis
Narrator and Point of View Why don't readers learn more about the details of the dog's accident?

Reading Check

What is the dog doing in the market?

such a way that I knew it must be broken. When I gently lifted his head, I saw that one eyelid was badly torn so that the eye was completely closed. But the other soft brown eye looked at me trustingly.

"Can you do anything for him, Mr. Herriot?" asked the policeman. "Can you save him?"

"I'll do my best," I replied.

I carried the little animal into the surgery and laid him on the table.

"There's an hour or two's work here, Helen," I said to my wife. "I'm very sorry, but we won't be able to go to the races."

"Never mind," she replied. "We must do what we can for this fellow."

Rather sadly she took off her fancy hat and I took off my good jacket. Dressed in our white coats we began to work.

Helen was used to helping me and she gave the anaesthetic,[5] then I set the broken leg in plaster and stitched up the wounds. The worst thing was the eye because even after I had stitched the eyelid it was still bruised and tightly closed and I was worried that he might lose the sight in that eye.

By the time we had finished, it was too late to go out anywhere, but Helen was quite cheerful. "We can still have our picnic," she said.

We carried the sleeping dog out to the garden and laid him on a mat on the lawn so that we could watch him as he came round from the anaesthetic.

Out there in the old high-walled garden the sun shone down on the flowers and the apple trees. Helen put on her fancy hat again and I put my smart jacket back on and as we sat there, enjoying the good things from the picnic basket, we felt that we were still having a day out. But Helen kept glancing <u>anxiously</u> at the little dog and I knew she was thinking the same thing as I was. Would he be all right after all that we had done for him and, even then, what was going to happen to him? Would his owners ever come to claim him, because if they didn't, he had nobody in the world to look after him.

Literary Analysis
Narrator and Point of View What information might you read here if this part of the story were told from Helen's point of view?

Vocabulary Builder
anxiously (aŋkʹ shəs lē) *adv.* in a worried or uneasy way

---

5. **anaesthetic** (an´es thetʹik) *n.* British spelling of **anesthetic**: a medicine that makes a patient fall asleep so that surgery can be performed without causing the patient pain.

Since he had been found by the police, he was classified as a stray and had to go into the kennels at the police station. When I visited him there two days later, he greeted me excitedly, balancing well on his plastered leg, his tail swishing. All his fear seemed to have gone. I was delighted to see that the injured eye was now fully open, and the swelling down.

The young policeman was as pleased as I was. "Look at that!" he exclaimed. "He's nearly as good as new again."

"Yes," I said, "he's done wonderfully well." I hesitated for a moment. "Has anybody enquired about him?"

He shook his head. "Nothing yet, but we'll keep hoping, and in the meantime we'll take good care of him here."

Reading Check

Why does the policeman bring the dog to the narrator's house?

▲ **Critical Viewing** What makes a garden, like the one in the picture, a nice place for a picnic? **[Analyze]**

I visited the kennels often, and each time the shaggy little creature jumped up to greet me, laughing into my face, mouth open, eyes shining. But nobody seemed to want him.

After a few more days it was clear that no owner was going to claim him, and my only hope was that somebody else would take him and give him a home.

There were other stray dogs in the kennels, and on one visit I saw a farmer calling to collect his wandering sheepdog.

Then a family was overjoyed at being reunited with their handsome golden retriever.

Finally a little old lady came in and tearfully gathered her tiny Yorkshire terrier into her arms. But nobody came for my little patient.

Various strangers came too, looking for a pet, but nobody seemed to be interested in him. Maybe it was because he was only a mongrel and the people who visited the kennels wanted a more elegant dog—yet I knew that he would make a perfect pet for anybody.

A week passed before I went again to the police station. The little dog's kennel was empty.

"What's happened?" I asked the policeman. "Has somebody taken him?"

The policeman looked very grave. "No," he replied, "I'm afraid he's been arrested."

"Arrested?" I said in astonishment. "What do you mean?"

▶ Critical Viewing What details in this picture indicate that the dog is recovering from its injuries? [Analyze]

"Well," he said, "it seems that it's against the law for a dog to go begging in the market square so he has been taken into police <u>custody</u>."

I was bewildered. "What are you talking about? A dog can't be arrested."

The policeman, still very solemn, shrugged his shoulders. "This dog was."

"I still don't know what this is all about," I said. "Where is he now?"

"I'll take you to him," the policeman replied.

We left the police station and walked a short way along the road to a pretty cottage.

We went inside and there, in the sitting-room, curled up in a big new doggy bed was my little friend. Two small girls were sitting by his side, stroking his coat.

The policeman threw back his head and laughed. "I've just been kidding you, Mr. Herriot. This is my house and I've taken him as a pet for my two daughters. They've been wanting a dog for some time and I've got so fond of this wee chap that I thought he'd be just right for them."

A wave of relief swept over me. "Well, that's wonderful," I said and I looked at his kind face gratefully. "What's your name?" I asked.

"Phelps," he replied. "PC Phelps. And they call me Funny Phelps at the police station because I like playing jokes on people."

"Well, you certainly took me in," I said. "Arrested indeed!"

He laughed again. "Well, you've got to admit he's in the hands of the law now!"

I laughed too. I didn't mind having the joke played on me because, funny Phelps or not, he was obviously a nice Phelps and would be a kind master for my doggy friend.

It was a happy day when I took the plaster off the little dog's leg and found that the break had healed perfectly. All the nasty cuts had healed, too, and when I lifted him down from the table, the small girls held up a beautiful new red collar with a lead to match. Their new pet liked the look of them because he sat up in that position I remembered so well, his paws dangling, his face looking up eagerly. The begging dog had found a home at last.

Vocabulary Builder
custody (kus′ tə dē) *n.* protection or supervision

Reading Skill
Make Predictions
Where do you think the police officer will take the narrator to see the dog? Read ahead to see if you are right.

Reading Skill
Make Predictions
Was your prediction about where the police officer would take the narrator correct? Explain.

Apply the Skills

The Market Square Dog

Thinking About the Selection

1. **Respond:** Were you surprised by the ending of this narrative? Why or why not?
2. **(a) Recall:** What event leads the narrator to help the dog?
   (b) Draw Conclusions: Why do you think the narrator visits the dog at the police station?
3. **(a) Interpret:** At the beginning of the story, why does the dog run away from people who try to pet him?
   (b) Compare and Contrast: How does this behavior change at the end of the story? **(c) Infer:** Why do you think the dog's behavior changes in this way?
4. **Hypothesize:** If the story were to continue, do you think the veterinarian and the police officer would become great friends? Why or why not?

Reading Skill

5. **(a)** What did you **predict** would happen to the dog?
   (b) On what details did you base your prediction?
6. As you read, did you change any predictions? Explain.

Literary Analysis

7. Make a chart like the one shown to note how Herriot's **point of view** affects what readers know about some events in the story.

Event	Details Provided by Narrator
The dog is begging for food in front of a stall.	The narrator thinks that dogs look very appealing when they sit up.

8. What details would you expect to find if the **narrator** were the police officer?

QuickReview

Story at a Glance
A veterinarian helps an injured stray dog.

Go Online
Assessment
For: Self-test
Visit: www.PHSchool.com
Web Code: ela-6106

Prediction: a reasonable guess about what will happen next in a story

Narrator: the voice that tells a story

Point of view: the perspective from which a story is told. A story will usually be told from either the *first-person* or the *third-person point of view.*

Vocabulary Builder

Practice **Synonyms** are words with similar meanings. For each item, choose a synonym from the vocabulary list on page 42.

1. ran, dashed, _____
2. protection, safekeeping, _____
3. nervously, worriedly, _____

Writing

Herriot's **autobiographical narrative** tells a story that is packed with details about an event in his own life. Write an autobiographical narrative about an animal that you know.

- First, brainstorm for details about animals you know. Then, narrow your topic to a single event involving one animal.
- List the details of the event. Then, number them in the order in which they occurred. Use your ordered list to write your autobiographical narrative.

For *Grammar, Vocabulary,* and *Assessment,* see **Build Language Skills,** pages 60–61.

Extend Your Learning

Listening and Speaking With a partner, act out a **conversation** between the narrator and his wife in which the narrator tells her about the police officer's adopting the dog. Use details from the story, as well as your own creative ideas, to invent an interesting dialogue.

Research and Technology With a partner, use the Internet and other reference materials to find more information about veterinary medicine. Then, work independently to write a **response** to the following statement: *Veterinarians do important but challenging work.* Use details from your research to support your response.

Build Language Skills

The Drive-In Movies • The Market Square Dog

Vocabulary Skill

Word Roots The word *support* contains the **Latin root** *-port-*, which means "to carry or bear." Knowing the meaning of the root helps you to understand and remember that *support* "holds something up." When you support an idea, you hold it up with details that show why the idea is valid.

➤ **Example:** Facts and statistics **support** my argument.

Practice Use each of the following phrases in a sentence.

1. support for a prior opinion
2. an example that supports
3. a letter of support
4. support for the wobbly table

Grammar Lesson

Singular and Plural Nouns **Singular nouns** refer to one person, place, or thing. **Plural nouns** refer to more than one. The **plural** form of most nouns is formed by adding the letter *-s* or the letters *-es* to the end of the word. Other nouns form their plurals differently.

➤ **Singular Nouns:** bell, canyon, tax, woman, mouse, strategy
➤ **Plural Nouns:** bells, canyons, taxes, women, mice, strategies

Practice Identify whether each word is singular or plural. Then, use each word in a sentence.

1. approaches
2. consequence
3. causes
4. strategies
5. prediction

MorePractice

For more practice with nouns, see the Grammar Handbook, p. R32.

W͗G Prentice Hall Writing and Grammar Connection: Chapter 29, Section 4.

Reading: Make Predictions

Directions: *Read the selection. Then, answer the questions.*

Juan and his brother Manny were busy getting ready for Julia's surprise party. Juan got a thick roll of paper and spread it out on the kitchen floor. Juan printed *happy graduation* carefully. Then, Manny looked at the clock. "We need to hurry!" he said. "Julia will be here in a half an hour. The guests will be here in ten minutes." The boys looked around in horror—the kitchen was a mess!

1. What will the boys probably do next?
   - A eat the cookies
   - B clean the kitchen
   - C call Julia
   - D sit and wait for the guests

2. What do you predict Juan will do with the sign?
   - A spend time adding more details
   - B start over
   - C throw it away
   - D quickly hang it up

3. Which prediction is most logical based on the passage?
   - A The guests will arrive before the boys are ready.
   - B Julia will be early.
   - C The boys will cancel the party.
   - D No one will come to the party.

4. Which detail would change a prediction about whether the boys will be ready for the party?
   - A It starts to rain.
   - B Juan's cousin arrives to help.
   - C Julia calls from the store.
   - D One of the guests cancels.

Timed Writing: Explanation

Review "The Drive-In Movies" or "The Market Square Dog." Write a brief explanation to show how the story was affected by the author's choice of narrator. As you write, identify story details that only the narrator could have known. Explain how the story would have been different without these details. **(20 minutes)**

 ## Writing Workshop: *Work in Progress*

Descriptive Essay

On the left side of your Place List, list the five senses. Next to each one of the senses, write a sentence describing the place, how it smells, how it looks, whether it is cold or warm, and so on. Put this work in your writing portfolio.

Reading Informational Materials

Web Sites

In Part 1, you are learning how to make predictions while reading literature. Making predictions is also important when you are using Web sites. When you need to find specific information fast, predicting which buttons or tools to use will help you to search more quickly. If you read "Stray," you will see that the Web site featured here could help Doris learn about pet care.

About Web Sites

Web sites are specific locations on the Internet. Each Web site has an address, or Universal Resource Locator (URL). The ending of a URL gives information about who maintains the site:

- **.edu**—site is maintained by an educational institution
- **.gov**—site is maintained by a government agency
- **.org**—site is maintained by a nonprofit organization
- **.com**—site is maintained by a commercial organization

A Web site can have many Web pages. You can move from one page to another by clicking your mouse on a *link.*

As you use Web sites, keep in mind that not all the information you find will be accurate, or correct. For this reason, make sure that your research comes from reliable sources.

Reading Skill

You can **use the text structure,** or special features, of Web sites to move quickly around a site and find the information you need. The chart shows some of the features that will help you find your way around a Web site.

Web Site Features	
Link	A connection to another spot on the same Web page or to a different Web page or Web site. A link can be underlined or highlighted text, an image, or a photograph. Links are what make the Web a "web."
Icon	An image or small drawing that may appear by itself or with text. Icons are often links as well.
Graphics	Pictures, maps, tables, and other graphic sources often featured on a Web site. These graphics often provide information, but they may also be links to other Web pages.

This is the home page for **www.animaland.org**, a starting point that will lead you to further information on other pages within the site or on related sites.

Each of these eight buttons leads to more information on a topic. By clicking on the button, you will open up a new page of the Web site.

http://www.animaland.org

pet care | animal encyclopedia | bookworms | ask azula | career center | real issues | humane education | games | legal info

Another way to navigate a Web site is to click on an underlined item, or link. Like buttons, links take you to specific types of information.

Reading Informational Materials

This page appears when you click on the button labeled "Pet Care Guide" and then click on "Dog."

These buttons are the same as the ones found on the Web site's home page. At any time, you can click on a button to go to a different Web page.

http://www.animaland.org/framesets/petcare_frameset.asp

ANIMAL ENCYCLOPEDIA   ASK AZULA   REAL ISSUES   GAMES & CARTOONS

BOOKWORMS   CAREER CENTER   HUMANE EDUCATION

PET CARE GUIDE

 Dog

 Cat

 Bird

 Rabbit

 Fish

 Gerbil

 Hamster

 Guinea Pig

Dog

The 411

Scientific name: Canis familiaris

Size: XS, S, M, L, XL!! Dogs range in size from tiny four-pound tea cup poodles to Irish wolfhounds, the tallest dogs at almost three feet high.

Lifespan: As a rule, smaller dogs tend to live longer than larger ones. A compact chihuahua can live to be 16, while giant breeds like bull mastiffs usually live to be about eight years old. And somewhere in the middle, the average, All-American mixed breed pooch has a lifespan of about 12 to 14 years.

Colors/varieties: There are more than 400 different breeds of dogs--spotted dalmatians, shiny black Labrador retrievers, brindle-coated boxers...to name just a few! But the most popular pooches of all are non-pedigree--that includes shaggy dogs, dogs with hairy ears, dogs with all-white socks dogs with fluffy tails and everything

more>>

CARE GUIDE

The 411

Chow Time!

Home, Sweet Home

Fun & Games

 Cartoon! Cleaning up after your dog.

 **Cartoon! Teaching your dog to sit.**

Print This Info

INFO TO GO >>>

YO, READ THIS!
Is your pet bright-eyed and alert? Are his ears clean and not stinky? Is he limping or bleeding? If your dog has refused food for more than a day, has been throwing up a lot or seems sick, consult your veterinarian for advice ASAP.

This is a list of links that connect to the different animals that are discussed in the Web site's "Pet Care Guide."

These links will lead to additional information on dogs, informative cartoons, and a printer-friendly version of the Web page.

Reading: Analyze Text Structure

Directions: *Choose the letter of the best answer to each question.*

1. What is the first page you see when you open this Web site?

   A the pet care guide

   B a brief history of the ASPCA

   C the home page, which has buttons and a list

   D the home page, which provides links to other Web sites

2. What page would most likely open if you clicked on the home page button labeled "Career Center"?

   A a page explaining how to take care of your pet

   B a page featuring games and cartoons

   C a page giving information about jobs related to animal care

   D a page giving important information about pet diseases

3. If you are on the pet care page for "Dog," what should you do to get more information?

   A go back to the home page and click on the doghouse

   B go to the top of the "Dog" page and click on "Humane Education"

   C go to the last line of the text and click on "more"

   D go to the left-hand list and click on "Gerbil"

Reading: Comprehension and Interpretation

Directions: *Write your answers on a separate sheet of paper.*

4. Why should you evaluate sources of information on the Internet?

5. The ASPCA is a national organization that rescues homeless animals and encourages people to adopt them. In your opinion, would the ASPCA Web site be a more reliable source of information on animal care than the Web site of a pet store? Explain.

Timed Writing: Explanation [Organizing]

Review what you have learned about using a Web site. Then, write a letter to a friend in which you summarize the features of www.animaland.org and explain how to find information about cat care. **(20 minutes)**

Fiction and Nonfiction

Fiction is writing that tells about imaginary people, animals, and events. Examples of fiction include short stories and folk tales. **Nonfiction** is writing that tells about real people, animals, places, events, and ideas. Examples of nonfiction include biographies and newspaper articles.

- A work of **fiction** contains one or more made-up elements, such as an animal that drives a car or a city under the ocean. Some writers base their fiction on actual events and people, adding invented characters, settings, or plots. If a piece of writing contains just one made-up element, the entire work is fiction.
- In a work of **nonfiction**, everything must be true. For example, animals must look and act like real animals, and all settings must exist in the real world.

Comparing Fiction and Nonfiction

The selections that follow were each inspired by the fact that some monkeys live in trees. "Why Monkeys Live in Trees" is fiction, and "The Case of the Monkeys That Fell From the Trees" is nonfiction. As you read each work, use a graphic organizer like the one shown to compare and contrast the way the monkeys in each selection are presented. An example has been provided for you.

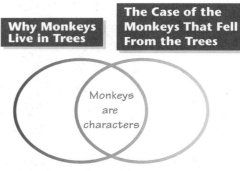

Vocabulary Builder

Why Monkeys Live in Trees

- **reflection** (ri flek´ shən) *n.* an image of one's self, as seen in a mirror (p. 68) *I saw a reflection of my face in the windowpane.*
- **regally** (rē´ gə lē) *adv.* in a stately manner, like a king or queen (p. 69) *The queen waved regally at the crowd.*
- **bellowed** (bel´ ōd) *v.* cried out in a low, loud voice (p. 69) *"Oh, no!" he bellowed. "My wallet is missing!"*

The Case of the Monkeys That Fell From the Trees

- **incidents** (in´ sə dənts´) *n.* events; occurrences (p. 72) *We had four incidents of forest fire near our house.*
- **abruptly** (ə brupt´ lē) *adv.* suddenly, without warning (p. 72) *The bus stopped so abruptly, I fell off my seat.*
- **distress** (di stres´) *n.* serious pain or sadness (p. 73) *She cried out in distress.*

Build Understanding

Connecting to the Literature

Reading/Writing Connection Jot down what you already know about monkeys—where they live, what they eat, and what special abilities they have. Use at least three of the following words: *reside, survive, demonstrate, select.* As you read, compare and contrast your notes with the new information the authors provide.

Meet the Authors

Julius **Lester** (b. 1939)

As a teenager, Julius Lester knew exactly what he wanted to be: a musician. "I was not a good writer," he recalls, "and I never dreamed I'd become an award-winning author."

Music, Civil Rights, and Writing After graduating from college, Lester had a successful musical career. He also became active in the civil rights movement and wrote books inspired by his African American heritage. The success of these books, which he wrote for adults, led him to write fifteen children's books.

Susan E. **Quinlan** (b. 1954)

Susan E. Quinlan and her husband, Bud Lehnhausen, have worked together for more than twenty-five years, conducting wildlife research and teaching natural history courses.

The Subject Is Nature Quinlan's work is inspired by her love of wildlife. "I write about nature and the work of scientists because I want to share my fascination in these topics with young readers. I hope that learning about some of the questions scientists ask, the techniques they use to seek answers, and their often surprising discoveries will encourage kids to be curious, ask questions, and learn more about nature and science," she says.

Go **Online**
Author Link

For: More about the authors
Visit: www.PHSchool.com
Web Code: ele-9106

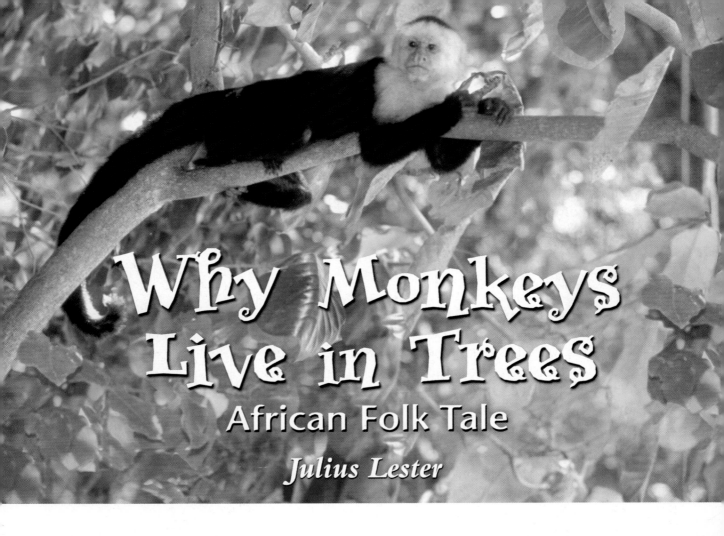

Why Monkeys Live in Trees

African Folk Tale

Julius Lester

One day Leopard was looking at his reflection in a pool of water. Looking at himself was Leopard's favorite thing in the world to do. Leopard gazed, wanting to be sure that every hair was straight and that all his spots were where they were supposed to be. This took many hours of looking at his <u>reflection</u>, which Leopard did not mind at all.

Finally he was satisfied that nothing was disturbing his handsomeness, and he turned away from the pool of water. At that exact moment, one of Leopard's children ran up to him.

"Daddy! Daddy! Are you going to be in the contest?"

"What contest?" Leopard wanted to know. If it was a beauty contest, of course he was going to be in it.

"I don't know. Crow the Messenger just flew by. She said that King Gorilla said there was going to be a contest."

▲ Critical Viewing
Based on the details here, why might a writer use monkeys in a tale meant to entertain? **[Analyze]**

Vocabulary Builder
reflection (ri flek´ shən) *n.* an image of one's self, as seen in a mirror

Without another word, Leopard set off. He went north-by-northeast, made a right turn at the mulberry bush and traveled east-by-south-by-west until he came to a hole in the ground. He went around in a circle five times, and headed north-by-somersault until he came to a big clearing in the middle of the jungle and that's where King Gorilla was.

King Gorilla sat at one end of the clearing on his throne. Opposite him, at the other side of the clearing, all the animals sat in a semicircle. In the middle, between King Gorilla and the animals, was a huge mound of what looked like black dust.

Leopard looked around with calm dignity. Then he strode regally over to his friend, Lion.

"What's that?" he asked, pointing to the mound of black dust.

"Don't know," Lion replied. "King Gorilla said he will give a pot of gold to whoever can eat it in one day. I can eat it in an hour."

Leopard laughed. "I'll eat it in a half hour."

It was Hippopotamus's turn to laugh. "As big as my mouth is, I'll eat that mound in one gulp."

The time came for the contest. King Gorilla had the animals pick numbers to see who would go in what order. To everybody's dismay, Hippopotamus drew Number 1.

Hippopotamus walked over to the mound of black dust. It was bigger than he had thought. It was much too big to eat in one gulp. Nonetheless, Hippopotamus opened his mouth as wide as he could, and that was very wide indeed, and took a mouthful of the black dust.

He started chewing. Suddenly he leaped straight into the air and screamed. He screamed so loudly that it knocked the ears off the chickens and that's why to this day chickens don't have ears.

Hippopotamus screamed and Hippopotamus yelled. Hippopotamus roared and Hippopotamus bellowed. Then he started sneezing and crying and tears rolled down his face like he was standing in the shower. Hippopotamus ran to the river and drank as much water as he could, and that was very much, indeed, to cool his mouth and tongue and throat.

Literary Analysis
Fiction and Nonfiction What details here show that this is a work of fiction?

Vocabulary Builder
regally (rē´ gə lē) *adv.* in a stately manner, like a king or queen

Vocabulary Builder
bellowed (bel´ ōd) *v.* cried out in a low, loud voice

Reading Check

What is Leopard's favorite pastime?

The animals didn't understand what had happened to Hippopotamus, but they didn't care. They were happy because they still had a chance to win the pot of gold. Of course, if they had known that the mound of black dust was really a mound of black pepper, maybe they wouldn't have wanted the gold.

Nobody was more happy than Leopard because he had drawn Number 2. He walked up to the black mound and sniffed at it.

"AAAAAAAACHOOOOOOO!" Leopard didn't like that but then he remembered the pot of gold. He opened his mouth wide, took a mouthful and started chewing and swallowing.

Leopard leaped straight into the air, did a back double flip and screamed. He yelled and he roared and he bellowed and, finally, he started sneezing and crying, tears rolling down his face like a waterfall. Leopard ran to the river and washed out his mouth and throat and tongue.

Lion was next, and the same thing happened to him as it did to all the animals. Finally only Monkey remained.

Monkey approached King Gorilla. "I know I can eat all of whatever that is, but after each mouthful, I'll need to lie down in the tall grasses and rest."

King Gorilla said that was okay.

Monkey went to the mound, took a tiny bit of pepper on his tongue, swallowed, and went into the tall grasses. A few minutes later, Monkey came out, took a little more, swallowed it, and went into the tall grasses.

Soon the pile was almost gone. The animals were astonished to see Monkey doing what they had not been able to do. Leopard couldn't believe it either. He climbed a tree and stretched out on a sturdy limb to get a better view. From his limb high in the tree Leopard could see into the tall grasses where Monkey went to rest. Wait a minute! Leopard thought something was suddenly wrong with his eyes because he thought he saw a hundred monkeys hiding in the tall grasses.

▲ Critical Viewing Based on this photograph, what human characteristics does this monkey seem to have? [Connect]

He rubbed his eyes and looked another look. There wasn't anything wrong with his eyes. There were a hundred monkeys in the tall grasses and they all looked alike!

Just then, there was the sound of loud applause. King Gorilla announced that Monkey had won the contest and the pot of gold.

Leopard growled a growl so scary that even King Gorilla was frightened. Leopard wasn't thinking about anybody except the monkeys. He took a long and beautiful leap from the tree right smack into the middle of the tall grasses where the monkeys were hiding.

The monkeys ran in all directions. When the other animals saw monkeys running from the grasses, they realized that the monkeys had tricked them and started chasing them. Even King Gorilla joined in the chase. He wanted his gold back.

The only way the monkeys could escape was to climb to the very tops of the tallest trees where no one else, not even Leopard, could climb.

And that's why monkeys live in trees to this very day.

Literary Analysis
Fiction and Nonfiction Identify a detail in this passage that is realistic, even though the story is fiction.

Thinking About the Selection

1. **Respond:** Which character or characters in this story do you find most entertaining? Explain.

2. **(a) Recall:** What must the animals do in the contest?
   (b) Infer: Why do the animals think it will be easy to win the contest? **(c) Support:** Explain why the contest proves to be more difficult than the animals thought.

3. **(a) Recall:** What does the monkey say he has to do between bites of pepper? **(b) Connect:** What does Leopard see in the tall grass? **(c) Deduce:** Why is the monkey able to eat all the pepper?

4. **(a) Summarize:** What two facts of nature does this tale pretend to explain? **(b) Respond:** Which of these two "explanations" do you feel is funnier? Explain.

5. **(a) Assess:** Is King Gorilla's contest a fair one? Explain.
   (b) Make a Judgment: Do the monkeys deserve to win? Why or why not?

The Case of the Monkeys That Fell From the Trees

Susan E. Quinlan

When the <u>incidents</u> began in August 1972, biologist Ken Glander and his wife, Molly, had been studying the eating habits of a troop of howling monkeys in northwestern Costa Rica for nearly three months. Then, over a two-week period, seven monkeys from various troops in the area fell out of trees and died. Another fell but climbed back up.

One morning the Glanders watched a female howling monkey with a ten-day-old baby turn in tight circles on a tree branch. <u>Abruptly</u>, she fell off the branch. For a moment she hung upside down, suspended by her long

Vocabulary Builder

incidents (in´sə dənts´) *n.* events; occurrences

abruptly (ə brupt´ lē) *adv.* suddenly, without warning

tail. Then her grip failed and she plunged thirty-five feet to the forest floor. Dazed but still alive, she climbed back up, carrying her clinging infant. She stopped on a thick branch and sat there without eating for the next twenty-four hours.

Normally, howling monkeys are skilled, nimble climbers. They often leap ten feet or more between tree limbs, and they almost never fall. Why were monkeys suddenly falling from trees?

Glander wondered if a disease or parasite[1] might be involved. He asked scientists in the microbiology department at the University of Costa Rica to examine some of the dead monkeys and look for clues. The scientists found no signs of disease or parasites. Nor had the monkeys starved. All had died in apparently healthy condition. Glander began to think they had been poisoned. But who or what would poison wild monkeys? Glander had several green, leafy suspects in mind, all of them tropical forest trees.

Many tropical trees have similar-looking leaves and trunks, so it is difficult to determine their species.[2] But tropical plant expert Paul Opler had identified all the trees in the Glanders' study area. Several poisonous species were present. Suspiciously, some of the monkeys that fell had been feeding in trees known to have poisonous leaves. Yet Glander knew this proved nothing.

All plants produce chemicals called secondary compounds, many of which are poisonous. Plants make these chemicals for a variety of purposes. Some ward off plant-eating animals, especially insects. But howling monkeys eat nothing except plants, so they could not survive unless they were able to digest or tolerate plant poisons. Other scientists had observed howlers eating leaves from many kinds of trees, including poisonous species, without any signs of <u>distress</u>. As a result, most scientists assumed that howling monkeys had an unlimited food supply in their lush tropical forest homes. Glander wasn't so sure.

Literary Analysis
Fiction and Nonfiction What factual problem are the scientists trying to solve?

Vocabulary Builder
distress (di stres´) *n.* serious pain or sadness

Reading Check

What do the scientists rule out as causes of the monkeys' strange behavior?

---

1. parasite (par´ə sīt) plant, animal, or insect that lives on or in another living thing, called "the host." The parasite gets its food from the blood or tissue of the host.
2. species (spē´ sēz) group of plants or animals, scientifically classified because of similar traits.

The monkeys that fell from the trees strengthened his belief that howling monkeys could not eat leaves from just any tree. He suspected that certain trees were monkey killers, but he needed evidence before he could point fingers. He and Molly began collecting the data they needed to make a case.

Their days started around 4 or 5 a.m. That's when the monkeys awoke, often greeting the day with roars and growls. The monkeys soon set off, alternating bouts of feeding with periods of crawling, leaping, and climbing through the treetops. Wherever the monkeys went, the Glanders followed on foot.

At midday, the monkeys settled down. Draping themselves over large branches, their arms and legs dangling, the howlers slept with their tails wrapped around branches to anchor them in place. Late in the day, when the air cooled a few degrees, the monkeys stirred. They climbed and fed until settling down for the night at sunset.

For twelve months, the Glanders endured long days, mosquitoes, heavy rains, and temperatures that sometimes soared over 100°F. They did this in order to make their observations of the monkey troop as continuous as possible. Throughout each day, they recorded how many minutes the monkeys spent sleeping, eating, and moving. They recorded which of 1,699 individually numbered trees the monkeys slept in and ate from, and exactly which parts the monkeys ate—leaves, fruits, flowers, or stems.

Each day, the scientists collected samples of leaves from every tree the monkeys fed in that day, and leaves from nearby trees of the same species. The monkeys had visited these trees but did not feed in them. The Glanders tagged the leaves with wire labels, noting the tree, the date, and the time that the sample was collected. Next, they dried the leaves in an oven, then packed them in zippered plastic bags for later study.

The Glanders soon noticed that the howlers ate new leaves whenever they could, only occasionally eating fruits, flowers, or mature leaves. In certain trees, the monkeys plucked off the leaves, then stripped and tossed away the leaf blades. They ate only the remaining leaf stems. Other scientists thought this messy feeding behavior meant that

> **Critical Viewing** Why do you think this monkey is called a howler monkey? **[Hypothesize]**

Literary Analysis
Fiction and Nonfiction What details here show that this work is nonfiction?

howling monkeys could afford to be wasteful in a forest where food was so abundant. Glander wasn't convinced.

After thousands of hours of field work, including nearly two thousand hours of observing monkeys, Glander reviewed all the records he and Molly had gathered. Their careful data showed that howlers had not eaten leaves from just any trees in the forest. Indeed, the monkeys had rarely eaten leaves from the most common tree species. Instead, they spent most of their feeding time in a few uncommon kinds of trees. All told, the monkeys had eaten from only 331 of the 1,699 trees in the area. More surprisingly, they had spent three-quarters of their feeding time in just 88 trees. The data showed that the monkeys selected only certain tree species for feeding.

Glander discovered something even more surprising. The monkeys had not eaten leaves from all the trees of favored species. Instead, they ate leaves from just a few individual trees of most species. For example, the monkeys traveled through most of the 149 madera negra trees in the area, but they ate mature leaves from only three of these. This pattern fascinated Glander, because the madera negra is one of the most toxic[3] trees in the forest. Its leaves are used to make rat poison.

To learn more, Glander chemically analyzed all the leaves he and Molly had collected from the madera negra trees in the study area during their field studies. The results were startling. The three individual trees from which the monkeys had eaten mature leaves showed no traces of poison alkaloids.[4] But leaves collected from the other madera negras were packed with these poisons. Somehow, the monkeys had picked out those very few trees whose leaves were not poisonous.

Chemical analyses of mature leaves from other kinds of trees revealed a similar pattern. The howling monkeys had consistently selected the most nutritious, most digestible, and least poisonous leaves available in their patch of forest. Glander noted that howlers ate only the leaf stems in some trees because the stems contained fewer poisons than the

Literary Analysis
Fiction and Nonfiction How do the Glanders find answers to their questions?

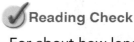
Reading Check

For about how long did the Glanders observe the monkeys?

---

3. **toxic** (täk′ sik) poisonous.
4. **alkaloids** (al′ kə loidz) group of chemical substances, some poisonous, found in plants.

leaves. His data showed that instead of being sloppy eaters awash in a sea of food, howling monkeys are cautious, picky eaters in a forest filled with poisons.

But the mystery of the monkeys that fell from the trees was not solved. If howling monkeys can identify and avoid the most toxic leaves, why would they ever become poisoned and fall? Glander uncovered more clues by studying plants and their poisons.

Literature in Context   Science Connection

Living Layers

Tropical rainforests cover seven percent of Earth's surface yet are home to fifty percent of the world's species. In the rainforest, the trees form distinct layers. Each layer is like a unique habitat. The chart shows the different species that live in each layer.

Colobus ▶ Monkey

▲ Macaw

◀ Butterfly

Tree ▶ Frog

◀ Toucan

Tarantula ▶

The **emergent** layer contains giant trees, some reaching as high as 200 feet.

The thick and leafy branches of the **canopy** layer block the sun and encourage the breeze.

Leafy bushes and the tops of small trees make up the first layer of the forest, called the **understory**. Nocturnal red-eyed tree frogs hide here during the day.

A carpet of dead leaves covers the **forest floor**.

Connect to the Literature How would an understanding of the layers help the biologists?

The concentration of poison is not uniform among those plants that produce poisonous secondary compounds. The kinds and amounts of poison present vary widely among plant species, among individual plants of a single species, and even within the parts of a single plant. In fact, individual plants make varying amounts of poisons at different times of year and under different growing conditions. Some plants produce more poisons after their leaves or twigs are eaten by plant-eating animals. These same plants make fewer poisons if they are not damaged by plant-eaters. Due to these constant changes, Glander realized that monkeys could not simply learn which trees had poisonous leaves and which had edible ones. Their task was far more complicated. How did the monkeys do it?

Again, Glander found an answer in his field records. Howlers had fed in 331 of the trees in the study area, but they made only one stop in 104 of these trees. In each case, a solitary adult monkey visited the tree briefly, ate just a little bit, and then moved on. Glander thinks these monkeys were "sampling" the leaves for poisons. If the plant parts were toxic, they probably tasted bad or made the monkey who sampled them feel slightly ill. He suspects that each monkey troop finds out which trees currently have the least poisonous leaves by regularly and carefully sampling from trees throughout the area. By using this technique, the monkeys would avoid eating too many of the most toxic plant poisons.

Considering the ever-changing toxicity of the leaves in a forest, however, Glander reasoned that individual monkeys may sometimes make mistakes. They may eat too many of the wrong leaves. More importantly, when edible leaves are scarce due to unusual conditions, monkeys may be forced to eat leaves they wouldn't otherwise choose. Glander first saw monkeys falling from trees during a severe drought[5] year, when the howlers' food choices were quite limited. Because some poisons produced by tropical plants affect animal muscles and nerves, eating the wrong leaves could certainly cause illness, dizziness, and deadly falls.

---

5. **drought** (drout) period of little or no rain.

Literary Analysis
Fiction and Nonfiction Which details in this paragraph are not often included in works of fiction?

Reading Check

According to Glander, how do the monkeys know which leaves are poisonous?

Today, after more than thirty years of studying monkeys, Ken Glander is convinced that the falling monkeys he and Molly observed were poisoned by eating leaves from the wrong trees at the wrong time. His work shows that a tropical forest is like a pantry filled with a mixture of foods and poisons. Only the most selective eaters can avoid the poisons and find enough edible food to survive.

However, the monkeys' poison-filled pantry has a silver lining. Poison chemicals used in small amounts often have medicinal value. Many human medicines contain plant poisons, including aspirin, quinine, atropine, morphine, digitoxin (a heart medicine), and cancer-fighting vincristine and paclitaxel. In fact, an estimated one-fourth of all medicines prescribed in the United States today come from plants.

Glander and other researchers have gathered some evidence that howlers and other monkeys sometimes select poisonous leaves for medicinal purposes, such as ridding themselves of parasites. Glander thinks scientists searching for new medicines for people might get some useful tips from howlers. The monkeys' behavior might help scientists select those plants most worth sampling.

Literary Analysis
Fiction and Nonfiction Is it a fact that monkeys eat leaves for medicinal purposes? Explain.

Thinking About the Selection

1. **(a) Recall:** What mystery do the scientists try to solve?
   (b) Cause and Effect: Why does Glander suspect the monkeys have been poisoned? **(c) Connect:** What eating habits of the monkeys are most puzzling? Why?

2. **(a) Recall:** Why is Glander fascinated that the monkeys eat madera negra leaves? **(b) Cause and Effect:** What evidence indicates that the monkeys he studies are "cautious, picky eaters"?

3. **(a) Recall:** What do the Glanders conclude about why some monkeys died, but others did not?
   (b) Cause and Effect: What makes Glander think that howler monkeys may provide useful tips to scientists?

Apply the Skills

Why Monkeys Live in Trees • The Case of the Monkeys That Fell From the Trees

Comparing Fiction and Nonfiction

1. **(a)** In a chart like the one shown, explain how three specific details in "Why Monkeys Live in Trees" prove that the selection is **fiction.** One detail is given as an example.

Detail	Why It Is Fiction
Leopard uses his reflection to see how he looks.	Real animals do not check their appearance.

(b) Next, create a new chart to explain how three specific details in "The Case of the Monkeys That Fell From the Trees" prove that the selection is **nonfiction.**

2. Use an example from each work to support the following:
   • A fictional story may contain details that seem realistic and true to real life.
   • A nonfiction selection may contain surprising facts.

Writing to Compare Literary Works

Write a paragraph comparing and contrasting the monkeys in these two selections. Use these questions to get started:
   • What can the monkeys in "Why Monkeys Live in Trees" do that real monkeys cannot do?
   • What real-life things do the monkeys in "The Case of the Monkeys That Fell From the Trees" do?
   • How are the monkeys in both selections alike? How are they different?

Vocabulary Builder

Practice For each item, write a sentence that uses the word pair correctly.

1. abruptly; shock
2. distress; earthquake
3. incidents; traffic
4. bellowed; umpire
5. regally; model
6. reflection; mirror

QuickReview

Fiction: writing that tells about events and characters from the writer's imagination

Nonfiction: writing that deals with real people, events, and ideas

Go Online
Assessment
For: Self-test
Visit: www.PHSchool.com
Web Code: ela-6107

Predicting

Directions: *Read the selection. Then, answer the questions.*

Karl and his sister Laurie were excited. Mom had finally agreed to let them get a puppy. She had waited until now because she was worried that a dog might trigger Karl's allergies. However, Karl and Laurie wanted a dog so much that Mom finally gave in.

Karl and Laurie decided to read about different kinds of dogs. Karl wanted to get a really big dog that didn't shed. Laurie didn't care about size—she just wanted a playful dog. Mom had a good suggestion, too. She hoped that Karl and Laurie would decide to adopt a dog from a shelter rather than buy a puppy at a pet store. She helped them find the Web site for the local shelter.

1. **What prior knowledge could help you predict the type of dog Karl and Laurie will get?**
   A knowing what kinds of dogs do not shed
   B knowing what dogs eat
   C knowing how much exercise dogs need
   D knowing what kinds of dogs bark a lot

2. **Which of the following is most likely?**
   A Karl and Laurie will decide to buy a dog that will upset Karl's allergies.
   B Karl and Laurie will adopt a dog from the shelter.
   C Laurie will persuade Karl to get a very large dog.
   D Karl and Laurie will decide to wait until their neighbor's dog has puppies.

3. **Which clue from the story supports the prediction that Karl and Laurie will get a dog that does not shed?**
   A Laurie wants a playful dog.
   B Karl has allergies.
   C Mom wants to go to the animal shelter.
   D Karl wants a big dog.

4. **What might cause you to revise your prediction?**
   A details about the size of the dog
   B prior knowledge about dogs that bark
   C new information about Karl's allergies
   D new information about the shelter Web site

5. **Which sentence would verify your prediction?**
   A Karl and Laurie researched dogs.
   B They found several types that do not shed.
   C They chose that type of dog when they went to the shelter.
   D The dog was very playful.

Assessment Practice

Vocabulary

Directions: *Choose the sentence that uses the underlined word **incorrectly**.*

6. **A** Can you <u>verify</u> that Thomas Jefferson was born in Virginia?
   B I will <u>verify</u> the meaning of the word.
   C He will <u>verify</u> his position by making the audience laugh.
   D We can <u>verify</u> the time by finding a schedule.

7. **A** The announcement was made <u>prior</u> to the arrival of the train.
   B You should edit your paper <u>prior</u> to turning it in.
   C Our <u>prior</u> appointment prevented us from making plans.
   D We learned <u>prior</u> information the next day.

8. **A** We were asked to <u>support</u> our school.
   B Find <u>support</u> for your answer.
   C <u>Support</u> demonstrates the difference in their situation.
   D <u>Support</u> the points in your thesis.

9. **A** It is necessary to <u>revise</u> your essay.
   B We have to <u>revise</u> it before handing it in.
   C <u>Revise</u> the essay for grammar and mechanics.
   D Demonstrate good <u>revise</u> skills on your essay.

10. **A** It helps to <u>predict</u> what will be on the test.
    B We <u>predict</u> that we will pass the test.
    C <u>Predict</u> is a skill that we learn and must practice.
    D Please <u>predict</u> what will happen next in the story.

Directions: *Choose the most likely meaning for each word.*

11. **portable**
    A large
    B inexpensive
    C easily broken
    D easily carried

12. **verify**
    A to tell something to someone
    B to make sure something is true
    C to find clues
    D to disprove

13. **verity**
    A happiness
    B pride
    C courage
    D truth

14. **porter**
    A a person who drives a taxi for pay
    B a person who carries luggage for pay
    C a person who rewrites stories for pay
    D a person who does research for pay

Description: Descriptive Essay

Descriptive writing creates a word picture by helping readers imagine the way something looks, feels, smells, tastes, or sounds. Follow the steps in this workshop to write a descriptive essay.

Assignment Write a descriptive essay about a place you know well, such as your grandparents' house or a park.

What to Include Your descriptive essay should feature the following elements:
- a main impression of the setting, supported by details that add specific information
- rich sensory details that appeal to the five senses
- an organization that helps readers picture the setting
- language that creates vivid images and comparisons
- error-free writing, including correct use of pronouns

To preview the criteria on which your descriptive essay may be judged, see the rubric on page 86.

Prewriting

Choosing Your Topic

Trigger Words Use trigger words to help you think of a place to describe. Think of three general words, such as *vacation, memories,* and *family*. Jot down specific places that you associate with each general word. Then, review what you have written, and choose the most interesting place.

Gathering Details

Use a sensory details chart to help you gather details about the sights, scents, textures, sounds, and tastes associated with your setting. This model shows details related to a campsite.

Sights	Scents	Textures	Sounds	Tastes
tall pine trees	spicy pines	crunchy pine	hoot of owls	(none)
campfire flames	fire smoke	needles underfoot	snap of logs burning	

Using the Form
You use elements of description in these writing types:
- letters
- short stories
- autobiographical essays
- advertisements

Work in Progress
Review the work you did on pages 13, 17, 41, and 61.

Drafting

Shaping Your Writing

Organize the details. Before you write, arrange the details in an order that will help the reader picture the setting. Arrange important elements in spatial order—left to right, front to back, or outward from the most important feature. For example, one writer used this diagram to organize the details about the campsite spatially.

Behind:
deep, dark forest; snow-covered mountains

Left:
tent; trees

Central detail:
blazing campfire

Right:
river; trees

Use figurative language. Figurative language is writing that is not meant to be taken literally. Use figurative language, such as similes and metaphors, to create vivid images and comparisons.

- **Simile:** a comparison using *like* or *as.* For example, "The campfire smoke was as thick as a curtain."

- **Metaphor:** a comparison in which one thing is referred to as if it were another. For example, "A curtain of smoke hung over us."

Revising

Revising Your Sentences

Vary sentence length. Make sure your writing does not repeat the same sentence structure over and over. Combine some sentences, or, to emphasize unusual or unique details, break a series of long sentences into shorter ones.

Reading **Writing** *Connection*

To read the complete student model, see page 85.

Student Model: Varying Sentence Length

Though there is so much darkness, ~~there is a small light.~~

~~It is a~~ streetlight. ~~It is~~ (tall) ~~and~~ shows off a silvery glow.

> The writer combined several short, choppy sentences to create one longer sentence.

Integrating Grammar Skills

Revising for Errors With Possessive Nouns

Possessive nouns are used to show ownership. Most errors occur when apostrophes are left out or placed incorrectly.

Identifying Errors in Possessive Nouns To form the possessive form of most singular nouns, add an apostrophe and an *s*.

➤ **Examples: Mary's** coat; the **boss's** desk

Most plural nouns end in -*s*. To form the possessive form of most plural nouns, simply add an apostrophe.

➤ **Examples:** the **Smiths'** car; the **girls'** basketball team

Some plural nouns do not end in -*s*. To make the possessive form of these nouns, add an apostrophe and an -*s*.

➤ **Examples:** the **children's** toys; the **women's** book club

Prentice Hall Writing and Grammar Connection: Chapter 26, Section 5

Type of Noun	Rule for Forming Possessive	Correct Possessive Form
singular noun	Add apostrophe -*s*.	*cat's* dish
singular noun ending in -*s*	Add apostrophe -*s*.	*dress's* hem
plural noun ending in -*s*	Add apostrophe.	*boys'* desks
plural noun that does not end in -*s*	Add apostrophe -*s*.	*mice's* nest

Fixing Errors To fix errors related to possessive nouns, follow these steps:

1. **Identify each noun that shows ownership.**
2. **Decide whether the noun is singular or plural.**
3. **Follow the rules for making possessive nouns to fix any errors.**

Apply It to Your Editing

Reread your essay and circle any possessive nouns that you find. Use the rules and examples to make the necessary corrections.

Student Model: Hailley White
Somerset, KY

The Night Life

As I sit here on my cold damp patio in early fall, I look at the dark sky. I see the beautiful bright stars as they twinkle. I am always in awe as I look up there, and my heart sometimes skips a beat. In such a vast sky, the expanse of it all makes me feel as though I am as small as a tiny ant. Also in the darkness is the moon, the big hunk of cheese. The man in the moon is clearly visible. He is smiling down on all of us, watching our every move.

While staring up, I feel a tug at my pant leg. It is my little chunky dog, Bridget. Her tail starts to wag as I scratch behind her ears. She is a good dog—that is a fact. I hear her barking sometimes when I am sleeping, probably at some cat. Bridget is my guard dog, but I wish I could make more time to spend with her.

I love the sounds of nature at nighttime. The sound of crickets rubbing their little legs together makes the most lovely noise. Then there is the big hoot owl in some distant tree, hooting a lonesome tune. Off in the distance there is the big bullfrog. All of these wonderful sounds are like a luring lullaby that could rock me to sleep.

There are small, medium, and large trees out in the wild. Each one makes the blackness a little more scary. Though there is so much darkness, a tall street light shows off a silvery glow. This is helpful for people who are coming home from a late night shift.

The air smells like freshly cut grass. In the dim light, the grass looks like asphalt, it is so black. When I take a step, it is really damp from the fallen dew, and the wetness gives everything a shimmery look. There is also the smell of decaying leaves. They make a crunching noise underneath my feet. I feel so free just running around my backyard barefoot in the dark. The leaves and the dew feel absolutely refreshing. You should really try it sometime.

House after house surrounds me. One has its lights on, showing that someone is still awake. The other houses' lights are completely out, and everyone is probably snug in their beds. I can see red blinking lights over the hills and valleys. They must be towers for cell phones, so people can communicate—even in the dark.

The sounds are not the same as they are in the daylight. It is really amazing that the world can be so quiet for a few hours. The sounds of nature are really peaceful to me. There is a slight breeze blowing, but that is okay. I wish that I could stand here forever, staring up at the total darkness, except for the light of a few stars.

In the first sentence, Hailley presents the setting she will describe.

The writer creates a vivid image with a simile that compares night sounds to a lullaby.

Hailley brings her setting to life by using images that appeal to smell, sight, touch, and sound.

By organizing her essay to focus on sensory images that surround her, the writer makes readers feel like they are in the setting she describes.

Editing and Proofreading

Check your essay for errors in grammar, spelling, and punctuation. **Focus on Comparative and Superlative Adjectives:** Be sure that you have used adjectives correctly.

- *Comparative adjectives compare two things:* The pine tree is <u>taller</u> than the oak tree. A sunset is <u>more beautiful</u> than a sunrise.

- *Superlative adjectives compare three or more things:* That pine tree is the <u>tallest</u> tree in the forest. This sunset is the <u>most beautiful</u> one I have ever seen.

Publishing and Presenting

Consider one of the following ways to share your writing:
Record it. Make an audio recording of your description. Ask classmates to imagine the setting as you play the tape.
Mail it. Send your descriptive essay to a friend or relative, either enclosed in a letter or an e-mail message.

Reflecting on Your Writing

Writer's Journal Jot down your thoughts on writing a descriptive essay. Begin by answering these questions:

- How did gathering details of your setting help you to revisit it?

- Which strategy would you use again? Why?

> *Prentice Hall Writing and Grammar Connection: Chapter 6*

Rubric for Self-Assessment

To assess your descriptive essay, use the following rubric:

Criteria	Rating Scale				
	not very				*very*
Focus: How clear is the main impression?	1	2	3	4	5
Organization: How clear is your organization?	1	2	3	4	5
Support/Elaboration: How effectively do you use sensory details in your description?	1	2	3	4	5
Style: How vivid is the language?	1	2	3	4	5
Conventions: How correct is your grammar, especially your use of possessive nouns?	1	2	3	4	5

Skills You Will Learn

Reading Skill: *Recognize Clues That Indicate an Opinion*
Literary Analysis: *Author's Perspective*

Reading Skill: *Use Resources to Check Facts*
Literary Analysis: *Tone*

Reading Skill: *Making Generalizations*

Literary Analysis: *Comparing Use of Symbolism*

Literature You Will Read

Reading and Vocabulary Skills Preview

Reading: Fact and Opinion

> A **fact** is a statement that can be proved. An **opinion** is a person's judgment or belief.

Skills and Strategies You Will Learn in Part 2

In Part 2, you will learn
- to **check facts** by using **reliable sources** (p. 106)
- to **distinguish between facts and opinions** by recognizing **clues that indicate opinions** (p. 90)
- to **make generalizations** based on facts (p. 124)

Using the Skills and Strategies in Part 2

In Part 2, you will learn the difference between a fact and an opinion, which will help you evaluate the statements that writers make. First, you will be able to understand which details are facts. Second, you will be able to recognize an opinion and then decide whether you agree with it.

The Philadelphia Zoo is the oldest zoo in the United States. I believe that it is also the best zoo. While many zoos restrain the animals in cages, the Philadelphia Zoo has created natural habitats where the animals can roam freely. Everyone agrees that this is the right way to organize a zoo.

Sentence	Fact	Opinion	Explanation
The Philadelphia Zoo is the oldest zoo in the United States.	yes	no	This statement can be proved true by checking a reference source.
I believe that it is also the best zoo.	no	yes	The phrase *I believe* and the judgment word *best* signal this is an opinion.

As you read the literature in this part, you will practice distinguishing between facts and opinions.

Academic Vocabulary: Words for Discussing Facts and Opinions

The following words will help you to talk and write about facts and opinions as you read the selections in this part.

Word	Definition	Example Sentence
fact *n.*	a statement that can be proved	A *fact* can be proved.
opinion *n.*	a statement that expresses a person's judgment or belief	In my *opinion*, North Carolina is a good place to live.
claim *n.*	a statement, as a fact	Their *claim* is true.
distinguish *v.*	tell the difference	*Distinguish* fact from opinion.
prove *v.*	show evidence	*Prove* that water contains oxygen and hydrogen.

Vocabulary Skills You Will Learn in Part 2

▶ The **origin** of a word is the word's history.

In Part 2, you will learn
- the word origin for **prove** (p. 122)
- the word origin for **claim** (p. 104)
- the word origin for **distinguish** (p. 104)
- the word origin for **fact** (p. 122)

The English language will never be complete. It continues to grow and change. A dictionary entry usually tells you a word's origin.

opinion comes from Middle English

o•pin•ion (əpin′yən) *n.* [[ME *opinioun* < OFr < L *opinio* <*opinari, to think,* akin to *optare, to select, desire:* see OPTION]] a belief not based on absolute certainty or positive knowledge but on what seems true, valid, or probable in one's own mind; a judgment

Languages that the word has come through are listed from most recent to earliest.

Activity Look up the word origin for each word in the chart in a dictionary. Then, explain how the origin of each word helps you to remember the meaning of the word.

These skills will help you become a better reader.
Practice them with either "Stage Fright" (p. 92) or
"My Papa, Mark Twain" (p. 97).

Reading Skill

Nonfiction works often include an author's opinion as
well as facts. A **fact** is information that can be
proved. An **opinion** is a person's judgment or belief.
To **recognize clues that indicate an opinion,** do this:
- Look for phrases that indicate an opinion, such as
  I believe or *in my opinion.*
- Look for words that indicate a personal judgment, such
  as *wonderful* or *terrible.*
- Be aware of words, such as *always, nobody, worst,* and *all,*
  that might indicate a personal judgment or viewpoint.

Detail:	Detail:

Author's Perspective:

_____
_____
_____
_____
_____

Literary Analysis

An **author's perspective** is the viewpoint from which he or she
writes. This perspective is based on the writer's beliefs and background. The author's perspective reveals his or her own feelings
or personal interest in a subject.

As you read, look for details that reveal the author's perspective. Use a diagram like the one shown.

Vocabulary Builder

Stage Fright

- **sympathy** (sim´pə thē) *n.* shared feeling
  (p. 92) *Nervous himself, Barry has
  sympathy for anyone who fears heights.*

- **compulsion** (kəm pul´shən) *n.* driving
  force (p. 92) *The desire to succeed was his
  compulsion in class.*

- **intently** (in tent´ lē) *adv.* purposefully; earnestly (p. 93) *The dog stared intently at the
  motionless ball.*

- **awed** (ôd) *adj.* filled with feelings of fear
  and wonder (p. 93) *Awed, the tourists
  stared at the canyon.*

My Papa, Mark Twain

- **absentminded** (ab´ sənt mīn´ did) *adj.*
  forgetful (p. 98) *Bob is absentminded and
  often forgets his key.*

- **incessantly** (in ses´ ənt lē) *adv.* constantly;
  continually (p. 98) *The car alarm blared
  incessantly.*

- **consequently** (kän´ si kwent´ lē) *adv.* as a
  result (p. 99) *She trained hard for the race
  and consequently won.*

Background

Stage Fright Many people experience a physical reaction to the stress of performing in public. Under stress, the heart beats faster, blood pressure rises, blood rushes to the muscles and brain, blood sugar increases for extra energy, sweat glands become active, and the mouth gets dry.

Connecting to the Literature

Reading/Writing Connection In "Stage Fright," author Mark Twain writes about the first time he made a speech in public. Make a list of some experiences that might cause stage fright in a person your age. Use at least three of the following words: *ignore, respond, complicate, react.*

Meet the Author | # Mark **Twain** (1835–1910)

Mark Twain was born with a much longer name— Samuel Langhorn Clemens. Growing up along the Mississippi River, in Hannibal, Missouri, Twain became a riverboat pilot at the age of twenty-three. Later, when he became an author, he adopted the pen name Mark Twain. This name comes from slang used by riverboat pilots and means "two fathoms (six feet) deep."

A Legendary Writer Mark Twain is considered one of the best American writers of the nineteenth century. In addition to writing books, Twain gave humorous lectures around the world. "Stage Fright" is the record of a speech he gave after his daughter's first public singing recital.

Fast Facts

▶ Twain's boyhood home in Missouri gave him the ideas for his best books.

▶ His novel *Tom Sawyer* (1876) is his most popular work.

▶ Its sequel, *The Adventures of Huckleberry Finn* (1884), is considered by many people to be America's greatest novel.

—Author Link

For: More about the author
Visit: www.PHSchool.com
Web Code: ele-9108

Stage Fright

Mark Twain

My heart goes out in <u>sympathy</u> to anyone who is making his first appearance before an audience of human beings. By a direct process of memory I go back forty years, less one month—for I'm older than I look.

I recall the occasion of my first appearance. San Francisco knew me then only as a reporter, and I was to make my bow to San Francisco as a lecturer. I knew that nothing short of <u>compulsion</u> would get me to the theater. So I bound myself by a hard-and-fast contract so that I could not escape. I got to the theater forty-five minutes before the hour set for the lecture. My knees were shaking so that I didn't know whether I could stand up. If there is an awful, horrible malady[1] in the world, it is stage fright—and sea-

---

1. **malady** (mal′ ə dē) *n.* illness.

sickness. They are a pair. I had stage fright then for the first and last time. I was only seasick once, too. It was on a little ship on which there were two hundred other passengers. I—was—sick. I was so sick that there wasn't any left for those other two hundred passengers.

It was dark and lonely behind the scenes in that theater, and I peeked through the little peek holes they have in theater curtains and looked into the big auditorium. That was dark and empty, too. By and by it lighted up, and the audience began to arrive.

I had got a number of friends of mine, stalwart[2] men, to sprinkle themselves through the audience armed with big clubs. Every time I said anything they could possibly guess I intended to be funny, they were to pound those clubs on the floor. Then there was a kind lady in a box up there, also a good friend of mine, the wife of the governor. She was to watch me <u>intently</u>, and whenever I glanced toward her she was going to deliver a gubernatorial laugh that would lead the whole audience into applause.

At last I began. I had the manuscript tucked under a United States flag in front of me where I could get at it in case of need. But I managed to get started without it. I walked up and down—I was young in those days and needed the exercise—and talked and talked.

Right in the middle of the speech I had placed a gem. I had put in a moving, pathetic part which was to get at the hearts and souls of my hearers. When I delivered it, they did just what I hoped and expected. They sat silent and <u>awed</u>. I had touched them. Then I happened to glance up at the box where the governor's wife was—you know what happened.

Well, after the first agonizing five minutes, my stage fright left me, never to return. I know if I was going to be hanged I could get up and make a good showing, and I intend to. But I shall never forget my feelings before the agony left me, and I got up here to thank you for her for helping my daughter, by your kindness, to live through her first appearance. And I want to thank you for your appreciation of her singing, which is, by the way, hereditary.

---

2. **stalwart** (stôl′ wərt) *adj.* strong; sturdy.

Reading Skill
Fact and Opinion
Name one fact and one opinion in this paragraph.

Vocabulary Builder
intently (in tent′ lē) *adv.* purposefully; earnestly

Vocabulary Builder
awed (ôd) *adj.* filled with feelings of fear and wonder

Literary Analysis
Author's Perspective
How would the story of Twain's first appearance be different if it were written by the governor's wife?

Apply the Skills

Stage Fright

Thinking About the Selection

1. **Respond:** How well do you think Mark Twain handles his own stage fright? Explain.
2. **(a) Recall:** What does Twain do to ensure that he will get a laugh during his first speech? **(b) Evaluate:** Do you think this is a good plan? Why or why not?
3. **(a) Recall:** What physical reactions does Mark Twain experience before giving his first speech? **(b) Draw Conclusions:** How might a little bit of stage fright help?
4. **(a) Recall:** What was the prearranged signal between Twain and the governor's wife? **(b) Speculate:** What probably happened when Twain delivered the "gem" in his speech?
5. **Make a Judgment:** Do you think Twain helped his daughter in her first public appearance? Why or why not?

Reading Skill

6. In a chart like the one shown, record three **opinions** that Twain gives. Then, list the clue words that helped you identify each opinion.

Opinion	Clue Word

7. What **facts** does Twain give about the theater where he makes his first appearance?

Literary Analysis

8. **(a)** Identify two feelings that Twain has about his first public-speaking engagement. **(b)** How does each detail convey his personal interest in his subject?
9. How might the **author's perspective** be different if Mark Twain's daughter had written "Stage Fright"?

QuickReview

Speech at a Glance
Mark Twain recalls the stage fright he experienced before his first public appearance.

Go Online
Assessment
For: Self-test
Visit: www.PHSchool.com
Web Code: ela-6108

Fact and Opinion: Facts can be proved. Opinions are a person's judgment or belief.

Author's Perspective: the writer's point of view, including the author's *attitudes, feelings,* and *personal interests*

Vocabulary Builder

Practice Describe each item by writing a sentence that uses a vocabulary word from the list on page 90.

1. an athlete's strong desire to compete
2. a student's feelings toward his classmates in summer school
3. the way a fan watches the ending of a close game
4. what a person felt during a powerful hurricane

Writing

Write a **dramatic scene** using Twain's description of his first public appearance. Add dialogue by imagining what the characters would say to each other. For example, you might add dialogue to Twain's description of talking to his "stalwart" friends. Use a script format as shown:

> **Twain:** Whenever I say something funny, pound your clubs on the floor to get the audience laughing.
> **Friends:** We'll do whatever we can to help you.

For *Grammar, Vocabulary,* and *Assessment,*
see **Build Language Skills,** pages 104–105.

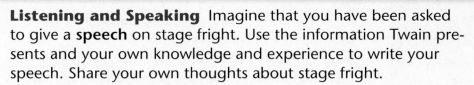

Extend Your Learning

Listening and Speaking Imagine that you have been asked to give a **speech** on stage fright. Use the information Twain presents and your own knowledge and experience to write your speech. Share your own thoughts about stage fright.

Research and Technology With a partner, use the Internet and library resources to find information about the anxiety, or fear, called stage fright. Use the information to make a **poster** or chart that explains these aspects of stage fright:
- what causes stage fright
- how the person with stage fright feels
- suggestions for coping with stage fright

Biography

Background

Family Biographer At age thirteen, Susy Clemens decided to secretly write a biography of her father, author Mark Twain. Susy kept her work-in-progress hidden in her bedroom. When her father saw the biography, he was delighted.

Connecting to the Literature

Reading/Writing Connection In "My Papa, Mark Twain," Susy Clemens records her perspective on and opinions of her father. List three things you would include in a biography of someone you admire. Use at least three of the following words: *define, identify, focus, conclude.*

Review

For **Reading Skill, Literary Analysis,** and **Vocabulary Builder,** see page 90.

Meet the Author

Susy **Clemens** (1872–1896)

Olivia Susan Clemens, called Susy, was the eldest daughter of American author Mark Twain. She was born in Elmira, New York, and grew up in her family's luxurious home in Hartford, Connecticut. There, her parents entertained famous people of the time— and Susy had the opportunity to meet them.

A Short Life It is said that Susy was her father's favorite daughter. After she died at age twenty-four, Twain's writing turned darker and more serious.

Fast Facts

▶ In 1906, Mark Twain included parts of Susy's biography in his autobiography.

▶ Susy Clemens's complete biography of her father, *Papa: An Intimate Biography of Mark Twain,* was not published until 1985. It keeps her misspellings and punctuation errors.

Go **Online** Author Link

For: More about the author
Visit: www.PHSchool.com
Web Code: ele-9109

My Papa, Mark Twain

Susy Clemens

◄ **Critical Viewing**
What details in this picture show the Clemens family's closeness? **[Analyze]**

We are a very happy family. We consist of Papa, Mamma, Jean, Clara and me. It is papa I am writing about, and I shall have no trouble in not knowing what to say about him, as he is a *very* striking character.

Papa's appearance has been described many times, but very incorrectly. He has beautiful gray hair, not any too thick or any too long, but just right; a Roman nose which greatly improves the beauty of his features; kind blue eyes and a small mustache. He has a wonderfully shaped head and profile. He has a very good figure—in short, he is an

Reading Skill
Fact and Opinion
Name one fact and one opinion here. What clue word helped you identify the opinion?

extrodinarily fine looking man. All his features are perfect except that he hasn't extrodinary teeth. His complexion is very fair, and he doesn't ware a beard. He is a very good man and a very funny one. He has got a temper, but we all of us have in this family. He is the loveliest man I ever saw or ever hope to see—and oh, so <u>absentminded</u>.

Papa's favorite game is billiards, and when he is tired and wishes to rest himself he stays up all night and plays billiards, it seems to rest his head. He smokes a great deal almost <u>incessantly</u>. He has the mind of an author exactly, some of the simplest things he can't understand. Our

burglar alarm is often out of order, and papa had been obliged to take the mahogany room off from the alarm altogether for a time, because the burglar alarm had been in the habit of ringing even when the mahogany-room window was closed. At length he thought that perhaps the burglar alarm might be in order, and he decided to try and see; accordingly he put it on and then went down and opened the window; <u>consequently</u> the alarm bell rang, it would even if the alarm had been in order. Papa went despairingly upstairs and said to mamma, "Livy the mahogany room won't go on. I have just opened the window to see."

"Why, Youth," mamma replied. "If you've opened the window, why of course the alarm will ring!"

"That's what I've opened it for, why I just went down to see if it would ring!"

Mamma tried to explain to papa that when he wanted to go and see whether the alarm would ring while the window was closed he *mustn't go* and open the window— but in vain, papa couldn't understand, and got very impatient with mamma for trying to make him believe an impossible thing true.

Papa has a peculiar gait we like, it seems just to suit him, but most people do not; he always walks up and down the room while thinking and between each coarse at meals.

Papa is very fond of animals particularly of cats, we had a dear little gray kitten once that he named

Vocabulary Builder
consequently (kän´ si kwent´ lē) *adv.* as a result

Literary Analysis
Author's Perspective How might Papa's retelling of the burglar alarm incident be different from Susy's version?

Reading Check

What is the relationship between the writer and her subject?

▲ **Critical Viewing** Susy is observing her two sisters in this picture. What do you think she might write about them in her journal? **[Speculate]**

"Lazy" (papa always wears gray to match his hair and eyes) and he would carry him around on his shoulder, it was a mighty pretty sight! the gray cat sound asleep against papa's gray coat and hair. The names that he has give our different cats are really remarkably funny, they are named Stray Kit, Abner, Motley, Fraeulein, Lazy, Buffalo Bill, Soapy Sall, Cleveland, Sour Mash, and Pestilence and Famine.

Papa uses very strong language, but I have an idea not nearly so strong as when he first married mamma. A lady acquaintance of his is rather apt to interrupt what one is saying, and papa told mamma he thought he should say to the lady's husband "I am glad your wife wasn't present when the Deity said Let there be light."

Papa said the other day, "I am a mugwump[1] and a mugwump is pure from the marrow out." (Papa knows that I am writing this biography of him, and he said this for it.) He doesn't like to go to church at all, why I never understood, until just now, he told us the other day that he couldn't bear to hear anyone talk but himself, but that he could listen to himself talk for hours without getting tired, of course he said this in joke, but I've no dought it was founded on truth.

One of papa's latest books is "The Prince and the Pauper" and it is unquestionably the best book he has ever written, some people want him to keep to his old style, some gentleman wrote him, "I enjoyed Huckleberry Finn immensely and am glad to see that you have returned to your old style." That enoyed me, that enoyed me greatly, because it trobles me to have so few people know papa, I mean realy know him, they think of Mark Twain as a

---

1. **mugwump** (mug´ wump´) *n.* Republican who refused to support the candidates of the party in the 1884 election.

Literature in Context

Literature Connection

Twain Makes His Mark At the 1890 stage premiere of *The Prince and the Pauper,* Mark Twain had no idea that it would someday be made into several movies. The first, a 1915 silent film, starred a woman in both lead roles. The second used identical twin boys.

The popularity of Twain's fiction did not make him wealthy, but at his death in 1910, he left behind a rich literary legacy.

Connect to the Literature

Why does Susy Clemens believe that *The Prince and the Pauper* is her father's best book?

humorist joking at everything; "And with a mop of reddish brown hair which sorely needs the barbar brush, a roman nose, short stubby mustache, a sad care-worn face, with maney crows' feet" etc. That is the way people picture papa, I have wanted papa to write a book that would reveal something of his kind sympathetic nature, and "The Prince and the Pauper" partly does it. The book is full of lovely charming ideas, and oh the language! It is perfect. I think that one of the most touching scenes in it is where the pauper is riding on horseback with his nobles in the "recognition procession" and he sees his mother oh and then what followed! How she runs to his side, when she sees him throw up his hand palm outward, and is rudely pushed off by one of the King's officers, and then how the little pauper's conscience troubles him when he remembers the shameful words that were falling from his lips when she was turned from his side "I know you not woman" and how his grandeurs were stricken valueless and his pride consumed to ashes. It is a wonderfully beautiful and touching little scene, and papa has described it so wonderfully. I never saw a man with so much variety of feeling as papa has; now the "Prince and the Pauper" is full of touching places, but there is always a streak of humor in them somewhere. Papa very seldom writes a passage without some humor in it somewhere and I don't think he ever will.

Clara and I are sure that papa played the trick on Grandma about the whipping that is related in "The Adventures of Tom Sawyer": "Hand me that switch." The switch hovered in the air, the peril was desperate—"My, look behind you Aunt!" The old lady whirled around and snatched her skirts out of danger. The lad fled on the instant, scrambling up the high board fence and disappeared over it.

We know papa played "Hookey" all the time. And how readily would papa pretend to be dying so as not to have to go to school! Grandma wouldn't make papa go to school, so she let him go into a printing office to learn the trade. He did so, and gradually picked up enough education to enable him to do about as well as those who were more studious in early life.

Literary Analysis
Author's Perspective
What details on this page show the author's feelings toward her subject?

Reading Skill
Fact and Opinion
What facts support Susy Clemens's opinion that her father did about as well as those who were more studious?

Apply the Skills

My Papa, Mark Twain

Thinking About the Selection

1. **Respond:** What questions do you have about Mark Twain after reading Susy Clemens's account of her father?
2. **Respond:** Make a three-column chart.
   - In the first column, write three details that reveal what Susy thinks of her father's appearance.
   - In the second column, list three words Susy would use to describe her father.
   - In the third column, list three words you would use to describe Mark Twain.
3. **(a) Recall:** What facts does the author give about her father's education? **(b) Deduce:** Explain how you think she feels about her father's lack of formal education.
4. **Speculate:** This essay contains many misspelled words. Why do you think it was published without the errors being corrected?

Reading Skill

5. **(a)** When the author says that *The Prince and the Pauper* is the best book Mark Twain has ever written, is she expressing a **fact or an opinion? (b)** What opinion do you think Susy has about her father as a writer? Explain.
6. In a chart like the one shown, record three opinions that Susy gives about her father. Then, list the clue words that helped you identify each opinion.

Opinion	Clue Word

Literary Analysis

7. **(a)** Identify two details of Susy Clemens's life that help you see the **author's perspective. (b)** How does each detail build her personal interest in her subject?
8. How might the author's perspective be different if someone outside Mark Twain's family had written this biography?

QuickReview

Who's Who?

Susy Clemens: the narrator of this biography

Papa: Susy's father, the famous writer Mark Twain

Mamma: Susy's mother

Jean and Clara: Susy's sisters

For: Self-test
Visit: www.PHSchool.com
Web Code: ela-6109

Fact and Opinion: Facts can be proved. Opinions are a person's judgment or belief.

Author's Perspective: the writer's point of view, including the author's *attitudes, feelings,* and *personal interests*

Vocabulary Builder

Practice Describe each item by writing a sentence that uses a vocabulary word from the list on page 90.

1. a person who never stops talking
2. a cause and a result
3. someone with a bad memory

Writing

Turn a passage from "My Papa, Mark Twain" into a **dramatic scene.** Use a script format as shown:

> **Papa:** I just opened the window to see if the alarm works.
> **Mamma:** If you've opened the window, why of course the alarm will ring!

- First, decide which characters are present in the scene.
- Then, imagine what the characters would say to each other during the scene, and write dialogue based on your ideas.

For *Grammar, Vocabulary,* and *Assessment,* see **Build Language Skills,** pages 104–105.

Extend Your Learning

Listening and Speaking Imagine that you have been asked to present a literary award to Mark Twain. Use Susy Clemens's biography and your own research to prepare a short **speech** about Twain. Be sure to tell the audience about Twain's books and why he has been chosen to receive the award.

Research and Technology With a partner, use the Internet and library resources to research some of the characters found in Mark Twain's books. Then, make a **poster** or chart that shows some of Twain's best-known works and characters.

Build Language Skills

Stage Fright • My Papa, Mark Twain

Vocabulary Skill

Word Origins The words *claim* and *exclaim* share a common **Latin origin**—*clamare,* which means "to cry out or shout." Words that share this origin have meanings related to stating or sharing information or feelings.

▶ **Examples:** claim, exclaim, clamor

The word **distinguish** comes from the Latin word *distinguere,* which means "separate." This word origin is helpful in visualizing that the word *distinguish* means to "tell the difference" between one thing and another.

▶ **Examples:** distinguish, distinct, distinction

Practice Use a dictionary to find the meanings of two words that are related to the word *claim* and one that is related to the word *distinguish.* Explain how the origin of the word is related to its current meaning. Then, use each word in a sentence that illustrates the word's meaning.

Grammar Lesson

Pronouns A *pronoun* is a word that takes the place of a noun or another pronoun. A *personal pronoun* refers to a specific noun that is named elsewhere in the sentence or paragraph. *Possessive pronouns* function as adjectives. They also answer the question *whose?* The chart below lists examples of the different types of pronouns.

Practice Complete each sentence with an appropriate pronoun. Then, identify the type of pronoun used.

1. Sharon lent me _____ pencil for the test.
2. "Where do _____ want to go?" Jen asked me.
3. "_____ report is on elephants," said Dan.
4. An elephant uses _____ trunk like a hand.
5. Dan always wears _____ favorite T-shirt to football games.

More Practice

For more practice with pronouns, see the Grammar Handbook, p. R32.

Personal Pronouns	Possessive Pronouns
I, he, she, him, her, you, they, them, it	my, his, her, your, their

W͞G Prentice Hall Writing and Grammar Connection: Chapter 14, Section 2.

Assessment Practice

Reading: Fact and Opinion

Directions: *Read the selection. Then, answer the questions.*

It was an uncomfortable situation. Tyrell and Marc, who were best friends, both made it to the final round of the math contest. Tyrell was last year's champion, and Marc had won the year before. This year, whoever won would have to beat his best friend. This was going to be the best math competition in history. Finally, the day of the competition arrived. No one could wait for the match to begin.

1. Which statement is *a fact*?
   A Tyrell was last year's champion.
   B It was an uncomfortable situation.
   C This was going to be the best math competition in history.
   D No one could wait for the competition to begin.

2. Which statement is an *opinion*?
   A Marc had won the year before.
   B Tyrell and Marc both made it to the final round.
   C Finally, the day of the competition arrived.
   D This was going to be the best math competition in history.

3. Which words are clues that indicate an opinion?
   A *whoever, his, finally*
   B *situation, friends, won*
   C *uncomfortable, best, no one*
   D *before, made, begin*

4. Which sentence best supports the author's opinion that it was an uncomfortable situation?
   A Marc and Tyrell are best friends.
   B Marc and Tyrell must compete against each other.
   C The competition was going to be entertaining.
   D Tyrell and Marc have both won in the past.

Timed Writing: Response to Literature

Review "My Papa, Mark Twain" or "Stage Fright." Write a brief profile of Mark Twain. **(20 minutes)**

 ## Writing Workshop: *Work in Progress*

Autobiographical Narrative

Make a list of events from your writing portfolio notes. Beside each event put the question "Why?" Answer each question in a few sentences. Put this work in your writing portfolio.

These skills will help you become a better reader. Practice them with either "The Lady and the Spider" (p. 108) or "Names/Nombres" (p. 115).

Reading Skill

To evaluate a work of nonfiction, you must understand the difference between **fact and opinion**. A *fact*, unlike an opinion, can be proved. An *opinion* expresses a judgment that can be supported but not proved. You can **check facts by using resources** such as the following:

- dictionaries
- encyclopedias
- reliable Web sites

To help you keep track of facts found in a nonfiction work, use a chart like the one shown.

Fact	Resource	True	False
Tigers live in only cold climates.	Internet		✓

Literary Analysis

The **tone** of a literary work is the writer's attitude toward his or her audience and subject. The tone can often be described in one word, such as *playful, serious,* or *humorous.* Factors that contribute to the tone are word choice, sentence structure, and sentence length. Notice how word choice can create a friendly tone:

If you plan ahead, I promise you, you'll have the best party ever!

As you read, look for details that convey a certain tone.

Vocabulary Builder

The Lady and the Spider

- **mode** (mōd) *n.* way of doing something (p. 108) *Her mode of dress is unique.*
- **frenzied** (fren´ zēd) *adj.* acting in a wild, uncontrolled way (p. 109) *The man ran from the bus in a frenzied rush.*
- **inhabited** (in hab´ it id) *adj.* lived in; occupied (p. 109) *The nest is inhabited by three birds.*

Names/Nombres

- **inevitably** (in ev´ i tə blē´) *adv.* unavoidably (p. 118) *Inevitably, her funny jokes made them laugh.*
- **chaotic** (kā ät´ ik) *adj.* completely confused (p. 118) *The crowd was chaotic.*
- **inscribed** (in skrībd´) *v.* had letters or writing put on (p. 119) *The jeweler inscribed their wedding rings.*

Essay

Background

Phobias The mere mention of certain animals—such as spiders—horrifies some people. An unreasonable fear is known as a *phobia*. The woman in "The Lady and the Spider" suffers from *arachnophobia,* a fear of spiders.

Connecting to the Literature

Reading/Writing Connection Like the woman in "The Lady and the Spider," you, or a person you know, may also suffer from *arachnophobia.* To prepare for the humor in this essay, list reasons why a spider might be afraid of a human. Use at least three of the following words: *capture, confront, contact, encounter, injure.*

Meet the Author

Robert **Fulghum** (b. 1937)

Ask Robert Fulghum what he has learned about life and he might say, "All I really need to know I learned in kindergarten." That is the title of his first bestseller, which includes funny essays like "The Lady and the Spider."

Many Careers Fulghum did not set out to be a writer. He worked as a ranch hand, a salesman, an art teacher, and a minister before becoming a full-time writer. Fulghum's seven books have sold more than 15 million copies worldwide.

Helping Others Fulghum believes in helping others. He raises money for charity by playing in a band called the Rock Bottom Remainders. His fellow musicians include authors Stephen King and Amy Tan and Matt Groening, the creator of *The Simpsons*. Fulghum has also donated money from one of his books to a human rights charity. "I don't think the thing is to be well known," he says, "but being worth knowing."

For: More about the author
Visit: www.PHSchool.com
Web Code: ele-9110

The Lady and the Spider

Robert Fulghum

This is my neighbor. Nice lady. Coming out her front door, on her way to work and in her "looking good" <u>mode</u>. She's locking the door now and picking up her daily luggage: purse, lunch bag, gym bag for aerobics, and the garbage bucket to take out. She turns, sees me, gives me the big, smiling Hello, takes three steps across her front porch. And goes "AAAAAAAAGGGGGGGGGGHHHHHHHHHH!!!!" (*That's a direct quote.*) At about the level of a fire engine at full cry. Spider web! She has walked full force into a spider web. And the pressing question, of course: Just where is the spider *now*?

She flings her baggage in all directions. And at the same time does a high-kick, jitterbug sort of dance—like a mating

▲ **Critical Viewing**
What details about this spider might make a person feel afraid? **[Analyze]**

Vocabulary Builder
mode (mōd) *n.* way of doing something

stork in crazed heat. Clutches at her face and hair and goes "AAAAAAAGGGGGGGHHHHHHHHH!!!!!" at a new level of intensity. Tries opening the front door without unlocking it. Tries again. Breaks key in the lock. Runs around the house headed for the back door. Doppler effect[1] of

"A A A A A G G G H H H H a a g g h . . ."

Now a different view of this scene. Here is the spider. Rather ordinary, medium gray, middle-aged lady spider. She's been up since before dawn working on her web, and all is well. Nice day, no wind, dew point just right to keep things sticky. She's out checking the moorings[2] and thinking about the little gnats she'd like to have for breakfast. Feeling good. Ready for action. All of a sudden— earthquake, tornado, volcano. The web is torn loose and is wrapped around a <u>frenzied</u> moving hay- stack, and a huge piece of raw- but-painted meat is making a sound the spider never heard before: "AAAAAAA-GGGGGGGGHHHHHHHHH!!!!!" It's too big to wrap up and eat later, and it's moving too much to hold down. Jump for it? Hang on and hope? Dig in?

Human being. She has caught a human being. And the pressing question is, of course: Where is it going and what will it do when it gets there?

The neighbor lady thinks the spider is about the size of a lob- ster and has big rubber lips and poisonous fangs. The neighbor lady will probably strip to the skin and take a full shower and shampoo just to make sure it's gone—and then put on a whole new outfit to make certain she is not <u>inhabited</u>.

The spider? Well, if she survives all this, she will really have something to talk about—the one that got away that was THIS BIG. "And you should have seen the JAWS on the thing!"

1. **Doppler effect** a change in the frequency and pitch of a sound, caused by the movement of the source or the listener.
2. **moorings** *n.* lines or cables that hold a ship or something else in place.

Literary Analysis
Tone How does the direct quotation from the lady indicate an informal tone?

Vocabulary Builder
frenzied (fren´ zēd) *adj.* acting in a wild, uncontrolled way

inhabited (in hab´ it əd) *adj.* lived in; occupied

Reading Check

Why is the speaker's neighbor screaming?

Spiders. Amazing creatures. Been around maybe 350 million years, so they can cope with about anything. Lots of them, too—sixty or seventy thousand per suburban acre. It's the web thing that I envy. Imagine what it would be like if people were equipped like spiders. If we had this little six-nozzled aperture[3] right at the base of our spine and we could make yards of something like glass fiber with

Reading Skill
Fact and Opinion
List one fact and one opinion in this paragraph.

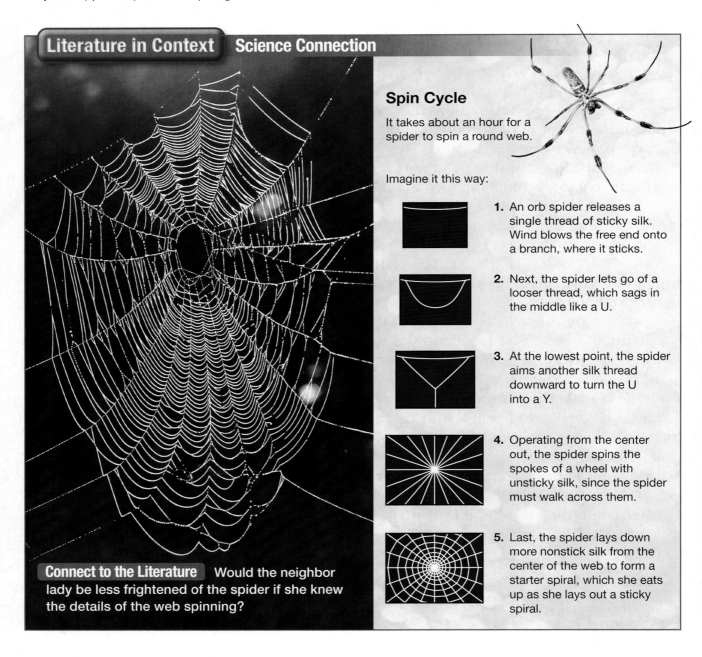

Literature in Context **Science Connection**

Spin Cycle

It takes about an hour for a spider to spin a round web.

Imagine it this way:

1. An orb spider releases a single thread of sticky silk. Wind blows the free end onto a branch, where it sticks.

2. Next, the spider lets go of a looser thread, which sags in the middle like a U.

3. At the lowest point, the spider aims another silk thread downward to turn the U into a Y.

4. Operating from the center out, the spider spins the spokes of a wheel with unsticky silk, since the spider must walk across them.

5. Last, the spider lays down more nonstick silk from the center of the web to form a starter spiral, which she eats up as she lays out a sticky spiral.

Connect to the Literature Would the neighbor lady be less frightened of the spider if she knew the details of the web spinning?

it. Wrapping packages would be a cinch! Mountain climbing would never be the same. Think of the Olympic events. And child rearing would take on new dimensions. Well, you take it from there. It boggles the mind. Cleaning up human-sized webs would be a mess, on the other hand.

All this reminds me of a song I know. And you know, too. And your parents and your children, they know. About the eensy-weensy spider. Went up the waterspout. Down came the rain and washed the spider out. Out came the sun and dried up all the rain. And the eensy-weensy spider went up the spout again. You probably know the motions, too.

What's the deal here? Why do we all know that song? Why do we keep passing it on to our kids? Especially when it puts spiders in such a favorable light? Nobody goes "AAAAAAAGGGGGGGGHHHHHHHHHH!!!!!" when they sing it. Maybe because it puts the life adventure in such clear and simple terms. The small creature is alive and looks for adventure. Here's the drainpipe—a long tunnel going up toward some light. The spider doesn't even think about it—just goes. Disaster befalls it—rain, flood, powerful forces. And the spider is knocked down and out beyond where it started. Does the spider say, "To heck with that"? No. Sun comes out—clears things up—dries off the spider. And the small creature goes over to the drainpipe and looks up and thinks it really wants to know what is up there. It's a little wiser now—checks the sky first, looks for better toeholds, says a spider prayer, and heads up through mystery toward the light and wherever.

Living things have been doing just that for a long, long time. Through every kind of disaster and setback and catastrophe. We are survivors. And we teach our kids about that. And maybe spiders tell their kids about it, too, in their spider sort of way.

So the neighbor lady will survive and be a little wiser coming out the door on her way to work. And the spider, if it lives, will do likewise. And if not, well, there are lots more spiders, and the word gets around. Especially when the word is "AAAAAAAGGGGGGGGHHHHHHHHHH!!!!"

Literary Analysis
Tone What do these questions suggest is the author's attitude toward the song?

Reading Skill
Fact and Opinion How could you check to see if "spiders tell their kids" about how to survive?

The Lady and the Spider

Thinking About the Selection

1. **Respond:** How would you react if you walked into a spider web?
2. **(a) Recall:** What does the lady do with her baggage? **(b) Infer:** What do her actions show about her feelings toward spiders?
3. **(a) Recall:** What are two thoughts the woman has about the situation? **(b) Recall:** What are two thoughts the spider has about the situation? **(c) Analyze:** Why do you think the narrator tells what both the lady and the spider are thinking?
4. **(a) Interpret:** How do you think the author feels about spiders? **(b) Analyze:** What makes you think this?
5. **Discuss:** Whose side are you on—the lady's or the spider's? In a small group, share your responses. Then, select one response to share with the class.

Reading Skill

6. **(a)** List two details about the lady's fear that the narrator presents as **facts**. **(b)** List two details about the lady's fear that the narrator presents as **opinions**.
7. What are two facts from the essay that you could prove true or false by checking on the Internet?

Literary Analysis

8. The passage in the chart has an informal, or friendly, **tone**. In a chart like the one shown, rewrite the passage in a more serious, or formal, tone.

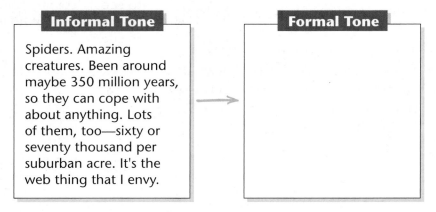

Informal Tone	Formal Tone
Spiders. Amazing creatures. Been around maybe 350 million years, so they can cope with about anything. Lots of them, too—sixty or seventy thousand per suburban acre. It's the web thing that I envy.	

QuickReview

Essay at a Glance

When the narrator sees a woman walk into a spider web, he thinks about the act from two points of view.

Go **O**nline
—Assessment
For: Self-test
Visit: www.PHSchool.com
Web Code: ela-6110

Fact: a statement that can be proved

Opinion: a judgment that can be supported but not proved

Tone: the writer's attitude toward the reader and subject

Vocabulary Builder

Practice In your notebook, explain why each statement is true or false.

1. Houses cannot be *inhabited*.
2. A person's *mode* of speaking is his or her own unique style.
3. A *frenzied* person is very calm and organized.

Writing

Write a **personal anecdote**, a brief story, about an encounter you have had with something in nature. Your anecdote can be funny or serious, but use vivid descriptions to make it come to life. Look at the example:

> **Details About the Storm:** Deafening thunder; darkness in the daytime; howling wind; bent-over trees
>
> **Details About My Reaction:** Trembling; holding hands over ears; turning on every light in the house

For *Grammar, Vocabulary,* and *Assessment,* see **Build Language Skills,** pages 122–123.

Extend Your Learning

Listening and Speaking Write a **monologue** that presents the thoughts of either the woman or the spider. You will be speaking as if you were one of these characters.
- Use the first-person point of view. Use the word *I.*
- Use vocabulary that reflects the personality of your character.

Research and Technology In a group, prepare a **presentation** on Robert Fulghum's life. Use the Internet and other library resources to find facts about his family, his career as a writer, and his hobbies and interests.

Build Understanding • *Names/Nombres*

Background

Languages In "Names/Nombres," Julia Alvarez tells how language differences have made her feel like an outsider. For example, in Spanish, the letter *j* is used for the sound English speakers associate with *h*. The letter *r* has a very different sound from its sound in English. Although many Spanish words have found their way into English, some of their pronunciations have changed over time.

Connecting to the Literature

Reading/Writing Connection In "Names/Nombres," Julia Alvarez writes about the shared experiences of emigrants from Latin America. Recall your experiences as a member of a group, such as a group of friends, a class, a club, or a team. List the benefits of belonging to a group. Use at least three of the following words: *contribute, identify, participate, promote.*

Review

For **Reading Skill, Literary Analysis,** and **Vocabulary Builder,** see page 106.

Meet the Author

Julia **Alvarez** (b. 1950)

Although Julia Alvarez was born in New York City, her family soon returned to the Dominican Republic. After Julia's father worked to overthrow the dictator there, he and his family fled the country. Julia was ten years old when they arrived in the United States.

Name Game From the moment young Julia arrived in New York City, she felt she had to "translate her experiences into English." Sometimes, as she shows in "Names/Nombres," it was the English speakers who did the translating.

Fast Facts

▶ Alvarez realized in high school that she wanted to pursue a career as a writer.

▶ The award-winning author says, "I write to find out what I'm thinking."

Go **O**nline
Author Link

For: More about the author
Visit: www.PHSchool.com
Web Code: ele-9111

Names/Nombres

Julia Alvarez

When we arrived in New York City, our names changed almost immediately. At Immigration,[1] the officer asked my father, *Mister Elbures*, if he had anything to declare. My father shook his head, "No," and we were waved through. I was too afraid we wouldn't be let in if I corrected the man's pronunciation, but I said our name to myself, opening my mouth wide for the organ blast of the *a*, trilling my tongue for the drum-roll of the *r*, *All-vah-rrr-es*! How could anyone get *Elbures* out of that orchestra of sound?

At the hotel my mother was *Missus Alburest*, and I was little girl, as in, "Hey, *little girl*, stop riding the elevator up and down. It's *not* a toy."

When we moved into our new apartment building, the super[2] called my father *Mister Alberase*, and the

---

1. Immigration government agency that processes people who have recently moved to the United States.
2. super *n.* superintendent; person who manages an apartment building.

neighbors who became mother's friends pronounced her name *Jew-lee-ah* instead of *Hoo-lee-ah*. I, her namesake, was known as *Hoo-lee-tah* at home. But at school, I was *Judy* or *Judith*, and once an English teacher mistook me for *Juliet*.

It took awhile to get used to my new names. I wondered if I shouldn't correct my teachers and new friends. But my mother argued that it didn't matter. "You know what your friend Shakespeare said, '*A rose by any other name would smell as sweet*.' " My father had gotten into the habit of calling any famous author "my friend" because I had begun to write poems and stories in English class.

By the time I was in high school, I was a popular kid, and it showed in my name. Friends called me *Jules* or *Hey Jude*, and once a group of troublemaking friends my mother forbade me to hang out with called me *Alcatraz*. I was *Hoo-lee-tah* only to Mami and Papi and uncles and aunts who came over to eat *sancocho* on Sunday afternoons—old world folk whom I would just as soon go back to where they came from and leave me to pursue whatever mischief I wanted to in America. JUDY ALCATRAZ: the name on the Wanted Poster would read. Who would ever trace her to me?

My older sister had the hardest time getting an American name for herself because *Mauricia* did not translate into English. Ironically, although she had the most foreign-sounding name, she and I were the Americans in the family. We had been born in New York City when our parents had first tried immigration and then gone back "home," too homesick to stay. My mother often told the story of how she had almost changed my sister's name in the hospital.

After the delivery, Mami and some other new mothers were cooing over their new baby sons and daughters and exchanging names and weights and delivery stories. My mother was embarrassed among the Sallys and Janes and Georges and Johns to reveal the rich, noisy name of *Mauricia*, so when her turn came to brag, she gave her baby's name as *Maureen*.

"Why'd ya give her an Irish name with so many pretty Spanish names to choose from?" one of the women asked.

Literary Analysis
Tone What attitude does the author have toward her different names?

Reading Skill
Fact and Opinion What opinion does the narrator give in this paragraph?

My mother blushed and admitted her baby's real name to the group. Her mother-in-law had recently died, she apologized, and her husband had insisted that the first daughter be named after his mother, *Mauran*. My mother thought it the ugliest name she had ever heard, and she talked my father into what she believed was an improvement, a combination of *Mauran* and her own mother's name, *Felicia*.

"Her name is *Mao-ree-shee-ah*," my mother said to the group of women.

"Why that's a beautiful name," the new mothers cried. "*Moor-ee-sha, Moor-ee-sha*," they cooed into the pink blanket. *Moor-ee-sha* it was when we returned to the States eleven years later. Sometimes, American tongues found even that mispronunciation tough to say and called her *Maria* or *Marsha* or *Maudy* from her nickname *Maury*. I pitied her. What an awful name to have to transport across borders!

My little sister, Ana, had the easiest time of all. She was plain *Anne*—that is, only her name was plain, for she turned out to be the pale, blond "American beauty" in the family. The only Hispanic thing about her was the affectionate nicknames her boyfriends sometimes gave her. *Anita*, or as one goofy guy used to sing to her to the tune of the banana advertisement, *Anita Banana*.[3]

Later, during her college years in the late '60s, there was a push to pronounce Third World names correctly. I remember calling her long distance at her group house and a roommate answering.

"Can I speak to Ana?" I asked, pronouncing her name the American way.

"Ana?" The man's voice hesitated. "Oh! you must mean *Ah-nah*!"

Collage (detail), 1992, Juan Sanchez,
Courtesy of Juan Sanchez and Guarighen, Inc., NYC

◀ **Critical Viewing** Of the three girls in this photo, which one best reflects the feelings of Alvarez as a child? **[Analyze]**

✔ **Reading Check**

What other names was Julia known by when she came to the United States?

---

3. **Anita Banana** play on the name *Chiquita Banana,* a character in a company's ad.

Our first few years in the States, though, ethnicity was not yet "in." Those were the blond, blue-eyed, bobby sock years of junior high and high school before the '60s ushered in peasant blouses, hoop earrings, serapes.[4] My initial desire to be known by my correct Dominican name faded. I just wanted to be Judy and merge with the Sallys and Janes in my class. But <u>inevitably</u>, my accent and coloring gave me away. "So where are you from, Judy?"

"New York," I told my classmates. After all, I had been born blocks away at Columbia Presbyterian Hospital.

"I mean, *originally*."

"From the Caribbean," I answered vaguely, for if I specified, no one was quite sure on what continent our island was located.

"Really? I've been to Bermuda. We went last April for spring vacation. I got the worst sunburn! So, are you from Portoriko?"

"No," I sighed. "From the Dominican Republic."

"Where's that?"

"South of Bermuda."

They were just being curious, I knew, but I burned with shame whenever they singled me out as a "foreigner," a rare, exotic friend.

"Say your name in Spanish, oh please say it!" I had made mouths drop one day by rattling off my full name, which according to Dominican custom, included my middle names, Mother's and Father's surnames for four generations back.

"Julia Altagracia María Teresa Álvarez Tavares Perello Espaillat Julia Pérez Rochet González," I pronounced it slowly, a name as <u>chaotic</u> with sounds as a Middle Eastern bazaar[5] or market day in a South American village.

My Dominican heritage was never more apparent than when my extended family attended school occasions. For my graduation, they all came, the whole lot of aunts and uncles and the many little cousins who snuck in without tickets. They sat in the first row in order to better understand the Americans' fast-spoken English. But how could they listen when they were constantly speaking among

---

4. serapes (sə rä´ pēz) *n.* colorful shawls worn in Latin America.
5. bazaar (bə zär´) *n.* marketplace; frequently, one held outdoors.

themselves in florid-sounding phrases, rococo[6] consonants, rich, rhyming vowels?

Introducing them to my friends was a further trial to me. These relatives had such complicated names and there were so many of them, and their relationships to myself were so convoluted. There was my Tía Josefina, who was not really an aunt but a much older cousin. And her daughter, Aida Margarita, who was adopted, *una hija de crianza.* My uncle of affection, Tío José, brought my *madrina* Tía Amelia and her *comadre* Tía Pilar. My friends rarely had more than a "Mom and Dad" to introduce.

After the commencement ceremony my family waited outside in the parking lot while my friends and I signed yearbooks with nicknames which recalled our high school good times: "Beans" and "Pepperoni" and "Alcatraz." We hugged and cried and promised to keep in touch.

Our goodbyes went on too long. I heard my father's voice calling out across the parking lot, "*Hoo-lee-tah! Vamonos!*"

Back home, my *tíos* and *tías* and *primas,* Mami and Papi, and *mis hermanas* had a party for me with *sancocho* and a storebought *pudín,* <u>inscribed</u> with *Happy Graduation, Julie.* There were many gifts—that was a plus to a large family! I got several wallets and a suitcase with my initials and a graduation charm from my godmother and money from my uncles. The biggest gift was a portable typewriter from my parents for writing my stories and poems.

Someday, the family predicted, my name would be well-known throughout the United States. I laughed to myself, wondering which one I would go by.

Vocabulary Builder
inscribed (in skrībd´)
v. written on

---

6. **rococo** (rə kō´ kō) *adj.* fancy style of art of the early eighteenth century.

Apply the Skills

Names/Nombres

Thinking About the Selection

1. **Respond:** Which name do you think best fits the author?
2. **(a) Recall:** How does Julia's family say her name?
   (b) Analyze Cause and Effect: Explain why some English speakers mispronounce her name. **(c) Connect:** What do you do or say when someone mispronounces your name?
3. **(a) Recall:** How does Julia respond when her classmates ask her from where she comes? **(b) Draw Conclusions:** Why does she respond as she does? **(c) Evaluate:** Would you make the same decision in the same situation? Why or why not?
4. **(a) Interpret:** Explain how the title captures the focus of Alvarez's narrative. **(b) Analyze:** How do Alvarez's feelings about the topic change over time? **(c) Synthesize:** What do names represent for Alvarez and others?
5. **Discuss:** How important are names in the way people view themselves and others? In a small group, share your responses. Then, select one response to share with the class.

Reading Skill

6. How might you check the fact that Julia Alvarez was born in New York City?
7. Alvarez relates the story of her sister's name by saying, "My mother thought it the ugliest name she had ever heard." Is her mother stating a **fact** or an **opinion**? Explain.

Literary Analysis

8. "Names/Nombres" is written in an informal, or friendly, **tone.** In a chart like the one shown, rewrite the two sentences in a more serious, or formal, tone.

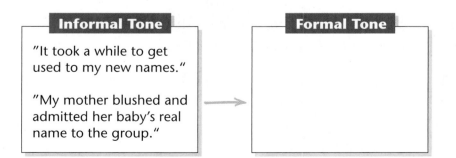

Informal Tone

"It took a while to get used to my new names."

"My mother blushed and admitted her baby's real name to the group."

Formal Tone

QuickReview

Essay at a Glance
A writer describes English speakers' inability to pronounce her family's Spanish names.

Go Online
Assessment
For: Self-test
Visit: www.PHSchool.com
Web Code: ela-6111

Fact: a statement that can be proved
Opinion: a judgment that can be supported but not proved

Tone: the writer's attitude toward the reader and subject

Vocabulary Builder

Practice In your notebook, explain why each statement is true or false.

1. A *chaotic* place is calm and relaxing.
2. A picture frame with initials etched onto it has been *inscribed* by someone.
3. If you do not study for a test, you will *inevitably* pass.

Writing

Write a **personal anecdote,** a brief story, about something from your family's past. It might be a funny story about a family experience or a story about an ancestor that has been passed down through your family. Include your own thoughts in your story.

For *Grammar, Vocabulary,* and *Assessment,* see **Build Language Skills,** pages 122–123.

Extend Your Learning

Listening and Speaking Using the information in "Names/Nombres," write a **monologue** that presents the thoughts of young Julia Alvarez as she first hears her name mispronounced.
- Stick to the first-person point of view. Use the word *I.*
- Use vocabulary that reflects Alvarez's personality.
- Give three reasons why it bothers you to have your name mispronounced.

Research and Technology Use the Internet and library sources to research the political and economic factors that caused Julia Alvarez's family to leave the Dominican Republic. Then, in a group, use your combined research to prepare a **presentation** for the class.

Build Language Skills

The Lady and the Spider • Names/Nombres

Vocabulary Skill

Word Origins The word *prove* comes from the Latin word *probare,* which means "test." Words that share this *origin* also have meanings related to testing or proving.

➤ **Examples:** prove, probable, probation

The word *fact* comes from the Latin word *factum,* which means "event." It means "something that is true." Like a fact, a real-life event actually happens; it is not made-up or imagined.

➤ **Example:** It is a **fact** that George Washington was the first president of the United States.

Practice Follow each of the directions.
1. Give one fact and one opinion about today.
2. Explain how you would prove how old you are.

Grammar Lesson

Pronouns A **pronoun** is a word that takes the place of a noun or another pronoun. Writers use pronouns to avoid the awkwardness of repeating the same noun over and over. **Interrogative pronouns** are used in questions. **Indefinite pronouns** can be plural or singular, depending on how they are used.

Interrogative Pronouns	Indefinite Pronouns
who, whom, whose, what, which	some, other, none

Practice Identify the type of each pronoun. Use each pronoun in a new sentence.

1. None of the children had difficulty.
2. Which player needed a helmet?
3. Who will come with me to the store?
4. Some like to watch television.
5. Whom should we thank?

MorePractice

For more practice with pronouns, see the Grammar Handbook, p. R32.

W̸G Prentice Hall Writing and Grammar Connection: Chapter 23, Section 1.

Reading: Fact and Opinion

Directions: *Read the selection. Then, answer the questions.*

"Be careful," warned the dealer. "That's the most valuable stamp in the shop. It's the prettiest, too. You'll never see another one of those. There are only five in the world. I found that stamp when I was traveling in North Africa. Stamp collecting is a hobby for the adventurous."

1. Which is a fact?
    A You'll never see another one of those.
    B That's the most valuable stamp in the shop.
    C It's the prettiest, too.
    D Stamp collecting is a hobby for the adventurous.

2. Which is an opinion?
    A That's the most valuable stamp in the shop.
    B It's the prettiest, too.
    C There are only five in the world.
    D when I was traveling in North Africa

3. Which can be checked using the Internet?
    A That's the most valuable stamp in the shop.
    B There are only five in the world.
    C It's the prettiest, too.
    D Stamp collecting is a hobby for the adventurous.

4. Which is an opinion that is based on facts?
    A You'll never see another one of those.
    B There are only five in the world.
    C That's the most valuable stamp in the shop.
    D I found the stamp when I was traveling in North Africa.

Timed Writing: Interpretation

Review "The Lady and the Spider" or "Names/Nombres." Write a brief description of the narrator's observations in the first paragraph of the selection. Then, explain how you think the narrator feels. Use details from the story to illustrate your explanation. **(20 minutes)**

 ## Writing Workshop: *Work in Progress*

Autobiographical Narrative

For an autobiographical narrative you may write, think of lessons that taught you how to be happier or more content. Make a web of one of these lessons. Put the web in your writing portfolio.

Reading Informational Materials

Atlas

In Part 2, you are learning how to distinguish between fact and opinion. In an atlas, you can find many useful facts that will help you understand aspects of a specific place. If you read "Names/Nombres," you can learn more about Julia Alvarez's Dominican heritage in the atlas entry that follows.

About Atlases

An **atlas** is a book of maps showing cities, mountains, rivers, and roads. Some atlases include facts about the places depicted, as well as brief articles on topics such as population and climate. Atlas maps usually contain the following:

- a *compass rose* that shows north, south, east, and west
- a *scale bar* that shows how many miles or kilometers are represented by one inch on the map
- a *legend,* or *key,* that explains the map's symbols and colors
- *labels* that indicate the location and name of each place
- an *inset map* showing a region's location on the globe

Reading Skill

A **generalization** is a broad statement based on many examples. A generalization that is supported by facts is a valid, or true, generalization. A generalization that is not well supported is a faulty generalization. The information in an atlas entry can help you make generalizations about a region. Use the checklist shown to help you make generalizations based on facts in an atlas:

Using an Atlas to Make Generalizations

- ❑ Use the compass rose to support generalizations about locations.
- ❑ Use the scale bar to support generalizations about distances.
- ❑ Use the key to support generalizations about such subjects as the size of cities and the height of mountains.

The Caribbean

The introductory section gives general information about the islands in the Caribbean Sea. The map below shows Hispaniola, an island made up of two separate countries.

The Caribbean Sea is enclosed by an arc of many hundreds of islands, islets, and offshore reefs that reach from Florida, in the US, round to Venezuela in South America. From 1492, Spain, France, Britain, and the Netherlands claimed the islands as colonies.

Hispaniola

Cap-Haïtien
Gonaïves
Île de la Gonâve
Jérémie
PORT-AU-PRINCE
Cayes
Jacmel
HAITI
Monte Cristi
Puerto Plata
Santiago
La Vega
San Francisco de Macorís
Pico Duarte 10,417ft
Cordillera Central
SANTO DOMINGO
La Romana
Isla Saona
Isla Beata
DOMINICAN REPUBLIC

The *compass rose* shows the directions north, south, east, and west. The *scale bar* shows that one inch on the map represents approximately 100 miles.

LAND HEIGHT
- 6,560–13,120ft
- 3,280–6,560ft
- 1,640–3,280ft
- 820–1,640ft
- 330–820ft
- 0–330ft

SEA DEPTH
- 0–820ft
- 820–1,640ft
- 1,640–3,280ft
- 3,280–6,560ft
- 6,560–9,840ft
- 9,840–13,120ft
- Below 13,120ft

CITIES AND TOWNS
- Over 500,000 people
- 100,000–500,000
- 50,000–100,000
- Less than 50,000

This key shows different colors representing different land heights and different depths of the sea. The other key lists the symbols that show populations.

N
W — E
S

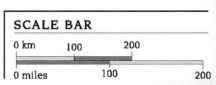

SCALE BAR

0 km	100	200
0 miles	100	200

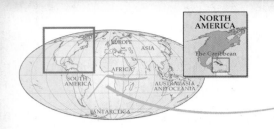

This inset map shows where the Caribbean Sea and its islands are located on the globe. To help you, a second inset shows them in relation to North America.

THE LANDSCAPE

The islands are formed from two main mountain chains: the Greater Antilles, which are part of a chain running from west to east, and the Lesser Antilles, which run from north to south. The mountains are now almost submerged under the Atlantic Ocean and Caribbean Sea. Only the higher peaks reach above sea level to form islands.

The information here describes the general landscape of the islands. It also provides details about the physical features of four of the island regions in the Caribbean.

The Bahamas
The Bahamas are low-lying islands formed from limestone rock. Their coastlines are fringed by coral reefs, lagoons, and mangrove swamps. Some of the bigger islands are covered with forests.

Hispaniola
Two countries, Haiti and the Dominican Republic, occupy the island of Hispaniola. The land is mostly mountainous, broken by fertile valleys.

Cuba
Cuba is the largest island in the Antilles. Its landscape is made up of wide, fertile plains with rugged hills and mountains in the southeast.

The Lesser Antilles
Most of these small volcanic islands have mountainous interiors. Barbados and Antigua are flatter, with some higher volcanic areas. Montserrat was evacuated in 1997, following volcanic eruptions on the island.

FARMING AND LAND USE

Agriculture is an important source of income, with over half of all produce exported. Many islands have fertile, well-watered land and large areas set aside for commercial crops such as sugarcane, tobacco, and coffee. Some islands rely heavily on a single crop; in Dominica, bananas provide over half the country's income. Cuba is one of the world's biggest sugar producers.

Havana

Kingston

Port-au-Prince

San Juan

FARMING AND LAND USE

- Cattle
- Fishing
- Pigs
- Poultry
- Shellfish
- Bananas
- Coffee
- Sugarcane
- Tobacco

- Cropland
- Forest
- Pasture
- • Major conurbation

The information in this paragraph is illustrated by a map. Note that the key contains symbols that show where various products are grown or raised. Additionally, the key shows that different colors on the map show different types of land use.

Reading: Making Generalizations

Directions: *Choose the letter of the best answer to each question.*

1. According to the "Cities and Towns" key and the map on page 125, which generalization is valid?

   A La Romana is the largest city in the Dominican Republic.

   B Jacmel has fewer people than Puerto Plata does.

   C Port-au-Prince is the largest city in Haiti.

   D La Vega is the second-largest city on Hispaniola.

2. According to the information in "The Landscape," which generalization is valid?

   A All of the Caribbean islands have tall mountains.

   B All of the mountains are in a chain that runs from west to east.

   C Most of the mountains are under the Atlantic and Caribbean.

   D Most of the islands have had recent volcanic eruptions.

3. According to the "Farming and Land Use" information, which generalization is valid?

   A Most of the land shown on the map is covered with forests.

   B None of the islands on the map use land for pastures.

   C At least half of the land on the islands shown is used for pastures and crops.

   D Urban areas take up most of the land on the islands shown.

Reading: Comprehension and Interpretation

Directions: *Write your answers on a separate sheet of paper.*

4. If you wanted to visit the Caribbean islands that are *not* mountainous, where might you go? Explain.

5. Why do you think the islands are prone to volcanic eruptions?

Timed Writing: Description

Describe the geography of Cuba based on the information in this atlas entry. In your description, make generalizations about the amount and type of land and water. **(20 minutes)**

Symbolism

A **symbol** is anything that stands for or represents something else. In literature, symbols often stand for ideas, such as love or hope.

Writers often use symbols to make a point or to reinforce the theme or message of a literary work. For example, in literature, a voyage might symbolize the journey of life. To find and interpret symbols, notice items that seem to be of special importance and analyze the types of details the writer uses to describe them.

Comparing Symbolism

The writers of "The Sound of Summer Running" and "Eleven" each use symbols to represent a larger theme. For the main character in each story, the symbol has either a negative or positive feeling attached to it. As you interpret symbols, keep these points in mind:

- The meaning of a symbol is often open to interpretation by the reader, but any interpretation should be based on story events and details.
- A symbol may have more than one meaning.

	The Sound of Summer Running	Eleven
Symbol	sneakers	red sweater
Descriptive words from story		
Details		
The symbol represents		

Compare the use of symbolism in "The Sound of Summer Running" and "Eleven" by using a chart like the one shown.

Vocabulary Builder

The Sound of Summer Running

- **seized** (sēzd) *v.* grabbed; taken hold of (p. 130) *He seized the railing to stop his fall.*

- **suspended** (sə spen´ did) *v.* stopped for a time (p. 130) *Classes are suspended due to bad weather.*

- **revelation** (rev´ ə lā´ shən) *n.* sudden rush of understanding (p. 135) *The scientist had a revelation as he finished his experiment.*

Eleven

- **raggedy** (rag´ i dē) *adj.* torn from wear (p. 138) *The doll's old dress was raggedy.*

- **alley** (al´ ē) *n.* narrow street between or behind buildings (p. 139) *Cars enter the garage from the alley.*

- **invisible** (in viz´ ə bəl) *adj.* not able to be seen (p. 139) *Though it is all around us, air is invisible.*

Build Understanding

Connecting to the Literature

Reading/Writing Connection In both of the following stories, the main characters are affected by objects in their lives. Write down three or four reasons why an object might take on importance in a person's life. Use three of the following words: *acquire, affect, attach, evoke.*

Meet the Authors

Ray **Bradbury** (b. 1920)

As a boy, Ray Bradbury nourished his imagination by attending circuses, watching magicians, and reading science-fiction novels. Bradbury once stated, "My life filled up with these wonderful events and people and images, and they stirred my imagination so that by the time I was twelve, I decided to become a writer. Just like that."

Although he is most famous for his science-fiction tales, his childhood fears and dreams fill the pages of his 1957 novel *Dandelion Wine,* which includes "The Sound of Summer Running."

Sandra **Cisneros** (b. 1954)

Sandra Cisneros writes about her life, her family, and her Mexican heritage. "I'm trying to write the stories that haven't been written," Cisneros once said about her own writing. ". . . I'm determined to fill a literary void." Her award-winning collection of short stories, *The House on Mango Street,* is about a young Mexican American girl growing up in Chicago. The book was inspired by the stories of the students Cisneros met while she was a teacher.

Go Online
Author Link

For: More about the authors
Visit: www.PHSchool.com
Web Code: ele-9112

The Sound of Summer Running

from Dandelion Wine

Ray Bradbury

Late that night, going home from the show with his mother and father and his brother Tom, Douglas saw the tennis shoes in the bright store window. He glanced quickly away, but his ankles were <u>seized</u>, his feet <u>suspended</u>, then rushed. The earth spun; the shop awnings slammed their canvas wings overhead with the thrust of his body running. His mother and father and brother walked quietly on both sides of him. Douglas walked backward, watching the tennis shoes in the midnight window left behind.

"It was a nice movie," said Mother.

Douglas murmured, "It was . . ."

It was June and long past time for buying the special shoes that were quiet as a summer rain falling on the walks. June and the earth full of raw power and everything everywhere in motion. The grass was still pouring in from the country, surrounding the sidewalks, stranding the houses. Any moment the town would capsize, go down and leave not a stir in the clover and weeds. And here Douglas

▲ Critical Viewing
How might the child in this picture feel while walking barefoot through the grass? **[Speculate]**

Vocabulary Builder
seized (sēzd) *v.* grabbed; taken hold of

suspended (sə spen´ did) *v.* stopped for a time

stood, trapped on the dead cement and the red-brick streets, hardly able to move.

"Dad!" He blurted it out. "Back there in that window, those Cream-Sponge Para Litefoot Shoes . . ."

His father didn't even turn. "Suppose you tell me why you need a new pair of sneakers. Can you do that?"

"Well . . ."

It was because they felt the way it feels every summer when you take off your shoes for the first time and run in the grass. They felt like it feels sticking your feet out of the hot covers in wintertime to let the cold wind from the open window blow on them suddenly and you let them stay out a long time until you pull them back in under the covers again to feel them, like packed snow. The tennis shoes felt like it always feels the first time every year wading in the slow waters of the creek and seeing your feet below, half an inch further downstream, with refraction, than the real part of you above water.

"Dad," said Douglas, "it's hard to explain."

Somehow the people who made tennis shoes knew what boys needed and wanted. They put marshmallows and coiled springs in the soles and they wove the rest out of grasses bleached and fired in the wilderness. Somewhere deep in the soft loam of the shoes the thin hard sinews of the buck deer were hidden. The people that made the shoes must have watched a lot of winds blow the trees and a lot of rivers going down to the lakes. Whatever it was, it was in the shoes, and it was summer.

Douglas tried to get all this in words.

"Yes," said Father, "but what's wrong with last year's sneakers? Why can't you dig *them* out of the closet?"

Well, he felt sorry for boys who lived in California where they wore tennis shoes all year and never knew what it was to get winter off your feet, peel off the iron leather shoes all full of snow and rain and run barefoot for a day and then lace on the first new tennis shoes of the season, which was better than barefoot. The magic was always in the new pair of shoes. The magic might die by the first of September, but now in late June there was still plenty of magic, and shoes like these could jump you over trees and rivers and houses. And if you wanted, they could jump you over fences and sidewalks and dogs.

Literary Analysis
Symbolism How does Douglas feel about the tennis shoes?

✓ Reading Check

Why are the shoes so appealing to Douglas?

New Shoes for H, 1973–1974, Don Eddy, The Cleveland Museum of Art

◀ **Critical Viewing**
Do you think Douglas would be drawn to any of the items in this store window? Why or why not? **[Speculate]**

"Don't you see?" said Douglas. "I just *can't* use last year's pair."

For last year's pair were dead inside. They had been fine when he started them out, last year. But by the end of summer, every year, you always found out, you always knew, you couldn't really jump over rivers and trees and houses in them, and they were dead. But this was a new year, and he felt that this time, with this new pair of shoes, he could do anything, anything at all.

They walked up on the steps to their house. "Save your money," said Dad. "In five or six weeks—"

"Summer'll be over!"

Lights out, with Tom asleep, Douglas lay watching his feet, far away down there at the end of the bed in the moonlight, free of the heavy iron shoes, the big chunks of winter fallen away from them.

"Reason. I've got to think of reasons for the shoes."

Well, as anyone knew, the hills around town were wild with friends putting cows to riot, playing barometer[1] to the atmospheric changes, taking sun, peeling like calendars each day to take more sun. To catch those friends, you must run much faster than foxes or squirrels. As for the

Literary Analysis
Symbolism How are old tennis shoes like the end of summer?

---

1. barometer (bə räm´ ət ər) *n.* device that measures air pressure, to predict weather changes.

town, it steamed with enemies grown irritable with heat, so remembering every winter argument and insult. *Find friends, ditch enemies!* That was the Cream-Sponge Para Litefoot motto. *Does the world run too fast? Want to catch up? Want to be alert, stay alert? Litefoot, then! Litefoot!*

He held his coin bank up and heard the faint small tinkling, the airy weight of money there.

Whatever you want, he thought, you got to make your own way. During the night now, let's find that path through the forest. . . .

Downtown, the store lights went out, one by one. A wind blew in the window. It was like a river going downstream and his feet wanting to go with it.

In his dreams he heard a rabbit running running running in the deep warm grass.

Old Mr. Sanderson moved through his shoe store as the proprietor of a pet shop must move through his shop where are kenneled animals from everywhere in the world, touching each one briefly along the way. Mr. Sanderson brushed his hands over the shoes in the window, and some of them were like cats to him and some were like dogs; he touched each pair with concern, adjusting laces, fixing tongues. Then he stood in the exact center of the carpet and looked around, nodding.

There was a sound of growing thunder.

One moment, the door to Sanderson's Shoe Emporium was empty. The next, Douglas Spaulding stood clumsily there, staring down at his leather shoes as if these heavy things could not be pulled up out of the cement. The thunder had stopped when his shoes stopped. Now, with painful slowness, daring to look only at the money in his cupped hand, Douglas moved out of the bright sunlight of Saturday noon. He made careful stacks of nickels, dimes, and quarters on the counter, like someone playing chess and worried if the next move carried him out into sun or deep into shadow.

"Don't say a word!" said Mr. Sanderson.

Douglas froze.

"First, I know just what you want to buy," said Mr. Sanderson. "Second, I see you every afternoon at my window; you think I don't see? You're wrong. Third, to give it its full name, you want the Royal

Literary Analysis
Symbolism How do the descriptions in this paragraph add other meanings to the shoes?

Reading Check

How does Douglas's father react when Douglas asks for the shoes?

Crown Cream-Sponge Para Litefoot Tennis Shoes: 'LIKE MENTHOL ON YOUR FEET!' Fourth, you want credit."

"No!" cried Douglas, breathing hard, as if he'd run all night in his dreams. "I got something better than credit to offer!" he gasped. "Before I tell, Mr. Sanderson, you got to do me one small favor. Can you remember when was the last time you yourself wore a pair of Litefoot sneakers, sir?"

Mr. Sanderson's face darkened. "Oh, ten, twenty, say, thirty years ago. Why . . . ?"

"Mr. Sanderson, don't you think you owe it to your customers, sir, to at least try the tennis shoes you sell, for just one minute, so you know how they feel? People forget if they don't keep testing things. United Cigar Store man smokes cigars, don't he? Candy-store man samples his own stuff, I should think. So . . ."

"You may have noticed," said the old man, "I'm wearing shoes."

"But not sneakers, sir! How you going to sell sneakers unless you can rave about them and how you going to rave about them unless you know them?"

Mr. Sanderson backed off a little distance from the boy's fever, one hand to his chin. "Well . . ."

"Mr. Sanderson," said Douglas, "you sell me something and I'll sell you something just as valuable."

"Is it absolutely necessary to the sale that I put on a pair of the sneakers, boy?" said the old man.

"I sure wish you could, sir!"

The old man sighed. A minute later, seated panting quietly, he laced the tennis shoes to his long narrow feet. They looked detached and alien[2] down there next to the dark cuffs of his business suit. Mr. Sanderson stood up.

"How do they *feel*?" asked the boy.

"How do they feel, he asks; they feel fine." He started to sit down.

Literary Analysis
Symbolism Why do you think Mr. Sanderson does not have the same reaction to the sneakers as Douglas?

"Please!" Douglas held out his hand. "Mr. Sanderson, now could you kind of rock back and forth a little, sponge around, bounce kind of, while I tell you the rest? It's this: I give you my money, you give me the shoes, I owe you a dollar. But, Mr. Sanderson, *but*—soon as I get those shoes on, you know what *happens*?"

---

2. alien (ā[′] yən) *adj.* foreign; unfamiliar.

"What?"

"Bang! I deliver your packages, pick up packages, bring you coffee, burn your trash, run to the post office, telegraph office, library! You'll see twelve of me in and out, in and out, every minute. Feel those shoes, Mr. Sanderson, *feel* how fast they'd take me? All those springs inside? Feel all the running inside? Feel how they kind of grab hold and can't let you alone and don't like you just *standing* there? Feel how quick I'd be doing the things you'd rather not bother with? You stay in the nice cool store while I'm jumping all around town! But it's not me really, it's the shoes. They're going like mad down alleys, cutting corners, and back! There they go!"

Mr. Sanderson stood amazed with the rush of words. When the words got going the flow carried him; he began to sink deep in the shoes, to flex his toes, limber[3] his arches, test his ankles. He rocked softly, secretly, back and forth in a small breeze from the open door. The tennis shoes silently hushed themselves deep in the carpet, sank as in a jungle grass, in loam and resilient clay. He gave one solemn bounce of his heels in the yeasty dough, in the yielding and welcoming earth. Emotions hurried over his face as if many colored lights had been switched on and off. His mouth hung slightly open. Slowly he gentled and rocked himself to a halt, and the boy's voice faded and they stood there looking at each other in a tremendous and natural silence.

A few people drifted by on the sidewalk outside, in the hot sun.

Still the man and boy stood there, the boy glowing, the man with <u>revelation</u> in his face.

"Boy," said the old man at last, "in five years, how would you like a job selling shoes in this emporium?"

"Gosh, thanks, Mr. Sanderson, but I don't know what I'm going to be yet."

"Anything you want to be, son," said the old man, "you'll be. No one will ever stop you."

The old man walked lightly across the store to the wall of ten thousand boxes, came back with some shoes for the boy, and wrote up a list on some paper while the boy was lacing the shoes on his feet and then standing there, waiting.

---

3. **limber** (lim´ bər) *v.* loosen up (a muscle or limb); make easy to bend.

Literary Analysis
Symbolism How are Mr. Sanderson's feelings for the shoes similar to Douglas's in this paragraph?

Vocabulary Builder
revelation (rev´ ə lā´ shən) *n.* sudden rush of understanding

Reading Check

What does Douglas ask Mr. Sanderson to do with the shoes?

The old man held out his list. "A dozen things you got to do for me this afternoon. Finish them, we're even Stephen, and you're fired."

"Thanks, Mr. Sanderson!" Douglas bounded away.

"Stop!" cried the old man.

Douglas pulled up and turned.

Mr. Sanderson leaned forward. "How do they *feel*?"

The boy looked down at his feet deep in the rivers, in the fields of wheat, in the wind that already was rushing him out of the town. He looked up at the old man, his eyes burning, his mouth moving, but no sound came out.

"Antelopes?" said the old man, looking from the boy's face to his shoes. "Gazelles?"

The boy thought about it, hesitated, and nodded a quick nod. Almost immediately he vanished. He just spun about with a whisper and went off. The door stood empty. The sound of the tennis shoes faded in the jungle heat.

Mr. Sanderson stood in the sun-blazed door, listening. From a long time ago, when he dreamed as a boy, he remembered the sound. Beautiful creatures leaping under the sky, gone through brush, under trees, away, and only the soft echo their running left behind.

"Antelopes," said Mr. Sanderson. "Gazelles."

He bent to pick up the boy's abandoned winter shoes, heavy with forgotten rains and long-melted snows. Moving out of the blazing sun, walking softly, lightly, slowly, he headed back toward civilization. . . .

Literary Analysis
Symbolism What three things in nature are used to describe the new shoes?

Thinking About the Selection

1. **Respond:** Is Douglas someone you admire? Why or why not?

2. **(a) Recall:** What are Douglas's feelings about last year's sneakers? **(b) Infer:** Why does he feel this way?

3. **(a) Recall:** What is Mr. Sanderson's reaction when Douglas asks him to try on the sneakers? **(b) Deduce:** Why does he react this way? **(c) Analyze:** Explain the change in Mr. Sanderson when he is wearing the sneakers.

4. **(a) Summarize:** Explain Douglas's plan, including why he thinks Mr. Sanderson must try on the sneakers.
   (b) Make a Judgment: Would this plan work on most store owners? Explain.

Eleven

SANDRA CISNEROS

Orange Sweater, 1955, Elmer Bischoff, San Francisco Museum of Modern Art, San Francisco, California

◀ **Critical Viewing**
Why might the girl in the picture be sitting alone? **[Speculate]**

What they don't understand about birthdays and what they never tell you is that when you're eleven, you're also ten, and nine, and eight, and seven, and six, and five, and four, and three, and two, and one. And when you wake up on your eleventh birthday you expect to feel eleven, but you don't. You open your eyes and everything's just like yesterday, only it's today. And you don't feel eleven at all. You feel like you're still ten. And you are—underneath the year that makes you eleven.

Like some days you might say something stupid, and that's the part of you that's still ten. Or maybe some days you might need to sit on your mama's lap because you're scared, and that's the part of you that's five. And one day when you're all grown up maybe you will need to cry like if you're three, and that's okay. That's what I tell Mama when she's sad and needs to cry. Maybe she's feeling three.

Because the way you grow old is kind of like an onion or like the rings inside a tree trunk or like my little wooden dolls that fit one inside the other, each year inside the next one. That's how being eleven years old is.

You don't feel eleven. Not right away. It takes a few days, weeks even, sometimes even months before you say eleven when they ask you. And you don't feel smart eleven, not until you're almost twelve. That's the way it is.

Only today I wish I didn't have just eleven years rattling inside me like pennies in a tin Band-Aid box. Today I wish I was one-hundred-and-two instead of eleven because if I was one-hundred-and-two I'd have known what to say when Mrs. Price put the red sweater on my desk. I would've known how to tell her it wasn't mine instead of just sitting there with that look on my face and nothing coming out of my mouth.

"Whose is this?" Mrs. Price says, and she holds the red sweater up in the air for all the class to see. "Whose? It's been sitting in the coatroom for a month."

"Not mine," says everybody. "Not me."

"It has to belong to somebody," Mrs. Price keeps saying, but nobody can remember. It's an ugly sweater with red plastic buttons and a collar and sleeves all stretched out like you could use it for a jump rope. It's maybe a thousand years old and even if it belonged to me I wouldn't say so.

Maybe because I'm skinny, maybe because she doesn't like me, that stupid Felice Garcia says, "I think it belongs to Rachel." An ugly sweater like that, all <u>raggedy</u> and old, but Mrs. Price believes her. Mrs. Price takes the sweater and puts it right on my desk, but when I open my mouth nothing comes out.

"That's not, I don't, you're not . . . not mine," I finally say in a little voice that was maybe me when I was four.

"Of course it's yours," Mrs. Price says, "I remember you wearing it once." Because she's older and the teacher, she's right and I'm not.

Portrait, From the Estate of Eloy Blanco, Collection of El Museo del Barrio, New York, NY

▲ **Critical Viewing**
Which character does the girl in this picture best represent? Why? **[Connect]**

Not mine, not mine, not mine, but Mrs. Price is already turning to page 32, and math problem number four. I don't know why but all of a sudden I'm feeling sick inside, like the part of me that's three wants to come out of my eyes, only I squeeze them shut tight and bite down on my teeth real hard and try to remember today I am eleven, eleven. Mama is making a cake for me for tonight, and when Papa comes home everybody will sing happy birthday, happy birthday to you.

But when the sick feeling goes away and I open my eyes, the red sweater's still sitting there like a big red mountain. I move the red sweater to the corner of my desk with my ruler. I move my pencil and books and eraser as far from it as possible. I even move my chair a little to the right. Not mine, not mine, not mine.

In my head I'm thinking how long till lunch time, how long till I can take the red sweater and throw it over the schoolyard fence, or leave it hanging on a parking meter, or bunch it up into a little ball and toss it in the <u>alley</u>. Except when math period ends Mrs. Price says loud and in front of everybody, "Now, Rachel, that's enough," because she sees I've shoved the red sweater to the tippy-tip corner of my desk and it's hanging all over the edge like a waterfall, but I don't care.

"Rachel," Mrs. Price says. She says it like she's getting mad. "You put that sweater on right now and no more non-sense."

"But it's not . . ."

"Now!" Mrs. Price says.

This is when I wish I wasn't eleven, because all the years inside of me—ten, nine, eight, seven, six, five, four, three, two, and one—are all pushing at the back of my eyes when I put one arm through one sleeve of the sweater that smells like cottage cheese, and then the other arm through the other and stand there with my arms apart as if the sweater hurts me and it does, all itchy and full of germs that aren't even mine.

That's when everything I've been holding in since this morning, since when Mrs. Price put the sweater on my desk, finally lets go, and all of a sudden I'm crying in front of everybody. I wish I was <u>invisible</u> but I'm not. I'm eleven

Literary Analysis
Symbolism How do Rachel's actions in this paragraph build the importance of the sweater?

Vocabulary Builder
alley (al′ ē) *n.* narrow street between or behind buildings

invisible (in viz′ ə bəl) *adj.* not able to be seen

Reading Check

How does the narrator feel about her eleventh birthday?

and it's my birthday today and I'm crying like I'm three in front of everybody. I put my head down on the desk and bury my face in my stupid clown sweater arms. My face all hot and spit coming out of my mouth because I can't stop the little animal noises from coming out of me, until there aren't any more tears left in my eyes, and it's just my body shaking like when you have the hiccups, and my whole head hurts like when you drink milk too fast.

But the worst part is right before the bell rings for lunch. That stupid Phyllis Lopez, who is even dumber than Felice Garcia, says she remembers the red sweater is hers! I take it off right away and give it to her, only Mrs. Price pretends like everything's okay.

Today I'm eleven. There's a cake Mama's making for tonight, and when Papa comes home from work we'll eat it. There'll be candles and presents and everybody will sing happy birthday, happy birthday to you, Rachel, only it's too late.

I'm eleven today. I'm eleven, ten, nine, eight, seven, six, five, four, three, two, and one, but I wish I was one-hundred-and-two. I wish I was anything but eleven, because I want today to be far away already, far away like a tiny kite in the sky, so tiny-tiny you have to close your eyes to see it.

Literary Analysis
Symbolism How are the red sweater and turning eleven years old alike for Rachel?

Thinking About the Selection

1. **Respond:** What would you like to say to Rachel? To Mrs. Price? To Felice Garcia?

2. **(a) Recall:** What is special about the day in this story? **(b) Analyze:** Explain how Rachel can be eleven and all her younger ages, too.

3. **(a) Analyze:** Why does Rachel wish she were "anything but eleven"? **(b) Connect:** How do the story's events suggest that Rachel's theory about ages has some truth to it?

4. **(a) Assess:** What are some advantages and disadvantages to "growing up"? **(b) Apply:** What disadvantages to growing up do Rachel's experiences illustrate? **(c) Make a Judgment:** Are Rachel's reactions understandable? Explain.

Apply the Skills

The Sound of Summer Running • *Eleven*

Comparing Symbolism

1. Explain what the new shoes in "The Sound of Summer Running" symbolize for Douglas.
2. Explain what the red sweater symbolizes for Rachel in "Eleven."
3. How are the feelings associated with each of the symbols different for Rachel and Douglas?

Writing to Compare Literary Works

Compare and contrast the ways symbols can be both positive and negative. Complete a chart like the one shown. Then, using the information you have gathered, write a paragraph explaining how the symbols in these stories help the authors express positive or negative feelings.

Story	Symbol	+ or − ?		Evidence
		❏	❏	
		❏	❏	

Vocabulary Builder

Practice Explain why each statement is true or false.

1. An *alley* is usually found behind a building.
2. If a bus service is *suspended,* the ride is free.
3. A person who has a *revelation* has a new insight or understanding.
4. Land *seized* by the government has been taken away.
5. The moon is *invisible* without a microscope.
6. A brand-new coat usually has *raggedy* sleeves.

QuickReview

Symbol: anything that stands for or represents something else

Go Online
Assessment
For: Self-test
Visit: www.PHSchool.com
Web Code: ela-6112

Fact and Opinion

Directions: *Questions 1–5 are based on the following selection.*

The platypus is a really funny-looking mammal. Most mammals have noses; a platypus, however, has a beak like a duck. Most mammals have hooves or feet with toes. The platypus has feet, but they are webbed, like the feet of a duck. The platypus does one other thing that is more like ducks than mammals; it lays eggs. Although the platypus shares some characteristics with a duck, they are actually very different. For example, the platypus has four feet, not two. Also, it is covered with beautiful brown fur, like the fur of a beaver. Everyone agrees that the platypus is the strangest, silliest animal on the planet!

1. **Which of the following statements is a fact?**
   A The platypus is funny-looking.
   B All ducks have brown fur.
   C The platypus has a beak like a duck's.
   D No mammals have webbed feet like a duck's.

2. **Which of the following statements is an opinion?**
   A Everyone agrees that the platypus is strange.
   B A platypus looks more like a duck than a mammal.
   C A platypus has webbed feet.
   D A platypus lays eggs, and most mammals do not.

3. **Which of the following statements contains both a fact and an opinion?**
   A Although the platypus is a mammal, it lays eggs.
   B Although the platypus is not a duck, it resembles a duck in many ways.

   C The fur of all platypuses and beavers is beautiful.
   D The platypus is a mammal, but it is a really funny-looking mammal.

4. **Based on the passage, which of the following claims can you prove?**
   A The platypus is one weird creature.
   B Nobody understands why a platypus is considered a mammal.
   C The platypus is a mammal, but it has features that most mammals do not have.
   D I think that the platypus is the most interesting mammal of all.

5. **What resource would be most useful for checking facts in this passage?**
   A a dictionary
   B a poem about animals
   C a Web site by an individual who loves animals
   D a Web site sponsored by a nature magazine

Assessment Practice

Vocabulary

Directions: *Choose the correct definition of the word.*

6. fact
- A an opinion that is popular
- B an opinion that can be challenged
- C a statement that can be proved
- D a statement that is experimental

7. opinion
- A a judgment or belief
- B a concern or worry
- C a common idea
- D a true statement

8. claim
- A state as a belief
- B question a belief
- C state as a fact
- D question a fact

9. distinguish
- A tell the difference between
- B put out with water
- C make extremely clean
- D be very sophisticated

10. prove
- A develop reasons that support an idea
- B evaluate the logic of an idea
- C show evidence something is true
- D question the truth of a statement

Directions: *Use what you have learned about word origins to choose the most likely meaning for each word.*

11. distinguishable
- A classifiable
- B separable
- C remarkable
- D extinguishable

12. claimant
- A a person who is perceptive
- B a person who calls for certain action
- C a person who works with the law
- D a person who decides on a course of action

13. proven
- A something that has been tested
- B something that is a major event
- C something that is separated from others in its class
- D something that is shouted

14. fact-finding
- A searching for ideas
- B academic research about a topic
- C finding the opinions that build an idea
- D finding that which is true

15. provable
- A to be able to be tested and shown to be true
- B to be able to be thought about and shown to be true
- C to be generally accepted as true
- D to be verified by an expert

Spelling Workshop

Easily Confused Words

Some words that you use often are easy to confuse with each other. They may sound almost the same or have similar spellings.

Do You Know Now? Like the words on the following list, *know* and *now* are easily confused. You most likely know the difference between words like these. In writing, though, you may forget and choose the wrong one. In addition, homonyms and homophones sound the same but are spelled differently. The spell-checker in a word-processing program will not find this kind of error, so proofread carefully.

You are blocking our light!

Study the Word List. Make sure you know when to use each word.

Practice Use words from the list to complete the sentences.

1. I am afraid I will _____ this ring because it is _____.

2. I can _____ all your reasons _____ the last one.

3. Jen likes the idea more now _____ she did _____.

4. _____ books _____ in the classroom.

5. The class did not _____ the schedule until _____.

Word List

Word List
our
are
than
then
know
now
lose
loose
accept
except

Directions: *Choose the sentence in which all words are spelled and used correctly.*

1. **A** There is a lose board in that floor.
   B Did Jose lose the race?
   C A screw on his glasses came lose.
   D She neatly cut off the lose button.

2. **A** This is are classroom.
   B We waited in are classroom for a while.
   C Are teacher came into the room.
   D We are waiting for the teacher.

3. **A** Everyone except Tina was late.
   B Did they except your invitation?
   C Please except my apology.
   D We hope you will except our offer.

4. **A** The baby was fussier then usual.
   B Al would rather hike than swim.
   C Dad wants to get home before than.
   D The test was harder then I expected.

Directions: *Choose the letter of the word that would be the correct spelling to fill in the blank.*

1. If we leave _____, we will be on time.
   A know
   B no
   C now
   D knew

2. Last year, Mr. Janzen was _____ favorite coach.
   A are
   B our
   C hour
   D or

3. If the plug comes _____, the toaster will not heat up.
   A lose
   B lost
   C loose
   D loos

4. The girls got there early, but _____ they had to wait.
   A then
   B than
   C thin
   D their

5. No one will be home to _____ the delivery.
   A except
   B expect
   C accept
   D acept

6. Do you _____ who won the election?
   A know
   B no
   C now
   D knew

Narration: Autobiographical Narrative

Some of the best stories are not made up; instead, they revolve around real events in the writer's life. This type of story is called an **autobiographical narrative.** Follow the steps outlined in this workshop to write an autobiographical narrative.

Assignment Write an autobiographical narrative about an event that taught you a lesson or helped you to grow.

What to Include Your autobiographical narrative should feature the following elements:
- an interest-grabbing first sentence or opening paragraph
- a clear sequence of events, using chronological order
- a central problem or conflict that you or someone else resolves
- vivid details that show the people, places, and events
- error-free writing, including correct use of pronouns and antecedents

To preview the criteria on which your autobiographical narrative may be judged, see the rubric on page 153.

 Writing Workshop: *Work in Progress*

Autobiographical Narrative

If you have completed the Work-in-Progress assignments, you already have several ideas you might use in your autobiographical narrative. Continue developing these ideas or explore a new topic as you complete the Writing Workshop.

Using the Form

You may use elements of this form in these writing situations:
- letters
- journals
- persuasive essays
- anecdotes

To get the feel for narrative nonfiction, read "Names / Nombres" by Julia Alvarez, p. 115.

Prewriting

Choosing Your Topic

To find the right topic for your autobiographical narrative, think of events that were really special for you. These strategies will help:

- **Freewriting** Write whatever thoughts occur to you about a general topic, such as *holidays, adventures,* or *a problem solved.* Focus more on getting your ideas down than on writing correctly. After five minutes, read over your thoughts, and choose a topic from among them.

- **Memory Quicklist** In the first column of a three-column chart, list special people, unique places, and memorable events. In the next column, describe each one. In the last column, give an example to support each description. Choose one memory as your topic.

Narrowing Your Topic

Once you have chosen a topic, narrow it by focusing on one significant part: a surprise, a problem, or some other aspect of the experience that really makes it stand out in your mind.

Gathering Details

Make a timeline. Begin to gather the details that you will use to develop your story. List the events and supporting details in the correct order on a timeline like the one shown.

Work in Progress
Review the work you did on pages 105 and 123.

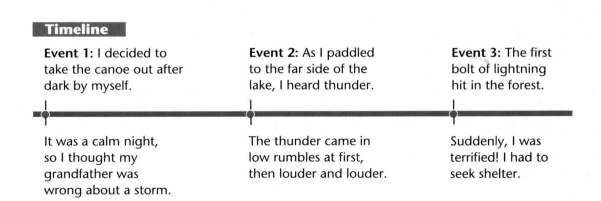

Timeline

Event 1: I decided to take the canoe out after dark by myself.

Event 2: As I paddled to the far side of the lake, I heard thunder.

Event 3: The first bolt of lightning hit in the forest.

It was a calm night, so I thought my grandfather was wrong about a storm.

The thunder came in low rumbles at first, then louder and louder.

Suddenly, I was terrified! I had to seek shelter.

Writing Workshop

Drafting

Shaping Your Writing

Decide on the order of events. Review your timeline. Then, make a decision about the order in which you will present the events.

- **Chronological Order:** Many stories start with the first event and then add the others in the order in which they occurred.

- **Chronological Order with Flashback:** Some stories begin at the end and flash back to the beginning. Then, through flashback, the writer tells the rest of the story in chronological order.

Plan to present your conflict. On a conflict map like this one, list each event that builds toward the **climax**, the story's highest point of tension. Then, list the events that reduce the tension until the last scene, or resolution, takes place. Use your conflict map as you draft.

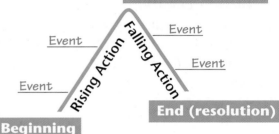

Providing Elaboration

Choose vivid language. You can add life and high-interest to your autobiographical narrative with vivid verbs, nouns, and adjectives.

Dull: As I went across the lake, I heard noises far away.
Vivid: As I paddled across the peaceful lake, I was suddenly aware of low rumbles of thunder rolling toward me.

Use dialogue. Dialogue will help to bring life to your characters. Do not report everything a character says. Instead, choose the important conversations that show a character's feelings and reactions.

To read the complete student model, see page 152.

Student Model: Using Dialogue

"Kyle," he said, "you have a rare condition called Osteochondritis Dissecans. It means part of your lower femur has died because there is no longer a blood supply to that area."

The writer effectively uses dialogue to explain his condition.

Jane Yolen

Jane Yolen

On Writing Narratives

I loved stories about King Arthur and Merlin since I was a child, so of course I wanted to write about them when I grew up. *Passager* and the two books after it that make up the Young Merlin Trilogy each began with a short story. Now, short stories can focus on a moment in time or a moment of emotion. A novel needs a longer narrative or story, in which a character grows, changes, or "gets wisdom."

"I write with both my head and my heart."

——————— *Jane Yolen*

Professional Model:

from *Passager,* Book 1 of the Young Merlin Trilogy

The whole time he had lived alone in the woods came to one easy winter, one very wet spring, one mild summer, and one brilliant fall.

In the old tales, Merlin went mad as an adult and ran off into the woods for a year. But I thought having him be a child was more interesting.

A year.

But for an eight-year-old that is a good portion of a lifetime. He remembered all of that year. What he could not recall clearly was how he had come to the woods, how he had come to be alone. What he could recall made him uneasy. He remembered it mostly at night. And in dreams.

My Merlin is a reader of dreams, which we find out in the second book. This is called foreshadowing, where the author puts down clues for later on in the story.

He remembered a large, smoky hearth and the smell of meat drippings. A hand slapped his—he remembered this, though he could not remember who had slapped him or why. That was not one of the bad dreams, though. He could clearly recall the taste of the meat before the slap, and it was good.

Authors write with a particular style or voice. In this kind of fantasy, I use a bardic (like the old bards or poet-singers) or Biblical voice. The phrase "and it was good" appears often in the beginning of the Bible.

Revising

Revising Your Overall Structure

Identify and strengthen connections. Draw an arrow from each paragraph to the next, and explain the relationship between the paragraphs it links. Then, ask yourself these questions:

- Do events in one paragraph cause those in the next?

- Does one paragraph give information that a reader needs in order to understand the next paragraph?

- Does one paragraph create curiosity or suspense about what might happen in the next paragraph?

If a paragraph is not clearly related to the ones before and after it, rewrite it or think about moving it or even deleting it.

Revising Your Paragraphs

Pack some punch into your lead. The first sentence of your autobiographical narrative is the **lead.** It should be an attention-grabber that makes your readers curious and committed to reading on to find out what happens. These ideas might help you to pack more power into that all-important sentence:

- Start with an exciting action. *Crash! A bolt of lightning hit somewhere on the island, with ear-splitting, terrifying power.*

- Start with a hint about a potential problem. *The sky darkened unexpectedly with storm clouds.*

- Start with some dramatic dialogue. *"Don't go out on that lake alone!" my grandfather warned.*

Peer Review: Work with a partner to discuss your lead, and revise if necessary.

Reading Writing Connection

To read the complete student model, see page 152.

Student Model: Using a Punchy Lead

~~Recently, I was diagnosed with Osteochondritis Dissecans, a serious bone condition.~~

My knee has been bothering me for quite a while.

> By rewriting his lead sentence, the writer hooks readers into wanting to read more of his story.

Integrating Language Skills

Revising for Pronoun/Antecedent Agreement

A **pronoun** takes the place of a noun. The noun that is replaced by the pronoun is called the **antecedent**.

Identifying Errors in Pronoun/Antecedent Agreement A pronoun and its antecedent must agree in number. Use a singular pronoun with a singular antecedent. Use a plural pronoun with a plural antecedent.

Prentice Hall Writing and Grammar Connection: Chapter 24, Section 2

> **Singular Pronoun and Antecedent**
> <u>North Carolina</u> is a popular vacation spot because ***it*** has many beautiful beaches.
>
> **Plural Pronoun and Antecedent**
> My <u>parents</u> said that ***they*** would attend my play.

Sometimes, the antecedent is not a noun, but an indefinite pronoun such as *anyone, everything, each, something,* or *nothing.* Most errors in pronoun/antecedent agreement occur when the antecedent is a singular indefinite pronoun.

> **Singular Indefinite Pronoun and Antecedent**
> <u>Somebody</u> on the boys' team left ***his*** catcher's mitt on the bus.
>
> **Plural Indefinite Pronoun and Antecedent**
> <u>Many</u> of the students brought ***their*** reports in on Thursday.

Fixing Errors To find and fix errors related to pronoun/antecedent agreement, follow these steps:

1. **Identify each pronoun/antecedent pair that you have used.**
2. **Decide whether the antecedent is singular or plural.** (Refer to R32–R47 for more on indefinite pronouns.)
3. **Follow the rules of agreement to fix any errors.**

Apply It to Your Editing

Reread your autobiographical narrative. Look for pronouns and their antecedents. Then, use the rules and examples above to make all necessary corrections.

Writing Workshop

Student Model: Kyle Shea
Clackamas, OR

A Time to Heal

My knee had been bothering me for quite a while. At first my parents weren't concerned. My mom said, "It's probably just growing pains." The pain continued so my parents took me to the doctor. The doctor took x-rays, bone scans, and MRI's. When we went back to the doctor for the results of the tests, the doctor entered the examining room looking very serious. "Kyle," he said, "you have a rare condition called Osteochondritis Dissecans. It means that part of your lower femur has died because there is no longer a blood supply to that area." He explained that this could be a very serious condition. My parents and I were in shock! I was very afraid.

The doctor gave me two options. He said, "You can have six months of complete rest—except walking or swimming—or you can have surgery to regenerate the blood supply to that area of the bone." The surgery involves drilling microscopic holes in the bone. I wasn't thrilled with either choice.

Faced with that decision, my parents and I decided to try resting before having the surgery. I couldn't finish my baseball season and was forced to sit out the football and basketball seasons also. It was really hard for me when friends would ask me why I hadn't tried out for the teams.

After six months of rest, I had more bad news—my leg had not gotten better so the doctor said, "Kyle, we have no other choice but to move forward with the surgery." The surgery will take about three months to heal. My recovery will require me to be on crutches for a month then gradually over the next two months start putting weight back on my leg. At the end of three months I will be back on my feet in time for spring baseball.

"Hey Kyle," my friend Alex asked, "isn't it hard not to play sports?"

"Alex," I said, "The thing I miss the most is just being around you guys. It's been really lonely. I can't wait to get back into it again."

I realize how fortunate I am. During my doctor visits I have met some really incredible people. I met a little girl that had to have her foot amputated because of a birth defect. She walks around as if she is no different than anyone else. She will be receiving a prosthetic foot when she is older so that she has better balance and can wear a shoe. I have been in the waiting area with kids that have cancer and other incurable diseases. Mine is an injury that can be corrected with surgery. I feel very lucky because I have an excellent chance of a complete recovery. A year off from sports taught me to appreciate what I took for granted like friends and being a part of a team.

This straightforward lead makes readers want to find out why Kyle's knee was bothering him.

Here, Kyle introduces the central problem that is the focus of his autobiographical narrative.

Transitions such as *before* and *after* help readers follow the chronological order of events.

Vivid details add impact. They support the closing sentence of the narrative.

Editing and Proofreading

Check your essay for errors in grammar, spelling, and punctuation.
Focus on Punctuating Dialogue: If you include conversations in your writing, follow the proper formatting rules.

- Enclose all direct quotations in quotation marks. *"You were right," I said to Jim.*
- Place a comma after the words that introduce the speaker. *Jim replied, "Well, you learned a lesson today."*
- Use commas and quotation marks before and after any interrupting words. *"Next time," I said, "I guess I'll listen."*

Publishing and Presenting

Consider one of the following ways to share your writing:
Deliver a speech. Use your autobiographical narrative as the basis for a dramatic presentation.
Get it published. Mail your narrative to a magazine that publishes student writing. Include a letter introducing your essay.

Reflecting on Your Writing

Writer's Journal Jot down your thoughts on writing an autobiographical narrative. Begin by answering these questions:

- How did gathering and using vivid details help you to express why the experience was so important to you?
- What new insights did you gain about this experience?

Prentice Hall Writing and Grammar Connection: Chapter 4

Rubric for Self-Assessment

To assess your autobiographical narrative, use the following rubric:

Criteria	Rating Scale *not very* → *very*
Focus: How clearly does the narrative present the problem or conflict?	1 2 3 4 5
Organization: How clearly is the sequence of events presented?	1 2 3 4 5
Support/Elaboration: How effective are details in describing people, places, and events?	1 2 3 4 5
Style: How well does the language grab readers' interest?	1 2 3 4 5
Conventions: How correct is your grammar, especially your use of pronouns and antecedents?	1 2 3 4 5

Communications Workshop

Following Oral Directions

Every day, you hear and follow oral directions and instructions. To understand and carry out **multistep oral directions,** or spoken directions with several steps, you need to listen carefully to the speaker and restate the directions in the correct sequence. The following strategies will help you demonstrate effective listening skills.

Listen Carefully

Following oral directions correctly requires understanding the speaker's message. To understand directions, follow these guidelines.

Notice action words and time-order words. Pay special attention to the key action word in each step. The key action words will help you remember what to do. For example, in these directions for a fire drill, the action words are underlined.

> ▶ **Example:** First, <u>close</u> the doors and windows. Then, <u>walk</u> to the nearest exit. When you are outside, <u>stand</u> with your class while the teacher counts the group.

Most directions are stated in chronological order and include words such as *first, then, next, finally,* and *last.*

Ask questions. Do not assume that the speaker will give you all the information you need. Identify missing information and ask questions to clarify.

Restate Directions

Repeating the directions allows the direction giver to correct any misunderstanding.

Use the action words and transition words. Repeat or restate the directions in your own words, using the action words to recall the action required. Use the transition words at the beginning of each step to restate multistep directions.

Checklist

Listen Carefully
- ☑ Focus on the speaker. Listen for main ideas.
- ☑ Notice the action word in each step.
- ☑ Notice time-order words.
- ☑ Ask questions.

Restate Carefully
- ☑ Repeat the directions in your own words.
- ☑ Use time-order words.

Tom Sawyer: An Adapted Classic

Mark Twain
Globe Fearon, 1996

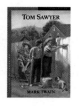

Novel The setting is 19th-century Mississippi. Tom Sawyer, Huckleberry Finn, and their friends love to explore caves, fantasize about being pirates, and dream of digging up treasures. Unknowingly and much to their guardians' and parents' concern, they run into dangerous situations.

Queen's Own Fool

Jane Yolen and Robert J. Harris
Penguin, 2003

Novel Written as historical fiction, *Queen's Own Fool* places readers in the courts of Europe during the 1500s, a time when the whims of royalty controlled the fates of countries. Nicola, the sensitive and clever confidante of Queen Mary, commits herself to a life of loyalty to a queen who is betrayed by almost everyone around her. History becomes adventure as Queen Mary tries to figure out how she can control her royal realm.

I, Juan de Pareja with Connected Readings

Elizabeth Borton de Trevino
Prentice Hall, 2000

Novel This Newbery–award-winning historical novel details the artistic awakening of a young apprentice to the great Renaissance Spanish painter, Diego de Velázquez.

Amelia Earhart: Courage in the Sky

Mona Kerby
Puffin, 1990

Biography When Amelia Earhart was young, she wanted to know why there were only heroes and no heroines in the adventure stories she read. She grew up to become a pioneer in aviation and a true heroine. This book takes the reader along on the journey of an exceptional woman who faced the world fearlessly until her mysterious disappearance in July 1937.

These titles are available in the Penguin/Prentice Hall Literature Library.
Consult your teacher before choosing one.

Think About It We all have parts of our personalities that we keep private because we are shy or just unsure of ourselves. Regardless of the reason, it is important to nurture our feelings of pride for what makes us different from everyone else. In this excerpt from his memoirs, Walter Dean Myers reflects on his love of both sports and books and the challenges he faced because of it.

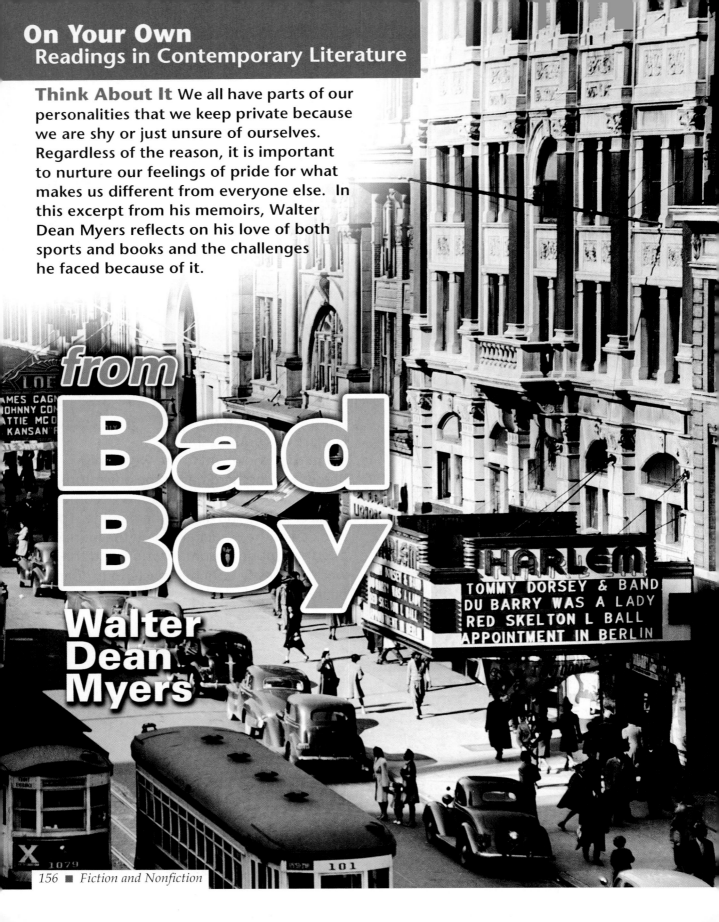

from
Bad
Boy

Walter Dean Myers

There were two categories of friends in my life: those with whom I played ball and everyone else. Athletes were highly respected in the black community, and boys my age were encouraged to play some sport. I loved playing ball. I would play basketball in the mornings with the boys who were just reaching their teens, and then stoop ball or punchball on the block with boys my age. Sometimes Eric and I would go down to the courts on Riverside Drive and play there. And I was a bad, bad loser. Most of my prayers, when they weren't for the Dodgers, were quick ones in the middle of a game, asking God to let me win. I liked other sports as well and even followed the New York Rangers hockey team in the papers for a while until I found out that all the references to ice meant just that, that they were skating on ice. There wasn't any ice to skate on in Harlem, so I gave up hockey.

With school out and me not having access to Mrs. Conway's cache of books, I rediscovered the George Bruce Branch of the public library on 125th Street. Sometimes on rainy days I would sit in the library and read. The librarians always suggested books that were too young for me, but I still went on a regular basis. I could never have afforded to buy the books and was pleased to have the library with its free supply.

Being a boy meant to me that I was not particularly like girls. Most of the girls I knew couldn't play ball, and that excluded them from most of what I wanted to do with my life. Dorothy Dodson, daughter of the Wicked Witch, read books, and I knew she did, but she couldn't stand me and was more than happy to tell me so on a number of occasions. Sometimes I would see other children on the trolley with books under their arms and suspected that they were like me somehow. I felt a connection with these readers but didn't know what the connection was. I knew there were things going on in my head, a fantasy life, that somehow corresponded to the books I read. I also felt a kind of comfort with books that I did not experience when I was away from them. Away from books I was, at times, almost desperate to fill up the spaces of my life. Books filled those spaces for me.

As much has I enjoyed reading, in the world in which I was living it had to be a secret vice. When I brought books home from the library, I would sometimes run into older kids who would tease me about my reading. It was, they made it clear, not what boys did. And though by now I was fighting older boys and didn't mind that one bit, for some reason I didn't want to fight about books. Books were

special and said something about me that I didn't want to reveal. I began taking a brown paper bag to the library to bring my books home in.

That year I learned that being a boy meant that I was supposed to do certain things and act in a certain way. I was very comfortable being a boy, but there were times when the role was uncomfortable. We often played ball in the church gym, and one rainy day, along with my brother Mickey and some of "my guys," I went to the gym, only to find a bevy of girls exercising on one half of the court. We wanted to run a full-court game, so we directed a few nasty remarks to the other side of the small gym. Then we saw that the girls were doing some kind of dance, so we imitated them, cracking ourselves up.

When the girls had finished their dancing, they went through some stretching exercises. A teenager, Lorelle Henry, was leading the group, and she was pretty, so we sent a few woo-hoos her way.

"I bet you guys can't even do these stretching exercises," Lorelle challenged.

We scoffed, as expected.

"If you can do these exercises, we'll get off the court," Lorelle said. "If not, you go through the whole dance routine with us."

It was a way to get rid of the girls, and we went over to do the exercises. Not one of us was limber enough to do the stretching exercises, and soon we were all trying to look as disgusted as we could while we hopped around the floor to the music.

They danced to music as a poem was being read. I liked the poem, which turned out to be "The Creation" by James Weldon Johnson. I liked dancing, too, but I had to pretend that I didn't like it. No big deal. I was already keeping reading and writing poems a secret; I would just add dancing.

Walter Dean Myers (b. 1937) was raised by foster parents in Harlem, a section of New York City populated mostly by African Americans. His foster mother taught him to read when he was just four years old. His love of reading has led him to write more than twenty-five books and short stories. Many of his works take place in Harlem and depict the problems and joys of being a teenager.

Readings in Contemporary Literature
Talk About It

Use these questions to guide a discussion of the excerpt from Bad Boy.

1. **(a)** What was Myers's attitude toward reading when he was a child? **(b)** Why did he think he had to keep this attitude a secret?

2. Myers loved to play sports. Think of an activity that you love and do well, such as playing basketball or dancing. Then, imagine that someone else with no experience in this area asks you to train him or her to do this skill. With a group, discuss the way you would approach the task of teaching.

3. What tone would you take toward the person you were training? Why?

4. How would you feel if the "student" did better than you? Explain. Choose a point person to share your group's ideas with the class.

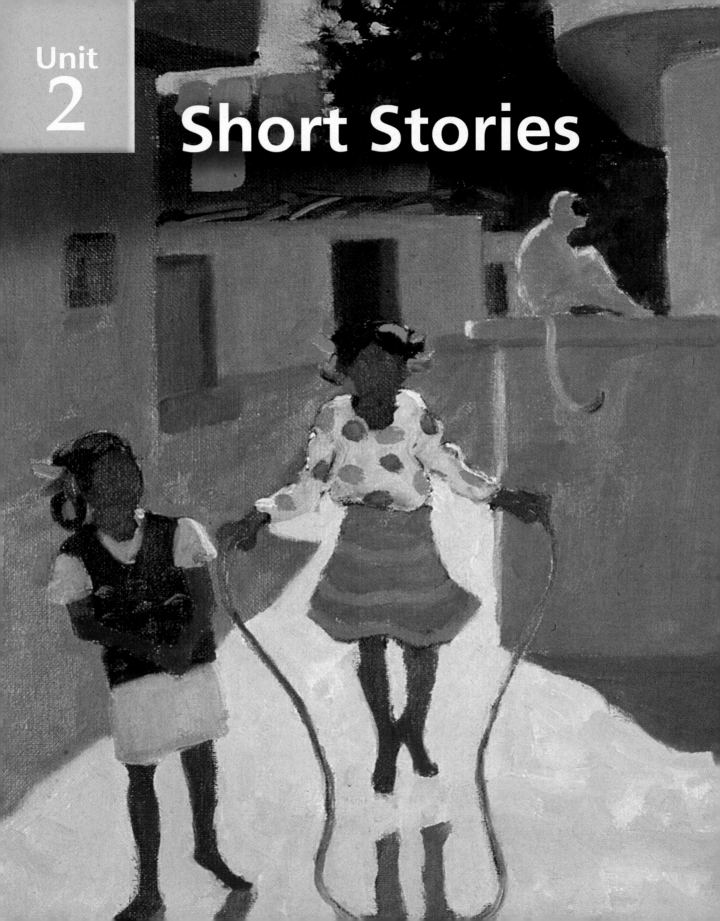

Unit
2

Short Stories

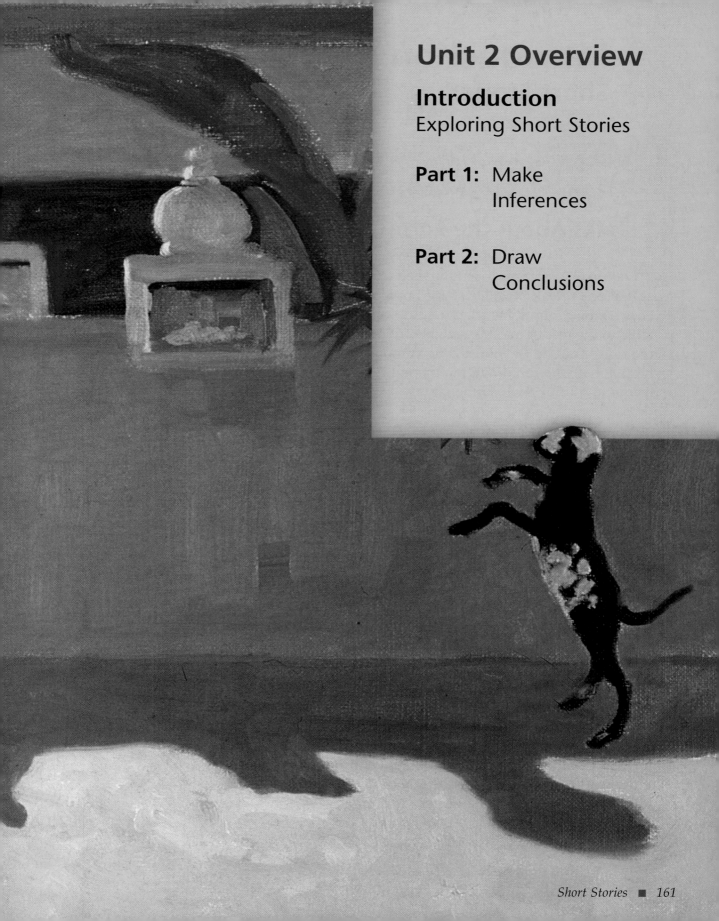

Unit 2 Overview

Introduction
Exploring Short Stories

Part 1: Make Inferences

Part 2: Draw Conclusions

Introduction:
Short Stories

Jean Craighead George

Talks About the Form

Jean Craighead
George

A squirrel was eager to eat the seeds on a bird feeder at the top of a tall pole. He started up the pole but slid back to the ground. He tried to jump from the picnic table to the feeder and missed. He tried hanging from the rain spout on the house, but found himself too high. Finally he ran down the tree limb above the feeder and hung by his hind claws.

The seeds were within his reach. He was about to eat when the house door opened and a boy stepped out. The squirrel jumped to the ground and ran. The boy threw out nuts and corn for the squirrel but he never came back. He had found a bird feeder in the next yard that was easy to climb.

▲ **Jean Craighead George** writes popular, prizewinning books about the adventures of young people forced to survive in the wilderness.

▼ **Critical Viewing** Jean Craighead George says that each author has an individual way of writing. In what ways does this illustration reflect that idea? **[Connect]**

A Short Story About a Squirrel

What you just read is a **short story.** It has a character. He is challenged and the challenges set us up for the ending. But where is the color a good short story needs? Where is the emotion and suspense and, finally, where is the dramatic ending we wait for?

A good writer will give those bare bones color, insight, and drama. The main character will become a wonderfully squirrelly squirrel. The back yard will be visible. The suspense will build up and up until the reader cannot wait to see how it all ends. If the reader smiles, rereads the tale or tells a friend to read it, the writer has spun art.

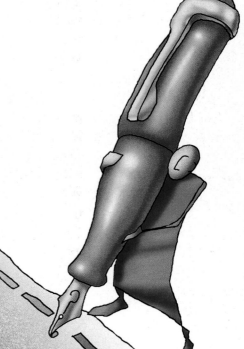

Different Writers Spin Different Stories

But the art of the short story is spun differently by each writer. Take my friend Joyce Carol Thomas. In one of her stories, the "I" is a single woman staking out a land claim in Oklahoma as was possible in 1889. The challenges are the hardships that Thomas's and other Black families faced in that raw hostile land.

Powerful Ending

Her ending is no squirrel finding easy access to food. Thomas's ending, shown here, carries the reader to greatness.

I have heard of a land
Where the pioneer woman still lives
Her possibilities reach as far
As her eyes can see
And as far as our imaginations can
  carry us.

from *I Have Heard of a Land*
—Joyce Carol Thomas

More About the Author

Jean Craighead George (b. 1919)

From her earliest days, Jean Craighead George has been fascinated by wild animals. Her first pet was a turkey vulture. She also has a special interest in wolves. During one summer spent at a research laboratory in Alaska, she learned to communicate with them. She has said, "The wolves are truly gentlemen, highly social and affectionate." George's human characters often have interesting animals as companions: a falcon, a weasel, and an alpha male wolf are some of them.

Fast Facts
▶ Jean Craighead George's brothers taught her falconry, the sport of using trained falcons to hunt game.
▶ Her novel *My Side of the Mountain* was made into a film in 1969.

Learning About Short Stories

Elements of Short Stories

The short story is a popular form of fiction. Like other types of fiction, a short story has a plot, characters, setting, and theme. Although all short stories are different, they all share the same basic elements.

Plot is the sequence of events in a story that are linked by cause and effect—earlier events advance the plot by bringing about later ones. As the problem in a short story gets worse, the plot builds to the point of greatest tension, called the **climax.** Then there is a **resolution**, or solving of the problem, and the story ends.

Conflict is a problem between opposing forces.

- An **internal conflict** takes place in the mind of a character. The character struggles to make a decision, take an action, or overcome an obstacle.

- An **external conflict** is one in which a character struggles with an outside force such as another character or a force of nature.

PEANUTS reprinted by permission of United Feature Syndicate, Inc.

Characters in a story are the people or animals who take part in the action.

- An author brings a character to life through methods of **characterization**—the act of creating and developing a character.

- A **character's traits**, or qualities, help readers understand the character and his or her actions. Character traits might include intelligence, stubbornness, or dependability.

- A **character's motives** are the reasons for his or her actions. Motives can include thoughts, feelings, or desires.

Setting is the time and place of the story's action. Details of setting can include the year, the time of day, or even the weather. The setting of a story can serve as the background for the plot and create a feeling or atmosphere.

- In a contemporary story, one that takes place in recent times, the made-up world of the setting usually includes details that are realistic.
- Stories based on events from history may include a mixture of fact and fiction.

Theme is a message about or insight into life. The theme of a story may be stated or implied.

- A **stated theme** is expressed directly by the author.
- An **implied theme** is suggested, or stated indirectly through what happens to the characters.

▼ **Critical Viewing**
What kind of conflict might this setting suggest? **[Connect]**

Check Your Understanding

For each item below, choose the letter of the short story element that matches the description.

1. a house at the beach during a hurricane
  a. setting
  b. character

2. an athlete who struggles to make the team
  a. theme
  b. conflict

3. a boy who enjoys studying dinosaurs
  a. character
  b. plot

4. sisters who learn the meaning of friendship
  a. theme
  b. setting

5. events that lead to the capture of a criminal
  a. setting
  b. plot

From the Author's Desk
Jean Craighead George Introduces "The Wounded Wolf"

"Wolves are friendly," I read in "The Wolves of Isle Royale" by Dr. L. David Mech, the world authority on wolves. I closed the book and headed out for wolf country to see if this were true. The year was 1970. The big bad wolf as portrayed in "Little Red Riding Hood" was the prevailing image of the wolf. He was a terrifying creature that ate babies and grandmothers.

Character Traits of the Wolf

I flew to Barrow, Alaska, where scientists at the Naval Arctic Research Lab had also found the wolf friendly, well organized, loyal, and devoted to their pups. Some of the scientists were communicating with the wolves in their own language of posture, voice, scent, and coloration. I watched in fascination.

When wolf student Gordon Haber invited me to Denali National Park to observe wolves in the wild, I hopped a ride with a bush pilot and joined Haber along the Sanctuary River. For ten days I lay on my belly watching the friendly, loving wolves and gathering details for **settings** and **characters.**

Characters and Conflicts in the Wild

Dramas unrolled: a grizzly bear threatened, a pup was briefly lost, ravens followed the adults on their hunts. "Hey," I said to myself. "The wolves are writing a story for me. I don't have to make it up." That afternoon Haber told me about Roko, an adolescent injured by a caribou. What happened to Roko took my breath away. I went home to write his story, "The Wounded Wolf."

Adding to the Basic Plot

To the basic **plot,** or story line, I added dramas I had seen in the Arctic—ravens pecking wounds, foxes nipping, grizzly bears threatening. I relived battles for survival, heard eerie sounds, saw bleak landscapes, then called upon the "humanity" of the wolf.

The Wounded Wolf

Jean Craighead George

A wounded wolf climbs Toklat Ridge,[1] a massive spine of rock and ice. As he limps, dawn strikes the ridge and lights it up with sparks and stars. Roko, the wounded wolf, blinks in the ice fire, then stops to rest and watch his pack run the thawing Arctic valley.

They plunge and turn. They fight the mighty caribou that struck young Roko with his hoof and wounded him. He jumped between the beast and Kiglo, leader of the Toklat pack. Young Roko spun and fell. Hooves, paws, and teeth roared over him. And then his pack and the beast were gone.

Gravely injured, Roko pulls himself toward the shelter rock. Weakness overcomes him. He stops. He and his pack are thin and hungry. This is the season of starvation. The

▲ **Critical Viewing**
What physical features could help this wolf survive in a cold, harsh environment? **[Analyze]**

Reading Check

What has Roko done to show he is a loyal pack member?

---

1. Toklat Ridge the top of a mountain located in Alaska's Denali National Park and Preserve.

winter's harvest has been taken. The produce of spring has not begun.

Young Roko glances down the valley. He droops his head and stiffens his tail to signal to his pack that he is badly hurt. Winds wail. A frigid blast picks up long shawls of snow and drapes them between young Roko and his pack. And so his message is not read.

A raven scouting Toklat Ridge sees Roko's signal. "Kong, kong, kong," he bells—death is coming to the ridge; there will be flesh and bone for all. His voice rolls out across the valley. It penetrates the rocky cracks where the Toklat ravens rest. One by one they hear and spread their wings. They beat their way to Toklat Ridge. They alight upon the snow and walk behind the wounded wolf.

"Kong," they toll[2] with keen excitement, for the raven clan is hungry, too. "Kong, kong"—there will be flesh and bone for all.

Roko snarls and hurries toward the shelter rock. A cloud of snow envelops him. He limps in blinding whiteness now.

A ghostly presence flits around. "Hahahahahahaha," the white fox states—death is coming to the Ridge. Roko smells the fox tagging at his heels.

The cloud whirls off. Two golden eyes look up at Roko. The snowy owl has heard the ravens and joined the deathwatch.

Roko limps along. The ravens walk. The white fox leaps. The snowy owl flies and hops along the rim of Toklat Ridge. Roko stops. Below the ledge out on the flats the musk-ox herd is circling. They form a ring and all face out, a fort of heads and horns and fur that sweeps down to their hooves. Their circle means to Roko that an enemy is present. He squints and smells the wind. It carries scents of thawing ice, broken grass—and earth. The grizzly bear is up! He has awakened from his winter's sleep. A craving need for flesh will drive him.

Roko sees the shelter rock. He strains to reach it. He stumbles. The ravens move in closer. The white fox boldly walks beside him. "Hahaha," he yaps. The snowy owl flies ahead, alights, and waits.

---

2. **toll** (tōl) *v.* announce.

Jean Craighead George
Author's Insight
Life and death rule this story. The wounded wolf is in trouble. I use my knowledge to paint his plight.

Fiction
Setting These descriptions of Toklat Ridge emphasize the harsh conditions of Roko's struggle.

▲ Critical Viewing
Does this raven seem as threatening as the birds in the story?
[Connect]

The grizzly hears the eager fox and rises on his flat hind feet. He twists his powerful neck and head. His great paws dangle at his chest. He sees the animal procession and hears the ravens' knell[3] of death. Dropping to all fours, he joins the march up Toklat Ridge.

Roko stops; his breath comes hard. A raven alights upon his back and picks the open wound. Roko snaps. The raven flies and circles back. The white fox nips at Roko's toes. The snowy owl inches closer. The grizzly bear, still dulled by sleep, stumbles onto Toklat Ridge.

Only yards from the shelter rock, Roko falls.

Instantly the ravens mob him. They scream and peck and stab at his eyes. The white fox leaps upon his wound. The snowy owl sits and waits.

Young Roko struggles to his feet. He bites the ravens. Snaps the fox. And lunges at the stoic[4] owl. He turns and warns the grizzly bear. Then he bursts into a run and falls against the shelter rock. The wounded wolf wedges down between the rock and barren ground. Now protected on three sides, he turns and faces all his foes.

The ravens step a few feet closer. The fox slides toward him on his belly. The snowy owl blinks and waits, and on the ridge rim roars the hungry grizzly bear.

Roko growls.

The sun comes up. Far across the Toklat Valley, Roko hears his pack's "hunt's end" song. The music wails and sobs, wilder than the bleating wind. The hunt song ends. Next comes the roll call. Each member of the Toklat pack barks to say that he is home and well.

"Kiglo here," Roko hears his leader bark. There is a pause. It is young Roko's turn. He cannot lift his head to answer. The pack is silent. The leader starts the count once more. "Kiglo here."—A pause. Roko cannot answer.

The wounded wolf whimpers softly. A mindful raven hears. "Kong, kong, kong," he tolls—this is the end. His booming sounds across the valley. The wolf pack hears the raven's message that something is dying. They know it is Roko, who has not answered roll call.

Jean Craighead George
Author's Insight
I bring in all the animals that would feed at a carcass. The story now calls for bravery on Roko's part—a last desperate effort before he dies. I use incidents I saw. I rewrote that scene five times. I wanted the incident to be short and swift like a bite.

Reading Check

What actions do the animals take to show their interest in Roko?

---

3. knell (nel) *n.* mournful sound, like a slowly ringing bell—usually indicating a death.
4. stoic (stō ik) *adj.* calm and unaffected by hardship.

The hours pass. The wind slams snow on Toklat Ridge. Massive clouds blot out the sun. In their gloom Roko sees the deathwatch move in closer. Suddenly he hears the musk-oxen thundering into their circle. The ice cracks as the grizzly leaves. The ravens burst into the air. The white fox runs. The snowy owl flaps to the top of the shelter rock. And Kiglo rounds the knoll.

In his mouth he carries meat. He drops it close to Roko's head and wags his tail excitedly. Roko licks Kiglo's chin to honor him. Then Kiglo puts his mouth around Roko's nose. This gesture says "I am your leader." And by mouthing Roko, he binds him and all the wolves together.

The wounded wolf wags his tail. Kiglo trots away.

Already Roko's wound feels better. He gulps the food and feels his strength return. He shatters bone, flesh, and gristle and shakes the scraps out on the snow. The hungry ravens swoop upon them. The white fox snatches up a bone. The snowy owl gulps down flesh and fur. And Roko wags his tail and watches.

For days Kiglo brings young Roko food. He <u>gnashes</u>, gorges, and shatters bits upon the snow.

A purple sandpiper winging north sees ravens, owl, and fox. And he drops in upon the feast. The long-tailed jaeger gull flies down and joins the crowd on Toklat Ridge. Roko wags his tail.

One dawn he moves his wounded leg. He stretches it and pulls himself into the sunlight. He walks—he romps. He runs in circles. He leaps and plays with chunks of ice. Suddenly he stops. The "hunt's end" song rings out. Next comes the roll call.

"Kiglo here."

"Roko here," he barks out strongly.

The pack is silent.

"Kiglo here," the leader repeats.

"Roko here."

Across the distance comes the sound of whoops and yips and barks and howls. They fill the dawn with celebration. And Roko prances down the Ridge.

Jean Craighead George
Author's Insight
And now, loving each word as I put it down, I come to the wonder of the wolf pack— altruism, or the unselfish concern for others.

Vocabulary Builder
gnashes (nash´ iz) *v.* bites with grinding teeth

▼ **Critical Viewing** According to the details in the story, why might a wolf like this howl? **[Interpret]**

From the Author's Desk
Jean Craighead George's Insights Into "The Wounded Wolf"

Q. **How much of the story is based on your observations?**

A. This is an event told to me by Dr. Gordon Haber, wolf expert, while we were stretched out on our bellies in Denali National Park, Alaska, observing the wolves of Sanctuary River. I embellished it with all the events I saw around a wolf kill.

Q. **How is writing about animals and humans different?**

A. Since animals share many of our behavioral traits—seeking food, fear, affection, rank, the need for sleep, to name a few— I read all that is in print about the animal I am writing about and then try to "read" what their behavior says. I also try to read the behavior of my human characters, although their range of emotions and ability to communicate are more complicated and longer lasting than the animals'—we think.

Writing about any character, be it human or beast, depends on the ability to put yourself in his or her place.

Student Corner

Q. **What might happen to Kiglo's wolf pack in the future?**
        —**Karen Chen, Niantic, Connecticut**

A. Since Kiglo's pack is in a National Park and cannot be hunted, the pack will probably remain constant in numbers of individuals. Kiglo will remain as leader as long as he lives or is healthy. He will be the only one to have pups. His duties are to lead the pack and make hunting decisions. His mate, the alpha female, will lead the pups and social activities. She will also participate in the hunt. As a pack they will keep the environment balanced and healthy.

Writing Workshop: *Work in Progress*

Review of a Short Story

List ideas and events in the story that you found most interesting. Then, use different-colored highlighters to group items that relate to plot, characters, setting, and ideas. Save this work in your writing portfolio.

Short Stories

Thinking About the Selection

1. **Respond:** Did you sympathize with Roko's struggle? Explain.

2. **(a) Recall:** How was Roko injured? **(b) Analyze:** What action does Roko take to save himself?

3. **(a) Recall:** How does Kiglo learn that Roko is hurt? **(b) Infer:** What does Kiglo's behavior show about how wolves take care of pack members?

Short Story Review

4. What is the main **conflict** in "The Wounded Wolf"? Explain.

5. When does it become clear how the story's conflict will be resolved?

6. **(a)** In the first column of a chart like the one shown, identify details that help you picture the **setting. (b)** In the second column, tell what those details mean to the struggle for survival. **(c)** With a partner, complete the third column with information that explains why the setting is important to the story.

Setting		
What it says	What it means	Why it is important

Research the Author

Using the Internet and library resources, prepare a **plan for a multimedia presentation** about Jean Craighead George.

- The card catalog in your local library or the online card catalog will help you locate titles of books by the author.
- Find at least three books to share with your classmates.
- Find images, such as book jackets or photographs, related to the subjects the author addresses. Find interesting information about the writer's life.
- Write a one-page report based on your research. Indicate where you would include art, illustrations, or photographs in a full multimedia presentation.

QuickReview

Story at a Glance

An injured animal struggles for survival in a harsh environment.

Go Online
Assessment

For: Self-test
Visit: www.PHSchool.com
Web Code: ela-6201

Short story: a brief work of fiction

Conflict: a problem or struggle between opposing forces

Setting: the time and place of a story's action

Make Inferences

Skills You Will Learn

Reading Skill: *Use Details to Make Inferences*
Literary Analysis: *Characterization*

Reading Skill: *Use Prior Knowledge to Make Inferences*

Literary Analysis: *Conflict and Resolution*

Reading Skill: *Using Text Aids and Text Features*

Literary Analysis: *Comparing Characters' Motives*

Literature You Will Read

Reading: Make Inferences

> When you make an **inference**, you use the information given in a text to make a logical assumption about information that is not stated.

Skills and Strategies You Will Learn in Part 1

In Part 1, you will learn
- to **refer to details** in the text to **make inferences** (p. 176)
- to **combine details** with your own **prior knowledge** to **make inferences** (p. 204)
- to **use text aids** and **features** to **make inferences** about information (p. 226)

Using the Skills and Strategies in Part 1

In Part 1, you will learn to find details in the text that act as clues to other information. Then, you will use text details and your own knowledge to speculate, or make logical assumptions, about what is not stated. Finally, you will use text aids and features to help you make inferences.

This example shows how you will apply the skills and strategies you will learn in Part 1.

> **Example:** Jack frowned when he saw his test score.

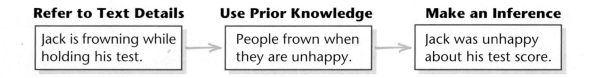

Refer to Text Details	Use Prior Knowledge	Make an Inference
Jack is frowning while holding his test.	People frown when they are unhappy.	Jack was unhappy about his test score.

Academic Vocabulary: Words for Discussing Inferences

The following words will help you to write and talk about inferences as you read the selections in this unit.

Word	Definition	Example Sentence
infer *v.*	assume something based on facts	You can *infer* from the music that something scary is going to happen.
refer *v.*	look back	*Refer* to the dictionary for the correct spelling.
speculate *v.*	make a prediction	We *speculate* that the main character will win the contest.
possible *adj.*	able to be done	Is it *possible* to describe the character more fully?
detail *n.*	a piece of information	The *details* in the story act as clues for the reader.

Vocabulary Skill: Roots

▶ A **root** is the most basic part of a word.

Knowing the meaning of common roots will help you understand and remember the meanings of words that contain the roots. In Part 1 you will learn the meaning of two common roots:
- the Latin root -*fer*- (p. 202)
- the Latin root -*spec*- (p. 224)

Most dictionary entries give you information about the root of the word. Look at the sample shown here.

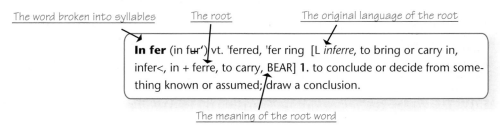

The word broken into syllables   The root   The original language of the root

In fer (in fʉr′) vt. 'ferred, 'fer ring [L *inferre*, to bring or carry in, infer<, in + ferre, to carry, BEAR] **1.** to conclude or decide from something known or assumed; draw a conclusion.

The meaning of the root word

Activity In a dictionary, find the root of the word. Then, explain how the root helps to form the meaning of the word.

- inference
- refer
- speculate
- inspector

These skills will help you become a better reader. Practice them with either "The Tail" (p. 178) or "Dragon, Dragon" (p. 191).

Reading Skill

When you **make inferences,** you make logical assumptions about something not directly stated. To make inferences, **use details** that the text provides.

▶ **Example:** Arnie *ran* to the mailbox to see if Jim's letter had *finally* arrived.

- You can infer from the word *finally* that Arnie has been waiting to hear from Jim.
- You can infer from *ran* that he is eager to get the letter.

Literary Analysis

Characterization is the way writers develop characters and reveal their traits, or qualities.

- With **direct characterization,** writers make straightforward statements about a character.
- With **indirect characterization,** writers present a character's thoughts, words, and actions and reveal what others say and think about the character.

As you read, use a graphic organizer like the one shown to note details that reveal what each character is like.

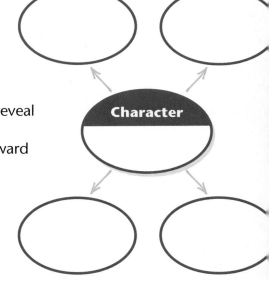

Vocabulary Builder

The Tail

- **gnawing** (nô´ iŋ) *v.* biting and cutting with the teeth (p. 185) *My dog was gnawing on a bone all afternoon.*
- **mauled** (môld) *v.* badly injured by being attacked (p. 186) *The fuzzy toy fell apart after it was mauled by my kitten.*
- **spasm** (spaz´ əm) *n.* a short, sudden burst (p. 187) *Nicole had a coughing spasm when smoke filled the room.*

Dragon, Dragon

- **ravaged** (rav´ ijd) *v.* violently destroyed; ruined (p. 191) *Rabbits ravaged my garden, leaving not one vegetable.*
- **reflecting** (ri flekt´ iŋ) *adj.* thinking seriously (p. 198) *Reflecting on Uncle Si's warning, I decided to stay home.*
- **craned** (krānd) *v.* stretched out for a better look (p. 198) *She craned her neck to get a better look at the president.*

Short Story

Background

Baby-sitting When parents go out and need someone to watch their young children, they may hire a baby sitter. In many communities, police departments and other service organizations offer courses for future baby sitters. These courses teach first aid, fire safety, and poison control. In some families, however, an older brother or sister may be responsible for "baby-sitting" a younger brother or sister. "The Tail" centers on the thoughts and actions of a teenage girl baby-sitting for her brother.

Connecting to the Literature

Reading/Writing Connection List reasons why baby-sitting for a brother or sister might be more difficult than baby-sitting for someone who is not a brother or sister. Use at least three of the following words: *accompany, consent, enforce, monitor, supervise.*

Meet the Author

Joyce **Hansen** (b. 1942)

Award-winning author Joyce Hansen was born in New York City, grew up and went to college there, and then spent twenty-two years teaching in the city's public schools. Her first three novels—*The Gift-Giver, Yellow Bird and Me,* and *Home Boy*—are all set in New York and focus on the lives of young people. Hansen now writes full time.

A Writer's Influences "I write about what I know and what moves me deeply," she says. "My characters are greatly influenced by my childhood and my students." During her childhood, Hansen learned to share her mother's love for books and writing. From her father, she learned how to tell stories. Hansen explains, "My father entertained my brothers and me with stories about his boyhood in the West Indies and his experiences as a young man in the Harlem of the 1920s and 1930s."

Go Online Author Link
For: More about the author
Visit: www.PHSchool.com
Web Code: ele-9202

The Tail — Joyce Hansen

It began as the worst summer of my life. The evening before the first day of summer vacation, my mother broke the bad news to me. I was in the kitchen washing dishes and dreaming about the wonderful things my friends and I would be doing for two whole months—practicing for the annual double-dutch[1] contest, which we would definitely win; going to the roller skating rink, the swimming pool, the beach; and sleeping as late in the morning as I wanted to.

"Tasha," my ma broke into my happy thoughts, "your father and I decided that you're old enough now to take on certain responsibilities."

My heart came to a sudden halt. "Responsibilities?"

"Yes. You do know what that word means, don't you?"

I nodded, watching her dice an onion into small, perfect pieces.

"You're thirteen going on fourteen and your father and I decided that you're old enough to watch Junior this summer, because I'm going to start working again."

"Oh, no!" I broke the dish with a crash. "Not that, Mama." Junior is my seven-year-old brother and has been following me like a tail ever since he learned how to walk. And to make matters worse, there are no kids Junior's age on our block. Everyone is either older or younger than he is.

---

1. **double-dutch** a jump-rope game in which two ropes are used at the same time.

Reading Skill
Make Inferences
Based on her words and actions, how does Tasha feel about baby-sitting for her brother?

I'd rather be in school than minding Junior all day. I could've cried.

"Natasha! There won't be a dish left in this house. You're not going to spend all summer ripping and roaring. You'll baby-sit Junior."

"But, Ma," I said, "it'll be miserable. That's not fair. All summer with Junior. I won't be able to play with my friends."

She wiped her hands on her apron. "Life ain't always fair."

I knew she'd say that.

"You'll still be able to play with your friends," she continued, "but Junior comes first. He is your responsibility. We're a family and we all have to help out."

Mama went to work that next morning. Junior and I both stood by the door as she gave her last-minute instructions. Junior held her hand and stared up at her with an innocent look in his bright brown eyes, which everyone thought were so cute. Dimples decorated his round cheeks as he smiled and nodded at me every time Ma gave me an order. I knew he was just waiting for her to leave so he could torment me.

"Tasha, I'm depending on you. Don't leave the block."

"Yes, Ma."

"No company."

"Not even Naomi? She's my best friend."

"No company when your father and I are not home."

"Yes, Ma."

"Don't let Junior hike in the park."

"Yes, Ma."

"Make yourself and Junior a sandwich for lunch."

"Yes, Ma."

"I'll be calling you at twelve, so you'd better be in here fixing lunch. I don't want you all eating junk food all day long."

"Yes, Ma."

"Don't ignore Junior."

"Yes, Ma."

"Clean the breakfast dishes."

"Yes, Ma."

Literary Analysis
Character In this dialogue, does the author use direct or indirect characterization to develop Tasha's personality? Explain.

Literary Analysis
Character Based on this dialogue, how would you describe Tasha's mother? Explain.

Reading Check

Why is Tasha unhappy with her mother's request?

"Don't open the door to strangers."

"Yes, Ma."

Then she turned to Junior. "Now you, young man. You are to listen to your sister."

"Yes, Mommy," he sang out.

"Don't give her a hard time. Show me what a big boy you can be."

"Mommy, I'll do whatever Tasha say."

She kissed us both good-bye and left. I wanted to cry. A whole summer with Junior.

Junior turned to me and raised his right hand. "This is a vow of obedience." He looked up at the ceiling. "I promise to do whatever Tasha says."

"What do you know about vows?" I asked.

"I saw it on television. A man—"

"Shut up, Junior. I don't feel like hearing about some television show. It's too early in the morning."

I went into the kitchen to start cleaning, when the downstairs bell rang. "Answer the intercom,[2] Junior. If it's Naomi, tell her to wait for me on the stoop," I called out. I knew that it was Naomi, ready to start our big, fun summer. After a few minutes the bell rang again.

"Junior!" I yelled. "Answer the intercom."

The bell rang again and I ran into the living room. Junior was sitting on the couch, looking at cartoons. "What's wrong with you? Why won't you answer the bell?"

He looked at me as if I were crazy. "You told me to shut up. I told you I'd do everything you say."

I pulled my hair. "See, you're bugging me already. Do something to help around here."

I pressed the intercom on the wall. "That you, Naomi?"

"Yeah."

"I'll be down in a minute. Wait for me out front."

"Okay."

I quickly washed the dishes. I couldn't believe how messed up my plans were. Suddenly there was a loud blast from the living room. I was so startled that I dropped a plate and it smashed to smithereens. Ma will kill me, I thought as I ran to the living room. It sounded like whole pieces of furniture were being sucked into the vacuum cleaner.

---

2. **intercom** *n.* a communication system used in apartment buildings.

Reading Skill
Make Inferences
Why do you think Tasha pulls her hair?

▶ **Critical Viewing**
Why might Tasha want to spend her summer in a park like this one? **[Analyze]**

"Junior," I screamed over the racket, "you have it on too high."

He couldn't even hear me. I turned it off myself.

"What's wrong?"

"Ma vacuumed the living room last night. It doesn't need cleaning."

"You told me to do something to help," he whined.

I finished the dishes in a hurry so that I could leave the apartment before Junior bugged out again.

I was so anxious to get outside that we ran down the four flights of stairs instead of waiting for the elevator. Junior clutched some comic books and his checkers game. He put his Mets baseball cap on backward as usual. Naomi sat on the stoop and Junior plopped right next to her like they were the best of friends.

"Hi, cutey." She smiled at him, turning his cap to the front of his head the way it was supposed to be.

"What are we going to do today, Naomi?" he asked.

"Junior, you're not going to be in our faces all day," I snapped at him.

"Mama said you have to watch me. So I have to be in your face."

"You're baby-sitting, Tasha?" Naomi asked.

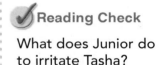

Reading Check

What does Junior do to irritate Tasha?

"Yeah." I told her the whole story.

"Aw, that's not so bad. At least you don't have to stay in the house. Junior will be good. Right, cutey?"

He grinned as she pinched his cheeks.

"See, you think he's cute because you don't have no pesty little brother or sister to watch," I grumbled.

"You ready for double-dutch practice?" she asked. "Yvonne and Keisha are going to meet us in the playground."

"Mama said we have to stay on the block," Junior answered before I could even open my mouth.

"No one's talking to you, Junior." I pulled Naomi up off the stoop. "I promised my mother we'd stay on the block, but the playground is just across the street. I can see the block from there."

"It's still not the block," Junior mumbled as we raced across the street.

We always went over to the playground to jump rope. The playground was just by the entrance to the park. There was a lot of space for us to do our fancy steps. The park was like a big green mountain in the middle of Broadway.

I'd figure out a way to keep Junior from telling that we really didn't stay on the block. "Hey, Tasha, can I go inside the park and look for caves?" People said that if you went deep inside the park, there were caves that had been used centuries ago when Native Americans still lived in northern Manhattan.

"No, Ma said no hiking in the park."

"She said no leaving the block, too, and you left the block."

"Look how close we are to the block. I mean, we can even see it. You could get lost inside the park."

"I'm going to tell Ma you didn't stay on the block."

"Okay, me and Naomi will hike with you up to the Cloisters later." That's a museum that sits at the top of the park, overlooking the Hudson River. "Now read your comic books."

"Will you play checkers with me too?"

"You know I hate checkers. Leave me alone." I spotted Keisha and Yvonne walking into the playground. All of us wore shorts and sneakers.

▶ **Critical Viewing**
Why does a crowd, like the one in the picture, make Tasha want to show off while jumping rope? **[Connect]**

Literary Analysis
Character What character trait does Tasha show by deciding to go to the playground?

Junior tagged behind me and Naomi as we went to meet them. "Remember you're supposed to be watching me," he said.

"How could I forget."

The playground was crowded. Swings were all taken and the older boys played stickball. Some little kids played in the sandboxes.

Keisha and Yvonne turned and Naomi and I jumped together, practicing a new routine. We were so good that some of the boys in the stickball game watched us. A few elderly people stopped to look at us too. We had an audience, so I really showed off—spinning and doing a lot of fancy footwork.

Suddenly Junior jumped in the ropes with us and people laughed and clapped.

"Junior!" I screamed. "Get out of here!"

"Remember, your job is to watch me." He grinned. My foot slipped and all three of us got tangled in the ropes and fell.

"Your feet are too big!" Junior yelled.

Everybody roared. I was too embarrassed. I tried to grab him, but he got away from me. "Get lost," I hollered after him as he ran toward the swings.

Reading Skill
Make Inferences
What are Tasha's feelings as the girls begin to jump? How do these feelings change when Junior joins in?

 Reading Check

What does Junior threaten to tell his mother?

I tried to forget how stupid I must've looked and went back to the ropes. I don't know how long we'd been jumping when suddenly a little kid ran by us yelling, "There's a wild dog loose up there!" He pointed to the steps that led deep inside the park.

People had been saying for years that a pack of abandoned dogs who'd turned wild lived in the park, but no one ever really saw them.

We forgot about the kid and kept jumping. Then one of the boys our age who'd been playing stickball came over to us. "We're getting out of here," he said. "A big yellow dog with red eyes just bit a kid."

I took the rope from Yvonne. It was time for me and Naomi to turn. "That's ridiculous. Who ever heard of a yellow dog with red eyes?"

Naomi stopped turning. "Dogs look all kind of ways. Especially wild dogs. I'm leaving."

"Me too," Yvonne said.

Keisha was already gone. No one was in the swings or the sandboxes. I didn't even see the old men who usually sat on the benches. "Guess we'd better get out of here too," I said. Then I realized that I didn't see Junior anywhere.

"Junior!" I shouted.

"Maybe he went home," Naomi said.

We dashed across the street. Our block was empty. Yvonne ran ahead of us and didn't stop until she reached her stoop. When I got to my stoop I expected to see Junior there, but no Junior.

"Maybe he went upstairs," Naomi said.

"I have the key. He can't get in the house."

"Maybe he went to the candy store?"

"He doesn't have any money, I don't think. But let's look."

We ran around the corner to the candy store, but no Junior.

As we walked back to the block, I remembered something.

"Oh, no, Naomi, I told him to get lost. And that's just what he did."

"He's probably hiding from us somewhere. You know how he likes to tease." She looked around as we walked up our block. "He might be hiding and watching us right now looking for him." She peeped behind parked cars, in doorways, and even opened the lid of a trash can.

"Junior," I called. "Junior!"

No answer. Only the sounds of birds and cars, sirens and a distant radio. I looked at the empty stoop where Junior should have been sitting. A part of me was gone and I had to find it. And another part of me would be gone if my mother found out I'd lost Junior.

I ran back toward the playground and Naomi followed me. "He's got to be somewhere right around here," she panted.

I ran past the playground and into the park. "Tasha, you're not going in there, are you? The dog."

I didn't answer her and began climbing the stone steps that wound around and through the park. Naomi's eyes stretched all over her face and she grabbed my arm. "It's dangerous up here!"

I turned around. "If you're scared, don't come. Junior's my only baby brother. Dear God," I said out loud, "please let me find him. I will play any kind of game he wants. I'll never yell at him again. I promise never to be mean to him again in my life!"

Naomi breathed heavily behind me. "I don't think Junior would go this far by himself."

I stopped and caught my breath. The trees were thick and the city street sounds were far away now.

"I know Junior. He's somewhere up here making believe he's the king of this mountain. Hey, Junior," I called, "I was just kidding. Don't get lost." We heard a rustling in the bushes and grabbed each other. "Probably just a bird," I said, trying to sound brave.

As we climbed some more, I tried not to imagine a huge yellow dog with red eyes <u>gnawing</u> at my heels.

The steps turned a corner and ended. Naomi screamed and pointed up ahead. "What's that?"

I saw a big brown and gray monstrous thing with tentacles reaching toward the sky, jutting out of the curve in the path. I screamed and almost ran.

Reading Skill
Make Inferences
How does Tasha feel about Junior's disappearance? How can you tell?

Vocabulary Builder
gnawing (nô´ iŋ) v.
biting and cutting with the teeth

Reading Check

Why is Tasha suddenly worried about Junior?

"What is that, Naomi?"

"I don't know."

"This is a park in the middle of Manhattan. It can't be a bear or anything." I screamed to the top of my lungs, "Junior!" Some birds flew out of a tree, but the thing never moved.

All Naomi could say was, "Dogs, Tasha."

I found a stick. "I'm going up. You wait here. If you hear growling and screaming, run and get some help." I couldn't believe how brave I was. Anyway, that thing, whatever it was, couldn't hurt me any more than my mother would if I didn't find Junior.

"You sure, Tasha?"

"No sense in both of us being <u>mauled</u>," I said.

Vocabulary Builder
mauled (môld) *v.*
badly injured by being attacked

I tipped lightly up the steps, holding the stick like a club. When I was a few feet away from the thing, I crumpled to the ground and laughed so hard that Naomi ran to me. "Naomi, look at what scared us."

She laughed too. "A dead tree trunk."

We both laughed until we cried. Then I saw one of Junior's comic books near a bush. I picked it up and started to cry. "See, he was here. And that animal probably tore him to pieces." Naomi patted my shaking shoulders.

Suddenly, there was an unbelievable growl. My legs turned to air as I flew down the steps. Naomi was ahead of me. Her two braids stuck out like propellers. My feet didn't even touch the ground. We screamed all the way down the steps. I tripped on the last step and was sprawled out on the ground. Two women passing by bent over me. "Child, are you hurt?" one of them asked.

Reading Skill
Make Inferences
What can you infer from Tasha's reaction to discovering Junior's comic book?

Then I heard a familiar laugh above me and looked up into Junior's dimpled face. He laughed so hard, he held his stomach with one hand. His checkers game was in the other. A little tan, mangy[3] dog stood next to him, wagging its tail.

I got up slowly. "Junior, I'm going to choke you."

He doubled over with squeals and chuckles. I wiped my filthy shorts with one hand and stretched out the other to snatch Junior's neck. The stupid little dog had the nerve to growl.

---

3. **mangy** (mān′ jē) *adj.* shabby and dirty.

"Me and Thunder hid in the bushes. We followed you." He continued laughing. Then he turned to the dog. "Thunder, didn't Tasha look funny holding that stick like she was going to beat up the tree trunk?"

I put my hands around Junior's neck. "This is the end of the tail," I said.

Junior grinned. "You promised. 'I'll play any game he wants. I'll never yell at him again. I promise never to be mean to him again in my life.' "

Naomi giggled. "That's what you said, Tasha." The mutt barked at me. Guess he called himself Junior's protector. I took my hands off Junior's neck.

Then Naomi had a laughing <u>spasm</u>. She pointed at the dog. "Is that what everyone was running from?"

"This is my trusted guard. People say he's wild. He just wants a friend."

"Thunder looks like he's already got a lot of friends living inside his fur," I said. We walked back to the block with the dog trotting right by Junior's side.

I checked my watch when we got to my building. "It's ten to twelve. I have to make lunch for Junior," I told Naomi. "But I'll be back out later."

The dog whined after Junior as we entered the building. "I'll be back soon, Thunder," he said, "after I beat my sister in five games of checkers."

Now he was going to blackmail me.

I heard Naomi giggling as Junior and I walked into the building. The phone rang just as we entered the apartment. I knew it was Ma.

"Everything okay, Tasha? Nothing happened?"

"No, Ma, everything is fine. Nothing happened at all."

Well, the summer didn't turn out to be so terrible after all. My parents got Thunder cleaned up and let Junior keep him for a pet. Me and my friends practiced for the double-dutch contest right in front of my building, so I didn't have to leave the block. After lunch when it was too hot to jump rope, I'd play a game of checkers with Junior or read him a story. He wasn't as pesty as he used to be, because now he had Thunder. We won the double-dutch contest. And Junior never told my parents that I'd lost him. I found out that you never miss a tail until you almost lose it.

Vocabulary Builder
spasm (spaz′ əm) *n.* a short, sudden burst

Literary Analysis
Character How does Tasha's character change by the end of the story?

The Tail ■ 187

Apply the Skills

The Tail

Thinking About the Selection

1. **Respond:** How would you feel if you had to watch a younger brother or sister during your summer vacation?
2. **(a) Recall:** What vow does Junior make to Tasha?
   (b) Generalize: Why is Tasha often frustrated when Junior "follows" her directions? Give an example. **(c) Analyze Cause and Effect:** What causes Junior to disappear?
3. **(a) Recall:** What information are Tasha and her friends given about a danger in the park? **(b) Draw Conclusions:** Why does this suddenly cause Tasha great worry?
4. **(a) Interpret:** What does Tasha mean when she says, "I found out that you never miss a tail until you almost lose it"? **(b) Analyze:** How does Tasha's statement show a change in her attitude?
5. **Discuss:** Tasha learns some important lessons from her experience. Discuss which lesson might help teenagers you know.

Reading Skill

6. Using a chart like the one shown, list the details that led you to **make an inference** about Tasha. One example is provided. Give at least two more examples.

Details	Inferences
Tasha tells Naomi, "If you're scared, don't come. Junior's my only baby brother."	Tasha is worried and is determined to find Junior, with or without Naomi's help.

Literary Analysis

7. List two examples of **direct characterization** from the story.
8. Identify two of Tasha's actions or thoughts. What character traits, or qualities, are revealed in these examples of **indirect characterization**?

QuickReview

Who's Who in the Story

Tasha: a thirteen-year-old girl

Junior: Tasha's seven-year-old brother

Naomi: Tasha's best friend

Thunder: a stray dog

Go Online
Assessment
For: Self-test
Visit: www.PHSchool.com
Web Code: ela-6202

Inference: a logical assumption about information not directly stated in a text

Characterization: the way authors develop characters and reveal their traits. Authors may use *direct characterization* or *indirect characterization*.

Vocabulary Builder

Practice Answer yes or no to each question, which contains a word from the vocabulary list on page 176. Explain your answer.

1. Would having a back <u>spasm</u> be pleasant?
2. Is a <u>gnawing</u> feeling a good feeling?
3. Should lion trainers be afraid of getting <u>mauled</u>?

Writing

Imagine you are the parent of a young child. Write a **help-wanted ad** for a baby sitter. Use your own knowledge to decide what character traits, abilities, and knowledge a baby sitter needs.

Help-wanted ads are usually short. Your ad should identify the job's specific responsibilities and the qualities you are looking for. Tell how much you will pay per hour and include your phone number.

For *Grammar, Vocabulary,* and *Assessment,* see **Build Language Skills,** pages 202–203.

Extend Your Learning

Listening and Speaking With a partner, present a **dramatic reading** of a scene in the story. For example, you might pick the scene in which Tasha's mother gives her instructions for baby-sitting. Vary your tone of voice to represent your character's feelings. Have other classmates watch and provide feedback.

Research and Technology Tasha wants her brother to find a way to entertain himself while she and her friends jump rope in the park. Do research on two or three games children can play outdoors. Use your data to make a **compare-and-contrast chart.** In your chart, categorize the games based on the level of difficulty, the average age to play, and the number of children needed to play.

Background

Dragon Stories Since ancient times, dragon stories have been told all over the world. Different cultures have different beliefs about these imaginary creatures. Although Asian dragons are believed to be wise and good, in other cultures dragons are thought to be greedy, evil creatures. In most European folklore, the hero who kills a dragon is a brave, strong warrior.

Connecting to the Literature

Reading/Writing Connection In "Dragon, Dragon," author John Gardner gives a twist to a traditional European dragon story to illustrate the power of advice—even advice that does not seem to make much sense at first. Write three sentences that tell why you might ask someone for advice. Use three of the following words: *consult, rely, seek, appeal, assist.*

Review

For **Reading Skill, Literary Analysis,** and **Vocabulary Builder,** see p. 176.

Meet the Author

John **Gardner** (1933–1982)

John Gardner loved old tales about dragons and other monsters. His first successful novel, *Grendel*, retells the Old English story of Beowulf, a famous monster-slaying hero. In an unusual twist, Gardner presents the monster's side of the story in *Grendel*.

Birthday Stories "I had two children," Gardner once said, "and from the time they were about four, on every birthday and every Christmas, I would write them a story, one for each of them."

Fast Facts

▶ Gardner always worked on several book projects at a time.

▶ His journal was published in 1999, seventeen years after his death.

Go **Online**
Author Link

For: More about the author
Visit: www.PHSchool.com
Web Code: ele-9203

DRAGON, DRAGON
John Gardner

There was once a king whose kingdom was plagued by a dragon. The king did not know which way to turn. The king's knights were all cowards who hid under their beds whenever the dragon came in sight, so they were of no use to the king at all. And the king's wizard could not help either because, being old, he had forgotten his magic spells. Nor could the wizard look up the spells that had slipped his mind, for he had unfortunately misplaced his wizard's book many years before. The king was at his wit's end.

Every time there was a full moon the dragon came out of his lair and <u>ravaged</u> the countryside. He frightened maidens and stopped up chimneys and broke store windows and set people's clocks back and made dogs bark until no one could hear himself think.

He tipped over fences and robbed graves and put frogs in people's drinking water and tore the last chapters out of novels and changed house numbers around so that people crawled into bed with their neighbors.

He stole spark plugs out of people's cars and put firecrackers in people's cigars and stole the clappers from all the church bells and sprung every bear trap for miles around so the bears could wander wherever they pleased.

And to top it all off, he changed around all the roads in the kingdom so that people could not get anywhere except by starting out in the wrong direction.

Vocabulary Builder
ravaged (rav´ ijd) *v.*
violently destroyed;
ruined

Literary Analysis
Character Based on his actions, what words would you use to describe the dragon?

Reading Check

What is the problem in the kingdom?

Dragon, Dragon ■ 191

"That," said the king in a fury, "is enough!" And he called a meeting of everyone in the kingdom.

Now it happened that there lived in the kingdom a wise old cobbler who had a wife and three sons. The cobbler and his family came to the king's meeting and stood way in back by the door, for the cobbler had a feeling that since he was nobody important there had probably been some mistake, and no doubt the king had intended the meeting for everyone in the kingdom except his family and him.

"Ladies and gentlemen," said the king when everyone was present, "I've put up with that dragon as long as I can. He has got to be stopped."

All the people whispered amongst themselves, and the king smiled, pleased with the impression he had made.

But the wise cobbler said gloomily, "It's all very well to talk about it—but how are you going to do it?"

And now all the people smiled and winked as if to say, "Well, King, he's got you there!"

The king frowned.

"It's not that His Majesty hasn't tried," the queen spoke up loyally.

Reading Skill
Make Inferences
How does the cobbler think he is different from most people in the kingdom?

▼ **Critical Viewing**
Why would the people of the kingdom fear a dragon like this one? **[Speculate]**

WARWICK GOBLE

"Yes," said the king, "I've told my knights again and again that they ought to slay that dragon. But I can't force them to go. I'm not a tyrant."[1]

"Why doesn't the wizard say a magic spell?" asked the cobbler.

"He's done the best he can," said the king.

The wizard blushed and everyone looked embarrassed. "I used to do all sorts of spells and chants when I was younger," the wizard explained. "But I've lost my spell book, and I begin to fear I'm losing my memory too. For instance, I've been trying for days to recall one spell I used to do. I forget, just now, what the deuce it was for. It went something like—

> *Bimble,*
> *Wimble,*
> *Cha, cha*
> CHOOMPF!

Suddenly, to everyone's surprise, the queen turned into a rosebush.

"Oh dear," said the wizard.

"Now you've done it," groaned the king.

"Poor Mother," said the princess.

"I don't know what can have happened," the wizard said nervously, "but don't worry, I'll have her changed back in a jiffy." He shut his eyes and racked his brain for a spell that would change her back.

But the king said quickly, "You'd better leave well enough alone. If you change her into a rattlesnake we'll have to chop off her head."

Meanwhile the cobbler stood with his hands in his pockets, sighing at the waste of time. "About the dragon . . . " he began.

"Oh yes," said the king. "I'll tell you what I'll do. I'll give the princess's hand in marriage to anyone who can make the dragon stop."

"It's not enough," said the cobbler. "She's a nice enough girl, you understand. But how would an ordinary person support her? Also, what about those of us that are already married?"

Literary Analysis
Character Based on his actions and words, how would you describe the wizard?

✓ **Reading Check**

Why is the wizard unable to get rid of the dragon?

---

1. **tyrant** (tī′ rənt) *n.* a cruel, unjust ruler.

"In that case," said the king, "I'll offer the princess's hand or half the kingdom or both—whichever is most convenient."

The cobbler scratched his chin and considered it. "It's not enough," he said at last. "It's a good enough kingdom, you understand, but it's too much responsibility."

"Take it or leave it," the king said.

"I'll leave it," said the cobbler. And he shrugged and went home.

But the cobbler's eldest son thought the bargain was a good one, for the princess was very beautiful and he liked the idea of having half the kingdom to run as he pleased. So he said to the king, "I'll accept those terms, Your Majesty. By tomorrow morning the dragon will be slain."

"Bless you!" cried the king.

"Hooray, hooray, hooray!" cried all the people, throwing their hats in the air.

The cobbler's eldest son beamed with pride, and the second eldest looked at him enviously. The youngest son said timidly, "Excuse me, Your Majesty, but don't you think the queen looks a little unwell? If I were you I think I'd water her."

"Good heavens," cried the king, glancing at the queen who had been changed into a rosebush, "I'm glad you mentioned it!"

Now the cobbler's eldest son was very clever and was known far and wide for how quickly he could multiply fractions in his head. He was perfectly sure he could slay the dragon by somehow or other playing a trick on him, and he didn't feel that he needed his wise old father's advice. But he thought it was only polite to ask, and so he went to his father, who was working as usual at his cobbler's bench, and said, "Well, Father, I'm off to slay the dragon. Have you any advice to give me?"

The cobbler thought a moment and replied, "When and if you come to the dragon's lair, recite the following poem:

Dragon, dragon, how do you do?
I've come from the king to murder you.

Say it very loudly and firmly and the dragon will fall, God willing, at your feet."

"How curious!" said the eldest son. And he thought to himself, "The old man is not as wise as I thought. If I say

Reading Skill
Make Inferences
What details support the inference that the cobbler is practical and has common sense?

Literary Analysis
Character Does the sentence starting "Now the cobbler's eldest son . . ." use direct or indirect characterization? Explain.

something like that to the dragon, he will eat me up in an instant. The way to kill a dragon is to out-fox him." And keeping his opinion to himself, the eldest son set forth on his quest.

When he came at last to the dragon's lair, which was a cave, the eldest son slyly disguised himself as a peddler and knocked on the door and called out, "Hello there!"

"There's nobody home!" roared a voice.

The voice was as loud as an earthquake, and the eldest son's knees knocked together in terror.

"I don't come to trouble you," the eldest son said meekly. "I merely thought you might be interested in looking at some of our brushes. Or if you'd prefer," he added quickly, "I could leave our catalogue with you and I could drop by again, say, early next week."

"I don't want any brushes," the voice roared, "and I especially don't want any brushes next week."

"Oh," said the eldest son. By now his knees were knocking together so badly that he had to sit down.

Suddenly a great shadow fell over him, and the eldest son looked up. It was the dragon. The eldest son drew his sword, but the dragon lunged and swallowed him in a single gulp, sword and all, and the eldest son found himself in the dark of the dragon's belly. "What a fool I was not to listen to my wise old father!" thought the eldest son. And he began to weep bitterly.

▲ **Critical Viewing**
Why would the king want to protect a kingdom like this one from a dragon? **[Speculate]**

Reading Skill
Make Inferences
What details support the inference that this is a humorous tale rather than a realistic or scary one?

✔ **Reading Check**

What does the father tell his eldest son to do when he gets to the dragon's lair?

Dragon, Dragon ■ 195

"Well," sighed the king the next morning, "I see the dragon has not been slain yet."

"I'm just as glad, personally," said the princess, sprinkling the queen. "I would have had to marry that eldest son, and he had warts."

Now the cobbler's middle son decided it was his turn to try. The middle son was very strong and he was known far and wide for being able to lift up the corner of a church. He felt perfectly sure he could slay the dragon by simply laying into him, but he thought it would be only polite to ask his father's advice. So he went to his father and said to him, "Well, Father, I'm off to slay the dragon. Have you any advice for me?"

The cobbler told the middle son exactly what he'd told the eldest.

"When and if you come to the dragon's lair, recite the following poem:
Dragon, dragon, how do you do?
I've come from the king to murder you.
Say it very loudly and firmly, and the dragon will fall, God willing, at your feet."

"What an odd thing to say," thought the middle son. "The old man is not as wise as I thought. You have to take these dragons by surprise." But he kept his opinion to himself and set forth.

When he came in sight of the dragon's lair, the middle son spurred his horse to a gallop and thundered into the entrance swinging his sword with all his might.

But the dragon had seen him while he was still a long way off, and being very clever, the dragon had crawled up on top of the door so that when the son came charging in he went under the dragon and on to the back of the cave and slammed into the wall. Then the dragon chuckled and got down off the door, taking his time, and strolled back to where the man and the horse lay unconscious from the terrific blow. Opening his mouth as if for a yawn, the dragon swallowed the middle son in a single gulp and put the horse in the freezer to eat another day.

"What a fool I was not to listen to my wise old father," thought the middle son when he came to in the dragon's belly. And he too began to weep bitterly.

Reading Skill
Make Inferences
How is the middle son different from the eldest son? Support your answer.

Literary Analysis
Character What new details about the dragon's character do you learn in this paragraph?

That night there was a full moon, and the dragon ravaged the countryside so terribly that several families moved to another kingdom.

"Well," sighed the king in the morning, "still no luck in this dragon business, I see."

"I'm just as glad, myself," said the princess, moving her mother, pot and all, to the window where the sun could get at her. "The cobbler's middle son was a kind of humpback."

Now the cobbler's youngest son saw that his turn had come. He was very upset and nervous, and he wished he had never been born. He was not clever, like his eldest brother, and he was not strong, like his second-eldest brother. He was a decent, honest boy who always minded his elders.

He borrowed a suit of armor from a friend of his who was a knight, and when the youngest son put the armor on it was so heavy he could hardly walk. From another knight he borrowed a sword, and that was so heavy that the only way the youngest son could get it to the dragon's lair was to drag it along behind his horse like a plow.

When everything was in readiness, the youngest son went for a last conversation with his father.

"Father, have you any advice to give me?" he asked.

"Only this," said the cobbler. "When and if you come to the dragon's lair, recite the following poem:

Dragon, dragon, how do you do?
I've come from the king to murder you.

Say it very loudly and firmly, and the dragon will fall, God willing, at your feet."

"Are you certain?" asked the youngest son uneasily.

"As certain as one can ever be in these matters," said the wise old cobbler.

And so the youngest son set forth on his quest. He traveled over hill and dale and at last came to the dragon's cave.

The dragon, who had seen the cobbler's youngest son while he was still a long way off, was seated up above the door, inside the cave, waiting and smiling to himself. But

▲ **Critical Viewing**
Does the boy in this picture look like a dragon slayer? Explain. **[Evaluate]**

Reading Check

What happens to the middle son when he arrives at the dragon's cave?

minutes passed and no one came thundering in. The dragon frowned, puzzled, and was tempted to peek out. However, <u>reflecting</u> that patience seldom goes unrewarded, the dragon kept his head up out of sight and went on waiting. At last, when he could stand it no longer, the dragon <u>craned</u> his neck and looked. There at the entrance of the cave stood a trembling young man in a suit of armor twice his size, struggling with a sword so heavy he could lift only one end of it at a time.

At sight of the dragon, the cobbler's youngest son began to tremble so violently that his armor rattled like a house caving in. He heaved with all his might at the sword and got the handle up level with his chest, but even now the point was down in the dirt. As loudly and firmly as he could manage, the youngest son cried—

Dragon, dragon, how do you do?
I've come from the king to murder you.

"What?" cried the dragon, flabbergasted. *"You? You? Murder Me???"* All at once he began to laugh, pointing at the little cobbler's son. *"He he he ho ha!"* he roared, shaking all over, and tears filled his eyes. *"He he he ho ho ho ha ha!"* laughed the dragon. He was laughing so hard he had to hang onto his sides, and he fell off the door and landed on his back, still laughing, kicking his legs helplessly, rolling from side to side, laughing and laughing and laughing.

The cobbler's son was annoyed. "I *do* come from the king to murder you," he said. "A person doesn't like to be laughed at for a thing like that."

"He he he!" wailed the dragon, almost sobbing, gasping for breath. "Of course not, poor dear boy! But really, *he he,* the *idea* of it, *ha, ha, ha!* And that simply ri*dic*ulous *poem!"* Tears streamed from the dragon's eyes and he lay on his back perfectly helpless with laughter.

"It's a good poem," said the cobbler's youngest son loyally. "My father made it up." And growing angrier he shouted, "I want you to stop that laughing, or I'll—I'll—" But the dragon could not stop for the life of him. And suddenly, in a terrific rage, the cobbler's son began flopping the sword end over end in the direction of the dragon. Sweat ran off the youngest son's forehead, but he labored on, blistering mad, and at last, with one supreme heave, he

Vocabulary Builder
reflecting (ri flekt′ iŋ)
adj. thinking seriously

craned (krānd) *v.*
stretched out for a better look

Reading Skill
Make Inferences
What do the dragon's words and laughter suggest about his feelings?

had the sword standing on its handle a foot from the dragon's throat. Of its own weight the sword fell, slicing the dragon's head off.

"He he ho huk," went the dragon—and then he lay dead.

The two older brothers crawled out and thanked their younger brother for saving their lives. "We have learned our lesson," they said.

Then the three brothers gathered all the treasures from the dragon's cave and tied them to the back end of the youngest brother's horse, and tied the dragon's head on behind the treasures, and started home. "I'm glad I listened to my father," the youngest son thought. "Now I'll be the richest man in the kingdom."

There were hand-carved picture frames and silver spoons and boxes of jewels and chests of money and silver compasses and maps telling where there were more treasures buried when these ran out. There was also a curious old book with a picture of an owl on the cover, and inside, poems and odd sentences and recipes that seemed to make no sense.

When they reached the king's castle the people all leaped for joy to see that the dragon was dead, and the princess ran out and kissed the youngest brother on the forehead, for secretly she had hoped it would be him.

"Well," said the king, "which half of the kingdom do you want?"

"My wizard's book!" exclaimed the wizard. "He's found my wizard's book!" He opened the book and ran his finger along under the words and then said in a loud voice, "Glmuzk, shkzmlp, blam!"

Instantly the queen stood before them in her natural shape, except she was soaking wet from being sprinkled too often. She glared at the king.

"Oh dear," said the king, hurrying toward the door.

Literature in Context

Literature Connection

Traditional Dragon Stories
Much of the humor in "Dragon, Dragon" comes from the way it turns traditional dragon stories upside down. For example, in *Beowulf*, one of the most famous dragon stories of all time, the king is a wise and noble man. A terrible dragon has been attacking his hall and killing his warriors. When brave Beowulf, a true hero, learns that the king needs help, he sails quickly to the rescue, humbly yet bravely presenting himself as the man for the job.

Connect to the Literature

Which of the cobbler's sons is most like Beowulf? Explain.

Apply the Skills

Dragon, Dragon

Thinking About the Selection

1. **Respond:** Do you think the cobbler is wise? Explain.
2. **(a) Recall:** Name two reasons why the king has not been able to get rid of the dragon at the beginning of the story. **(b) Distinguish:** Why are these details surprising?
3. **(a) Recall:** What advice does the cobbler give to his sons? **(b) Connect:** Why do the sons doubt his advice?
4. **(a) Recall:** What happens to the two elder sons when they attempt to slay the dragon? **(b) Interpret:** What might their fate say about people who do not listen to advice?
5. **(a) Recall:** How does the youngest son succeed in slaying the dragon? **(b) Analyze:** Why is he successful? **(c) Deduce:** What does the cobbler seem to know all along about his sons and about the dragon?
6. **Discuss:** What is the difference between listening to advice and letting others do your thinking for you?

Reading Skill

7. Using a chart like the one shown, list the details that led you to **make an inference** about the youngest son. One example is provided. Give at least two more examples.

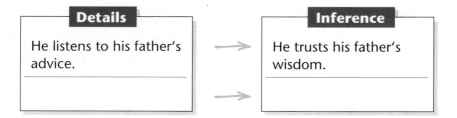

Details		Inference
He listens to his father's advice.	→	He trusts his father's wisdom.
	→	

Literary Analysis

8. List two examples of **direct characterization** from the story.
9. Identify two actions or thoughts of the youngest son. What character traits are revealed in these examples of **indirect characterization**?

QuickReview

Story at a Glance
Three brothers discover that their father's advice about slaying a dragon has unexpected results.

Go **O**nline
—Assessment
For: Self-test
Visit: www.PHSchool.com
Web Code: ela-6203

Inference: a logical assumption about information not directly stated

Characterization: the way authors develop characters and reveal their traits. Authors may use *direct characterization* or *indirect characterization*.

Vocabulary Builder

Practice Answer yes or no to each question, which contains a word from the vocabulary list on page 176. Explain your answer.

1. Is a person who is <u>reflecting</u> on something childish?
2. Does a house that a storm has <u>ravaged</u> need repairs?
3. If a turtle <u>craned</u> its neck, was it hiding its head?

Writing

Imagine you are the king and are looking for someone to kill the dragon. Write a **help-wanted ad** to find a dragon slayer. Think about what character traits, abilities, and knowledge the dragon slayer should have.

Help-wanted ads are usually short. First, identify the job's specific challenges. Then list qualifications required. Finally, offer a reward.

For *Grammar, Vocabulary,* and *Assessment,* see **Build Language Skills,** pages 202–203.

Extend Your Learning

Listening and Speaking With a partner, present a **dramatic reading** of the scene in which the youngest son approaches the cave. Vary the volume and tone of your voice to show levels of feeling, such as annoyance or rage. Then give each other feedback on the techniques used to show the characters' feelings. Perform the scene again, using the feedback to improve your reading.

Research and Technology Make a **compare-and-contrast chart** about dragons in world literature. Using the word *dragon,* search online databases for information about dragon tales in various cultures. In your chart, categorize the tales based on the dragon's physical features and potential for good and evil and on the types of tales (legends, myths, folk tales) in which the dragons appear.

Build Language Skills

The Tail • Dragon, Dragon

Vocabulary Skill

Roots *-fer-* The **Latin root** *-fer-* means "to bring or carry." **Infer** contains *-fer-*. When you infer something, you "bring in" the details and your own knowledge to make an assumption. The root *-fer-* is also found in the word *refer.* When you *refer* to something, you "bring back" previous information.

➤ **Example:** I had to **refer** to the notes I made earlier.

Practice Answer the following questions. Use the italicized word in your answer.

1. In what situation might you *refer* to a map?
2. What would you *infer* if you saw rain dripping through a ceiling?
3. What does a *ferry*boat do?
4. What is the purpose of a *conference*?

Grammar Lesson

Verbs A **verb** is a word that shows an action or a state of being in a sentence. An **action verb,** such as *jump* or *dance,* names an action of a person or thing.

➤ **Example:** He jumped over the rock. (*The action is jumping.*)

A **linking verb,** such as *is* or *feels,* connects a noun or pronoun to a word that identifies, renames, or describes the noun or pronoun. Other common linking verbs are *seem, look,* and *become.*

➤ **Example:** *Katie* is *an artist.* (Artist *renames* Katie.)
　　　　　　The *blanket* feels *soft.* (Soft *describes the noun* blanket.)

Practice Write the verbs and identify each as either an action verb or a linking verb. Then rewrite each sentence using a different action or linking verb. Notice how changing the verb changes the meaning of the sentence.

1. This pizza tastes good.
2. Mrs. Ramirez was my second-grade teacher.
3. We walked to the park after school.
4. I became tired after soccer practice.
5. Birds nested in the old spruce tree.

MorePractice

For more practice with verbs, see Grammar Handbook, p. R32.

*W*_G *Prentice Hall Writing and Grammar Connection: Chapter 15, Section 1*

Reading: Make Inferences

Directions: *Read the selection. Then, answer the questions.*

When the director called her name, Yvonne felt a cold shiver and her knees felt a little shaky. However, she smiled bravely. Then, she cleared her throat and nodded to the piano player. Suddenly, her shakes and jitters were gone. As her lovely voice floated out into the auditorium, the director smiled. "WOW!" he said to his assistant. "I don't need to see any more people."

1. Why did Yvonne feel a cold shiver run down her back?
   A It was cold in the room.
   B She was feeling ill.
   C She was nervous and scared.
   D The director was unkind to her.

2. Which is the best inference to make?
   A She has not met this director before.
   B Her best friend is the piano player.
   C Yvonne is hoping to become an assistant to the director.
   D She is trying out for a musical.

3. Which is the best inference to make?
   A She feels more shaky as she sings.
   B Yvonne stops feeling frightened.
   C Her voice sounds low and scratchy.
   D Yvonne wants to be a princess.

4. What do the director's words and actions suggest?
   A He wants Yvonne to play the piano.
   B He likes Yvonne because she smiled so bravely.
   C He thinks Yvonne will be perfect for a part in his play.
   D He thinks that Yvonne seems too nervous to be in a play.

Timed Writing: Description [Interpretation]

Review "The Tail" or "Dragon, Dragon." Write a brief description of your favorite character. Explain what the character's words and actions suggest about the character. **(20 minutes)**

 ## Writing Workshop: *Work in Progress*

Review of a Short Story

Brainstorm the ideas and events that were most interesting in the story you read. Then, using a different color highlighter for each category, group each story element. Choose the category that has the most items and write that category name on the top of your paper. Put your notes in your writing portfolio.

These skills will help you become a better reader. Practice them with either "Zlateh the Goat" (p. 206) or "The Old Woman Who Lived With the Wolves" (p. 217).

Reading Skill

An **inference** is a logical assumption about information not directly stated. It is based on information the text gives and your own thoughts. To make an inference, combine text clues with your **prior knowledge,** or what you already know. For example, from the sentence "Tina smiled when she saw the snow," you might infer that Tina is happy. This inference is based on your prior knowledge that people smile when they are happy. Because the text states that Tina is smiling at the snow, you can infer that the snow is the reason she is happy.

To help make inferences as you read, use a chart like this one.

Details

↓

Prior Knowledge

↓

Inference

Literary Analysis

A **conflict** is a struggle between opposing forces. In a short story, the conflict drives the action. Events in the story contribute to the conflict or to the **resolution**—the way in which the conflict is settled. A conflict can be *external* or *internal*.

- **External conflict:** a character struggles against an outside force, such as another person or an element of nature.
- **Internal conflict:** a character struggles within him- or herself to make a choice, take an action, or overcome a feeling.

A story may have several conflicts, which may be related.

Vocabulary Builder

Zlateh the Goat

- **bound** (bound) *v.* tied (p. 207) *They bound the lifeboat to the ship.*
- **exuded** (eg zy͞ood′ əd) *v.* gave off; oozed (p. 210) *The clown exuded happiness.*
- **trace** (trās) *n.* mark left behind by something (p. 213) *We cleaned until there was not a trace of dirt.*

The Old Woman Who Lived With the Wolves

- **coaxed** (kōkst) *v.* persuaded by gentle urging (p. 219) *She coaxed him to eat.*
- **traversed** (trə vʉrst′) *v.* went across (p. 220) *They traversed a lake to get home.*
- **offensive** (ə fen′siv) *adj.* unpleasant (p. 221) *The odor of garbage was offensive.*

Build Understanding • *Zlateh the Goat*

Background

Hypothermia In "Zlateh the Goat," a young boy is lost out-doors in a winter storm. He runs the risk of frostbite and hypoth-ermia. When hypothermia occurs, the body temperature drops below normal and breathing slows. If the victim is not warmed, he or she becomes unconscious.

Connecting to the Literature

Reading/Writing Connection In this story, snow becomes a deadly enemy for a boy and a goat, who must help each other survive a blizzard. Write several sentences about problems or dan-gerous situations that you know weather can cause. Use at least three of the following words: *expose, injure, isolate, restrict.*

Meet the Author

Isaac Bashevis **Singer** (1904–1991)

He lived in the United States for more than half his life, but Isaac Bashevis Singer never forgot the Polish villages of his youth. He brought those neighbor-hoods to life again and again in the stories and novels he wrote during his career.

Keeper of the Culture Prejudice against Jews prompted Singer to leave Poland for New York in 1935. Soon after, World War II devastated the Jewish neighborhoods of Eastern Europe. Yet Singer kept writing stories about the vanished world he remem-bered. Throughout his life, Singer wrote in his native language of Yiddish, translating many of his stories into English afterward. He explained, "I always knew that a writer has to write in his own language or not at all." In 1978 he won the Nobel Prize for Literature, the first Yiddish-language author to be so honored.

Go **Online**
Author Link

For: More about the author
Visit: www.PHSchool.com
Web Code: ele-9204

ISAAC BASHEVIS SINGER

At Hanukkah[1] time the road from the village to the town is usually covered with snow, but this year the winter had been a mild one. Hanukkah had almost come, yet little snow had fallen. The sun shone most of the time. The peasants complained that because of the dry weather there would be a poor harvest of winter grain. New grass sprouted, and the peasants sent their cattle out to pasture.

For Reuven the furrier it was a bad year, and after long hesitation he decided to sell Zlateh the goat. She was old and gave little milk. Feivel the town butcher had offered eight gulden[2] for her. Such a sum would buy Hanukkah candles, potatoes and oil for pancakes, gifts for the children, and other holiday necessaries for the house. Reuven told his oldest boy Aaron to take the goat to town.

Literary Analysis
Conflict What conflict is resolved by Reuven's decision to sell Zlateh?

---

1. **Hanukkah** (khä´ noo kä) Jewish festival celebrated for eight days in early winter. Hanukkah is also called the "festival of lights" because a candle is lit on each of the eight days.
2. **gulden** (gool´ dən) *n.* unit of money.

Illustrations copyright © 1966 by Maurice Sendak, copyright renewed 1994 by Maurice Sendak.
Printed with permission from HarperCollins Publishers.

◀ Critical Viewing
What do you think
life is like in a village
like the one in this
picture? [Speculate]

Aaron understood what taking the goat to Feivel meant, but had to obey his father. Leah, his mother, wiped the tears from her eyes when she heard the news. Aaron's younger sisters, Anna and Miriam, cried loudly. Aaron put on his quilted jacket and a cap with earmuffs, <u>bound</u> a rope around Zlateh's neck, and took along two slices of bread with cheese to eat on the road. Aaron was supposed

Vocabulary Builder
bound (bound) *v.* tied

✓ Reading Check

Why is Aaron taking the goat to Feivel?

to deliver the goat by evening, spend the night at the butcher's, and return the next day with the money.

While the family said goodbye to the goat, and Aaron placed the rope around her neck, Zlateh stood as patiently and good-naturedly as ever. She licked Reuven's hand. She shook her small white beard. Zlateh trusted human beings. She knew that they always fed her and never did her any harm.

When Aaron brought her out on the road to town, she seemed somewhat astonished. She'd never been led in that direction before. She looked back at him questioningly, as if to say, "Where are you taking me?" But after a while she seemed to come to the conclusion that a goat shouldn't ask questions. Still, the road was different. They passed new fields, pastures, and huts with thatched roofs. Here and there a dog barked and came running after them, but Aaron chased it away with his stick.

The sun was shining when Aaron left the village. Suddenly the weather changed. A large black cloud with a bluish center appeared in the east and spread itself rapidly over the sky. A cold wind blew in with it. The crows flew low, croaking. At first it looked as if it would rain, but instead it began to hail as in summer. It was early in the day, but it became dark as dusk. After a while the hail turned to snow.

In his twelve years Aaron had seen all kinds of weather, but he had never experienced a snow like this one. It was so dense it shut out the light of the day. In a short time their path was completely covered. The wind became as cold as ice. The road to town was narrow and winding. Aaron no longer knew where he was. He could not see through the snow. The cold soon penetrated his quilted jacket.

At first Zlateh didn't seem to mind the change in weather. She, too, was twelve years old and knew what winter meant. But when her legs sank deeper and deeper into the snow, she began to turn her head and look at Aaron in wonderment. Her mild eyes seemed to ask, "Why are we out in such a storm?" Aaron hoped that a peasant would come along with his cart, but no one passed by.

▶ **Critical Viewing**
What does Zlateh's posture in the picture say about her feelings? **[Infer]**

Literary Analysis
Conflict In what two ways are the snow and wind in conflict with Aaron?

The snow grew thicker, falling to the ground in large, whirling flakes. Beneath it Aaron's boots touched the softness of a plowed field. He realized that he was no longer on the road. He had gone astray. He could no longer figure out which was east or west, which way was the village, the town. The wind whistled, howled, whirled the snow about in eddies.[3] It looked as if white imps were playing tag on the fields. A white dust rose above the ground. Zlateh stopped. She could walk no longer. Stubbornly she anchored her cleft hooves in the earth and bleated as if pleading to be taken home. Icicles hung from her white beard, and her horns were glazed with frost.

Aaron did not want to admit the danger, but he knew just the same that if they did not find shelter they would freeze to death. This was no ordinary storm. It was a mighty blizzard. The snowfall had reached his knees. His hands were numb, and he could no longer feel his toes. He choked when he breathed. His nose felt like wood, and he rubbed it with

Illustrations copyright © 1966 by Maurice Sendak, copyright renewed 1994 by Maurice Sendak. Printed with permission from HarperCollins Publishers.

 Reading Check

What surprises Zlateh when she and Aaron reach the road?

---

3. eddies (ed′ ēz) *n.* currents of air moving in circular motions like little whirlwinds.

bleating began to sound like crying. Those humans in whom she had so much confidence had dragged her into a trap. Aaron began to pray to God for himself and for the innocent animal.

Suddenly he made out the shape of a hill. He wondered what it could be. Who had piled snow into such a huge heap? He moved toward it, dragging Zlateh after him. When he came near it, he realized that it was a large haystack which the snow had blanketed.

Aaron realized immediately that they were saved. With great effort he dug his way through the snow. He was a village boy and knew what to do. When he reached the hay, he hollowed out a nest for himself and the goat. No matter how cold it may be outside, in the hay it is always warm. And hay was food for Zlateh. The moment she smelled it she became contented and began to eat. Outside, the snow continued to fall. It quickly covered the passageway Aaron had dug. But a boy and an animal need to breathe, and there was hardly any air in their hideout. Aaron bored a kind of a window through the hay and snow and carefully kept the passage clear.

Zlateh, having eaten her fill, sat down on her hind legs and seemed to have regained her confidence in man. Aaron ate his two slices of bread and cheese, but after the difficult journey he was still hungry. He looked at Zlateh and noticed her udders were full. He lay down next to her, placing himself so that when he milked her he could squirt the milk into his mouth. It was rich and sweet. Zlateh was not accustomed to being milked that way, but she did not resist. On the contrary, she seemed eager to reward Aaron for bringing her to a shelter whose very walls, floor, and ceiling were made of food.

Through the window Aaron could catch a glimpse of the chaos outside. The wind carried before it whole drifts of snow. It was completely dark, and he did not know whether night had already come or whether it was the darkness of the storm. Thank God that in the hay it was not cold. The dried hay, grass, and field flowers <u>exuded</u> the warmth of the summer sun. Zlateh ate frequently; she nibbled from above, below, from the left and right. Her body gave forth an animal warmth, and Aaron cuddled up to her. He had

▶ Critical Viewing
Why does Aaron look sad in this picture? [Connect]

Literary Analysis
Conflict and Resolution How has the discovery of the haystack temporarily resolved Aaron's problem?

Vocabulary Builder
exuded (eg zyo͞od′ əd) v. gave off; oozed

always loved Zlateh, but now she was like a sister. He was alone, cut off from his family, and wanted to talk. He began to talk to Zlateh. "Zlateh, what do you think about what has happened to us?" he asked.

"Maaaa," Zlateh answered.

"If we hadn't found this stack of hay, we would both be frozen stiff by now," Aaron said.

"Maaaa," was the goat's reply.

"If the snow keeps on falling like this, we may have to stay here for days," Aaron explained.

"Maaaa," Zlateh bleated.

"What does 'maaaa' mean?" Aaron asked. "You'd better speak up clearly."

"Maaaa, maaaa," Zlateh tried.

"Well, let it be 'maaaa' then," Aaron said patiently. "You can't speak, but I know you understand. I need you and you need me. Isn't that right?"

"Maaaa."

Aaron became sleepy. He made a pillow out of some hay, leaned his head on it, and dozed off. Zlateh, too, fell asleep.

When Aaron opened his eyes, he didn't know whether it was morning or night. The snow had blocked up his window. He tried to clear it, but

Illustrations copyright © 1966 by Maurice Sendak, copyright renewed 1994 by Maurice Sendak. Printed with permission from HarperCollins Publishers.

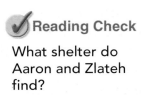

Reading Check

What shelter do Aaron and Zlateh find?

when he had bored through to the length of his arm, he still hadn't reached the outside. Luckily he had his stick with him and was able to break through to the open air. It was still dark outside. The snow continued to fall and the wind wailed, first with one voice and then with many. Sometimes it had the sound of devilish laughter. Zlateh, too, awoke, and when Aaron greeted her, she answered, "Maaaa." Yes, Zlateh's language consisted of only one word, but it meant many things. Now she was saying, "We must accept all that God gives us—heat, cold, hunger, satisfaction, light, and darkness."

Aaron had awakened hungry. He had eaten up his food, but Zlateh had plenty of milk.

For three days Aaron and Zlateh stayed in the haystack. Aaron had always loved Zlateh, but in these three days he loved her more and more. She fed him with her milk and helped him keep warm. She comforted him with her patience. He told her many stories, and she always cocked her ears and listened. When he patted her, she licked his hand and his face. Then she said, "Maaaa," and he knew it meant, I love you, too.

The snow fell for three days, though after the first day it was not as thick and the wind quieted down. Sometimes Aaron felt that there could never have been a summer, that the snow had always fallen, ever since he could remember. He, Aaron, never had a father or mother or sisters. He was a snow child, born of the snow, and so was Zlateh. It was so quiet in the hay that his ears rang in the stillness. Aaron and Zlateh slept all night and a good part of the day. As for Aaron's dreams, they were all about warm weather. He dreamed of green fields, trees covered with blossoms, clear brooks, and singing birds. By the third night the snow had stopped, but Aaron did not dare to find his way home in the darkness. The sky became clear and the moon shone, casting silvery nets on the snow. Aaron dug his way out and looked at the world. It was all white, quiet, dreaming dreams of heavenly splendor. The stars were large and close. The moon swam in the sky as in a sea.

On the morning of the fourth day Aaron heard the ringing of sleigh bells. The haystack was not far from the road. The peasant who drove the sleigh pointed out the way to him—

Literary Analysis
Conflict In what way are Aaron and Zlateh still in danger from the storm?

Reading Skill
Make Inferences Using your own experience, what inference can you make about how Aaron feels based on the details in this passage?

not to the town and Feivel the butcher, but home to the village. Aaron had decided in the haystack that he would never part with Zlateh.

Aaron's family and their neighbors had searched for the boy and the goat but had found no <u>trace</u> of them during the storm. They feared they were lost. Aaron's mother and sisters cried for him; his father remained silent and gloomy. Suddenly one of the neighbors came running to their house with the news that Aaron and Zlateh were coming up the road.

There was great joy in the family. Aaron told them how he had found the stack of hay and how Zlateh had fed him with her milk. Aaron's sisters kissed and hugged Zlateh and gave her a special treat of chopped carrots and potato peels, which Zlateh gobbled up hungrily.

Nobody ever again thought of selling Zlateh, and now that the cold weather had finally set in, the villagers needed the services of Reuven the furrier once more. When Hanukkah came, Aaron's mother was able to fry pancakes every evening, and Zlateh got her portion, too. Even though Zlateh had her own pen, she often came to the kitchen, knocking on the door with her horns to indicate that she was ready to visit, and she was always admitted. In the evening Aaron, Miriam, and Anna played dreidel.[4] Zlateh sat near the stove watching the children and the flickering of the Hanukkah candles.

Once in a while Aaron would ask her, "Zlateh, do you remember the three days we spent together?"

And Zlateh would scratch her neck with a horn, shake her white bearded head, and come out with the single sound which expressed all her thoughts, and all her love.

Vocabulary Builder
trace (trās) *n.* mark left behind by something

Literary Analysis
Conflict How is the family's conflict over selling Zlateh resolved?

---

4. dreidel (drā´ dəl) *n.* small top with Hebrew letters on each of four sides, spun in a game played by children.

Apply the Skills

Zlateh the Goat

Thinking About the Selection

1. **Respond:** What questions do you have about the story? Write them in the first column of a three-column chart. Trade charts with a partner.
   - In the second column, answer your partner's questions. Discuss your responses.
   - In the third column, explain how the discussion affected your understanding of the work.
2. **(a) Recall:** What happens to Aaron and Zlateh on the way to town? **(b) Deduce:** Why is their situation dangerous?
3. **(a) Draw Conclusions:** Why does the stay in the haystack change Aaron's mind about selling Zlateh? **(b) Apply:** What is this story's message about friendship and trust?

Reading Skill

4. Aaron's mother and sisters cry over selling Zlateh. Based on what you know of human behavior, what **inference** can you make about their feelings for the goat?
5. What details in the story support the inference that Aaron is quick-thinking and brave?

Literary Analysis

6. Copy the chart. For each **conflict** listed, tell whether it is internal or external and explain how it was resolved.

Conflict	What Kind?	Resolution
Reuven needs the money he could get for Zlateh, but he loves Zlateh.		
Aaron and Zlateh need food and shelter but are caught in a blizzard.		

7. Explain how the **resolution** of the first conflict is influenced by the second conflict.

QuickReview

Story at a Glance

A snowstorm both creates a problem and solves a problem for a young boy and his goat.

Go Online
Assessment
For: Self-test
Visit: www.PHSchool.com
Web Code: ela-6204

Inference: a logical assumption about information that is not directly stated in a text

Conflict: a struggle between opposing forces that can be *internal* or *external*

Resolution: the way the conflict is settled

Vocabulary Builder

Practice Answer each question using a word from the vocabulary list on page 204. Explain your choice.

1. Which word could describe footprints left in the snow?
2. How else can you say that you attached one thing to another?
3. How else can you say that a stove gave off heat?

Writing

Write a short **persuasive speech** that Aaron might give to urge his father to keep Zlateh. In the first paragraph, state your position in favor of keeping the goat. Then support your position with reasons that will appeal to Reuven. Revise to remove less persuasive details.

For *Grammar, Vocabulary,* and *Assessment,*
see **Build Language Skills,** pages 224–225.

Extend Your Learning

Listening and Speaking A **monologue** is a speech given by one person. Speaking as Zlateh, deliver a monologue in which you say what you think about the humans' behavior. Change the tone and volume of your voice to show feelings such as puzzlement or annoyance, and use facial expressions to reflect the meanings of your words.

Research and Technology With a small group, find out about *shtetls,* Jewish villages of Eastern Europe. Use the word *shtetl* as a keyword to search the Internet. Prepare a **chart** that shows what Aaron's day-to-day life might have been like. Answer the following questions:
- What were the homes like?
- What responsibilities might a twelve-year-old boy have had?
- How did most people make a living?

Short Story

Background

The Sioux This story comes from the Sioux, a Native American people of the northern plains. The Sioux moved frequently from place to place, settling where they could find good supplies of fresh water and buffalo, their main source of food. Their lives were linked to the cycles of the natural world, so they had a special understanding of the animals in their world.

Connecting to the Literature

Reading/Writing Connection In "The Old Woman Who Lived With the Wolves," a young Sioux woman becomes lost in the wilderness. List the challenges and feelings a person in this situation would face. Use at least three of the following words: *obtain, survive, locate, rely, isolate.*

Review

For **Reading Skill, Literary Analysis,** and **Vocabulary Builder,** see p. 204.

Meet the Author

Chief Luther **Standing Bear** (1868–1939)

A member of the Oglala Sioux, Chief Luther Standing Bear was a writer who fought for Native American rights. In his work, he describes the customs and beliefs of the Sioux, including their special relationship with nature. In *Land of the Spotted Eagle,* Chief Standing Bear wrote, "Earth was bountiful and we were surrounded with the blessings of the great mystery."

Fast Facts

▶ In addition to being a writer, Luther Standing Bear was an actor and a leader of his people.

▶ His family named him *Ota K'Te* (Plenty Kill), but he later called himself Standing Bear because it was his father's name.

▶ Standing Bear was a graduate of the Carlisle Indian School in Pennsylvania.

Go Online **Author Link**
For: More about the author
Visit: www.PHSchool.com
Web Code: ele-9205

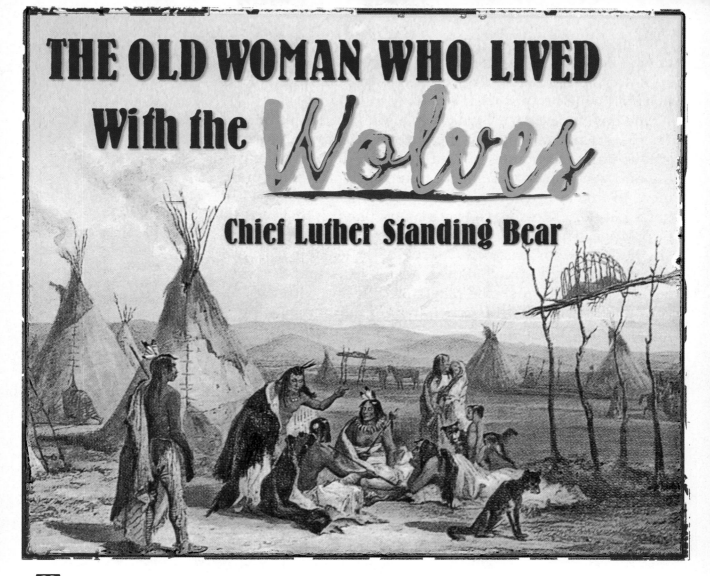

THE OLD WOMAN WHO LIVED With the *Wolves*

Chief Luther Standing Bear

The Sioux were a people who traveled about from place to place a great deal within the borders of their own country. They did not trespass upon the territory of their neighbor Indians, but liked to make their home first here and then there upon their own ground, just as they pleased. It was not like moving from one strange town to another, but wherever they settled it was home. Taking down and putting up the tipis was not hard for them to do.

The reasons for their moving were many. Perhaps the grass for their ponies ran short, or the water in the creek became low. Maybe the game had gone elsewhere, and

Reading Skill
Make Inferences
Explain how the details in these paragraphs support the inference that the Sioux enjoy traveling.

▲ Critical Viewing Based on the picture and title, what do you already know about the story? **[Preview]**

maybe the people just moved the camp to a fresh green spot, for the Sioux loved pure water, pure air, and a clean place on which to put their tipis.

One day, long ago, a Sioux village was on the march. There were many people in the party, and many children. A great number of horses carried the tipis, and herds of racing and war horses were being taken care of by the young men. In this crowd was a young woman who carried with her a pet dog. The dog was young and playful, just past the puppy age. The young woman was very fond of her pet, as she had cared for it since it was a wee little thing with eyes still closed. She romped along with the pup, and the way seemed short because she played with it and with the young folks when not busy helping her mother with the packing and unpacking.

One evening Marpiyawin missed her dog. She looked and she called, but he was not to be found. Perhaps someone liked her playful pet and was keeping him concealed, but after a search she became satisfied that no one in camp

Reading Skill
Make Inferences
What do the details here tell you about how the Sioux feel about animals? Explain.

Literature in Context | Social Studies Connection

Home on the Range

Tipi (or *teepee*) is the Sioux word for "dwelling place." Tipis were about fourteen feet tall and faced east to greet the rising sun.

Assembling a tipi took about fifteen minutes, a job performed by the tribe's women, who also owned the tipis. ▶

The poles supporting the hides were usually made of lodgepole pine because the wood was tall, thin, and tough. ▶

Moving the tipis was relatively easy. Horses or dogs would drag the tipi poles with the rest of the tribe's belongings. ▼

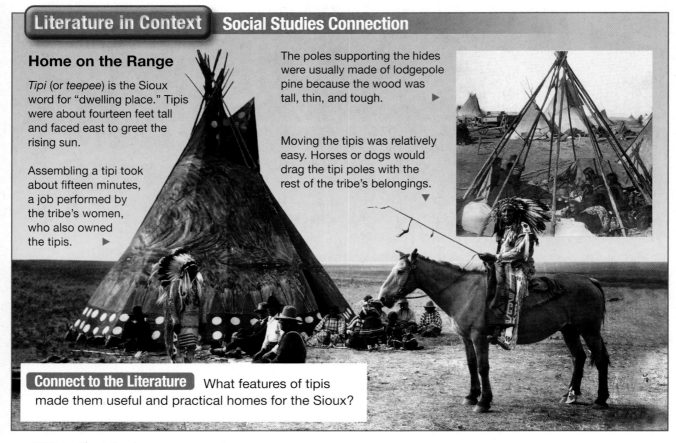

Connect to the Literature What features of tipis made them useful and practical homes for the Sioux?

was hiding him. Then she thought that perhaps he had lain down to sleep somewhere along the way and had been left behind. Then, lastly, she thought that the wolves had enticed him to join their pack. For oftentimes the Sioux dogs were <u>coaxed</u> away and ran with the wolf-pack, always returning, however, in a few days or weeks to the village.

So Marpiyawin, thinking the matter over, decided that she would go back over the way her people had journeyed and that somewhere she would find her dog. She would then bring him back to camp with her. Without a word to anyone, she turned back, for she had no fear of becoming lost. Nothing could befall her, so why should she fear? As she walked back, she came to the foothills at the base of the mountains where her village people had spent the summer. As she slept that night, the first snowfall of the autumn came so silently that it did not awaken her. In the morning everything was white with snow, but it was not far to the place where the village had been in camp and so determined was she to find her dog that she decided to keep going. Marpiyawin now felt that her pet had gone back to the old camping-ground, as dogs often do, and was now there howling and crying to be found.

That afternoon the snow fell thicker and faster and Marpiyawin was forced to seek shelter in a cave, which was rather dark, but warm and comfortable. She was not hungry, for in her little rawhide[1] bag was still some *wasna*.[2] She was tired, however, so it was not long till she fell asleep, and while she slept she had a most wonderful vision. In her dream the wolves talked to her and she understood them, and when she talked to them they understood her too. They told her that she had lost her way, but that she should trust them and they would not see her suffer from cold or hunger. She replied that she would not worry, and when she awoke it was without fear, even though in the cave with her were the wolves sitting about in a friendly manner.

The blizzard raged outside for many days, still she was contented, for she was neither cold nor hungry. For meat

---

1. rawhide (rô´ hīd) *n.* rough leather.
2. wasna (wäs´ nuh) *n.* meat and berries pounded and pressed together in flat strips to make a nutritious food that is easy to carry.

Vocabulary Builder
coaxed (kōkst) *v.* persuaded by gentle urging

Literary Analysis
Conflict What conflict is developed here?

Literary Analysis
Conflict How has the snow increased the conflict in the story?

Reading Check

Why does Marpiyawin get separated from the rest of her tribe?

the wolves supplied her with tender rabbits and at night they kept her body warm with their shaggy coats of fur. As the days wore on, she and the wolves became fast friends.

But clear days finally came and the wolves offered to lead her back to her people, so they set out. They <u>traversed</u> many little valleys and crossed many creeks and streams; they walked up hills and down hills, and at last came to one from which she could look down upon the camp of her people. Here she must say "Good-bye" to her friends and companions—the wolves. This made her feel very sad, though she wanted to see her people again. Marpiyawin thanked all the wolves for their kindness to her and asked what she might do for them. All they asked was that, when the long winter months came and food was scarce, she bring to the top of the hill some nice fat meat for them to eat. This she gladly promised to do and went down the hill toward the camp of her people.

Vocabulary Builder
traversed (trə vʉrst´)
v. went across

◀ Critical Viewing
Why would Marpiyawin approach a wolf like the one in this painting without fear? **[Speculate]**

As Marpiyawin neared the village, she smelled a very unpleasant odor. At first it mystified her, then she realized it was the smell of human beings. At once the knowledge came to her that the smell of humans was very different from the smell of animals. This was why she now knew that animals so readily track human beings and why the odor of man is oftentimes so <u>offensive</u> to them. She had been with the wolves so long that she had lost the odor of her people and now was able to see that, while man often considers the animal offensive, so do animals find man offensive.

Marpiyawin came to the camp of her people and they were happy to see her, for they had considered her lost and thought she had been taken by an enemy tribe. But she pointed to the top of the hill in the distance, and there sat her friends, their forms black against the sky. In great surprise her people looked, not knowing what to say. They thought she must have just escaped a great danger. So she explained to them that she had been lost and would have perished had not the wolves saved her life. She asked them to give her some of their fat meat that she might carry it to the top of the hill. Her people were so grateful and happy that a young man was sent about the camp telling of the safe return of Marpiyawin and collecting meat from each tipi. Marpiyawin took the meat, placed the bundle on her back, and went up the hill, while the village people looked on in wonder. When she reached the hilltop she spread the meat on the ground and the wolves ate it.

Ever after that, when the long winter months came and food was scarce and hard to find, Marpiyawin took meat to her friends the wolves. She never forgot their language and oftentimes in the winter their voices calling to her would be heard throughout the village. Then the people would ask the old woman what the wolves were saying. Their calls would be warnings that a blizzard was coming, or that the enemy was passing close, and to send out a scout or to let the old woman know that they were watching her with care.

And so Marpiyawin came to be known to the tribe as "The Old Woman Who Lived with the Wolves," or, in the Sioux language as, "Win yan wan si k'ma nitu ompi ti."

Vocabulary Builder
offensive (ə fen´ siv)
adj. unpleasant

Reading Skill
Make Inferences
How do the Sioux feel about wolves, based on their reaction to Marpiyawin's story?

Apply the Skills

The Old Woman Who Lived With the Wolves

Thinking About the Selection

1. **Respond:** What questions do you have about the story? Write them in the first column of a three-column chart. Trade charts with a partner.
   - In the second column, answer your partner's questions. Discuss your responses.
   - In the third column, explain how the discussion affected your understanding of the work.

2. **(a) Recall:** How did Marpiyawin come to spend time living with the wolves? **(b) Analyze:** Why do you think she is not afraid of the wolves?

3. **(a) Draw Conclusions:** Would Marpiyawin have survived without the wolves? Support your answer. **(b) Generalize:** What does her experience suggest about the way the Sioux view nature?

Reading Skill

4. **(a)** Think of a time when you lost something. Make an **inference** about how Marpiyawin feels as she sets out to find her dog. **(b)** Explain how your prior knowledge and experience helped you make the inference.

Literary Analysis

5. Copy the chart. For each **conflict** listed, tell whether it is internal or external and explain how it was resolved.

Conflict	What Kind?	Resolution
Marpiyawin needs food and shelter, but she is lost.		
She is sad to leave the wolves but misses her people.		

6. Explain how the **resolution** of the first conflict leads to the second conflict.

QuickReview

Story at a Glance

A young Sioux woman becomes separated from her people but finds she is not alone in her struggle to survive.

Go Online
Assessment

For: Self-test
Visit: www.PHSchool.com
Web Code: ela-6205

Inference: a logical assumption about information not directly stated in a text

Conflict: a struggle between opposing forces that can be *internal* or *external*

Resolution: the way the conflict is settled

Vocabulary Builder

Practice Answer each of the following questions using a word from the vocabulary list on page 204.

1. Which word could describe a skunk's odor?

2. Which word could be used to say you persuaded someone to do something?

3. How else could you say that you crossed the desert?

Writing

Write a short **persuasive speech** that Marpiyawin might give to urge her people to help the wolves.

- List three reasons for trusting the wolves that will appeal to her people.
- State your position clearly in the first paragraph. Present reasons that support your position.
- Revise your speech to remove less persuasive details.

For *Grammar, Vocabulary,* and *Assessment,* see **Build Language Skills,** pages 224–225.

Extend Your Learning

Listening and Speaking A **monologue** is a speech given by one person. Speaking as one of the wolves, deliver a brief monologue that represents what you think about the humans' behavior. Change the tone and volume of your voice to show feelings such as puzzlement or annoyance, and use facial expressions to reflect the meanings of your words.

Research and Technology With a small group, find out about Sioux settlements. Use the words *Sioux settlements* as keywords to begin a search on the Internet. Prepare a **chart** that shows the Sioux people's day-to-day life. Answer these questions:

- What were the settlements like?
- What responsibilities would a Sioux girl have had?

Build Language Skills

Vocabulary Skill

Roots -spec- The **Latin root** -*spec*- means "look or see."
Speculate comes from the Latin root -*spec*-. When you
speculate about something, you use what you know to "see"
details that have not yet been revealed.

▶ **Example:** They speculated about the reasons for the unusual
weather.

Practice Use a dictionary to look up the meaning of each of the
following words. Explain how each meaning relates to the idea of
"look or see." Then use each word in a sentence.

1. speculation
2. spectacle
3. inspector
4. conspicuous

Grammar Lesson

Principal Parts of Verbs Every verb has four main forms, or
principal parts. These parts are used to form verb tenses that
show time. The example shows the four principal parts. Notice
that regular verbs form their past tense and past participles by
adding -*ed* or -*d*. Irregular verbs, such as *be,* form their past tense
and/or past participles in different ways.

Present	talk
Present Participle (am)	talking
Past	talked
Past Participle (have)	talked

Practice Rewrite each sentence, replacing the italicized verb
with the principal part indicated in parentheses.

1. I *look* for my pencil. (present participle)
2. We *be* to this store before. (past participle)
3. The girls *change* their phone numbers. (past)
4. I think our neighbor *move*. (past participle)
5. We *walk* to get exercise. (present participle)

MorePractice

For more practice
with pronouns, see
Grammar Hand-
book, p. R32.

*W*G *Prentice Hall Writing and Grammar Connection: Chapter 22, Section 1*

Reading: Inferences

Directions: *Read the selection. Then, answer the questions.*

Sitting inside the tent, George listened to the wind howling down the mountain. He was eager to reach the top of the mountain, but he knew that the weather made climbing dangerous. Although he could probably finish the climb, the less experienced climbers on his team would have great difficulty. George heaved a sigh, then went to tell the group that they would turn back.

1. Based on your prior knowledge, what inference can you make about the weather?
   A It is warm.
   B It is cloudy.
   C It is stormy.
   D It is very hot.

2. Which inference is supported by details in the selection?
   A George is an experienced climber.
   B There are ten people in George's climbing team.
   C This is George's third time climbing the mountain.
   D George is a reckless climber.

3. Which detail supports the inference that George is disappointed?
   A He listens.
   B He sighs.
   C He thinks.
   D He sits.

4. Which inference is supported by details in the selection?
   A It is dangerous to climb a mountain during a storm.
   B George is tired of climbing.
   C George's team is not interested in climbing mountains.
   D Climbers do not need to be concerned about the weather.

Timed Writing: Explanation [Critical Stance]

Review "The Old Woman Who Lived With the Wolves" or "Zlateh the Goat." Explain the importance of the relationship between humans and animals in the story. Use details from the text to support your answer. **(20 minutes)**

 Writing Workshop: *Work in Progress*

Review of a Short Story

For several minutes, freewrite about the story you chose. As you write, include as many of your responses as possible. Choose the idea you think best captures your response. Put this in your writing portfolio.

Reading Informational Materials

Textbooks

In Part 1, you are learning about making inferences in literature. Inferences are also helpful when reading textbooks. If you read "Zlateh the Goat," you made inferences about village life in Poland at the time of the story. You can make inferences about the population and land of modern Poland using the textbook article, maps, and charts that follow.

About Textbooks

A **textbook** gives factual information about a specific subject, such as math or world history. The purpose of a textbook is to help students learn new information. The information is typically organized into units, chapters, and sections. Questions and activities throughout the textbook help students review what they have read. Textbooks also include text aids and text features, such as the following, to help readers understand and use the information given.

Text Aids	Text Features
• chapter titles • main headings and subheadings • highlighted vocabulary	• maps, graphs, and charts • photographs, drawings, and diagrams with captions

Reading Skill

Text aids and text features organize details in a textbook and highlight important information. Here are some tips for using text aids and text features effectively.

Tips for Using Text Aids and Text Features

❑ Headings and subheadings tell you the main ideas of the chapters.

❑ Maps, graphs, and charts help you understand the main ideas of the chapters.

❑ Pictures and diagrams with captions give examples or make clear the main ideas of the chapters.

POLAND

> The chapter title and the heading highlight the main idea of the chapter.

Tradition in Poland

Since Poland's communist government fell, the country has moved away from a communist economy in which the government owned and ran all the businesses. Instead, Poland has adopted the **free enterprise** system, or capitalism. In it, people can run their own businesses. But not all of life in Poland has changed. As you travel in the countryside, you see signs of a way of life that existed long before communist rule.

Farms dot the countryside on the way to the Tatra Mountains in Poland.

> The vocabulary term is highlighted to indicate it is an important idea. The word *capitalism* helps you understand its meaning.

The Polish Countryside   For a look at tradition in Poland, you might visit the northeast corner of the country. Here, the Polish border has shifted many times. Again and again, other countries have seized this area. Sometimes, it belonged to Russia. At other times, it was controlled by Lithuania (lith oo ay nee uh) or Germany. There were even times when other countries took over all of Poland. But no matter what happened, the traditions of Polish life stayed the same. This is true even today.

After World War II, Poland became a communist nation. At public festivals, Poles had to pledge loyalty to communism. When crops did not grow, Poles relied on money from the communist government. When Poles were sick, they went to doctors who were paid by the government. When they were too old to farm, they knew they would receive a government pension.

Now all that has changed. It is up to the farmer to save money for old age. If the crops fail, the farmer must try to borrow money to start again. Learning this new way of life has been hard for some Poles.

The Polish Language Like Roman Catholicism, the language of the Poles has also stood the test of time. Some foreign rulers banned the use of Polish in schools and in the government. The communists did not ban Polish but did force Polish schoolchildren to learn Russian, the main language of the Soviet Union.

Today, the Polish language is alive and well. It ties the people of the nation together and it gives them the strong feeling that being Polish is something different and special. As a Slavic language, it also links the nation to other Slavic nations in Eastern Europe.

The large feature includes a map of Poland and charts to help you understand more about the geography, land use, and sources of income in Poland.

The pie chart gives information about the labor force, and the line graph gives information about money received from exports.

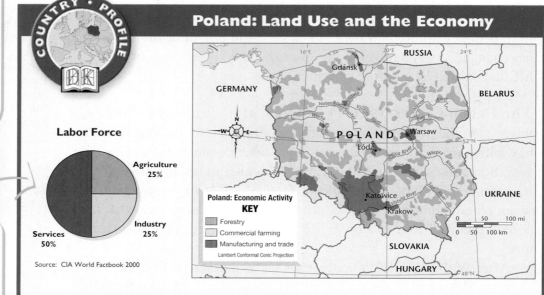

COUNTRY · PROFILE

Poland: Land Use and the Economy

Labor Force

- Agriculture 25%
- Industry 25%
- Services 50%

Source: CIA World Factbook 2000

Poland: Economic Activity
KEY
- Forestry
- Commercial farming
- Manufacturing and trade

Lambert Conformal Conic Projection

Income From Agricultural Exports

Millions of Dollars: 3,000 / 2,500 / 2,000 / 1,500 / 1,000 / 500 / 0

Year: 1965, 1970, 1975, 1980, 1985, 1990, 1995, 1999

Source: Food and Agriculture Organization of the United Nations

Economics The map and charts show the importance of agriculture in Poland. **Map and Chart Study** (a) Look at the information on this page and list three pieces of evidence that show agriculture is important to Poland.
(b) How much money did Poland make from agricultural exports in 1999?

Reading: Using Text Aids and Text Features

Directions: *Choose the letter of the best answer to each question.*

1. According to the map of Poland, which statement is true?
   A Most of the land is used for commercial farming.
   B Most of the land is used for forestry.
   C Poland shares a border with Hungary.
   D Germany is east of Poland.

2. According to the "Labor Force" pie chart, which statement is true?
   A More people work in agriculture than in industry.
   B About twice as many people work in industry than in agriculture.
   C About half of the labor force works in services.
   D Today, there are only twenty-five agricultural workers in Poland.

3. Which statement can be proved true by making inferences from the **headings** and **subheadings** in this chapter?
   A Two important parts of Polish tradition come from its country-side and its language.
   B Poland's economy has switched to capitalism.
   C The communists forced Polish students to learn Russian.
   D The income from Poland's agricultural exports has risen.

Reading: Comprehension and Interpretation

Directions: *Write your answers on a separate sheet of paper.*

4. According to this chapter, in what specific ways has life in Poland changed since it went from communism to capitalism?

5. Which is more widespread in Poland—forestry or manufacturing and trade? What text feature helped you find the answer?

Timed Writing: Explanation [Generating]

Explain why agriculture (also called commercial farming) is important to the people and the economy of Poland. Support your answer with details from text aids and features. **(20 minutes)**

Characters' Motives

Writers make their stories believable by creating characters with needs and desires. Then, they put the characters into situations that drive their behavior. A **character's motives** are the reasons behind his or her actions. These motivations can be based on internal and external factors.

- *Internal factors* include thoughts and feelings, such as jealousy, pride, or love.
- *External factors* are events or actions, such as a natural disaster or winning money.

Characters often have more than one motivation. For example, a character might be motivated to win a contest for the prize money but also to gain someone's approval.

Comparing Characters' Motives

These stories feature young characters who are motivated by several factors. To identify the reasons behind the characters' actions, ask yourself these questions:

- What do the characters want?
- What do the characters need?
- What do they do to get what they want or need?

As you read, use a chart like the one shown to track the motivations of the stories' main characters, Becky and Janet.

Character

↓

Action

↓

Motivation

Vocabulary Builder

Becky and the Wheels-and-Brake Boys

- **menace** (men´ əs) *n.* threat; danger (p. 234) *The pothole is a menace to cars.*

- **reckless** (rek´ lis) *adj.* not careful; taking chances (p. 236) *Reckless driving may cause an accident.*

- **envy** (en´ vē) *n.* unhappy feeling of wanting what someone else has (p. 239) *Terry's envy over Lynn's new bike was clear to all.*

The Southpaw

- **former** (fôr´ mər) *adj.* existing in an earlier time; past (p. 240) *Their former math teacher visited their school.*

- **unreasonable** (un rē´ zən i bəl) *adj.* not fair; not sensible (p. 242) *Asking for more allowance is an unreasonable request.*

Build Understanding

Connecting to the Literature

Reading/Writing Connection In these stories, the characters have skills that make them proud. List several skills or accomplishments that would make someone your age proud. Explain the difficulty or challenge of each achievement. Use three of these words: *accomplish, obtain, participate, perceive.*

Meet the Authors

James **Berry** (b. 1925)

In his writing, James Berry often celebrates the richness of his Jamaican heritage.

Inspiration Berry once explained the inspiration for his writing this way: "[the stories] were straight out of my own childhood and later observations. . . . No one has reported our stories, or the way we saw things. It's the function of writers and poets to bring in the left-out side of the human family."

Judith **Viorst** (b. 1931)

Born in Newark, New Jersey, Judith Viorst knew as a child that she wanted to be a writer. She kept writing until she found success with her stories and poetry.

Family Characters Viorst's three sons are sometimes characters in her books. Of a musical based on her book *Alexander and the Terrible, Horrible, No Good, Very Bad Day,* Viorst said, "I watched seven young men and women, playing multiple roles, become flesh-and-blood versions of my son Alexander, his brothers and friends. . . . This was a truly weird and truly thrilling thing to see."

Go **Online**
Author Link

For: More about the authors
Visit: www.PHSchool.com
Web Code: ele-9206

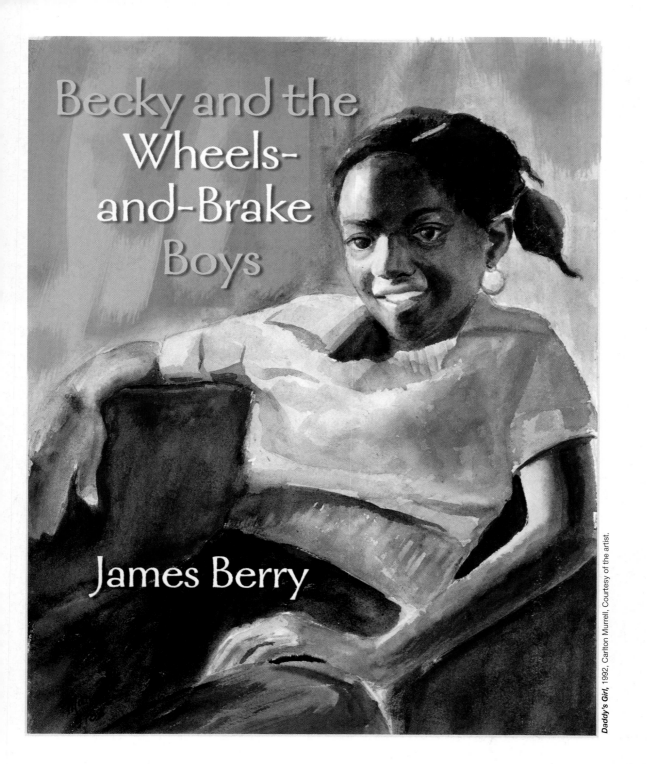

Becky and the Wheels-and-Brake Boys

James Berry

Daddy's Girl, 1992, Carlton Murrell, Courtesy of the artist.

Even my own cousin Ben was there—riding away, in the ringing of bicycle bells down the road. Every time I came to watch them—see them riding round and round enjoying themselves—they scooted off like crazy on their bikes.

They can't keep doing that. They'll see!

▲ Critical Viewing
Based on her expression and posture, what do you think this girl is like?
[Analyze]

I only want to be with Nat, Aldo, Jimmy, and Ben. It's no fair reason they don't want to be with me. Anybody could go off their head for that. Anybody! A girl can not, not, let boys get away with it all the time.

Bother! I have to walk back home, alone.

I know total-total that if I had my own bike, the Wheels-and-Brake Boys wouldn't treat me like that. I'd just ride away with them, wouldn't I?

Over and over I told my mum I wanted a bike. Over and over she looked at me as if I was crazy. "Becky, d'you think you're a boy? Eh? D'you think you're a boy? In any case, where's the money to come from? Eh?"

Of course I know I'm not a boy. Of course I know I'm not crazy. Of course I know all that's no reason why I can't have a bike. No reason! As soon as I get indoors I'll just have to ask again—ask Mum once more.

At home, indoors, I didn't ask my mum.

It was evening time, but sunshine was still big patches in yards and on housetops. My two younger brothers, Lenny and Vin, played marbles in the road. Mum was taking measurements of a boy I knew, for his new trousers and shirt. Mum made clothes for people. Meggie, my sister two years younger than me, was helping Mum on the veranda. Nobody would be pleased with me not helping. I began to help.

Granny-Liz would always stop fanning herself to drink up a glass of ice water. I gave my granny a glass of ice water, there in her rocking chair. I looked in the kitchen to find shelled coconut pieces to cut into small cubes for the fowls' morning feed. But Granny-Liz had done it. I came and started tidying up bits and pieces of cut-off material around my mum on the floor. My sister got nasty, saying she was already helping Mum. Not a single good thing was happening for me.

With me even being all so thoughtful of Granny's need of a cool drink, she started up some botheration[1] against me.

Listen to Granny-Liz: "Becky, with you moving about me here on the veranda, I hope you dohn have any centipedes or scorpions[2] in a jam jar in your pocket."

Literary Analysis
Characters' Motives
Why does Becky want a bike?

✓ **Reading Check**

What is one reason why Becky cannot have a bicycle?

---

1. botheration (bäth′ ər ā′ shən) n. trouble.
2. scorpions (skôr′ pē ənz) n. close relatives of spiders, with a poisonous stinger at the end of their tails; scorpions are found in warm regions.

"No, mam," I said sighing, trying to be calm. "Granny-Liz," I went on, "you forgot. My centipede and scorpion died." All the same, storm broke against me.

"Becky," my mum said. "You know I don't like you wandering off after dinner. Haven't I told you I don't want you keeping company with those awful riding-about bicycle boys? Eh?"

"Yes, mam."

"Those boys are a <u>menace</u>. Riding bicycles on sidewalks and narrow paths together, ringing bicycle bells and braking at people's feet like wild bulls charging anybody, they're heading for trouble."

"They're the Wheels-and-Brake Boys, mam."

"The what?"

"The Wheels-and-Brake Boys."

"Oh! Given themselves a name as well, have they? Well, Becky, answer this. How d'you always manage to look like you just escaped from a hair-pulling battle? Eh? And don't I tell you not to break the backs down and wear your canvas shoes like slippers? Don't you ever hear what I say?"

"Yes, mam."

"D'you want to end up a field laborer? Like where your father used to be overseer?"[3]

"No, mam."

"Well, Becky, will you please go off and do your homework?"

Everybody did everything to stop me. I was allowed no chance whatsoever. No chance to talk to Mum about the bike I dream of day and night! And I knew exactly the bike I wanted. I wanted a bike like Ben's bike. Oh, I wished I still had even my scorpion on a string to run up and down somebody's back!

I answered my mum. "Yes, mam." I went off into Meg's and my bedroom.

I sat down at the little table, as well as I might. Could homework stay in anybody's head in broad daylight outside? No. Could I keep a bike like Ben's out of my head? Not one bit. That bike took me all over the place. My beautiful bike jumped every log, every rock, every fence. My beautiful bike did everything cleverer than a clever cowboy's horse,

Vocabulary Builder
menace (men´ əs) *n.* threat; danger

Literary Analysis
Characters' Motives Is Becky's dream of having a bike an internal or external motivation? Explain.

---

3. **overseer** (ō´ vər sē´ ər) *n.* supervisor of workers.

Mother, I Love to Ride, 1992, Carlton Murrell, Courtesy of the artist.

with me in the saddle. And the bell, the bell was such a glorious gong of a ring!

If Dad was alive, I could talk to him. If Dad was alive, he'd give me money for the bike like a shot.

I sighed. It was amazing what a sigh could do. I sighed and tumbled on a great idea. Tomorrow evening I'd get Shirnette to come with me. Both of us together would be sure to get the boys interested to teach us to ride. Wow! With Shirnette they can't just ride away!

Next day at school, everything went sour. For the first time, Shirnette and me had a real fight, because of what I hated most.

Shirnette brought a cockroach to school in a shoe-polish tin. At playtime she opened the tin and let the cockroach fly into my blouse. Pure panic and disgust nearly killed me. I crushed up the cockroach in my clothes and practically ripped my blouse off, there in open sunlight. Oh, the smell of a cockroach is the nastiest ever to block your nose! I

▲ Critical Viewing
What do you think the girl in this picture would tell Becky's mother about riding a bike? **[Speculate]**

✓ Reading Check

How does Becky's mother feel about the Wheels-and-Brake Boys?

started running with my blouse to go and wash it. Twice I had to stop and be sick.

I washed away the crushed cockroach stain from my blouse. Then the stupid Shirnette had to come into the toilet, falling about laughing. All right, I knew the cockroach treatment was for the time when I made my centipede on a string crawl up Shirnette's back. But you put fair-is-fair aside. I just barged into Shirnette.

When it was all over, I had on a wet blouse, but Shirnette had one on, too.

Then, going home with the noisy flock of children from school, I had such a new, new idea. If Mum thought I was scruffy, Nat, Aldo, Jimmy, and Ben might think so, too. I didn't like that.

After dinner I combed my hair in the bedroom. Mum did her machining[4] on the veranda. Meggie helped Mum. Granny sat there, wishing she could take on any job, as usual.

I told Mum I was going to make up a quarrel with Shirnette. I went, but my friend wouldn't speak to me, let alone come out to keep my company. I stood alone and watched the Wheels-and-Brake Boys again.

This time the boys didn't race away past me. I stood leaning against the tall coconut palm tree. People passed up and down. The nearby main road was busy with traffic. But I didn't mind. I watched the boys. Riding round and round the big flame tree, Nat, Aldo, Jimmy, and Ben looked marvelous.

At first each boy rode round the tree alone. Then each boy raced each other round the tree, going round three times. As he won, the winner rang his bell on and on, till he stopped panting and could laugh and talk properly. Next, most reckless and fierce, all the boys raced against each other. And, leaning against their bicycles, talking and joking, the boys popped soft drinks open, drank, and ate chipped bananas.

I walked up to Nat, Aldo, Jimmy, and Ben and said, "Can somebody teach me to ride?"

"Why don't you stay indoors and learn to cook and sew and wash clothes?" Jimmy said.

---

4. **machining** (mə shēn´ iŋ) *n.* sewing.

Literary Analysis
Characters' Motives
What is Becky's motivation for fixing her hair?

Vocabulary Builder
reckless (rek´ lis) *adj.* not careful; taking chances

I grinned. "I know all that already," I said. "And one day perhaps I'll even be mum to a boy child, like all of you. Can you cook and sew and wash clothes, Jimmy? All I want is to learn to ride. I want you to teach me."

I didn't know why I said what I said. But everybody went silent and serious.

One after the other, Nat, Aldo, Jimmy, and Ben got on their bikes and rode off. I wasn't at all cross with them. I only wanted to be riding out of the playground with them. I knew they'd be heading into the town to have ice cream and things and talk and laugh.

Mum was sitting alone on the veranda. She sewed buttons onto a white shirt she'd made. I sat down next to Mum. Straightaway, "Mum," I said, "I still want to have a bike badly."

"Oh, Becky, you still have that foolishness in your head? What am I going to do?"

Mum talked with some sympathy. Mum knew I was honest. "I can't get rid of it, mam," I said.

Reading Check

Why do Becky and Shirnette have a fight?

Biking for Fun, 1992, Carlton Murrell, Courtesy of the artist.

◄ Critical Viewing How do the boys in this picture compare to those in the story? [Connect]

Mum stopped sewing. "Becky," she said, staring in my face, "how many girls around here do you see with bicycles?"

"Janice Gordon has a bike," I reminded her.

"Janice Gordon's dad has acres and acres of coconuts and bananas, with a business in the town as well."

I knew Mum was just about to give in. Then my granny had to come out onto the veranda and interfere. Listen to that Granny-Liz. "Becky, I heard your mother tell you over and over she cahn[5] afford to buy you a bike. Yet you keep on and on. Child, you're a girl."

"But I don't want a bike because I'm a girl."

"D'you want it because you feel like a bwoy?" Granny said.

"No. I only want a bike because I want it and want it and want it."

Granny just carried on. "A tomboy's like a whistling woman and a crowing hen, who can only come to a bad end. D'you understand?"

I didn't want to understand. I knew Granny's speech was an awful speech. I went and sat down with Lenny and Vin, who were making a kite.

By Saturday morning I felt real sorry for Mum. I could see Mum really had it hard for money. I had to try and help. I knew anything of Dad's—anything—would be worth a great mighty hundred dollars.

I found myself in the center of town, going through the busy Saturday crowd. I hoped Mum wouldn't be too cross. I went into the fire station. With lots of luck I came face to face with a round-faced man in uniform. He talked to me. "Little miss, can I help you?"

I told him I'd like to talk to the head man. He took me into the office and gave me a chair. I sat down. I opened out my brown paper parcel. I showed him my dad's sun helmet. I told him I thought it would make a good fireman's hat. I wanted to sell the helmet for some money toward a bike, I told him.

The fireman laughed a lot. I began to laugh, too. The fireman put me in a car and drove me back home.

---

5. **cahn** can't.

Literary Analysis
Characters' Motives
How does Becky feel about Granny-Liz's ideas?

Literary Analysis
Characters' Motives
What two possible motives does Becky have for trying to sell her father's helmet?

Mum's eyes popped to see me bringing home the fireman. The round-faced fireman laughed at my adventure. Mum laughed, too, which was really good. The fireman gave Mum my dad's hat back. Then—mystery, mystery—Mum sent me outside while they talked.

My mum was only a little cross with me. Then—mystery and more mystery—my mum took me with the fireman in his car to his house.

The fireman brought out what? A bicycle! A beautiful, shining bicycle! His nephew's bike. His nephew had been taken away, all the way to America. The bike had been left with the fireman-uncle for him to sell it. And the good, kind fireman-uncle decided we could have the bike—on small payments. My mum looked uncertain. But in a big, big way, the fireman knew it was all right. And Mum smiled a little. My mum had good sense to know it was all right. My mum took the bike from the fireman Mr. Dean.

And guess what? Seeing my bike much, much newer than his, my cousin Ben's eyes popped with <u>envy</u>. But he took on the big job. He taught me to ride. Then he taught Shirnette.

I ride into town with the Wheels-and-Brake Boys now. When she can borrow a bike, Shirnette comes too. We all sit together. We have patties and ice cream and drink drinks together. We talk and joke. We ride about, all over the place.

And, again, guess what? Fireman Mr. Dean became our best friend, and Mum's especially. He started coming around almost every day.

Vocabulary Builder
envy (en´ vē) *n.* unhappy feeling of wanting what someone else has

Literary Analysis
Characters' Motives
What motivates the fireman to sell the bicycle to Becky?

Thinking About the Selection

1. **Respond:** Do you think Becky should have taken her father's sun helmet to sell? Why or why not?

2. **(a) Infer:** Why don't Becky's mother and grandmother want her to join the Wheels-and-Brake Boys? **(b) Analyze:** What other reasons keep Becky from getting a bike?

3. **(a) Infer:** How would you describe Becky's personality? **(b) Analyze:** Which parts of Becky's personality help her achieve her goal?

★The★Southpaw★ JUDITH VIORST

Dear Richard,
    Don't invite me to your birthday party because I'm not coming. And give back the Disneyland sweatshirt I said you could wear.
    If I'm not good enough to play on your team, I'm not good enough to be friends with.
        Your *former* friend,
        Janet

P.S. I hope when you go to the dentist he finds 20 cavities.

Dear Janet,
    Here is your stupid Disneyland sweatshirt, if that's how you're going to be. I want my comic books now—finished or not. No girl has ever played on the Mapes Street baseball team, and as long as I'm captain, no girl ever will.
Your former friend,
    Richard

P.S. I hope when you go for your checkup you need a tetanus shot.

Dear Richard,
    I'm changing my goldfish's name from Richard to Stanley. Don't count on my vote for class president next year. Just because I'm a member of the ballet club doesn't mean I'm not a terrific ballplayer.
Your former friend,
    Janet

P.S. I see you lost your first game 28–0.

Dear Janet,
    I'm not saving any more seats for you on the bus. For all I care you can stand the whole way to school. Why don't you just forget about baseball and learn something nice like knitting?
Your former friend,
    Richard

P.S. Wait until Wednesday.

Dear Richard,
    My father said I could call someone to go with us for a ride and hot-fudge sundaes. In case you didn't notice, I didn't call you.
Your former friend,
    Janet

P.S. I see you lost your second game, 34–0.

Dear Janet,
    Remember when I took the laces out of my blue-and-white sneakers and gave them to you? I want them back.
Your former friend,
    Richard

P.S. Wait until Friday.

Dear Richard,
    Congratulations on your un-broken record. Eight straight losses, wow! I understand you're the laughingstock of New Jersey.
    Your former friend,
    Janet

P.S. Why don't you and your team forget about baseball and learn something nice like knitting maybe?

Dear Janet,
    Here's the silver horseback riding trophy that you gave me. I don't think I want to keep it anymore.
Your former friend,
    Richard

P.S. I didn't think you'd be the kind who'd kick a man when he's down.

Literary Analysis
Characters' Motives
Is Janet's motivation for writing to Richard external or internal? Explain.

Dear Richard,
    I wasn't kicking exactly. I was kicking back.
Your former friend,
    Janet

P.S. In case you were wondering, my batting average is .345.

Dear Janet,
    Alfie is having his tonsils out tomorrow. We might be able to let you catch next week.
    Richard

Dear Richard,
    I pitch.
Janet

Dear Janet,
    Joel is moving to Kansas and Danny sprained his wrist. How about a permanent place in the outfield?
    Richard

✓ Reading Check

What are Richard and Janet fighting about?

Dear Richard,
    I pitch.
Janet

Dear Janet,
    Ronnie caught the chicken pox and Leo broke his toe and Elwood has these stupid violin lessons. I'll give you first base, and that's my final offer.
        Richard

Dear Richard,
    Susan Reilly plays first base, Marilyn Jackson catches, Ethel Kahn plays center field, I pitch. It's a package deal.
        Janet

P.S. Sorry about your 12-game losing streak.

Dear Janet,
    Please! Not Marilyn Jackson.
    Richard

Dear Richard,
    Nobody ever said that I was unreasonable. How about Lizzie Martindale instead?
        Janet

Dear Janet,
    At least could you call your goldfish Richard again?
Your friend,
        Richard

Literary Analysis
Characters' Motives
What motivations do Janet and Richard share?

Vocabulary Builder
unreasonable (un rē´ zən i bəl) *adj.* not fair; not sensible

Thinking About the Selection

1. **Respond:** Do you think Janet and Richard can be friends again? Why or why not?

2. **(a) Recall:** Why is Janet angry with Richard?
   (b) Analyze: Using two examples, explain how each friend shows anger.

3. **(a) Recall:** What position does Janet want to play? **(b) Infer:** What agreement do Janet and Richard reach about her demands? **(c) Evaluate:** Do you think this arrangement suits both of them? Explain.

4. **Speculate:** Do you think that Richard's baseball team will finally win a game? Explain.

Apply the Skills

Becky and the Wheels-and-Brake Boys • The Southpaw

Comparing Characters' Motives

1. Use a graphic organizer like the one shown to compare the **motivations** of Becky and Janet.

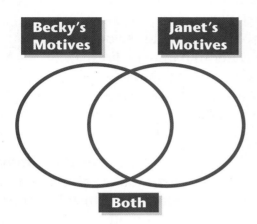

2. What internal motivation do Becky and Janet share? How does it affect the events in each story?

Writing to Compare Literary Works

Compare and contrast the motives of Becky and Janet. In a brief essay, explain how each girl's motivations help or hinder her in reaching her goals. Use these questions to get started:

- What does each girl want?
- What are each girl's reasons for wanting to reach her goal?
- How might their internal motivations prevent them from reaching their goals?

Vocabulary Builder

Practice Answer each question with either *yes* or *no.* Then explain your answer.

1. If a person is a *menace,* is he or she well-behaved?
2. Would a *former* president be discussed in a history book?
3. Is it *unreasonable* to want to protect the environment?
4. If people are filled with *envy,* are they jealous of something?
5. Would *reckless* behavior be rewarded?

QuickReview

Motives: reasons why a character acts in a certain way

Go Online
—Assessment
For: Self-test
Visit: www.PHSchool.com
Web Code: ela-6206

Reading

Directions: *Read the selection. Then, answer the questions.*

In 1906, a powerful earthquake struck San Francisco. The initial shaking lasted about 40 seconds, and many buildings collapsed. The earthquake tore apart water pipes and gas lines, and power lines fell everywhere. But the worst was yet to come. Fires broke out all over the city. Sadly, firefighters had little water to battle the fires with. The blazes raged for three days. In the end, nearly 500 city blocks burned. More than 28,000 buildings were destroyed, and 250,000 people were left homeless. It is believed that 3,000 people died, although no one knows the exact number.

1. **What is the most likely reason that no one knows for sure how many people died in the earthquake?**
   A No one cared to take an exact count.
   B Many bodies could not be recovered.
   C Victims did not live in the city.
   D The records were lost in other earthquakes.

2. **Which of the following details would help you infer that San Francisco had electricity in 1906?**
   A Fires broke out all over the city.
   B Approximately 3,000 people died.
   C Power lines fell everywhere.
   D Almost 500 city blocks burned.

3. **Which of the following details would *not* help you infer that the earthquake was destructive?**
   A Almost 500 city blocks burned.
   B More than 28,000 buildings were destroyed.
   C The earthquake occurred in 1906.
   D Thousands were left homeless.

4. **Based on your prior knowledge of earthquakes and the details in the selection, which inference is most reasonable?**
   A The initial shaking in less powerful earthquakes is less than 30 seconds.
   B Fires are common with less powerful earthquakes.
   C Three days of fires are common with earthquakes.
   D The initial shaking is not an indication of an earthquake's power.

5. **What can you infer from details in the passage?**
   A The fires left more people homeless than the earthquake.
   B The earthquake did more damage than the fires.
   C The earthquake was not damaging.
   D The fires did not destroy many buildings.

Assessment Practice

Vocabulary

Directions: *Choose the word that best completes each of the following sentences.*

6. I _____ that you're in a good mood.
   A refer
   B confer
   C deter
   D speculate

7. I _____ that you are very tired.
   A infer
   B refer
   C ferry
   D fertile

8. It is _____ to get the homework finished in two hours.
   A probable
   B spectacle
   C possible
   D detailed

9. Many speakers _____ to notecards while they are talking.
   A infer
   B refer
   C speculate
   D inspector

10. The _____ in a story are one basis of forming an inference.
   A references
   B inferences
   C details
   D spectators

Directions: *Use your knowledge of roots to choose the best definition for each word.*

11. inference
   A a strange or remarkable sight
   B a new decision
   C the act of bringing about
   D the act of looking

12. spectacle
   A a strange or remarkable sight
   B a new decision
   C the act of bringing about
   D the act of looking

13. transfer
   A change completely
   B switch
   C bring from one place to another
   D remove from one place

14. aspect
   A the way a person thinks
   B the way a person looks
   C the way a person reacts
   D the way a person functions

15. circumspect (circum = *around*)
   A decide without asking around
   B look around at all the choices
   C work around any problems
   D determine what might be around

Writing Workshop

Response to Literature: Review

When you read a literary work, the characters, the plot, and the writing itself can spark a reaction in you. In a **response to literature** or a **review,** you tell or write about this reaction. Follow the steps outlined in the workshop to write a review.

Assignment Write a review of a book, short story, essay, article, or poem that you read recently.

What to Include Your review should feature these elements:
- a summary of important features of the work
- a strong, interesting focus on some aspect of the work
- clear organization based on several ideas, patterns, or images
- supporting details for each main idea
- your own feelings about or judgment of the work
- error-free grammar, including troublesome verbs

To preview the criteria on which your review may be judged, see the rubric on page 250.

Prewriting

Choosing Your Topic

Book Talk In a group, discuss literary works you have enjoyed. Jot down titles that spark a response in you. Choose your topic from these titles.

Gathering Details

Jot down details to support your position. For the literary work you choose, think about the topic you will write about. For example, consider the story's plot, characters, or message. Then, reread the work to find the details to support a single idea you want to develop.

Topic: Greyling's parents should have told him that he was a selchie.

Greyling often looked at the sea sadly.

Greyling chooses to stay out at sea.

Using the Form
You may use elements of this form in these types of writing:
- book or film reviews
- letters to authors
- comparisons of works

Work in Progress
Review the work you did on pages 171, 203, and 225.

Drafting

Shaping Your Writing

Organize your response. A well-organized draft has these connected parts as the graphic shows:

- First, the **introduction** includes a brief summary, which describes the central problem in the work. State your main idea about the literature here.

- The **body** offers evidence to support your idea, including quotations, examples, and specific references to the text.

- Finally, the **conclusion** restates your interpretation and may include your feelings or opinions about what you have read. You might explain whether this story has had a lasting impression on you, or whether you would recommend the story.

Introduction

Identify your response.

Body

Support your response.

Conclusion

Summarize your ideas and make a recommendation.

Providing Elaboration

Justify your response. Elaborate on your general ideas by including details that support your opinion.

General Idea:	This story is full of suspense.
Specific Support:	Every time the clock chimes, the reader knows the hour of decision is closer.

Revising

Revising Your Overall Structure

Color-code related details. Review your draft to be sure that you have supported each point you have made. Circle each of your main points in a different color. Use the same color to underline the supporting points as you did for the main point. If a paragraph contains a few different colors, revise by moving sentences to the paragraph they support. If a sentence is neither circled nor underlined, delete it or use it in a new paragraph.

Revising Your Paragraphs

Add a quotation or two. Review the work to search for quotations that might serve as good examples to strengthen your draft. Then, insert quotations to support each point you make.

Integrating Grammar Skills

Correcting Errors With Verbs

Irregular verbs are those in which the past tense and past participle are not formed by adding *-ed* or *-d* to the present. **Troublesome** verbs are verb pairs that are easily confused.

Identifying Incorrect Forms of Irregular Verbs Memorize these verb forms that occur frequently in reading and writing.

Prentice Hall Writing and Grammar Connection: Chapter 22, Sections 1 and 3

Examples of Irregular Verbs

Present	Present Participle	Past	Past Participle
drink	(am) drinking	drank	(have) drunk
do	(am) doing	did	(have) done
bring	(am) bringing	brought	(have) brought

Identifying Incorrect Forms of Troublesome Verbs The two verbs in each of these pairs are often confused:

Lay/lie *Lay* means "to put or place something." It takes a direct object. Example: *Shelly laid the guitar on the table. Lie* means "to rest in a reclining position" or "to be situated." Example: *Barb is lying in the hammock. I have lain in the shade most of the day.*

Raise/rise *Raise* means "to lift up" or "to cause to rise." It takes a direct object. Example: *The wind has raised a cloud of dust. Rise* means "to get up" or "to go up." It does not take a direct object. Example: *My neighbors rise very early in the morning. The temperature has risen ten degrees.*

Fixing Errors To fix incorrect irregular verbs, identify which principal part of the verb is needed. Then, use these methods:

1. **Recall the correct use from the chart of principal parts.**
2. **Use a dictionary to determine the correct form.**

To fix an incorrectly used troublesome verb, use these methods:

1. **Remember the meaning of the verb.**
2. **Use a dictionary to determine which verb to use.**

Apply It to Your Editing

Choose two paragraphs in your draft. Circle the verbs in each sentence of the paragraphs. If any irregular verbs or troublesome verbs are used incorrectly, fix them using the methods above.

Student Model: Chris Harshfield
Louisville, KY

Response to *Tuck Everlasting*

Imagine finding a way to stay young forever! That's what the characters in *Tuck Everlasting,* a novel by Natalie Babbit, do. The novel makes the idea especially interesting by presenting it in a story that makes a realistic situation out of a very unrealistic idea.

Winnie, the main character, meets a strange family, the Tucks. She soon discovers that they have a secret: All of them have drunk from a spring of water that makes them live forever. Because Winnie has a crush on Jesse, one of the Tucks, she is tempted to drink from the spring, too, when she is old enough to marry him. Based on things the characters say and do, we know that this will not be an easy decision for Winnie. The question is very important to readers.

Should Winnie drink from the spring? The theme of this story is not a new one, but the way it is presented is better than in other stories. Like most of the other writers, Babbit suggests that living forever is not a good idea. Unlike other stories I have read about this theme, however, *Tuck Everlasting* really convinced me by showing examples I could understand. The novel also helped show the theme through characters who seem like real people. Even though I know there is no spring like the one in the book, the book made it seem real enough to get me thinking about the problem Winnie faces.

The final outcome of the story settles the question as far as Winnie is concerned. When Jesse returns years later, he finds her marker in the cemetery. Because she is dead, we know that she decided to not drink from the spring. The words on her marker suggest that she had a happy life, and that she got over Jesse. For Winnie, in any case, Mr. Tuck's memorable and mysterious words prove true: ". . . the stream keeps moving on, taking it all back again" (Babbit 31).

I was glad to see the mystery of Winnie's life solved for readers. However, the questions that do not get answered left me a little disappointed. I would have preferred to know how Winnie reached her decision, not just what she decided. Overall, though, *Tuck Everlasting* tells a good story and raises interesting questions. In the end, Tuck gives the answer, "Life. Moving, growing, changing, never the same two minutes together" (Babbit 30).

In the introduction, the writer indicates the focus of his response.

Enough of a summary is given so that readers can understand the writer's response.

The response is organized mainly around the theme.

Here, Chris gives his interpretation of the theme and supports it with an example from the novel.

In the conclusion, Chris shares his own feelings and judgments. He finishes with a general impression and a quotation from the novel.

Writing Workshop

Editing and Proofreading

Check your paper for errors in spelling, punctuation, and grammar.

Focus on Punctuating Quotations: Check any quotation against the original text to make sure you have copied the words exactly. Use quotation marks and commas to separate a quotation from the rest of the sentences.

Publishing and Presenting

Choose one of these ideas for sharing your writing:

Organize a literature discussion day. Arrange a day for you and your classmates to present and discuss your responses to literature.

Write a letter to an author. Turn your review into a letter to the author. Tell what you liked about the work and ask questions about his or her writing, using examples from the book. Share your letter and any response to it with your classmates.

Reflecting on Your Writing

Writer's Journal Jot down your thoughts on writing a literary review. Begin by answering these questions:

- In what way is jotting down notes while reading helpful in preparing a response to literature?
- As you wrote your review, what new insights into the work did you have?

Prentice Hall Writing and Grammar Connection: Chapter 12, Section 6

Rubric for Self-Assessment

To assess your review of a work, use the following rubric:

Criteria	Rating Scale (not very → very)				
	1	2	3	4	5
Focus: How clearly have you focused on an interesting aspect of the story?	1	2	3	4	5
Organization: How well are ideas, patterns, or images organized?	1	2	3	4	5
Support/Elaboration: How convincing are the supporting details for each main idea?	1	2	3	4	5
Style: How well have you stated your feelings or judgments?	1	2	3	4	5
Conventions: How correct is your grammar, especially your use of irregular verbs?	1	2	3	4	5

Skills You Will Learn

Reading Skill: *Ask Questions to Identify Supporting Details*
Literary Analysis: *Theme*

Reading Skill: *Use Prior Knowledge to Draw Conclusions*
Literary Analysis: *Setting*

Reading Skill: *Compare-and-Contrast Organization*

Literary Analysis: *Comparing Character Traits and Theme*

Literature You Will Read

Reading: Drawing Conclusions

▶ A **conclusion** is a decision or an opinion you reach by drawing together details in a text.

Skills and Strategies You Will Learn in Part 2

In Part 2, you will learn

- to **ask questions** about details to reach a **conclusion** (p. 256).
- to **use your prior knowledge** to support a **conclusion** (p. 280).
- to **draw conclusions** based on **comparing and contrasting** (p. 308).

Using the Skills and Strategies in Part 2

In Part 2, you will learn to ask questions about details in a text and combine the answers with your own knowledge to reach a conclusion. You will also use comparison and contrast to draw conclusions. Drawing conclusions helps you interpret information and ideas that are not directly stated in the text.

This diagram shows how to ask questions and use prior knowledge to draw a conclusion.

▶ **Example:** Max dieted and was careful about the foods he ate. He exercised every day for an hour. By January, he was pleased that he saw results.

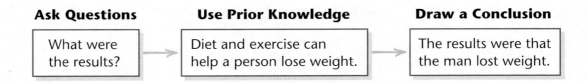

Ask Questions	Use Prior Knowledge	Draw a Conclusion
What were the results?	Diet and exercise can help a person lose weight.	The results were that the man lost weight.

Academic Vocabulary: Words for Drawing Conclusions

The following words will help you to write and talk about conclusions as you read the selections in this unit.

Word	Definition	Example Sentence
apparently *adv.*	appearing to be	*Apparently* the author wanted to surprise the reader.
identifiable *adj.*	recognizable; able to be identified	There are *identifiable* stereotypes in the work.
conclude *v.*	form an opinion	I *conclude* that the character will succeed.
support *v.*	provide evidence for	These details *support* my point.
support *n.*	evidence or reasons for	Give *support* for your position.
examine *v.*	look at carefully	*Examine* the character's motives.

Vocabulary Skill: Suffixes

▶ A **suffix** is a letter or group of letters added to the end of a word to form a new word with a slightly different meaning.

In Part 2 you will learn
- how the suffix *-ly* forms adverbs (p. 278)
- how the suffix *-able* forms adjectives (p. 306)
- how the suffix *-ible* forms adjectives (p. 306)

Adding a suffix to a word often changes its part of speech.

Suffix	Meaning	Part of speech	Example Words
-ly	in a way	adverb	slowly, happily
-able, -ible	able to be	adjective	identifiable, movable

Activity Use each word in a sentence. Explain how the function of the word in the sentence changes when the suffix is added.

- apparent/apparently
- eventual/eventually
- move/movable
- believe/believable

These skills will help you become a better reader. Practice them with either "The All-American Slurp" (p. 256) or "The Circuit" (p. 269).

Reading Skill

A **conclusion** is a decision or opinion you reach based on details in a literary work. To identify the details that will help you draw conclusions, **ask questions** such as *Why is this detail included in the story?* For example, if a boy falls off his bicycle and then says he does not want to ride anymore, you might ask why he makes that decision. You could conclude that he is afraid.

Literary Analysis

The **theme**, or central idea of a story, is a thought about life that the story conveys. Sometimes the theme is directly stated. Other times you must figure it out by considering the events in the story, the characters' thoughts and feelings, and the story's title. Completing a graphic organizer such as the one shown can help you identify the theme of a story.

Key Events — *Characters' Thoughts* — **Theme** — *Story's Title*

Vocabulary Builder

The All-American Slurp

- **emigrated** (em´ i grāt´ id) *v.* left one country to settle in another (p. 256) *His family emigrated from Iran to France.*

- **smugly** (smug´ lē) *adv.* in a way that shows satisfaction with oneself (p. 259) *Jan smiled smugly after winning the game.*

- **systematic** (sis´ tə mat´ ik) *adj.* orderly (p. 261) *Carlos has a systematic way of cooking.*

- **etiquette** (et´ i kit) *n.* acceptable social manners (p. 262) *It is bad etiquette to talk with food in your mouth.*

- **consumption** (kən sump´ shən) *n.* eating; drinking; using up (p. 263) *Gregory's consumption of popcorn is amazing.*

The Circuit

- **drone** (drōn) *n.* continuous humming sound (p. 273) *The engine's drone made us sleepy.*

- **instinctively** (in stiŋk´ tiv lē) *adv.* done automatically, without thinking (p. 273) *Kim instinctively ducked as the ball flew past.*

- **savoring** (sā´ vər iŋ) *v.* enjoying; tasting with delight (p. 274) *Ellis was savoring the fresh bread.*

Short Story

Background

Chinese Customs Every culture has unique customs and rituals surrounding food and meals. In this story, the habits of a Chinese family newly arrived in the United States surprise their neighbors. According to Chinese customs, food is often served on large platters in the center of the table and handled with slender sticks called chopsticks.

Connecting to the Literature

Reading/Writing Connection Eating customs are just the beginning of cultural differences. However, meeting new people also opens the door to new experiences. Write a few sentences of advice you might give to a family from a different culture who has recently moved to your neighborhood. Use three of the following words: *appreciate, respond, conflict, conclude.*

Meet the Author

Lensey **Namioka** (b. 1929)

Authors often write about their own experiences. In "The All-American Slurp," Lensey Namioka based the main character on herself. Like her character, Namioka discovered big differences between Chinese and American eating habits.

Writing for Herself Namioka completed her first book, *Princess with a Bamboo Sword,* at the age of eight. As an adult, Namioka began writing the kind of stories she herself enjoyed reading, rather than writing specifically for young people. "Maybe I write these books because I never really grew up," she says.

Fast Facts

▶ Namioka's father made up the name *Lensey*.
▶ Namioka's husband is Japanese, which is why she has a Japanese last name. For this reason, Namioka has written books about both China and Japan.

For: More about the author
Visit: www.PHSchool.com
Web Code: ele-9208

The All-American Slurp

Lensey Namioka

The first time our family was invited out to dinner in America, we disgraced ourselves while eating celery. We had <u>emigrated</u> to this country from China, and during our early days here we had a hard time with American table manners.

In China we never ate celery raw, or any other kind of vegetable raw. We always had to disinfect the vegetables in boiling water first. When we were presented with our first relish tray, the raw celery caught us unprepared.

Vocabulary Builder
emigrated (em´ i grāt´ id) *v.* left one country to settle in another

We had been invited to dinner by our neighbors, the Gleasons. After arriving at the house, we shook hands with our hosts and packed ourselves into a sofa. As our family of four sat stiffly in a row, my younger brother and I stole glances at our parents for a clue as to what to do next.

Mrs. Gleason offered the relish tray to Mother. The tray looked pretty, with its tiny red radishes, curly sticks of carrots, and long, slender stalks of pale green celery. "Do try some of the celery, Mrs. Lin," she said. "It's from a local farmer, and it's sweet."

Mother picked up one of the green stalks, and Father followed suit. Then I picked up a stalk, and my brother did too. So there we sat, each with a stalk of celery in our right hand.

Mrs. Gleason kept smiling. "Would you like to try some of the dip, Mrs. Lin? It's my own recipe: sour cream and onion flakes, with a dash of Tabasco sauce."

Most Chinese don't care for dairy products, and in those days I wasn't even ready to drink fresh milk. Sour cream sounded perfectly revolting. Our family shook our heads in unison.

Mrs. Gleason went off with the relish tray to the other guests, and we carefully watched to see what they did. Everyone seemed to eat the raw vegetables quite happily.

Mother took a bite of her celery. *Crunch.* "It's not bad!" she whispered.

Father took a bite of his celery. *Crunch.* "Yes, it is good," he said, looking surprised.

I took a bite, and then my brother. *Crunch, crunch.* It was more than good; it was delicious. Raw celery has a slight sparkle, a zingy taste that you don't get in cooked celery. When Mrs. Gleason came around with the relish tray, we each took another stalk of celery, except my brother. He took two.

There was only one problem: long strings ran through the length of the stalk, and they got caught in my teeth. When I help my mother in the kitchen, I always pull the string out before slicing celery.

I pulled the strings out of my stalk. *Z-z-zip, z-z-zip.* My brother followed suit. *Z-z-zip, z-z-zip, z-z-zip.* To my left, my parents were taking care of their own stalks. *Z-z-zip, z-z-zip, z-z-zip.*

Reading Skill
Draw Conclusions
How do you think the narrator feels at this point in the dinner? Explain.

Reading Check

Why don't the Lins know how to eat celery?

Suddenly I realized that there was dead silence except for our zipping. Looking up, I saw that the eyes of everyone in the room were on our family. Mr. and Mrs. Gleason, their daughter Meg, who was my friend, and their neighbors the Badels— they were all staring at us as we busily pulled the strings of our celery.

That wasn't the end of it. Mrs. Gleason announced that dinner was served and invited us to the dining table. It was lavishly covered with platters of food, but we couldn't see any chairs around the table. So we helpfully carried over some dining chairs and sat down. All the other guests just stood there.

Mrs. Gleason bent down and whispered to us, "This is a buffet dinner. You help yourselves to some food and eat it in the living room."

Our family beat a retreat back to the sofa as if chased by enemy soldiers. For the rest of the evening, too mortified to go back to the dining table, I nursed a bit of potato salad on my plate.

Next day Meg and I got on the school bus together. I wasn't sure how she would feel about me after the spectacle our family made at the party. But she was just the same as usual, and the only reference she made to the party was, "Hope you and your folks got enough to eat last night. You certainly didn't take very much. Mom never tries to figure out how much food to prepare. She just puts everything on the table and hopes for the best."

I began to relax. The Gleasons' dinner party wasn't so different from a Chinese meal after all. My mother also puts everything on the table and hopes for the best.

Meg was the first friend I had made after we came to America. I eventually got acquainted with a few other kids in school, but Meg was still the only real friend I had.

Reading Skill
Draw Conclusions
What can you conclude about the narrator, based on this paragraph?

My brother didn't have any problems making friends. He spent all his time with some boys who were teaching him baseball, and in no time he could speak English much faster than I could—not better, but faster.

I worried more about making mistakes, and I spoke carefully, making sure I could say everything right before opening my mouth. At least I had a better accent than my parents, who never really got rid of their Chinese accent, even years later. My parents had both studied English in school before coming to America, but what they had studied was mostly written English, not spoken.

Father's approach to English was a scientific one. Since Chinese verbs have no tense, he was fascinated by the way English verbs changed form according to whether they were in the present, past imperfect, perfect, pluperfect,[1] future, or future perfect tense. He was always making diagrams of verbs and their inflections,[2] and he looked for opportunities to show off his mastery of the pluperfect and future perfect tenses, his two favorites. "I shall have finished my project by Monday," he would say <u>smugly</u>.

Vocabulary Builder
smugly (smug´ lē) *adv.* in a way that shows satisfaction with oneself

Mother's approach was to memorize lists of polite phrases that would cover all possible social situations. She was constantly muttering things like "I'm fine, thank you. And you?" Once she accidentally stepped on someone's foot, and hurriedly blurted, "Oh, that's quite all right!" Embarrassed by her slip, she resolved to do better next time. So when someone stepped on *her* foot, she cried, "You're welcome!"

In our own different ways, we made progress in learning English. But I had another worry, and that was my appearance. My brother didn't have to worry, since Mother bought him blue jeans for school, and he dressed like all the other boys. But she insisted that girls had to wear skirts. By the time she saw that Meg and the other girls were wearing jeans, it was too late. My school clothes were bought already, and we didn't have money left to buy new outfits for me. We had too many other things to buy first, like furniture, pots, and pans.

The first time I visited Meg's house, she took me upstairs to her room, and I wound up trying on her clothes. We were

Reading Check

Why is the narrator worried about her appearance?

---

1. **pluperfect** (plōō´ pʉr´ fikt) *adj.* the past perfect tense of verbs in English.
2. **inflections** (in flek´ shəns) *n.* changes in the forms of words to show different tenses.

pretty much the same size, since Meg was shorter and thinner than average. Maybe that's how we became friends in the first place. Wearing Meg's jeans and T-shirt, I looked at myself in the mirror. I could almost pass for an American—from the back, anyway. At least the kids in school wouldn't stop and stare at me in my white blouse and navy blue skirt that went a couple of inches below the knees.

When Meg came to my house, I invited her to try on my Chinese dresses, the ones with a high collar and slits up the sides. Meg's eyes were bright as she looked at herself in the mirror. She struck several sultry poses, and we nearly fell over laughing.

The dinner party at the Gleasons' didn't stop my growing friendship with Meg. Things were getting better for me in other ways too. Mother finally bought me some jeans at the end of the month, when Father got his paycheck. She wasn't in any hurry about buying them at first, until I worked on her. This is what I did. Since we didn't have a car in those days, I often ran down to the neighborhood store to pick up things for her. The groceries cost less at a big supermarket, but the closest one was many blocks away. One day, when she ran out of flour, I offered to borrow a bike from our neighbor's son and buy a ten-pound bag of flour at the supermarket. I mounted the boy's bike and waved to Mother. "I'll be back in five minutes!"

Before I started pedaling, I heard her voice behind me. "You can't go out in public like that! People can see all the way up to your thighs!"

"I'm sorry," I said innocently. "I thought you were in a hurry to get the flour." For dinner we were going to have pot-stickers (fried Chinese dumplings), and we needed a lot of flour.

"Couldn't you borrow a girl's bicycle?" complained Mother. "That way your skirt won't be pushed up."

"There aren't too many of those around," I said. "Almost all the girls wear jeans while riding a bike, so they don't see any point buying a girl's bike."

Literary Analysis
Theme What theme is hinted at by the narrator's response to her reflection in the mirror?

Reading Skill
Draw Conclusions What can you conclude about the narrator based on why she helps her mother?

We didn't eat pot-stickers that evening, and Mother was thoughtful. Next day we took the bus downtown and she bought me a pair of jeans. In the same week, my brother made the baseball team of his junior high school, Father started taking driving lessons, and Mother discovered rummage sales.

We soon got all the furniture we needed, plus a dart board and a 1,000-piece jigsaw puzzle (fourteen hours later, we discovered that it was a 999-piece jigsaw puzzle). There was hope that the Lins might become a normal American family after all.

Then came our dinner at the Lakeview restaurant.

The Lakeview was an expensive restaurant, one of those places where a headwaiter dressed in tails conducted you to your seat, and the only light came from candles and flaming desserts. In one corner of the room a lady harpist played tinkling melodies.

Father wanted to celebrate, because he had just been promoted. He worked for an electronics company, and after his English started improving, his superiors decided to appoint him to a position more suited to his training. The promotion not only brought a higher salary but was also a tremendous boost to his pride.

Up to then we had eaten only in Chinese restaurants. Although my brother and I were becoming fond of hamburgers, my parents didn't care much for western food, other than chow mein.[3] But this was a special occasion, and Father asked his coworkers to recommend a really elegant restaurant. So there we were at the Lakeview, stumbling after the headwaiter in the murky dining room.

At our table we were handed our menus, and they were so big that to read mine I almost had to stand up again. But why bother? It was mostly in French, anyway.

Father, being an engineer, was always <u>systematic</u>. He took out a pocket French dictionary. "They told me that most of the items would be in French, so I came prepared." He

---

3. chow mein (chou´ mān´) *n.* thick stew of meat, celery, and Chinese vegetables.

Literary Analysis
Theme How might the activities listed here relate to the theme?

Vocabulary Builder
systematic (sis´ tə mat´ ik) *adj.* orderly

Reading Check

Why does Mr. Lin take his family to a fancy restaurant?

even had a pocket flashlight, the size of a marking pen. While Mother held the flashlight over the menu, he looked up the items that were in French.

"*Pâté en croûte*," (pä tā´ än kro͞ot) he muttered. "Let's see . . . *pâté* is paste . . . *croûte* is crust . . . hmm . . . a paste in crust."

The waiter stood looking patient. I squirmed and died at least fifty times.

At long last Father gave up. "Why don't we just order four complete dinners at random?" he suggested.

"Isn't that risky?" asked Mother. "The French eat some rather peculiar things, I've heard."

"A Chinese can eat anything a Frenchman can eat," Father declared.

The soup arrived in a plate. How do you get soup up from a plate? I glanced at the other diners, but the ones at the nearby tables were not on their soup course, while the more distant ones were invisible in the darkness.

Fortunately my parents had studied books on western <u>etiquette</u> before they came to America. "Tilt your plate," whispered my mother. "It's easier to spoon the soup up that way."

She was right. Tilting the plate did the trick. But the etiquette book didn't say anything about what you did after the soup reached your lips. As any respectable Chinese knows, the correct way to eat your soup is to slurp. This helps to cool the liquid and prevent you from

Vocabulary Builder
etiquette (et´ i ket) *n.* acceptable social manners

Reading Skill
Draw Conclusions
How does this information about slurping help you understand the story's central problem?

burning your lips. It also shows your appreciation.

We showed our appreciation. *Shloop*, went my father. *Shloop* went my mother. *Shloop, shloop,* went my brother, who was the hungriest.

The lady harpist stopped playing to take a rest. And in the silence, our family's <u>consumption</u> of soup suddenly seemed unnaturally loud. You know how it sounds on a rocky beach when the tide goes out and the water drains from all those little pools? They go *shloop, shloop, shloop.* That was the Lin family, eating soup.

At the next table a waiter was pouring wine. When a large *shloop* reached him, he froze. The bottle continued to pour, and red wine flooded the tabletop and into the lap of a customer. Even the customer didn't notice anything at first, being also hypnotized by the *shloop, shloop, shloop.*

It was too much. "I need to go to the toilet," I mumbled, jumping to my feet. A waiter, sensing my urgency, quickly directed me to the ladies' room.

I splashed cold water on my burning face, and as I dried myself with a paper towel, I stared into the mirror. In this perfumed ladies' room, with its pink-and-silver wallpaper and marbled sinks, I looked completely out of place. What was I doing here? What was our family doing in the Lakeview restaurant? In America?

The door to the ladies' room opened. A woman came in and glanced curiously at me. I retreated into one of the toilet cubicles and latched the door.

Time passed—maybe half an hour, maybe an hour. Then I heard the door open again, and my mother's voice. "Are you in there? You're not sick, are you?"

There was real concern in her voice. A girl can't leave her family just because they slurp their soup. Besides, the toilet cubicle had a few drawbacks as a permanent residence. "I'm all right," I said, undoing the latch.

Mother didn't tell me how the rest of the dinner went, and I didn't want to know. In the weeks following, I managed to push the whole thing into the back of my mind, where it jumped out at me only a few times a day. Even now, I turn hot all over when I think of the Lakeview restaurant.

But by the time we had been in this country for three months, our family was definitely making progress toward

Vocabulary Builder
consumption (kən sump′ shen) *n.* eating; drinking; using up

Reading Skill
Draw Conclusions
How does the narrator feel about her family's behavior? How can you tell?

Reading Check

Why do the Lins slurp their soup?

becoming Americanized. I remember my parents' first PTA meeting. Father wore a neat suit and tie, and Mother put on her first pair of high heels. She stumbled only once. They met my homeroom teacher and beamed as she told them that I would make honor roll soon at the rate I was going. Of course Chinese etiquette forced Father to say that I was a very stupid girl and Mother to protest that the teacher was showing favoritism toward me. But I could tell they were both very proud.

The day came when my parents announced that they wanted to give a dinner party. We had invited Chinese friends to eat with us before, but this dinner was going to be different. In addition to a Chinese-American family, we were going to invite the Gleasons.

"Gee, I can hardly wait to have dinner at your house," Meg said to me. "I just *love* Chinese food."

That was a relief. Mother was a good cook, but I wasn't sure if people who ate sour cream would also eat chicken gizzards stewed in soy sauce.

Mother decided not to take a chance with chicken gizzards. Since we had western guests, she set the table with large dinner plates, which we never used in Chinese meals. In fact we didn't use individual plates at all, but picked up food from the platters in the middle of the table and brought it directly to our rice bowls. Following the practice of Chinese-American restaurants, Mother also placed large serving spoons on the platters.

The dinner started well. Mrs. Gleason exclaimed at the beautifully arranged dishes of food: the colorful candied fruit in the sweet-and-sour pork dish, the noodle-thin shreds of chicken meat stir-fried with tiny peas, and the glistening pink prawns in a ginger sauce.

At first I was too busy enjoying my food to notice how the guests were doing. But soon I remembered my duties. Sometimes guests were too polite to help themselves and you had to serve them with more food.

I glanced at Meg, to see if she needed more food, and my eyes nearly popped out at the sight of her plate. It was piled with food: the sweet-and-sour meat pushed right against the chicken shreds, and the chicken sauce ran into the

Literary Analysis
Theme In what way does Mother's dinner plan show that the family has adjusted to life in America?

Reading Skill
Draw Conclusions What can you conclude about the Lins' eating customs from the narrator's reactions to what the Gleasons do?

prawns. She had been taking food from a second dish before she finished eating her helping from the first!

Horrified, I turned to look at Mrs. Gleason. She was dumping rice out of her bowl and putting it on her dinner plate. Then she ladled prawns and gravy on top of the rice and mixed everything together, the way you mix sand, gravel, and cement to make concrete.

I couldn't bear to look any longer, and I turned to Mr. Gleason. He was chasing a pea around his plate. Several times he got it to the edge, but when he tried to pick it up with his chopsticks, it rolled back toward the center of the plate again. Finally he put down his chopsticks and picked up the pea with his fingers. He really did! A grown man!

All of us, our family and the Chinese guests, stopped eating to watch the activities of the Gleasons. I wanted to giggle. Then I caught my mother's eyes on me. She frowned and shook her head slightly, and I understood the message: the Gleasons were not used to Chinese ways, and they were just coping the best they could. For some reason I thought of celery strings.

When the main courses were finished, Mother brought out a platter of fruit. "I hope you weren't expecting a sweet dessert," she said. "Since the Chinese don't eat dessert, I didn't think to prepare any."

"Oh, I couldn't possibly eat dessert!" cried Mrs. Gleason. "I'm simply stuffed!"

Meg had different ideas. When the table was cleared, she announced that she and I were going for a walk. "I don't know about you, but I feel like dessert," she told me, when we were outside. "Come on, there's a Dairy Queen down the street. I could use a big chocolate milkshake!"

Although I didn't really want anything more to eat, I insisted on paying for the milkshakes. After all, I was still hostess.

Meg got her large chocolate milkshake and I had a small one. Even so, she was finishing hers while I was only half done. Toward the end she pulled hard on her straws and went *shloop, shloop*.

"Do you always slurp when you eat a milkshake?" I asked, before I could stop myself.

Meg grinned. "Sure. All Americans slurp."

Literary Analysis
Theme What lesson is the narrator learning about people's experiences?

Reading Skill
Draw Conclusions What can you conclude about the narrator's manners from her insistence on paying?

Apply the Skills

The All-American Slurp

Thinking About the Selection

1. **Respond:** What advice would you give the narrator about adjusting to life in the United States? Why?
2. **(a) Recall:** Describe the way in which each Lin family member learns English. **(b) Infer:** What does each person's way of learning English show about his or her personality?
3. **(a) Recall:** How do the Lins embarrass themselves at the restaurant? **(b) Compare and Contrast:** In what ways are the Gleasons' actions at the Lins' house similar to those of the Lins at the Gleasons' house?
4. **Discuss:** Based on this story, what qualities might a person need to adjust to life in a new country? Share your answers with a partner. Then, discuss how your ideas grew or changed after hearing someone else's response.

Reading Skill

5. Complete a chart like the one shown to **draw conclusions** about the story.

Question	Details That Answer Question	Conclusion
Why do the Gleasons stare as the Lins pull celery strings?		
Why do people in the restaurant stare when the Lins slurp their soup?		
What makes the narrator uneasy when the Gleasons come to dinner?		

Literary Analysis

6. **(a)** What **theme** about cultural differences does the story illustrate? **(b)** What details or events support the theme?
7. How does the title relate to the story's theme?

Story at a Glance

Members of a Chinese family, new to America, adjust to their new life.

Go Online
Assessment
For: Self-test
Visit: www.PHSchool.com
Web Code: ela-6207

Conclusion: a decision or an opinion based on details in a text

Theme: the central idea or message of a story

Vocabulary Builder

Practice Match each situation with a vocabulary word from the list on page 254.

1. an organized way to clean house
2. how a winner might talk
3. moved from Peru to Egypt
4. thanking your host
5. eating a large meal

Writing

Write a brief **description** of a character in the story.

- Begin by listing details that describe the character's appearance, actions, and personality.
- At the beginning of your description, introduce the character and identify one or two words that capture the character's personality, such as *brave, smart,* or *mean.*
- Use clear, specific language to support your description. For example, give details showing that the narrator is uncomfortable: "The narrator feels too embarrassed to eat."

For *Grammar, Vocabulary,* and *Assessment,*
see **Build Language Skills,** pages 278–279.

Extend Your Learning

Listening and Speaking With a partner, prepare and role-play an **interview** with the narrator of the story. Decide who will play each role.

- Use story details to gather information for your interview.
- Prepare a list of questions to ask in the interview. Rehearse responses to the questions.
- Conduct your interview in front of the class.

Research and Technology Use the Internet and library resources to research Lensey Namioka's life. Focus your research on a specific topic. For example, find out more about her connections to China, Japan, and the United States, the story behind the name *Lensey,* or her work as an author. Present your findings in a **report** to the class.

Build Understanding • *The Circuit*

Background

Migrant Workers "The Circuit" is about a family of migrant farmworkers. Most migrant workers in the United States move often to follow the demands of seasonal harvesting. The whole family usually travels together, with children helping adults on the farms. Children may start school late in the fall or leave early in the spring to help with the harvest.

Connecting to the Literature

Reading/Writing Connection The children of migrant workers are always "the new kids" at school because they move so often. List three or four ways that changing schools might affect schoolwork and friendships. Use at least three of these words: *adjust, affect, encounter, establish.*

Review

For **Reading Skill, Literary Analysis,** and **Vocabulary Builder,** see page 254.

Meet the Author

Francisco **Jiménez** (b. 1943)

Born in Mexico, Francisco Jiménez (hē mā´ nez) came with his family to the United States when he was four. The family settled in California and became migrant workers. Like the narrator in "The Circuit," Jiménez could not go to school before the harvest ended. He once said, "I came to realize that learning and knowledge were the only stable things in my life. Whatever I learned in school, that knowledge would stay with me no matter how many times we moved."

The Path to Success In high school, Jiménez supported himself by working as a janitor. His excellent grades won him three college scholarships. He went on to become an outstanding teacher and college official, as well as an award-winning writer.

Fast Facts

▶ Jiménez was one of nine children in his family.
▶ He taught himself by studying while in the fields and by reading whenever he had a chance.

Go Online
Author Link
For: More about the author
Visit: www.PHSchool.com
Web Code: ele-9209

The Circuit

Francisco Jiménez

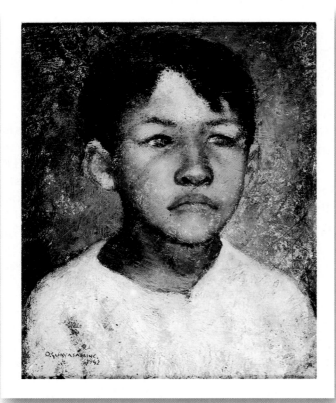

My Brother, 1942, Guayasamin (Oswaldo Guayasamin Calero) Collection, The Museum of Modern Art, New York

◀ **Critical Viewing**
If this painting represents a character in the story, how do you think that character feels? **[Analyze]**

It was that time of year again. Ito, the strawberry share-cropper,[1] did not smile. It was natural. The peak of the strawberry season was over and the last few days the workers, most of them *braceros*,[2] were not picking as many boxes as they had during the months of June and July.

As the last days of August disappeared, so did the number of *braceros*. Sunday, only one—the best picker—came

---

1. **sharecropper** (sher´ kräp´ ər) *n.* one who works for a share of a crop; tenant farmer.
2. ***braceros*** (brä ser´ os) *n.* migrant Mexican farm laborers who harvest crops.

to work. I liked him. Sometimes we talked during our half-hour lunch break. That is how I found out he was from Jalisco, the same state in Mexico my family was from. That Sunday was the last time I saw him.

When the sun had tired and sunk behind the mountains, Ito signaled us that it was time to go home. "*Ya esora*,"[3] he yelled in his broken Spanish. Those were the words I waited for twelve hours a day, every day, seven days a week, week after week. And the thought of not hearing them again saddened me.

As we drove home Papá did not say a word. With both hands on the wheel, he stared at the dirt road. My older brother, Roberto, was also silent. He leaned his head back and closed his eyes. Once in a while he cleared from his throat the dust that blew in from outside.

Yes, it was that time of year. When I opened the front door to the shack, I stopped. Everything we owned was neatly packed in cardboard boxes. Suddenly I felt even more the weight of hours, days, weeks, and months of work. I sat down on a box. The thought of having to move to Fresno[4] and knowing what was in store for me there brought tears to my eyes.

That night I could not sleep. I lay in bed thinking about how much I hated this move.

A little before five o'clock in the morning, Papá woke everyone up. A few minutes later, the yelling and screaming of my little brothers and sisters, for whom the move was a great adventure, broke the silence of dawn. Shortly, the barking of the dogs accompanied them.

While we packed the breakfast dishes, Papá went outside to start the "Carcanchita."[5] That was the name Papá gave his old '38 black Plymouth. He bought it in a used-car lot in Santa Rosa in the winter of 1949. Papá was very proud of his little jalopy. He had a right to be proud of it. He spent a lot of time looking at other cars before buying this one. When he finally chose the "Carcanchita," he checked it thoroughly before driving it out of the car lot. He examined every inch of the car. He listened to the motor, tilting his head from side to side like a parrot, trying to detect any

Literary Analysis
Theme What clues do this event and the narrator's actions give you about the theme?

---

3. *Ya esora* (yä es ô rä) Spanish for "It's time" (*Ya es hora*).
4. **Fresno** (frez′ nō) *n.* city in central California.
5. **Carcanchita** (kär kän chē′ tä) affectionate name for the car.

noises that spelled car trouble. After being satisfied with the looks and sounds of the car, Papá then insisted on knowing who the original owner was. He never did find out from the car salesman, but he bought the car anyway. Papá figured the original owner must have been an important man because behind the rear seat of the car he found a blue necktie.

Papá parked the car out in front and left the motor running. "*Listo*,"[6] he yelled. Without saying a word, Roberto and I began to carry the boxes out to the car. Roberto carried the two big boxes and I carried the two smaller ones. Papá then threw the mattress on top of the car roof and tied it with ropes to the front and rear bumpers.

Everything was packed except Mamá's pot. It was an old large galvanized[7] pot she had picked up at an army surplus store in Santa María the year I was born. The pot had many dents and nicks, and the more dents and nicks it acquired the more Mamá liked it. "*Mi olla*,"[8] she used to say proudly.

I held the front door open as Mamá carefully carried out her pot by both handles, making sure not to spill the cooked beans. When she got to the car, Papá reached out to help her with it. Roberto opened the rear car door and Papá gently placed it on the floor behind the front seat. All of us then climbed in. Papá sighed, wiped the sweat off his forehead with his sleeve, and said wearily: "*Es todo*."[9]

As we drove away, I felt a lump in my throat. I turned around and looked at our little shack for the last time.

At sunset we drove into a labor camp near Fresno. Since Papá did not speak English, Mamá asked the camp foreman if he needed any more workers. "We don't need no more," said the foreman, scratching his head. "Check with Sullivan down the road. Can't miss him. He lives in a big white house with a fence around it."

When we got there, Mamá walked up to the house. She went through a white gate, past a row of rose bushes, up the stairs to the front door. She rang the doorbell. The porch light went on and a tall husky man came out. They exchanged a few words. After the man went in, Mamá

Reading Skill
Draw Conclusions
What do the details so far tell you about the family's attitude toward moving again?

Reading Check

Why is Papá proud of "Carcanchita"?

---

6. *Listo* (lēs´ to) Spanish for "Ready."
7. galvanized (gal´ və nīzd) *adj.* coated with zinc to prevent rusting.
8. *Mi olla* (mē ō´ yä) Spanish for "My pot."
9. *Es todo* (es tō´ thō) Spanish for "That's everything."

clasped her hands and hurried back to the car. "We have work! Mr. Sullivan said we can stay there the whole season," she said, gasping and pointing to an old garage near the stables.

The garage was worn out by the years. It had no windows. The walls, eaten by termites, strained to support the roof full of holes. The dirt floor, populated by earthworms, looked like a gray road map.

That night, by the light of a kerosene lamp, we unpacked and cleaned our new home. Roberto swept away the loose dirt, leaving the hard ground. Papá plugged the holes in the walls with old newspapers and tin can tops. Mamá fed my little brothers and sisters. Papá and Roberto then brought in the mattress and placed it on the far corner of the garage. "Mamá, you and the little ones sleep on the mattress. Roberto, Panchito, and I will sleep outside under the trees," Papá said.

Early next morning Mr. Sullivan showed us where his crop was, and after breakfast, Papá, Roberto, and I headed for the vineyard to pick.

Around nine o'clock the temperature had risen to almost one hundred degrees. I was completely soaked in sweat and my mouth felt as if I had been chewing on a handkerchief. I walked over to the end of the row, picked up the jug of water we had brought, and began drinking. "Don't drink too much; you'll get sick," Roberto shouted. No sooner had he said that than I felt sick to my stomach. I dropped to my knees and let the jug roll off my hands. I remained motionless with my eyes glued on the hot sandy ground. All I could hear

Literature in Context

Geography Connection

Agricultural Seasons With sunny weather and a favorable climate, California produces more crops than any other state. At every point in the year, there is a different crop ready to be harvested in some part of the state. Migrant workers, such as Panchito's family, migrate from place to place to harvest the available crop. Grapes are picked in the summer and fall in the lush valleys of central and northern California, peak strawberry season hits the southern coastal regions in the spring, and cotton is harvested in the dry valleys of central and southern California during the winter.

Connect to the Literature

Identify two ways the agricultural seasons affect the characters in this story.

was the <u>drone</u> of insects. Slowly I began to recover. I poured water over my face and neck and watched the dirty water run down my arms to the ground.

I still felt a little dizzy when we took a break to eat lunch. It was past two o'clock and we sat underneath a large walnut tree that was on the side of the road. While we ate, Papá jotted down the number of boxes we had picked. Roberto drew designs on the ground with a stick. Suddenly I noticed Papá's face turn pale as he looked down the road. "Here comes the school bus," he whispered loudly in alarm. <u>Instinctively</u>, Roberto and I ran and hid in the vineyards. We did not want to get in trouble for not going to school. The neatly dressed boys about my age got off. They carried books under their arms. After they crossed the street, the bus drove away. Roberto and I came out from hiding and joined Papá. "*Tienen que tener cuidado,*"[10] he warned us.

After lunch we went back to work. The sun kept beating down. The buzzing insects, the wet sweat, and the hot dry dust made the afternoon seem to last forever. Finally the mountains around the valley reached out and swallowed the sun. Within an hour it was too dark to continue picking. The vines blanketed the grapes, making it difficult to see the bunches. "*Vámonos,*"[11] said Papá, signaling to us that it was time to quit work. Papá then took out a pencil and began to figure out how much we had earned our first day. He wrote down numbers, crossed some out, wrote down some more. "*Quince,*"[12] he murmured.

When we arrived home, we took a cold shower underneath a waterhose. We then sat down to eat dinner around some wooden crates that served as a table. Mamá had cooked a special meal for us. We had rice and tortillas with "*carne con chile,*"[13] my favorite dish.

The next morning I could hardly move. My body ached all over. I felt little control over my arms and legs. This feeling went on every morning for days until my muscles finally got used to the work.

It was Monday, the first week of November. The grape season was over and I could now go to school. I woke up

---

10. *Tienen que tener cuidado* (tē en´en kā ten er´ kwē thä´ thō) Spanish for "You have to be careful."
11. *Vámonos* (vä´ mō nōs) Spanish for "Let's go."
12. *Quince* (kēn´ sā) Spanish for "Fifteen."
13. "*carne con chile*" (kär´ nā kən chil´ ā) dish of ground meat, hot peppers, beans, and tomatoes.

Vocabulary Builder
drone (drōn) *n.* continuous humming sound

Vocabulary Builder
instinctively (in stiŋk´ tiv lē) *adv.* done automatically, without thinking

✔ **Reading Check**

What makes work in the vineyard hard for Panchito?

early that morning and lay in bed, looking at the stars and savoring the thought of not going to work and of starting sixth grade for the first time that year. Since I could not sleep, I decided to get up and join Papá and Roberto at breakfast. I sat at the table across from Roberto, but I kept my head down. I did not want to look up and face him. I knew he was sad. He was not going to school today. He was not going tomorrow, or next week, or next month. He would not go until the cotton season was over, and that was sometime in February. I rubbed my hands together and watched the dry, acid stained skin fall to the floor in little rolls.

When Papá and Roberto left for work, I felt relief. I walked to the top of a small grade next to the shack and watched the "Carcanchita" disappear in the distance in a cloud of dust.

Two hours later, around eight o'clock, I stood by the side of the road waiting for school bus number twenty. When it arrived I climbed in. Everyone was busy either talking or yelling. I sat in an empty seat in the back.

When the bus stopped in front of the school, I felt very nervous. I looked out the bus window and saw boys and girls carrying books under their arms. I put my hands in my pant pockets and walked to the principal's office. When I entered I heard a woman's voice say: "May I help you?" I was startled. I had not heard English for months. For a few seconds I remained speechless. I looked at the lady who waited for my answer. My first instinct was to answer her in Spanish, but I held back. Finally, after struggling for English words, I managed to tell her that I wanted to enroll in the sixth grade. After answering many questions, I was led to the classroom.

Mr. Lema, the sixth-grade teacher, greeted me and assigned me a desk. He then introduced me to the class. I was so nervous and scared at that moment when every-one's eyes were on me that I wished I were with Papá and Roberto picking cotton. After taking roll, Mr. Lema gave the class the assignment for the first hour. "The first thing we have to do this morning is finish reading the story we began yesterday," he said enthusiastically. He walked up to

Vocabulary Builder
savoring (sā′ vər iŋ)
v. enjoying; tasting with delight

Literary Analysis
Theme How does the sentence that begins "He would not go" suggest that the family's life follows a cycle? How might this relate to the story's theme?

Reading Skill
Draw Conclusions Why is the narrator startled when he first hears English spoken?

me, handed me an English book, and asked me to read. "We are on page 125," he said politely. When I heard this, I felt my blood rush to my head; I felt dizzy. "Would you like to read?" he asked hesitantly. I opened the book to page 125. My mouth was dry. My eyes began to water. I could not begin. "You can read later," Mr. Lema said understandingly.

For the rest of the reading period I kept getting angrier and angrier at myself. I should have read, I thought to myself.

During recess I went into the restroom and opened my English book to page 125. I began to read in a low voice, pretending I was in class. There were many words I did not know. I closed the book and headed back to the classroom.

Mr. Lema was sitting at his desk correcting papers. When I entered he looked up at me and smiled. I felt better. I walked up to him and asked if he could help me with the new words. "Gladly," he said.

The rest of the month I spent my lunch hours working on English with Mr. Lema, my best friend at school.

One Friday during lunch hour Mr. Lema asked me to take a walk with him to the music room. "Do you like music?" he asked me as we entered the building.

"Yes, I like *corridos*,"[14] I answered. He then picked up a trumpet, blew on it and handed it to me. The sound gave me goose bumps. I knew that sound. I had heard it in many corridos. "How would you like to learn how to play it?" he asked. He must have read my face because before I could answer, he added: "I'll teach you how to play it during our lunch hours."

That day I could hardly wait to get home to tell Papá and Mamá the great news. As I got off the bus, my little brothers and sisters ran up to meet me. They were yelling and screaming. I thought they were happy to see me, but when I opened the door to our shack, I saw that everything we owned was neatly packed in cardboard boxes.

Reading Skill
Draw Conclusions
What do the details in this paragraph lead you to conclude about Mr. Lema's character?

---

14. *corridos* (kō rē´ thōs) *n.* ballads.

Apply the Skills

The Circuit

Thinking About the Selection

1. **Respond:** What do you admire about Panchito? Why?
2. **(a) Recall:** What does Panchito do on his school lunch hours? **(b) Infer:** Why do you think Panchito calls Mr. Lema his "best friend at school"? **(c) Interpret:** Based on the information in the story, how would you describe Panchito's personality?
3. **(a) Infer:** What is the best thing that happens to Panchito on the last day of school? **(b) Infer:** What is the worst thing?
4. **Discuss:** What, if anything, might be done to ease the hardships faced by families like Panchito's? Share your answer with a partner. Then, discuss how your ideas grew or changed after you heard someone else's response.

Reading Skill

5. Complete a chart like the one shown to **draw conclusions** about the story.

Question	Details That Answer Question	Conclusion
Why does Panchito work so much?		
Why does Panchito not read aloud on the first day of school?		
Why are the family's belongings packed in boxes?		

Literary Analysis

6. **(a)** What **theme**, or message about life, does the story illustrate? **(b)** What details or events support the theme?
7. How does the title relate to the story's theme?

QuickReview

Who's Who in the Story
Panchito: a young migrant worker
Roberto: Panchito's older brother
Mr. Lema: Panchito's sixth-grade teacher

Go Online
Assessment
For: Self-test
Visit: www.PHSchool.com
Web Code: ela-6208

Conclusion: a decision or opinion based on details in a text

Theme: the central idea or message of a story

Vocabulary Builder

Practice Match each situation with a vocabulary word from the list on page 254.

1. eating a delicious meal
2. how mother animals protect their young
3. the sound of bees buzzing

Writing

Write a brief **description** of a character in the story.

- Begin by listing details that describe the character's appearance, actions, and personality.
- At the beginning of your description, introduce the character and identify one or two words that capture the character's personality, such as *brave, smart*, or *mean*.
- Use clear, specific language to support your description. For example, give details to show that Papá is kind: "Papá lets Mamá and the children sleep on the mattress."

For *Grammar, Vocabulary,* and *Assessment,* see **Build Language Skills,** pages 278–279.

Extend Your Learning

Listening and Speaking With another student, prepare and role-play an **interview** about life as a migrant worker. Decide who will play the worker and the reporter.

- Use story details to gather information about migrant workers.
- Prepare a list of questions to ask in the interview. Rehearse responses to the questions.
- Conduct your interview in front of the class.

Research and Technology In a small group, research the lives of migrant workers. Use the information to prepare a brief **report**. In your report, include specific information on topics such as places where they work, their length of stay in one place, their living conditions, and their average wages.

Build Language Skills

The All-American Slurp • The Circuit

Vocabulary Skill

Suffixes: The **suffix** -*ly* means "in a way." Almost any adjective becomes an adverb when you add the suffix -*ly*. The suffix -*ly* is found in the word **apparently**. If something is *apparently* true, it is presented *in a way* that is *apparent*, or evident.

> adjective + -*ly* = adverb

Practice Add the suffix -*ly* to the following words. Then, use each word in a sentence. Use a dictionary if necessary.

1. final

2. quick

3. identifiable

4. year

5. loud

6. slow

Grammar Lesson

Simple Verb Tenses A verb is a word that expresses an action or a state of being. A **verb tense** shows the time of the action or state of being the verb expresses.

Form the past tense of regular verbs with -*ed* or -*d*. Memorize the past tense of irregular verbs. All future tenses use the helping verb *will*.

More Practice

For more practice in verb tense, see Grammar Handbook, p. R32.

Tenses	Regular Verb: Cheer	Irregular Verb: Sit	Irregular Verb: Be
Present	I cheer.	I sit.	I am.
Past	I cheered.	I sat.	I was.
Future	I will cheer.	I will sit.	I will be.

Practice Write the past and future tense for each present-tense verb. Then, use each tense of each verb in a sentence.

1. support

2. examine

3. know

4. conclude

5. draw

WG Prentice Hall Writing and Grammar Connection: Chapter 22, Section 1

Reading: Draw Conclusions

Directions: *Questions 1–4 are based on the following selection.*

Sally Peck saw a crime in progress in a field near her farm. Two men were trying to steal a dinosaur fossil that scientists had been digging up. Sally called the police. The police caught the would-be thieves before the fossil was damaged. When the local community heard the news, people became interested in the skeleton. The citizens quickly raised $50,000 to build a museum to house the skeleton. They felt that the dinosaur was part of the community history and belonged to all the residents.

1. Which conclusion can you draw?
   A The thieves live in the community.
   B Dinosaur fossils are valuable.
   C Sally Peck is a scientist.
   D The skeleton is very large.

2. Which questions would you answer before concluding that the citizens think the fossil belongs to all the residents of the community?
   A Why did thieves want the fossil?
   B Why did the citizens want to put the fossil in a museum?
   C How did they catch the thieves?
   D How much did the museum cost?

3. Which of these is a conclusion, based on the end of the passage?
   A The residents did not know about the fossil before the attempted theft.
   B The residents want to learn more about dinosaur fossils.
   C The police told the residents about the attempted theft.
   D The skeleton is in a museum.

4. Which of these is a valid conclusion?
   A The town will sell the skeleton.
   B Many residents are scientists.
   C Sally is a leader of the community.
   D The community has pride.

Timed Writing: Interpretation [Critical Stance]

Review either "The All-American Slurp" or "The Circuit." Discuss the reasons the narrator would or would not agree with the statement. *Change is a wonderful part of life.* **(30 minutes)**

 Writing Workshop: *Work in Progress*

Short Story

For a short story you will write later, work in pairs to list ten conflicts or disagreements that occur between people or groups of people. Then, underline the conflicts that you think are most important. Put your notes in your writing portfolio.

These skills will help you become a better reader. Practice them with either "The King of Mazy May" (p. 282) or "Aaron's Gift" (p. 295).

Reading Skill

Drawing conclusions means making decisions or forming opinions about what has happened in a literary work. Base your conclusions on details in the text and on your own **prior knowledge,** or things you know from your own experience. For example, if a dog in a story wags its tail, you might conclude that the dog is friendly because you have seen this behavior in your own pet.

As you read, use a graphic organizer like the one shown to record the conclusions you draw from the text. Check to see that your conclusions make sense. If they do not, think of new conclusions.

Literary Analysis

The **setting** of a literary work is the time and place of the action. The time may be a historical era, the present or future, the season of the year, or the hour of the day. The place can be as general as outer space or as specific as a particular street. As you read, notice the impact of the setting on characters and events in a story.

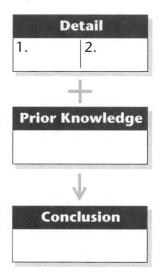

Detail	
1.	2.

Prior Knowledge

Conclusion

Vocabulary Builder

The King of Mazy May

- **endured** (en d̄oord´) *v.* suffered through (p. 283) *The team endured a long losing streak.*

- **liable** (lī´ə bəl) *adj.* likely to do something or to happen (p. 284) *Our dog is liable to bark at anything.*

- **declined** (dē klīnd´) *v.* refused (p. 287) *We declined his offer of a ride home.*

- **summit** (sum´ it) *n.* highest part (p. 290) *The climbers' goal was to reach the mountain's summit.*

Aaron's Gift

- **thrashing** (thrash´ iŋ) *n.* wild moving (p. 297) *The fish's thrashing broke the fisherman's line.*

- **pleaded** (plēd´ id) *v.* begged (p. 299) *Jason pleaded for a new skateboard.*

- **consoled** (kən sōld´) *v.* comforted (p. 300) *She consoled the crying child with a hug.*

- **hesitated** (hez´i tāt´ id) *v.* stopped because of indecision (p. 301) *Maria hesitated before jumping into the pool.*

Background

Klondike Gold In 1896, George Carmack found gold in the Klondike region of northwestern Canada. His find began with a quarter ounce of the precious metal—equal in value to what an average worker could earn in a week! Thousands of other prospectors followed Carmack. Most found hardship, but no gold.

Connecting to the Literature

Reading/Writing Connection In "The King of Mazy May," a young boy protects the property of a friend from thieves. List situations in which you would defend someone who is being treated unfairly. Write sentences using at least three of the following words: *abandon, challenge, dedicate, plead.*

Meet the Author

Jack **London** (1876–1916)

Jack London lived an adventurous life. Before this Californian was out of his teens, he had worked in a factory, traveled as a hobo, captained a pirate ship, and searched for gold. London's love of reading and his own adventures inspired him to write.

The Story Behind the Story In 1897, London went to northwestern Canada, where gold had just been discovered. He did not find any gold, but he did have adventures on the way to Dawson. Once, for instance, he made a boat from trees and ran the dangerous White Horse rapids. In "The King of Mazy May," London writes about a young miner who also has a thrilling trip to Dawson.

Fast Facts

▶ Altogether, London wrote more than fifty books, including *The Call of the Wild* and *White Fang.*
▶ London built a boat and sailed it around the world.

Go **Online**
Author Link

For: More about the author
Visit: www.PHSchool.com
Web Code: ele-9210

THE King of Mazy May

JACK LONDON

Walt Masters is not a very large boy, but there is manliness in his make-up, and he himself, although he does not know a great deal that most boys know, knows much that other boys do not know. He has never seen a train of cars nor an elevator in his life, and for that matter he has never once looked upon a cornfield, a plow, a cow, or even a

▼ **Critical Viewing** What can you tell about the story's setting, based on this photograph?
[Draw Conclusions]

chicken. He has never had a pair of shoes on his feet, nor gone to a picnic or a party, nor talked to a girl. But he has seen the sun at midnight, watched the ice jams on one of the mightiest of rivers, and played beneath the northern lights,[1] the one white child in thousands of square miles of frozen wilderness.

Walt has walked all the fourteen years of his life in sun-tanned, moose-hide moccasins, and he can go to the Indian camps and "talk big" with the men, and trade calico and beads with them for their precious furs. He can make bread without baking powder, yeast, or hops, shoot a moose at three hundred yards, and drive the wild wolf dogs fifty miles a day on the packed trail.

Last of all, he has a good heart, and is not afraid of the darkness and loneliness, of man or beast or thing. His father is a good man, strong and brave, and Walt is growing up like him.

Walt was born a thousand miles or so down the Yukon,[2] in a trading post below the Ramparts. After his mother died, his father and he came up on the river, step by step, from camp to camp, till now they are settled down on the Mazy May Creek in the Klondike country. Last year they and several others had spent much toil and time on the Mazy May, and <u>endured</u> great hardships; the creek, in turn, was just beginning to show up its richness and to reward them for their heavy labor. But with the news of their discoveries, strange men began to come and go through the short days and long nights, and many unjust things they did to the men who had worked so long upon the creek.

Si Hartman had gone away on a moose hunt, to return and find new stakes driven and his claim jumped.[3] George Lukens and his brother had lost their claims in a like manner, having delayed too long on the way to Dawson to record them. In short, it was the old story, and quite a number of the earnest, industrious prospectors had suffered similar losses.

Literary Analysis
Setting What does the setting of frozen wilderness tell you about Walt's life?

Vocabulary Builder
endured (en dōord′) v. suffered through

 Reading Check

Why would someone jump another person's claim?

But Walt Masters's father had recorded his claim at the start, so Walt had nothing to fear now that his father had gone on a short trip up the White River prospecting for quartz. Walt was well able to stay by himself in the cabin, cook his three meals a day, and look after things. Not only did he look after his father's claim, but he had agreed to keep an eye on the adjoining one of Loren Hall, who had started for Dawson to record it.

Loren Hall was an old man, and he had no dogs, so he had to travel very slowly. After he had been gone some time, word came up the river that he had broken through the ice at Rosebud Creek and frozen his feet so badly that he would not be able to travel for a couple of weeks. Then Walt Masters received the news that old Loren was nearly all right again, and about to move on afoot for Dawson as fast as a weakened man could.

Walt was worried, however; the claim was <u>liable</u> to be jumped at any moment because of this delay, and a fresh stampede had started in on the Mazy May. He did not like the looks of the newcomers, and one day, when five of them came by with crack dog teams and the lightest of camping outfits, he could see that they were prepared to make speed, and resolved to keep an eye on them. So he locked up the cabin and followed them, being at the same time careful to remain hidden.

He had not watched them long before he was sure that they were professional stampeders, bent on jumping all the claims in sight. Walt crept along the snow at the rim of the creek and saw them change many stakes, destroy old ones, and set up new ones.

In the afternoon, with Walt always trailing on their heels, they came back down the creek, unharnessed their dogs, and went into camp within two claims of his cabin. When he saw them make preparations to cook, he hurried home to get something to eat himself, and then hurried back. He crept so close that he could hear them talking quite plainly, and by pushing the underbrush aside he could catch occasional glimpses of them. They had finished eating and were smoking around the fire.

"The creek is all right, boys," a large, black-bearded man, evidently the leader, said, "and I think the best thing we

Literary Analysis
Setting How does the time of the story affect travel and communications?

Vocabulary Builder
liable (lī′ə bəl) *adj.* likely to do something or to happen

Reading Skill
Draw Conclusions What does Walt's behavior tell you about his attitude toward the men?

"Cold" Rush

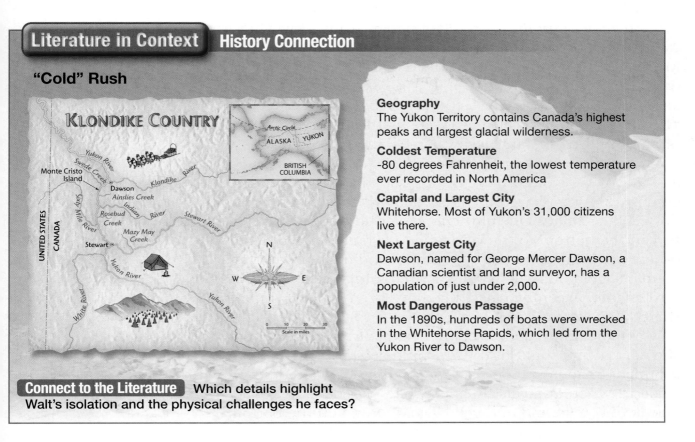

KLONDIKE COUNTRY

Geography
The Yukon Territory contains Canada's highest peaks and largest glacial wilderness.

Coldest Temperature
-80 degrees Fahrenheit, the lowest temperature ever recorded in North America

Capital and Largest City
Whitehorse. Most of Yukon's 31,000 citizens live there.

Next Largest City
Dawson, named for George Mercer Dawson, a Canadian scientist and land surveyor, has a population of just under 2,000.

Most Dangerous Passage
In the 1890s, hundreds of boats were wrecked in the Whitehorse Rapids, which led from the Yukon River to Dawson.

Connect to the Literature   Which details highlight Walt's isolation and the physical challenges he faces?

can do is to pull out tonight. The dogs can follow the trail; besides, it's going to be moonlight. What say you?"

"But it's going to be beastly cold," objected one of the party. "It's forty below zero now."

"An' sure, can't ye keep warm by jumpin' off the sleds an' runnin' after the dogs?" cried an Irishman. "An' who wouldn't? The creek's as rich as a United States mint! Faith, it's an ilegant chanst to be gettin' a run fer yer money! An' if ye don't run, it's mebbe you'll not get the money at all, at all."

"That's it," said the leader. "If we can get to Dawson and record, we're rich men; and there's no telling who's been sneaking along in our tracks, watching us, and perhaps now off to give the alarm. The thing for us to do is to rest the dogs a bit, and then hit the trail as hard as we can. What do you say?"

Evidently the men had agreed with their leader, for Walt Masters could hear nothing but the rattle of the tin dishes

Reading Check

According to the Irishman, what can a sled driver do to keep warm?

The King of Mazy May ■ 285

which were being washed. Peering out cautiously, he could see the leader studying a piece of paper. Walt knew what it was at a glance—a list of all the unrecorded claims on Mazy May. Any man could get these lists by applying to the gold commissioner at Dawson.

"Thirty-two," the leader said, lifting his face to the men. "Thirty-two isn't recorded, and this is thirty-three. Come on; let's take a look at it. I saw somebody had been working on it when we came up this morning."

Three of the men went with him, leaving one to remain in camp. Walt crept carefully after them till they came to Loren Hall's shaft. One of the men went down and built a fire on the bottom to thaw out the frozen gravel, while the others built another fire on the dump and melted water in a couple of gold pans. This they poured into a piece of canvas stretched between two logs, used by Loren Hall in which to wash his gold.

In a short time a couple of buckets of dirt were sent up by the man in the shaft, and Walt could see the others grouped anxiously about their leader as he proceeded to wash it. When this was finished, they stared at the broad streak of black sand and yellow gold grains on the bottom of the pan, and one of them called excitedly for the man who had remained in camp to come. Loren Hall had struck it rich and his claim was not yet recorded. It was plain that they were going to jump it.

Walt lay in the snow, thinking rapidly. He was only a boy, but in the face of the threatened injustice to old lame Loren Hall he felt that he must do something. He waited and watched, with his mind made up, till he saw the men begin to square up new stakes. Then he crawled away till out of hearing, and broke into a run for the camp of the stampeders. Walt's father had taken their own dogs with him prospecting, and the boy knew how impossible it was for him to undertake the seventy miles to Dawson without the aid of dogs.

Gaining the camp, he picked out, with an experienced eye, the easiest running sled and started to harness up the stampeders' dogs. There were three teams of six each, and from these he chose ten of the best. Realizing how necessary it was to have a good head dog, he strove to discover a

Reading Skill
Draw Conclusions
Why is the leader interested in the unrecorded claim?

Reading Skill
Draw Conclusions
Why would it be impossible to travel seventy miles to Dawson without dogs?

leader amongst them; but he had little time in which to do it, for he could hear the voices of the returning men. By the time the team was in shape and everything ready, the claim-jumpers came into sight in an open place not more than a hundred yards from the trail, which ran down the bed of the creek. They cried out to Walt, but instead of giving heed to them he grabbed up one of their fur sleeping robes, which lay loosely in the snow, and leaped upon the sled.

"Mush! Hi! Mush on!" he cried to the animals, snapping the keen-lashed whip among them.

The dogs sprang against the yoke straps, and the sled jerked under way so suddenly as to almost throw him off. Then it curved into the creek, poising perilously on the runner. He was almost breathless with suspense, when it finally righted with a bound and sprang ahead again. The creek bank was high and he could not see the men, although he could hear their cries and knew they were running to cut him off. He did not dare to think what would happen if they caught him; he just clung to the sled, his heart beating wildly, and watched the snow rim of the bank above him.

Suddenly, over this snow rim came the flying body of the Irishman, who had leaped straight for the sled in a desperate attempt to capture it; but he was an instant too late. Striking on the very rear of it, he was thrown from his feet, backward, into the snow. Yet, with the quickness of a cat, he had clutched the end of the sled with one hand, turned over, and was dragging behind on his breast, swearing at the boy and threatening all kinds of terrible things if he did not stop the dogs; but Walt cracked him sharply across the knuckles with the butt of the dog whip till he let go.

It was eight miles from Walt's claim to the Yukon—eight very crooked miles, for the creek wound back and forth like a snake, "tying knots in itself," as George Lukens said. And because it was so crooked the dogs could not get up their best speed, while the sled ground heavily on its side against the curves, now to the right, now to the left.

Travelers who had come up and down the Mazy May on foot, with packs on their backs, had <u>declined</u> to go round all the bends, and instead had made shortcuts across the

Literary Analysis
Setting What conditions make it difficult for Walt to get to Dawson?

Vocabulary Builder
declined (dē klīnd´) *v.* refused

Reading Check

How does Walt escape the grasp of the Irishman?

narrow necks of creek bottom. Two of his pursuers had gone back to harness the remaining dogs, but the others took advantage of these shortcuts, running on foot, and before he knew it they had almost overtaken him.

▲ Critical Viewing
What might it be like to live in this cabin, with only dogs for company?
[Speculate]

"Halt!" they cried after him. "Stop, or we'll shoot!"

But Walt only yelled the harder at the dogs, and dashed around the bend with a couple of revolver bullets singing after him. At the next bend they had drawn up closer still, and the bullets struck uncomfortably near him but at this point the Mazy May straightened out and ran for half a mile as the crow flies. Here the dogs stretched out in their long wolf swing, and the stampeders, quickly winded, slowed down and waited for their own sled to come up.

Looking over his shoulder, Walt reasoned that they had not given up the chase for good, and that they would soon be after him again. So he wrapped the fur robe about him to shut out the stinging air, and lay flat on the empty sled, encouraging the dogs, as he well knew how.

At last, twisting abruptly between two river islands, he came upon the mighty Yukon sweeping grandly to the north. He could not see from bank to bank, and in the quick-falling twilight it loomed a great white sea of frozen stillness. There was not a sound, save the breathing of the dogs, and the churn of the steel-shod sled.

Literary Analysis
Setting Why is it good for Walt that it hasn't snowed recently?

No snow had fallen for several weeks, and the traffic had packed the main river trail till it was hard and glassy as glare ice. Over this the sled flew along, and the dogs kept the trail fairly well, although Walt quickly discovered that he had made a mistake in choosing the leader. As they were driven in single file, without reins, he had to guide them by his voice, and it was evident the head dog had never learned the meaning of "gee" and "haw."[4] He hugged the inside of the curves too closely, often forcing his comrades

---

4. **"gee" and "haw"** (jē) and (hô) commands used to tell an animal to turn to the right or the left.

After Dinner Music, 1988, Scott Kennedy, Courtesy of the Greenwich Workshop Inc.

behind him into the soft snow, while several times he thus capsized[5] the sled.

There was no wind, but the speed at which he traveled created a bitter blast, and with the thermometer down to forty below, this bit through fur and flesh to the very bones. Aware that if he remained constantly upon the sled he would freeze to death, and knowing the practice of Arctic travelers, Walt shortened up one of the lashing thongs, and whenever he felt chilled, seized hold of it, jumped off, and ran behind till warmth was restored. Then he would climb on and rest till the process had to be repeated.

Looking back he could see the sled of his pursuers, drawn by eight dogs, rising and falling over the ice hummocks like a boat in a seaway. The Irishman and the black-bearded leader were with it, taking turns in running and riding.

Night fell, and in the blackness of the first hour or so Walt toiled desperately with his dogs. On account of the poor lead dog, they were continually floundering off the beaten track into the soft snow, and the sled was as often riding on its side or top as it was in the proper way. This work and strain tried his strength sorely. Had he not been in such haste he could have avoided much of it, but he feared the stampeders would creep up in the darkness and overtake him. However, he could hear them yelling to their

Reading Skill
Draw Conclusions
What do Walt's actions to stay warm tell you about his determination?

 Reading Check

What advantage do Walt's pursuers have over him?

---

5. capsized (kap´ sīzd´) *v.* overturned.

dogs, and knew from the sounds they were coming up very slowly.

When the moon rose he was off Sixty Mile, and Dawson was only fifty miles away. He was almost exhausted, and breathed a sigh of relief as he climbed on the sled again. Looking back, he saw his enemies had crawled up within four hundred yards. At this space they remained, a black speck of motion on the white river breast. Strive as they would, they could not shorten this distance, and strive as he would, he could not increase it.

Walt had now discovered the proper lead dog, and he knew he could easily run away from them if he could only change the bad leader for the good one. But this was impossible, for a moment's delay, at the speed they were running, would bring the men behind upon him.

When he was off the mouth of Rosebud Creek, just as he was topping a rise, the report of a gun and the ping of a bullet on the ice beside him told him that they were this time shooting at him with a rifle. And from then on, as he cleared the <u>summit</u> of each ice jam, he stretched flat on the leaping sled till the rifle shot from the rear warned him that he was safe till the next ice jam was reached.

Now it is very hard to lie on a moving sled, jumping and plunging and yawing[6] like a boat before the wind, and to shoot through the deceiving moonlight at an object four hundred yards away on another moving sled performing equally wild antics. So it is not to be wondered at that the black-bearded leader did not hit him.

After several hours of this, during which, perhaps, a score of bullets had struck about him, their ammunition began to give out and their fire slackened. They took greater care, and shot at him at the most favorable opportunities. He was also leaving them behind, the distance slowly increasing to six hundred yards.

Lifting clear on the crest of a great jam off Indian River, Walt Masters met with his first accident. A bullet sang past his ears, and struck the bad lead dog.

Reading Skill
Draw Conclusions
How would having the proper lead dog help Walt?

Vocabulary Builder
summit (sum′ it) *n.* highest part

---

6. yawing (yô′ iŋ) *adj.* swinging from side to side.

The poor brute plunged in a heap, with the rest of the team on top of him.

Like a flash Walt was by the leader. Cutting the traces with his hunting knife, he dragged the dying animal to one side and straightened out the team.

He glanced back. The other sled was coming up like an express train. With half the dogs still over their traces, he cried "Mush on!" and leaped upon the sled just as the pursuers dashed abreast[7] of him.

The Irishman was preparing to spring for him—they were so sure they had him that they did not shoot—when Walt turned fiercely upon them with his whip.

He struck at their faces, and men must save their faces with their hands. So there was no shooting just then. Before they could recover from the hot rain of blows, Walt reached out from his sled, catching their wheel dog by the forelegs in midspring, and throwing him heavily. This snarled the team, capsizing the sled and tangling his enemies up beautifully.

Away Walt flew, the runners of his sled fairly screaming as they bounded over the frozen surface. And what had seemed an accident proved to be a blessing in disguise. The proper lead dog was now to the fore, and he stretched low and whined with joy as he jerked his comrades along.

By the time he reached Ainslie's Creek, seventeen miles from Dawson, Walt had left his pursuers, a tiny speck, far behind. At Monte Cristo Island he could no longer see them. And at Swede Creek, just as daylight was silvering the pines, he ran plump into the camp of old Loren Hall.

Almost as quick as it takes to tell it, Loren had his sleeping furs rolled up, and had joined Walt on the sled. They permitted the dogs to travel more slowly, as there was no sign of the chase in the rear, and just as they pulled up at the gold commissioner's office in Dawson, Walt, who had kept his eyes open to the last, fell asleep.

And because of what Walt Masters did on this night, the men of the Yukon have become proud of him, and speak of him now as the King of Mazy May.

Reading Skill
Draw Conclusions
Based on your own experiences, what do you think gives Walt the strength to continue?

Reading Skill
Draw Conclusions
Why does Walt fall asleep when the sled pulls into Dawson?

---

7. abreast (ə brest´) adv. alongside.

Apply the Skills

The King of Mazy May

Thinking About the Selection

1. **Respond:** What do you think is the most important event in the story? Explain your answer.
2. **(a) Recall:** What are Walt's responsibilities while his father is away? **(b) Compare and Contrast:** How are Walt's responsibilities different from those of other children his age?
3. **Evaluate:** This story suggests that "manliness" is based on strength and bravery. Explain why you agree or disagree.
4. **(a) Extend:** As this story illustrates, the discovery of gold in the Klondike brought out the best and the worst in people. Why do you think that the discovery of gold had such a major impact on people? **(b) Apply:** If you had lived during that time, would you have been tempted to travel to the Klondike in search of gold? Explain.

Reading Skill

5. List three story details that support the following **conclusion**: *At the time of this story, life in the Klondike was dangerous and challenging.*
6. Based on your prior knowledge, how do you think Walt feels when people call him the "King of Mazy May"?

Literary Analysis

7. **(a)** Describe the **setting** of "The King of Mazy May." **(b)** Why is the setting important to the story?
8. **(a)** Use a chart like the one shown to list ways in which details of the setting affect events in the story. **(b)** With a partner, explain your responses. Then discuss how your ideas grew or changed based on your work together.

Details of Setting		Story Events
Time		
Place		

Vocabulary Builder

Practice Write a sentence to respond to each item using a word from the vocabulary list on page 280.

1. Explain why Klondike claims were likely to be jumped.
2. Propose the placement for a lookout tower in a hilly region.
3. Describe an offer that has been refused.
4. Describe a boy who had suffered through many hardships.

Writing

You may not have foiled stampeders like Walt does, but you have probably had the experience of struggling to meet a goal. Choose one such experience, and use it as the topic for a brief **personal narrative**—a story that captures the details of the experience, along with your thoughts and feelings about it.

- Use a timeline to list events in the order in which they occurred. Add details that describe the events.
- Refer to your timeline as you write your narrative. Include details about each event and tell how you felt at each stage.

For *Grammar, Vocabulary,* and *Assessment,* see **Build Language Skills,** pages 306–307.

Extend Your Learning

Listening and Speaking As Walt, give a **speech** accepting an award for courage from Dawson.

- Make an outline of what you want to say.
- Vary the volume, or loudness, of your voice. Increase volume as you build toward an exciting moment or important idea.
- Deliver the speech to your classmates.

Research and Technology In a small group, prepare a **presentation** on gold mining. Use resources such as the Internet and nonfiction books to research the life of a miner. Do a keyword search for "gold mining in Canada." Use visuals to show where gold was mined. Share your findings with the class.

Build Understanding • *Aaron's Gift*

Background

Carrier Pigeons Today, carrier pigeons like the one in "Aaron's Gift" may seem unusual. However, carrier pigeons have been used throughout history to carry messages over long distances. The ancient Romans used pigeons to report chariot race results. Pigeons also carried vital messages during World War I.

Connecting to the Literature

Reading/Writing Connection Using pigeons to carry messages is a unique solution to a problem. The boy in "Aaron's Gift" also tries to solve a problem by finding a new way to look at it. Connect to Aaron's experience by writing a few sentences about times when you found a new approach or viewpoint that helped you solve a problem. Use three of these words: *rely, accomplish, adjust, resolve.*

Review

For **Reading Skill, Literary Analysis,** and **Vocabulary Builder,** see page 280.

Meet the Author

Myron **Levoy** (b. 1930)

Myron Levoy has loved reading and writing ever since he was a boy growing up in New York City. In a passage about his childhood, he wrote, "Times were hard and toys were few, but I remember from a very early age constant trips to the library with my mother and brother, and the smell and feel of books."

Inspiration Strikes The New York Public Library never lost its appeal for Levoy. When he was sixteen, he got a summer job there. One day Levoy viewed an exhibit of handwritten poems by Edward Arlington Robinson. Seeing poems before him in paper and ink had a strong impact. "Such power, an entire world, on that one small sheet!" Levoy says. "It was absolute and final: yes, I would become a writer above all else!"

Go Online
Author Link

For: More about the author
Visit: www.PHSchool.com
Web Code: ele-9211

Aaron's GIFT

Myron Levoy

Aaron Kandel had come to Tompkins Square Park to roller-skate, for the streets near Second Avenue were always too crowded with children and peddlers and old ladies and baby buggies. Though few children had bicycles in those days, almost every child owned a pair of roller skates. And Aaron was, it must be said, a Class A, triple-fantastic roller skater.

Aaron skated back and forth on the wide walkway of the park, pretending he was an aviator in an air race zooming around pylons, which were actually two lampposts. During his third lap around the racecourse, he noticed a pigeon on the grass, behaving very strangely. Aaron skated to the line of benches, then climbed over onto the lawn.

The pigeon was trying to fly, but all it could manage was to flutter and turn round and round in a large circle, as if it were performing a frenzied dance. The left wing was only half open and was beating in a clumsy, jerking fashion; it was clearly broken.

Luckily, Aaron hadn't eaten the cookies he'd stuffed into his pocket before he'd gone clacking down the three flights of stairs from his apartment, his skates already on. He broke a cookie into small crumbs and tossed some toward the pigeon. "Here pidge, here pidge," he called. The pigeon

▲ **Critical Viewing**
How would you compare this bird to the bird described in the third paragraph? **[Compare and Contrast]**

Reading Check

What makes Aaron stop to call the pigeon?

spotted the cookie crumbs and, after a moment, stopped thrashing about. It folded its wings as best it could, but the broken wing still stuck half out. Then it strutted over to the crumbs, its head bobbing forth-back, forth-back, as if it were marching a little in front of the rest of the body—perfectly normal, except for that half-open wing which seemed to make the bird stagger sideways every so often.

The pigeon began eating the crumbs as Aaron quickly unbuttoned his shirt and pulled it off. Very slowly, he edged toward the bird, making little kissing sounds like the ones he heard his grandmother make when she fed the sparrows on the back fire escape.

Then suddenly Aaron plunged. The shirt, in both hands, came down like a torn parachute. The pigeon beat its wings, but Aaron held the shirt to the ground, and the bird couldn't escape. Aaron felt under the shirt, gently, and gently took hold of the wounded pigeon.

"Yes, yes, pidge," he said, very softly. "There's a good boy. Good pigeon, good."

The pigeon struggled in his hands, but little by little Aaron managed to soothe it. "Good boy, pidge. That's your new name. Pidge. I'm gonna take you home, Pidge. Yes, yes, *ssh*. Good boy. I'm gonna fix you up. Easy, Pidge, easy does it. Easy, boy."

Aaron squeezed through an opening between the row of benches and skated slowly out of the park, while holding the pigeon carefully with both hands as if it were one of his mother's rare, precious cups from the old country. How fast the pigeon's heart was beating! Was he afraid? Or did all pigeons' hearts beat fast?

It was fortunate that Aaron was an excellent skater, for he had to skate six blocks to his apartment, over broken pavement and sudden gratings and curbs and cobblestones. But when he reached home, he asked Noreen Callahan, who was playing on the stoop, to take off his skates for him. He would not chance going up three flights on roller skates this time.

Reading Skill
Draw Conclusions
Do you think Aaron would be a good friend? Why or why not?

Literary Analysis
Setting List three details that show the setting.

"Is he sick?" asked Noreen.

"Broken wing," said Aaron. "I'm gonna fix him up and make him into a carrier pigeon or something."

"Can I watch?" asked Noreen.

"Watch what?"

"The operation. I'm gonna be a nurse when I grow up."

"OK," said Aaron. "You can even help. You can help hold him while I fix him up."

Aaron wasn't quite certain what his mother would say about his new-found pet, but he was pretty sure he knew what his grandmother would think. His grandmother had lived with them ever since his grandfather had died three years ago. And she fed the sparrows and jays and crows and robins on the back fire escape with every spare crumb she could find. In fact, Aaron noticed that she sometimes created crumbs where they didn't exist, by squeezing and tearing pieces of her breakfast roll when his mother wasn't looking.

Aaron didn't really understand his grandmother, for he often saw her by the window having long conversations with the birds, telling them about her days as a little girl in the Ukraine.[1] And once he saw her take her mirror from her handbag and hold it out toward the birds. She told Aaron that she wanted them to see how beautiful they were. Very strange. But Aaron did know that she would love Pidge, because she loved everything.

To his surprise, his mother said he could keep the pigeon, temporarily, because it was sick, and we were all strangers in the land of Egypt,[2] and it might not be bad for Aaron to have a pet. *Temporarily.*

The wing was surprisingly easy to fix, for the break showed clearly and Pidge was remarkably patient and still, as if he knew he was being helped. Or perhaps he was just exhausted from all the <u>thrashing</u> about he had done. Two Popsicle sticks served as splints, and strips from an old undershirt were used to tie them in place. Another strip held the wing to the bird's body.

1. **Ukraine** (yōō krān´) country located in Eastern Europe. From 1924 to 1991, Ukraine was part of the former Soviet Union.

2. **we were all . . . land of Egypt** a reference to the biblical story of the enslavement of the Hebrew people in Egypt. Around 1300 B.C., the Hebrews were led out of Egypt by Moses.

Reading Skill
Draw Conclusions
Why does Aaron's grandmother feed the birds?

Vocabulary Builder
thrashing (thrash´ iŋ)
n. wild moving

Reading Check

How does Aaron "fix up" Pidge?

Aaron's father arrived home and stared at the pigeon. Aaron waited for the expected storm. But instead, Mr. Kandel asked, "Who *did* this?"

"Me," said Aaron. "And Noreen Callahan."

"Sophie!" he called to his wife. "Did you see this! Ten years old and it's better than Dr. Belasco could do. He's a genius!"

As the days passed, Aaron began training Pidge to be a carrier pigeon. He tied a little cardboard tube to Pidge's left leg and stuck tiny rolled-up sheets of paper with secret messages into it: THE ENEMY IS ATTACKING AT DAWN. Or: THE GUNS ARE HIDDEN IN THE TRUNK OF THE CAR. Or: VINCENT DEMARCO IS A BRITISH SPY. Then Aaron would set Pidge down at one end of the living room and put some popcorn at the other end. And Pidge would waddle slowly across the room, cooing softly, while the ends of his bandages trailed along the floor.

At the other end of the room, one of Aaron's friends would take out the message, stick a new one in, turn Pidge around, and aim him at the popcorn that Aaron put down on his side of the room.

And Pidge grew fat and contented on all the popcorn and crumbs and corn and crackers and Aaron's grandmother's breakfast rolls.

Aaron had told all the children about Pidge, but he only let his very best friends come up and play carrier-pigeon with him. But telling everyone had been a mistake. A group of older boys from down the block had a club—Aaron's mother called it a gang—and Aaron had longed to join as he had never longed for anything else. To be with them and share their secrets, the secrets of older boys. To be able to enter their clubhouse shack on the empty lot on the next street. To know the password and swear the secret oath. To belong.

Pigeons, John Sloan, The The Hayden Collection, Courtesy, Museum of Fine Arts, Boston, Massachusetts

▼ **Critical Viewing**
What details in this painting suggest freedom? **[Interpret]**

About a month after Aaron had brought the pigeon home, Carl, the gang leader, walked over to Aaron in the street and told him he could be a member if he'd bring the pigeon down to be the club mascot.[3] Aaron couldn't believe it; he immediately raced home to get Pidge. But his mother told Aaron to stay away from those boys, or else. And Aaron, miserable, argued with his mother and <u>pleaded</u> and cried and coaxed. It was no use. Not with those boys. No.

Aaron's mother tried to change the subject. She told him that it would soon be his grandmother's sixtieth birthday, a very special birthday indeed, and all the family from Brooklyn and the East Side would be coming to their apartment for a dinner and celebration. Would Aaron try to build something or make something for Grandma? A present made with his own hands would be nice. A decorated box for her hairpins or a crayon picture for her room or anything he liked.

In a flash Aaron knew what to give her: Pidge! Pidge would be her present! Pidge with his wing healed, who might be able to carry messages for her to the doctor or his Aunt Rachel or other people his grandmother seemed to go to a lot. It would be a surprise for everyone. And Pidge would make up for what had happened to Grandma when she'd been a little girl in the Ukraine, wherever that was.

Often, in the evening, Aaron's grandmother would talk about the old days long ago in the Ukraine, in the same way that she talked to the birds on the back fire escape. She had lived in a village near a place called Kishinev with hundreds of other poor peasant families like her own. Things hadn't been too bad under someone called Czar Alexander the Second,[4] whom Aaron always pictured as a tall handsome man in a gold uniform. But Alexander the Second was assassinated, and Alexander the Third, whom Aaron pictured as an ugly man in a black cape, became the Czar. And the Jewish people of the Ukraine had no peace anymore.

One day, a thundering of horses was heard coming toward the village from the direction of Kishinev. *The*

Vocabulary Builder
pleaded (plēd´ id) *v.* begged

Literary Analysis
Setting In your own words, describe the setting of Aaron's grandmother's childhood.

Reading Check

Why does Aaron want to give Pidge to his grandmother?

Cossacks! The Cossacks! someone had shouted. The Czar's horsemen! Quickly, quickly, everyone in Aaron's grandmother's family had climbed down to the cellar through a little trapdoor hidden under a mat in the big central room of their shack. But his grandmother's pet goat, whom she'd loved as much as Aaron loved Pidge and more, had to be left above, because if it had made a sound in the cellar, they would never have lived to see the next morning. They all hid under the wood in the woodbin and waited, hardly breathing.

Suddenly, from above, they heard shouts and calls and screams at a distance. And then the noise was in their house. Boots pounding on the floor, and everything breaking and crashing overhead. The smell of smoke and the shouts of a dozen men.

The terror went on for an hour and then the sound of horses' hooves faded into the distance. They waited another hour to make sure, and then the father went up out of the cellar and the rest of the family followed. The door to the house had been torn from its hinges and every piece of furniture was broken. Every window, every dish, every stitch of clothing was totally destroyed, and one wall had been completely bashed in. And on the floor was the goat, lying quietly. Aaron's grandmother, who was just a little girl of eight at the time, had wept over the goat all day and all night and could not be <u>consoled</u>.

But they had been lucky. For other houses had been burned to the ground. And everywhere, not goats alone, nor sheep, but men and women and children lay quietly on the ground. The word for this sort of massacre, Aaron had learned, was *pogrom*. It had been a pogrom. And the men on the horses were Cossacks. Hated word. Cossacks.

Vocabulary Builder
consoled (kän sōld')
v. comforted

And so Pidge would replace that goat of long ago. A pigeon on Second Avenue where no one needed trapdoors or secret escape passages or woodpiles to hide under. A pigeon for his grandmother's sixtieth birthday. *Oh wing, heal quickly so my grandmother can send you flying to everywhere she wants!*

But a few days later, Aaron met Carl in the street again. And Carl told Aaron that there was going to be a meeting that afternoon in which a map was going to be drawn up to show where a secret treasure lay buried on the empty lot. "Bring the pigeon and you can come into the shack. We got a badge for you. A new kinda membership badge with a secret code on the back."

Aaron ran home, his heart pounding almost as fast as the pigeon's. He took Pidge in his hands and carried him out the door while his mother was busy in the kitchen making stuffed cabbage, his father's favorite dish. And by the time he reached the street, Aaron had decided to take the bandages off. Pidge would look like a real pigeon again, and none of the older boys would laugh or call him a bundle of rags.

Gently, gently he removed the bandages and the splints and put them in his pocket in case he should need them again. But Pidge seemed to hold his wing properly in place.

When he reached the empty lot, Aaron walked up to the shack, then <u>hesitated</u>. Four bigger boys were there. After a moment, Carl came out and commanded Aaron to hand Pidge over.

"Be careful," said Aaron. "I just took the bandages off."

"Oh sure, don't worry," said Carl. By now Pidge was used to people holding him, and he remained calm in Carl's hands.

"OK," said Carl. "Give him the badge." And one of the older boys handed Aaron his badge with the code on the back. "Now light the fire," said Carl.

"What . . . what fire?" asked Aaron.

"The fire. You'll see," Carl answered.

"You didn't say nothing about a fire," said Aaron. "You didn't say nothing to—"

"Hey!" said Carl. "I'm the leader here. And you don't talk unless I tell you that you have p'mission. Light the fire, Al."

Vocabulary Builder
hesitated (hez′ i tāt′ id)
v. stopped because of indecision

Reading Check

Why does Aaron bring Pidge to the meeting?

The boy named Al went out to the side of the shack, where some wood and cardboard and old newspapers had been piled into a huge mound. He struck a match and held it to the newspapers.

"OK," said Carl. "Let's get 'er good and hot. Blow on it. Everybody blow."

Aaron's eyes stung from the smoke, but he blew alongside the others, going from side to side as the smoke shifted toward them and away.

"Let's fan it," said Al.

In a few minutes, the fire was crackling and glowing with a bright yellow-orange flame.

"Get me the rope," said Carl.

One of the boys brought Carl some cord and Carl, without a word, wound it twice around the pigeon, so that its wings were tight against its body.

"What . . . what are you *doing*!" shouted Aaron. "You're hurting his wing!"

"Don't worry about his wing," said Carl. "We're gonna throw him into the fire. And when we do, we're gonna swear an oath of loyalty to—"

"No! *No*!" shouted Aaron, moving toward Carl.

"Grab him!" called Carl. "Don't let him get the pigeon!"

But Aaron had leaped right across the fire at Carl, taking him completely by surprise. He threw Carl back against the shack and hit out at his face with both fists. Carl slid down to the ground and the pigeon rolled out of his hands. Aaron scooped up the pigeon and ran, pretending he was on roller skates so that he would go faster and faster. And as he ran across the lot he pulled the cord off Pidge and tried to find a place, *any* place, to hide him. But the boys were on top of him, and the pigeon slipped from Aaron's hands.

"Get him!" shouted Carl.

Aaron thought of the worst, the most horrible thing he could shout at the boys. "Cossacks!" he screamed. "You're all Cossacks!"

Two boys held Aaron back while the others tried to catch the pigeon. Pidge fluttered along the ground just out of reach, skittering one way and then the other. Then the boys came at him from two directions. But suddenly Pidge beat

Reading Skill
Draw Conclusions
What can you conclude about Aaron from his actions to save Pidge?

his wings in rhythm, and rose up, up over the roof of the nearest tenement, up over Second Avenue toward the park.

With the pigeon gone, the boys turned toward Aaron and tackled him to the ground and punched him and tore his clothes and punched him some more. Aaron twisted and turned and kicked and punched back, shouting "Cossacks! Cossacks!" And somehow the word gave him the strength to tear away from them.

When Aaron reached home, he tried to go past the kitchen quickly so his mother wouldn't see his bloody face and torn clothing. But it was no use; his father was home from work early that night and was seated in the living room. In a moment Aaron was surrounded by his mother, father, and grandmother, and in another moment he had told them everything that had happened, the words tumbling out between his broken sobs. Told them of the present he had planned, of the pigeon for a goat, of the gang, of the badge with the secret code on the back, of the shack, and the fire, and the pigeon's flight over the tenement roof.

And Aaron's grandmother kissed him and thanked him for his present which was even better than the pigeon.

"What present?" asked Aaron, trying to stop the series of sobs.

And his grandmother opened her pocketbook and handed Aaron her mirror and asked him to look. But all Aaron saw was his dirty, bruised face and his torn shirt.

Aaron thought he understood and then, again, he thought he didn't. How could she be so happy when there really was no present? And why pretend that there was?

Later that night, just before he fell asleep, Aaron tried to imagine what his grandmother might have done with the pigeon. She would have fed it, and she certainly would have talked to it, as she did to all the birds, and . . . and then she would have let it go free. Yes, of course. Pidge's flight to freedom must have been the gift that had made his grandmother so happy. Her goat has escaped from the Cossacks at last, Aaron thought, half dreaming. And he fell asleep with a smile.

Literary Analysis
Setting How might Pidge see the difference between the tenement yard and the open sky?

Reading Skill
Draw Conclusions What conclusion can you draw about Aaron based on his desire to replace his grandmother's beloved goat?

Apply the Skills

Aaron's Gift

Thinking About the Selection

1. **Respond:** What do you think is the most important event in the story? Explain your answer.
2. **(a) Recall:** What happened to Aaron's grandmother as a child? **(b) Analyze Cause and Effect:** How does the childhood experience help Aaron decide what to give her for her birthday?
3. **(a) Recall:** What does Carl want to do with Pidge? **(b) Compare and Contrast:** How are Carl and the boys like the Cossacks?
4. **(a) Evaluate:** Which is the better gift for Aaron's grandmother: the pigeon or the pigeon's freedom? Explain. **(b) Apply:** What are two other "gifts" that are not physical objects that one person can give another? Explain.

Reading Skill

5. List three story details that support the following **conclusion:** *Aaron is a sensitive and thoughtful boy.*
6. Based on your prior knowledge, why do you think Aaron's mother forbids him to play with Carl and the other boys?

Literary Analysis

7. **(a)** Describe the **setting** of "Aaron's Gift." **(b)** Why is the setting important to the story?
8. **(a)** Use a chart like the one shown to list ways in which details of the setting affect events in the story. **(b)** With a partner, explain your responses. Then discuss how your ideas grew or changed based on your work together.

Details of Setting		Story Events
Time		
Place		

QuickReview

Story at a Glance
By helping an injured bird, a boy gives his grandmother an unexpected gift.

Go **Online**
Assessment
For: Self-test
Visit: www.PHSchool.com
Web Code: ela-6210

Conclusion: a decision or opinion that is based on details in a literary work

Setting: time and place of the action in a story

Vocabulary Builder

Practice Write a sentence for each item that uses a word from the "Aaron's Gift" vocabulary list on page 280.

1. Describe a girl who begged her friends to go to the movies.
2. Explain how you responded to someone whose pet died.
3. Describe a bird that tries to escape from a cage.
4. Describe a shy person who finally entered a new classroom.

Writing

You may not have rescued a bird like Aaron does, but you have probably had the experience of struggling to meet a goal. Choose one such experience, and use it as the topic for a brief **personal narrative**—a story that captures the details of the experience, along with your thoughts and feelings about the experience.

- Use a timeline to list events in the order in which they occurred. Add details that describe the events.
- Refer to your timeline as you write your narrative. Include details about each event and tell how you felt at each stage.

For *Grammar, Vocabulary,* and *Assessment,* see **Build Language Skills,** pages 306–307.

Extend Your Learning

Listening and Speaking As Aaron, give a **speech** honoring his grandmother on her birthday.

- Plan your speech by making an outline of what you want to say.
- Vary the volume, or loudness, of your voice. Increase the volume as you build toward an exciting moment. Call attention to important points by pausing before making a statement.
- Deliver the speech to classmates.

Research and Technology In a small group, prepare a **presentation** on carrier pigeons and how they are trained. Use resources such as the Internet and library to research information. Do a keyword search for "carrier pigeons" or "homing pigeons." Share your findings with the class.

Build Language Skills

Vocabulary Skill

Suffixes *-able, -ible* The **suffixes** *-able* and *-ible* mean "able to be." The word *identifiable* contains the suffix *-able.* When an animal is *identifiable,* it means it is able to be identified.

▶ **Example:** People are *identifiable* by their fingerprints.

Practice Use a dictionary to help you explain the meaning of each word. Include the words *able to be* in your definition.

1. lovable
2. changeable

3. breakable
4. flammable

Grammar Lesson

Verbs: Perfect Tenses The **perfect verb tenses** of verbs combine a form of *have* with the past participle.

- The **present perfect tense** shows an action that began in the past and continues into the present.
- The **past perfect tense** shows a past action or condition that ended before another past action began.
- The **future perfect tense** shows a future action or condition that will have ended before another begins.

MorePractice

For more practice with perfect tenses, see Grammar Handbook, p. R32.

Present Perfect	Past Perfect	Future Perfect
have, has + past participle	had + past participle	will have + past participle
They have voted.	They had voted by the time we arrived.	The council will have voted by summer.

Practice Rewrite each sentence using the tense in parentheses. You may have to change other verbs in the sentence or add to the sentence.

1. Teens *have ridden* skateboards for years. (past perfect)
2. People *had wanted* to find cleaner forms of transportation. (future perfect)
3. Teens *will have found* new transportation by the time you get older. (past perfect)
4. Many environmentalists believe people *will have adopted* electric cars. (present perfect)
5. I *had traded* in my bike for skates. (present perfect)
6. She *has brought* her bike helmet for you to wear. (future perfect)

W͞G *Prentice Hall Writing and Grammar Connection: Chapter 22, Section 2.*

Reading: Draw Conclusions

Directions: *Questions 1–4 are based on the following selection.*

For years, people have dreamed of having robots to do household chores. While this has not happened, robots are doing many important jobs. Surgeons use robots to make precise movements that are difficult for a human hand. Robots pick apples from the tops of trees. Scientists have used robots to explore dangerous places, such as, inside active volcanoes and on the surface of Mars.

1. Which conclusion is most logical?
   A Robots are cheaper than human surgeons.
   B Robots are stronger than humans.
   C Robots are not as reliable as humans.
   D Robots can survive higher temperatures than humans.

2. What can you conclude from the passage about the future of robots?
   A Robots will no longer be useful.
   B Robots will become even more important.
   C Robots will be expensive.
   D Humans will be able to do everything a robot can do.

3. Which word best describes the way robots are discussed in this passage?
   A useful
   B dangerous
   C frightening
   D serious

4. What can you conclude about robots' uses?
   A Robots will never do household chores.
   B Robots help build scientific knowledge.
   C Robots are used only in science fiction.
   D Robots would not be useful in schools.

Timed Writing: Description [Interpretation]

Review "Aaron's Gift" or "The King of Mazy May." Write a description of the setting in one of the works. Describe the setting as you picture it, adding details that the author did not supply. **(20 minutes)**

 ## Writing Workshop: *Work in Progress*

Short Story

Using the conflict list, write the names of two characters who might be involved in this conflict and jot down key words to describe their personalities. Put this work in your portfolio.

Comparison-and-Contrast Articles

In Part 2, you are learning to compare and contrast. Comparison-and-contrast-organization is also used in some nonfiction. If you read "The King of Mazy May," you may enjoy this article about two explorers who raced each other in a similar setting.

About Comparison-and-Contrast Articles

A **comparison-and-contrast article** is expository writing that identifies and examines similarities and differences. There are two common ways of organizing these articles.

- **Block organization:** The writer presents all the details of one subject, then all the details of the other subject.
- **Point-by-point organization:** The writer presents one detail about both subjects and then presents another detail about both subjects.

The writer of "Race to the End of the Earth" uses elements of block and point-by-point organization to describe two men who competed to reach the South Pole first. The article compares and contrasts the men's backgrounds, how they prepared for the trip, and what strategies they used to reach their goals.

Reading Skill

Read comparison-and-contrast articles critically by **identifying and analyzing the organization.** Use the pattern—block or point-by-point—to find and understand the author's main points about how the subjects are alike and different. Then analyze the information by breaking it into parts or categories. Evaluate comparisons in the article by asking yourself questions like the ones in the chart.

Questions for evaluating comparison-and-contrast organization
Are the same categories covered for each half of the comparison?
Are an approximately equal number of details supplied for each category?
Does the writer support compare-and-contrast statements with examples and facts?

Race to the End of the Earth

William G. Scheller

Amundsen's team proving South Pole location

Two explorers competed against each other and a brutal environment to reach the South Pole.

The drifts were so deep and the snow was falling so heavily that the team of five Norwegian explorers could hardly see their sled dogs a few feet ahead of them. Behind rose a monstrous mountain barrier. The men had been the first to cross it. But now they and their dogs were stumbling toward a stark and desolate plateau continually blasted by blizzards. The landscape was broken only by the towering peaks of mountains that lay buried beneath a mile of ancient ice. Led by Roald Amundsen, the men were still 300 miles from their goal: the South Pole.

On that same day, a party of 14 British explorers was also struggling across a similarly terrifying landscape toward the same destination. But they were almost twice as far from success. Their commander was Capt. Robert Falcon Scott, a naval officer. Amundsen was Scott's rival.

Preparation Both expedition leaders had long been preparing for their

> The heading signals that the writer will compare the subjects' methods of preparation.

Reading Informational Materials

race to the South Pole. Amundsen came from a family of hardy sailors, and he had decided at the age of 15 to become a polar explorer. He conditioned himself by taking long ski trips across the Norwegian countryside and by sleeping with his windows open in winter.

By the time of his South Pole attempt, Amundsen was an experienced explorer. He had sailed as a naval officer on an expedition in 1897 that charted sections of the Antarctic coast. Between 1903 and 1906 he commanded the ship that made the first voyage through the Northwest Passage, the icy route that threads its way through the Canadian islands separating the Atlantic and Pacific Oceans. During that long journey Amundsen learned how the native people of the Arctic dress and eat to survive in extreme cold. He also learned that the dogsled was the most efficient method of polar transportation. These lessons would serve him well at Earth's frozen southern end.

Robert Scott was an officer in the British Navy. He had decided that leading a daring expedition of discovery would be an immediate route to higher rank. He heard that Great Britain's Royal Geographical Society was organizing such an exploration, and he volunteered in 1899 to be its commander. Now he was in command again.

The two expedition leaders had different styles. Scott followed a British tradition of brave sacrifice. He felt that he and his men should be able to reach the South Pole with as little help as possible from sled dogs and special equipment. He did bring dogs to Antarctica, as well as 19 ponies and three gasoline-powered sledges, or sturdy sleds. But his plan was for his team to "man-haul," or carry, all of their own supplies along the final portion of the route.

Here, the differences that affected the outcome of the race are analyzed.

◀ Scott's ill-fated team

This paragraph ends with a point-by-point comparison of the teams' attitudes toward skis.

Each heading begins a new section that highlights more similarities and differences.

Roald Amundsen had spent much time in the far north, and he was a practical man. He'd seen how useful dogs were to Arctic inhabitants. He would be traveling in one of the most dangerous places on Earth, and he knew that sled dogs would be able to get his party all the way to the South Pole and make a safe return. Amundsen also placed great faith in skis, which he and his Norwegian team members had used since childhood. The British explorers had rarely used skis before this expedition and did not understand their great value.

The two leaders even had different ideas about diet. Scott's men would rely on canned meat. But Amundsen's plan made more sense. He and his men would eat plenty of fresh seal meat. Amundsen may not have fully understood the importance of vitamins, but fresh meat is a better source of vitamin C, which prevents scurvy, a painful and sometimes deadly disease.

The Race Is On! After making long sea voyages from Europe, Scott and Amundsen set up base camps in January on opposite edges of the Ross Ice Shelf. Each team spent the dark winter months making preparations to push on to the Pole when spring would arrive in Antarctica. Amundsen left base camp on October 20, 1911, with a party of four. Scott, accompanied by nine men, set off from his camp 11 days later. Four others had already gone ahead on the motorized sledges.

Scott's Final Diary Entry

Things went wrong for Scott from the beginning. The sledges broke down and had to be abandoned. Scott and his men soon met up with the drivers, who were traveling on foot. Blizzards then struck and lasted several weeks into December. Scott's ponies were proving to be a poor choice for Antarctic travel as well. Their hooves sank deep into the snow, and their perspiration froze on their bodies, forming sheets of ice. (Dogs do not perspire; they pant.) On December 9, the men shot the last of the surviving weak and frozen ponies. Two days later Scott sent his remaining dogs back to base camp along with several members of the expedition. Over the next month, most of the men returned to the camp. Scott's plan from here on was for the five men remaining to man-haul supplies the rest of the way to the Pole and back.

For Scott and his men, the journey was long and brutal. To cover only ten miles each day, the team toiled like dogs—like the dogs they no longer had. Food and fuel were in short supply, so the men lacked the energy they needed for such a crushing task.

Roald Amundsen's careful planning and Arctic experience were paying off. Even so, there's no such thing as easy travel by land in Antarctica. To the men who had just crossed those terrible mountains, the Polar Plateau might have looked easy. But Amundsen's team still had to cross a

long stretch they later named the "Devil's Ballroom." It was a thin crust of ice that concealed crevasses, or deep gaps, that could swallow men, sleds, and dogs. Stumbling into one crevasse, a team of dogs dangled by their harnesses until the men could pull them up to safety.

Reaching the Goal

On skis, with the "ballroom" behind them and well-fed dogs pulling their supply sleds, Amundsen and his men swept across the ice. The going was smooth for them, and the weather was fine. The Norwegians' only worry was that they'd find Scott had gotten to the Pole first. On the afternoon of December 14, 1911, it was plain that no one was ahead of them. At three o'clock, Amundsen skied in front of the team's sleds, then stopped to look at his navigation instruments. There was no point further south. He was at the South Pole!

> This paragraph shows that the two teams suffered similar problems.

Reading: Comparison and Contrast

Directions: *Choose the letter of the best answer to each question.*

1. Which statement accurately identifies a similarity in the backgrounds of Amundsen and Scott?

   A They were both Norwegians.

   B They were both naval officers.

   C They were both excellent skiers.

   D They had both taken voyages through the Northwest Passage.

2. Which is a major difference between the men?

   A Amundsen was more experienced at exploring icy settings.

   B Scott was more experienced at exploring icy settings.

   C Amundsen brought sled dogs, but Scott did not.

   D Amundsen brought ponies and sledges, but Scott did not.

3. Which statement accurately describes a difference that had a great effect on the outcome of the race?

   A Amundsen was Norwegian, and Scott was British.

   B By winning the race, Amundsen hoped to gain fame as an explorer, but Scott wanted to write a book.

   C Scott decided his men would carry most of the supplies, but Amundsen decided to use dog sleds.

   D Scott decided that his men would use skis, but Amundsen decided to use motorized sleds.

Reading: Comprehension and Interpretation

Directions: *Write your answers on a separate sheet of paper.*

4. Contrast the strategies used by each team. **[Organizing]**

5. Evaluate the organization of "Race to the End of the Earth." Comment on the balance of details and the effectiveness of support for the comparisons and contrasts. **[Evaluating]**

Timed Writing: Analysis [Connections]

Write an analysis of Amundsen's trip. In your analysis, identify the reasons his team reached the South Pole before Scott's team. Support your reasons with details from the article. **(20 minutes)**

Theme

The **theme** of a story is the central thought, message, or lesson about life that the story conveys. Sometimes the theme is stated directly. Other times, you must figure it out yourself by considering the events in the story, the characters' thoughts and feelings, and the story's title.

To help you figure out a story's theme, ask yourself the following questions:

- What traits are revealed by the characters' actions?
- How do the characters' actions reflect a possible theme?

As you read "Business at Eleven" and "Feathered Friend," look at what the characters say and do, where the story takes place, and which objects seem important. On a chart like the one shown, record details of the characters' traits and actions in order to identify the theme of each story.

Comparing Themes

The writers of the following stories use the characters and events to develop a theme. Both selections feature characters at work. However, they work in very different ways. As you read, notice the message each story conveys about jobs, ambition, and working with others to achieve a goal.

Trait

↓

Action

↓

Result

↓

Theme

Vocabulary Builder

Business at Eleven

- **proposition** (präp´ ə zish´ ən) *n.* an offer (p. 316) *The salesman gave us a proposition: If we bought early, we could save the shipping costs.*

- **satisfactorily** (sat´ is fak´ tə rə lē) *adv.* in a way that fulfills a need or a goal (p. 317) *Our room was comfortable once we rearranged the furniture satisfactorily.*

- **sorting** (sôrt´ iŋ) *v.* arranging materials into groups based on similar traits; classifying (p. 318) *Mom was sorting the coins into piles—nickels, dimes, and quarters.*

- **ambition** (am bish´ ən) *n.* an important goal for the future (p. 319) *Her ambition was to graduate, so Jan studied.*

Feathered Friend

- **regulation** (reg´ yə lā´ shən) *n.* rule (p. 322) *Our school had a regulation against wearing shorts.*

- **fusing** (fyoo´ ziŋ) *n.* joining permanently (p. 323) *The fusing of metal beams requires intense heat.*

- **ceased** (sēst) *v.* stopped (p. 323) *I was late because my watch had ceased to work.*

Build Understanding

Connecting to the Literature

Reading/Writing Connection Whether we enjoy our jobs or not, work is an important factor of life. Jot down a few sentences to explain why people may choose to work hard. Use at least three of the following words: *define, establish, achieve, invest, participate, seek.*

Meet the Authors

Toshio **Mori** (1910–1980)

Toshio Mori was born in Oakland, California, and spent most of his life working in a flower nursery. He wrote many novels and short stories about the lives of ordinary Japanese Americans in California.

Relocated to Utah Mori was one of many Japanese Americans who were kept against their will in camps during World War II. He spent four years in a relocation camp in Topaz, Utah. Because of this internment, his first novel, *Yokahama, California,* was not published until 1949, although it was ready in 1942.

Arthur C. **Clarke** (b. 1917)

Arthur C. Clarke was born in Somerset, England. He became interested in science at an early age and built his first telescope at age thirteen. His first science-fiction story was published in 1946 in the magazine *Astounding Science.*

Television Firsts Clarke became the first television owner on Sri Lanka, the island off India where he lives. He holds another, more important television "first." He was the first to think of sending television and radio signals around the world by bouncing them off satellites.

Go **Online**
Author Link

For: More about the authors
Visit: www.PHSchool.com
Web Code: ele-9212

BUSINESS AT ELEVEN
TOSHIO MORI

When he came to our house one day and knocked on the door and immediately sold me a copy of *The Saturday Evening Post*,[1] it was the beginning of our friendship and also the beginning of our business relationship.

His name is John. I call him Johnny and he is eleven. It is the age when he should be crazy about baseball or football or fishing. But he isn't. Instead he came again to our door and made a business <u>proposition</u>.

"I think you have many old magazines here," he said.

"Yes," I said, "I have magazines of all kinds in the basement."

"Will you let me see them?" he said.

"Sure," I said.

I took him down to the basement where the stacks of magazines stood in the corner. Immediately this little boy went over to the piles and lifted a number of magazines and examined the dates of each number and the names.

---

1. *The Saturday Evening Post* a popular weekly magazine containing nonfiction articles, short stories by famous writers, and cartoons.

▲ **Critical Viewing** Based on his expression and the way he is standing, what kind of personality might this boy have? **[Analyze]**

Vocabulary Builder
proposition (präp´ ə zish´ ən) *n.* an offer

"Do you want to keep these?" he said.

"No. You can have them," I said.

"No. I don't want them for nothing," he said. "How much do you want for them?"

"You can have them for nothing," I said.

"No, I want to buy them," he said. "How much do you want for them?"

This was a boy of eleven, all seriousness and purpose.

"What are you going to do with the old magazines?"

"I am going to sell them to people," he said.

We arranged the financial matters <u>satisfactorily</u>. We agreed he was to pay three cents for each copy he took home. On the first day he took home an *Esquire*, a couple of old *Saturday Evening Posts*, a *Scribner's*, an *Atlantic Monthly*, and a *Collier's*. He said he would be back soon to buy more magazines.

When he came back several days later, I learned his name was John so I began calling him Johnny.

"How did you make out, Johnny?" I said.

"I sold them all," he said. "I made seventy cents altogether."

"Good for you," I said. "How do you manage to get seventy cents for old magazines?"

Johnny said as he made the rounds selling *The Saturday Evening Post*, he also asked the folks if there were any back numbers they particularly wanted. Sometimes, he said, people will pay unbelievable prices for copies they had missed and wanted very much to see some particular articles or pictures, or their favorite writers' stories.

"You are a smart boy." I said.

"Papa says, if I want to be a salesman, be a good salesman," Johnny said. "I'm going to be a good salesman."

"That's the way to talk," I said. "And what does your father do?"

"Dad doesn't do anything. He stays at home," Johnny said.

"Is he sick or something?" I said.

"No, he isn't sick," he said. "He's all right. There's nothing wrong with him."

"How long have you been selling *The Saturday Evening Post*?" I asked.

"Five years," he said. "I began at six."

Vocabulary Builder
satisfactorily (sat′ is fak′ tə rə lē) *adv.* in a way that fulfills a need or a goal

Literary Analysis
Theme What character traits does Johnny demonstrate?

Reading Check

Why are some people willing to pay a lot for back numbers of *The Saturday Evening Post*?

"Your father is lucky to have a smart boy like you for a son," I said.

That day he took home a dozen or so of the old magazines. He said he had five standing orders, an *Esquire* issue of June 1937, *Atlantic Monthly* February 1938 number, a copy of December 11, 1937 issue of *The New Yorker*, *Story Magazine* of February 1934, and a *Collier's* of April 2, 1938. The others, he said, he was taking a chance at.

"I can sell them," Johnny said.

Several days later I saw Johnny again at the door.

"Hello, Johnny," I said. "Did you sell them already?"

"Not all," he said. "I have two left. But I want some more."

"All right," I said. "You must have good business."

"Yes," he said, "I am doing pretty good these days. I broke my own record selling *The Saturday Evening Post* this week."

"How much is that?" I said.

"I sold 167 copies this week," he said. "Most boys feel lucky if they sell seventy-five or one hundred copies. But not for me."

"How many are there in your family, Johnny?" I said.

"Six counting myself," he said. "There is my father, three smaller brothers, and two small sisters."

"Where's your mother?" I said.

"Mother died a year ago," Johnny said.

He stayed in the basement a good one hour <u>sorting</u> out the magazines he wished. I stood by and talked to him as he lifted each copy and inspected it thoroughly. When I asked him if he had made a good sale with the old magazines recently, he said yes. He sold the *Scribner's* Fiftieth Anniversary Issue for sixty cents. Then he said he made several good sales with *Esquire* and a *Vanity Fair* this week.

"You have a smart head, Johnny," I said. "You have found a new way to make money."

Johnny smiled and said nothing. Then he gathered up the fourteen copies he picked out and said he must be going now.

"Johnny," I said, "hereafter you pay two cents a copy. That will be enough."

Johnny looked at me.

"No," he said. "Three cents is all right. You must make a profit, too."

An eleven-year-old boy—I watched him go out with his short business-like stride.

Next day he was back early in the morning. "Back so soon?" I said.

"Yesterday's were all orders," he said. "I want some more today."

"You certainly have a good trade," I said.

"The people know me pretty good. And I know them pretty good," he said. And about ten minutes later he picked out seven copies and said that was all he was taking today.

"I am taking Dad shopping," he said. "I am going to buy a new hat and shoes for him today."

"He must be tickled,"[2] I said.

"You bet he is," Johnny said. "He told me to be sure and come home early."

So he said he was taking these seven copies to the customers who ordered them and then run home to get Dad.

Two days later Johnny wanted some more magazines. He said a Mr. Whitman who lived up a block wanted all the magazines with Theodore Dreiser's stories inside. Then he went on talking about other customers of his. Miss White, the schoolteacher, read Hemingway, and he said she would buy back copies with Hemingway stories anytime he brought them in. Some liked Sinclair Lewis, others Saroyan, Faulkner, Steinbeck, Mann, Faith Baldwin, Fannie Hurst, Thomas Wolfe. So it went. It was amazing how an eleven-year-old boy could remember the customers' preferences and not get mixed up.

One day I asked him what he wanted to do when he grew up. He said he wanted a book shop all his own. He said he would handle old books and old magazines as well as the new ones and own the biggest bookstore around the Bay Region.[3]

"That is a good <u>ambition</u>," I said. "You can do it. Just keep up the good work and hold your customers."

On the same day, in the afternoon, he came around to the house holding several packages.

"This is for you," he said, handing over a package.

2. **tickled** (tik´ əld) *adj.* greatly pleased or delighted.
3. **Bay Region** the area that surrounds San Francisco Bay in the state of California, including such major cities as San Francisco, Oakland, San Jose, and Sausalito.

Literary Analysis
Theme Based on what you have read so far, why do you think Johnny works so hard?

Vocabulary Builder
ambition (am bish´ ən) *n.* an important goal for the future

Reading Check

How many people are in Johnny's family, and who are they?

"What is this?" I said.

Johnny laughed. "Open up and see for yourself," he said.

I opened it. It was a book rest, a simple affair but handy.

"I am giving these to all my customers," Johnny said.

"This is too expensive to give away, Johnny," I said. "You will lose all your profits."

"I picked them up cheap," he said. "I'm giving these away so the customers will remember me."

"That is right, too," I said. "You have good sense."

After that he came in about half a dozen times, each time taking with him ten or twelve copies of various magazines. He said he was doing swell. Also, he said he was now selling *Liberty* along with the *The Saturday Evening Post*s.

Then for two straight weeks I did not see him once. I could not understand this. He had never missed coming to the house in two or three days. Something must be wrong, I thought. He must be sick, I thought.

One day I saw Johnny at the door. "Hello, Johnny," I said. "Where were you? Were you sick?"

"No. I wasn't sick," Johnny said.

"What's the matter? What happened?" I said.

"I'm moving away," Johnny said. "My father is moving to Los Angeles."

"Sit down, Johnny," I said. "Tell me all about it."

THE SATURDAY EVENING POST

Nov. 10, '23

5 cts

Alice Duer Miller—Samuel G. Blythe—John A. Moroso—Charles Brackett
Kenneth L. Roberts—Elsie Singmaster—Isaac F. Marcosson—Hal G. Evarts

©*The Curtis Publishing Company,* Illustrator: Norman Rockwell

▲ Critical Viewing
Why might covers like this one have made people want to read *The Saturday Evening Post*? **[Connect]**

He sat down. He told me what had happened in two weeks. He said his dad went and got married to a woman he, Johnny, did not know. And now, his dad and this woman say they are moving to Los Angeles. And about all there was for him to do was to go along with them.

"I don't know what to say, Johnny," I said.

Johnny said nothing. We sat quietly and watched the time move.

"Too bad you will lose your good trade," I finally said.

"Yes. I know," he said. "But I can sell magazines in Los Angeles."

"Yes, that is true," I said.

Then he said he must be going. I wished him good luck. We shook hands. "I will come and see you again," he said.

"And when I visit Los Angeles some day," I said, "I will see you in the largest bookstore in the city."

Johnny smiled. As he walked away, up the street and out of sight, I saw the last of him walking like a good business-man, walking briskly, energetically, purposefully.

Literary Analysis
Theme What do Johnny's smile and the narrator's description in the last sentence suggest about Johnny? Explain.

Thinking About the Selection

1. **Respond:** Do you think the narrator is a good friend to Johnny? Explain your answer.

2. **(a) Recall:** How do the narrator and Johnny meet?
   (b) Infer: What does the narrator find surprising about Johnny, compared to other eleven-year-old boys he knows?

3. **(a) Recall:** Describe Johnny's business. **(b) Infer:** What do Johnny's business attitudes and skills suggest about his personality?

4. **(a) Recall:** What conditions in the present lead Johnny to work so hard? **(b) Connect:** How might he use what he has learned through this business to reach his goals for a future career? **(c) Speculate:** Do you think Johnny will succeed in the future? Explain.

5. **(a) Assess:** What are some advantages and disadvantages of having a job at age eleven? **(b) Analyze:** Why do you think many countries have passed child labor laws aimed at pre-venting children from working on a full-time basis?

feathered friend

Arthur C. Clarke

To the best of my knowledge, there's never been a
<u>regulation</u> that forbids one to keep pets in a space station.
No one ever thought it was necessary—and even had such
a rule existed, I am quite certain that Sven Olsen would
have ignored it.

With a name like that, you will picture Sven at once as a
six-foot-six Nordic giant, built like a bull and with a voice to
match. Had this been so, his chances of getting a job in
space would have been very slim. Actually he was a wiry
little fellow, like most of the early spacers, and managed to

Vocabulary Builder
regulation (reg´ yə lā´
shən) *n.* rule

Literary Analysis
Theme What
possible theme does
the first paragraph
suggest?

qualify easily for the 150-pound bonus[1] that kept so many of us on a reducing diet.

Sven was one of our best construction men, and excelled at the tricky and specialized work of collecting assorted girders[2] as they floated around in free fall, making them do the slow-motion, three-dimensional ballet that would get them into their right positions, and <u>fusing</u> the pieces together when they were precisely dovetailed into the intended pattern: it was a skilled and difficult job, for a space suit is not the most convenient of garbs in which to work. However, Sven's team had one great advantage over the construction gangs you see putting up skyscrapers down on Earth. They could step back and admire their handiwork without being abruptly parted from it by gravity. . . .

Don't ask me why Sven wanted a pet, or why he chose the one he did. I'm not a psychologist, but I must admit that his selection was very sensible. Claribel weighed practically nothing, her food requirements were tiny—and she was not worried, as most animals would have been, by the absence of gravity.

I first became aware that Claribel was aboard when I was sitting in the little cubbyhole laughingly called my office, checking through my lists of technical stores to decide what items we'd be running out of next. When I heard the musical whistle beside my ear, I assumed that it had come over the station intercom, and waited for an announcement to follow. It didn't; instead, there was a long and involved pattern of melody that made me look up with such a start that I forgot all about the angle beam just behind my head. When the stars had <u>ceased</u> to explode before my eyes, I had my first view of Claribel.

She was a small yellow canary, hanging in the air as motionless as a hummingbird—and with much less effort, for her wings were quietly folded along her sides. We stared at each other for a minute; then, before I had quite recovered my wits, she did a curious kind of backward loop I'm sure no earthbound canary had ever managed, and departed with a few leisurely flicks. It was quite obvious

---

1. 150-pound bonus extra money for being lightweight.
2. girders (gʉr′ dərz) *n.* long, thick pieces of metal.

Vocabulary Builder
fusing (fyo͞o′ ziŋ) *n.*
joining permanently

Vocabulary Builder
ceased (sēst) *v.*
stopped

Reading Check

Where does Sven do his construction work?

that she'd already learned how to operate in the absence of gravity, and did not believe in doing unnecessary work.

Sven didn't confess to her ownership for several days, and by that time it no longer mattered, because Claribel was a general pet. He had smuggled her up on the last ferry from Earth, when he came back from leave— partly, he claimed, out of sheer scientific curiosity. He wanted to see just how a bird would operate when it had no weight but could still use its wings.

Claribel thrived and grew fat. On the whole, we had little trouble concealing our guest when VIP's from Earth came visiting. A space station has more hiding places than you can count; the only problem was that Claribel got rather noisy when she was upset, and we sometimes had to think fast to explain the curious peeps and whistles that came from ventilating shafts and storage bulkheads. There were a couple of narrow escapes—but then who would dream of looking for a canary in a space station?

We were now on twelve-hour watches, which was not as bad as it sounds, since you need little sleep in space. Though of course there is no "day" and "night" when you are floating in permanent sunlight, it was still convenient to stick to the terms. Certainly when I woke that "morning" it felt like 6:00 a.m. on Earth. I had a nagging headache, and vague memories of fitful, disturbed dreams. It took me ages to undo my bunk straps, and I was still only half awake when I joined the remainder of the duty crew in the mess. Breakfast was unusually quiet, and there was one seat vacant.

▲ **Critical Viewing**
Do you think these crew members get along with one another? Explain. **[Infer]**

Literary Analysis
Theme What do the details about Claribel tell people about birds in space?

"Where's Sven?" I asked, not very much caring.

"He's looking for Claribel," someone answered. "Says he can't find her anywhere. She usually wakes him up."

Before I could retort that she usually woke me up, too, Sven came in through the doorway, and we could see at once that something was wrong. He slowly opened his hand, and there lay a tiny bundle of yellow feathers, with two clenched claws sticking pathetically up into the air.

"What happened?" we asked, all equally distressed.

"I don't know," said Sven mournfully. "I just found her like this."

"Let's have a look at her," said Jock Duncan, our cook-doctor-dietitian. We all waited in hushed silence while he held Claribel against his ear in an attempt to detect any heartbeat.

Presently he shook his head. "I can't hear anything, but that doesn't prove she's dead. I've never listened to a canary's heart," he added rather apologetically.

"Give her a shot of oxygen," suggested somebody, point-ing to the green-banded emergency cylinder in its recess beside the door. Everyone agreed that this was an excellent idea, and Claribel was tucked snugly into a face mask that was large enough to serve as a complete oxygen tent for her.

To our delighted surprise, she revived at once. Beaming broadly, Sven removed the mask, and she hopped onto his finger. She gave her series of "Come to the cookhouse, boys" trills—then promptly keeled over again.

"I don't get it," lamented Sven. "What's wrong with her? She's never done this before."

For the last few minutes, something had been tugging at my memory. My mind seemed to be very sluggish that morning, as if I was still unable to cast off the burden of sleep. I felt that I could do with some of that oxygen—but before I could reach the mask, understanding exploded in my brain. I whirled on the duty engineer and said urgently:

"Jim! There's something wrong with the air! That's why Claribel's passed out. I've just remembered that miners used to carry canaries down to warn them of gas."

"Nonsense!" said Jim. "The alarms would have gone off. We've got duplicate circuits, operating independently."

Literary Analysis
Theme What do the words and actions of the crew members reveal about their attitude toward Claribel?

Reading Check

What did the crew members do to wake up Claribel?

"Er—the second alarm circuit isn't connected up yet," his assistant reminded him. That shook Jim; he left without a word, while we stood arguing and passing the oxygen bottle around like a pipe of peace.

He came back ten minutes later with a sheepish expression. It was one of those accidents that couldn't possibly happen; we'd had one of our rare eclipses by Earth's shadow that night; part of the air purifier had frozen up, and the single alarm in the circuit had failed to go off. Half a million dollars' worth of chemical and electronic engineering had let us down completely. Without Claribel, we should soon have been slightly dead.

So now, if you visit any space station, don't be surprised if you hear an inexplicable snatch of birdsong. There's no need to be alarmed; on the contrary, in fact. It will mean that you're being doubly safeguarded, at practically no extra expense.

Literary Analysis
Theme What details here suggest the idea that birds can be useful companions in unsafe situations?

Thinking About the Selection

1. **Respond:** Do you think it was a good idea for Sven to smuggle Claribel into space? Why or why not?

2. **(a) Recall:** Where does the story take place? **(b) Compare and Contrast:** Name two features of life in the story that differ from life on Earth.

3. **(a) Synthesize:** Explain three events or factors that help the narrator figure out that something is wrong with the air. **(b) Make a Judgment:** Who is responsible for saving the crew's lives: Claribel or the narrator? Explain.

4. **(a) Analyze Cause and Effect:** What prevented the alarm from warning the crew about the problem? **(b) Speculate:** What are some potential problems with using a canary instead of an electric alarm? **(c) Evaluate:** Which do you think is the better alarm? Why?

5. **Generalize:** Do you think it would be good for humans to have pets living with them in space stations? Why or why not?

Apply the Skills

Comparing Themes

1. Complete a chart like the one shown to analyze each narrator's change in attitude toward the main character.

Attitude Toward	Beginning	End	Reason
Claribel			
Johnny			

2. What theme about young people and self-direction does "Business at Eleven" convey? Explain.

3. What theme about relying on others does "Feathered Friend" convey? Explain.

Writing to Compare Literary Works

In an essay, compare the theme each story presents about the importance of work. Consider these questions:

- In each story, is the group or the individual more important?
- In what ways does each character depend on others for his success?
- What challenges does each character face?
- How does each character's job affect the way he feels about himself?

In your essay, decide which message more closely matches your feelings about the importance of work.

Vocabulary Builder

Practice For each item, write a single sentence correctly using the words indicated.

1. ambition; business
2. sorting; socks
3. proposition; agree
4. satisfactorily; completed
5. fusing; pieces
6. ceased; action
7. regulation; army

QuickReview

Theme: the central insight or message of a story

Go Online
Assessment
For: Self-test
Visit: www.PHSchool.com
Web Code: ela-6211

Reading

Directions: *Questions 1–6 are based on the following selection.*

In July 2002, nine coal miners became trapped in an underground mine in western Pennsylvania. A mine wall gave way, bringing in millions of gallons of rainwater from an old mine next to it. The water flooded and cornered the men. Rescue workers above ground sent air down to the men through a long pipe. Then they dug an escape hole 245 feet deep to take the miners through. During that time, the miners wrote out their wills and lived off a single sandwich that they shared. Although they were hungry and dehydrated, all nine men survived. However, only one of them was willing to return to working in underground mines.

1. **Based on the first part of the passage why do you think that air was sent down into the mine?**
   A There was too much air in the mine.
   B The miners had little air to breathe.
   C The air would fill the old mine next to it.
   D They had to check to see if the pipe worked.

2. **What conclusion can you draw about the men?**
   A They were wealthy.
   B They wanted to stay together as a group.
   C They wished to make time pass quickly.
   D They thought they might die in the mine.

3. **Why do you think the men shared a single sandwich?**
   A It was the only food they had.
   B They all liked the same food.
   C They weren't very hungry.
   D The men always shared their food.

4. **Based on details in the passage and on your prior knowledge, why do you think only one miner returned to work afterward?**
   A The others found better jobs.
   B The others were afraid to return.
   C The others did not get along well.
   D The ninth miner owned the mine.

5. **Which of these conclusions cannot be drawn from the article?**
   A The rescue took time.
   B Pennsylvania mines are more dangerous than other mines.
   C The water had cut off the usual ways out of the mine.
   D The men were frightened.

6. **What conclusion can you draw about other mining accidents?**
   A Men sometimes die.
   B The rescue is always successful.
   C Water poses the greatest danger.
   D They usually occur in the summer.

Assessment Practice

Vocabulary

Directions: *Choose the word that best completes the sentence.*

7. _____ your conclusion with evidence.
   A Identify
   B Examine
   C Support
   D Refer

8. _____, the singer was sick.
   A Identifiably
   B Conclusively
   C Happily
   D Apparently

9. To formulate a valid conclusion, _____ the details of a story.
   A ignore
   B examine
   C support
   D refer

10. The story has an _____ theme.
    A identifiable
    B apparently
    C supported
    D examined

11. You can _____ that the writer enjoys nature.
    A conclude
    B examine
    C identifiable
    D appeal

12. _____ the students studied well, for they all did very well on the test.
    A Apparently
    B Understandable
    C Regrettably
    D Eventually

13. Despite the numerous steps in this process we will finish _____.
    A apparently
    B understandable
    C regrettable
    D eventually

14. That rock is so heavy it is simply not _____.
    A apparent
    B movable
    C understandably
    D understandable

15. We were _____ playing when she reminded us that there was homework to do.
    A deniably
    B understandable
    C eventually
    D happily

16. The child was nervous in a store filled with so many _____ objects.
    A breakable
    B changeable
    C replaceable
    D reusable

SPELLING

Adding Suffixes

Adding a suffix to a word can change its spelling. Knowing the rules can help you spell words with suffixes correctly.

By day he was a mild-mannered teacher of adjectives, by night he was Adverb Man!

Rules for Adding Suffixes

- Change the *y* to *i* and add the suffix if there is a consonant followed by a *y*. *(happy + ly = happily)*

- Do not change the *y* to *i* before the suffix when the original word ends in *y* and you are adding the suffix *-ing*. *(copy + ing = copying)*

- Double the last letter when the word is one syllable and ends in a consonant. *(sun + y = sunny)*

- Double the last letter if the last syllable is stressed and ends in a single consonant. *(begin + ing = beginning)*

- DO NOT double the last letter if the last syllable is unstressed. *(remember + ed = remembered)*

- Never double the last letter when a word ends in more than one consonant. *(work + able = workable)*

Practice

For each word on the word list, explain which rule is followed when adding the suffix. If a word does not follow any of the rules, explain that it is an exception. Copy the words, organizing them into groups of words that follow the same rule. Add one word to each list to show another example of a word that follows the rule.

Word List
calmly
quietly
traveling
canceling
appealing
admirable
notable
workable
responsibly
typically

Monitor Your Progress

Assessment Practice

Directions: *Write the letter of the word and suffix combination that is spelled correctly.*

1. demonstrate + ing
A demonstrateing
B demonstrating
C demonstratting
D demonstratying

2. direct + ly
A directely
B directtly
C directly
D directily

3. general + ly
A generaly
B generally
C generalily
D generaley

4. cancel + able
A cancelable
B cancellable
C canceliable
D cancelyable

5. cry + ing
A crying
B criing
C cring
D cryeing

Directions: *Write the letter of the word that is spelled correctly.*

6. A joked
B permited
C beged
D stoped

7. A occured
B cried
C judgeing
D happening

8. A abandonnment
B establishment
C developement
D regment

9. A mannly
B likly
C instensely
D friendly

10. A dependeable
B alloweble
C understandeable
D tolerable

Narration: Short Story

Short stories are brief works of fiction meant to entertain, explore ideas, or tell truths about life. They often feature a conflict, or problem, faced by one or more characters. Follow the steps outlined in the workshop to write your own short story.

Assignment Write a short story about a person who faces a difficult challenge.

What to Include Your short story should feature these elements:
- one or more well-drawn characters
- an interesting conflict or problem
- a plot that moves toward the resolution of the conflict
- a clear and accurate point of view, or perspective
- concrete and sensory details that establish the setting
- dialogue, or conversations between characters
- error-free grammar, including the use of consistent verb tenses

To preview the criteria on which your short story may be judged, see the rubric on page 339.

Writing Workshop: *Work in Progress*

If you have completed the Work-in-Progress assignments, you already have a wealth of ideas in your portfolio to use in your short story. You may continue to develop these ideas or explore a new idea as you complete the Writing Workshop.

Using the Form

You may use elements of this form in these types of writing:
- letters
- scripts and screenplays

To get a feel for short stories, read "Stray" by Cynthia Rylant on page 24.

Prewriting

Choosing Your Topic

Use one of these strategies to help choose a topic for your short story:

Freewriting Set a timer and freewrite for five minutes. Start with an image—a person in a boat in the middle of the ocean—or a feeling—curiosity, fear, or loneliness. During freewriting, focus more on the flow of ideas than on spelling or grammar. After five minutes, review your freewriting. Circle ideas to use in your story.

Art and Photo Review Look at several pieces of fine art or photography in your textbooks or other sources. For each, imagine a story based on what the image suggests. Choose one of these ideas as the basis of a story.

Narrowing Your Topic

Once you have a general idea of the story you will tell, get a better idea of its conflict—the struggle between two opposing forces. To identify the conflict, ask yourself these questions:

- What does my main character want?
- Who or what is getting in the way?
- What will the character do to overcome this obstacle?

Work in Progress
Review the work you did on pages 279 and 307.

Gathering Details

Create your main character. Fill in a chart like the one shown to help you get to know your main character.

Title your story.
With a clear idea of your topic and your main character, list possible appropriate titles for your story. Scan your list and choose the title that best captures the heart of what your story will convey.

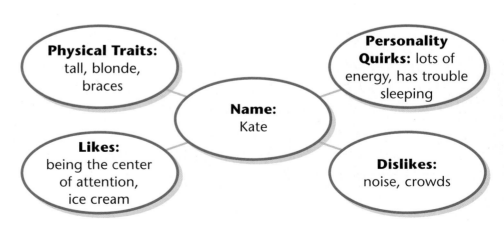

Physical Traits: tall, blonde, braces

Personality Quirks: lots of energy, has trouble sleeping

Name: Kate

Likes: being the center of attention, ice cream

Dislikes: noise, crowds

Writing Workshop

Drafting

Shaping Your Writing

Develop your plot. Use a plot diagram like the one shown to organize the sequence of events in your short story. Plot often follows this pattern:

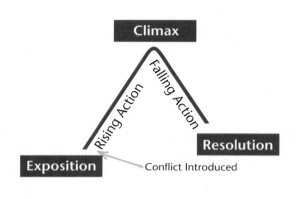

- **Exposition** introduces characters and situation, including the conflict.

- The **conflict** develops during the rising action, which leads to the climax of the story.

- The **climax,** or point of greatest tension, is when the story turns out one way or another.

- In the **falling action,** events and emotions wind down.

- In the **resolution,** the conflict is resolved and loose ends are tied up.

Providing Elaboration

Use sensory details. As you draft your story, make your characters and setting come alive by including sensory details—language that describes how things look, sound, feel, taste, and smell.

Dull: The sky *looked stormy.*
Vivid: The sky *boiled with black clouds and loud thunder.*

Write from a specific point of view. Tell your story from a single point of view, either as a participant—first-person point of view— or an observer—third-person point of view.

To read the complete student model, see page 338.

Student Model: Choose a Point of View

I sat staring blankly at the sheet of notebook paper in front of me.
My teacher had just finished explaining how to divide fractions.
I didn't understand it at all. I hated math, and now in sixth
grade, math was much harder.

> The writer tells the story from the first-person point of view.

From the Author's Desk

Jean Craighead George
on Revising a Story

Jean Craighead
George

My Side of the Mountain is the story of Sam, who leaves a very crowded city home to live off the land and survive in the wilds of the Catskill Mountains, New York. I wrote the book in two weeks. When it was done, I started writing the story all over again. What follows is a look at my changes to the second manuscript. Sam is in his home in a big hemlock tree reading a journal entry from the previous winter. The entry is shown in quotation marks, and "The Baron" is a weasel.

"Live, note all things around you, and write out of love."
—Jean Craighead George

Professional Model:
from *My Side of the Mountain*

"Tomorrow I hope The Baron and I can tunnel out into the sunlight. I wonder if I should dig ~~it~~ ^the snow. But that would mean I would have to put it somewhere, and the only place to put it is in my nice snug tree. Maybe I can pack it^with ^my hands as I go. I've always dug into the snow from the top, never up from under ~~the snow.~~

"The Baron must dig up from under the snow. I wonder where he puts^what he digs ~~the extra.~~ Well, I guess I'll know in the morning."

When I wrote that last winter, I was scared and thought maybe I'd never get out of my tree. I had been scared for two days — ever since^the ~~first that~~ blizzard hit the Catskill Mountains ⊙— ~~but w~~When I came up to the sunlight, which I did by simply poking my head into the soft snow and standing up, I laughed at my dark fears.

In the first version, the book began with Sam telling his Dad goodbye. I thought a flashback to an earlier time, with the journal entry, was much more exciting.

I am Sam now, finding consolation in my wild friend, The Baron Weasel.

I realized that "I wonder where he puts the extra" was not on scene enough for my style of writing so inserted "what he digs." Now I could visualize pawsful of snow and wonder where I would put them if I were Sam.

Writing Workshop

Revising

Revising Your Overall Structure

Create logical connections between events. The first step in revising your story is to make sure that your plot makes sense. Use a bead chart to make sure that events are logically connected.

- Underline each major event in your story.
- Summarize each event in a "bead" on a chart like the one shown. Show the connections between events by writing a word or phrase in the connector string, as shown in the chart.
- Review the chart and add events if most of your connectors say *next*. If you cannot think of a good connection between two events, delete or reshape one of the events.
- Consider using literary devices such as suspense, foreshadowing, or flashback to add variety to your "string" of events.

Troy doesn't hear any response from Leonard. — he starts to worry

Revising Your Paragraphs

Using dialogue to "show" rather than "tell." Bring your story to life with dialogue—words you have written as though the characters have said them. Realistic dialogue can include slang and interrupted speech. Review your draft for places to add dialogue.

Troy starts wondering where Leonard is. — he's curious, annoyed — Troy yells to Leonard to stop searching. — next — Troy goes into woods to look for Leonard.

1   2   3

Peer Review: Have a classmate make suggestions for improving your story with dialogue. Then, consider making revisions.

Reading · Writing Connection

To read the complete student model, see page 338.

Student Model: Using Dialogue

He whipped out a deck of cards. I raised my eyebrows at him.

I couldn't see how a deck of cards could help me with math.

"Do you know how to play Go Fish?" asked Math Mackerel.

"Yes, but how is…" I tried to ask.

"Good, I'll go first." and he began to deal the cards with his fins.

> Adding dialogue here brings the reader into the scene and allows insight into the characters' personalities.

Integrating Grammar Skills

Revising to Maintain Verb Tense

A **verb tense** tells the time—past, present, or future—of an action or a state of being. Using different verb tenses in a story can help explain causes and effects, but it can also lead to errors.

Present tense indicates an action or a condition in the present. It may also indicate an action or a condition that occurs regularly.

> Ian *is helping* his uncle build a deck. Carla *teaches* swimming.

Past tense tells that an action took place in the past.

> The Lanfords *traveled* to Turkey last March.

Future tense tells that an action will take place in the future.

> I *will rearrange* my bedroom furniture this weekend.

Identifying Errors Jumping from one verb tense to another can confuse readers. Look at these examples:

> **Incorrect use of verb tenses:**
> PAST   PRESENT
> As Carlos *waited* outside the gym, he *sees* his friend Raul.

> **Correction:**
> As Carlos *waited* outside the gym, he *saw* his friend Raul.

> **Correct use of different tenses to show sequence of events:**
> PAST   FUTURE
> Because Amy *finished* her report early, she *will attend* the concert.

Fixing Errors Follow these steps to fix errors in verb tenses:

1. **Review your story, noting shifts in verb tenses within a sentence or paragraph.**
2. **Make sure that you have used changes in verb tenses for a good reason.** You may have chosen to show a relationship between ideas or to show the order of events.
3. **Rewrite sentences that contain incorrect shifts in tenses.**

Apply It to Your Editing

Choose two paragraphs in your draft. Circle the verbs in each sentence of the paragraphs and review the vocabulary. If you find any incorrect shifts in verb tenses, fix them using the previously described methods.

Prentice Hall Writing and Grammar Connection: Chapter 22, Section 2

Student Model:
Karina McCorkle
Raleigh, NC

Math Mackerel

I sat staring blankly at the sheet of notebook paper in front of me. My teacher had just finished explaining how to divide fractions. I didn't understand it at all. I hated math, and now in sixth grade, math was much harder.

"I wish someone could help me understand math." I whispered.

Suddenly, a fish appeared out of thin air. I stared at him. He was standing on his tail with a flowing red cape and on his chest, he had a yellow emblem with the red letters "MM."

"W-who are you?" I stammered.

"I am Math Mackerel. I thought I heard someone asking for help with math," the fish stated proudly.

"Oh, that was me," I said.

"I'll see you at recess." Math Mackerel said as he disappeared with a swish of his tail. And a flick of fins.

My teacher called out, "Time to put your math in your notebooks."
I realized I hadn't written down a single problem on my paper.

"Drat!" I thought and put away my paper.

Outside, I sat in a secluded spot behind a bush and waited. Suddenly, Math Mackerel appeared.

"Greetings," said Math Mackerel happily. "I am here to help you with math."

"Are you going to give me all the knowledge I need?" I asked curiously.

"I could do that, but that would be cheating," scoffed Math Mackerel. He whipped out a deck of cards. I raised my eyebrows at him. I couldn't see how a deck of cards could help me with math.

"Do you know how to play Go Fish?" asked Math Mackerel.

"Yes, but how is…" I tried to ask.

"Good, I'll go first." And he began to deal the cards with his fins.
Twenty minutes later, we were still playing a hearty game of Go Fish.

"Got any nines?" I asked peering over my cards.

"Yes, what is one and seven ninths divided by two thirds?" he asked.

"Two and two thirds" I answered.

"Good job!" Math Mackerel said as he slammed his nines on the ground.
Suddenly I heard my teacher's whistle. It was time to go inside.

"I will see you tomorrow," Math Mackerel called as he disappeared.

Math Mackerel and I played Go Fish for three weeks, and I got better and better at math. Then one day, my teacher announced a math test to review what we had learned. Suddenly, all my confidence evaporated. Playing with Math Mackerel was something I could handle easily, but a test was a different matter.

At recess, Math Mackerel was already waiting for me.

"Time to continue yesterday's game," Math Mackerel said happily.

"There is going to be a math test on Friday! You have to be there!" I gasped.

"Just remember Go Fish, and you'll be fine." And he disappeared as his cape swirled around him.

All week, I dreaded Friday. I gulped as the teacher passed out papers. I worked through the problems and found them easy as I thought about Go Fish. My teacher returned the tests on Monday. I picked mine up and saw an A!

The conflict of the story is introduced in the first paragraph of Karina's story.

Karina chooses to write her story from the first-person point of view.

The writer adds dialogue between the two central characters.

The plot moves forward toward the climax.

Karina includes an exciting climax and ends with the resolution.

Editing and Proofreading

Check your paper to correct errors in spelling, punctuation, and grammar.

Focus on Punctuating Dialogue: Pay particular attention to proofreading your story's dialogue. Note these examples of different ways of showing—and punctuating—the words your characters say.

> *"You can have three wishes," the genie said.*
> *Victor announced, "I will not go one step farther!"*
> *"May I have a word with you?" asked Sylvia.*
> *"Everyone is here," noted Trenell, "except Keisha."*

Publishing and Presenting

Consider one of the following ways to share your writing:
Submit your story. Submit your story to your school's literary magazine, a national magazine, an e-zine, or a contest that publishes student writing. Ask your teacher for suggestions.
Give a reading. Get together with a group of classmates and present a literary reading for an audience at your school.

Reflecting on Your Writing

Writer's Journal Jot down your thoughts on writing a short story. Begin by answering these questions:
- What part of the process did you like most? Why?
- The next time you write a story, what do you think you might do differently as a result of this experience?

Rubric for Self-Assessment

To assess your short story, use the following rubric:

Criteria	Rating Scale
	not very · · · very
Focus: How well drawn are the characters?	1 2 3 4 5
Organization: How clearly organized is the story's plot?	1 2 3 4 5
Support/Elaboration: How well do the details and language establish the setting?	1 2 3 4 5
Style: How consistently have you used point of view?	1 2 3 4 5
Conventions: How correct is your grammar, especially your use of verb tenses?	1 2 3 4 5

Evaluating a Persuasive Message

A persuasive message encourages the audience to think or act in a certain way.

Evaluating the Message

Identify the source delivering the message. Think about who is delivering the "information" and their purpose. Facts supplied by the person or group may be slanted to favor a point of view.

Evaluate the content of the message. A fact is something that can be proved or demonstrated. An opinion can be supported but not proved.

Recognize propaganda. When the information is completely one-sided, it is called *propaganda*. Propaganda is the spreading of misleading ideas.

Evaluate the delivery of the message. Persuasive messages can be delivered in a variety of formats— writing, radio, television, film, or billboards. Ask yourself if the words, sounds, and pictures are meant to make you *feel* a certain way or *think* a certain way.

Recognizing Persuasive Techniques

Be aware of persuasive techniques that are used in place of factual information.

- **Emotional appeal** An emotional appeal tries to influence your choice through feelings rather than information.

- **Bandwagon appeal** This technique relies on the idea that people make choices to be part of a crowd.

- **Testimonial** Famous people give their opinion or are shown doing something.

Technique	Example
Bandwagon appeal	Every sixth-grader thinks this, so you should too.
Testimonial	Famous people use this product, so it must be good.
Loaded language (words meant to give a positive or negative slant to a statement)	My opponent is wavering. I am considering the options. . .

Activity ▶ *Prepare and Deliver a Speech* ▶ In a small group, evaluate a television advertisement by answering these questions:

1. Who is presenting the information? **2.** How reliable is the information? **3.** Are emotional pictures and music used? **4.** Are persuasive techniques used? Share your answers with the rest of the class.

The Heart of a Chief

Joseph Bruchac
Puffin Books, 1998
Novel Eleven-year-old Chris Nicola is a member of the Penacook nation. Chris lives on the Penacook Indian Reservation and goes to school in town. At school, things are going well—he has been selected to lead a group project on using Indian names for sports teams. However, at home there is controversy. The Penacook are divided over whether or not to build a casino on a beautiful island Chris thinks of as his own. Readers of this novel will be moved by Chris's pride in his culture and his simple message of respect.

The Secret Garden

Frances Hodgson Burnett
Signet Classics, 1986
Novel Orphaned Mary Lennox is sent to live at her uncle's house on the Yorkshire moors in England. Mary finds the huge house full of secrets. At night, she hears the sound of crying down one of the long corridors. Outside, she meets Dickon, a magical boy who can charm and talk to animals. Then, one day, with the help of a friendly robin, Mary discovers the most mysterious wonder of all—a secret garden, walled and locked, which has been completely forgotten for many years.

My Side of the Mountain

Written and illustrated by Jean Craighead George
Puffin Books, 1988
Novel Sam Gribley is tired of living in a crowded New York City apartment, so, with his parents' permission, he runs away to the Catskill Mountain wilderness to make a life of his own. No one takes his plans seriously—except Sam himself. With only a penknife, a ball of cord, an ax, forty dollars, and some flint and steel, he must rely on his intelligence and the resources of the land to survive. Sam learns about courage, danger, and independence during his year in the wilderness.

Sea Otter Rescue: The Aftermath of an Oil Spill

Roland Smith
Puffin Books, 1999
Nonfiction When the *Exxon Valdez,* an oil tanker, struck the rocks in Prince William Sound, Alaska, nearly 11 million gallons of crude oil spilled into the water. The result was an oil slick, which threatened all of the area wildlife, especially the sea otters. This is the story of the animal rescue experts who went to Alaska to lend a hand. This book is a fascinating first-hand account of the heroic measures taken to save the lives of hundreds of sea otters.

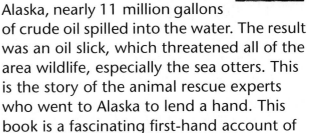

These titles are available in the Penguin/Prentice Hall Literature Library.
Consult your teacher before choosing one.

Think About It Sometimes we are kind to others because we genuinely like them. At other times, we are nice in the hope that we can get something in return. In his novel *Stargirl*, author Jerry Spinelli explores the reasons behind the ways people treat one another. This excerpt from the novel shows the narrator and Stargirl discussing their very different ideas about doing nice things for other people.

from **Stargirl**

Jerry Spinelli

JERRY SPINELLI

Jacket Illustration ©2000 by Alfred A. Knopf

I tagged along on missions. One day she bought a small plant, an African violet in a plastic pot on sale for ninety-nine cents at a drugstore.

"Who's it for?" I asked her.

"I'm not exactly sure," she said. "I just know that someone at an address on Marion Drive is in the hospital for surgery, so I thought whoever's back home could use a little cheering up."

"How do you know this stuff?" I said.

She gave me a mischievous grin. "I have my ways."

We went to the house on Marion Drive. She reached into the saddle pack behind her bicycle seat. She pulled out a handful of ribbons. She chose a pale violet one that matched the color of the tiny blossoms and stuffed the remaining ribbons back into the seat pack. She tied the violet ribbon around the pot. I held her bike while she set the plant by the front door.

Riding away, I said, "Why don't you leave a card or something with your name on it?"

The question surprised her. "Why should I?"

Her question surprised me. "Well, I don't know, it's just the way people do things. They expect it. They get a gift, they expect to know where it came from."

"Is that important?"

"Yeah, I guess—"

I never finished that thought. My tires shuddered as I slammed my bike to a halt. She stopped ahead of me. She backed up. She stared.

"Leo, what is it?"

I wagged my head. I grinned. I pointed to her. "It was you."

"Me what?"

"Two years ago. My birthday. I found a package on my front step. A porcupine necktie. I never found out who gave it to me."

She walked her bike alongside mine. She grinned. "A mystery."

"Where did you find it?" I said.

"I didn't. I had my mother make it."

She didn't seem to want to dwell on the subject. She started pedaling and we continued on our way.

"Where were we?" she said.

"Getting credit," I said.

"What about it?"

"Well, it's nice to get credit."

The spokes of her rear wheel spun behind the curtain of her long skirt. She looked like a photograph from a hundred years ago. She turned her wide eyes on me. "Is it?" she said.

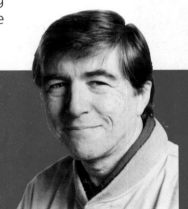

Meet the Author

Jerry Spinelli (b. 1941) writes realistic fiction about teenagers. He regrets not reading much when he was younger. To make up for that fact, Spinelli made the title character of his Newbery award–winning book, *Maniac McGee*, an enthusiastic reader who always has a book in his hand.

Readings in Contemporary Fiction
Talk About It

Use these questions to guide a discussion of this excerpt.

1. What do you see in Stargirl that sets her apart from others?

2. In a group, discuss the following questions:
- Why might someone do a good deed but not take credit?
- If you could help others without their knowing, would you?

Choose a point-person from the group and share your ideas with the class.

Types of Nonfiction
Narrative, Expository, and Reflective

Unit 3 Overview

Introduction
Exploring Types of
Nonfiction

Part 1: Author's Purpose

Part 2: Main Idea

Introduction:
Exploring Types of Nonfiction

Zlata Filipović

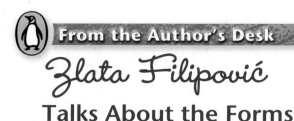

From the Author's Desk

Zlata Filipović

Talks About the Forms

The world we live in is swirling with information and ideas. We are constantly learning new facts and becoming aware of people's thoughts and opinions.

▲ Zlata Filipović (zlä´ tä fē lē pō´ vich) began writing her now-famous diary as an 11-year-old during the Bosnian War.

Articles and Essays

Two common forms for communicating ideas and information are **articles** and **essays.** Both are nonfiction compositions dealing with a particular topic.

Articles, which tend to be shorter, can be found in newspapers, magazines, and encyclopedias. Readers usually go to articles for information and explanations. Essays, especially **personal essays,** are often longer and reflect more of the author's personality than articles do. Readers appreciate them as much for their **literary style,** or way of using words, as for the information they convey.

While I enjoy getting information from articles in newspapers and magazines, I really love getting to know authors through their more personal writings, like essays. I feel privileged to listen to what they want to tell me in their own special style of writing.

◄ **Critical Viewing** Zlata Filipović says that she writes to inform, persuade, provoke, and inspire readers. Which of those purposes does this picture illustrate? **[Connect]**

Passion Is as Important as Research

I have written essays and articles myself. While I know that research and the organization of thoughts and ideas are the basis for such writing, I believe that my passion for what I am trying to convey is the most important ingredient. For me, the special element that makes the writing mine can only be something from deep inside me that I am trying to address and communicate to others.

In writing essays and articles, I feel honored that I can achieve these important **purposes:** informing people, provoking them into thinking, convincing them of something, or inspiring them to support a cause.

The author of the quotation shown here was a teenage girl in hiding from the Nazis during World War II. She truly believed that writing can give one strength at times of deep sorrow and is a way of upholding one's own ideals and of sharing them with the world. I, too, believe these things.

It is really a wonder that I haven't dropped all my ideals, because they seem so absurd and impossible to carry out. Yet I keep them, because in spite of everything, I still believe that people are really good at heart... I think that all will come right... and that peace and tranquillity will return again.

from Anne Frank: The Diary of a Young Girl
— Anne Frank

More About the Author

Zlata **Filipović** (b. 1980)

When asked why she began her diary, **Zlata Filipović** responded, "I wanted to have one place where I could put my memories." These "memories" were a young girl's day-to-day impressions of life in the war-torn city of Sarajevo (sar′ ə yā′ vō). From 1992 to 1996, this city in southeastern Europe was under attack during the civil war in the former Yugoslavia. Filipović has used proceeds from the sale of her book to help victims of this war.

Fast Facts

▶ Zlata called her diary Mimmy after a pet goldfish.
▶ In 1998, she was a featured speaker at an exhibition devoted to Anne Frank in Mostar, a town in Bosnia and Herzegovina.

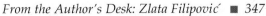

Learning About Types of Nonfiction

Elements of Nonfiction Writing

Nonfiction writing is about real people, places, ideas, and experiences.

Organization Most essays and articles are organized in a way that presents information clearly.

- **Chronological organization** presents details in time order, from first to last—or sometimes from last to first.
- **Cause-and-effect organization** shows the relationship among events.
- **Comparison-and-contrast organization** shows the ways in which two or more subjects are similar and different.

CALVIN AND HOBBS © 1992 Watterson. Reprinted with permission of UNIVERSAL PRESS SYNDICATE. All rights reserved.

The Importance of the Author From background experience to word choice, the way a writer approaches a subject is an important part of nonfiction writing.

- An **author's influences** include the author's heritage, culture, and personal beliefs.
- The **author's style** is the way he or she puts ideas into words. An author's style might be formal, friendly, or humorous.
- Both the author's influences and the author's style can have a strong impact on the **mood,** or overall feeling, created by the essay or article.
- The **author's purpose,** or reason for writing, will help the writer decide what details to include. Common purposes include to entertain, to inform, and to persuade.

Types of Nonfiction Writing

Some examples of nonfiction writing include the following:

Letters, journals, and **diaries** contain personal thoughts and reflections.

Biographies and **autobiographies** tell life stories. A **biography** is the life story of someone written by another person. An **autobiography** is the writer's account of his or her own life.

Media accounts are nonfiction works written for newspapers, magazines, television, or radio.

Essays and **articles** are short nonfiction works that focus on a particular subject. Both may fall into these categories:

- **Historical writing** gives facts, explanations, and insights about historical events.
- **Persuasive writing** is meant to persuade the reader or listener to adopt a particular point of view or take a particular course of action.
- **Descriptive writing** appeals to the five senses.
- **Expository writing** presents facts, discusses ideas, or explains a process.
- **Narrative writing** tells the story of real-life experiences.
- **Visual writing** combines text and images to share information.
- **Reflective writing** addresses an event in the writer's life and provides insight about why the event is important.

▼ **Critical Viewing**
This photograph shows Sarajevo, Zlata Filipović's hometown in Bosnia and Herzegovina. How might this area have changed during the war that overran the city nine years later ? **[Speculate]**

Check Your Understanding

Which organization would you expect each of these works of nonfiction to follow? Explain your answers.
1. an account of a baseball championship
2. an expository essay explaining why the team won
3. an analysis of the winning and losing team.

Back in 1992, when I started writing my **diary,** I was eleven, living a happy and carefree life in my native Sarajevo, looking forward to each day. It never crossed my mind that a war would happen to me and turn everything upside down.

Author's Influences: What Inspired Me to Write

Some of my older girlfriends were keeping a diary, and in an attempt to be "older" and like them, I began writing mine. I had also read the famous diary kept by Anne Frank when she was in hiding from the Nazis. Still another inspiration was the fictional work entitled *The Secret Diary of Adrian Mole,* the charming creation of British author Sue Townsend.

My Diary: A Record of Terrible Events

I thought my diary would be my personal treasure, something to turn back to in years to come and laugh at my innocence and the happy days of my childhood. Unfortunately, brutally and suddenly, war entered my life and my diary took on a new **purpose.** It became a war diary, a record of terrible events happening to my family, my neighbors, my city, and my country.

Eventually, that diary got published and became a record of the siege of Sarajevo and a testament to a child's life under gunfire.

The Diary Itself Is the Audience and "a friend"

But my diary was also more than just a place to record events around me. It was a friend. The paper it was made of was patient, ready, and willing to accept anything and everything I had to say, without judging me. It was a sort of therapy for dealing with everything that was going on.

I also discovered the beauty of writing—when one can pour oneself onto a great white emptiness and fill it with emotions and thoughts and leave them there forever.

Zlata Filipović

Monday, March 30, 1992

Hey, Diary! You know what I think? Since Anne Frank[1] called her diary Kitty, maybe I could give you a name too. What about:

ASFALTINA PIDZAMETA
SEFIKA HIKMETA
SEVALA MIMMY

or something else???
I'm thinking, thinking . . .
I've decided! I'm going to call you
MIMMY
All right, then, let's start.

Dear Mimmy,
It's almost half-term. We're all studying for our tests. Tomorrow we're supposed to go to a classical music concert at the Skenderija Hall. Our teacher says we shouldn't go because there will be 10,000 people, pardon me, children, there, and somebody might take us as hostages or plant a bomb in the concert hall. Mommy says I shouldn't go. So I won't.

Hey! You know who won the Yugovision Song Contest?! EXTRA NENA!!!???

---

1. Anne Frank In 1942, 13-year-old Anne Frank began a diary that she kept for the two years that she and her family and some others hid from the Nazis in an attic in Amsterdam. Anne died in a concentration camp in 1945. Her father published parts of the diary in 1947, and it has since become a classic.

▲ **Critical Viewing**
What does this picture of Zlata sitting in rubble tell you about her daily life? **[Generalize]**

Zlata Filipović
Author's Insight
I wanted to give my diary a name so I could imagine a friend I could tell everything to.

✓ **Reading Check**

Why does Zlata's teacher advise against going to the concert?

I'm afraid to say this next thing. Melica says she heard at the hairdresser's that on Saturday, April 4, 1992, there's going to be BOOM—BOOM, BANG—BANG, CRASH Sarajevo. Translation: they're going to bomb Sarajevo.

Love,
Zlata

Sunday, April 12, 1992

Dear Mimmy,
The new sections of town—Dobrinja, Mojmilo, Vojnicko polje—are being badly shelled. Everything is being destroyed, burned, the people are in shelters. Here in the middle of town, where we live, it's different. It's quiet. People go out. It was a nice warm spring day today. We went out too. Vaso Miskin Street was full of people, children. It looked like a peace march. People came out to be together, they don't want war. They want to live and enjoy themselves the way they used to. That's only natural, isn't it? Who likes or wants war, when it's the worst thing in the world?

I keep thinking about the march I joined today. It's bigger and stronger than war. That's why it will win. The people must be the ones to win, not the war, because war has nothing to do with humanity. War is something inhuman.

Zlata

▲ **Critical Viewing**
What does her expression reveal about how Zlata feels about the soldier? **[Interpret]**

Tuesday, April 14, 1992

Dear Mimmy,
People are leaving Sarajevo. The airport, train and bus stations are packed. I saw sad pictures on TV of people parting. Families, friends separating. Some are leaving, others staying. It's so sad. Why? These people and children aren't guilty of anything. Keka and Braco[2] came early this morning. They're in the kitchen with Mommy and Daddy, whispering.

---

2. Keka and Braco nicknames of a husband and wife who are friends of Zlata's parents.

Keka and Mommy are crying. I don't think they know what to do—whether to stay or to go. Neither way is good.

Zlata

Saturday, May 2, 1992

Dear Mimmy,

Today was truly, absolutely the worst day ever in Sarajevo. The shooting started around noon. Mommy and I moved into the hall. Daddy was in his office, under our apartment, at the time. We told him on the intercom to run quickly to the downstairs lobby where we'd meet him. We brought Cicko[3] with us. The gunfire was getting worse, and we couldn't get over the wall to the Bobars',[4] so we ran down to our own cellar.

The cellar is ugly, dark, smelly. Mommy, who's terrified of mice, had two fears to cope with. The three of us were in the same corner as the other day. We listened to the pounding shells, the shooting, the thundering noise overhead. We even heard planes. At one moment I realized that this awful cellar was the only place that could save our lives. Suddenly, it started to look almost warm and nice. It was the only way we could defend ourselves against all this terrible shooting. We heard glass shattering in our street. Horrible. I put my fingers in my ears to block out the terrible sounds. I was worried about Cicko. We had left him behind in the lobby. Would he catch cold there? Would something hit him? I was terribly hungry and thirsty. We had left our half-cooked lunch in the kitchen.

When the shooting died down a bit, Daddy ran over to our apartment and brought us back some sandwiches. He said he could smell something burning and that the phones weren't working. He brought our TV set down to the cellar. That's when we learned that the main post office (near us) was on fire and that they had kidnapped our President. At around 8:00 we went back up to our apartment. Almost every window in our street was broken. Ours were all right, thank God. I saw the post office in flames. A terrible sight.

---

3. **Cicko** (chēk′ ō) Zlata's canary.
4. **Bobars'** (Bō′ bërs) next-door neighbors.

Zlata Filipović
Author's Insight
It is difficult to determine when exactly the war began. Here, I am writing about that strange in-between period and how the war was slowly creeping into our town and into our lives.

Diaries
Personal Reflections
In these paragraphs, Zlata gives the reader a realistic sense of how close the war is coming to her home.

Reading Check

Which of their actions show that Zlata and her family are afraid?

The fire-fighters battled with the raging fire. Daddy took a few photos of the post office being devoured by the flames. He said they wouldn't come out because I had been fiddling with something on the camera. I was sorry. The whole apartment smelled of the burning fire. God, and I used to pass by there every day. It had just been done up. It was huge and beautiful, and now it was being swallowed up by the flames. It was disappearing. That's what this neighborhood of mine looks like, my Mimmy. I wonder what it's like in other parts of town? I heard on the radio that it was awful around the Eternal Flame.[5] The place is knee-deep in glass. We're worried about Grandma and Granddad. They live there. Tomorrow, if we can go out, we'll see how they are. A terrible day. This has been the worst, most awful day in my eleven-year-old life. I hope it will be the only one. Mommy and Daddy are very edgy. I have to go to bed.

Ciao![6]
Zlata

Diaries
Mood The frightening details in this entry clearly show why Zlata declares May 2, 1992, the most awful day of her 11 years.

Tuesday, May, 5, 1992

Dear Mimmy,
The shooting seems to be dying down. I guess they've caused enough misery, although I don't know why. It has something to do with politics. I just hope the "kids" come to some agreement. Oh, if only they would, so we could live and breathe as human beings again. The things that have happened here these past few days are terrible. I want it to stop forever. PEACE! PEACE!

I didn't tell you, Mimmy, that we've rearranged things in the apartment. My room and Mommy and Daddy's are too dangerous to be in. They face the hills, which is where they're shooting from. If only you knew how scared I am to go near the windows and into those rooms. So, we turned a safe corner of the sitting room into a "bedroom." We sleep on mattresses on the floor. It's strange and awful. But, it's safer that way. We've turned everything around for safety. We put Cicko in the kitchen. He's safe there, although once the

Zlata Filipović
Author's Insight
For safety, we moved everything in our apartment. I write about it as a mark of the adaptability of a family that wants to survive. It is also a sign of our acceptance of anything.

---

5. Eternal Flame Sarajevo landmark that honors those who died resisting the Nazi occupation during World War II.
6. Ciao! (chou) *interj.* hello or goodbye.

shooting starts there's nowhere safe except the cellar. I suppose all this will stop and we'll all go back to our usual places.

Ciao!
Zlata

▲ **Critical Viewing**
Though Zlata and her father seem to be able to get their errands done, what does this picture say about the safety of the streets?
[Connect]

Thursday, May 7, 1992

Dear Mimmy,
I was almost positive the war would stop, but today . . . Today a shell fell on the park in front of my house, the park where I used to play and sit with my girlfriends. A lot of people were hurt. From what I hear Jaca, Jaca's mother, Selma, Nina, our neighbor Dado and who knows how many other people who happened to be there were wounded. Dado, Jaca and her mother have come home from the hospital, Selma lost a kidney but I don't know how she is, because she's still in the hospital. AND NINA IS DEAD. A piece of shrapnel lodged in her brain and she died. She was such a sweet, nice little girl. We went to kindergarten together, and we used to play together in the park. Is it possible I'll never see Nina again? Nina, an innocent eleven-year-old little girl—the victim of a stupid war. I feel sad. I cry and wonder why? She didn't do anything. A disgusting war has destroyed a young child's life. Nina, I'll always remember you as a wonderful little girl.

Love, Mimmy,
Zlata

✓ **Reading Check**

What two important events has Zlata endured?

Monday, June 29, 1992

Dear Mimmy,
BOREDOM!!! SHOOTING!!! SHELLING!!! PEOPLE BEING KILLED!!! DESPAIR!!! HUNGER!!! MISERY!!! FEAR!!!

    That's my life! The life of an innocent eleven-year-old schoolgirl!! A schoolgirl without a school, without the fun and excitement of school. A child without games, without friends, without the sun, without birds, without nature, without fruit, without chocolate or sweets, with just a little powdered milk. In short, a child without a childhood. A wartime child. I now realize that I am really living through a war, I am witnessing an ugly, disgusting war. I and thousands of other children in this town that is being destroyed, that is crying, weeping, seeking help, but getting none. God, will this ever stop, will I ever be a schoolgirl again, will I ever enjoy my childhood again? I once heard that childhood is the most wonderful time of your life. And it is. I loved it, and now an ugly war is taking it all away from me. Why? I feel sad. I feel like crying. I am crying.

Your Zlata

Thursday, October 29, 1992

Dear Mimmy,
Mommy and Auntie Ivanka (from her office) have received grants to specialize in Holland. They have letters of guarantee,[7] and there's even one for me. But Mommy can't decide. If she accepts, she leaves behind Daddy, her parents, her brother. I think it's a hard decision to make. One minute I think—no, I'm against it. But then I remember the war, winter, hunger, my stolen childhood and I feel like going. Then I think of Daddy, Grandma and Granddad, and I don't want to go. It's hard to know what to do. I'm really on edge, Mimmy, I can't write anymore.

Your Zlata

---

7. letters of guarantee letters from people or companies promising to help individuals who wanted to leave the country during the war.

Zlata Filipović
Author's Insight
I thought about the details of my life and I was very angry so I wrote this in capital letters.

Zlata Filipović
Author's Insight
The loss of my innocence and childhood is something that I came to realize very early on. I wanted so desperately to be a child, but circumstances were not allowing me to be one. I was very sad.

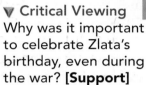
Monday, November 2, 1992

Dear Mimmy,
Mommy thought it over, talked to Daddy, Grandma and Granddad, and to me, and she's decided to go. The reason for her decision is—ME. What's happening in Sarajevo is already too much for me, and the coming winter will make it even harder. All right. But . . . well, I suppose it's better for me to go. I really can't stand it here anymore. I talked to Auntie Ivanka today and she told me that this war is hardest on the children, and that the children should be got out of the city. Daddy will manage, maybe he'll even get to come with us.

                                            Ciao!
                                            Zlata

▼ **Critical Viewing**
Why was it important to celebrate Zlata's birthday, even during the war? [**Support**]

Thursday, December 3, 1992

Dear Mimmy,
Today is my birthday. My first wartime birthday. Twelve years old. Congratulations. Happy birthday to me!

The day started off with kisses and congratulations. First Mommy and Daddy, then everyone else. Mommy and Daddy gave me three Chinese vanity cases—with flowers on them!

As usual there was no electricity. Auntie Melica came with her family (Kenan, Naida, Nihad) and gave me a book. And Braco Lajtner came, of course. The whole neighborhood got together in the evening. I got chocolate, vitamins, a heart-shaped soap (small, orange), a key chain with a picture of Maja and Bojana, a pendant made of a stone from Cyprus, a ring (silver) and earrings (bingo!).

The table was nicely laid, with little rolls, fish and rice salad, cream cheese (with Feta), canned corned beef, a pie, and, of course—a birthday cake. Not how it used to be, but there's a war on. Luckily there was no shooting, so we could celebrate.

✓ **Reading Check**

What major decision has Zlata's mother made?

It was nice, but something was missing. It's called peace!

Your Zlata

Tuesday, July 27, 1993

Dear Mimmy,

Journalists, reporters, TV and radio crews from all over the world (even Japan). They're interested in you, Mimmy, and ask me about you, but also about me. It's exciting. Nice. Unusual for a wartime child.

My days have changed a little. They're more interesting now. It takes my mind off things. When I go to bed at night I think about the day behind me. Nice, as though it weren't wartime, and with such thoughts I happily fall asleep.

But in the morning, when the wheels of the water carts wake me up, I realize that there's a war on, that mine is a wartime life. SHOOTING, NO ELECTRICITY, NO WATER, NO GAS, NO FOOD. Almost no life.

Zlata

Diaries

Chronological Organization Nearly seven months have passed. In the July 27 entry, Zlata has become less anxious, though the war is still an uncomfortable reality.

▼ **Critical Viewing** Although there is no electricity and Zlata must read by candlelight, what can you tell about her mood? **[Infer]**

Thursday, October 7, 1993

Dear Mimmy,

Things are the way they used to be, lately. There's no shooting (thank God), I go to school, read, play the piano . . .

Winter is approaching, but we have nothing to heat with.

I look at the calendar and it seems as though this year of 1993 will again be marked by war. God, we've lost two years listening to gunfire, battling with electricity, water, food, and waiting for peace.

I look at Mommy and Daddy. In two years they've aged ten. And me? I haven't aged, but I've grown, although I honestly don't know how. I don't eat fruit or vegetables, I don't drink juices, I don't eat meat . . . I am a child of rice, peas and spaghetti. There I am talking about food again. I often catch myself dreaming about chicken, a good cutlet, pizza, lasagna . . . Oh, enough of that.

Zlata

Diaries
Author's Style
Zlata weaves together her immediate desire for food and her observation of how her parents have aged. This combination in the text shows that she can be both childlike and mature.

Tuesday, October 12, 1993

Dear Mimmy,

I don't remember whether I told you that last summer I sent a letter through school to a pen-pal in America. It was a letter for an American girl or boy.

Today I got an answer. A boy wrote to me. His name is Brandon, he's twelve like me, and lives in Harrisburg, Pennsylvania. It really made me happy.

I don't know who invented the mail and letters, but thank you whoever you are. I now have a friend in America, and Brandon has a friend in Sarajevo. This is my first letter from across the Atlantic. And in it is a reply envelope, and a lovely pencil.

A Canadian TV crew and journalist from *The Sunday Times* (Janine) came to our gym class today. They brought me two chocolate bars. What a treat. It's been a long time since I've had sweets.

Love,
Zlata

Reading Check

What are some of the things that have cheered Zlata?

Dear Mimmy,

PARIS. There's electricity, there's water, there's gas. There's, there's . . . life, Mimmy. Yes, life; bright lights, traffic, people, food . . . Don't think I've gone nuts, Mimmy. Hey, listen to me, Paris!? No, I'm not crazy, I'm not kidding, it really is Paris and (can you believe it?) me in it. Me, my Mommy and my Daddy. At last. You're 100% sure I'm crazy, but I'm serious, I'm telling you, dear Mimmy, that I have arrived in Paris. I've come to be with you. You're mine again now and together we're moving into the light. The darkness has played out its part. The darkness is behind us; now we're bathed in light lit by good people. Remember that—good people. Bulb by bulb, not candles, but bulb by bulb, and me bathing in the lights of Paris. Yes, Paris. Incredible. You don't understand. You know, I don't think I understand either. I feel as though I must be crazy, dreaming, as though it's a fairy tale, but it's all TRUE.

Diaries
Mood This section of the diary is upbeat, as Zlata and her family find safety.

▼ **Critical Viewing**
What details in the December 1993 entry show why Zlata is happy to be in Paris? **[Connect]**

Q. Did you write in your diary every day?

A. No, I wrote whenever I felt like writing. I was not really a strict diary-keeper, more someone who did it for pleasure.

Q. How did your diary become so well known?

A. My diary was first published by a French humanitarian organization in Bosnia during the war. Since there were many journalists in Bosnia at the time, they wrote about me and that is how the rest of the world came to know about me and my writing! What followed were offers from publishers around the world, and finally my parents and I decided on a publisher in France who then promoted it in many countries.

Q. Do you still keep a diary or journal?

A. After my diary was first published, I stopped writing for a while—I guess I needed a break. But some years on, I was worried or sad about something and I knew that the best thing I could do was to keep a diary again, pouring my thoughts and worries onto the page. And this is still the case!

StudentCorner

Q. Is there a specific message you want your readers to get from your diary?

—**Mackenna Geary, Hobart, Indiana**

A. I hope that in reading my diary people will be able to understand at least a little of what it is like for a child to grow up during a war. Then maybe no children in the future will have to live that fate.

 Writing Workshop: *Work in Progress*

How-to Essay

For a how-to essay you may write, list tasks that you know how to do. Consider sports, crafts, and other skills that you know well. Give yourself four minutes to make this list. Save this Task Sheet in your writing portfolio.

Apply the Skills

Nonfiction

Thinking About the Selection

1. **Respond:** Which details recorded in Zlata Filipović's diary did you find most interesting? Explain.

2. **(a) Recall:** What hardships did Zlata and her family endure during the war? **(b) Infer:** How did these hardships change Zlata's life? **(c) Analyze Cause and Effect:** Why did Zlata have mixed feelings about leaving Sarajevo?

3. **(a) Analyze:** What do you learn about Zlata's interests through the diary? **(b) Generalize:** How would you describe her personality? **(c) Infer:** Does Mimmy have the same personality as Zlata? Support your answer.

Nonfiction Review

4. **(a)** Using a chart like the one shown, find examples of **nonfiction** writing in the diary. **(b)** Share your responses with a partner to see if there are similarities and differences in your choices. **(c)** Did your partner's responses change your ideas? Explain.

Examples of Nonfiction Writing

Narration	
Description	

QuickReview

Selection at a Glance
A girl keeps a diary about her wartime experiences in Sarajevo.

Go Online
Assessment

For: Self-Test
Visit: www.PHSchool.com
Web Code: ela-6301

Nonfiction: writing about real people, places, ideas, and experiences. It can be developed through *narration, description, exposition, persuasion, or reflection.*

Research the Author

Develop a short **biographical sketch** of Zlata Filipović after her arrival in Paris in 1993. Using what you learned in "More About the Author," and from library resources, write a profile of the author. Include answers to the questions below.
- What is Zlata's life like in her new home?
- What projects has Zlata supported while in exile?
- How can you communicate directly with Zlata?

Share your findings with classmates.

Unit 3
Part 1

Author's Purpose

Reading: Author's Purpose

> An **author's purpose** is the main reason the author writes a work.

Skills and Strategies You Will Learn in Part 1

In Part 1, you will learn to

- **recognize details** that indicate an **author's purpose** (p. 366)
- **ask questions** to help you determine the **author's purpose** (p. 386)
- **evaluate evidence** that an author has used to **determine the author's purpose** (p. 402)

Using the Skills and Strategies in Part 1

In Part 1, you will learn to determine an author's purpose that is, to recognize the author's main reason for writing. You will practice using details in the text as clues to the author's purpose. In addition, you will ask questions that lead you to recognize and think about the author's reasons for writing. Finally, you will apply what you have learned to make judgments about the support an author provides to achieve his or her purpose.

The table shown lists some reasons, or purposes, that many authors write.

To Entertain	To Inform	To Persuade
I tried "sit." I tried "stay." Fido paused his destructive rampage only long enough to bark at me. I think he was busy saying "Not now, I'm busy making trouble."	Say the word "sit" in a firm voice. Hold the leash in your left hand to prevent your dog from running.	An untrained dog is an unhappy dog. Training your dog to obey simple commands like "sit" and "stay" will make both you and your dog calmer.

Academic Vocabulary: Words for Discussing Author's Purpose

The following words will help you write and talk about the author's purpose.

Word	Definition	Sample Sentence
achievement *n.*	result of achieving or accomplishing	She won an award for her *achievement.*
intent *n.*	purpose, objective, or aim	My *intent* was to finish my homework early.
direction *n.*	act of directing or supervising	The *directions* were exact.
influence *n.*	power to affect others	That book *influenced* many people.
strategy *n.*	a plan for a specific outcome	The author's *strategy* was to make the reader laugh.

Vocabulary Skill: Suffixes

▶ **Suffixes** A **suffix** is a letter or group of letters added to the end of a word to form a new word.

In Part 1, you will learn suffixes that form nouns.
- the suffix *-ment* (p. 384)
- the suffix *-tion* (p. 400)

achieve	verb "succeed"
+ ment	forms nouns
achievement	**noun** meaning "result of success"

participate	verb "take part"
+ tion	forms nouns
participation	**noun** meaning "act of taking part"

Activity For each pair, look up the first word in the dictionary. Then, explain how the suffix changes the meaning.

1. accomplish—accomplishment

2. intent—intention

3. enjoy—enjoyment

These skills will help you become a better reader. Practice them with either "Hard as Nails" (p. 368) or "Water" (p. 379).

Reading Skill

An **author's purpose** is the main reason the author writes a work. An author can have more than one purpose. For example, in an article about trees, the author's purposes may be to inform readers about fir trees and to persuade readers that fir trees should be protected.

 Learn to recognize details that indicate the author's purpose.
- Facts and statistics are used to inform or persuade.
- Stories about experiences are used to entertain.
- Opinions and thoughts are used to reflect on an experience.

 Use a chart like the one shown to help you determine an author's purpose.

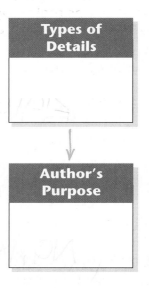

Literary Analysis

In a **narrative essay,** the author tells the true story of real events that happened to real people. An **autobiographical narrative** tells about an event or a time in the author's own life. The author may therefore include his or her own thoughts, feelings, and reactions.

 Authors also include specific details to achieve a purpose. For example, authors may share lessons they have learned from mistakes they have made.

Vocabulary Builder

Hard as Nails

- **embedded** (em bed´ əd) *adj.* firmly fixed in surrounding material (p. 369) *The builders embedded special stones in the cement.*

- **exhaust** (eg zôst´) *v.* use up (p. 370) *Running far will exhaust my energy.*

- **immense** (i mens´) *adj.* huge (p. 375) *Teaching fifty dancers was an immense job.*

Water

- **imitate** (im´ i tāt´) *v.* copy; mimic (p. 379) *We whistle to imitate the sounds of birds.*

- **persisted** (pər sist´ id) *v.* refused to give up (p. 380) *The child persisted in whining.*

- **sentiment** (sen´ tə mənt) *n.* a gentle feeling (p. 380) *My mother's warm smile carries the sentiment of love.*

Build Understanding • *Hard as Nails*

Background

Newspaper Boys Like the writer of "Hard as Nails," newspaper delivery boys working in cities in the 1930s had routes that covered many blocks. At that time, a daily newspaper cost only a few cents. Paperboys might make a dime a week for each subscriber and a penny for each paper they sold on the street.

Connecting to the Literature

Reading/Writing Connection In "Hard as Nails," Russell Baker learns that having a job requires responsibility. List ways people learn about being responsible or show that they are responsible. Use at least three of the following words: *undertake, maintain, participate, contribute.*

Meet the Author

Russell **Baker** (b. 1925)

Russell Baker was born in rural Virginia in 1925. After the death of his father in 1931, Baker's mother moved the family to New Jersey. Six years later, Baker and his family settled in Baltimore, Maryland, where he became a newspaper delivery boy. From then on, Baker worked mainly in the newspaper business. He became a reporter and then a columnist at *The New York Times,* a widely respected newspaper.

Career Goals Baker was determined to become a writer as far back as the seventh grade, when he decided that "making up stories must surely be almost as fun as reading them." His essay "Hard as Nails" comes from his book *Growing Up,* which has been called "a wondrous book, funny, sad, and strong." Baker won a Pulitzer Prize both for his newspaper "Observer" column in the *Times* and for *Growing Up.*

Go **Online**
Author Link

For: More about the author
Visit: www.PHSchool.com
Web Code: ele-9302

Hard as Nails

Russell Baker

My mother started me in newspaper work in 1937 right after my twelfth birthday. She would have started me younger, but there was a law against working before age twelve. She thought it was a silly law, and said so to Deems.

Deems was boss of a group of boys who worked home delivery routes for the *Baltimore News-Post*. She found out about him a few weeks after we got to Baltimore. She just went out on the street, stopped a paperboy, and asked how he'd got his job.

▼ **Critical Viewing** What details show that the newspaper reporters in this photograph lived and worked in earlier times? Explain. **[Analyze]**

"There's this man Deems . . ."

Deems was short and plump and had curly brown hair. He owned a car and a light gray suit and always wore a necktie and white shirt. A real businessman, I thought the first time I saw him. My mother was talking to him on the sidewalk in front of the Union Square Methodist Church and I was standing as tall as I could, just out of earshot.

"Now, Buddy, when we get down there keep your shoulders back and stand up real straight," she had cautioned me after making sure my necktie was all right and my shirt clean.

Watching the two of them in conversation, with Deems glancing at me now and then, I kept my shoulders drawn back in the painful military style I'd seen in movies, trying to look a foot taller than I really was.

"Come over here, Russ, and meet Mister Deems," she finally said, and I did, managing to answer his greeting by saying, "The pleasure's all mine," which I'd heard people say in the movies. I probably blushed while saying it, because meeting strangers was painfully embarrassing to me.

"If that's the rule, it's the rule," my mother was telling Deems, "and we'll just have to put up with it, but it still doesn't make any sense to me."

As we walked back to the house she said I couldn't have a paper route until I was twelve. And all because of some foolish rule they had down here in Baltimore. You'd think if a boy wanted to work they would encourage him instead of making him stay idle so long that laziness got <u>embedded</u> in his bones.

That was April. We had barely finished the birthday cake in August before Deems came by the apartment and gave me the tools of the newspaper trade: an account book for keeping track of the customers' bills and a long, brown web belt. Slung around one shoulder and across the chest, the belt made it easy to balance fifteen or twenty pounds of papers against the hip. I had to buy my own wire cutters for opening the newspaper bundles the trucks dropped at Wisengoff's store on the corner of Stricker and West Lombard streets.

In February my mother had moved us down from New Jersey, where we had been living with her brother Allen

Literary Analysis
Narrative Essay What details so far indicate that this is a narrative essay? Explain.

Vocabulary Builder
embedded (em bed´ əd) *adj.* firmly fixed in surrounding material

Reading Check

Why is Russ's mother so concerned about how Russ looks and stands?

ever since my father died in 1930. This move of hers to Baltimore was a step toward fulfilling a dream. More than almost anything else in the world, she wanted "a home of our own." I'd heard her talk of that "home of our own" all through those endless Depression years when we lived as poor relatives dependent on Uncle Allen's goodness. "A home of our own. One of these days, Buddy, we'll have a home of our own."

That winter she had finally saved just enough to make her move, and she came to Baltimore. There were several reasons for Baltimore. For one, there were people she knew in Baltimore, people she could go to if things got desperate. And desperation was possible, because the moving would <u>exhaust</u> her savings, and the apartment rent was twenty-four dollars a month. She would have to find a job quickly. My sister Doris was only nine, but I was old enough for an after-school job that could bring home a few dollars a week. So as soon as it was legal I went into newspaper work.

Vocabulary Builder
exhaust (eg zôst´) *v.*
use up

The romance of it was almost unbearable on my first day as I trudged west along Lombard Street, then south along Gilmor, and east down Pratt Street with the bundle of newspapers strapped to my hip. I imagined people pausing to admire me as I performed this important work, spreading the news of the world, the city, and the racetracks onto doorsteps, through mail slots, and under door jambs. I had often gazed with envy at paperboys; to be one of them at last was happiness sublime.

Reading Skill
Author's Purpose
Based on the details in this paragraph, what do you think is Baker's purpose for writing this essay? Explain.

Very soon, though, I discovered drawbacks. The worst of these was Deems. Though I had only forty customers, Deems sent papers for forty-five. Since I was billed for every paper left on Wisengoff's corner, I had to pay for the five extra copies out of income or try to hustle them on the street. I hated standing at streetcar stops yelling, "Paper! Paper!" at people getting off trolleys.[1] Usually, if my mother wasn't around to catch me, I stuck the extras in a dark closet and took the loss.

Deems was constantly baiting new traps to dump more papers on me. When I solved the problem of the five extras by getting five new subscribers for home delivery, Deems

---

1. trolleys (träl´ ēz) *n.* electric passenger trains, also called streetcars, running on rails in the city streets. These were discontinued in most American cities in the mid-1930s.

announced a competition with mouth-watering prizes for the newsboys who got the most new subscribers. Too innocent to cope with this sly master of private enterprise,[2] I took the bait.

"Look at these prizes I can get for signing up new customers," I told my mother. "A balloon-tire bicycle. A free pass to the movies for a whole year."

The temptation was too much. I reported my five new subscribers to help me in the competition.

Whereupon Deems promptly raised my order from forty-five to fifty papers, leaving me again with the choice of hustling to unload the five extras or losing money.

I won a free pass to the movies, though. It was good for a whole year. And to the magnificent Loew's Century located downtown on Lexington Street. The passes were good only for nights in the middle of the week when I usually had too

---

2. **private enterprise** *n.* business run for profit.

▲ **Critical Viewing**
Why might it be hard to concentrate in a newspaper office like this one? **[Infer]**

✓ **Reading Check**
Why does Baker say that Deems was the worst drawback to being a paperboy?

much homework to allow for movies. Still, in the summer with school out, it was thrilling to go all the way downtown at night to sit in the Century's damask[3] and velvet splendor and see MGM's glamorous stars in their latest movies.

To collect my prize I had to go to a banquet the paper gave for its "honor carriers" at the Emerson Hotel. There were fifty of us, and I was sure the other forty-nine would all turn out to be slicksters wised up to the ways of the world, who would laugh at my doltish ignorance of how to eat at a great hotel banquet. My fear of looking foolish at the banquet made me lie awake nights dreading it and imagining all the humiliating mistakes I could make.

I had seen banquets in movies. Every plate was surrounded by a baffling array of knives, forks, and spoons. I knew it would be the same at the Emerson Hotel. The Emerson was one of the swankiest hotels in Baltimore. It was not likely to hold down on the silverware. I talked to my mother.

"How will I know what to eat what with?"

The question did not interest her.

"Just watch what everybody else does, and enjoy yourself," she said.

I came back to the problem again and again.

"Do you use the same spoon for your coffee as you do for dessert?"

"Don't worry about it. Everybody isn't going to be staring at you."

"Is it all right to butter your bread with the same knife you use to cut the meat?"

"Just go and have a good time."

Close to panic, I showed up at the Emerson, found my way to the banquet, and was horrified to find that I had to sit beside Deems throughout the meal. We probably talked about something, but I was so busy sweating with terror and rolling my eyeballs sidewise to see what silverware Deems was using to eat with that I didn't hear a word all night. The following week, Deems started sending me another five extras.

Reading Skill
Author's Purpose
Why might Baker have included these details about his feelings before going to the banquet?

Literary Analysis
Narrative Essay What real event from the author's life is described here?

---

3. damask (dam´ əsk) *adj.* made of damask, a shiny cloth often used for curtains and to cover seat cushions in old-time movie theaters.

Now and then he also provided a treat. One day in 1938 he asked if I would like to join a small group of boys he was taking to visit the *News-Post* newsroom. My mother, in spite of believing that nothing came before homework at night, wasn't coldhearted enough to deny me a chance to see the city room[4] of a great metropolitan newspaper. I had seen plenty of city rooms in the movies. They were glamorous places full of exciting people like Lee Tracey, Edmund Lowe, and Adolphe Menjou[5] trading wisecracks and making mayors and cops look like saps. To see such a place, to stand, actually stand, in the city room of a great newspaper and look at reporters who were in touch every day with killers and professional baseball players—that was a thrilling prospect.

Because the *News-Post* was an afternoon paper, almost everybody had left for the day when we got there that night. The building, located downtown near the harbor, was disappointing. It looked like a factory, and not a very big factory either. Inside there was a smell compounded of ink, pulp, chemicals, paste, oil, gasoline, greasy rags, and hot metal. We took an elevator up and came into a long room filled with dilapidated[6] desks, battered telephones, and big blocky typewriters. Almost nobody there, just two or three men in shirt-sleeves. It was the first time I'd ever seen Deems look awed.

"Boys, this is the nerve center of the newspaper," he said, his voice heavy and solemn like the voice of Westbrook Van Voorhis, the *March of Time*[7] man, when he said, "Time marches on."

I was confused. I had expected the newsroom to have glamour, but this place had nothing but squalor. The walls hadn't been painted for years. The windows were filthy. Desks were heaped with mounds of crumpled paper, torn sheets of newspaper, overturned paste pots, dog-eared telephone directories. The floor was ankle deep in newsprint, carbon paper, and crushed cigarette packages. Waist-high cans overflowed with trash. Ashtrays were buried under

Reading Skill
Author's Purpose
Why might Baker have included the contrast between newspaper city rooms in movies and the real city room he visits?

✓ **Reading Check**

How is the inside of the *News-Post* building different from what the author expects?

---

4. **city room** the office at a newspaper used by those who report on city events.
5. **Lee Tracey, Edmund Lowe, and Adolphe Menjou** actors in movies of the time.
6. **dilapidated** (də lap´ ə dāt´ id) *adj.* rundown; in poor condition.
7. the *March of Time* a newsreel series that ran from 1935 to 1951, showing current news events along with interviews. Newsreels were shown between feature films at movie theaters.

cigarette ashes and butts. Ugly old wooden chairs looked ready for the junk shop.

It looked to me like a place that probably had more cockroaches than we had back home on Lombard Street, but Deems was seeing it through rose-colored glasses.[8] As we stood looking around at the ruins, he started telling us how lucky we were to be newsboys. Lucky to have a foot on the upward ladder so early in life. If we worked hard and kept expanding our paper routes we could make the men who ran this paper sit up and notice us. And when men like that noticed you, great things could happen, because they were important men, the most important of all being the man who owned our paper: Mr. Hearst Himself, William Randolph Hearst, founder of the greatest newspaper organization in America. A great man, Mr. Hearst, but not so great that he didn't appreciate his newsboys, who were the backbone of the business. Many of whom would someday grow up and work at big jobs on this paper. Did we realize that any of us, maybe all of us, could end up one of these days sitting right here in this vitally important room, the news-room, the nerve center of the newspaper?

Yes, Deems was right. Riding home on the streetcar that night, I realized I was a lucky boy to be getting such an early start up the ladder of journalism. It was childish to feel let down because the city room looked like such a dump instead of like city rooms in the movies. Deems might be a slave driver, but he was doing it for my own good, and I ought to be grateful. In *News Selling*, the four-page special paper Mr. Hearst published just for his newsboys, they'd run a piece that put it almost as beautifully as Deems had.

YOU'RE A MEMBER OF THE FOURTH ESTATE was the headline on it. I was so impressed

---

8. **seeing it through rose-colored glasses** ignoring its unappealing features or drawbacks.

that I put the paper away in a safe place and often took it out to read when I needed inspiration. It told how "a great English orator" named Edmund Burke "started a new name for a new profession—the Fourth Estate[9] . . . the press . . . NEWSPAPER MEN."

And it went on to say:

"The Fourth Estate was then . . . and IS now . . . a great estate for HE-men . . . workers . . . those who are proud of the business they're in!"

(Mr. Hearst always liked plenty of exclamation marks, dots, and capital letters.)

"Get that kick of pride that comes from knowing you are a newspaper man. That means something!

"A newspaper man never ducks a dare. YOU are a newspaper man. A salesman of newspapers . . . the final cog[10] in the <u>immense</u> machine of newspaper production—a SERVICE for any man to be proud of.

"So throw back the chest. Hit the route hard each day. Deliver fast and properly. Sell every day. Add to your route because you add to the NEWSPAPER field when you do. And YOU MAKE MONEY DOING IT. It is a great life—a grand opportunity. Don't boot it—build it up. Leave it better than when you came into it."

"It is a great life." I kept coming back to that sentence as I read and reread the thing. No matter how awful it got, and it sometimes got terrible, I never quit believing it was a great life. I kept at it until I was almost sixteen, chest thrown back, delivering fast and properly, selling every day and adding to my route. At the end I'd doubled its size and was making as much as four dollars a week from it.

A few months after he took us down to see the city room, Deems quit. My mother said he'd found a better job. Later, when I thought about him, I wondered if maybe it wasn't because he hated himself for having to make life hell for boys. I hoped that wasn't the reason because he was the first newspaperman I ever knew, and I wanted him to be the real thing. Hard as nails.

9. Edmund Burke . . . Fourth Estate Edmund Burke (1729–1797) was an English political figure famous for his speeches and essays. He called the press the "Fourth Estate," meaning it was a base of political power just as were the three social classes in England during that period.
10. cog (cäg) *n.* gear.

Literary Analysis
Narrative Essay
William Randolph Hearst was a powerful publisher who owned many newspapers. What details about this real person does Baker include?

Vocabulary Builder
immense (i mens´) *adj.* huge

Reading Skill
Author's Purpose
Why do you think Baker quoted parts of Hearst's special paper for newsboys?

Apply the Skills

Hard as Nails

Thinking About the Selection

1. **Respond:** Would you like to work for Deems? Explain.
2. **(a) Recall:** At the beginning of the selection, what does Baker's mother want her son to do? **(b) Compare and Contrast:** Explain how Baker's dreams for himself are similar to and different from his mother's dreams for him. **(c) Draw Conclusions:** Why do you think their dreams differ? Support your answer with details from the narrative.
3. **(a) Recall:** What does Deems do when Russ sells all his papers? **(b) Infer:** What lesson do you think Deems is teaching Russ? **(c) Draw Conclusions:** At the end of the essay, why does Russ want to believe that Deems really was "hard as nails"?
4. **(a) Evaluate:** Does Deems treat the newsboys fairly or unfairly? **(b) Discuss:** In a small group, share your responses. Then, share one response with the class.

Reading Skill

5. What are two **purposes** Baker may have had for writing this narrative essay?
6. What details from the essay indicate each purpose?

Literary Analysis

7. Complete a chart like the one shown to think about why Baker includes particular events in his **autobiographical narrative**.

Event From Narrative	Author's Thoughts and Feelings	Why Is It Included?
Baker and his family move to Baltimore.		
Baker goes to the banquet.		

8. What do you know about the banquet that you would not have known if Deems had told the story?

QuickReview

Essay at a Glance
At twelve, Russell Baker learns the difficulties and rewards of delivering newspapers.

Go Online
Assessment
For: Self-test
Visit: www.PHSchool.com
Web Code: ela-6302

Author's Purpose: an author's main reason for writing. General purposes are *to inform, to entertain, to persuade,* or *to reflect.*

Autobiographical Narrative: a brief nonfiction work that tells a true story from the writer's own life

Vocabulary Builder

Practice Use a word from the "Hard as Nails" vocabulary list on page 366 to write a sentence for each numbered item.

1. Tell about something that is too big for you to carry.
2. Tell about a situation in which something gets used up.
3. Describe a necklace with many diamonds.

Writing

Assume the role of Russell Baker and write a **letter** to Deems. Pretend Baker is sixteen and is giving up his delivery route. In your letter, explain why you want to stay in the newspaper business, using details such as what you learned from Deems.

For *Grammar, Vocabulary,* and *Assessment,* see **Build Language Skills,** pages 384–385.

Extend Your Learning

Listening and Speaking With a partner, prepare a **presentation** for young children about the experiences that Baker shares in "Hard as Nails." Help the children understand the significance of these experiences. Include background information to illustrate the difficulties of Baker's job. Use vocabulary young children can understand.

Research and Technology In a small group, find out about jobs in print journalism, such as reporting, editing, photographing, cartooning, and proofreading. Each student should search a different kind of source for information—for example, career guides, encyclopedias, online news groups, and Web sites. Then prepare a **project,** such as a brochure, a poster, or an oral report, that relates to career development.

Autobiographical Essay

Background

Helen Keller and Anne Sullivan A serious illness left Helen Keller, the author of "Water," blind and deaf before she was two years old. When teacher Anne Sullivan entered her life, seven-year-old Keller did not even know what words were. She did not understand that objects and ideas have "names." Sullivan herself had lost almost all of her sight and became a student at the Perkins Institute, a school for the blind. Although surgery restored some of Sullivan's sight, her experience inspired her to bring language to Keller.

Connecting to the Literature

Reading/Writing Connection In "Water," Helen Keller tells the story of the breakthrough moment when a new approach helped her understand language. Write several sentences about a time when you discovered and used a new or unique approach to a problem. Use at least three of the following words: *utilize, implement, investigate, resolve.*

Review

For **Reading Skill, Literary Analysis,** and **Vocabulary Builder,** see page 366.

Meet the Author

Helen **Keller** (1880–1968)

When Helen Keller's mother learned that her baby daughter would never again hear or see, she consulted the Perkins Institute director, who recommended Anne Sullivan as the girl's teacher.

Early Lessons In "Water," from her autobiography, Keller describes her early lessons with Sullivan. Eventually, Keller learned to read by using Braille (raised dots that stand for letters), to type, and to speak.

Fast Facts

▶ Helen Keller gained international fame as the first deaf and blind person to graduate from college.

▶ She wrote several books, articles, and essays about her struggle and her incredible teacher.

Go **Online**
Author Link

For: More about the author
Visit: www.PHSchool.com
Web Code: ele-9303

Water

HELEN KELLER

The morning after my teacher came she led me into her room and gave me a doll. The little blind children at the Perkins Institution had sent it and Laura Bridgman had dressed it; but I did not know this until afterward. When I had played with it a little while, Miss Sullivan slowly spelled into my hand the word "d-o-l-l." I was at once interested in this finger play and tried to <u>imitate</u> it. When I finally succeeded in making the letters correctly I was flushed with childish pleasure and pride. Running downstairs to my mother I held up my hand and made the letters for doll. I did not know that I was spelling a word or even that words existed; I was simply making my fingers go in monkey-like imitation. In the days that followed I learned to spell in this uncomprehending way a great many words, among them *pin, hat, cup* and a few verbs like *sit, stand* and *walk.* But my teacher had been with me several weeks before I understood that everything has a name.

Vocabulary Builder
imitate (im´i tāt´) *v.*
copy; mimic

Literary Analysis
Narrative Essay
What details so far indicate that this is a narrative essay?

One day, while I was playing with my new doll, Miss Sullivan put my big rag doll into my lap also, spelled "d-o-l-l" and tried to make me understand that "d-o-l-l" applied to both. Earlier in the day we had had a tussle over the words "m-u-g" and "w-a-t-e-r." Miss Sullivan had tried to impress it upon me that "m-u-g" is *mug* and that "w-a-t-e-r" is *water*, but I <u>persisted</u> in confounding the two. In despair she had dropped the subject for the time, only to renew it at the first opportunity. I became impatient at her repeated attempts and, seizing the new doll, I dashed it upon the floor. I was keenly delighted when I felt the fragments of the broken doll at my feet. Neither sorrow nor regret followed my passionate outburst. I had not loved the doll. In the still, dark world in which I lived there was no strong <u>sentiment</u> or tenderness. I felt my teacher sweep the fragments to one side of the hearth,[1] and I had a sense of satisfaction that the cause of my discomfort was removed. She brought me my hat, and I knew I was going out into the warm sunshine. This thought, if a wordless sensation may be called a thought, made me hop and skip with pleasure.

We walked down the path to the well-house, attracted by the fragrance of the honeysuckle with which it was covered. Some one was drawing water and my teacher placed my hand under the spout. As the cool stream gushed over one hand she spelled into the other the word *water*, first slowly, then rapidly. I stood still, my whole attention fixed upon the motions of her fingers. Suddenly I felt a misty consciousness as of something forgotten—a thrill of returning thought; and somehow the mystery of language was revealed to me. I knew then that "w-a-t-e-r" meant the wonderful cool something that was flowing over my hand. That living word awakened my soul, gave it light, hope, joy, set it free! There were barriers still, it is true, but barriers that could in time be swept away.

I left the well-house eager to learn. Everything had a name, and each name gave birth to a new thought. As we returned to the house every object which I touched seemed to quiver with life. That was because I saw everything with the strange, new sight that had come to me. On entering

---

1. hearth (härth) *n.* the stone or brick floor of a fireplace, sometimes extending into the room.

Vocabulary Builder
persisted (pər sist′ id)
v. refused to give up

Vocabulary Builder
sentiment (sen′ tə mənt) *n.* a gentle feeling

Reading Skill
Author's Purpose
Based on the details in this paragraph, what do you think is Helen Keller's purpose for writing? Explain.

the door I remembered the doll I had broken. I felt my way to the hearth and picked up the pieces. I tried vainly to put them together. Then my eyes filled with tears; for I realized what I had done, and for the first time I felt repentance and sorrow.

I learned a great many new words that day. I do not remember what they all were; but I do know that *mother*, *father*, *sister*, *teacher* were among them—words that were to make the world blossom for me, "like Aaron's rod, with flowers." It would have been difficult to find a happier child than I was as I lay in my crib at the close of that eventful day and lived over the joys it had brought me, and for the first time longed for a new day to come.

▲ **Critical Viewing**
How would you describe the expressions on the faces of the woman and girl? **[Analyze]**

Reading Skill
Author's Purpose
What purpose do the details in this paragraph best support?

Apply the Skills

Water

Thinking About the Selection

1. **Respond:** Before she learned to communicate, Helen Keller shows impatience and anger by smashing her doll. Should she be excused for such behavior? Explain.

2. **(a) Recall:** Which event helps Helen to recognize the meaning of *w-a-t-e-r*? **(b) Compare and Contrast:** Explain how water from the pump is the same as and different from water in the mug. **(c) Draw Conclusions:** What does "Water" illustrate about teaching someone an idea?

3. **(a) Recall:** How does Keller feel when she goes to bed on the night she learned about *w-a-t-e-r*? **(b) Infer:** Why does she feel that way? **(c) Draw Conclusions:** What will Keller want to do when she wakes up? Support your answer.

4. **(a) Evaluate:** What do you think is the most valuable part of being able to communicate? **(b) Discuss:** In a small group, share your responses. Then, as a group, share one response with the class.

Reading Skill

5. What are two **purposes** Keller may have had for writing this narrative essay?

6. What details from the essay indicate each purpose?

Literary Analysis

7. Complete a chart like the one shown to think about why Keller includes particular events in her **autobiographical narrative**.

Event From Narrative	Author's Thoughts and Feelings	Why Is It Included?
Helen breaks her doll.		
Helen connects the word *w-a-t-e-r* with water from the pump.		

8. What do you know about the doll breaking that you would not have known if Anne Sullivan had told the story?

Vocabulary Builder

Practice Use a word from the "Water" vocabulary list on page 366 to write a sentence for each numbered item.

1. Explain why a person would send flowers to a loved one.
2. Tell about a person who called every day about a broken streetlight until the city fixed it.
3. Tell an actor to act like a bird.

Writing

Assume the role of Anne Sullivan and write a **letter** to the director of the school for the blind where Sullivan had been a student. Pretend you are writing on the day Keller learns what *w-a-t-e-r* means. Explain why you want to stay on the job or give it up.

For *Grammar, Vocabulary,* and *Assessment,*
see **Build Language Skills,** pages 384–385.

Extend Your Learning

Listening and Speaking With a partner, prepare a **presentation** for young children about the experiences Keller shares in "Water." Help the children understand the significance of these experiences. Include background information to illustrate the difficulties created by Keller's disabilities. Use vocabulary young children can understand.

Research and Technology In a small group, find out about careers in educating people who are blind. To gather information, each member should search a different kind of source—for example, newspapers, encyclopedias, online news groups, and Web sites. Then prepare a **project,** such as a brochure, a poster, or a radio news story, that relates to career development.

Build Language Skills

Hard as Nails • Water

Vocabulary Skill

Suffixes The **suffix** *-ment* means "the state, act, or result of." Adding *-ment* to a word makes the new word a noun that means "the state or result" of the original action. For example, the verb *accomplish* can be turned into the noun *accomplishment.* An *accomplishment* is the result of what a person *accomplishes.*

▶ **Example:** It is a great *accomplishment* for an author to achieve his or her purpose for writing.

A word's use in a sentence determines its part of speech. Some words can act as both a noun and a verb, depending on their use. For example, *document* can act as a verb or a noun.

Practice Write the new word that is formed by adding *-ment* to each word below. Then explain what the new word means.

1. enchant
2. excite
3. govern
4. disappoint
5. enjoy

Grammar Lesson

Adjectives and Articles An **adjective** is a word that describes a person, place, or thing. An adjective answers one of the following questions: *What kind? Which one? How many? How much?* Adjectives are often called modifiers because they modify, or make clearer, the meaning of a noun or pronoun. An **article** is a special kind of adjective. There are three articles: *a, an,* and *the.*

Practice Write each sentence. Underline the adjective, circle the article, and draw an arrow to the word each modifies. After each sentence, tell which question the adjective answers: *What kind? Which one? How many?* or *How much?*

1. The nest held four birds.
2. There is a red pencil on the desk.
3. He had an accident and dented the front door of the car.

MorePractice

For more practice with adjectives and articles, see the Grammar Handbook, p. R31.

𝒲𝒢 *Prentice Hall Writing and Grammar Connection: Chapter 16, Section 1*

Reading: Author's Purpose

Directions: *Read the selection. Then, answer the questions.*

I don't like pickles. In fact, even thinking about pickles makes me crazy. Looking back, the beginning of my pickle phobia started about seven years ago. My family and I went to a party. Our neighbor, Mrs. Scott, brought her homemade pickles. I was only four, and I couldn't reach the pickle dish. So I asked each person who came to the table to please pass me a pickle. At the end of the day, my stomach felt like a big balloon that was ready to burst. I had eaten every single one of Mrs. Scott's pickles.

1. Which phrase helps the reader determine the author's purpose?
   A Looking back
   B Our neighbor, Mrs. Scott
   C every single one
   D At the end of the day

2. What is the author's general purpose for writing this essay?
   A to inform
   B to persuade
   C to reflect on a memory
   D to describe a good pickle

3. What shows that the author's purpose is to entertain?
   A In fact, even thinking about pickles makes me crazy.
   B My family and I went to a party.
   C Our neighbor, Mrs. Scott, brought her homemade pickles.
   D I couldn't reach the pickle dish.

4. What is the author's specific purpose?
   A to share a personal experience
   B to tell why pickles are dangerous
   C to describe good pickles
   D to describe a bad stomachache

Timed Writing: Interpretation [Critical Stance]

Review "Water" or "Hard as Nails." Identify the author's purpose and his or her specific message. Support your interpretation with details from the work. **(20 minutes)**

 ## Writing Workshop: *Work in Progress*

How-to Essay

Review the Task Sheet from your writing portfolio and choose three tasks. Imagine explaining this skill to someone else and then decide who your audience might be. For each task, note the audience and write a word or two to describe the audience's knowledge level. Save this work in your writing portfolio.

These skills will help you become a better reader. Practice them with either "The Shutout" (p. 388) or "Jackie Robinson: Justice at Last" (p. 395).

Reading Skill

An **author's purpose** is his or her reason for writing. To understand an author's specific purpose, **ask questions.**

- What kinds of details am I given?
- How are the details presented?
- Why does the author present these details in this way?

The chart shows the answers to these questions for two different works about building a doghouse. Although both works are on the same topic, the answers to the questions reveal that they have different purposes. Use a chart like this one as you read.

Literary Analysis

An **essay** is a short piece of nonfiction about a specific subject. An **expository essay** has one or more of these general purposes:

- Provides information
- Discusses ideas and opinions
- Explains how to do or make something

As you read an expository essay, notice how the subject of the essay gives a focus to one or more of these general purposes.

What Kinds of Details?	
Directions for building a doghouse	Author tries to build a doghouse
How Presented?	
Numbered steps	Exaggerated stories
Why?	
To make the directions easy to follow	To make the situation funny
Purpose	
To inform	To entertain

Vocabulary Builder

The Shutout

- **anecdotes** (an´ ik dōts´) *n.* short, entertaining tales (p. 388) *Grandpa told us many funny anecdotes about his youth.*

- **evolved** (ē välvd´) *v.* grew gradually; developed (p. 389) *Many modern stories have evolved from ancient myths and legends.*

- **diverse** (də vʉrs´) *adj.* various; with differing characteristics (p. 389) *Mammals are a diverse group of animals.*

- **irrational** (i rash´ ə nəl) *adj.* unreasonable (p. 390) *His fear of spiders is irrational.*

Jackie Robinson: Justice at Last

- **integrate** (in´ tə grāt´) *v.* remove all barriers and allow access to all (p. 395) *Laws were passed to integrate the schools.*

- **petition** (pə tish´ən) *n.* a document that people sign to express demands (p. 396) *Students signed a petition asking for an after-school program.*

- **retaliated** (ri tal´ ē āt ´id) *v.* punished in return for an injury or a wrong done (p. 397) *He has never retaliated against anyone who tried to hurt him.*

Expository Essay

Background

The Shutout In the earliest days of baseball, African American and white players played side by side. Eventually, however, baseball became segregated, or separated, into teams of "blacks" and "whites." As this essay shows, however, segregation could not "shut out" African Americans from playing the game and creating baseball legends as amazing as those of their white counterparts.

Connecting to the Literature

Reading/Writing Connection "The Shutout" describes an unfair situation that African American ballplayers faced in the early days of baseball. Write briefly about what you think a person should do when faced with an unfair situation. Use at least three of the following words: *confront, contend, prevail, proceed, pursue.*

Meet the Authors

Patricia C. **McKissack** (b. 1944)
Fredrick **McKissack**, Jr. (b. 1965)

Patricia McKissack began her career first as an English teacher and then as an editor of children's books. While working as an editor, she decided to become a writer. "I write because there's a need to have books for, by, and about the African American experience and how we helped to develop this country," says McKissack. She is now author of more than seventy-five books for children and young adults.

The Family Business McKissack co-wrote many of her books with her husband Fredrick McKissack. Together, the couple has won countless awards. Their son, Fredrick McKissack, Jr., is also a writer. With her son, Patricia McKissack wrote *Black Diamond: The Story of the Negro Baseball Leagues,* from which "The Shutout" was taken. *Black Diamond* focuses on the talents and triumphs of leading Negro League baseball players. The book brings to life an important period in the history of baseball.

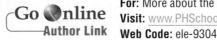

Go Online
Author Link

For: More about the authors
Visit: www.PHSchool.com
Web Code: ele-9304

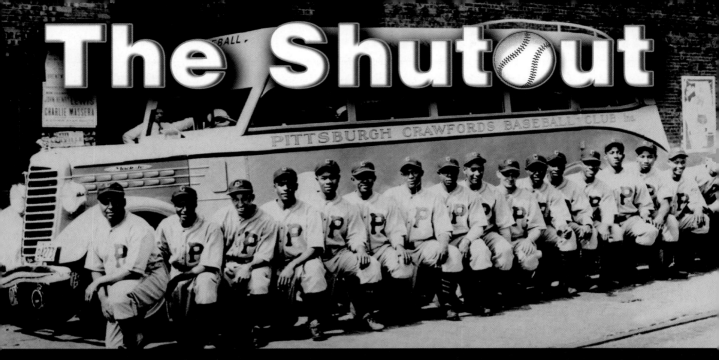

The Shutout

Patricia C. McKissack and Fredrick McKissack, Jr.

The history of baseball is difficult to trace because it is embroidered with wonderful <u>anecdotes</u> that are fun but not necessarily supported by fact. There are a lot of myths that persist about baseball—the games, the players, the owners, and the fans—in spite of contemporary research that disproves most of them. For example, the story that West Point cadet Abner Doubleday "invented" baseball in 1839 while at Cooperstown, New York, continues to be widely accepted, even though, according to his diaries, Doubleday never visited Cooperstown. A number of records and documents show that people were playing stick-and-ball games long before the 1839 date.

Albigence Waldo, a surgeon with George Washington's troops at Valley Forge, wrote in his diary that soldiers were "batting balls and running bases" in their free time. Samuel Hopkins Adams (1871–1958), an American historical novelist, stated that his grandfather "played baseball on Mr. Mumford's pasture" in the 1820's.

Although baseball is a uniquely American sport, it was not invented by a single person. Probably the game

▲ **Critical Viewing**
How is this team similar to and different from the baseball teams of today? **[Compare and Contrast]**

Vocabulary Builder
anecdotes (an´ ik dōts´) *n.* short, entertaining tales

Literary Analysis
Expository Essay
What clues in the picture and these paragraphs indicate that this is an expository essay?

<u>evolved</u> from a variety of stick-and-ball games that were played in Europe, Asia, Africa, and the Americas for centuries and brought to the colonies by the most <u>diverse</u> group of people ever to populate a continent. More specifically, some historians believe baseball is an outgrowth of its first cousin, *rounders,* an English game. Robin Carver wrote in his *Book of Sports* (1834) that "an American version of rounders called *goal ball* was rivaling cricket in popularity."

It is generally accepted that by 1845, baseball, as it is recognized today, was becoming popular, especially in New York. In that year a group of baseball enthusiasts organized the New York Knickerbocker Club. They tried to standardize the game by establishing guidelines for "proper play."

The Knickerbockers' rules set the playing field—a diamond-shaped infield with four bases (first, second, third, and home) placed ninety feet apart. At that time, the pitching distance was forty-five feet from home base and the "pitch" was thrown under-handed. The three-strikes-out rule, the three-out inning, and the ways in which a player could be called out were also specified. However, the nine-man team and nine-inning game were not established until later. Over the years, the Knickerbockers' basic rules of play haven't changed much.

In 1857–1858, the newly organized National Association of Base Ball Players was formed, and baseball became a business. Twenty-five clubs—mostly from eastern states—formed the Association for the purpose of setting rules and guidelines for club and team competition. The Association defined a professional player as a person who "played for money, place or emolument (profit)." The Association also authorized an admission fee for one of the first "all-star" games between Brooklyn and New York. Fifteen hundred people paid fifty cents to see that game. Baseball was on its way to becoming the nation's number-one sport.

By 1860, the same year South Carolina seceded from the Union, there were about sixty teams in the Association. For obvious reasons none of them were from the South. Baseball's development was slow during the Civil War years, but teams continued to compete, and military records show that,

Vocabulary Builder
evolved (ē välvd´) *v.* grew gradually; developed

diverse (də vʉrs´) *adj.* various; with differing characteristics

Reading Skill
Authors' Purpose
Based on what you have read, what do you think is the authors' purpose in writing this essay?

Reading Check

Who set early guidelines for playing baseball?

sometimes between battles, Union soldiers chose up teams and played baseball games. It was during this time that records began mentioning African-American players. One war journalist noted that black players were "sought after as teammates because of their skill as ball handlers."

Information about the role of African Americans in the early stages of baseball development is slight. Several West African cultures had stick-and-ball and running games, so at least some blacks were familiar with the concept of baseball. Baseball, however, was not a popular southern sport, never equal to boxing, wrestling, footracing, or horse racing among the privileged landowners.

Slave owners preferred these individual sports because they could enter their slaves in competitions, watch the event from a safe distance, pocket the winnings, and personally never raise a sweat. There are documents to show that slave masters made a great deal of money from the athletic skills of their slaves.

Free blacks, on the other hand, played on and against integrated[1] teams in large eastern cities and in small midwestern hamlets. It is believed that some of the emancipated[2] slaves and runaways who served in the Union Army learned how to play baseball from northern blacks and whites who had been playing together for years.

After the Civil War, returning soldiers helped to inspire a new interest in baseball all over the country. Teams sprung up in northern and midwestern cities, and naturally African Americans were interested in joining some of these clubs. But the National Association of Base Ball Players had other ideas. They voted in December 1867 not to admit any team for membership that "may be composed of one or more colored persons." Their reasoning was as irrational as the racism that shaped it: "If colored clubs were admitted," the Association stated, "there would be in all probability some division of feeling whereas, by excluding them no injury could result to anyone . . . and [we wish] to keep out of the convention the discussion of any subjects having a political bearing as this [admission of blacks on the Association teams] undoubtedly would."

1. **integrated** (in´ tə grāt´ id) *adj.* open to both African Americans and whites.
2. **emancipated** (ē man´ sə pāt´ id) *adj.* freed from slavery.

Reading Skill
Authors' Purpose
Based on what you have read so far, what is the authors' general purpose for writing this essay? What is the authors' specific purpose?

Vocabulary Builder
irrational (i rash´ ə nəl) *adj.* unreasonable

So, from the start, organized baseball tried to limit or exclude African-American participation. In the early days a few black ball players managed to play on integrated minor league teams. A few even made it to the majors, but by the turn of the century, black players were shut out of the major leagues until after World War II. That doesn't mean African Americans didn't play the game. They did.

Black people organized their own teams, formed leagues, and competed for championships. The history of the old "Negro Leagues" and the players who barnstormed[3] on black diamonds is one of baseball's most interesting chapters, but the story is a researcher's nightmare. Black baseball was outside the mainstream of the major leagues, so team and player records weren't well kept, and for the most part, the white press ignored black clubs or portrayed them as clowns. And for a long time the Baseball Hall of Fame didn't recognize any of the Negro League players. Because of the lack of documentation, many people thought the Negro Leagues' stories were nothing more than myths and yarns, but that is not the case. The history of the Negro Leagues is a patchwork of human drama and comedy, filled with legendary heroes, infamous owners, triple-headers, low pay, and long bus rides home—not unlike the majors.

---

3. **barnstormed** v. went from one small town to another, putting on an exhibition.

▲ **Critical Viewing**
Based on the clothing and buildings shown here, during what period in U.S. history might this scene have taken place? **[Deduce]**

Literary Analysis
Expository Essay
This final paragraph contains some of the essay's most important ideas. State them in your own words.

Apply the Skills

The Shutout

Thinking About the Selection

1. **Respond:** What questions do you have about the essay? Write them in the first column of a three-column chart. Trade charts with a partner.
   - In the second column, answer your partner's questions. Discuss your responses.
   - In the third column, explain how the discussion changed your understanding of the work.

Questions	Answers	Change

2. **(a) Recall:** When did baseball become popular, and who created the playing rules? **(b) Analyze:** Give specific examples of the changes that occurred following the creation of baseball as a professional sport. **(c) Generalize:** What is one reason baseball rules and regulations were created?
3. **(a) Recall:** What were the team owners' reasons for not letting African Americans play? **(b) Identify Cause and Effect:** What effect did this exclusion have on the history of baseball? **(c) Connect:** What attitudes and conditions contributed to this exclusion?
4. **Make a Judgment:** Do you think that sports today are segregated in any way? Explain.

Reading Skill

5. What kinds of details are included in the essay?
6. What is the general **purpose** of the essay?

Literary Analysis

7. What is the focus of this **expository essay**?
8. What is the author's specific purpose in focusing on this topic?

QuickReview

Essay at a Glance
After the Civil War, African Americans formed their own leagues because they were "shut out" of major-league baseball.

For: Self-test
Visit: www.PHSchool.com
Web Code: ela-6304

Author's Purpose: an author's main reason for writing. Possible purposes are *to inform, to entertain, to persuade,* or *to reflect on a personal experience.*

Expository Essay: nonfiction that gives information, discusses ideas, or explains how to do something

Vocabulary Builder

Practice Write a sentence explaining why each statement is true or false without using the underlined word.

1. Golf <u>evolved</u> from bowling.

2. Canines do not consist of a <u>diverse</u> group of dogs.

3. The belief that men from outer space are in our classroom today is totally <u>irrational</u>.

4. <u>Anecdotes</u> explain how water turns into ice.

Writing

Write a **persuasive letter** to a friend encouraging him or her to read "The Shutout." Your purpose is to convince your friend that the essay is interesting and worthwhile. Present your reasons, supported by examples from the essay and your reactions to it.

For *Grammar, Vocabulary,* and *Assessment,* see **Build Language Skills,** pages 400–401.

Extend Your Learning

Listening and Speaking Invite a baseball coach to your class to explain how to swing a bat, steal a base, bunt, and set up a double play. Then, in a small group, prepare instructional presentations for younger students that **give directions** for each activity. Summarize the coach's ideas, demonstrate each step, and explain key terms. Use language younger students can understand.

Research and Technology In a group, prepare a **visual timeline** to tell the story that begins with "The Shutout" and extends through the creation of the Negro Leagues. Choose visuals that represent the highlights of this part of baseball history. Find information by using the Internet, databases, and CD-ROMs. Organize these visuals in the order in which the events they represent happened. Label each visual clearly and accurately.

Expository Essay

Background

Jackie Robinson In the early 1900s, major-league baseball excluded African American players. Therefore, these players formed their own teams and, in the 1920s, organized the Negro Leagues. Although they did not become as widely known as their white counterparts, some of the best players in baseball history played in the Negro Leagues. Jackie Robinson, the topic of the following essay, began his professional baseball career on a Negro Leagues team, the Kansas City Monarchs.

Connecting to the Literature

Reading/Writing Connection Jackie Robinson overcame huge roadblocks on the road to success. List some problems and roadblocks you face as you try to achieve the things that mean the most to you. Use at least three of the following words: *confront, contend, prevail, proceed, pursue.*

Review

For **Reading Skill, Literary Analysis,** and **Vocabulary Builder,** see page 386.

Meet the Authors

Geoffrey C. **Ward** (b. 1940)

The author of many award-winning books, Geoffrey C. Ward is also a screenwriter and a former editor of *American Heritage* magazine. With Ken Burns, whom he has worked with for almost twenty years, Ward has written award-winning television documentaries, including *Baseball, The Civil War,* and *The West.*

Ken **Burns** (b. 1953)

Ken Burns has co-written, produced, and directed several television documentaries and miniseries and has directed movies that have been nominated for Academy Awards. "Jackie Robinson: Justice at Last" is from a book based on Ward and Burns's 1994 television documentary *Baseball.* This documentary won numerous awards, including an Emmy.

Go Online
Author Link

For: More about the authors
Visit: www.PHSchool.com
Web Code: ele-9305

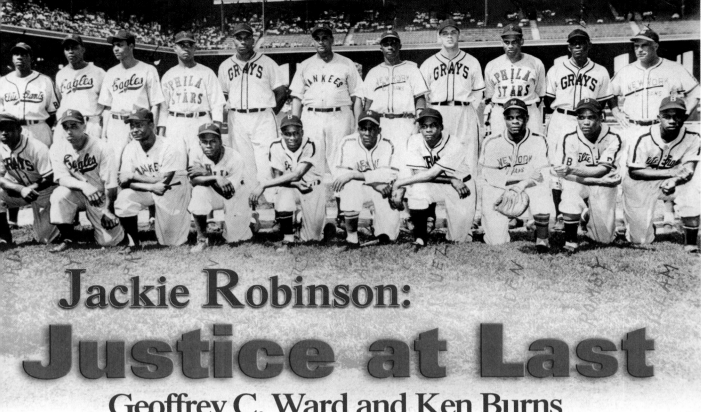

Jackie Robinson:
Justice at Last

Geoffrey C. Ward and Ken Burns

It was 1945, and World War II had ended. Americans of all races had died for their country. Yet black men were still not allowed in the major leagues. The national pastime was loved by all America, but the major leagues were for white men only.

Branch Rickey of the Brooklyn Dodgers thought that was wrong. He was the only team owner who believed blacks and whites should play together. Baseball, he felt, would become even more thrilling, and fans of all colors would swarm to his ballpark.

Rickey decided his team would be the first to <u>integrate</u>. There were plenty of brilliant Negro league players, but he knew the first black major leaguer would need much more than athletic ability.

Many fans and players were prejudiced—they didn't want the races to play together. Rickey knew the first black player would be cursed and booed. Pitchers would throw at him; runners would spike him. Even his own teammates might try to pick a fight.

▲ Critical Viewing
What details in this 1948 picture of the Negro League East All-Stars indicate their desire to compete? **[Analyze]**

Vocabulary Builder
integrate (in´ tə grāt´) v. remove all barriers and allow access to all

But somehow this man had to rise above that. No matter what happened, he must never lose his temper. No matter what was said to him, he must never answer back. If he had even one fight, people might say integration wouldn't work.

When Rickey met Jackie Robinson, he thought he'd found the right man. Robinson was 28 years old, and a superb athlete. In his first season in the Negro leagues, he hit .387. But just as importantly, he had great intelligence and sensitivity. Robinson was college-educated, and knew what joining the majors would mean for blacks. The grandson of a slave, he was proud of his race and wanted others to feel the same.

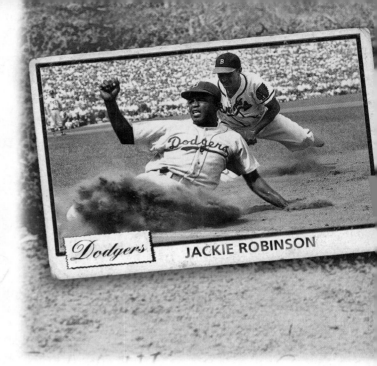

JACKIE ROBINSON

In the past, Robinson had always stood up for his rights. But now Rickey told him he would have to stop. The Dodgers needed "a man that will take abuse."

At first Robinson thought Rickey wanted someone who was afraid to defend himself. But as they talked, he realized that in this case a truly brave man would have to avoid fighting. He thought for a while, then promised Rickey he would not fight back.

Robinson signed with the Dodgers and went to play in the minors in 1946. Rickey was right—fans insulted him, and so did players. But he performed brilliantly and avoided fights. Then, in 1947, he came to the majors.

Many Dodgers were angry. Some signed a <u>petition</u> demanding to be traded. But Robinson and Rickey were determined to make their experiment work.

On April 15—Opening Day—26,623 fans came out to Ebbets Field. More than half of them were black—Robinson was already their hero. Now he was making history just by being on the field.

The afternoon was cold and wet, but no one left the ballpark. The Dodgers beat the Boston Braves, 5–3. Robinson went hitless, but the hometown fans didn't seem to care—they cheered his every move.

Reading Skill
Authors' Purpose
Based on what you have read so far, what is the authors' general purpose for writing this essay?

Vocabulary Builder
petition (pə tish´ən) *n.* a document that people sign to express demands

Literary Analysis
Expository Essay
What situation do the writers explain in the essay so far?

◄ **Critical Viewing**
What qualities of
Jackie Robinson do
you think are
demonstrated in
these two pictures?
Explain. **[Analyze]**

Robinson's first season was difficult. Fans threatened to kill him; players tried to hurt him. The St. Louis Cardinals said they would strike if he took the field. And because of laws separating the races in certain states, he often couldn't eat or sleep in the same places as his teammates.

Yet through it all, he kept his promise to Rickey. No matter who insulted him, he never <u>retaliated</u>.

Robinson's dignity paid off. Thousands of fans jammed stadiums to see him play. The Dodgers set attendance records in a number of cities.

Slowly his teammates accepted him, realizing that he was the spark that made them a winning team. No one was more daring on the base paths or better with the glove. At the plate, he had great bat control—he could hit the ball anywhere. That season, he was named baseball's first Rookie of the Year.

Jackie Robinson went on to a glorious career. But he did more than play the game well—his bravery taught Americans a lesson. Branch Rickey opened a door, and Jackie Robinson stepped through it, making sure it could never be closed again. Something wonderful happened to baseball—and America—the day Jackie Robinson joined the Dodgers.

Vocabulary Builder
retaliated (ri tal´ē āt´id)
v. punished in return
for an injury or a
wrong done

Reading Skill
Authors' Purpose
How does the final
sentence help you
understand the
authors' specific
purpose in writing
this essay?

Apply the Skills

Jackie Robinson: Justice at Last

Thinking About the Selection

1. **Respond:** What questions do you have about the essay? Write them in the first column of a three-column chart. Trade charts with a partner.
   - In the second column, answer your partner's questions. Discuss your responses.
   - In the third column, explain how the discussion affected your understanding of the work.

Questions	Answers	Has Understanding Changed? Explain.

2. **(a) Recall:** Who was Branch Rickey? **(b) Analyze:** Why is Rickey given a great deal of credit in this essay?
3. **(a) Recall:** What advice did Rickey give Robinson?
   (b) Interpret: Why was this important advice?
   (c) Evaluate: How important was the advice? Explain.
4. **(a) Recall:** Name three difficult situations that Jackie Robinson and the Dodgers faced during Robinson's first season. **(b) Analyze:** How did Robinson and the team overcome these difficulties?
5. **(a) Recall:** Why did Robinson's teammates eventually accept him? **(b) Speculate:** Why did everyone else eventually accept Robinson and the integration of baseball?

Reading Skill

6. What kinds of details are included in the **essay**?
7. What is the general **purpose** of the essay?

Literary Analysis

8. What is the focus of this **expository essay**?
9. What is the author's specific purpose in focusing on this topic?

QuickReview

Essay at a Glance
Baseball star Jackie Robinson becomes the first African American to play major-league baseball.

Go Online
Assessment
For: Self-test
Visit: www.PHSchool.com
Web Code: ela-6305

Author's Purpose: an author's main reason for writing. Possible purposes are *to inform, to entertain, to persuade,* or *to reflect on a personal experience.*

Expository Essay: nonfiction that gives information, discusses ideas, or explains how to do something

Vocabulary Builder

Practice Write a sentence telling why each statement is true or false without using the underlined word.

1. Branch Rickey did not want to <u>integrate</u> baseball.
2. People have never <u>retaliated</u> against social injustices.
3. One way to get something done is to sign a <u>petition</u>.

Writing

Write a **persuasive letter** to a friend encouraging him or her to read "Jackie Robinson: Justice at Last." Your purpose is to convince your friend that the essay is interesting and worthwhile. Present your reasons, supported by examples from the essay and from your reactions to it.

For *Grammar, Vocabulary,* and *Assessment,* see **Build Language Skills,** pages 400–401.

Extend Your Learning

Listening and Speaking Invite a baseball coach to your class to explain how to swing a bat, steal a base, bunt, and set up a double play. Then, in a small group, prepare instructional presentations for younger students that **give directions** for each activity. Summarize the coach's ideas and tips, demonstrate each step, and explain key terms. Use language a younger audience can understand.

Research and Technology In a group, prepare a **visual timeline** to tell the story of Jackie Robinson's baseball career. Find information by using the Internet, databases, and CD-ROMs. Choose visuals that represent the highlights of Robinson's career. Organize these visuals in the order in which the events they represent happened. Label each visual clearly and accurately.

Build Language Skills

The Shutout • Jackie Robinson: Justice at Last

Vocabulary Skill

Suffix The **suffix** -*tion* means "the state, act, or result of." Adding the suffix -*tion* to a word forms a noun that names the state, act, or result of the original word. For example, when you determine the author's *intent,* you define the author's *intention.*

Practice Answer each question with a complete sentence that includes a form of the underlined word.

▶ **Example:** How does a store manager create a price <u>reduction</u>?
A store manager reduces prices to create a price reduction.

1. What should people do to practice good <u>communication</u>?
2. What does a person who gives <u>directions</u> do?
3. What do you get from a hero who <u>inspires</u> you?

Grammar Lesson

Comparisons With Adjectives Most adjectives have different forms—the **positive**, the **comparative**, and the **superlative**. *Comparative adjectives* compare two people, places, or things. *Superlative adjectives* compare three or more people, places, or things. If a positive adjective contains one or two syllables, add the ending -*er* or -*est.* If the positive adjective contains three or more syllables, usually use the words *more* or *most.*

More Practice

For more practice with Comparison of Adjectives, see the Grammar Handbook, p. R31.

Positive Adjectives	Comparative Adjectives	Superlative Adjectives
I have a **big** dog.	My dog is **bigger** than her dog.	My dog is the **biggest** dog in our neighborhood.
It is a **beautiful** day.	Today is **more beautiful** than yesterday.	Monday was the **most beautiful** day of the week.

Practice Write each sentence using the comparative or superlative form of the adjective. Explain what quantity is being compared.

1. That is the _____ building in our city. (tall)
2. This chair is _____ than that one. (comfortable)
3. This movie is _____ than the one I saw last week. (exciting)

Reading: Author's Purpose

Directions: *Read the selection. Then, answer the questions.*

Fenway Park, the home of the Boston Red Sox, is the oldest professional baseball stadium in the United States. It opened on April 20, 1912. Fenway Park is the second home field for the Red Sox. The team was established in 1901, with a different name—the Boston Americans—and a different home field. In 1904, General Charles Henry Taylor, a Civil War veteran, bought the team. In 1907, he changed the team name to the Red Sox, and three years later, he began the construction for their new field, Fenway Park.

1. What kinds of details are emphasized?
   A descriptions of Fenway Park
   B reasons to visit Fenway Park
   C facts about historical Fenway Park
   D thoughts about the importance of Fenway Park

2. The presentation of the details is
   A chronological.
   B in order of importance.
   C random.
   D emotional.

3. What is the author's general purpose?
   A to inform
   B to persuade
   C to reflect on a memory
   D to analyze history

4. What is the author's specific purpose?
   A to praise the Red Sox
   B to point out the Red Sox were once the Boston Americans
   C to provide facts about Fenway Park and the Boston Red Sox
   D to prove that Civil War veterans were enthusiastic baseball fans

Timed Writing: Explanation [Critical Stance]

Review "Jackie Robinson: Justice at Last" or "The Shutout." Identify the authors' purpose. Then, explain how the authors use evidence to achieve the purpose. **(25 minutes)**

 ## Writing Workshop: *Work in Progress*

How-to Essay

Use the notes from your writing portfolio to choose one task and audience. Then, consider the type of language you would use for that audience. Write three details you would want to convey in your essay. Save this work in your writing portfolio.

Persuasive Speeches

In Part 1, you are learning about determining an author's purpose in literature. Determining an author's purpose is also important when reading persuasive texts. The persuasive speech featured here connects to two selections about baseball: "Jackie Robinson: Justice at Last" and "The Shutout."

About Persuasive Speeches

A **persuasive speech** is a public presentation that argues for or against a particular position. A powerful persuasive speech can change people's thinking about an issue. Examples of persuasive speeches include campaign speeches, fundraising speeches, and sermons. An effective persuasive speech has these characteristics:

- an issue with two sides
- a clear statement of the speaker's purpose and position
- clear organization of the text into sections
- facts, statistics, and reasons to support the position
- powerful language intended to persuade

Reading Skill

When you **evaluate an author's argument,** you look closely at the evidence that supports the author's position. An effective argument is backed up by facts and sound ideas. Look for a clear statement of the author's argument and note supporting information. Use a checklist such as the one shown to evaluate the following speech.

Checklist for Evaluating an Author's Argument

- ☐ Does the author present a clear argument?
- ☐ Is the argument supported by evidence?
- ☐ Is the evidence believable?
- ☐ Does the author use sound reasoning to develop the argument?
- ☐ Do I agree with the message? Why or why not?

Preserving a Great American Symbol

Richard Durbin

Congressman Richard Durbin gave the following humorous speech in the House of Representatives on July 26, 1989. While most speeches to Congress are serious, Durbin's is humorous yet persuasive and "drives home" the point that wooden baseball bats should not be replaced with metal ones.

In his introduction, Durbin clearly introduces his topic and his purpose for delivering the speech.

Mr. Speaker, I rise to condemn the desecration of a great American symbol. No, I am not referring to flagburning; I am referring to the baseball bat.
Several experts tell us that the wooden baseball bat is doomed to extinction, that major league baseball players will soon be standing at home plate with aluminum bats in their hands.

Reading Informational Materials

Baseball fans have been forced to endure countless indignities by those who just cannot leave well enough alone: designated hitters,[1] plastic grass, uniforms that look like pajamas, chicken-clowns dancing on the base lines, and, of course, the most heinous sacrilege, lights in Wrigley Field.[2]

> Durbin uses humor to persuade and entertain.

Are we willing to hear the crack of a bat replaced by the dinky ping? Are we ready to see the Louisville Slugger replaced by the aluminum ping dinger? Is nothing sacred?

Please do not tell me that wooden bats are too expensive, when players who cannot hit their weight are being paid more money than the President of the United States.

Please do not try to sell me on the notion that these metal clubs will make better hitters.

> Durbin closes with a dramatic statement, which serves as a final persuasive argument.

What will be next? Teflon baseballs? Radar-enhanced gloves? I ask you.

I do not want to hear about saving trees. Any tree in America would gladly give its life for the glory of a day at home plate.

I do not know if it will take a constitutional amendment to keep our baseball traditions alive, but if we forsake the great Americana of broken-bat singles and pine tar,[3] we will have certainly lost our way as a nation.

---

1. designated hitter player who bats in place of the pitcher and does not play any other position. The position was created in 1973 in the American League. Some fans argue that it has changed the game for the worse.

2. Wrigley Field historic baseball field in Chicago. It did not have lights for night games until 1988. Some fans regretted the change.

3. broken-bat singles . . . pine tar When a batter breaks a wooden bat while hitting the ball and makes it to first base, it is a notable event in a baseball game. Pine tar is a substance used to improve the batter's grip on a wooden bat.

Reading: Evaluating an Author's Argument

Directions: *Choose the letter of the best answer to each question about the persuasive speech.*

1. Which of these best states the position of the author in this speech?

   A Metal bats should not replace wooden ones.

   B Nothing is sacred in baseball.

   C Wrigley Field should not have lights.

   D Metal bats make better hitters.

2. Which statement supports the author's argument?

   A Wooden bats are too expensive.

   B Baseball players make too much money.

   C Wooden bats are part of American tradition.

   D Baseball fans oppose changes to the game.

3. Which claim in support of the author's argument cannot be proved?

   A Metal bats make a pinging sound.

   B The nation's well-being is tied to baseball.

   C Wrigley Field has lights.

   D Some baseball players earn more than the president.

Reading: Comprehension and Interpretation

Directions: *Write your answers on a separate sheet of paper.*

4. Identify the author's purpose in delivering this speech. **[Generating]**

5. Explain how the author ties baseball to America's well-being in his speech. **[Integrating]**

6. Analyze the author's use of humorous images and language to appeal to his audience's emotions. Support your answer with details from the speech. **[Evaluating]**

Timed Writing: Response [20 minutes]

Respond to the speech "Preserving a Great American Symbol." Tell why you do or do not agree with the author's argument. Cite specific details from the speech and support your response with reasons.

Biography and Autobiography

Biography is a form of nonfiction in which a writer tells the life story of another person. Biographies often present the experiences and actions of famous people. They may also explain the challenges, successes, or failures a person faced.

In contrast, an **autobiography** is a form of nonfiction in which a person narrates his or her own life story. In autobiographies, writers may explain their actions, offer their insights and feelings about events, or reveal the private side of public events.

Comparing Biography and Autobiography

Biography and autobiography have these differences:

- Biography uses the pronouns *he* and *she,* relies on research, and may be a more objective work.

- Autobiography uses the pronoun *I*, relies on firsthand thoughts, and is a more personal presentation.

However, these forms also have similarities. For example, writers of both forms have a wide array of facts and events from which to choose. When they are writing short essays, rather than full-length books, writers must narrow their topic to present a specific side of their subject.

As you read, note the details about each subject on a chart like the one shown. Then decide what each writer conveys to you about the subject.

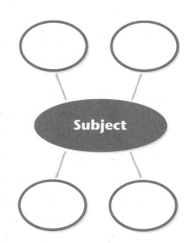

Vocabulary Builder

from Something to Declare

- **concludes** (kən kloōdz´) *v.* comes to an end (p. 408) *When the play concludes, the curtain will drop.*

- **perplexities** (pər plek´ sə tēz) *n.* things that confuse or puzzle (p. 408) *We discussed the rules and other perplexities.*

- **quandaries** (kwän´ də rēz) *n.* problems; uncertainties (p. 408) *The immigrants faced many quandaries in their new country.*

A Backwoods Boy

- **regarded** (ri gärd´ əd) *v.* thought of; considered (p. 414) *Teens in the 1960s regarded the Beatles as the best.*

- **intrigued** (in trēgd´) *v.* fascinated (p. 419) *The book of mystery tales intrigued me, so I asked for another.*

- **treacherous** (trech´ ər əs) *adj.* dangerous (p. 420) *Those rocks are treacherous—especially when wet.*

Build Understanding

Connecting to the Literature

Reading/Writing Connection In writing an autobiography or biography, writers must decide which parts of the subject's life to cover—childhood, adolescence, jobs, other parts, or all the parts. Choose a person and write three sentences about the parts of his or her life that you might cover in a brief biographical essay. Use three of these words: *emphasize, research, concentrate, elaborate, investigate.*

Meet the Authors

Julia **Alvarez** (b. 1950)

Although born in New York City, Julia Alvarez was raised until age ten in the Dominican Republic. She is the author of novels, short stories, poems, and nonfiction.

Play on Words The title *Something to Declare* is a play on a question Alvarez, as a child, heard officials ask people entering the United States: "Do you have anything to declare?" The question means "Are you bringing in any items that we need to know about?" The verb *declare* also means "say forcefully." The following selection, the introduction to Alvarez's book of essays, is her answer.

Russell **Freedman** (b. 1929)

Russell Freedman developed research skills as a reporter and went on to write more than thirty nonfiction books. "A Backwoods Boy" is from *Lincoln: A Photobiography.*

Highlighting History Freedman began writing books about history for young readers because his own children were not interested in the past. He is committed to making actual events come alive through vivid, revealing writing and fascinating, authentic photos.

Go **Online**
Author Link

For: More about the authors
Visit: www.PHSchool.com
Web Code: ele-9306

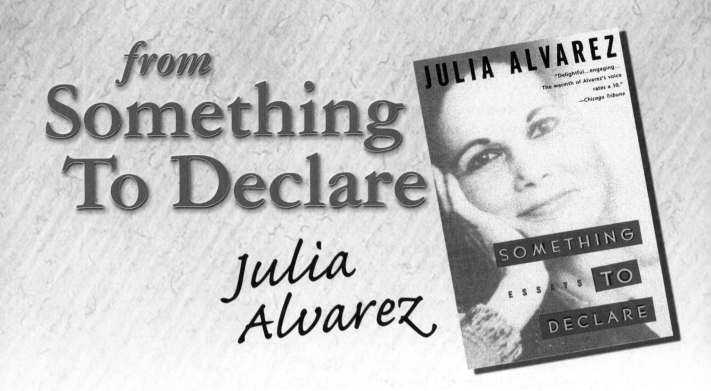

from Something To Declare

Julia Alvarez

The first time I received a letter from one of my readers, I was surprised. I had just published my first book of poems, *Homecoming*, which <u>concludes</u> with a sonnet sequence titled "33." My reader wanted to know why I had included forty-one sonnets when the title of the sequence was "33."

I considered not answering. Often, it is the little <u>perplexities</u> and curiosities and <u>quandaries</u> that remain after I have finished reading a book that send me to buy another book by that author. If I want to know more, the best way to find out is to read all the books that the author has written.

In the end, though, I couldn't resist. I wrote back, explaining how thirty-three represented my age at the time I wrote the sequence, how I had meant to include only thirty-three sonnets but I kept writing them and writing them, how the sonnets were not sonnets in the traditional sense. . . . Before I knew it, I had written my reader not just a note on my sonnet sequence but a short essay.

Many of the essays in this book began in just that way— as answers to such queries. Jessica Peet, a high-school

Vocabulary Builder
concludes (kən klōōdz´) *v.* comes to an end

perplexities (pər plek´ sə tēz) *n.* things that confuse or puzzle

quandaries (kwän´ də rēz) *n.* problems; uncertainties

Literary Analysis
Biography and Autobiography
Which of her own actions is Alvarez explaining?

student, read my first novel, *How the García Girls Lost Their Accents*, in her Vermont Authors class and wanted to know if I considered myself a Vermonter. The Lane Series, our local arts and entertainment series, wanted to know what I might have to say about opera. Share Our Strength was putting together a fund-raising anthology. Did I have anything at all to declare about food?

I could not really say to any of them, "Read my novels or my poems or my stories." These folks wanted what my boarding-school housemother used to call a straight answer. Which is where essays start. Not that they obey housemothers. Not that they list everything you are supposed to list on that Customs Declaration form. (How could the wild, multitudinous, daily things in anyone's head be inventoried in a form?) But that is the pretext of essays: *we have something to declare.*

And so this essay book is dedicated to you, my readers, who have asked me so many good questions and who want to know more than I have told you in my novels and poems. About my experience of immigration, about switching languages, about the writing life, the teaching life, the family life, about all of those combined.

Your many questions boil down finally to this one question: Do you have anything more to declare?

Yes, I do.

Literary Analysis
Biography and Autobiography
What do you know about Alvarez's life based on the many organizations listed in this paragraph?

Thinking About the Selection

1. **Respond:** The piece you just read is the introduction to the autobiographical book *Something to Declare.* Would you want to read the rest of the book? Why or why not?

2. **(a) Recall:** Why does Alvarez consider not answering the reader's question about the sonnets in *Homecoming*? **(b) Infer:** What do her reasons reveal about her?

3. **(a) Recall:** What does Alvarez realize about her readers and their questions about her? **(b) Connect:** Where does this realization lead Alvarez?

4. **(a) Interpret:** How is the book *Something to Declare* different from Alvarez's other books? **(b) Speculate:** Do you think Alvarez enjoys writing essays more than she enjoys writing novels or poems? Explain.

A Backwoods Boy

Russell Freedman

"It is a great piece of folly to attempt to make anything out of my early life. It can all be condensed into a simple sentence, and that sentence you will find in Gray's Elegy[1]—'the short and simple annals[2] of the poor.' That's my life, and that's all you or anyone else can make out of it."[3]

Abraham Lincoln never liked to talk much about his early life. A poor backwoods farm boy, he grew up swinging an ax on frontier homesteads in Kentucky, Indiana, and Illinois.

He was born near Hodgenville, Kentucky, on February 12, 1809, in a log cabin with one window, one door, a chimney, and a hardpacked dirt floor. His parents named him after his pioneer grandfather. The first Abraham Lincoln had been shot dead by hostile Indians in 1786, while planting a field of corn in the Kentucky wilderness.

Young Abraham was still a toddler when his family packed their belongings and moved to another log-cabin

▲ **Critical Viewing**
Is it surprising that a president of the United States was born in a cabin like this? Why or why not? **[Assess]**

**Literary Analysis
Biography and Autobiography**
Which words here indicate that Freedman is using the third-person point of view?

---

1. **elegy** (el′ ə jē) *n.* poem praising someone who has died.
2. **annals** (an′ əlz) *n.* historical records.
3. **"It is a great . . . out of it"** This is a quotation from Lincoln.

farm a few miles north, on Knob Creek. That was the first home he could remember, the place where he ran and played as a barefoot boy.

He remembered the bright waters of Knob Creek as it tumbled past the Lincoln cabin and disappeared into the Kentucky hills. Once he fell into the rushing creek and almost drowned before he was pulled out by a neighbor boy. Another time he caught a fish and gave it to a passing soldier.

Lincoln never forgot the names of his first teachers— Zachariah Riney followed by Caleb Hazel—who ran a windowless log schoolhouse two miles away. It was called a "blab school." Pupils of all ages sat on rough wooden benches and bawled out their lessons aloud. Abraham went there with his sister Sarah, who was two years older, when they could be spared from their chores at home. Holding hands, they would walk through scrub trees and across creek bottoms to the schoolhouse door. They learned their numbers from one to ten, and a smattering of reading, writing, and spelling.

Their parents couldn't read or write at all. Abraham's mother, Nancy, signed her name by making a shakily drawn mark. He would remember her as a thin, sad-eyed woman who labored beside her husband in the fields. She liked to gather the children around her in the evening to recite prayers and Bible stories she had memorized.

His father, Thomas, was a burly, barrel-chested farmer and carpenter who had worked hard at homesteading since marrying Nancy Hanks in 1806. A sociable fellow, his greatest pleasure was to crack jokes and swap stories with his chums. With painful effort, Thomas Lincoln could scrawl his name. Like his wife, he had grown up without education, but that wasn't unusual in those days. He supported his family by living off his own land, and he watched for a chance to better himself.

In 1816, Thomas decided to pull up stakes again and move north to Indiana, which was about to join the Union as the nation's nineteenth state. Abraham was seven. He remembered the one-hundred-mile journey as the hardest experience of his life. The family set out on a cold morning in December, loading all their possessions on two horses.

Literary Analysis
Biography and Autobiography Why might Freedman have included facts about the fish and about Lincoln's school memories?

Reading Check

What prevented Abraham Lincoln from attending school every day?

They crossed the Ohio River on a makeshift ferry, traveled through towering forests, then hacked a path through tangled underbrush until they reached their new homesite near the backwoods community of Little Pigeon Creek.

Thomas put up a temporary winter shelter—a crude, three-sided lean-to of logs and branches. At the open end, he kept a fire burning to take the edge off the cold and scare off the wild animals. At night, wrapped in bearskins and huddled by the fire, Abraham and Sarah listened to wolves howl and panthers scream.

Abraham passed his eighth birthday in the lean-to. He was big for his age, "a tall spider of a boy," and old enough to handle an ax. He helped his father clear the land. They planted corn and pumpkin seeds between the tree stumps. And they built a new log cabin, the biggest one yet, where Abraham climbed a ladder and slept in a loft beneath the roof.

Soon after the cabin was finished, some of Nancy's kinfolk arrived. Her aunt and uncle with their adopted son Dennis had decided to follow the Lincolns to Indiana. Dennis Hanks became an extra hand to Thomas and a big brother to Abraham, someone to run and wrestle with.

A year later, Nancy's aunt and uncle lay dead, victims of the dreaded "milk sickness" (now known to be caused by a poisonous plant called white snake root). An epidemic of the disease swept through the Indiana woods in the summer of 1818. Nancy had nursed her relatives until the end, and then she too came down with the disease. Abraham watched his mother toss in bed with chills, fever, and pain for seven days before she died at the age of thirty-four. "She knew she was going to die," Dennis Hanks recalled. "She called up the children to her dying side and told them to be good and kind to their father, to one another, and to the world."

Thomas built a coffin from black cherry wood, and nine-year-old Abraham whittled the pegs that held the wooden planks together. They buried Nancy on a windswept hill, next to her aunt and uncle. Sarah, now eleven, took her mother's place, cooking, cleaning, and mending clothes for her father, brother, and cousin Dennis in the forlorn and lonely cabin.

Literary Analysis
Biography and Autobiography
What do these details about the temporary home tell you about Lincoln's childhood?

Literary Analysis
Biography and Autobiography Why do you think the writer includes this information about Nancy Lincoln's death?

Thomas Lincoln waited for a year. Then he went back to Kentucky to find himself a new wife. He returned in a four-horse wagon with a widow named Sarah Bush Johnston, her three children, and all her household goods. Abraham and his sister were fortunate, for their stepmother was a warm and loving person. She took the motherless children to her heart and raised them as her own. She also spruced up the neglected Lincoln cabin, now shared by eight people who lived, ate, and slept in a single smoky room with a loft.

Abraham was growing fast, shooting up like a sunflower, a spindly youngster with big bony hands, unruly black hair, a dark complexion, and luminous gray eyes. He became an expert with the ax, working alongside his father, who also hired him out to work for others. For twenty-five cents a day, the boy dug wells, built pigpens, split fence rails, felled trees. "My how he could chop!" exclaimed a friend. "His ax would flash and bite into a sugar tree or a sycamore, and down it would come. If you heard him felling trees in a clearing, you would say there were three men at work, the way the trees fell."

Meanwhile, he went to school "by littles," a few weeks one winter, maybe a month the next. Lincoln said later that all his schooling together "did not amount to one year." Some fragments of his schoolwork still survive, including a verse that he wrote in his homemade arithmetic book: "Abraham Lincoln/his hand and pen/he will be good but/god knows When."

Mostly, he educated himself by borrowing books and newspapers. There are many stories about Lincoln's efforts to find enough books to satisfy him in that backwoods country. Those he liked he read again and again, losing himself in the adventures of *Robinson Crusoe* or the magical tales of *The Arabian Nights*. He was thrilled by a biography of George Washington, with its stirring account of the Revolutionary War. And he came to love the rhyme and rhythm of poetry, reciting passages from Shakespeare or the Scottish poet Robert Burns at the drop of a hat. He would carry a book out to the field with him, so he could read at the end of each plow furrow, while the horse was getting its breath. When noon came, he would sit under a

Literary Analysis
Biography and Autobiography
What details here show Lincoln was smart, even though he had little schooling?

 **Reading Check**

What physical work does Lincoln do to help support his family?

tree and read while he ate. "I never saw Abe after he was twelve that he didn't have a book in his hand or in his pocket," Dennis Hanks remembered. "It didn't seem natural to see a feller read like that."

By the time he was sixteen, Abraham was six feet tall— "the gangliest awkwardest feller . . . he appeared to be all joints," said a neighbor. He may have looked awkward, but hard physical labor had given him a tough, lean body with muscular arms like steel cables. He could grab a woodsman's ax by the handle and hold it straight out at arm's length. And he was one of the best wrestlers and runners around.

He also had a reputation as a comic and storyteller. Like his father, Abraham was fond of talking and listening to talk. About this time he had found a book called *Lessons in Elocution*, which offered advice on public speaking. He practiced before his friends, standing on a tree stump as he entertained them with fiery imitations of the roving preachers and politicians who often visited Little Pigeon Creek.

Folks liked young Lincoln. They <u>regarded</u> him as a good-humored, easy-going boy—a bookworm maybe, but smart and willing to oblige. Yet even then, people noticed that he could be moody and withdrawn. As a friend put it, he was "witty, sad, and reflective by turns."

At the age of seventeen, Abraham left home for a few months to work as a ferryman's helper on the Ohio River. He was eighteen when his sister Sarah died early in 1828, while giving birth to her first child.

That spring, Abraham had a chance to get away from the backwoods and see something of the world. A local merchant named James Gentry hired Lincoln to accompany his son Allen on a twelve-hundred-mile flatboat voyage to New Orleans. With their cargo of country produce, the two boys floated down the Ohio River and into the Mississippi, maneuvering with long poles to avoid snags and sandbars, and to navigate in the busy river traffic.

New Orleans was the first real city they had ever seen. Their eyes must have popped as the great harbor came into view, jammed with the masts of sailing ships from distant ports all over the world. The city's cobblestone streets teemed with sailors, traders, and adventurers speaking

Literary Analysis
Biography and Autobiography
What impression of Lincoln does the writer convey with the information in this paragraph?

Vocabulary Builder
regarded (ri gärd′ əd) *v.* thought of; considered

Literary Analysis
Biography and Autobiography
Which details tell why Lincoln's eyes "must have popped" in New Orleans?

strange languages. And there were gangs of slaves everywhere. Lincoln would never forget the sight of black men, women, and children being driven along in chains and auctioned off like cattle. In those days, New Orleans had more than two hundred slave dealers.

The boys sold their cargo and their flatboat and returned up river by steamboat. Abraham earned twenty-four dollars—a good bit of money at the time—for the three-month trip. He handed the money over to his father, according to law and custom.

Thomas Lincoln was thinking about moving on again. Lately he had heard glowing reports about Illinois, where instead of forests there were endless prairies with plenty of rich black soil. Early in 1830, Thomas sold his Indiana farm. The Lincolns piled everything they owned into two ox-drawn wagons and set out over muddy roads, with Abraham, just turned twenty-one, driving one of the wagons himself. They traveled west to their new homesite in central Illinois, not far from Decatur. Once again, Abraham helped his father build a cabin and start a new farm.

He stayed with his family through their first prairie winter, but he was getting restless. He had met an enterprising fellow named Denton Offutt, who wanted him to take another boatload of cargo down the river to New Orleans. Abraham agreed to make the trip with his stepbrother, John Johnston, and a cousin, John Hanks.

When he returned to Illinois three months later, he paid a quick farewell visit to his father and stepmother. Abraham was twenty-two now, of legal age, free to do what he wanted. His parents were settled and could get along without him. Denton Offutt was planning to open a general store in the flourishing village of New Salem, Illinois, and he had promised Lincoln a steady job.

Lincoln arrived in New Salem in July 1831 wearing a faded cotton shirt and blue jeans too short for his long legs—a "friendless, uneducated, penniless boy," as he later described himself. He tended the counter at Denton Offutt's store and slept in a room at the back.

▲ **Critical Viewing**
How does this image of Thomas Lincoln compare with your image of him as he is described in the text? **[Connect]**

Literary Analysis
Biography and Autobiography How do his experiences in New Orleans and cargo-boating change Lincoln's life?

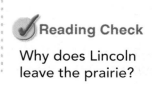

Reading Check
Why does Lincoln leave the prairie?

The village stood in a wooded grove on a bluff above the Sangamon River. Founded just two years earlier, it had about one hundred people living in one- and two-room log houses. Cattle grazed behind split-rail fences, hogs snuffled along dusty lanes, and chickens and geese flapped about underfoot. New Salem was still a small place, but it was growing. The settlers expected it to become a frontier boom town.

With his gifts for swapping stories and making friends, Lincoln fit easily into the life of the village. He showed off his skill with an ax, competed in footraces, and got along with everyone from Mentor Graham, the schoolmaster, to Jack Armstrong, the leader of a rowdy gang called the Clary's Grove boys. Armstrong was the wrestling champion of New Salem. He quickly challenged Lincoln to a match.

On the appointed day, an excited crowd gathered down by the river, placing bets as the wrestlers stripped to the waist for combat. They circled each other, then came to grips, twisting and tugging until they crashed to the ground with Lincoln on top. As he pinned Armstrong's shoulders to the ground, the other Clary's Grove boys dived in to join the scuffle. Lincoln broke away, backed against a cliff, and defiantly offered to take them all on—one at a time. Impressed, Armstrong jumped to his feet and offered Lincoln his hand, declaring the match a draw. After that, they were fast friends.

Lincoln also found a place among the town's intellectuals. He joined the New Salem Debating Society, which met once a week in James Rutledge's tavern. The first time he debated, he seemed nervous. But as he began to speak in his high, reedy voice, he surprised everyone with the force and logic of his argument. "He was already a fine speaker," one debater recalled. "All he lacked was culture."

Lincoln was self-conscious about his meager education, and ambitious to improve himself. Mentor Graham, the schoolmaster and a fellow debater, took a liking to the young man, lent him books, and offered to coach him in the fine points of English grammar. Lincoln had plenty of time to study. There wasn't much business at Offutt's store, so he could spend long hours reading as he sat behind the counter.

Literary Analysis
Biography and Autobiography
What does this anecdote about wrestling reveal about Lincoln?

When the store failed in 1832, Offutt moved on to other schemes. Lincoln had to find something else to do. At the age of twenty-three, he decided to run for the Illinois state legislature. Why not? He knew everyone in town, people liked him, and he was rapidly gaining confidence as a public speaker. His friends urged him to run, saying that a bright young man could go far in politics. So Lincoln announced his candidacy and his political platform. He was in favor of local improvements, like better roads and canals. He had made a study of the Sangamon River, and he proposed that it be dredged and cleared so steamboats could call at New Salem—insuring a glorious future for the town.

Before he could start his campaign, an Indian war flared up in northern Illinois. Chief Black Hawk of the Sauk and Fox tribes had crossed the Mississippi, intending, he said, to raise corn on land that had been taken from his people thirty years earlier. The white settlers were alarmed, and the governor called for volunteers to stop the invasion.

Literary Analysis
Biography and Autobiography
What important career decision does the author relate here?

✓ **Reading Check**

How does Lincoln improve his public-speaking skills?

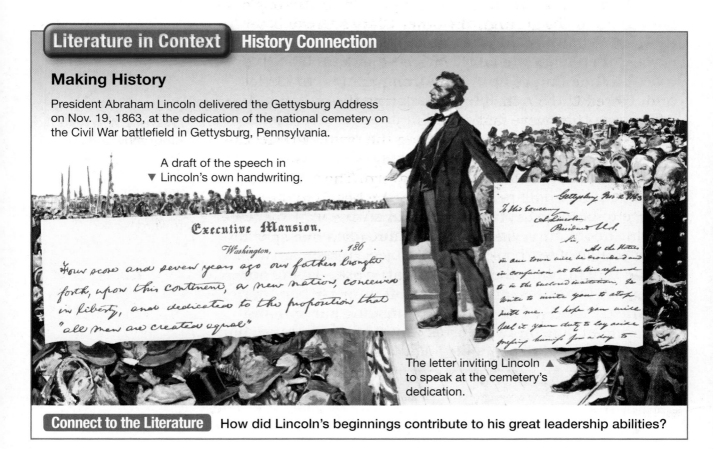

Literature in Context   **History Connection**

Making History

President Abraham Lincoln delivered the Gettysburg Address on Nov. 19, 1863, at the dedication of the national cemetery on the Civil War battlefield in Gettysburg, Pennsylvania.

A draft of the speech in
▼ Lincoln's own handwriting.

The letter inviting Lincoln ▲ to speak at the cemetery's dedication.

Connect to the Literature   How did Lincoln's beginnings contribute to his great leadership abilities?

Lincoln enlisted in a militia company made up of his friends and neighbors. He was surprised and pleased when the men elected him as their captain, with Jack Armstrong as first sergeant. His troops drilled and marched, but they never did sight any hostile Indians. Years later, Lincoln would joke about his three-month stint as a military man, telling how he survived "a good many bloody battles with mosquitoes."

By the time he returned to New Salem, election day was just two weeks off. He jumped into the campaign—pitching horseshoes with voters, speaking at barbecues, chatting with farmers in the fields, joking with customers at country stores. He lost, finishing eighth in a field of thirteen. But in his own precinct,[4] where folks knew him, he received 227 votes out of 300 cast.

Defeated as a politician, he decided to try his luck as a frontier merchant. With a fellow named William Berry as his partner, Lincoln operated a general store that sold everything from axes to beeswax. But the two men showed little aptitude for business, and their store finally "winked out," as Lincoln put it. Then Berry died, leaving Lincoln saddled with a $1,100 debt—a gigantic amount for someone who had never earned more than a few dollars a month. Lincoln called it "the National Debt," but he vowed to repay every cent. He spent the next fifteen years doing so.

To support himself, he worked at all sorts of odd jobs. He split fence rails, hired himself out as a farmhand, helped at the local gristmill.[5] With the help of friends, he was appointed postmaster of New Salem, a part-time job that paid about fifty dollars a year. Then he was offered a chance to become deputy to the local surveyor.[6] He knew nothing about surveying, so he bought a compass, a chain, and a couple of textbooks on the subject. Within six weeks, he had taught himself enough to start work—laying out roads and townsites, and marking off property boundaries.

As he traveled about the county, making surveys and delivering mail to faraway farms, people came to know him as an honest and dependable fellow. Lincoln could be

---

4. precinct (prē′ siŋkt) *n.* election district.
5. gristmill (grist′ mil′) *n.* place where grain is ground into flour.
6. surveyor (sər vā′ ər) *n.* person who identifies or marks the boundaries of land.

Literary Analysis
Biography and Autobiography
Which character traits does this information about campaigning show?

Literary Analysis
Biography and Autobiography
What do the facts here suggest about Lincoln's attitude toward work?

counted on to witness a contract, settle a boundary dispute, or compose a letter for folks who couldn't write much themselves. For the first time, his neighbors began to call him "Abe."

In 1834, Lincoln ran for the state legislature again. This time he placed second in a field of thirteen candidates, and was one of four men elected to the Illinois House of Representatives from Sangamon County. In November, wearing a sixty-dollar tailor-made suit he had bought on credit, the first suit he had ever owned, the twenty-five-year-old legislator climbed into a stagecoach and set out for the state capital in Vandalia.

In those days, Illinois lawmakers were paid three dollars a day to cover their expenses, but only while the legislature was in session. Lincoln still had to earn a living. One of his fellow representatives, a rising young attorney named John Todd Stuart, urged Lincoln to take up the study of law. As Stuart pointed out, it was an ideal profession for anyone with political ambitions.

And in fact, Lincoln had been toying with the idea of becoming a lawyer. For years he had hung around frontier courthouses, watching country lawyers bluster and strut as they cross-examined witnesses and delivered impassioned speeches before juries. He had sat on juries himself, appeared as a witness, drawn up legal documents for his neighbors. He had even argued a few cases before the local justice of the peace.

Yes, the law intrigued him. It would give him a chance to rise in the world, to earn a respected place in the community, to live by his wits instead of by hard physical labor.

Yet Lincoln hesitated, unsure of himself because he had so little formal education. That was no great obstacle, his friend Stuart kept telling him. In the 1830's, few American lawyers had ever seen the inside of a law school. Instead, they "read law" in the office of a practicing attorney until they knew enough to pass their exams.

▲ Critical Viewing
Which side of Lincoln's life does this portrait illustrate? [Interpret]

Vocabulary Builder
intrigued (in trēgd′) v. fascinated

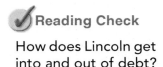 Reading Check

How does Lincoln get into and out of debt?

Lincoln decided to study entirely on his own. He borrowed some law books from Stuart, bought others at an auction, and began to read and memorize legal codes[7] and precedents.[8] Back in New Salem, folks would see him walking down the road, reciting aloud from one of his law books, or lying under a tree as he read, his long legs stretched up the trunk. He studied for nearly three years before passing his exams and being admitted to practice on March 1, 1837.

By then, the state legislature was planning to move from Vandalia to Springfield, which had been named the new capital of Illinois. Lincoln had been elected to a second term in the legislature. And he had accepted a job as junior partner in John Todd Stuart's Springfield law office.

In April, he went back to New Salem for the last time to pack his belongings and say goodbye to his friends. The little village was declining now. Its hopes for growth and prosperity had vanished when the Sangamon River proved too treacherous for steamboat travel. Settlers were moving away, seeking brighter prospects elsewhere.

By 1840, New Salem was a ghost town. It would have been forgotten completely if Abraham Lincoln hadn't gone there to live when he was young, penniless, and ambitious.

---

7. legal codes body of law, as for a nation or a city, arranged systematically.
8. precedents (pres´ ə dents) *n.* legal cases that may serve as a reference.

Thinking About the Selection

1. **Respond:** What would you say was the greatest challenge Lincoln overcame to become a state legislator?

2. **(a) Recall:** What two facts about Lincoln between the ages of eight and twenty-one can you recall? **(b) Generalize:** What words would you use to describe Lincoln at that time in his life?

3. **(a) Analyze:** In what ways did his life change in New Salem? **(b) Connect:** How is the Lincoln of New Salem similar to or different from the Lincoln whom most people know in American history?

4. **(a) Interpret:** How did Lincoln continue to develop and change after he was elected to office? **(b) Speculate:** In what ways did these experiences help him become a great leader?

Apply the Skills

from *Something to Declare* • *A Backwoods Boy*

Comparing Biography and Autobiography

1. **(a)** What facts about her writing life does Julia Alvarez include in the selection from *Something to Declare*? **(b)** How does she feel about these experiences? Explain.

2. **(a)** What details in "A Backwoods Boy" help Freedman show that Lincoln had a difficult childhood? **(b)** What details show that Lincoln chose his own path to build success for himself?

3. What do you think each author wanted readers to know about his or her subject after reading these works? Explain.

Writing to Compare Literary Works

Compare and contrast what you learned about Julia Alvarez with what you learned about Abraham Lincoln. In an essay, discuss how the autobiography and biography helped you get to know these two people. Complete a chart like the one shown to get started.

Overall Impression	Details	My Further Questions

Vocabulary Builder

Practice Respond to each item. Then explain your answer.

1. Describe someone you *regarded* as a hero when you were little.
2. Name something that is full of *perplexities*.
3. Name a television show that *intrigued* you recently.
4. Would you cross a *treacherous* street against the light?
5. What would you do if you faced *quandaries* in a new school?
6. How do you feel when a vacation *concludes*?

QuickReview

Biography: nonfiction in which a writer tells part or all of the life story of another person
Autobiography: nonfiction in which a person tells part or all of his or her own life story

Go Online
Assessment
For: Self-test
Visit: www.PHSchool.com
Web Code: ela-6306

Reading

Directions: *Questions 1–5 are based on this selection.*

It is important that everyone who is eligible to vote do so in all elections. It does not matter whether it is a local, state, or national election.

In some countries, citizens are denied the right to vote. Here in the United States, we have that right. It is important that we live in a country where leaders are chosen by the people. Therefore, voting is a responsibility as well as a right. Many Americans think, "My one vote doesn't really matter." Yet that's not true. Some elections have been very close. Every vote does count. Make sure your vote is one of them.

1. **What is the author's specific purpose for writing?**
   A to explain how the election process works
   B to praise our government
   C to teach the history of the United States
   D to get people to vote

2. **Which statement most clearly indicates the author's purpose?**
   A It is important that everyone who is eligible to vote do so in all elections.
   B It does not matter whether it is a local, state, or national election.
   C Some elections have been very close.
   D Make sure your vote is one of them.

3. **Which detail provides effective evidence that helps the author achieve her purpose?**
   A It is important that everyone who is eligible to vote do so in all elections.
   B It does not matter whether it is a local, state, or national election.
   C Some elections have been very close.
   D Make sure your vote is one of them.

4. **Who is the intended audience for this writing?**
   A adults over 50 years old
   B teenagers under 16
   C women only
   D any eligible voter

5. **The author presents details**
   A in chronological order.
   B with emotional appeal.
   C in order of importance.
   D with descriptions of voting.

Assessment Practice

Vocabulary

Directions *Choose the best definition for the word.*

6. achievement
- A without achieving
- B achieving again
- C the result of achieving
- D achieving before

7. intent
- A the state of an intent
- B after an intent
- C having no aim
- D purpose of

8. direction
- A directing after
- B the act of directing
- C with more directing
- D directing before

9. influence
- A affect
- B deliver
- C exaggerate
- D sickness

10. strategy
- A a plan
- B a military term
- C a game term
- D layers

Directions *Choose the best definition.*

11. disappointment
- A disappoint again
- B never disappoint
- C the result of being disappointed
- D one who disappoints

12. excitement
- A without being excited
- B less than excited
- C one who excites
- D the act of being excited

13. government
- A the result of governing
- B the people who govern
- C the act of governing
- D the people who are governed

14. election
- A a formal contest
- B qualification to vote
- C the counting of choices
- D the act of making a choice

15. information
- A the act of telling or instructing
- B the printed instructions in a text
- C instructions that are specific
- D persuasive language

Exposition: How-to Essay

Expository writing is writing that explains or informs. In a **how-to essay,** you explain how to do or make something. Follow the steps outlined in this workshop to write your own how-to essay.

Assignment Write a how-to essay to explain a process.

What to Include To succeed, your how-to essay should feature the following elements:

- a specific, achievable result
- a list of all the materials needed
- a clear sequence of steps, presented in exact order
- transitional words and phrases to make the order clear
- illustrations or diagrams, as needed, to provide further explanation of any complicated steps
- a clear organizational format
- error-free writing, especially the correct use of modifiers

To preview the criteria on which your how-to essay may be judged, see the rubric on page 428.

Prewriting

Choosing Your Topic

Brainstorming Think about skills you have mastered, games that you like to play, and crafts or recipes you enjoy. Jot down every idea that comes to mind. After five minutes, review your notes. Select an activity that you would enjoy teaching someone to do.

Gathering Details

Begin by making two simple lists: one for the materials your reader will need to complete the task, and one for the steps he or she must follow. In the examples shown here, the writer prepares to write about making spaghetti. Before you begin your draft, review your lists to add any items you may have left out.

Using the Form
You may use elements of this form in these writing situations:
- recipes
- manuals
- travel directions

Work in Progress
Review the work you did on pages 361, 385, and 401.

STEPS	MATERIALS
1. Fill pot with water.	1. large pot with lid
2. Add salt.	2. spaghetti
3. Bring water to boil.	3. teaspoon of salt
4.	4.

Drafting

Shaping Your Writing

Plan your draft so that it has a clear beginning, middle, and end.

- **Include a catchy introduction.** First, identify the task and build your reader's interest. Then, transition into the procedure.

- **Present a step-by-step guide.** Next, list the materials in the order in which they will be used. Present the steps in exact order, adding details and illustrations as needed. Use transitional words and phrases such as *first, next, after, then,* and *finally,* to keep the order clear.

- **Finish with a summary and a send-off.** Sum up the process and encourage your readers to enjoy the finished product.

Revising

Revising Your Overall Structure

Strengthen your opening. To make sure that your essay begins with a strong introduction, keep these questions in mind:
- Does it clearly define the task?
- Does it make the readers want to keep reading?
- Does it make a transition into the steps of the process?

Use your answers to these questions to guide your revision.

Revising Your Word Choice

Check your use of transitions. In a how-to essay, transitional words and phrases help readers follow the steps correctly. Refer to the numbered list of steps you prepared. As you review your draft, make sure that a transitional word or phrase occurs where each number appears on your list. Consult the list of common transitions shown here.

Useful chronological transitions	
first	once you have . . .
next	at the same time
then	while you . . .
after you have . . .	finally

Integrating Grammar Skills

Revising for Correct Use of Troublesome Modifiers

Modifiers are adjectives and adverbs that add details and description to your writing. Most errors occur when writers mistake adjectives for adverbs.

> *Prentice Hall Writing and Grammar Connection: Chapter 25, Section 2*

- **Adjectives:** Use adjectives to modify nouns or pronouns.
  Examples: *This is a <u>tasty</u> meal. It was <u>easy</u> to prepare.*

- **Adverbs:** Use adverbs to modify action verbs.
  Example: *They set the table <u>perfectly</u>.*

Errors Involving *Good* and *Well* To identify and fix errors related to the modifiers *good* and *well*, review these rules:

- ***Good*** is an adjective that modifies only nouns and pronouns.
  Example: *This meal is <u>good</u>. (Good* modifies <u>meal</u>.)

- ***Well*** is an adverb that modifies action verbs, such as **stir**.
  Example: *Stir the spaghetti <u>well</u>. (Well* modifies <u>stir</u>.)

Errors Involving *Better* and *Best* To identify and fix errors related to the modifiers *better* and *best*, determine the number of things or actions.

- Use ***better*** when two things or actions are being compared.
  Example: *I think spaghetti is <u>better</u> than rice.*

- Use ***best*** when three or more things or actions are being compared.
  Example: *I think spaghetti is the <u>best</u> food of all.*

Fixing Errors To correct errors involving troublesome modifiers:

1. **Find the modifiers in your writing.**
2. **For *good* and *well*, determine whether the words are used as adjectives or adverbs.** Using the rules on this page, replace words you have used incorrectly.
3. **For *good, better, best,* choose the modifier that suits the number of items being compared.**

Apply It to Your Editing

Reread your draft and circle the modifiers *good, well, better,* and *best*. Use the rules above to make all necessary corrections.

Student Model: Sara Noē
La Porte, Indiana

How to Write a Poem

The technique of writing poetry varies among different poets. My format depends on the mood I'm in, the environment around me, and what my inspiration is. I can't think of a poem whenever I want to; I have to let it come to me on its own. However, there are many other ways to write poems that rhyme. The most common process I've seen follows these steps:

1. picking a topic you're good at or having knowledge about the subject
2. brainstorming for words that relate to your topic
3. thinking up more words that rhyme with your first list and that also describe your topic
4. creating phrases that include your rhyming words at the end
5. finally, combining your phrases into one and trying to get the words to flow together

> Sara numbers her steps to show their clear sequence.

If you choose a topic you don't like or don't know a lot about, your poem may end up being dull or boring. Sometimes there's a topic you can't get off your mind, and research may help you find out enough to write about it. Word webs and lists are the best way to brainstorm for words. If another way helps you more, go for it!

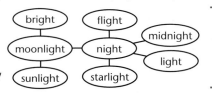

> She uses a diagram to explain the use of a word web.

Remember to make sure your words relate to your topic. For rhyming words, just go through the alphabet until you have plenty. Once you have your list done, sit down in a quiet place and begin organizing the words into phrases. The rhyming words from your list should be at the end of each phrase. Here is where the words and ideas need to flow together. Finally, put all of your phrases together. When you are finished, your words should blend together in one smooth poem.

Those are the steps for rhyming poems, but free-form poems don't rhyme. For these, the best I can tell you is to use your imagination. A thesaurus might help you with finding majestic words or just the right ones for your needs. Poetry is very cheap; the only materials you need are paper, a pencil, and your imagination. Pretty much anybody can write poetry, but it takes dedication and a lot of determination to make it a good poem. Some people write poetry for competition, while others just write in their spare time. Some people, like me, do both. Competition is fun occasionally, but if that's the only reason you write poems, then that may take all the excitement out of it. Poetry is my hobby, and it can easily be yours. Just do your best, and be proud of what you accomplish. Go for it!

> Sara lists all of the materials needed for the process she is explaining.

> She describes a specific result of following the directions in her essay.

Writing Workshop

Editing and Proofreading

Check your essay to correct errors in grammar, punctuation, and spelling.

Focus on Punctuating Transitions: In a how-to essay, many sentences may begin with transitions. Place a comma after each one. In addition, place a comma after introductory phrases or clauses. Look at these examples:

Next, add a teaspoon of salt.

Before stirring, make sure the spoon is clean.

Publishing and Presenting

Consider the following possibilities for sharing your work:

Give a demonstration. Using the information in your essay, give a demonstration. Make visual aids such as posters, diagrams, and photographs to use with your presentation.

Create a "how-to" Web page. Work with a teacher to design a Web page presenting the how-to essays of your class.

Reflecting on Your Writing

Writer's Journal Jot down your thoughts on the experience of writing a how-to essay. Begin by answering these questions:

- As you wrote, what did you learn about the activity or skill that you were explaining?
- Do you think that the part of the activity that was hardest to explain is the hardest to do? Explain your answer.

Prentice Hall Writing and Grammar: Chapter 10

Rubric For Self-Assessment

To assess your how-to essay, use the following rubric:

Criteria	Rating Scale not very　　　　very
How well have you focused your topic?	1　2　3　4　5
How organized are the sequence of steps and list of materials?	1　2　3　4　5
How helpful are illustrations or diagrams?	1　2　3　4　5
How well do you use transitions to make the steps clear?	1　2　3　4　5
How correct is your grammar, especially your use of modifiers?	1　2　3　4　5

Unit 3 Part 2 Main Idea

Skills You Will Learn

Reading Skill: *Using Key Details to Determine the Main Idea*

Literary Analysis: *Author's Influences*

Reading Skill: *Evaluate Author's Purpose*

Reading Skill: *Distinguish Between Important and Unimportant Details*

Literary Analysis: *Mood*

Literary Analysis: *Authors' Styles*

Literature You Will Read

Reading: Main Idea

> The **main idea** in a text is the most significant point that the author makes.

Skills and Strategies You Will Learn in Part 2

In Part 2, you will learn

- to **distinguish between important and unimportant details** to determine the **main idea** (p. 454)
- to **identify key details** that help you determine the **main idea** (p. 432)
- to use these strategies to evaluate an **author's purpose** (p. 450)

Using the Skills and Strategies in Part 2

In Part 2, you will learn to determine the main idea by identifying the most important points that the author makes. You will also learn to find these key details by distinguishing between important and unimportant details. Then, you will apply these strategies to evaluate an author's purpose.

The important details are identified in the following passage.

The Salton Sea is California's biggest inland lake. *Although the heat is unbearable, and the shoreline swarms with insects*, this ugly duckling of a lake harbors some surprises. *Biological surveys show a rich diversity of wildlife.* Although the water temperature is 90 degrees, the lake is crowded with fish. In fact, some local people describe being able to scoop them up in trash bags. *The abundant fish attract an astonishing variety of bird species.* So, *although the lake is* **unattractive for humans, it is a paradise for wildlife.**

Academic Vocabulary: Words for Discussing the Main Idea

The following words will help you write and talk about the main idea as you read the selections in this unit.

Word	Definition	Sample Sentence
essential *adj.*	basic; necessary	The main idea states the *essential* idea of an essay.
key *adj.*	important	The secret document held *key* information.
determine *v.*	decide or figure out	Try to *determine* the author's key points.
identify *v.*	recognize or point out	I can *identify* a mistake that the author made.
significant *adj.*	important	Every detail in the essay should be *significant*.

Vocabulary Skill: Words With Multiple Meanings

▶ **Words With Multiple Meanings** A word with multiple meanings has more than one definition and use.

In your reading, you may notice that a word you know is used in an unexpected way. For example, the word *essential* can be an adjective that describes something, or it can be a noun that names a thing or place.

Word	Part of Speech	Meaning
essential	*adj.*	basic; fundamental
essential	*n.*	something necessary

Activity Use each word in a sentence.

1. box (noun)

2. box (verb)

3. essential (noun)

4. essential (adjective)

5. key (noun)

6. key (adjective)

These skills will help you become a better reader. Practice them with either "Langston Terrace" (p. 434) or "Turkeys" (p. 441).

Reading Skill

The **main idea** is the most important point in a literary work. Sometimes the main idea is stated directly. Other times, you must figure it out by **identifying key details** in the text.

- Key details often reveal what a work is about.
- They are sometimes repeated throughout a literary work.
- They are related to other details in a work.

As you read, use a graphic organizer like the one shown to record key details. Then use those details to determine the main idea.

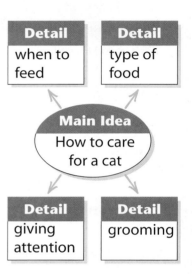

Literary Analysis

An **author's influences** are the cultural and historical factors that affect his or her writing. These factors may include the time and place of an author's birth, the author's cultural background, or world events that happened during the author's lifetime. For example, the gold rush of 1849 might have influenced the ideas of an author who grew up in California in the 1850s. As you read, look for details that indicate an author's influences.

Vocabulary Builder

Langston Terrace

- **applications** (ap´ li kā´ shənz) *n.* forms filled out to make a request (p. 434) *The manager reviewed many job applications.*
- **community** (kə myoo´ nə tē) *n.* group of people living in the same area (p. 436) *Grandma lives in a retirement community.*
- **resident** (rez´ i dənt) *adj.* living in a place (p. 436) *Resident students live on campus.*
- **reunion** (rē yoon´ yən) *n.* a gathering of people who have been separated (p. 437) *I saw many old friends at my class reunion.*

Turkeys

- **dilution** (di loo´ shən) *n.* process of weakening by mixing with something else (p. 442) *Through dilution, the water mixed with the chlorine.*
- **methods** (meth´ ədz) *n.* ways of doing something (p. 443) *People have different methods of studying for an exam.*
- **sensible** (sen´ sə bəl) *adj.* wise; intelligent (p. 444) *Fruit is a sensible snack.*
- **vigilance** (vij´ ə ləns) *n.* watchfulness (p. 445) *The officer's vigilance prevented a crime.*

Background

Langston Terrace Langston Terrace was the first public housing project in Washington, D.C., and the second in the nation. Built in 1938, it housed 274 African American working-class families. Eloise Greenfield's family was among the first to move in. Today, Langston Terrace is a national historic landmark.

Connecting to the Literature

Reading/Writing Connection In "Langston Terrace," the author describes the factors that gave her a sense of community as a child. Make a list of the factors that you think are needed to make up a community. Use three of the following words: *cooperate, establish, identify, reinforce, participate, reside.*

Meet the Author

Eloise **Greenfield** (b. 1929)

Eloise Greenfield spent many hours reading in the library, which was a two-minute walk from her back door. Although she loved books, she did not love writing.

A Love of Words One day, however, Greenfield sat down and began to write. Since then, she has published more than thirty books, including picture books, collections of poetry, and biographies. Greenfield once said, "I love words . . . sometimes they make me laugh. Other times, I feel a kind of pain in struggling to find the right ones. But I keep struggling, because I want to do my best, and because I want children to have the best."

Fast Facts

▶ "Langston Terrace" comes from the book *Childtimes*, which tells the story of Greenfield's family.

▶ Greenfield wrote *Childtimes* with her mother, Lessie Jones Little.

Go Online
Author Link

For: More about the author
Visit: www.PHSchool.com
Web Code: ele-9308

Langston Terrace

Eloise Greenfield

I fell in love with Langston Terrace the very first time I saw it. Our family had been living in two rooms of a three-story house when Mama and Daddy saw the newspaper article telling of the plans to build it. It was going to be a low-rent housing project in northeast Washington, and it would be named in honor of John Mercer Langston, the famous black lawyer, educator, and congressman.

So many people needed housing and wanted to live there, many more than there would be room for. They were all filling out <u>applications</u>, hoping to be one of the 274 families chosen. My parents filled out one, too.

I didn't want to move. I knew our house was crowded—there were eleven of us, six adults and five children—but I didn't want to leave my friends, and I didn't want to go to a strange place and be the new person in a neighborhood and a school where most of the other children already knew each other. I was eight years old, and I had been to three schools. We had moved five times since we'd been in Washington, each time trying to get more space and a better place to live.

▲ Critical Viewing
How do these family members appear to feel about their new home? [Speculate]

Vocabulary Builder
applications (ap´ li kā´ shənz) *n.* forms filled out to make a request

But rent was high so we'd always lived in a house with relatives and friends, and shared the rent.

One of the people in our big household was Lillie, Daddy's cousin and Mama's best friend. She and her husband also applied for a place in the new project, and during the months that it was being built, Lillie and Mama would sometimes walk fifteen blocks just to stand and watch the workmen digging holes and laying bricks. They'd just stand there watching and wishing. And at home, that was all they could talk about. "When we get our new place . . ." "If we get our new place . . ."

Lillie got her good news first. I can still see her and Mama standing at the bottom of the hall steps, hugging and laughing and crying, happy for Lillie, then sitting on the steps, worrying and wishing again for Mama.

Finally, one evening, a woman came to the house with our good news, and Mama and Daddy went over and picked out the house they wanted. We moved on my ninth birthday. Wilbur, Gerald, and I went to school that morning from one house, and when Daddy came to pick us up, he took us home to another one. All the furniture had been moved while we were in school.

Langston Terrace was a lovely birthday present. It was built on a hill, a group of tan brick houses and apartments with a playground as its center. The red mud surrounding the concrete walks had not yet been covered with black soil and grass seed, and the holes that would soon be homes for young trees were filled with rainwater. But it still looked beautiful to me.

We had a whole house all to ourselves. Upstairs and downstairs. Two bedrooms, and the living room would be my bedroom at night. Best of all, I wasn't the only new per-

✓ **Reading Check**

Why is the move to Langston Terrace exciting for the whole family?

son. Everybody was new to this new little <u>community</u>, and by the time school opened in the fall, we had gotten used to each other and had made friends with other children in the neighborhood, too.

I guess most of the parents thought of the new place as an in-between place. They were glad to be there, but their dream was to save enough money to pay for a house that would be their own. Saving was hard, though, and slow, because each time somebody in a family got a raise on the job, it had to be reported to the manager of the project so that the rent could be raised, too. Most people stayed years longer than they had planned to, but they didn't let that stop them from enjoying life.

They formed a <u>resident</u> council to look into any neighbor-hood problems that might come up. They started a choral group and presented music and poetry programs on Sunday evenings in the social room or on the playground. On weekends, they played horseshoes and softball and other games. They had a reading club that met once a week at the Langston branch of the public library, after it opened in the basement of one of the apartment buildings. The library was very close to my house. I could leave by my back door and be there in two minutes. The playground was right in front of my house, and after my sister Vedie was born and we moved a few doors down to a three-bedroom house, I could just look out of my bedroom window to see if any of my friends were out playing.

There were so many games to play and things to do. We played hide-and-seek at the lamppost, paddle tennis and shuffleboard, dodge ball and jacks. We danced in fireplug showers, jumped rope to rhymes, played "Bouncy, Bouncy, Bally," swinging one leg over a bouncing ball, played baseball on a nearby field, had parties in the social room and bus trips to the beach. In the playroom, we played Ping-Pong and pool, learned to sew and embroider and crochet.

For us, Langston Terrace wasn't an in-between place. It was a growing-up place, a good growing-up place. Neighbors who cared, family and friends, and a lot of fun. Life was good. Not perfect, but good. We knew about problems, heard about them, saw them, lived through some hard ones ourselves, but our community wrapped itself around us, put itself between us and the hard knocks, to cushion the blows.

It's been many years since I moved away, but every once in a long while I go back, just to look at things and remember. The large stone animals that decorated the playground are still there. A walrus, a hippo, a frog, and two horses. They've started to crack now, but I remember when they first came to live with us. They were friends, to climb on or to lean against, or to gather around in the evening. You could sit on the frog's head and look way out over the city at the tall trees and rooftops.

Nowadays, whenever I run into old friends, mostly at a funeral, or maybe a wedding, after we've talked about how we've been and what we've been doing, and how old our children are, we always end up talking about our childtime in our old neighborhood. And somebody will say, "One of these days we ought to have a Langston <u>reunion</u>." That's what we always called it, just "Langston," without the "Terrace." I guess because it sounded more homey. And that's what Langston was. It was home.

Literary Analysis
Author's Influences
How do the author's childhood experiences influence her attitude about the importance of family and friends?

Vocabulary Builder
reunion (rē yōōn′ yən) *n.* a gathering of people who have been separated

Apply the Skills

from _Langston Terrace_

Thinking About the Selection

1. **Respond:** What questions would you like to ask Eloise Greenfield about her childhood? Explain your answers.
2. **(a) Recall:** Why does Eloise's family move many times before moving to Langston Terrace? **(b) Compare and Contrast:** How is the family's new home similar to the old home? How is it different?
3. **(a) Recall:** On what day does Eloise's family move to Langston Terrace? **(b) Draw Conclusions:** How does Eloise feel on this day? Explain.
4. **(a) Recall:** Why do some of the parents think of Langston Terrace as an "in-between place"? **(b) Speculate:** How might the author's story have been different if Langston Terrace had been an in-between place for her family?
5. **(a) Recall:** As an adult, how does Eloise Greenfield feel about Langston Terrace? **(b) Speculate:** Why might former residents of Langston Terrace want to have a reunion? Explain.

Reading Skill

6. Eloise Greenfield's thoughts and feelings about Langston Terrace make up the main idea of this essay. List four **key details** that show Greenfield's thoughts and feelings.
7. In your own words, state the **main idea** of this essay.

Literary Analysis

8. In a chart like the one shown, list cultural and historical factors that may have **influenced** Greenfield's writing of "Langston Terrace."

Time and Place	Cultural Background	World Events

9. Which factors on your completed chart do you think influenced the author's writing the most? Explain.

Vocabulary Builder

Practice Answer each of the following questions with either *yes* or *no*. Then explain your answer.

1. Should someone who wants a job fill out an <u>application</u>?
2. Can a <u>community</u> help someone in need?
3. Does a <u>resident</u> apartment dweller need a place to live?
4. If you want to see an old friend, should you go to a <u>reunion</u>?

Writing

Write a **journal entry** as if you were a young Eloise Greenfield. Describe an event from the essay and, as Eloise, include your own thoughts and feelings about the event. First, choose an event in the essay as your topic. Jot down notes about Eloise's reaction to the event. Then tell what happened. Include how you feel about the event, rather than just reporting it.

For *Grammar, Vocabulary,* and *Assessment,* see **Build Language Skills,** pages 448–449.

Extend Your Learning

Listening and Speaking With a partner, perform a **dramatic reading** of the last two paragraphs of "Langston Terrace." Use your voice to communicate meaning. Pause before an important point and speak slowly to show the author's thoughtfulness as she thinks back on her childhood. Ask your partner to provide feedback on your presentation. Then revise your reading to incorporate his or her comments.

Research and Technology With a group, use the Internet and library resources to prepare a **presentation** about one of your communities. For example, you might choose your school, neighborhood, or city.

- Research your community's history.
- Make a map of your community and its landmarks.
- Prepare a poster that highlights the community's features.

Narrative Essay

Background

Conservation "Turkeys" tells of the efforts of conservationists to preserve a population of wild turkeys. Conservation became an issue in the United States in the early 1900s when President Theodore Roosevelt established the first wildlife refuge at Pelican Island, Florida. He later set aside more than 140 million acres nationwide as forest reserves.

Connecting to the Literature

Reading/Writing Connection In "Turkeys," Bailey White shows how people make connections with the world around them. Make a list of ways you connect with the natural world. Use three of the following words: *evoke, affect, focus, respond.*

Review

For **Reading Skill, Literary Analysis,** and **Vocabulary Builder,** see page 432.

Meet the Author

Bailey **White** (b. 1950)

Bailey White's father, Robb, was a writer of children's stories and television and movie scripts. Inspired by his love of words, Bailey White began writing in her teen years. Her mother, Rosalie, was a farmer. Through her mother, White gained an admiration for nature.

Letting the Story Roll As a teacher in Thomasville, Georgia, White did not expect to become famous. However, as an essayist on National Public Radio, she shared her observations with listeners across the country. About fiction, White states, "I liked the idea of starting with just anything . . . and being free to just let the story roll out from there."

Fast Facts

▶ White's first collection of essays, *Mama Makes Up Her Mind and Other Dangers of Southern Living,* was on the bestseller list for 55 weeks.

▶ In 1999, she began to write full time.

For: More about the author
Visit: www.PHSchool.com
Web Code: ele-9309

TURKEYS

Bailey White

Something about my mother attracts ornithologists.[1] It all started years ago when a couple of them discovered she had a rare species of woodpecker coming to her bird feeder. They came in the house and sat around the window, exclaiming and taking pictures with big fancy cameras. But long after the red cockaded woodpeckers had gone to roost, the ornithologists were still there. There always seemed to

---

1. **ornithologists** (ôr′ nə thäl′ ə jists) *n.* people who study birds.

be three or four of them wandering around our place and staying for supper.

In those days, during the 1950's, the big concern of ornithologists in our area was the wild turkey. They were rare, and the pure-strain wild turkeys had begun to interbreed with farmers' domestic stock. The species was being degraded. It was extinction by <u>dilution</u>, and to the ornithologists it was just as tragic as the more dramatic demise of the passenger pigeon or the Carolina parakeet.

Vocabulary Builder
dilution (di lo͞oʹ shən)
n. process of weakening by mixing with something else

Literature in Context   Science Connection

Leaving the Nest

Most birds' eggs need to be kept at a regular temperature between 99 and 102 degrees F in order to hatch. For most birds, this means incubating, or warming, the eggs, usually by sitting on them. For some birds in extremely hot climates, though, the parent bird may actually have to cool the egg to keep it at the correct temperature. The parent bird cools the egg by shading it or dripping water on it.

Ostrich egg ▼

	Wild Turkey	Ruby-throated Hummingbird	Ostrich
Nest	Rough pile of leaves, twigs, brush on ground	Cup made of moss, fluff, and spiderwebs in a tree	Shallow hole in ground
Incubation time	28 days	14 days	42 days
Egg size	2 1/2 to 3 inches wide—less than a pound (a little larger than a chicken's egg)	Size of a bean	6 inches wide—3 lbs. (the equivalent of two dozen chicken eggs)
Young leave nest and feed themselves	12–24 hours after hatching	3 weeks after hatching	Almost immediately
Fledged (having all the feathers needed to fly)	10 days old	2–3 weeks old	Ostriches never fly, but they have all their feathers when they hatch.

◀ Young turkeys are called "poults." Although they can walk and feed themselves, they stay with the parent birds until they can fly and escape on their own from predators. Even then, they may continue to travel as a group.

Chicken egg ▼

Hummingbird egg ▼

Connect to the Literature (a) The ornithologists in this story are watching and protecting a nest of wild turkey eggs. Based on the information provided, why might the eggs need to be protected? (b) Would the other types of eggs described need the same protection? Explain.

One ornithologist had devised a formula to compute the ratio of domestic to pure-strain wild turkey in an individual bird by comparing the angle of flight at takeoff and the rate of acceleration. And in those sad days, the turkeys were flying low and slow.

It was during that time, the spring when I was six years old, that I caught the measles. I had a high fever, and my mother was worried about me. She kept the house quiet and dark and crept around silently, trying different <u>methods</u> of cooling me down.

Even the ornithologists stayed away—but not out of fear of the measles or respect for a household with sickness. The fact was, they had discovered a wild turkey nest. According to the formula, the hen was pure-strain wild— not a taint of the sluggish domestic bird in her blood—and the ornithologists were camping in the woods, protecting her nest from predators and taking pictures.

One night our phone rang. It was one of the ornithologists. "Does your little girl still have measles?" he asked.

"Yes," said my mother. "She's very sick. Her temperature is 102."

"I'll be right over," said the ornithologist.

In five minutes a whole carload of them arrived. They marched solemnly into the house, carrying a cardboard box. "A hundred and two, did you say? Where is she?" they asked my mother.

They crept into my room and set the box down on the bed. I was barely conscious, and when I opened my eyes, their worried faces hovering over me seemed to float out of the

Reading Skill

Main Idea How do these details support the main idea that pure-strain wild turkeys are becoming rare?

Vocabulary Builder

methods (meth´ ədz) *n.* ways of doing something

◀ **Critical Viewing** Compare this turkey's appearance with that of another bird you know. **[Compare and Contrast]**

✔ Reading Check

What happened to the author when she was six years old?

darkness like giant, glowing eggs. They snatched the covers off me and felt me all over. They consulted in whispers.

"Feels just right, I'd say."

"A hundred two—can't miss if we tuck them up close and she lies still."

I closed my eyes then, and after a while the ornithologists drifted away, their pale faces bobbing up and down on the black wave of fever.

The next morning I was better. For the first time in days I could think. The memory of the ornithologists with their whispered voices was like a dream from another life. But when I pulled down the covers, there staring up at me with googly eyes and wide mouths were sixteen fuzzy baby turkeys, and the cracked chips and caps of sixteen brown speckled eggs.

I was a <u>sensible</u> child. I gently stretched myself out. The eggshells crackled, and the turkey babies fluttered and cheeped and snuggled against me. I laid my aching head back on the pillow and closed my eyes. "The ornithologists," I whispered. "The ornithologists have been here."

It seems the turkey hen had been so disturbed by the elaborate protective measures that had been undertaken on her behalf that she had abandoned her nest on the night the eggs were due to hatch. It was a cold night. The ornithologists, not having an incubator on hand, used their heads and came up with the next best thing.

The baby turkeys and I gained our strength together. When I was finally able to get out of bed and feebly creep around the house, the turkeys peeped and cheeped around my ankles, scrambling to keep up with me and tripping over their own big spraddle-toed feet. When I went outside for the first time, the turkeys tumbled after me down the steps and scratched around in the yard while I sat in the sun.

Finally, in late summer, the day came when they were ready to fly for the first time as adult birds. The ornithologists gathered. I ran down the hill, and the turkeys ran too. Then, one by one, they took off. They flew high and fast. The ornithologists made Vs with their thumbs and forefingers, measuring angles. They consulted their stopwatches

Reading Skill
Main Idea What key detail do you learn here that is important to the ornithologists' plan?

Vocabulary Builder
sensible (sen´ sə bil) *adj.* wise; intelligent

Literary Analysis
Author's Influence How do you think this experience has influenced the author's feelings about wild turkeys?

and paced off distances. They scribbled in their tiny note-books. Finally they looked at each other. They sighed. They smiled. They jumped up and down and hugged each other. "One hundred percent pure wild turkey!" they said.

Nearly forty years have passed since then. Now there's a vaccine for measles. And the woods where I live are full of pure wild turkeys. I like to think they are all descendants of those sixteen birds I saved from the <u>vigilance</u> of the ornithologists.

◄ **Critical Viewing**
How old do you think this turkey is? How can you tell? **[Infer]**

Apply the Skills

Turkeys

Thinking About the Selection

1. **Respond:** How would you react if you woke up to find newly hatched turkeys in your bed?
2. **(a) Recall:** Where do the events in "Turkeys" take place? **(b) Analyze:** What problem threatens the wild turkey at this time?
3. **(a) Recall:** Why are the ornithologists around the author's home? **(b) Interpret:** At the beginning of the essay, what is the relationship between the author and the ornithologists?
4. **(a) Recall:** What event brings the wild turkey and the author together? **(b) Evaluate:** Why is the author's fever important to the ornithologists? **(c) Analyze:** What is amusing about the solution to the ornithologists' problem?
5. **(a) Make a Judgment:** Do you think the actions of the ornithologists in this narrative are important? Why or why not? **(b) Interpret:** How do you think White feels when she watches the turkeys take off? Explain.

Reading Skill

6. Bailey White's thoughts and feelings about the ornithologists make up the main idea of this essay. List four **key details** that show White's thoughts and feelings.
7. In your own words, state the **main idea** of this essay.

Literary Analysis

8. In a chart like the one shown, list cultural and historical factors that may have **influenced** White's writing of "Turkeys."

Time and Place	Cultural Background	World Events

9. Which factors on your completed chart do you think influenced the author's writing the most? Explain.

QuickReview

Essay at a Glance
The author describes an interesting and funny event from her childhood.

Go Online
Assessment
For: Self-test
Visit: www.PHSchool.com
Web Code: ela-6308

Main Idea: the most important point in a literary work or passage

Author's Influences: the cultural and historical factors that affect an author's writing

Vocabulary Builder

Practice Answer each of the following questions with either *yes* or *no*. Then explain your answer.

1. Is a <u>dilution</u> of bleach stronger than plain bleach?
2. Are there many <u>methods</u> in the study of science?
3. Is it <u>sensible</u> to wear sneakers when mountain climbing?
4. Will a town's <u>vigilance</u> increase the crime rate?

Writing

Write a **journal entry** as if you were a young Bailey White. Describe an event from the essay and, as White, include your own thoughts and feelings about the event. First, choose an event in the essay as your topic. Jot down notes about White's reaction to the event. Then tell what happened. Include how you feel about the event, rather than just reporting it.

For *Grammar, Vocabulary,* and *Assessment,* see **Build Language Skills,** pages 448–449.

Extend Your Learning

Listening and Speaking With a partner, perform a **dramatic reading** of the morning when Bailey awakes to find baby turkeys in her bed. Use your voice to communicate meaning. Pause before an important point and speak slowly to show Bailey's bewilderment. Ask your partner for feedback on your presentation. Then revise it to incorporate his or her comments.

Research and Technology With a group, use the Internet and library resources to prepare a **presentation** on conservation. For example, you might choose land or animal conservation.

- Research the history of your topic.
- Investigate problems and solutions associated with your topic.
- Prepare a poster to promote conservation.

Build Language Skills

Vocabulary Skill

Words With Multiple Meanings Some words have more than one meaning. Clarify the meaning by looking at the context, or the situation, in which the word is used. The word *dashed* commonly means "ran quickly." Here, the word has a different meaning:

We dashed the coconut on the rock to crack it open.

The fact that the coconut is cracked is a clue that *dashed* probably means "threw down with force."

Practice Explain two meanings each word can have. Then, write a sentence that shows how the word is used with each meaning you identify.

1. close
2. lap
3. extension
4. following
5. sign

MorePractice

For more practice with adverbs, see the Grammar Handbook, p. R31.

Grammar Lesson

Adverbs An **adverb** is a word that modifies—or describes—a verb, an adjective, or another adverb. Adverbs answer the questions *where?, when?, how?,* and *to what extent?*

He ran <u>slowly</u>.	modifies *ran*	*How* did he run?
She walked <u>extremely</u> slowly.	modifies *slowly*	*To what extent* did she walk slowly?
Maples are <u>very</u> tall trees.	modifies *tall*	*To what extent* are they tall?

Practice Write the adverb that modifies the underlined word in each sentence. Explain what question it answers. Then, rewrite the sentence using a different adverb.

1. They <u>rehearsed</u> every day until they knew their parts.
2. Juanita spoke too <u>softly</u>.
3. Ricky, in a very <u>kind</u> manner, reminded Juanita to speak loudly.
4. The audience <u>applauded</u> appreciatively.
5. Congratulations to the students for a job well <u>done</u>.

W͓G Prentice Hall Writing and Grammar Connection: Chapter 16, Section 2

Reading: Main Idea

Directions: *Read the selection. Then, answer the questions.*

The world's tropical rain forests are filled with treasures more valuable than gold or jewels. Rain forests include many varieties of fruit, thousands of species of animals, many plants with healing properties, and trees. The trees give off oxygen, which is necessary to humans. Rubber trees yield natural rubber, which is used in many products. The sap of one kind of tree is similar to diesel oil.

1. According to the passage, which are treasures of the rain forests?
   A oxygen, fruit, gold
   B fruits, rubber, oxygen
   C diesel fuel, animals, jewels
   D fruits, animals, plants

2. Why are the rain forests important for the study of medicine?
   A They have an abundance of fruit.
   B The sap of one kind of tree is like diesel oil.
   C They have many plants with healing properties.
   D They contain useful resources.

3. What is the main idea?
   A Rain forests include many varieties of fruits.
   B There are thousands of species of animals in rain forests.
   C Tropical rain forests are valuable.
   D Oxygen is necessary to humans.

4. Which detail does not support the main idea?
   A Rain forests contain many plants with healing properties.
   B Trees in the rain forests give off oxygen.
   C Rubber is used in many products.
   D One tree's sap is like diesel oil.

Timed Writing: Explanation [Critical Stance]

Review either "Langston Terrace" or "Turkeys" and write a brief explanation of the main idea of the essay. Include key details from the essay that point to the main idea. **(20 minutes)**

 ## Writing Workshop: *Work in Progress*

Persuasive Essay

Work with a small group to generate a list of five things that could be changed in your community. Write one sentence for each point that clearly states what should be changed. Save this Change List in your writing portfolio.

Reading Informational Materials

Magazine Articles

In Part 2, you are learning about author's purpose. Knowing an author's purpose is important when reading magazine articles. If you read "Turkeys," you learned how one person saved turkeys from harm. The magazine article that follows shows a method that is quite different.

About Magazine Articles

A **magazine** is a periodical, a collection of articles published at regular time periods—usually weekly or monthly. The articles in magazines focus on topics of interest at the time the magazine is published. Magazine articles usually have these characteristics:

- pictures and graphics
- headings to break up text
- a title meant to capture readers' interest

Reading Skill

An **author's purpose** is his or her main reason for writing. Authors of nonfiction texts, such as magazine articles, write for one or more of these purposes:

- to inform readers about a person or topic
- to state a viewpoint
- to persuade readers to take a specific action
- to entertain readers

As you read, look for details in the text that indicate the author's purpose. Then judge whether the author is successful in achieving that purpose. Use a graphic organizer like the one shown to list details and language that help you **recognize and evaluate an author's purpose.**

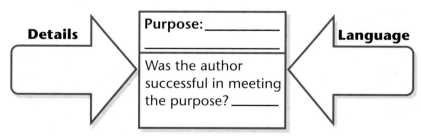

Photographs illustrate the topic of the magazine article. Here, President Harry Truman pardons a turkey in the 1940s.

Where Do **Turkeys** Go After **Being Pardoned** by the **President?**

Bijal P. Trivedi

Presidential turkeys spend their entire life bettering themselves in anticipation of that glorious presidential pardon; that ethereal moment when they are forever reprieved from the roasting rack.

It all begins in April when about 2,500 toms hatch from their shell. These turkeys, already a notch above the common variety destined for the dinner plate, are raised in an air-conditioned barn with fluffy piles of sawdust up to their knees, said National Turkey Federation Chairman Nick Weaver.

In August, when the toms have reached about 25 pounds (11 kilograms), six are chosen as presidential candidates. Weaver, as chairman of the NTF, will raise and choose the final pair of birds destined for the appointment at the White House.

Birds Chosen for Looks

These six elite specimens, chosen for their fine plumage, poise and portly figure, are moved to a separate building where they are groomed for their future executive tasks.

From August through November and up until the day before the pardon, the goal is to familiarize the birds with people so that they don't lose their composure during the ceremony with the President.

Weaver came up with a particularly unique way to do this. The six birds are exposed to people dressed in long-sleeved, dark-blue overalls to simulate the dark-blue suits of the officials and security personnel present at the White House.

This year Weaver chose the presidential and vice presidential

The magazine's name and issue date often appear at the bottom of the page.

November 20, 2001 • *National Geographic Today*

turkeys from the half dozen eager toms in Goldsboro, North Carolina, two days before the ceremony in the nation's capital.

Weaver chose the tom he thought was the "most regal"—the bird with the most beautiful white plumage, the best behavior and poise. The First Bird, Liberty, and his back-up, Freedom, were placed in crates and driven to Washington.

> A heading helps break up the text and provides a clue to the main idea.

The Good Life

For the presidential pair, their road trip to the White House is where the good life begins. The birds spend the night before the White House ceremony at the Hotel Washington, a plush establishment with a terrace restaurant that over-looks the President's mansion. The unlikely guests spend the night on the terrace level in a service corridor.

What the President Said

After leaving the Hotel Washington the birds were whisked to the White House Rose Garden. When the President appeared, Liberty was hoisted onto a pedestal.

"I'm not going to speak too long, because our guest of honor looks a little nerv-ous," said Bush. "Nobody's told him yet that I'm going to give him a pardon."

Then the pardon: "For this turkey and his traveling companion, this will not be their last Thanksgiving," said the President. "By virtue of an unconditional presidential pardon, they are safe from harm."

He then invited the children to pet Liberty. Within a couple of minutes of pardoning the turkey, a few turkey embraces, and a few autographs, the President hurried back inside the White House.

For Liberty it was the pinnacle of a career. Liberty and Freedom were whisked off to Frying Pan Park's Kidwell Farm in Herndon, Virginia—about 30 minutes west of Washington—where the pardoned turkeys live.

> Authors of magazine articles often use quo-tations to add interest to their stories. Note that the author identi-fies the source of each quotation in the article. Here, he identifies President George W. Bush but uses only his last name, because readers in 2001 would have known to whom the author was referring.

November 20, 2001 • *National Geographic Today*

Reading: Evaluating an Author's Purpose

Directions: *Choose the letter of the best answer to each question.*

1. Which conclusion can you draw from the article's title?
   A The author takes the subject seriously.
   B This is a scientific article.
   C The article is probably humorous.
   D This is a fictional article.

2. Which detail suggests one of the author's purposes?
   A the number of turkeys born each year
   B the name of the representative of the National Turkey Federation
   C the description of the process for choosing a turkey
   D the description of the Hotel Washington

3. Which sentence from the article suggests that one purpose of the author is to entertain readers?
   A Presidential turkeys spend their entire life bettering themselves in anticipation of that glorious presidential pardon.
   B It all begins in April when about 2,500 toms hatch.
   C Weaver came up with a particularly unique way to do this.
   D Liberty was hoisted onto a pedestal.

Reading: Comprehension and Interpretation

Directions: *Write your answers on a separate sheet of paper.*

4. Aside from being entertained, what purpose might someone have for reading this article? **[Generative]**

5. Do you think the author achieves the purpose of entertaining the reader? Why or why not? **[Evaluate]**

6. What is the purpose of pardoning the turkey? **[Generative]**

Timed Writing: Explanation

Explain at least three ways the author of this article uses humor to entertain readers. Use specific examples in your explanation.
(20 minutes)

These skills will help you become a better reader. Practice them with either "La Leña Buena" (p. 456) or the excerpt from *The Pigman & Me* (p. 461).

Reading Skill

The **main idea** is the most important point in a literary work. Individual paragraphs or sections may also have a central idea that supports the main idea of the work. To determine the main idea, **distinguish between important and unimportant details.** Important details are small pieces of information that tell more about the main idea. They are also called *supporting details.*

- Ask yourself questions such as these about details in a literary work: *Why did the author include this detail? Does this detail help readers understand the main idea of the work?*
- Keep in mind that not all details support the main idea.

To track details as you read, use a chart like the one shown.

Selection: "U.S. Completes Gold Run"	
Detail	Important?
Hamm's team beat Brazil in 2004 Olympics.	√
Wambach scored winning goal for U.S.	
Hamm said she was proud of Olympic win.	√
Husband plays baseball.	
Main Idea: Mia Hamm was a key player on the U.S. soccer team that won gold in 2004 Olympics.	

Literary Analysis

Mood is the overall feeling a literary work produces in a reader. For example, the mood of a work may be happy, sad, scary, or hopeful. To create a particular mood, writers carefully choose words and create word pictures that appeal to the reader's senses.

Some literary works present a single mood throughout a selection. In other works, the mood changes within the piece.

Vocabulary Builder

La Leña Buena

- **engulfing** (en gulf′ iŋ) *adj.* swallowing up; overwhelming (p. 456) *The engulfing fog hid the tops of skyscrapers.*
- **fragrant** (frā′ grənt) *adj.* having a pleasant odor (p. 456) *I prefer fragrant roses to tulips with no scent.*
- **confiscated** (kän′ fis kāt′ id) *v.* seized, usually by governmental authority (p. 457) *Police confiscated the illegally parked car.*

from The Pigman & Me

- **exact** (eg zakt′) *v.* demand with force or authority (p. 462) *District attorneys exact punishment for convicts.*
- **undulating** (un′ jə lāt′ iŋ) *adj.* moving in waves, like a snake (p. 467) *The banner was undulating in the breeze.*
- **distorted** (di stôrt′ id) *adj.* twisted out of normal shape (p. 467) *The fun house mirror distorted our images.*

Build Understanding • *La Leña Buena*

Background

Mexico in the Early 1900s "La Leña Buena" tells why some Mexicans left Mexico in the early 1900s. The Mexican Revolution, a violent civil war, lasted from 1910 to 1920 and left the country in a condition that was difficult for all but the wealthiest citizens. Most urban workers as well as farmers and peasants were very poor. Large numbers of Mexicans, eager for better opportunities, crossed the border into the United States.

Connecting to the Literature

Reading/Writing Connection In this essay, the author recalls stories told by the brother of his great-grandfather about life in Mexico before he left. In a few sentences, explain how young people can benefit from stories told by older family members. Use at least three of the following words: *benefit, enable, contribute, enrich.*

Meet the Author

John Phillip **Santos** (b. 1957)

John Phillip Santos began writing poetry when he was young and developed a love of words. He went on to become a writer, journalist, filmmaker, and producer.

Stories to Tell In speaking to students, Santos reminds them that America is home to people from all over the world and that all these people have stories to tell. He encourages young people to find their own stories by studying their past.

Fast Facts

▶ Santos has written and produced more than forty television documentaries. Two of his films have earned Emmy nominations.

▶ Most of his documentaries have focused on culture, religion, and politics.

▶ He is the first American of Mexican descent to win a Rhodes scholarship, an honor for college students.

Go Online
Author Link

For: More about the author
Visit: www.PHSchool.com
Web Code: ele-9310

La Leña Buena
John Phillip Santos

Good wood is like a jewel, Tío Abrán, my great-grandfather Jacobo's twin brother, used to say. Huisache burns fast, in twisting yellow flames, <u>engulfing</u> the log in a cocoon of fire. It burns brightly, so it is sought after for Easter bonfires. But it does not burn hot, so it's poor wood for home fires. On a cold morning in the sierra, you can burn a whole tree by noon. Mesquite, and even better, cedar—these are noble, hard woods. They burn hot and long. Their smoke is <u>fragrant</u>. And if you know how to do it, they make exquisite charcoal.

Vocabulary Builder
engulfing (en gulf´ iŋ)
adj. swallowing up; overwhelming

fragrant (frā´ grənt)
adj. having a pleasant odor

"La leña buena es como una joya"

Good wood is like a jewel. And old Tío Abrán knew wood the way a jeweler knows stones, and in northern Coahuila, from Múzquiz to Rosita, his charcoal was highly regarded for its sweet, long-burning fire.

Abrán was one of the last of the Garcias to come north. Somewhere around 1920, he finally had to come across the border with his family. He was weary of the treacheries[1] along the roads that had become a part of life in the sierra towns since the beginning of the revolution ten years earlier. Most of the land near town had been deforested and the only wood he could find around Palaú was huisache. To find any of the few pastures left with arbors of mesquite trees, he had to take the unpaved mountain road west from Múzquiz, along a route where many of the militantes[2] had their camps. Out by the old Villa las Rusias, in a valley far off the road, there were mesquite trees in every direction as far as you could see. He made an arrangement with the owner of the villa to give him a cut from the sale of charcoal he made from the mesquite. But many times, the revolucionarios <u>confiscated</u> his day's load of wood, leaving him to return home, humiliated, with an empty wagon.

Aside from Tía Pepa and Tío Anacleto, who had returned to Mexico by then, he had been the last of the Garcias left in Mexico, and he had left reluctantly. On the day he arrived in San Antonio with his family, he had told his brother Abuelo Jacobo, "If there was still any mesquite that was easy to get to, we would've stayed."

---

1. treacheries (trech´ ər ēz) *n.* acts of betrayal.
2. *militantes* (mil´ ē tan´ tās) *n.* Spanish for "militants"—people who fight or are willing to fight.

Apply the Skills

La Leña Buena

Thinking About the Selection

1. **Respond:** What qualities of Tío Abrán do you admire? Why?
2. **(a) Recall:** How does Tío Abrán earn his living in Mexico? **(b) Connect:** What are the "treacheries" that the author mentions in this work? **(c) Infer:** Why do you think the revolutionaries take Tío Abrán's wood?
3. **(a) Recall:** Where were most members of the Garcia family living while Tío Abrán was still in Mexico? **(b) Interpret:** What role do trees play in Tío Abrán's decision to stay and then to leave Mexico? **(c) Speculate:** Do you think that he continues in the same line of work after he moves? Explain.
4. **(a) Recall:** What does Tío Abrán say on the day of his arrival in San Antonio, Texas? **(b) Infer:** What does this remark tell you about his feelings toward Mexico?
5. **(a) Take a Position:** Do you think that Tío Abrán's decision to leave Mexico was a wise one for his family? Why or why not? **(b) Speculate:** How do you think the author has been affected by his great-uncle's decision? **(c) Discuss:** Share your response with a partner. Then discuss whether someone else's response affected your thinking.

Reading Skill

6. What is the **main idea** of this essay?
7. Identify two important **details** that support this main idea.
8. What is one **unimportant detail**?

Literary Analysis

9. What is one **mood** that is created in this essay?
10. Complete a chart like the one shown to analyze which words and images create the mood in "La Leña Buena."

Words		Images		Mood

Vocabulary Builder

Practice Write sentences that correctly use each word pair.

1. confiscated; purses
2. fragrant; laundry
3. engulfing; crowd

Writing

When Tío Abrán arrived in San Antonio, he had family there to help him adjust to a new culture. Write a **problem-and-solution essay** to help immigrants adjust to one aspect of life in the United States.

- First, clearly state one problem immigrants might face.
- Then, provide step-by-step solutions to the problem.
- Give evidence that supports your suggested solutions.

For *Grammar, Vocabulary,* and *Assessment,* see **Build Language Skills,** pages 472–473.

Extend Your Learning

Listening and Speaking In a small group, hold an **informal discussion** to consider these questions:

- What are the pros and cons of having aunts, uncles, and grandparents living near you?
- What are the pros and cons of relatives living in different cities, states, or countries?

Each person in the group should offer an opinion backed up with facts. Offer your opinion without dominating the discussion. Use good listening skills while each person is talking. At the end of the discussion, summarize the group's ideas.

Research and Technology To learn more about 21st-century immigration to the United States, use a library catalog or an Internet search engine. Select at least two sources and write **annotated bibliography entries**. Include publication information and explain why the source is valuable.

Build Understanding • from *The Pigman & Me*

Background

Ground Rules Every place and situation has its own set of rules. Some of these rules are formal and printed. Sometimes, though, the unwritten rules may be just as important as the written ones. For example, an unwritten rule is to support your friends. In this excerpt, the author recalls a time when he had to figure out how to manage unwritten rules.

Connecting to the Literature

Reading/Writing Connection This selection deals with the ways rules influence our lives. In a journal entry, write one written or unwritten rule that is important at school, in the library, or in your home. Use at least three of the following words: *benefit, enable, contribute, enrich.*

Meet the Author

Paul **Zindel** (1936–2003)

As a teenager, Paul Zindel lived for a while on Staten Island, New York, with his mother and sister. Before he wrote the novel *The Pigman,* Zindel taught high school science while writing in his spare time. After the success of *The Pigman,* Zindel started writing full time.

Writing for Teens "I felt I could do more for teenagers by writing for them," he once said. He discovered that most young adult books did not relate to the teenagers he knew. Zindel made a list of pointers and then wrote another novel, following his own advice.

Fast Facts

► On Staten Island, Zindel met Frankie Vivona. Although they were not relatives, Zindel used the title *nonno,* "grandfather" in Italian, for Vivona.
► Vivona inspired the character Angelo Pignati in the novel *The Pigman.* Zindel then used his *nonno*'s real name in his memoir, *The Pigman & Me,* from which the excerpt comes.

Go Online Author Link

For: More about the author
Visit: www.PHSchool.com
Web Code: ele-9311

from The Pigman & Me
Paul Zindel

When trouble came to me, it didn't involve anybody I thought it would. It involved the nice, normal, smart boy by the name of John Quinn. Life does that to us a lot. Just when we think something awful's going to happen one way, it throws you a curve and the something awful happens another way. This happened on the first Friday, during gym period, when we were allowed to play games in the school yard. A boy by the name of Richard Cahill, who lived near an old linoleum factory, asked me if I'd like to play paddle ball with him, and I said, "Yes." Some of the kids played softball, some played warball, and there were a few other games where you could sign out equipment and do what you wanted. What I didn't know was that you were allowed to sign out the paddles for only fifteen minutes per period so more kids could get a chance to use them. I just didn't happen to know that

▲ **Critical Viewing**
What are some conflicts among students that might occur in a scene like this one? **[Analyze]**

✔ **Reading Check**

Why do students need to sign out the paddles in fifteen-minute intervals?

little rule, and Richard Cahill didn't think to tell me about it. Richard was getting a drink from the water fountain when John Quinn came up to me and told me I had to give him my paddle.

"No," I said, being a little paranoid about being the new kid and thinking everyone was going to try to take advantage of me.

"Look, you *have* to give it to me," John Quinn insisted.

That was when I did something berserk. I was so wound up and frightened that I didn't think, and I struck out at him with my right fist. I had forgotten I was holding the paddle, and it smacked into his face, giving him an instant black eye. John was shocked. I was shocked. Richard Cahill came running back and he was shocked.

"What's going on here?" Mr. Trellis, the gym teacher, growled.

"He hit me with the paddle," John moaned, holding his eye. He was red as a beet, as Little Frankfurter, Conehead, Moose, and lots of the others gathered around.

"He tried to take the paddle away from me!" I complained.

"His time was up," John said.

Mr. Trellis set me wise to the rules as he took John over to a supply locker and pulled out a first-aid kit.

"I'm sorry," I said, over and over again.

Then the bell rang, and all John Quinn whispered to me was that he was going to get even. He didn't say it like a nasty rotten kid, just more like an all-American boy who knew he'd have to regain his dignity about having to walk around school with a black eye. Before the end of school, Jennifer came running up to me in the halls and told me John Quinn had announced to everyone he was going to <u>exact</u> revenge on me after school on Monday. That was the note of disaster my first week at school ended on, and I was terrified because I didn't know how to fight. I had never even been in a fight. What had happened was all an accident. It really was.

When Nonno Frankie arrived on Saturday morning, he found me sitting in the apple tree alone. Mom had told him it was O.K. to walk around the whole yard now, as long as he didn't do any diggings or mutilations other than weed-

Reading Skill
Main Idea What details support the main idea that the narrator did not expect or intend to injure John?

Vocabulary Builder
exact (eg zakt´) *v.* demand with force or authority

Literary Analysis
Mood What mood does the author create with the words *revenge, disaster,* and *terrified*?

pulling on her side. I was expecting him to notice right off the bat that I was white with fear, but instead he stood looking at the carvings Jennifer and I had made in the trunk of the tree. I thought he was just intensely curious about what "ESCAPE! PAUL & JENNIFER!" meant. Of course, the twins, being such copycats, had already added their names so the full carving away of the bark now read, "ESCAPE! PAUL & JENNIFER! & NICKY & JOEY!" And the letters circled halfway around the tree.

"You're killing it," Nonno Frankie said sadly.

"What?" I jumped down to his side.

"The tree will die if you cut any more."

I thought he was kidding, because all we had done was carve off the outer pieces of bark. We hadn't carved deep into the tree, not into the *heart* of the tree. The tree was too important to us. It was the most crucial place to me and Jennifer, and the last thing we'd want to do was hurt it.

"The heart of a tree isn't deep inside of it. Its heart and blood are on the *outside*, just under the bark," Nonno Frankie explained. "That's the living part of a tree. If you carve in a circle all around the trunk, it's like slitting its throat. The water and juices and life of the tree can't move up from the roots!" I knew about the living layer of a tree, but I didn't know exposing it would kill the whole tree. I just never thought about it, or I figured trees patched themselves up.

"Now it can feed itself from only half its trunk," Nonno Frankie explained. "You must not cut any more."

"I won't," I promised. Then I felt worse than ever. Not only was I scheduled to get beat up by John Quinn after school on Monday, I was also a near tree-killer. Nonno Frankie finally looked closely at me.

"Your first week at school wasn't all juicy meatballs?" he asked.

That was all he had to say, and I spilled out each and every horrifying detail. Nonno Frankie let me babble on and on. He looked as if he understood exactly how I felt and wasn't going to call me stupid or demented or a big yellow coward. When I didn't have another word left in me, I just shut up and stared down at the ground.

Reading Skill
Main Idea Is the detail about "the twins, being such copycats" important to the main idea of the paragraph? Why or why not?

Literary Analysis
Mood What words create a threatening mood in this paragraph?

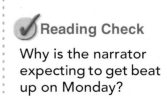
Reading Check

Why is the narrator expecting to get beat up on Monday?

from *The Pigman & Me* ■ 463

"Stab nail at ill Italian bats!" Nonno Frankie finally said.

"What?"

He repeated the weird sentence and asked me what was special about it. I guessed, "It reads the same backward as forward?"

"Right! Ho! Ho! Ho! See, you learn! You remember things I teach you. So today I will teach you how to fight, and you will smack this John Quinn around like floured pizza dough."

"But I can't fight."

"I'll show you Sicilian combat tactics."

"Like what?"

"Everything about Italian fighting. It has to do with your mind and body. Things you have to know so you don't have to be afraid of bullies. Street smarts my father taught me. Like 'Never miss a good chance to shut up!'"

VAROOOOOOOOOOM!

A plane took off over our heads. We walked out beyond the yard to the great field overlooking the airport.

Nonno Frankie suddenly let out a yell. "Aaeeeeeyaaaay-eeeeeh!" It was so blood-curdlingly weird, I decided to wait until he felt like explaining it.

"Aaeeeeeyaaaayeeeeeh!" he bellowed again. "It's good to be able to yell like Tarzan!" he said. "This confuses your enemy, and you can also yell it if you have to retreat. You run away roaring and everyone thinks you at least have guts! It confuses everybody!"

"Is that all I need to know?" I asked, now more afraid than ever of facing John Quinn in front of all the kids.

"No. Tonight I will cut your hair."

"Cut it?"

"Yes. It's too long!"

"It is?"

"Ah," Nonno Frankie said, "you'd be surprised how many kids lose fights because of their hair. Alexander the Great always ordered his entire army to shave their heads. Long hair makes it easy for an enemy to grab it and cut off your head."

▲ Critical Viewing
How does this boy's expression connect to the narrator's conversation with Nonno Frankie? [Connect]

Reading Skill
Main Idea What details support the main idea that Nonno Frankie is an unusual character?

"John Quinn just wants to beat me up!"

"You can never be too sure. This boy might have the spirit of Genghis Khan!"

"Who was Genghis Khan?"

"Who? He once killed two million enemies in one hour. Some of them he killed with yo-yos."

"Yo-yos?"

"See, these are the things you need to know. The yo-yo was first invented as a weapon. Of course, they were as heavy as steel pipes and had long rope cords, but they were still yo-yos!"

"I didn't know that," I admitted.

"That's why I'm telling you. You should always ask about the rules when you go to a new place."

"I didn't think there'd be a time limit on handball paddles."

"That's why you must ask."

"I can't ask everything," I complained.

"Then you *read.* You need to know all the rules wherever you go. Did you know it's illegal to hunt camels in Arizona?"

"No."

"See? These are little facts you pick up from books and teachers and parents as you grow older. Some facts and rules come in handy, some don't. You've got to be observant. Did you know that Mickey Mouse has only *four* fingers on each hand?"

"No."

"All you have to do is look. And rules change! You've got to remember that. In ancient Rome, my ancestors worshipped a god who ruled over mildew. Nobody does anymore, but it's an interesting thing to know. You have to be connected to the past and present and future. At NBC, when they put in a new cookie-cutting machine, I had to have an open mind. I had to prepare and draw upon everything I knew so that I didn't get hurt."

Nonno Frankie must have seen my mouth was open so wide a baseball could have flown into my throat and choked me to death. He stopped at the highest point in the rise of land above the airport. "I can see you want

Literary Analysis
Mood How does the author create a humorous mood?

Reading Check

Why does Nonno Frankie insist that the narrator always know the rules?

some meat and potatoes. You want to know exactly how to beat this vicious John Quinn."

"He's not vicious."

"Make believe he is. It'll give you more energy for the fight. When he comes at you, don't underestimate the power of negative thinking! You must have only positive thoughts in your heart that you're going to cripple this monster. Stick a piece of garlic in your pocket for good luck. A woman my mother knew in Palermo did this, and she was able to fight off a dozen three-foot-tall muscular Greeks who landed and tried to eat her. You think this is not true, but half her town saw it. The Greeks all had rough skin and wore backpacks and one-piece clothes. You have to go with what you feel in your heart. One of my teachers in Sicily believed the Portuguese man-of-war jellyfish originally came from England. He felt that in his heart, and he eventually proved it. He later went on to be awarded a government grant to study tourist swooning sickness in Florence."

"But how do I hold my hands to fight? How do I hold my fists?" I wanted to know.

"Like this!" Nonno Frankie demonstrated, taking a boxing stance with his left foot and fist forward.

"And then I just swing my right fist forward as hard as I can?"

"No. First you curse him."

"Curse him?"

"Yes, you curse this John Quinn. You tell him, 'May your left ear wither and fall into your right pocket!' And you tell him he looks like a fugitive from a brain gang! And tell him he has a face like a mattress! And that an espresso coffee cup would fit on his head like a sombrero. And then you just give him the big Sicilian surprise!"

"What?"

"You kick him in the shins!"

By the time Monday morning came, I was a nervous wreck. Nonno Frankie had gone back to New York the night before, but had left me a special bowl of pasta and steamed octopus that he said I should eat for breakfast so I'd have "gusto" for combat. I had asked him not to discuss my

Reading Skill
Main Idea What is the main idea of this paragraph?

upcoming bout with my mother or sister, and Betty didn't say anything so I assumed she hadn't heard about it.

Jennifer had offered to get one of her older brothers to protect me, and, if I wanted, she was willing to tell Miss Haines so she could stop anything from happening. I told her, "No." I thought there was a chance John Quinn would have even forgotten the whole incident and wouldn't make good on his revenge threat. Nevertheless, my mind was numb with fear all day at school. In every class I went to, it seemed there were a dozen different kids coming over to me and telling me they heard John Quinn was going to beat me up after school.

At 3 P.M. sharp, the bell rang.

All the kids started to leave school.

I dawdled.

I cleaned my desk and took time packing up my books. Jennifer was at my side as we left the main exit of the building. There, across the street in a field behind Ronkewitz's Candy Store, was a crowd of about 300 kids standing around like a big, <u>undulating</u> horseshoe, with John Quinn standing at the center bend glaring at me.

"You could run," Jennifer suggested, tossing her hair all to the left side of her face. She looked much more than pretty now. She looked loyal to the bone.

"No," I said. I just walked forward toward my fate, with the blood in my temples pounding so hard I thought I was going to pass out. Moose and Leon and Mike and Conehead and Little Frankfurter were sprinkled out in front of me, goading me forward. I didn't even hear what they said. I saw only their faces <u>distorted</u> in ecstasy and expectation. They looked like the mob I had seen in a sixteenth-century etching where folks in London had bought tickets to watch bulldogs attacking water buffalo.

John stood with his black eye, and his fists up.

I stopped a few feet from him and put my fists up. A lot of kids in the crowd started to shout, "Kill him, Johnny!" but I may have imagined that part.

John came closer. He started to dance on his feet like all father-trained fighters do. I danced, too, as best I could.

The crowd began to scream for blood. Jennifer kept shouting, "Hey, there's no need to fight! You don't have to fight, guys!"

But John came in for the kill. He was close enough now so any punch he threw could hit me. All I thought of was Nonno Frankie, but I couldn't remember half of what he told me and I didn't think any of it would work anyway.

"*Aaeeeeeyaaaayeeeeeh!*" I suddenly screamed at John. He stopped in his tracks and the crowd froze in amazed silence. Instantly, I brought back my right foot, and shot it forward to kick John in his left shin. The crowd was shocked, and booed me with mass condemnation for my Sicilian fighting technique. I missed John's shin, and kicked vainly again. He threw a punch at me. It barely touched me, but I was so busy kicking, I tripped myself and fell down. The crowd cheered. I realized everyone including John thought his punch had floored me. I decided to go along with it. I groveled in the dirt for a few moments, and then stood up slowly holding my head as though I'd received a death blow. John put his fists down. He was satisfied justice had been done and his black eye had been avenged. He turned to leave, but Moose wasn't happy.

"Hey, ya didn't punch him enough," Moose complained to John.

"It's over," John said, like the decent kid he was.

"No, it's not," Moose yelled, and the crowd began to call for more blood. Now it was Moose coming toward me, and I figured I was dead meat. He came closer and closer. Jennifer shouted for him to stop and threatened to pull his eyeballs out, but he kept coming. And that was when something amazing happened. I was aware of a

Literary Analysis
Mood A fight scene would normally be scary. What details give this scene a humorous mood?

figure taller than me, running, charging. The figure had long blond hair, and it struck Moose from behind. I could see it was a girl and she had her hands right around Moose's neck, choking him. When she let him go, she threw him about ten feet, accidentally tearing off a religious medal from around his neck. Everyone stopped dead in their tracks, and I could see my savior was my sister.

"If any of you tries to hurt my brother again, I'll rip your guts out," she announced.

Moose was not happy. Conehead and Little Frankfurter were not happy. But the crowd broke up fast and everyone headed home. I guess that was the first day everybody learned that if nothing else, the Zindel kids stick together. As for Nonno Frankie's Sicilian fighting technique, I came to realize he was ahead of his time. In fact, these days it's called karate.

Reading Skill
Main Idea What is the main idea of this final paragraph?

◀ **Critical Viewing** How are these boys similar to John and his friends? **[Compare]**

Apply the Skills

from *The Pigman & Me*

Thinking About the Selection

1. **Respond:** Do you think Paul should have backed out of the fight? Why or why not?
2. **(a) Recall:** Identify two pieces of advice that Nonno Frankie gives Paul. **(b) Analyze:** Does any of Frankie's advice apply to more than the fight itself? Explain.
3. **(a) Recall:** What does Paul do after he falls down during the fight? **(b) Infer:** Why does he do this? **(c) Analyze:** Is his strategy a good one? Explain.
4. **(a) Compare and Contrast:** Explain the difference between John's attitude and the attitude of the other students after Paul falls down. **(b) Analyze:** What problems does the attitude of the other students create for John and for Paul?
5. **(a) Evaluate:** Is resorting to fighting when there is a conflict ever justified? Explain. **(b) Discuss:** Share your response with a partner. Then discuss whether someone else's response did or did not change your thinking.

Reading Skill

6. What is the **main idea** of this selection?
7. What are two **important details** in the selection that support this main idea?
8. What is one **unimportant detail** that does not support the main idea?

Literary Analysis

9. What is one **mood**, or overall feeling, that the author creates in this selection?
10. Complete a chart like the one shown to analyze which words and images create the mood of this selection.

QuickReview

Who's Who in the Essay

Paul: the author as a boy

John: the boy whom Paul fights

Nonno Frankie: Paul's grandfatherly friend

Jennifer: Paul's friend

Betty: Paul's sister

Go Online
—Assessment
For: Self-test
Visit: www.PHSchool.com
Web Code: ela-6310

Main Idea: the most important point in a literary work

Mood: the overall feeling a literary work produces in a reader

Vocabulary Builder

Practice Write sentences that correctly use each word pair.

1. exact (as a verb); payment
2. undulating; necklace
3. distorted; ideas

Writing

When Paul unintentionally broke the rule about paddles, he had to face some attitudes about student behavior. Write a **problem-and-solution essay** to help new students adjust to one aspect of life at your school.

- First, clearly state one problem new students might face. The problem might relate to finding their way around or understanding school rules.
- Then, provide step-by-step solutions to the problem.
- Give evidence that supports your suggested solutions.

For *Grammar, Vocabulary,* and *Assessment,* see **Build Language Skills,** pages 472–473.

Extend Your Learning

Listening and Speaking In a small group, hold an **informal discussion** to consider these questions:

- If students are new to a school, what actions should they take?
- What actions should new students avoid?

Each person in the group should offer an opinion backed up with facts. Offer your opinions without dominating the group discussion. Use good listening skills while each person is talking. At the end of the discussion, summarize the group's ideas.

Research and Technology Frankie Vivona is proud of Italy, his family's native country. To learn more about twenty-first century immigration to the United States, use a library catalog or an Internet search engine. Select at least two sources and write **annotated bibliography entries**. Include publication information and explain why the source is valuable.

Build Language Skills

Vocabulary Skill

Words With Multiple Meanings A single word can have many different meanings. The meaning of a word depends on how it is used in a sentence. For example, the word *key* can mean "important," as in a key idea. It can also mean "a device that opens a lock" or "a low island."

▶ **Example:** The story's *key* point was that if you live alone on a *key*, you don't need to lock up anything with a *key*.

Practice Write the meaning of *key* that applies in each sentence. Then, write your own sentence using key in the same way.

1. The sailor's ship washed up on the *key*.
2. The speaker made a *key* point just now.
3. You can duplicate a *key* at a hardware store.

Grammar Lesson

Conjunctions and Interjections **Conjunctions** connect sentence parts and help show the relationship of information in the sentence. **Interjections** express feelings.

- Conjunctions such as *and, or, but, nor, for, yet,* and *so* connect words, groups of words, and whole sentences.

▶ **Example:** *The cousins swam* and *watched movies together.*

- Interjections such as *ah, aha, golly, hey, oh, oops, shh,* and *whew* express sudden excitement or strong feeling.

▶ **Example:** *Oh, now I see how the puzzle works.*
  Hurray! I finished my chores.

MorePractice

For more practice with conjunctions and interjections, see the Grammar Handbook, p. R31.

Practice Write a conjunction or an interjection that fits each sentence.

1. Angel is small _____ strong.
2. We can ride our bikes _____ walk to the store.
3. _____! Ken is the fastest runner in the school.
4. _____, I see you collect old coins.

WG Prentice Hall Writing and Grammar Connection, Chapter 18, Section 1

Reading: Main Idea

Directions: *Read the selection. Then, answer the questions.*

(1) Traditionally, Americans valued thrift. They bought mainly what they needed. Until the 1920s, shopping centers did not exist. Food was not "fast." There were few advertisements.

(2) The decade of the 1920s gave birth to much of the popular culture we know in modern America. The nation's first shopping center opened in Kansas City, giving consumers a more convenient way to shop. The first fast-food chain, A&W Root Beer, began selling burgers and soft drinks. Advertising became big business in the 1920s.

(3) The 1920s saw the development of a consumer economy, one that depends on a large amount of spending by consumers—individuals who use, or consume, products.

1. Where is the selection's main idea?
   A in the first paragraph
   B in the second paragraph
   C in the third paragraph
   D in the second and third paragraphs

2. Which begins a topic sentence?
   A The decade of the 1920s . . .
   B The nation's first shopping . . .
   C The first fast-food . . .
   D Advertising became . . .

3. Which detail supports the main idea?
   A people bought what they needed
   B shops opened in Kansas City
   C burgers and soft drinks sold
   D advertising became big business

Timed Writing: Description [Cognition]

Write a description of either Tío Abrán from "La Leña Buena" or Paul Zindel from *The Pigman & Me.* **(20 minutes)**

 ## Writing Workshop: *Work in Progress*

Persuasive Essay
Use the Change List from your writing portfolio. For one of the items, list two factual reasons to support your idea. Then, name one emotional appeal that might be used to convince your audience that you are correct. Save this work in your writing portfolio.

Author's Style

An **author's style** is his or her usual way of writing. You can see an author's style in his or her use of the following elements:

- **Word choice** (also called *diction*): Authors can choose words that are formal or informal, fancy or plain, technical or ordinary.
- **Arrangement of words:** Some writers prefer short sentences, whereas others write long, involved sentences.
- **Emotion/Tone:** The author's attitude toward a subject affects the way a work conveys its ideas.
- **Figurative language:** Some writers use poetic language to present ideas in innovative ways. Others choose words so that every one means exactly what it says.

Comparing Authors' Styles

"Letter From a Concentration Camp" is a letter written by a fictional character named Jimbo. "Letter to Scottie" was written by a father to his daughter. As you will see, the letters reflect two very different styles. For each letter, use a chart like the one shown to note the words, patterns, and personality that each of the writers conveys to the reader.

Word choice
Emotion/Tone
Sentence length
Figurative language

Vocabulary Builder

Letter From a Concentration Camp

- **regret** (ri gret´) *v.* be sorry about (p. 478) *If I get a stomachache I regret overeating.*

- **hearing** (hir´ iŋ) *n.* chance to give evidence and testimony (p. 479) *The council held a hearing about the new mall.*

Letter to Scottie

- **documentation** (däk´ yoō mən tā´ shən) *n.* supporting evidence (p. 480) *We had documentation proving our identity.*

- **misery** (miz´ ər ē) *n.* great sorrow (p. 481) *The team lost the championship game, causing us misery.*

- **composed** (kəm pōzd´) *v.* made up (p. 481) *The art is composed of paper and wood.*

- **rudimentary** (roō´ də men´ tər ē) *adj.* incompletely developed (p. 482) *My essay was too rudimentary for a good grade.*

Build Understanding

Connecting to the Literature

Reading/Writing Connection A personal letter usually reports a writer's feelings, but some letters can go beyond feelings to tell about the events that are happening in a specific time and place. In a short paragraph, tell which kind of letter you like to get. Use three of these words: *consist, appreciate, respond, identify, focus.*

Meet the Authors

Yoshiko **Uchida** (1921–1992)

Yoshiko Uchida was born in California to parents who had emigrated from Japan. When Japan and the United States went to war during World War II, Uchida and her family were forced to live in an internment, or prison, camp.

History Brought to Life As an adult, Uchida took pride in her heritage and decided to write works for children and adults. She dealt with her own wartime experience in two autobiographies as well as in fiction.

F. Scott **Fitzgerald** (1896–1940)

A distant relative of the author of the national anthem, Francis Scott Key Fitzgerald was born in Minnesota. At age twenty-three, he published his first novel, *This Side of Paradise,* which became an instant success. Fitzgerald went on to write short stories, screenplays, and more novels.

The Personal Side Fitzgerald married and in 1921 had a daughter, Frances Scott Fitzgerald, whose nicknames were "Scottie" and "Pie." Because of her parents' travels, Scottie spent much of her youth in boarding schools and at summer camp. She was at camp when her father wrote her the following letter.

Go Online
Author Link

For: More about the authors
Visit: www.PHSchool.com
Web Code: ele-9312

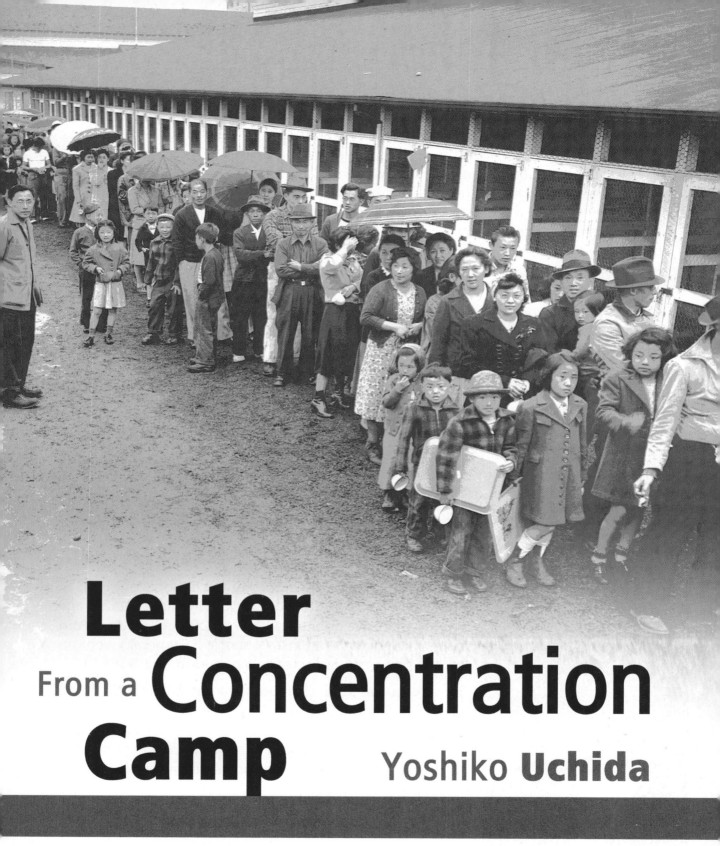

Letter
From a Concentration Camp
Yoshiko **Uchida**

Background Although World War II had begun in 1939, the United States entered the war in December 1941, right after Japan attacked Pearl Harbor, a U.S. Navy base in Hawaii. President Franklin Roosevelt signed Executive Order 9066 in February 1942, moving people of Japanese heritage to internment camps—also called concentration camps—to make sure they did not aid the enemy. Yoshiko Uchida, who had to spend part of her youth in such a camp, created this letter, which is fictional.

Mailing Address: Barrack 16, Apartment 40
                  Tanforan Assembly Center
                  San Bruno, California
Actual Address: Stable 16, Horse stall 40
                  Tanforan Racetrack

May 6, 1942

Dear Hermie:

Here I am sitting on an army cot in a smelly old horse stall, where Mama, Bud, and I have to live for who knows how long. It's pouring rain, the wind's blowing in through all the cracks, and Mama looks like she wants to cry. I guess she misses Papa. Or maybe what got her down was that long, muddy walk along the racetrack to get to the mess hall for supper.

Anyway, now I know how it feels to stand in line at a soup kitchen with hundreds of hungry people. And that cold potato and weiner they gave me sure didn't make me feel much better. I'm still hungry, and I'd give you my last nickel if you appeared this minute with a big fat hamburger and a bagful of cookies.

You know what? It's like being in jail here—not being free to live in your own house, do what you want, or eat what you want. They've got barbed wire all around this racetrack and guard towers at each corner to make sure we can't get out. Doesn't that sound like a prison? It sure feels like one!

Literary Analysis
Author's Style What language here is informal?

✔ **Reading Check**

What details about his surroundings make the letter writer feel as if he is in a prison?

◀ **Critical Viewing** Based on the buildings, the faces of these families, and the items some are carrying, what might be happening in this picture? **[Infer]**

◄ **Critical Viewing**
What emotions do you think these boys share with Jimbo, the writer of this letter? **[Connect]**

What I want to know is, What am I doing here anyway? Me—a genuine born-in-California citizen of the United States of America stuck behind barbed wire, just because I look like the enemy in Japan. And how come you're not in here too, with that German blood in your veins and a name like Herman Schnabel. We're at war with Germany too, aren't we? And with Italy? What about the people at Napoli Grocers?

My brother, Bud, says the US government made a terrible mistake that they'll <u>regret</u> someday. He says our leaders betrayed us and ignored the Constitution. But you know what I think? I think war makes people crazy. Why else would a smart man like President Franklin D. Roosevelt sign an executive order to force us Japanese Americans out of our homes and lock us up in concentration camps? Why else would the FBI take Papa off to a POW camp[1] just because he worked for a Japanese company? Papa—who loves America just as much as they do.

Literary Analysis
Author's Style
Would you say the author's style is informal or formal? Explain.

Vocabulary Builder
regret (ri gret') *v.* be sorry about

---

1. **POW camp** prisoner-of-war camp, where persons captured in war are confined.

Hey, ask Mrs. Wilford what that was all about. I mean that stuff she taught us in sixth grade about the Bill of Rights and due process of law. If that means everybody can have a <u>hearing</u> before being thrown in prison, how come nobody gave us a hearing? I guess President Roosevelt forgot about the Constitution when he ordered us into concentration camps. I told you war makes people crazy!

Well, Hermie, I gotta go now. Mama says we should get to the showers before the hot water runs out like it did when she went to do the laundry. Tomorrow she's getting up at 4:00 a.m. to beat the crowd. Can you imagine having to get up in the middle of the night and stand in line to wash your sheets and towels? By hand too! No luxuries like washing machines in this dump!

Hey, do me a favor? Go pet my dog, Rascal, for me. He's probably wondering why I had to leave him with Mrs. Harper next door. Tell him I'll be back to get him for sure. It's just that I don't know when. There's a rumor we're getting shipped to some desert—probably in Utah. But don't worry, when this stupid war is over, I'm coming home to California and nobody's ever going to kick me out again! You just wait and see! So long, Hermie.

> Your pal,
> Jimbo Kurasaki

Vocabulary Builder
hearing (hir´ in) *n.* chance to give evidence and testimony

Literary Analysis
Author's Style What is Jimbo's attitude toward his situation?

Thinking About the Selection

1. **Respond:** What did you find most difficult about Jimbo's situation?

2. **(a) Recall:** According to Jimbo, what does Bud think about holding Japanese Americans in the camps? **(b) Infer:** Why does Jimbo conclude that "war makes people crazy"?

3. **(a) Recall:** Why does Jimbo mention Mrs. Wilford's lessons about the Bill of Rights? **(b) Infer:** Why did the U.S. government deny Japanese Americans a hearing before sending them to camps?

4. **(a) Recall:** Name some rights that Jimbo and his family have lost. **(b) Speculate:** When Jimbo is released from the camp, might his attitude toward those rights be different? Explain.

Letter to Scottie

F. Scott Fitzgerald

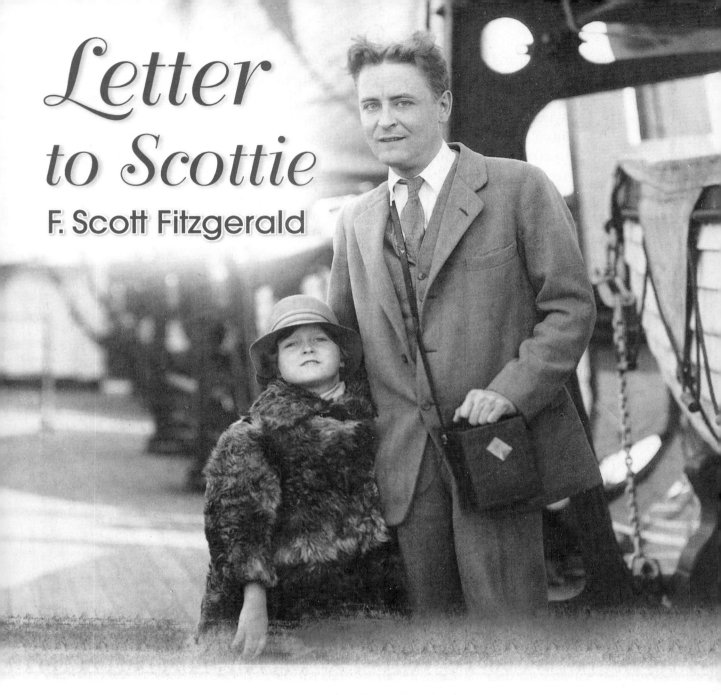

La Paix, Rodgers' Forge
Towson, Maryland
August 8, 1933

Dear Pie:

I feel very strongly about you doing [your] duty. Would you give me a little more <u>documentation</u> about your reading in French? I am glad you are happy—but I never believe

Vocabulary Builder
documentation (däk´
yōo mən tā´ shən) *n.*
supporting evidence

much in happiness. I never believe in <u>misery</u> either. Those are things you see on the stage or the screen or the printed page, they never really happen to you in life.

All I believe in in life is the rewards for virtue (according to your talents) and the *punishments* for not fulfilling your duties, which are doubly costly. If there is such a volume in the camp library, will you ask Mrs. Tyson to let you look up a sonnet of Shakespeare's in which the line occurs *"Lilies that fester smell far worse than weeds."*

Have had no thoughts today, life seems <u>composed</u> of getting up a *Saturday Evening Post*[1] story. I think of you, and always pleasantly; but if you call me "Pappy" again I am going to take the White Cat out and beat his bottom hard, *six times for every time you are impertinent.* Do you react to that?

> I will arrange the camp bill.
> Halfwit, I will conclude.

Things to worry about:
> Worry about courage
> Worry about cleanliness
> Worry about efficiency
> Worry about horsemanship
> Worry about . . .

Things not to worry about:
> Don't worry about popular opinion
> Don't worry about dolls
> Don't worry about the past
> Don't worry about the future
> Don't worry about growing up
> Don't worry about anybody getting ahead of you
> Don't worry about triumph
> Don't worry about failure unless it comes through
>   your own fault
> Don't worry about mosquitoes
> Don't worry about flies
> Don't worry about insects in general
> Don't worry about parents
> Don't worry about boys

---

1. *Saturday Evening Post* a weekly magazine for which Fitzgerald wrote.

◀ **Critical Viewing**
What details in this photograph suggest that Fitzgerald and his daughter feel affection for each other? **[Analyze]**

Vocabulary Builder
misery (miz´ ər ē) *n.* great sorrow

composed (kəm pōzd´) *v.* made up

Literary Analysis
Author's Style What makes this section of the letter straightforward and uncomplicated?

Reading Check
Which items in the "Don't worry" list have to do with competition?

Don't worry about disappointments
Don't worry about pleasures
Don't worry about satisfactions
Things to think about:
What am I really aiming at?
How good am I really in comparison to my contemporaries in regard to:
(a) Scholarship
(b) Do I really understand about people and am I able to get along with them?
(c) Am I trying to make my body a useful instrument or am I neglecting it?

With dearest love,
[Daddy]

P.S. My come-back to your calling me Pappy is christening you by the word Egg, which implies that you belong to a very <u>rudimentary</u> state of life and that I could break you up and crack you open at my will and I think it would be a word that would hang on if I ever told it to your contemporaries. "Egg Fitzgerald." How would you like that to go through life with—"Eggie Fitzgerald" or "Bad Egg Fitzgerald" or any form that might occur to fertile minds? Try it once more and I swear I will hang it on you and it will be up to you to shake it off. Why borrow trouble?
Love anyhow.

Literary Analysis
Author's Style Is the author's style here humorous, serious, or both? Explain.

Vocabulary Builder
rudimentary (ro͞o′ də men′ tər ē) *adj.* incompletely developed

Thinking About the Selection

1. **Respond:** How would you react if you received this letter?

2. **(a) Recall:** What is Scottie's nickname for her father?
   (b) Infer: How does he feel about this? How do you know?

3. **(a) Recall:** How does Fitzgerald end the letter, just before he signs it? **(b) Speculate:** What kind of relationship do you think Fitzgerald had with his daughter?

4. **(a) Speculate:** Why does Fitzgerald advise his daughter not to worry about the past or the future? **(b) Take a Position:** Which item on the list of things to worry about do you think is most important? Explain.

Apply the Skills

Letter From a Concentration Camp • Letter to Scottie

Comparing Authors' Styles

1. **(a)** In "Letter From a Concentration Camp," which words show an informal word choice? **(b)** In "Letter to Scottie," which words demonstrate formal word choice?
2. How would you describe the sentence style in each letter? Find an example sentence in each letter to support your answer.
3. Which writer uses more figurative language? Explain.
4. Complete a chart like the one shown to show how each author's style suits each letter's purpose.

	Letter From a Concentration Camp	Letter to Scottie
Purpose		
Emotion/ Tone		
Style elements		

QuickReview

Author's style: the way an author writes—including *word choice and arrangement, emotion and tone,* and *figurative language*

Go Online
———Assessment
For: Self-test
Visit: www.PHSchool.com
Web Code: ela-6311

Writing to Compare Literary Works

Compare and contrast the authors' styles in these two letters. In an essay, discuss the ways that the authors reveal their styles. Use these questions to get started:

- Is the tone of each letter formal or conversational?
- What images, or "word pictures," does each author convey?
- What can you tell about the personalities of the writers— either real or fictional—from their writing?

Vocabulary Builder

Practice Use the following word pairs correctly in sentences.

1. composed; team
2. hearing; judge
3. rudimentary; skills
4. misery; hurricane
5. regret; angry
6. documentation; camera

Reading

Directions: *Questions 1–5 are based on the following selection.*

The best way to maintain good health is through proper diet and exercise. Eating the right foods gives you the energy and strength you need to function. Healthful foods such as fruits and vegetables provide the vitamins and minerals that a body needs to perform properly. For example, oranges and tomatoes provide Vitamin C. Getting sufficient exercise also helps to keep the body in shape. Exercise helps your muscles and your cardiovascular system. Activities such as running, biking, swimming, and tennis are excellent workouts. A sport like baseball, however, does not provide the sustained benefits to the heart and lungs.

1. **What is the main idea of the passage?**
   A Food gives your body energy.
   B Exercise keeps you in shape.
   C Sports are a form of exercise.
   D Diet and exercise lead to good health.

2. **Which of the following details is unimportant in the overall passage?**
   A Vegetables provide vitamins and minerals.
   B Tomatoes provide Vitamin C.
   C Running is an excellent workout.
   D Food gives you energy and strength.

3. **Which of the following is a key detail in the passage?**
   A Baseball is a group sport.
   B Running and biking are activities.
   C Fruits and vegetables promote health.
   D Running is not a group sport.

4. **What detail supports the idea that proper diet is important for good health?**
   A Exercise is as important as diet.
   B Fruits contain vitamins and minerals.
   C Biking and tennis keep you in shape.
   D Foods give you the energy and strength to function.

5. **What detail supports the idea that exercise is important for good health?**
   A Basketball is a group sport.
   B Exercise keeps the body in shape.
   C Swimming is a fun activity.
   D Weightlifting is a difficult activity.

Assessment Practice

Vocabulary

Directions: *Choose the correct definition of the italicized word in the sentence.*

6. **The girl *identified* several descriptive phrases in the novel.**
   A   to make similar
   B   to recognize
   C   to fingerprint
   D   to change significantly

7. **Each paragraph should have an *essential* idea to focus writing.**
   A   structural element of a novel
   B   the first sentence of a paragraph
   C   contributing to the meaning
   D   central or important

8. **There was a *significant* protest when the play was censored.**
   A   of some importance
   B   of little consequence
   C   important
   D   minor

9. **We are trying to *determine* the main idea by listing the key details.**
   A   to explain in detail
   B   to end an argument
   C   to discourage
   D   to recognize

10. **There are *key* points that the author did not mention.**
   A   necessary for basic understanding
   B   necessary for a logical argument
   C   important to the argument
   D   unimportant to the argument

Directions: *Choose the definition that matches the way the word is used in the sentence.*

11. **Shana was *close* to her brother and missed him when she was at camp.**
   A   shut
   B   be shut away from
   C   near in interests or affection
   D   to bring to an end

12. ***Close* your books and put them away.**
   A   shut
   B   be shut away from
   C   near in interests or affection
   D   to bring to an end

13. **My *key* got stuck in the door.**
   A   a device that unlocks a lock
   B   a reef or low island
   C   important
   D   a part of a computer keyboard

14. **She was a *key* athlete in the Olympics.**
   A   a device that unlocks a lock
   B   a reef or low island
   C   important
   D   a part of a computer keyboard

Base Words and Endings

Some words require spelling changes when endings like *-ed* and *-ing* are added. Other words do not. Some words also have irregular plural forms. There are several rules that can help you form words like these.

Review the Rules Nearly all base words follow specific rules for adding *-ed* and *-ing.* Some plural words have irregular spellings, but there are rules for these words, too.

Words with one syllable	Words with several syllables	Irregular plurals
SPELLED	DEFEATED	OXEN
WORKED		GEESE
		WIVES

Rules for Adding *-ed* and *-ing*
- For most verbs, do not double the final consonant.
- For most one-syllable verbs ending in one vowel and one consonant, double the final consonant.
- For verbs that end in a vowel + *y,* generally keep the *y.*
- For verbs that end in a consonant + *y,* keep the *y* when adding *-ing.* Change *y* to *i* when adding *-ed.*

Spelling Irregular Plurals
- For many words ending in *f,* change *f* to *v* and add *-es.*
- For some plurals, use the same spelling as the singular.
- For some irregular plurals, add a special ending to the word.

Practice Add *-ed* and *-ing* to each of the following words.

1. hurry
2. leak
3. occur
4. delay

Word List
carried
carrying
benefiting
leaped
delayed
stopped
ourselves
oxen
deer
teeth

Assessment Practice

A. Directions: *Write the letter of the sentence in which the underlined word is spelled correctly.*

1. **A** In the past, <u>oxes</u> were used for many tasks.
   B They pulled wagons that <u>carried</u> families to the West.
   C If a wagon train was <u>delayied</u>, the animals waited patiently.
   D They could travel many miles before they <u>stoped</u> to rest.

2. **A** Julia spotted three <u>deers</u> in the woods.
   B The deer <u>stoped</u> eating when they heard her approach.
   C One of the deer had a leaf stuck in its <u>teeth</u>.
   D Suddenly, the deer <u>leapped</u> quickly through the forest.

3. **A** The clown <u>carryed</u> a huge ball in his arms.
   B He <u>leapped</u> onto the back of a silly-looking cart.
   C Then a dog burst out of the ball he was <u>carrying</u>.
   D The audience applauded so loudly that the show was <u>delaid</u>.

4. **A** Were you <u>refering</u> to us when you made that comment?
   B You said you had <u>stoppied</u> criticizing us.
   C We keep <u>ourselfs</u> busy and try to stay out of trouble.
   D Is someone else <u>benefiting</u> from our hard work?

B. Directions: *Apply the rules for base words and endings. Choose the correct spelling for each word.*

1. The mouse _____ under the table.
   A scurryed   **C** scurried
   B scurryied   **D** scurreyied

2. We put three new _____ on the wall.
   A shelfs   **C** shelvies
   B shelfves   **D** shelves

3. Jack is in so much trouble that he may be _____.
   A expeld   **C** expeled
   B expelled   **D** expelied

4. Mom has been _____ about you all day.
   A worring   **C** worrying
   B worreying   **D** worryieng

5. Use that _____ to cut the paper.
   A scissors   **C** scissorses
   B scissores   **D** scissor

6. They _____ many miles to reach their new home.
   A journeyed   **C** journeied
   B journeyied   **D** journyied

Exposition: Persuasive Essay

A **persuasive essay** argues the case for or against a particular position or urges a specific course of action. Follow the steps outlined in this workshop to write your own persuasive essay.

Assignment Write a persuasive essay to convince readers to improve their lives in a specific way.

What to Include An effective persuasive essay features the following elements:
- a clear thesis or statement that presents a position on an issue that has at least two sides
- facts, examples, and reasons that support the position
- powerful language to appeal to a specific audience
- evidence and arguments to address readers' concerns
- a clear organization, including an introduction, a body, and a strong conclusion
- error-free writing, including correct use of coordinating conjunctions

To preview the criteria on which your persuasive essay may be judged, see the rubric on page 495.

Writing Workshop: *Work in Progress*

If you have completed the Work-in-Progress assignments, you have several ideas in your portfolio you might use in your persuasive essay. Continue developing these ideas, or you might choose to explore a new idea as you complete the Writing Workshop.

Using the Form
You may use elements of persuasion in these types of writing:
- speeches
- advertisements
- problem-solution essays

Reading Writing Connection

To get the feel for persuasion, read the editorial "Music for All?" on page 861.

Prewriting

Choosing Your Topic

The best topic is one that is important to you and has two perspectives—one that you can support and one that you can oppose. Use the following strategies to help you find a suitable topic:

- **Conduct a media review.** Think about the local issues in the news now. Look through the newspaper for stories, read the letters to the editor, and watch and listen to local television and radio news programs to list all the topics that appeal to you. Then, choose one for your essay.

- **Organize a round table.** Gather classmates for a discussion of places and groups that are important to you. Think of issues that affect the locations and people you have listed. Jot down any ideas that interest you, and choose a topic.

Work in Progress
Review the work you did on pages 449 and 473.

Narrowing Your Topic

Once you choose a topic, make sure it is not too big for a short persuasive essay. Use a graphic organizer like the one shown to narrow your topic.

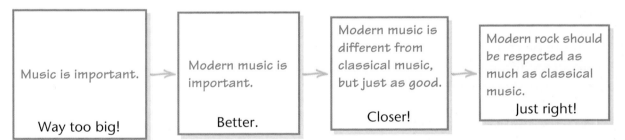

Music is important.

Way too big!

→

Modern music is important.

Better.

→

Modern music is different from classical music, but just as good.

Closer!

→

Modern rock should be respected as much as classical music.

Just right!

Gathering Details

Collect evidence. Identify facts, examples, statistics, quotations, and personal observations that support your position. Take notes on the sources of your information, because you need to credit any ideas or words that are not your own.

Anticipate counterarguments. Look ahead to identify readers' questions and points of view that might differ from your position. Be prepared to include facts that you think will successfully overcome these criticisms.

Writing Workshop

Drafting

Shaping Your Writing

Write a thesis statement. The evidence you have gathered will help support your position. Prepare a thesis statement—one sentence that names your issue and expresses your position.

Sample Thesis Statements

1. Our school should have recycling bins.
2. Young people should exercise twenty minutes every day.

Create a clear organization. Review the chart shown here to organize your thoughts clearly and concisely. Include your thesis statement in your introduction. Support your thesis statement in the body. Organize supporting information into paragraphs. Each paragraph should focus on one reason you give for your position. Conclude with a restatement of your thesis.

Providing Elaboration

Support each point. As you develop each piece of evidence, be sure that you support it fully. Use the following techniques:

- Find and use examples.
  Main idea: Vegetables are healthy snacks.
  Supporting example: Carrots are a source of Vitamin A.

- Use facts or statistics.
  Main idea: Rock music is often loud, but it is still music.
  Supporting fact: Rock follows a rhythmic pattern.

- Include quotations and expert opinions.
  Main idea: Our nation depends on volunteers.
  Supporting quotation: "Ask not what your country can do for you; ask what you can do for your country."
  —President John F. Kennedy

- Include personal observations to appeal to emotions.
  Main idea: Doctors agree that daily exercise is important.
  Supporting observation: I always feel better after jogging.

Target your audience. Consider your readers' ages and their knowledge about your topic. Then, develop your draft with this information in mind.

Introduction

Thesis statement

↓

Body

Main point followed by facts, details, arguments, statistics, expert opinions. Explanations and evidence for the readers' concerns and counterarguments.

↓

Conclusion

Summary of arguments. Strong restatement of position.

From the Author's Desk

Zlata Filipović

On Writing Persuasively

Zlata
Filipović

Reading my diary inspired a large group of American high school students to write diaries about their life in a dangerous neighborhood of Los Angeles. Their book, published in 1999, became known as *The Freedom Writers Diary*. I was very moved by their project and wrote a foreword for their book, which is so full of enthusiasm about life and writing, and the power of both!

> *"My thoughts seem so much clearer when I write them down."*
> ———— Zlata Filipović

Professional Model:

from Foreword to
The Freedom Writers Diary

Sometimes we suffer because of many things over which we have no control: the color of our skin, poverty, our religion, our family situation, war. It would be easy to become a victim of our circumstances and continue feeling sad, scared or angry; or instead, we could choose to deal with the injustice humanely and break the chains of negative thoughts and ~~actions~~ ^energies,

I connected problems of war with problems of racism or violence in what are considered peaceful countries to show that everywhere in the world people face difficulties.

. . . Writing about the things that happen to us allows us to look objectively at what's going on around us and turn a negative experience into something positive and useful. This process requires a lot of work, effort and greatness, but it is possible, and the Freedom Writers have proved it—they've chosen a difficult, but powerful, path. . . . I have heard people say that it is not what happens to us that matters, but how we deal with it. . .

I am fascinated by how people transform their experiences through writing, and by how powerful writing can be. Now I wish I had left in the word *actions*. It is more concrete than *energies*.

One always hears interesting quotes and ideas — they can all be an inspiration for writing and an effective way of making a point.

Revising

Revising Your Paragraphs

Revise to improve support. Review your draft to find places where you might need to strengthen arguments that support your thesis. Follow these steps:

1. Underline your thesis statement.

2. Put a star next to each supporting point. Add more support if you have only one star.

3. Draw attention to a well-supported point by adding charged language or a colorful comparison.

4. If you find a paragraph without support, review your prewriting notes and add support. If necessary, do extra research to find the support you need.

To read the complete student model, see page 494.

Student Model: Revising to Improve Support

Music can be classified as any group of organized sounds. Yet while the roars of today's lead vocalists don't seem to make sense, even they are organized and related to the message of the song. Is it music? Yes.* It follows a precise rhythmic pattern. It repeats. You might not like the style, but you cannot deny it is music. Just because howls from a modern vocalist don't follow any pitches doesn't mean they can't be classified as perfectly good music.

Isaac adds more support to strengthen his argument.

Revising Your Sentences

Revise to strengthen images and observations. Look for places where you can add or improve an image or personal observation that illustrates your point. Use words that call specific pictures or sensory details to mind. Vivid language will appeal to your readers' emotions and help you to persuade them to agree with you.

Peer Review: Ask a partner to identify places in your draft that spark emotional reactions, such as fear, pride, anger, or happiness. Consider adding more details to get the response you want.

Integrating Grammar Skills

Combining Sentences Using Coordinating Conjunctions

If your draft has too many sentences that are short and similar, you can fix that problem by choosing and using the right coordinating conjunction.

Coordinating conjunctions such as *and, but, or,* and *so* connect words or groups of words that are similar in form. They can connect noun with noun, phrase with phrase, and sentence with sentence.

Identifying Which Coordinating Conjunction to Use As the chart shows, each coordinating conjunction has its own distinct meaning and purpose. To use a conjunction to join a pair of related sentences, first determine the relationship between the ideas in each sentence.

Prentice Hall Writing and Grammar Connection: Chapter 3, Section 1

Coordinating Conjunction	Purpose	Use
and	to join similar or related ideas	I live in an apartment, **and** it is on the fourth floor.
but	to highlight difference or contrast	I like soccer, **but** my brother does not.
or	to show choices	You can have your lunch now, **or** you can wait for Molly.
so	to show cause and effect	I enjoy adventure stories, **so** I loved *Treasure Island*.

Using Coordinating Conjunctions To use coordinating conjunctions, follow these steps:

1. **Identify the relationship between the sentences you wish to combine.**
2. **Choose a coordinating conjunction based on your purpose.**
3. **Join the two sentences using a comma and the coordinating conjunction you selected.**

You may need to rephrase your sentences to make them work.

Apply It to Your Editing

Reread the draft of your persuasive essay, looking for short sentences that present related ideas. Then, use the rules and examples above to make the necessary adjustments.

Writing Workshop

Student Model: Isaac Tetenbaum
Reseda, CA

Modern Rock Is Music, Too

Maybe you think Chopin is really cool—the blissful tones of the piano, played to serenade and mesmerize, the dazzling cadenzas and glistening high notes. For a change, though, why don't you pop in a modern rock CD? Contemporary music gets very little respect, yet most of the people who put it down haven't even listened to it. Modern rock deserves to be regarded and respected as music.

Music can be classified as any group of organized sounds. Yet while the roars of today's lead vocalists don't seem to make sense, even they are organized and related to the message of the song. Is it music? Yes. It follows a precise rhythmic pattern. It repeats. Just because howls from a modern vocalist don't follow any pitches doesn't mean they can't be classified as perfectly good music. You might not like the style, but you cannot deny it is music.

Once you've accepted rock as music, you might say all rock songs are in the same key—E. Just because the lowest string of the guitar is an E doesn't mean modern rock musicians continuously strum that string and open and end a tune with it. Nowadays, as new musicians experiment with different pitches, the common E of rock has almost disappeared.

In a technique called "dropping," guitarists and bassists of modern rock bands have been able to use lower pitches in their songs. In fact, a well-known modern guitarist has successfully created a seven-string guitar. Its seventh string has the default pitch of a B. Although you might have to listen a little harder to hear the evidence, the musicians of contemporary bands know their music. How else could they come up with "dropping" and the seven string guitar?

I think anyone, even the most classical music lover, can appreciate today's sounds if given a chance. (Notice I didn't say love, just appreciate.) I listen to Chopin and modern rock. I respect both kinds of music because each one has its place. Chopin is like elegant figure skating—rock is like snowboarding. I feel free when I listen to my favorite rock group. Why don't you listen with me?

Isaac clearly establishes the two sides—those who like contemporary music and those who prefer classical. The last sentence in the introduction is the thesis.

The writer provides evidence that contemporary artists would be considered musical even by classical definitions.

Here, the writer admits that readers might think that all rock music is written in the same key—an argument he says is no longer true.

A powerful image helps readers understand Isaac's opinion.

Editing and Proofreading

Review your draft to fix errors in grammar, spelling, and punctuation.

Focus on Sentence Fragments: Correct any incomplete sentences that lack either a subject or a predicate or that do not express a complete thought.

> **Fragment:** Although I agree with you. We should learn more.
>
> **Complete sentence:** Although I agree with you, we should learn more.

Publishing and Presenting

Consider one of the following ways to share your writing:

Deliver a speech. Use your persuasive composition as the basis for a speech that you give to your classmates.

Post your essay. Post your persuasive composition on a class or community bulletin board so that others can read it and discuss your position.

Reflecting on Your Writing

Writer's Journal Jot down your thoughts on writing a persuasive essay. Begin by answering these questions:

- How did gathering evidence to support your position change or deepen your feelings about the issue?
- In the course of writing your essay, what insights did you gain about how to build an effective and fair argument?

> *Prentice Hall Writing and Grammar Connection: Chapter 7*

Rubric for Self-Assessment

To assess your persuasive essay, use the following rubric:

Criteria	Rating Scale
	not very *very*
How clearly is your position stated?	1 2 3 4 5
How organized is the introduction, body, and conclusion?	1 2 3 4 5
How well are facts, statistics, examples, and reasons presented?	1 2 3 4 5
How powerful are the images and language?	1 2 3 4 5
How correct is your grammar, especially your use of coordinating conjunctions?	1 2 3 4 5

Problem–Solution Proposal

A **problem–solution proposal** is a formal plan that suggests a course of action for solving a problem. The following strategies can help you present a convincing problem–solution proposal.

Preparing and Delivering the Proposal

Organize your ideas. First, identify the problem and make a list of its causes. Use statistics and examples to demonstrate these causes. Then, describe your proposed solution and list the reasons you think the solution will work. Add details that provide evidence for each point of your solution.

Establish connections and provide evidence. Use visual aids to show connections or provide evidence. A bar graph, pictures, or charts can show the connection between the problem you defined and the solution you are proposing. In the example shown, the bar graph illustrates the increase in accidents each year and provides support for the solution of installing a traffic light. Draw your visual aids or create them on a computer.

Problem: Accidents have increased each year.
Solution: Replace stop signs with a traffic light.

Practice your presentation. Practice delivering your presentation effectively. A well-delivered presentation will be more effective. Speak slowly so that your audience will understand each word.

Adjust your speaking rate by pausing after you make an important point. Refer to items on your visuals to emphasize your points.

Delivering Your Proposal

Have your notes and visual aids prepared and in order. Make eye contact with members of the audience to engage them. Deliver the presentation as you have practiced it. Use gestures to emphasize your points.

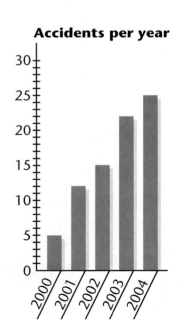

Accidents per year

Activity ⟩ *Problem-Solution Proposal* Prepare a proposal to solve a problem or improve a situation in your neighborhood or community. Present your proposal to a group of classmates. Use at least one visual aid.

20,000 Leagues Under the Sea

Jules Verne
Pacemaker Classics, 1973
Novel One of Jules Verne's most exciting novels, *20,000 Leagues Under the Sea* describes a strange underwater world that no one in the 1800s had ever seen. The survivors of a ship explosion find themselves swallowed up by a submarine called the *Nautilus* that is commanded by the madman Captain Nemo. Readers go along on the submarine trip around the world.

Where the Red Fern Grows

Wilson Rawls
Laurel-Leaf, 2001
Novel Billy and his two dogs roam the dark hills and river bottoms of Cherokee country in the Ozarks of northeastern Oklahoma. Old Dan had the brawn, Little Anne had the brains, and Billy had the will to train them to be the finest hunting team in the valley. Glory and sadness follow Billy and the dogs through the land where the legendary red fern grows as they hunt racoons and find adventure.

Brady

Jean Fritz
Penguin Group, 1992
Novel *Brady* takes place in 1836, during the period before the Civil War when tensions were heating up about the subject of slavery in the United States. The story is set on a farm in Pennsylvania, which is not far from the slave state Virginia. This novel traces the path that the young Brady takes, one that leads him to the underground railroad and dangerous adventures.

The Red Pony

John Steinbeck
Penguin, 1992
Novel *The Red Pony* is made up of four interrelated stories about the coming of age of a boy named Jody. Raised on a ranch in northern California, Jody is well-schooled in the hard work and demands of a rancher's life. He is accustomed to the way of horses; but nothing has prepared him for the special connection he will forge with Galiban, the hot-tempered pony his father gives him. Jody discovers that there are still lessons to be learned about the ways of nature and the ways of man.

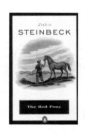

These titles are available in the Penguin/Prentice Hall Literature Library.
Consult your teacher before choosing one.

Think About It People often find themselves in situations in which they must introduce strangers to each other. Not knowing everyone's names, not knowing what to say, feeling the pressure to get it right—these complications can make introductions difficult. In the following reading, you will learn about the current customs of proper etiquette—the rules of polite behavior—for introductions.

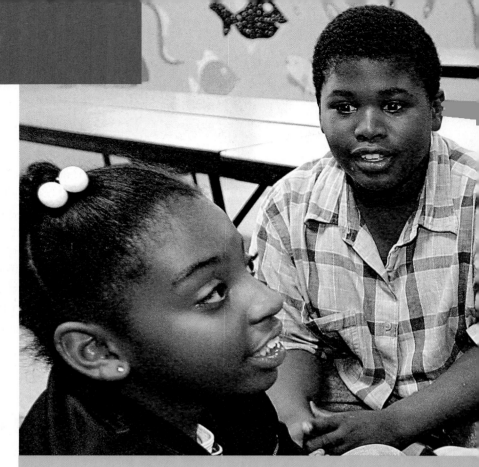

Social Interactions 101
The Rituals of Relating

Alex J. Packer

Unless you're a hermit, a castaway, or a monk who has taken a vow of silence, you experience many social interactions each day. Some are brief and anonymous, such as holding a door for a stranger or giving money to a sales clerk. Others are intimate and meaningful, such as consoling a friend or confiding in a parent. Yet they all have one thing in common: They are acted out according to certain unspoken rules and expectations for behavior. These rules and expectations govern everything from gift giving to eating, job hunting to baby-sitting, greeting people to meeting people. Your ability to "play the game" will help you to feel confident, and others to feel comfortable, in virtually any situation.

An Introduction to Introductions

Like it or not, first impressions count. You can make a lifetime of good first impressions by learning how to give and receive introductions.

Introducing Yourself

This is the simplest introduction. All you have to do is remember your own name. At school or parties, or when others have neglected to introduce you, look the person you want to meet in the eye, smile, extend your right hand, and say "Hi, I'm _____." If the person doesn't respond with his or her name, you can continue with "And you're . . .?"

Introducing Others

Let's start with the adult world, where things tend to be a bit more formal. If you're making the introduction, simply say "Mother, I'd like to present my friend, Sticky Fingers." It's not necessary to add "Sticky, this is my mother." Life is too short for such double-talk.

Social Interactions 101: The Rituals of Relating ■ *499*

You may also use such phrases as "Mother, I'd like to introduce Sticky," or, if you're in a hurry, "Mom, this is Sticky."

If you think that the people might know each other but you're not sure, you can turn your introduction into a question: "Mother, have you met Sticky?"

Sometimes kids and parents have different last names. In which case you would say, after presenting Sticky to your mom, "Sticky, this is my mother, Mrs. Her-Last-Name." That way, he'll know not to call her Mrs. Your-Last-Name.

Piece of cake.

But how do you know *who* to present to *whom*? Here's the rule: You present the person of "lesser" status to the person of "greater" status. You address the person of "greater" status by saying his or her name first:

"Your Highness, I'd like to present Simon the Stableboy."

"Warden, I'd like to introduce my cellmate, Lucky."

"Professor Glockenspiel, this is my poodle, Puddles."

Since *who* outranks *whom* can be as confusing as knowing *when* to say *which*, the chart on the following page will help you to keep things straight.

Please don't have a fit about this status thing. It doesn't mean that royals are better than commoners, women are better than men, or adults are better than children. It's just the way things are done. And don't worry about making a mistake. If you present whoever to whomever when whomever should have been presented to whoever, few people will notice, since they'll be delighted that you made any introduction at all. And your own status will be tops in everyone's eyes.

When you make an introduction, try to include a little information about the person you're introducing. Otherwise, the people you've just introduced may stare at their feet with nothing to say.

You can try things like:

"Grandma, this is my friend Harry Houdini. He does magic tricks."

"Ms. Grier, I'd like to present my sister Charlotte. She designs Web sites."

"Dad, this is Ron Gomez. He's on the swim team with me."

You can see how these introductory add-ons provide openings for further conversation. Be discreet, though. The idea is to offer an enticing tidbit of information, not to reveal any secrets.

"Greater" Status	"Lesser" Status
Adults	Children
Teachers	Students
Longtime friends	New friends
Females	Males
Relatives	Non-relatives
Bosses	Employees
Queen of England	The town dogcatcher

"How do you introduce people if you've forgotten their names?"
With difficulty. "Dr. Femur, I'd like you to meet . . . er, ah, um, uh . . ." is inadequate as an introduction. But we all forget names sometimes. Since it's worse to make *no* introduction, you have three choices when memory fails you:

1. be up-front
2. bluff, or
3. cheat.

Being up-front means coming clean about your mental lapse. You begin the introduction ("Dad, this is a friend from math class"), then turn to your friend and say "I'm so sorry, I've forgotten your name." At this point, your friend will supply her name.

If you're introducing yourself, you can say "Hi, we've met before, but I'm afraid I've forgotten your name. I'm _____."

What if you're introducing two people to each other and you've forgotten *both* of their names? The up-front approach would be "I'm sorry. I'm so terrible with names I'd forget my own if it wasn't sewn into my underwear. Do you think you could introduce yourselves?"

With the bluffing method, you hope to avoid detection by getting those people whose names you've forgotten to introduce

themselves. Begin by looking warmly at both people. Then say "Do you two know each other?" If the bluff works, they reply "No" and introduce themselves. If it doesn't, they say "No" and turn to you with expectant looks on their faces. Uh-oh!

If you've forgotten just one person's name, turn to him and say "Have you met Mrs. Dickens? She was my eighth-grade English teacher." With any luck, he'll reply "No, I haven't had the pleasure. Hi, I'm Nicholas Nickleby."

You can even use the bluff technique when introducing yourself to someone whose name you've forgotten. Smile, stick out your hand, and say "Hi. It's good to see you again. I'm _____." Then hope that person will respond with her name.

Cheating isn't nice, but sometimes it's necessary. Assume a frantic air and invent an emergency: "Oh, dear, I think the dog just ate my gerbil." Then say "Could you please introduce yourselves?" as you rush from the room.

Like it or not, first impressions count. You can make a lifetime of good first impressions by learning how to give and receive introductions.

Group Introductions

Situations may arise that call for group introductions. For example, let's say your cousin joins you and some friends for a movie. If the group is small (five people or fewer), you can introduce him to everyone. If the group is large, individual introductions will take forever and you'll miss the movie. At times like these, it's perfectly acceptable to make an efficient group presentation: "Hey, everybody, this is my cousin Alfredo Fettucine. He's visiting from Rome."

Alfredo can smile and say "Hi." The rest of you can smile and say "Hey" or "How's it goin'?" Physical gestures are also acceptable—a wave, a friendly salute, a tip of the baseball cap—anything that makes Alfredo feel welcome.

Handshakes and standing up (if you are sitting down) are unnecessary in such informal situations. Individual members of the group should introduce themselves to Alfredo as they talk with him.

Meet the Author

Alex J. Packer has written many books to help young people manage the tricky rules of behavior and manners. Among these books are *Bringing Up Parents: The Teenager's Handbook* and the book from which this excerpt was taken, *How Rude! The Teenagers' Guide to Good Manners, Proper Behavior, and Not Grossing People Out.*

Readings in Culture
Talk About It

Use these questions to guide a discussion of the selection.

1. Why is it important to introduce yourself?

2. Using Packer's tips, break into small groups and take turns introducing yourselves. Then, discuss with your group how you would introduce the following people to each other:
   - your friend, Mikey, and your piano teacher, Mrs. Keys
   - your mail carrier, Mr. Post, and a person whose name you've forgotten
   - your best friend, Louisa, and your entire art class

   Choose a point-person to share your group's ideas with the class.

Poetry

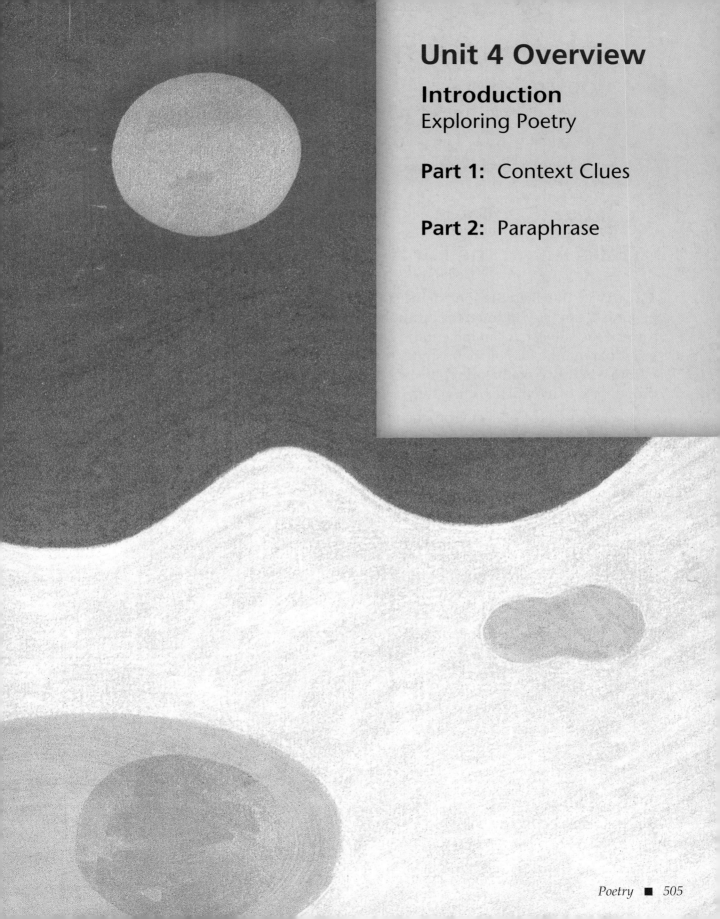

Unit 4 Overview

Introduction
Exploring Poetry

Part 1: Context Clues

Part 2: Paraphrase

Introduction:
Poetry

Gary Soto
Talks About the Form

Poetry can be called the song of the soul. The song, of course, can vary in **tone,** the attitude it expresses toward the subject. It can lament the death of a grandparent, the loss of friendship, our personal failures on the basketball or volleyball court, or a brooding day in which nothing went right.

Or a poem may reflect the other end of our emotional scale—the happy feeling of liking another person, owning a puppy, receiving a birthday gift you truly love, the rush of braving a monstrous ride at the amusement park, rock climbing, dancing, and other exhilarating moments. Poetry, then, is an emotional response to the world around us.

A poem doesn't resemble a story in which the sentences flow evenly from margin to margin. A poem doesn't look like a play with its cast of characters confined to a space called the stage. A poem is not an essay with its logic and heavy words. No, a poem has its own meaning and shape.

▲ **Gary Soto** is an award-winning poet who has also made films and written fiction and nonfiction.

▶ Critical Viewing
Which details in this picture support Gary Soto's idea that poetry is "the song of the soul"? **[Connect]**

How Can We Recognize Poetry?

Poetry can have established formal structures, such as a pattern of **rhymes,** repeated sounds at the ends of lines. These structures often make it easier to recite and memorize poems, and also please the listener's ear. Or a poem may take the shape of irregular lines on the page. We may call this **free verse,** a catch-all phrase for poems that are not written in rhyme and **meter,** or regular rhythm. Overall, one of the best definitions of poetic form I've ever heard is the remark by Leonard Nathan, shown here.

A Compliment

A poet decides on his or her subject by what touches the heart. We look around and we look into ourselves. We write what pains us or what we care about deeply. The result is an eerie satisfaction. And what's one of the best compliments a poet can receive? I recall a sixth grader telling me, "Mr. Soto, your poems sound like you." I had to smile and think, "I have caught myself in words."

"Poems are pattern in motion, like music but gifted with human speech."

— **Leonard Nathan,**
contemporary poet

More About the Author

Gary **Soto** (b. 1952)

Gary Soto has gathered ideas for his poetry, fiction, and nonfiction from his experience growing up in a Mexican American community in California. Often his work uses realistic details to tell about the everyday lives of Mexican American boys and girls. His poetry was honored when he became one of the youngest authors chosen to appear in the *Norton Anthology of American Poetry.*

Fast Facts
► Soto's hobbies include karate and Aztec dancing.
► The Soto household includes two cats: Corky and Sharkie.

Learning About Poetry

Elements of Poetry

Poets use language imaginatively to create images, tell stories, explore feelings, and describe experiences. To do this, poets use a variety of specific elements and techniques.

Sound devices add a musical quality to poetry. Poets use these devices to enhance a poem's mood and meaning.

- **Rhyme** is the repetition of sounds at the ends of words, such as *pool, rule,* and *fool.*
- **Rhythm** is the beat created by the pattern of stressed and unstressed syllables: *Thĕ cát săt ón thĕ mát.*
- **Repetition** is the use of any element of language—a sound, word, phrase, clause, or sentence—more than once.
- **Onomatopoeia** is the use of words that imitate sounds: *crash, bang, hiss, splat.*
- **Alliteration** is the repetition of consonant sounds in the beginning of words: *lovely lonely lights.*

Figurative language is writing or speech that is not meant to be taken literally. The many types of figurative language are called **figures of speech**. Writers use these figures of speech to state ideas in a vivid and imaginative way.

- **Metaphors** describe one thing as if it were something else. They often point out a similarity between two unlike things: *The snow was a white blanket over the town.*
- **Similes** use *like* or *as* to compare two apparently unlike things and show similarities between the two: *She is as slow as a turtle.*
- **Personification** gives human qualities to something that is nonhuman: *The ocean crashed angrily during the storm.*

Sensory language is writing or speech that appeals to one or more of the five senses—sight, sound, smell, taste, and touch. This language creates word pictures, or **images.** Poets often use these word pictures to help the reader experience a poem fully.

Forms of Poetry

Narrative poetry tells a story in verse. Narrative poems often have elements similar to those in a short story, such as plot and characters.

Lyric poetry expresses the thoughts and feelings of a single speaker, often in highly musical verse.

Concrete poems are shaped to look like their subjects. The poet arranges the lines to create a picture on the page.

Haiku is a three-line Japanese verse form. The first and the third lines each have five syllables, and the second line has seven.

Limerick is a humorous, rhyming, five-line poem with a specific

Check Your Understanding

rhythm pattern and rhyme scheme.
For each item below, identify the element of poetry illustrated by the underlined portion.

1. The honeybee <u>buzzed</u> by and landed on a nearby flower.

2. <u>Moonlight crept slowly</u> into the boy's room at night.

3. The <u>baby's cry was a siren</u> alerting her father it was time for dinner.

4. The <u>silver stars swirled</u> in the <u>summer sky</u>.

5. He was <u>as hungry as a bear</u> after school.

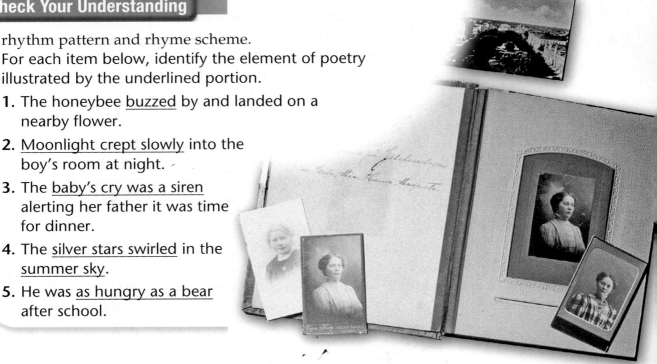

From the Author's Desk
Gary Soto Introduces His Poetry

My poems are an emotional response to the world around me. I write in free verse and use my instincts to determine line breaks and stanza breaks. I'm certainly aware of structure, but what propels my poetry are **narrative**, or story, and **imagery**, words I use to make you see what I see.

Imagery: Detailed Pictures in Poems

I feel like a painter standing before a white canvas. And just what do I want you to view once this canvas is filled? I have a long list, but for years I was particularly engaged in reconstructing my childhood. I liked going back, so to speak. I liked recalling my dog, Brownie, and other pets. I liked recalling the baseball diamond, the chinaberry tree, the church I attended, the canal tipped white with small waves, and the dull, sweaty times when I weeded a neighbor's yard for a quarter.

I loved my neighborhood, poor as it was, and wanted others to love it as well. To convince the reader, I knew that I had to provide detailed pictures, otherwise I would lose you on the way.

A Narrative Poem and a Lyric Poem

Some of these pictures appear in the **narrative poem** "Oranges," which I hope has stirred the hearts of would-be couples. Here a boy, age twelve, sets out from his home and walks over to a young girl's house. I'm often asked if the poem is autobiographical. Yes, the figure in the poem is me, and the girl is Margarita, a classmate at Jefferson Elementary School in Fresno. But parts of the poem are not factually true.

"Ode to Family Photographs" is a **lyric poem** expressing thoughts and feelings rather than telling a story. It is a playful comment about all the horrible photographs parents and relatives take.

▲ **Critical Viewing**
What other images
might suit this poem?
[Extend]

Gary Soto

The first time I walked
With a girl, I was twelve,
Cold, and weighted down
With two oranges in my jacket.
5   December. Frost cracking
Beneath my steps, my breath
Before me, then gone,
As I walked toward
Her house, the one whose
10   Porch light burned yellow
Night and day, in any weather.
A dog barked at me, until
She came out pulling
At her gloves, face bright
15   With <u>rouge</u>. I smiled,

Poetry
Sensory Language
The sound of frost
crunching beneath
the boy's feet shows
the cold.

Vocabulary Builder
rouge (ro͞ozh) n.
reddish cosmetic
used to color cheeks

Touched her shoulder, and led
Her down the street, across
A used car lot and a line
Of newly planted trees,
20 Until we were breathing
Before a drugstore. We
Entered, the tiny bell
Bringing a saleslady
Down a narrow aisle of goods.
25 I turned to the candies
Tiered like bleachers,
And asked what she wanted—
Light in her eyes, a smile
Starting at the corners
30 Of her mouth. I fingered
A nickel in my pocket,
And when she lifted a chocolate
That cost a dime,
I didn't say anything.
35 I took the nickel from
My pocket, then an orange,
And set them quietly on
The counter. When I looked up,
The lady's eyes met mine,
40 And held them, knowing
Very well what it was all
About.
          Outside,
A few cars hissing past,
45 Fog hanging like old
Coats between the trees.
I took my girl's hand
In mine for two blocks,
Then released it to let
50 Her unwrap the chocolate.
I peeled my orange
That was so bright against
The gray of December
That, from some distance,
55 Someone might have thought
I was making a fire in my hands.

Gary Soto
Author's Insight
I see now how shy we
were. We are both
scared of saying the
wrong thing.

Vocabulary Builder
tiered (tērd) *adj.*
arranged in levels
placed one above
another

Poetry
Simile Lines 25 and
26 compare rows of
candy to seats in a
sports stadium.

Gary Soto
Author's Insight
The orange is bright
against the cold
winter sky, to show
that there is hope
and love against the
darker realities of the
world.

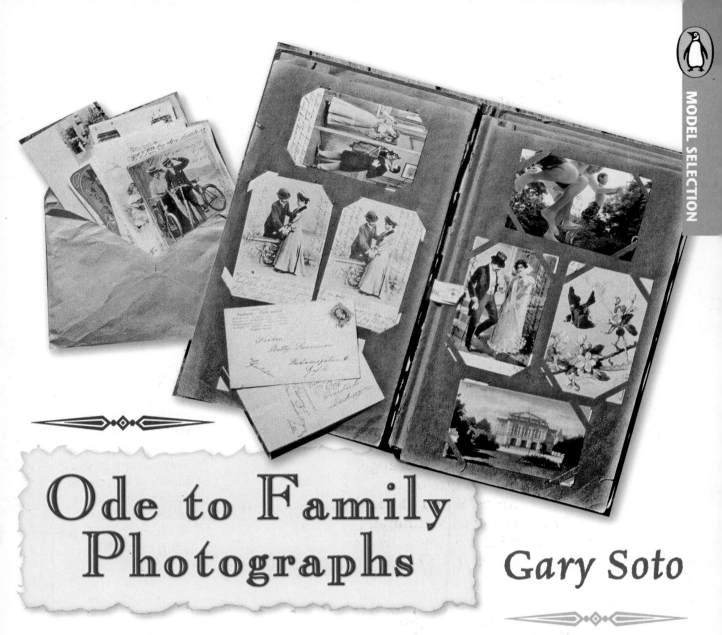

Ode to Family Photographs

Gary Soto

This is the pond, and these are my feet.
This is the rooster, and this is more of my feet.

Mamá was never good at pictures.

This is a statue of a famous general who lost an
    arm
5   And this is me with my head cut off.

This is a trash can chained to a gate,
This is my father with his eyes half-closed.

▲ **Critical Viewing**
What do these old
photographs suggest
about the subject of
this poem? **[Infer]**

◀ **Critical Viewing**
In what way does this active photograph capture the mood of the poem? **[Draw Conclusions]**

This is a photograph of my sister
And a giraffe looking over her
    shoulder.

10 This is our car's front bumper.
This is a bird with a pretzel in its
    beak.
This is my brother Pedro standing
    on one leg on a rock,
With a smear of chocolate on his
    face.

Mamá sneezed when she looked
15 *Behind the camera: the snapshots*
    are blurry,
The angles dizzy as a spin on a
    merry-go-round.

But we had fun when Mamá picked
    up the camera.
How can I tell?
Each of us laughing hard.
20 Can you see? I have candy in my
    mouth.

Gary Soto
Author's Insight
Actually I'm Pedro standing on the rock. Somewhere in our family photograph album, we have a snapshot of me mugging goofily on a log.

Gary Soto
Author's Insight
Notice how the tone of the poem is boyish, even though the poem was written by an adult poet.

From the Author's Desk
Gary Soto's Insights Into His Poetry

Q. Was "Oranges" hard to write?

A. I remember getting a first draft done fairly quickly, and then I had to go back to tighten the writing. By "tighten" I mean revise, which for me is stripping unnecessary words from the poem. I have yet to meet a poet who doesn't tinker with a poem. In fact, I know a good many poets who do it endlessly.

Q. Are poems about family similar to family photographs?

A. Yes. In some ways, poems are like photographs, and photographs are like poems—they evoke in us strange feelings that are difficult to express. We can't call back the past to live it over again, but we can view it through photographs and sometimes poems in order to relive those moments. With a photograph, the image is caught forever. With a poem, you can recreate the moment with words and then change the words. In short, my poems are using both memory *and* imagination.

Student Corner

Q. Do you write about things that have happened to you?
    —William Hartsfield, Tallahassee, Florida

A. "Write about yourself," is what my first creative writing teacher in college said. I took his instructions to heart and got busy writing about what I knew best—my neighborhood, family, best friend, would-be girlfriends, places where I'd gone. Confident, I had material that engaged me. Over the years, however, I have turned to fiction, which, as you can guess, is built from the imagination. Of the ten novels I've written, I would say that I never met any of my characters in real life.

 Writing Workshop: *Work in Progress*

Writing for Assessment
Some tests assess how well you can write an answer to a specific question. Write this prompt on the top of your paper: *Describe a place that has been important to you.* Jot down two ideas you might discuss in an essay. Save this Topic List in your writing portfolio.

Apply the Skills

Poetry

Thinking About the Poems

1. **Respond:** What details in "Oranges" seem especially realistic to you?

2. **(a) Recall:** What does the saleslady know about the 12-year-old boy that the girl does not? **(b) Speculate:** How would the girl react if she knew what the saleslady knows? **(c) Infer:** Does the poem "Oranges" describe a successful first date? Explain.

3. **(a) Recall:** Describe one picture in "Ode to Family Photographs." **(b) Draw Conclusions:** Based on the poem, what are the speaker's feelings about his mother?

Poetry Review

4. Analyze the **sensory language** in the poems by completing a chart like the one shown. In the first column, identify images that use sensory language. In the second, explain what the language means. In the third, explain why the image is important to the poem.

What It Says	What It Means	Why It Is Important
"Frost cracking/ Beneath my steps, my breath/ Before me, then gone/	It is very cold.	The relationship is new and uncertain. At the end of the poem there is an image of warmth.

5. **(a)** What do these poems have in common? **(b)** How are they different?

Research the Author

Using the Internet and library sources, choose three poems by Gary Soto for a **poster** you design.

- Include a photo of the author and list facts about his career as a poet.
- Under each poem, include a short explanation of its meaning.
- Write a brief evaluation of the poems. Tell what you liked about each work and why you chose it.

Skills You Will Learn

Reading Skill: *Preview to Identify Unfamiliar Words*
Literary Analysis: *Rhythm and Rhyme*

Reading Skill: *Using Context to Understand Specialized or Technical Language*

Reading Skill: *Read Ahead to Find Context Clues*
Literary Analysis: *Figurative Language: Simile, Metaphor, Personification*

Literary Analysis: *Comparing Imagery*

Literature You Will Read

Reading: Context Clues

> **Context** is the situation in which a word is used. Context clues are the words and phrases around an unfamiliar word that can help you figure out its meaning.

Skills and Strategies you will learn in Part 1

In Part 1, you will learn

- to **ask questions** that help you recognize the meaning suggested by **context clues** (p. 520)
- to **reread and read ahead** to find **context clues** (p. 544)
- to **use context clues** to help you clarify the meaning of specialized **terms of technical language** (p. 540)

Using the Skills and Strategies in Part 1

In Part 1, you will learn to use context clues to figure out the meanings of unfamiliar words. To find and use these clues, you will sometimes reread a passage or read ahead to look for clues. You will also practice asking questions that help you use context clues.

Read the statement below. Then, refer to the examples which show how different kinds of context clues give clues that help you figure out a word's meaning.

Statement Instead of cooperating, the mule was quite **obstinate**.

Restatement The mule was **obstinate**. He would not *cooperate*.

Contrast The pony was *cooperative*, but the mule was **obstinate**.

Description The **obstinate** mule stood *stubbornly* without moving.

Examples The mule was **obstinate**. We soon realized he would *not do anything* we wanted him to do.

Meaning **Obstinate** means "uncooperative" or "stubborn." It describes someone or something that will not cooperate.

Academic Vocabulary: Words for Discussing Context Clues

The following words will help you talk and write about the selections in Part 1.

Word	Definition	Example Sentence
preview *v.*	view, or look at, beforehand	*Preview* to get an idea of the topic.
restate *v.*	state again	*Restate* the topic in your own words.
context *n.*	situation in which a word is used	Figure out the definition from its *context*.
define *v.*	state the meaning	A dictionary will *define* that word.
explain *v.*	make clear or understandable	Can you *explain* that idea to me?

Vocabulary Skill: Prefixes

▶ A **prefix** is a letter or a group of letters added to the beginning of a word to form a new word.

In Part 1, you will learn
- the prefix *pre-* (p. 538) • the prefix *re-* (p. 556)

Prefix	Meaning	Words With the Prefix
pre-	"before" or "toward"	preview, predict, preface
re-	"back" or "again"	restate, react, readjust

Activity Use the meaning to decide whether each definition refers to a word that begins with *pre-* or *re-*. Then, use a dictionary to identify a word that fits each meaning.

1. establish again
2. decided ahead of time
3. an opening statement
4. bring to mind again

You can apply the instruction on this page to these poems.

Poetry Collection 1
Adventures of Isabel,
page 522
Ankylosaurus, page 523
*Wilbur Wright and
Orville Wright,* page 524

Poetry Collection 2
A Dream Within a Dream,
page 529
Life Doesn't Frighten Me,
page 530
The Walrus and the Carpenter,
page 532

Reading Skill

Context clues are found in the text surrounding an unfamiliar word. They may be words with the same meaning, or descriptions or explanations. To use context clues, **ask questions**.

- *What kind of word is it?*
- *What word can I use in place of the unfamiliar word?*
- *Does the new sentence make sense?*

The chart helps you find out the meaning of *stride* in this sentence:

▶ **Example:** He lengthened his *stride* to catch up with his friend.

Unfamiliar Word
stride

Question
What kind of word?

Answer
It names a way you move to catch up.

Meaning
"step"

Literary Analysis

Rhythm and **rhyme** add a musical quality to poems.
- **Rhythm:** the sound pattern created by stressed and unstressed syllables.

  ▶ **Example:** JACK and JILL went UP the HILL
  (4 stressed/3 unstressed)

- **Rhyme:** the repetition of sounds at the ends of words, such as *delight* and *excite*. Once a rhyme pattern, or *scheme,* is established, you come to expect rhymes.

Vocabulary Builder

Poetry Collection 1

- **ravenous** (rav′ ə nəs) *adj.* greedily hungry (p. 522) *The ravenous boy ate everything.*
- **rancor** (raŋ′ kər) *n.* bitter hate or ill will (p. 522) *Rancor showed in his mean face.*
- **inedible** (in ed′ ə bəl) *adj.* not fit to be eaten (p. 523) *A clam's shell is inedible.*

Poetry Collection 2

- **deem** (dēm) *v.* judge (p. 529) *We deem it necessary to cancel the election.*
- **beseech** (bē sēch′) *v.* beg (p. 533) *The children always beseech her for a snack.*
- **dismal** (diz′ məl) *adj.* causing gloom or misery (p. 535) *We heard dismal news.*

Connecting to the Literature

Reading/Writing Connection The three poems in this group use humor. Write three sentences about what makes something funny. Use at least three of these words: *display, distort, emphasize, focus.*

Meet the Authors

Ogden **Nash** (1902–1971)
Adventures of Isabel (p. 522)

Ogden Nash, one of America's best-loved poets and humorists, threw away his first poetry attempt. Luckily, he pulled it out of the trash and sent it to *The New Yorker* magazine—which published it immediately! During his forty-year career, Nash wrote more than thirty poetry books.

Jack **Prelutsky** (b. 1940)
Ankylosaurus (p. 523)

As a child, Jack Prelutsky was not a fan of poetry. As an adult, however, he decided to write some poems to accompany his drawings of imaginary creatures. Prelutsky soon published his first book of poems. He went on to write many more books of humorous verse.

Rosemary (1898–1962) and Stephen Vincent **Benét** (1898–1943)
Wilbur Wright and Orville Wright (p. 524)

In 1933, this husband-and-wife team wrote a poetry collection called *A Book of Americans,* from which "Wilbur Wright and Orville Wright" is taken. Rosemary Benét was a frequent contributor to many important magazines. Stephen Vincent Benét won the Pulitzer Prize for Poetry—twice!

 Go **Online** Assessment

For: More about these authors
Visit: www.PHSchool.com
Web Code: ele-9402

ADVENTURES of ISABEL

OGDEN NASH

Isabel met an enormous bear,
Isabel, Isabel, didn't care;
The bear was hungry, the bear was <u>ravenous</u>,
The bear's big mouth was cruel and cavernous.
5 The bear said, Isabel, glad to meet you,
How do, Isabel, now I'll eat you!
Isabel, Isabel, didn't worry,
Isabel didn't scream or scurry.
She washed her hands and she straightened her
    hair up,
10 Then Isabel quietly ate the bear up.

Once in a night as black as pitch
Isabel met a wicked old witch.
The witch's face was cross and wrinkled,
The witch's gums with teeth were sprinkled.
15 Ho ho, Isabel! the old witch crowed,
I'll turn you into an ugly toad!
Isabel, Isabel, didn't worry,
Isabel didn't scream or scurry,
She showed no rage and she showed no <u>rancor</u>,
20 But she turned the witch into milk and drank her.

Isabel met a hideous giant,
Isabel continued self-reliant.
The giant was hairy, the giant was horrid,
He had one eye in the middle of his forehead.
25 Good morning Isabel, the giant said,
I'll grind your bones to make my bread.
Isabel, Isabel, didn't worry,
Isabel didn't scream or scurry.
She nibbled the zwieback that she always fed off,
30 And when it was gone, she cut the giant's head off.

Vocabulary Builder
ravenous (rav´ ə nəs)
adj. greedily hungry

Vocabulary Builder
rancor (raŋ´ kər) *n.*
bitter hate or ill will

Literary Analysis
Rhythm and Rhyme
What two-word
rhymes are used in
lines 29 and 30?

Isabel met a troublesome doctor,
He punched and he poked till he really shocked her.
The doctor's talk was of coughs and chills
And the doctor's satchel bulged with pills.
35 The doctor said unto Isabel,
Swallow this, it will make you well.
Isabel, Isabel, didn't worry,
Isabel didn't scream or scurry.
She took those pills from the pill concocter,
40 And Isabel calmly cured the doctor.

Reading Skill
Context Clues
What clues help you understand that a satchel is something that holds things?

Ankylosaurus

Jack Prelutsky

Clankity Clankity Clankity Clank!
Ankylosaurus was built like a tank,
its hide was a fortress as sturdy as steel,
it tended to be an <u>inedible</u> meal.

5 It was armored in front, it was armored behind,
there wasn't a thing on its minuscule mind,
it waddled about on its four stubby legs,
nibbling on plants with a mouthful of pegs.

Ankylosaurus was best left alone,
10 its tail was a cudgel of gristle and bone,
Clankity Clankity Clankity Clank!
Ankylosaurus was built like a tank.

Vocabulary Builder
inedible (in ed´ ə bəl)
adj. not fit to be eaten

Literary Analysis
Rhythm and Rhyme
What is the pattern of rhymes at the ends of lines in each stanza?

Wilbur Wright AND Orville Wright

Rosemary and Stephen Vincent Benét

Said Orville Wright to Wilbur Wright,
"These birds are very trying.
I'm sick of hearing them cheep-cheep
About the fun of flying.
5 A bird has feathers, it is true.
That much I freely grant.
But, must that stop us, W?"
Said Wilbur Wright, "It shan't."

And so they built a glider, first,
10 And then they built another.
—There never were two brothers more
Devoted to each other.
They ran a dusty little shop

▼ **Critical Viewing**
The picture shows the Wright brothers flying the first power-driven, heavier-than-air machine in 1903, near Kitty Hawk, North Carolina. Compare this machine to today's airplanes. **[Compare]**

For bicycle-repairing,
15 And bought each other soda-pop
and praised each other's daring.

They glided here, they glided there,
They sometimes skinned their noses.
—For learning how to rule the air
20 Was not a bed of roses—
But each would murmur, afterward,
While patching up his bro,
"Are we discouraged, W?"
"Of course we are not, O!"

25 And finally, at Kitty Hawk
In Nineteen-Three (let's cheer it!)
The first real airplane really flew
With Orville there to steer it!
—And kingdoms may forget their kings
30 And dogs forget their bites,
But, not till Man forgets his wings,
Will men forget the Wrights.

▲ **Critical Viewing**
Based on this 1908 photo of Wilbur Wright, what words would you use to describe him? **[Analyze]**

Reading Skill
Context Clues How are *W* and *O* used here? What words would you use in their place?

Apply the Skills

Poetry Collection 1

Thinking About the Selections

1. **Respond:** Which poem did you find most humorous? Why?
2. **(a) Support:** Describe Isabel's personality, using details from "Adventures of Isabel" to support your answer.
   (b) Assess: Is Isabel someone you would want to have as a friend? Explain.
3. **(a) Recall:** In "Ankylosaurus," what was Ankylosaurus built like? **(b) Analyze:** Which sound words help reinforce this image? **(c) Speculate:** Why do you think Prelutsky begins the poem with these words and this image?
4. **(a) Support:** What details in "Wilbur Wright and Orville Wright" reveal that the authors admire the Wright brothers? **(b) Evaluate:** Do you think the Wright brothers earned their fame? Why or why not?

Reading Skill

5. For each of the following lines of poetry, write a question that you would ask to help you understand the underlined word. Then explain how the italicized **context clues** help you figure out the meaning of the word.
   (a) *nibbling* on plants with a *mouthful* of <u>pegs</u>
   (b) These birds are very <u>trying</u>. I'm *sick of* hearing them
   (c) She showed no *rage* and she *showed* no <u>rancor</u>.

Literary Analysis

6. How many stressed syllables are in these lines of poetry?

   They glided here, they glided there
   They sometimes skinned their noses.

7. Complete a chart like the one shown to give examples of **rhyming** words each poet uses. One example is given.

Poem	Rhyming Words		
"Ankylosaurus"	clank/tank		
"Wilbur Wright . . ."			
"Adventures of Isabel"			

QuickReview

Poems at a Glance
Adventures of Isabel: a humorous poem about a brave, young girl

Ankylosaurus: a humorous poem about a dinosaur

Wilbur Wright and Orville Wright: a poem about the first airplane flight

Go Online
Assessment
For: Self-test
Visit: www.PHSchool.com
Web Code: ela-6402

Context Clues: the words and phrases around an unfamiliar word that help you find its meaning

Rhythm: pattern of stressed and unstressed syllables

Rhyme: repetition of sounds at the ends of words

Vocabulary Builder

Practice Write a sentence about each numbered item using a word from the *Poetry Collection 1* vocabulary list on page 520.

1. a person who has not eaten all day
2. a person who must confront an enemy
3. a dinner that has been burned

Writing

One way to respond to literature is to write a **letter to an author**—even if you never mail it. Write a letter to one of the poets in the collection. Tell whether you like the poem and whether you would recommend it to others.

- Begin with a sentence that states your overall reaction.
- Then, develop your reasons and give examples.

For *Grammar, Vocabulary,* and *Assessment,* see **Build Language Skills,** pages 538–539.

Extend Your Learning

Listening and Speaking With a partner, plan an interview with one of the Wright brothers.

- Develop a list of questions you will ask.
- Organize the questions into categories.
- Do research to find the answers.
- Act out the interview.

Research and Technology Use library resources to gather a variety of poems and stories about dinosaurs. Organize them in a **booklet,** making sure to include illustrations. Write an annotation—a descriptive comment—for each poem or story, comparing or contrasting it with "Ankylosaurus."

Poetry

Connecting to the Literature

Reading/Writing Connection In their works, the poets in this collection describe their thoughts and feelings about the world, based on observation and imagination. List ways in which people form opinions about the world. Use at least three of these words: *interpret, perceive, respond, distinguish, react.*

Review

For **Reading Skill, Literary Analysis,** and **Vocabulary Builder,** see page 520.

Meet the Authors

Edgar Allan **Poe** (1809–1849)
A Dream Within a Dream (p. 529)
    Edgar Allan Poe, one of America's best-known writers, led a troubled life. His father deserted him, his mother died before he was three, and his wife died young. Despite his problems, Poe produced a large body of work, including short stories, essays, and poems.

Maya **Angelou** (b. 1928)
Life Doesn't Frighten Me (p. 530)
    Maya Angelou changed her childhood name (she was born Marguerite Johnson), and she has never stopped exploring who she is. In addition to being a poet and best-selling author, Angelou has been an educator, historian, actress, playwright, civil-rights activist, producer, and director.

Lewis **Carroll** (1832–1898)
The Walrus and the Carpenter (p. 532)
    Lewis Carroll is the pen name of Englishman Charles Lutwidge Dodgson, a math professor. Carroll wrote two children's classics, *Alice's Adventure in Wonderland* (1865) and *Through the Looking Glass* (1872), which contains "The Walrus and the Carpenter."

Go Online
Assessment
For: More about these authors
Visit: www.PHSchool.com
Web Code: ele-9403

A Dream Within a Dream
Edgar Allan Poe

Take this kiss upon the brow!
And, in parting from you now,
Thus much let me avow—
You are not wrong, who <u>deem</u>
5   That my days have been a dream;
Yet if hope has flown away
In a night, or in a day,
In a vision, or in none,
Is it therefore the less *gone*?
10 *All* that we see or seem
Is but a dream within a dream.
I stand amid the roar
Of a surf-tormented shore,
And I hold within my hand
15 Grains of the golden sand—
How few! yet how they creep
Through my fingers to the deep,
While I weep—while I weep!
O God! can I not grasp
20 Them with a tighter clasp?
O God! can I not save
One from the pitiless wave?
Is *all* that we see or seem
But a dream within a dream?

Vocabulary Builder
deem (dēm) *v.* judge

Literary Analysis
Rhythm and Rhyme
What is the pattern of stressed and unstressed syllables in most of the lines of this poem?

Life Doesn't Frighten Me

Maya Angelou

Shadows on the wall
Noises down the hall
Life doesn't frighten me at all
Bad dogs barking loud
5 Big ghosts in a cloud
Life doesn't frighten me at all.

Mean old Mother Goose
Lions on the loose
They don't frighten me at all
10 Dragons breathing flame
On my counterpane[1]
That doesn't frighten me at all.

I go boo
Make them shoo
15 I make fun
Way they run
I won't cry
So they fly
I just smile
20 They go wild
Life doesn't frighten me at all.

Literary Analysis
Rhythm and Rhyme
The poet uses lists of things to build rhythm and rhyme. What things does she list in the first stanza?

Reading Skill
Context Clues What words help you know the meaning of *shoo* in line 14? What does *shoo* mean?

---

1. counterpane *n.* bedspread.

Tough guys in a fight
All alone at night
Life doesn't frighten me at all.

25 Panthers in the park
Strangers in the dark
No, they don't frighten me at all.

That new classroom where
Boys all pull my hair
30 (Kissy little girls
With their hair in curls)
They don't frighten me at all.

Don't show me frogs and snakes
And listen for my scream,
35 If I'm afraid at all
It's only in my dreams.

I've got a magic charm
That I keep up my sleeve,
I can walk the ocean floor
40 And never have to breathe.

Life doesn't frighten me at all
Not at all
Not at all.
Life doesn't frighten me at all.

Literary Analysis
Rhythm and Rhyme
What repeated words help create rhythm in this poem?

◀ **Critical Viewing**
What details show that this girl is confident and determined?
[Analyze]

The Walrus and the Carpenter

Lewis Carroll

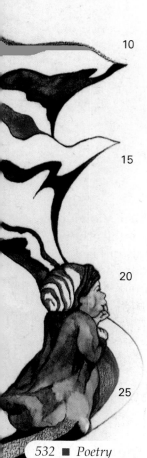

The sun was shining on the sea,
    Shining with all his might:
He did his very best to make
    The billows smooth and bright—
5 And this was odd, because it was
    The middle of the night.

The moon was shining sulkily,
    Because she thought the sun
Had got no business to be there
10   After the day was done—
"It's very rude of him," she said,
    "To come and spoil the fun!"

The sea was wet as wet could be,
    The sands were dry as dry.
15 You could not see a cloud, because
    No cloud was in the sky:
No birds were flying overhead—
    There were no birds to fly.

The Walrus and the Carpenter
20   Were walking close at hand:
They wept like anything to see
    Such quantities of sand:
"If this were only cleared away,"
    They said, "it would be grand!"

25 "If seven maids with seven mops
    Swept it for half a year,

Reading Skill

Context Clues What words and phrases here help you determine the meaning of the word *sulkily*? What does *sulkily* mean?

Do you suppose," the Walrus said,
    "That they could get it clear?"
"I doubt it," said the Carpenter,
30   And shed a bitter tear.

"O Oysters, come and walk with us!"
    The Walrus did <u>beseech</u>.
"A pleasant walk, a pleasant talk,
    Along the briny beach:
35 We cannot do with more than four,
    To give a hand to each."

The eldest Oyster looked at him,
    But never a word he said:
The eldest Oyster winked his eye,
40   And shook his heavy head—
Meaning to say he did not choose
    To leave the oyster-bed.

But four young Oysters hurried up,
    All eager for this treat:
45 Their coats were brushed, their faces
45   washed,
45   Their shoes were clean and neat—
And this was odd, because, you know,
    They hadn't any feet.

Vocabulary Builder
beseech (bē sēch´)
v. beg

Four other Oysters followed them,
50   And yet another four;
And thick and fast they came at last,
        And more, and more, and more—
All hopping through the frothy waves,
        And scrambling to the shore.

55 The Walrus and the Carpenter
        Walked on a mile or so,
And then they rested on a rock
        Conveniently low:
And all the little Oysters stood
60   And waited in a row.

"The time has come," the Walrus said,
        "To talk of many things:
Of shoes—and ships—and sealing wax—
        Of cabbages—and kings—
65 And why the sea is boiling hot—
        And whether pigs have wings."

"But wait a bit," the Oysters cried,
        "Before we have our chat;
For some of us are out of breath,
70   And all of us are fat!"
"No hurry!" said the Carpenter.
        They thanked him much for that.

"A loaf of bread," the Walrus said,
        "Is what we chiefly need:

Reading Skill
Context Clues What word does *frothy* describe? What actions here help you know it means "churning or foamy"?

Literary Analysis
Rhythm and Rhyme How many syllables should you pronounce in *conveniently* to keep the poem's rhythmic pattern?

◄ Critical Viewing
In what way does this illustration reflect the feeling of the poem?
[Connect]

75 Pepper and vinegar besides
    Are very good indeed—
Now, if you're ready, Oysters dear,
    We can begin to feed."

"But not on us!" the Oysters cried,
80   Turning a little blue.
"After such kindness, that would be
    A <u>dismal</u> thing to do!"
"The night is fine," the Walrus said.
    "Do you admire the view?"

85 "It was so kind of you to come!
    And you are very nice!"
The Carpenter said nothing but
    "Cut us another slice.
I wish you were not quite so deaf—
90   I've had to ask you twice!"

"It seems a shame," the Walrus said,
    "To play them such a trick.
After we've brought them out so far,
    And made them trot so quick!"
95 The Carpenter said nothing but
    "The butter's spread too thick!"

"I weep for you," the Walrus said:
    "I deeply sympathize."
With sobs and tears he sorted out
100   Those of the largest size,
Holding his pocket-handkerchief
    Before his streaming eyes.

"O Oysters," said the Carpenter,
    "You've had a pleasant run!
105 Shall we be trotting home again?"
    But answer came there none—
And this was scarcely odd, because
    They'd eaten every one.

Vocabulary Builder
dismal (diz´ məl) *adj.*
causing gloom or
misery

Literary Analysis
Rhythm and Rhyme
In each six-line stanza
of this poem, which
lines rhyme?

Apply the Skills

Poetry Collection 2

Thinking About the Selections

1. **Respond:** Which speaker would you like to meet? Why?
2. **(a) Analyze:** What is the speaker doing in lines 13–19 of "A Dream Within a Dream"? **(b) Connect:** How are these actions related to the idea of dreaming? **(c) Interpret:** Explain the title. What dream is within what dream?
3. **(a) Recall:** Name three things that do not frighten the speaker of "Life Doesn't Frighten Me." **(b) Infer:** Why does the speaker smile at frightening things? **(c) Analyze:** What does this reveal about the speaker's personality?
4. **(a) Recall:** How does the "eldest Oyster" react to the Walrus and the Carpenter? **(b) Predict:** What does this oyster's reaction hint about the events to come?

Reading Skill

5. For each of the following lines of poetry, write a question that you would ask to help you understand the underlined word. Then explain how the italicized **context clues** help you figure out the meaning of the word.
   (a) I go *boo* / Make them <u>shoo</u> / I *make fun* / When they *run*
   (b) And I *hold within* my *hand* / <u>Grains</u> of the *golden sand*
   (c) "I *weep* for you," the Walrus said: / "I *deeply* <u>sympathize</u>."

Literary Analysis

6. How many stressed syllables are in these lines of poetry?

   "If seven maids with seven mops / Swept it for half a year

7. Complete a chart like the one shown to give examples of **rhyming** words each poet uses. One example is given.

Poem	Rhyming Words		
"Life Doesn't Frighten Me"	wall/hall/all		
"A Dream Within a Dream"			
"The Walrus and the Carpenter"			

QuickReview

Poems at a Glance

A Dream Within a Dream: a man faces the passing of time

Life Doesn't Frighten Me: a girl shows confidence

The Walrus and the Carpenter: oysters are tricked by a hungry walrus and carpenter

Go Online
Assessment

For: Self-test
Visit: www.PHSchool.com
Web Code: ela-6403

Context Clues: the words and phrases around an unfamiliar word that help you find its meaning

Rhythm: pattern of stressed and unstressed syllables
Rhyme: repetition of sounds at the ends of words

Vocabulary Builder

Practice Write a sentence about each numbered item using a word from the *Poetry Collection 2* vocabulary list on page 520.

1. a person who wants his friends to help him move his sofa
2. a decision to cancel an exam
3. weather of drizzly rain and gray skies

Writing

One way to respond to literature is to write a **letter to an author**—even if you never mail it. Write a letter to one of the poets in the collection. Tell whether you like the poem and whether you would recommend it to others.

- Begin with a sentence that states your overall reaction.
- Then, develop your reasons and give examples.

For *Grammar, Vocabulary,* and *Assessment,* see **Build Language Skills,** pages 538–539.

Extend Your Learning

Listening and Speaking With a partner, plan an interview with one of the poets in this collection—Maya Angelou, Edgar Allan Poe, or Lewis Carroll.

- Develop a list of questions you will ask.
- Organize the questions into categories.
- Do research to find the answers.
- Act out the interview.

Research and Technology Using the Internet and other resources, gather a variety of poems and stories written by Lewis Carroll. Organize them in a **booklet**, making sure to include illustrations. Write an annotation—a descriptive comment—for each poem or story, comparing or contrasting it with "The Walrus and the Carpenter."

Build Language Skills

Poetry Collection 1 • Poetry Collection 2

Vocabulary Skill

Prefixes The **prefix** *pre-* means "before" or "toward." The prefix *pre-* is found in the word *preview,* which means "to view in advance." When you preview a chapter in a textbook, you look at the heading and charts before you read the chapter.

➤ **Example:** Before baking the cake, *preheat* the oven to 350°.

Practice Answer each question in a complete sentence. Use the italicized word in your response.

1. Would a book's *preface* come at the beginning or the end?
2. When would you complete a *preliminary* activity?
3. What do you do when you *predict* an event?

Grammar Lesson

Sentences: Simple and Compound Subjects A simple sentence can contain a simple subject or a compound subject. A **simple subject** is the person, place, or thing about which a sentence is written. A **compound subject** is made up of two or more nouns. Compound subjects are connected by conjunctions such as *and.*

More Practice

For more practice with simple and compound subjects, see the Grammar Handbook, p. R33.

Example	Simple Subject
Ricardo skis every winter.	Ricardo

Example	Compound Subject
Ricardo and Pablo ski every winter.	Ricardo and Pablo

Practice Rewrite the sentences, changing simple subjects to compound subjects and compound subjects to simple subjects.

1. Devon and Bob asked the coach about practice.
2. While walking, Anita found a lost dog.
3. Brad is going to call the movie theater.
4. The boys' track teams are divided by ability, not by grade.
5. The hockey team and the soccer team are going to have a fundraiser on Tuesday.

*W*_G *Prentice Hall Writing and Grammar Connection: Chapter 19, Section 3*

Reading: Context Clues

Directions: *Read the selection. Then, answer the questions.*

When you exercise, drink plenty of water to keep your body <u>hydrated</u>. As you exercise, you sweat. The <u>perspiration</u> you wipe from your face is your body losing water. If you lose too much water, you become <u>dehydrated</u>. A water loss of as little as ten percent can make you sick. Drink water before, during, and after exercise to replace the water your body loses.

1. The underlined word *hydrated* means
   A cool.
   B having enough water.
   C filled with oxygen.
   D clean and healthy.

2. Which phrase is the best context clue to help you know the meaning of *hydrated*?
   A your body
   B drink plenty of water
   C you sweat
   D can make you sick

3. Which word shows a contrast with *replenish*?
   A lose
   B during
   C replace
   D after

4. The best clue to the meaning of *perspiration* is in
   A the same sentence.
   B the previous sentence.
   C the following sentence.
   D the first sentence.

Timed Writing: Persuasion [Connections]

Review either *Poetry Collection 1* or *Poetry Collection 2*. Then, write a brief letter to the editor of your school newspaper persuading him or her to reprint your favorite poem. Give reasons why people should read the poem. Support your ideas with details from the poem. **(20 minutes)**

Writing Workshop: *Work in Progress*

Writing for Assessment
Review your Topic List and the writing prompt on page 515. Of the places you have identified, decide which one has been more important to you. Jot down 3–5 details to help you describe the place. Consider the sights, sounds, and smells you associate with this place. Put this work in your writing portfolio.

Reading Informational Materials

Instruction Manuals

In Part 1, you are learning about using context clues in literature. Using context clues is also helpful in reading informational materials such as recipes, user's guides, and instruction manuals. If you read the poem "Ankylosaurus," you might enjoy making a paper dinosaur.

About Instruction Manuals

An **instruction manual** presents a step-by-step process for completing a certain task. The text explains how to put something together, how to perform a procedure, or how to use a product.

Most instruction manuals have these features:

- a specific result that the reader can accomplish by following the directions
- a list of the materials needed
- a series of steps explained in logical order

Reading Skill

In an instruction manual, you may come across unfamiliar words or words that are used in a unique way. **Use context clues to understand specialized and technical language.** The surrounding words and the diagrams can help clarify the intended meaning. Use a graphic organizer like the one shown to list context clues for each unfamiliar word or phrase.

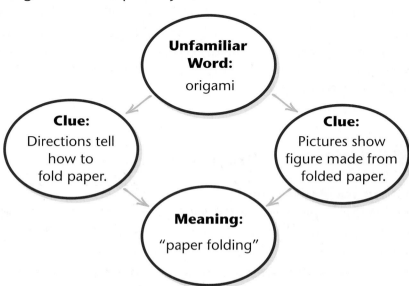

Unfamiliar Word: origami

Clue: Directions tell how to fold paper.

Clue: Pictures show figure made from folded paper.

Meaning: "paper folding"

ORIGAMI

APATOSAURUS by Rachel Katz

Begin with a 9 inch by 12 inch piece of construction paper or an 8½ inch by 11 inch sheet of copy paper.

The directions tell what kind of paper you need to complete the project.

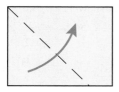

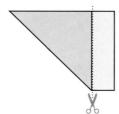

1 Place the rectangle sideways. Valley fold the left-hand side up to meet the top, thereby making a triangle.

2 Cut along the side of the triangle.

3 Save the rectangular piece of paper for the dinosaur's legs.

4 Open out the triangle into a square. Turn the square around to look like a diamond, making sure the existing fold-line is running horizontally across the paper.

Visual aids provide context clues that help you understand specialized terms like *valley fold*.

Body

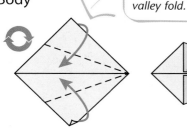

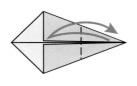

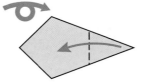

5 From the right-hand corner, valley fold the top and bottom sloping edges over to meet the middle fold-line, thereby making the kite base.

6 Valley fold the right-hand point over to meet the vertical edges. Press it flat and unfold it.

7 Turn the paper over. Valley fold the right-hand point over along the fold-line made in step 6.

8 Valley fold the point over back out toward the right.

Numbered steps show the order in which directions should be followed.

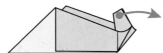

9 Valley fold the paper in half from bottom to top.

10 Reach inside the model and pull out the . . .

11 dinosaur's neck. Press it flat, into the position shown in step 12.

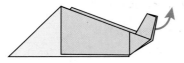

12 Reach inside the neck and pull out the . . .

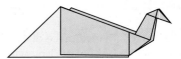

13 Head. Press it flat, into the position shown, thereby completing the body.

Headings help you see how tasks are organized.

Legs

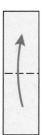

1 Use the remaining rectangle. Fold bottom up to the top.

2 Unfold.

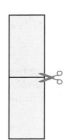

3 Cut in half along crease.

4 Fold in half.

Diagrams and pictures help you check whether you are completing the steps correctly.

5 Fold top down.

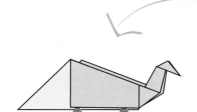

6 Staple as shown.

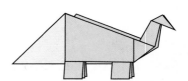

7 Here is the completed Apatosaurus.

Reading: Context Clues

Directions: *Choose the letter of the best answer to each question about the instruction manual.*

1. What clues help you clarify the meaning of *valley fold*?
   A knowing that a valley is an area of low land between mountains
   B looking at the diagrams
   C reading the directions
   D all of the above

2. Which of these helps you understand the meaning of *horizontally*?
   A the diagrams in steps 3 and 4
   B the diagrams in steps 4 and 5
   C the instructions in step 5
   D the instructions in step 6

3. Why do you think the shape shown in step 6 on page 541 is called a "kite base"?
   A It can fly.
   B It is attached to a string.
   C It is shaped like a kite.
   D It is made out of paper.

Reading: Comprehension and Interpretation

Directions: *Write your answers on a separate sheet of paper.*

4. Why do you begin the project with a rectangular piece of paper instead of a square piece of paper? [**Generating**]

5. Explain how the diagrams help you understand the instructions. [**Analysis**]

6. How do the red arrows used in the diagrams make the instructions easier to follow? [**Analysis**]

Timed Writing: Explanation [Cognition]

Describe the finished origami product. Use and define at least one word or phrase from the instruction manual whose meaning you determined from context clues. (**20 minutes**)

You can apply the instruction on this page to these poems.

Reading Skill

Context is the situation in which a word or expression is used. Details in the surrounding text give you clues to the word's meaning. Some words have more than one meaning. **Reread and read ahead** to find context clues that clarify meanings of words with multiple meanings. The examples show how context clarifies the meaning of *hide*.

➤ **Example:** The children tried to <u>hide</u> the broken vase.

The elephant's gray <u>hide</u> was tough and leathery.

Literary Analysis

Figurative language is language that is not meant to be taken literally. Authors use figurative language to state ideas in fresh ways. They may use one or more of the following types of figurative language:

- **Similes** compare two unlike things using *like* or *as*.
- **Metaphors** compare two unlike things by stating that one thing is another.
- **Personification** compares an object or animal to a human by giving the object or animal human characteristics.

Use a chart like this to unlock the meaning of figurative language.

Figurative Language
a day as soft as silk

↓

Type
simile

↓

What the Language Does
compares weather to soft fabric to show that the weather is gentle

Vocabulary Builder

Poetry Collection 1

- **chorus** (kôr´əs) *n.* the sound produced by many voices singing or speaking at the same time (p. 546) *A <u>chorus</u> of birdsong filled the air.*

- **thrives** (thrīvs) *v.* grows well (p. 546) *Cactus <u>thrives</u> in the desert.*

Poetry Collection 2

- **billowing** (bil´ ō iŋ) *v.* filling with wind (p. 553) *The sails were <u>billowing</u> in the wind.*

- **plunging** (plunj´ iŋ) *v.* throwing oneself (p. 553) *The children were <u>plunging</u> themselves into the pool.*

Build Understanding • *Poetry Collection 1*

Poetry

Connecting to the Literature

Reading/Writing Connection Poets paint unexpected pictures of people, places, and things. Write three sentences about how to describe something common in an uncommon way. Use three of these words: *alter, contrast, distort, emphasize.*

Meet the Authors

Eve **Merriam** (1916–1992)
Simile: Willow and Ginkgo (p. 546)

Eve Merriam fell in love very early with the music of language. She wrote award-winning poetry for adults and children, and she also wrote and directed musical theater productions. Among her many books for young readers are *There Is No Rhyme for Silver, It Doesn't Always Have to Rhyme, Out Loud,* and *Rainbow Writing.*

Emily **Dickinson** (1830–1886)
Fame Is a Bee (p. 547)

After one year of college, Emily Dickinson was homesick and returned to her parents' house in Amherst, Massachusetts. For her remaining years, she seldom traveled or received guests. Dickinson read many books and wrote more than 1,700 poems, which form a kind of lifelong diary of her deepest thoughts. She is considered one of the leading voices of American poetry.

Langston **Hughes** (1902–1967)
April Rain Song (p. 547)

Award-winning poet, dramatist, and novelist Langston Hughes traveled to Africa and Europe as a young man before settling in Harlem in New York City. In the 1920s, he was one of the leaders of the Harlem Renaissance, a period in which African American writers, artists, and musicians produced brilliant works.

Go **Online**
Assessment

For: More about these authors
Visit: www.PHSchool.com
Web Code: ele-9404

Simile: Willow and Ginkgo

Eve Merriam

The willow is like an etching,[1]
Fine-lined against the sky.
The ginkgo is like a crude sketch,
Hardly worthy to be signed.

5 The willow's music is like a soprano,
Delicate and thin.
The ginkgo's tune is like a <u>chorus</u>
With everyone joining in.

The willow is sleek as a velvet-nosed calf;
10 The ginkgo is leathery as an old bull.
The willow's branches are like silken thread;
The ginkgo's like stubby rough wool.

The willow is like a nymph[2] with streaming hair;
Wherever it grows, there is green and gold and fair.
15 The willow dips to the water,
Protected and precious, like the king's favorite
     daughter.

The ginkgo forces its way through gray concrete;
Like a city child, it grows up in the street.
Thrust against the metal sky,
20 Somehow it survives and even <u>thrives</u>.

My eyes feast upon the willow,
But my heart goes to the ginkgo.

---

1. etching (ech´ iŋ) *n.* print of a drawing made on metal, glass, or wood.
2. nymph (nimf) *n.* goddess of nature, thought of as a beautiful maiden.

▲ **Critical Viewing**
Ginkgo trees have large, upright branches and fan-shaped leaves. How do these willow trees differ from ginkgos? **[Contrast]**

Vocabulary Builder
chorus (kôr´ əs) *n.* the sound produced by many voices singing or speaking at the same time

thrives (thrīvz) *v.* grows well

Literary Analysis
Figurative Language
What kind of figurative language tells how the ginkgo grows?

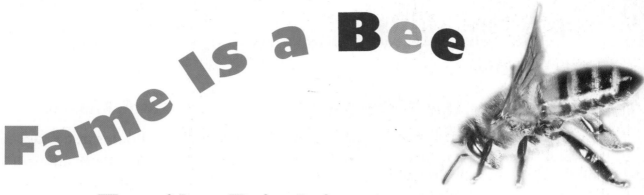

Fame Is a Bee

Emily Dickinson

Fame is a bee.
It has a song—
It has a sting—
Ah, too, it has a wing.

Literary Analysis
Figurative Language
What type of figurative language is used to compare fame to a bee?

April Rain Song

Langston Hughes

Let the rain kiss you.
Let the rain beat upon your head with silver liquid drops.
Let the rain sing you a lullaby.

The rain makes still pools on the sidewalk.
5   The rain makes running pools in the gutter.
The rain plays a little sleep-song on our roof at night—

And I love the rain.

Reading Skill
Context Clues
Which meaning of *running* does the poet use in line 5? How can you tell?

Apply the Skills

Poetry Collection 1

Thinking About the Selections

1. **Respond:** Which poem did you enjoy the most? Explain.
2. **(a) Recall:** Merriam first compares both the willow and the ginkgo to drawings. Name two other categories to which the poet compares both trees. **(b) Compare and Contrast:** What overall impression do you get of each tree?
3. **(a) Interpret:** Fill out a three-column chart like the one shown. Complete the first two columns in response to the ideas in "Fame Is a Bee." **(b) Discuss:** Trade charts with a partner and discuss your responses. **(c) Respond:** In the third column of your chart, evaluate how your response has or has not changed based on your discussion.

Good Things About Fame	Bad Things About Fame	Final Response to Poem

4. **(a) Recall:** In "April Rain Song," what kind of song does the rain sing? **(b) Infer:** What does the kind of song tell you about the poet's feelings about rain? **(c) Speculate:** How would the poem be different if it were about the rain that comes with a hurricane?

Reading Skill

5. In "Simile: Willow and Ginkgo," does the word *thin* mean "skinny" or "fragile"? What **context clues** help you decide?
6. In "April Rain Song," what is the meaning of "beat"? What context clues help you decide?

Literary Analysis

7. Find an example of each kind of **figurative language** in the poems in this collection. Explain your choice.
   (a) metaphor
   (b) personification
   (c) simile

QuickReview

Poems at a Glance

Simile: Willow and Ginkgo: a comparison of two kinds of beauty

Fame Is a Bee: a reflection on fame

April Rain Song: a celebration of the gentle spring rain

Go Online
Assessment
For: Self-test
Visit: www.PHSchool.com
Web Code: ela-6404

Context Clues: the words and phrases around an unfamiliar word that help you find its meaning

Figurative Language: language that is not meant to be taken literally. Types of figurative language include *personification, metaphor,* and *simile.*

Vocabulary Builder

Practice Answer each question with either *yes* or *no.* Then explain your answer.

1. Is a song in which only one person sings called a *chorus*?
2. If an animal *thrives* in a certain environment, is it doing well?

Writing

Write a **poem** with figurative language.

- Pick a subject that you have positive feelings about, such as sunshine, breezes, stars, or moonlight. Make a cluster diagram by jotting down qualities of your subject.
- Brainstorm for other things or people that have those qualities that could be used in a comparison.
- Using your notes, draft a poem with at least one example of figurative language.

For *Grammar, Vocabulary,* and *Assessment,* see **Build Language Skills,** pages 556–557.

Extend Your Learning

Listening and Speaking Prepare a **poetry reading**. Select one of the poems in this group or one that you have read elsewhere. Practice reading the poem aloud, using expression and pauses. Pay attention to end-of-line punctuation. Memorize and present your selected poem to the class. Speak slowly.

Research and Technology With a small group, research and prepare a **multimedia report** on characteristics of a tree that grows in your community.

- Find art or pictures that you can use as visual aids to accompany the oral report.
- Prepare an outline for your presentation, making each member of the group responsible for one section of the report.
- Present your report to the class. Then display the artwork on a bulletin board.

Poetry

Connecting to the Literature

Reading/Writing Connection Poets use vivid details to write about love and friendship. Write three sentences about how it feels to care deeply for another person, such as a grandparent, uncle, or best friend. Use three of the following words: *aid, assist, contribute, demonstrate, participate.*

Review

For **Reading Skill, Literary Analysis,** and **Vocabulary Builder,** see page 544.

Meet the Authors

Sandra **Cisneros** (b. 1954)
Abuelito Who (p. 551)

Sandra Cisneros was born in Chicago, but her family often traveled to Mexico to live with her grandfather, the *abuelito* in her poem "Abuelito Who." The frequent moves left Cisneros with few friends, but she remembers that she "retreated inside" herself, reading books and writing. She has won several awards for her poetry and short stories.

Nikki **Giovanni** (b. 1943)
The World Is Not a Pleasant Place to Be (p. 552)

Born in Knoxville, Tennessee, Nikki Giovanni has become one of America's most popular poets. Her awards include the National Association for the Advancement of Colored People (NAACP) Image Award for Literature and the Langston Hughes Award for Distinguished Contributions to Arts and Letters. She is a college professor.

Theodore **Roethke** (1908–1963)
Child on Top of a Greenhouse (p. 553)

Theodore Roethke was born and raised in Saginaw, Michigan, where his father and uncle grew and sold plants. As a child, Roethke spent hours in their greenhouse, which inspired the poem in this collection. In 1954, his book of poems entitled *The Waking* won a Pulitzer Prize.

Go Online
Assessment
For: More about these authors
Visit: www.PHSchool.com
Web Code: ele-9405

Ezra Davenport, 1929, Clarence Holbrook Carter, Courtesy of the artist

Abuelito • Who •

Sandra Cisneros

Abuelito[1] who throws coins like rain
and asks who loves him
who is dough and feathers
who is a watch and glass of water
5 whose hair is made of fur
is too sad to come downstairs today
who tells me in Spanish you are my diamond
who tells me in English you are my sky
whose little eyes are string
10 can't come out to play
sleeps in his little room all night and day
who used to laugh like the letter k
is sick
is a doorknob tied to a sour stick
15 is tired shut the door
doesn't live here anymore
is hiding underneath the bed
who talks to me inside my head
is blankets and spoons and big brown shoes
20 who snores up and down up and down up and down
        again
is the rain on the roof that falls like coins
asking who loves him
who loves him who?

Reading Skill
Context Clues What meaning of the word *watch* does the poet use in line 4?

Literary Analysis
Figurative Language What type of figurative language does the poet use to describe Abuelito in lines 14–19?

---

1. Abuelito (ä bwä lē´ tō) *n.* in Spanish, an affectionate term for a grandfather.

The World Is Not a Pleasant Place to Be

Nikki Giovanni

the world is not a pleasant place
to be without
someone to hold and be held by

a river would stop
5   its flow if only
a stream were there
to receive it

an ocean would never laugh
if clouds weren't there
10   to kiss her tears

the world is not
a pleasant place to be without
someone

Literary Analysis
Figurative Language
What type of figurative language is used in lines 8–10? What do you think the poet means?

552 ■ *Poetry*

Child on Top of a Greenhouse

Theodore Roethke

The wind <u>billowing</u> out the seat of my britches,
My feet crackling splinters of glass and dried putty,
The half-grown chrysanthemums staring up like accusers,
Up through the streaked glass, flashing with sunlight,
A few white clouds all rushing eastward,
A line of elms <u>plunging</u> and tossing like horses,
And everyone, everyone pointing up and shouting!

Vocabulary Builder
billowing (bil´ ō iŋ) *v.*
filling with wind

plunging (plunj´ iŋ) *v.*
moving suddenly
forward or downward

Apply the Skills

Poetry Collection 2

Thinking About the Selections

1. **Respond:** Which poem did you enjoy the most? Explain.
2. **(a) Recall:** Whom is Cisneros's poem about? **(b) Interpret:** Why does the speaker feel as if Abuelito is "hiding underneath the bed"? **(c) Connect:** Based on the descriptions of Abuelito, how does the speaker feel about him?
3. **(a) Interpret:** Fill out a three-column chart like the one shown. Complete the first two columns in response to the ideas in "The World Is Not a Pleasant Place to Be."
   (b) Discuss: Trade charts with a partner and discuss your responses. **(c) Respond:** In the third column of your chart, evaluate how your response to the poem has or has not changed based on your discussion.

Good Things About Friends	Life Without Friends	Final Response to Poem

4. **(a) Recall:** Describe the weather in "Child on Top of a Greenhouse." **(b) Connect:** What feelings seem to be behind the speaker's words?

Reading Skill

5. In "Child on Top of a Greenhouse," does the word *britches* mean "pants" or "trousers"? What **context clue** or clues help you decide?
6. In "The World Is Not a Pleasant Place to Be," what is the meaning of *flow*? What context clues help you decide?

Literary Analysis

7. Find an example of each kind of **figurative language** in the poems in this collection. Explain your choice.
   (a) metaphor
   (b) personification
   (c) simile

QuickReview

Poems at a Glance

Abuelito Who: a girl's description of her grandfather

The World Is Not a Pleasant Place . . . : reflections on friendship

Child on Top of a Greenhouse: a memory of a daring stunt

Go Online
Assessment
For: Self-test
Visit: www.PHSchool.com
Web Code: ela-6405

Context Clues: the words and phrases around an unfamiliar word that help you find its meaning
Figurative Language: language that is not meant to be taken literally. Types of figurative language include *personification, metaphor,* and *simile.*

Vocabulary Builder

Practice Answer each question with either *yes* or *no.* Then explain your answer.

1. If a sail is *billowing,* is it moving?
2. Should a person who is *plunging* into the deep end of a pool know how to swim?

Writing

Write a **poem** with figurative language.

- Pick a subject that you have positive feelings about, such as sunshine, breezes, stars, or moonlight. Make a cluster diagram by jotting down qualities of your subject.
- Brainstorm for other things or people that have those qualities that could be used in a comparison.
- Using your notes, draft a poem with at least one example of figurative language.

For *Grammar, Vocabulary,* and *Assessment,*
see **Build Language Skills,** pages 556–557.

Extend Your Learning

Listening and Speaking Prepare a **poetry reading**. Select one of the poems in this group or one that you have read elsewhere. Practice reading the poem aloud, using expression and pauses. Pay attention to end-of-line punctuation. Memorize and present your selected poem to the class. Speak slowly.

Research and Technology With a small group, research and prepare a **multimedia report** on greenhouses.

- Find art or pictures that you can use as visual aids to accompany the oral report.
- Prepare an outline for your presentation, making each member of the group responsible for one section of the report.
- Present your report to the class. Then display the artwork on a bulletin board.

Build Language Skills

Poetry Collection 1 • Poetry Collection 2

Vocabulary Skill

Prefixes The **prefix *re-*** means "back" or "again." Words that begin with this prefix have meanings related to something being brought back or done again. For example, when you *restate* something, you say it again.

▶ **Example:** I will **restate** the main idea for those who didn't understand it.

Practice Write the meaning of each word below. Explain how each meaning relates to the idea of "back" or "again." Then, use each word in a sentence.

1. reread
2. return
3. rephrase
4. reorganize

Grammar Lesson

Sentence Types Sentences can be classified according to what they do. This chart shows the four types of sentences.

Type of Sentence	Sample Sentence	Function	Punctuation
Declarative	The sky is blue.	states an idea	period
Interrogative	What time is it?	asks a question	question mark
Imperative	Do not enter!	gives an order or direction	period or exclamation mark
Exclamatory	This is amazing!	expresses strong emotion	exclamation mark

Practice Write a brief paragraph about an event in your school. Include at least one declarative, one interrogative, one imperative, and one exclamatory sentence. Label each sentence type.

MorePractice

For more practice with sentence types, see the Grammar Handbook, p. R33.

WG Prentice Hall Writing and Grammar Connection: Chapter 20, Section 2

Reading: Context Clues

Directions: *Read the selection. Then, answer the questions.*

It was quite a <u>predicament</u>. I needed a costume for the school play, but I couldn't find one at any of the stores. One night, I told my grandmother my problem. "I can <u>remedy</u> that!" Grandma offered. Over the next week, Grandma attacked the <u>arduous</u> task, shopping for supplies, making a pattern, and staying up late each night after work to snip and sew and trim. She created an <u>outrageous</u> costume. It had a velvet robe, a golden crown, and a long purple cape. I was proud of my costume—and of Grandma!

1. What is the meaning of *predicament*?

  A store

  B problem

  C play or dramatic scene

  D knight

2. Which word or phrase provides the best clue to the meaning of *remedy*?

  A One night

  B told

  C problem

  D offered

3. Which word could replace *arduous*?

  A proud

  B easy

  C difficult

  D convenient

4. What is the meaning of *outrageous* in the context of this passage?

  A unacceptable

  B surprising

  C amazing

  D humorous

Timed Writing: Interpretation [Connections]

Review *Poetry Collection 1* or *Poetry Collection 2*. Choose a musical group that you would recommend to set one of the poems to music. Use details related to style and theme to justify your choice. **(20 minutes)**

 ## Writing Workshop: *Work in Progress*

Writing for Assessment

The practice writing prompt on page 515 asks you to describe a place that is important to you. Review the work you have done. In a sentence, explain why this place is important to you.

Imagery

An **image** is a word or phrase that appeals to the five senses of sight, hearing, smell, taste, and touch. Writers use this sensory language—**imagery**—to create word pictures.

- Images can create a feeling of movement. For example, "the autumn leaves floated to the ground" shows the reader *how* the leaves fell.
- Imagery helps a writer express moods or emotions.
- An image can appeal to more than one sense. "Soft carpet of yellow prairie flowers" appeals to both touch and sight.

Comparing Imagery

Poets often use imagery to generate mood in their work. **Mood,** or atmosphere, is the feeling that a poem creates in a reader. For example, a poem's mood might be fanciful, frightening, thoughtful, or lonely.

In the following poems, each poet uses imagery to achieve a different effect. As you read each poem, follow these steps:

- Think about the pictures the poem creates in your mind.
- Identify which sense or senses each image appeals to.
- Determine the overall mood or emotion the poet expresses through imagery.

For each poem, use a chart like the one shown to analyze imagery.

	Poem Title
sight	
hearing	
smell	
taste	
touch	

Vocabulary Builder

Dust of Snow

- **rued** (ro͞od) *v.* regretted (p. 561) *I rued my decision to lend her my skateboard, so I looked for ways to get it back.*

who knows if the moon's

- **steeples** (stē′ pəls) *n.* towers rising above churches or other structures (p. 562) *The steeples of the town's churches rose above the trees.*

Build Understanding

Connecting to the Literature

Reading/Writing Connection Both of these poems use imagery to describe important changes. Jot down a change you have experienced that has affected you. Then, describe a sight, sound, smell, touch, or taste that you associate with the change. Use three of the following words: *interpret, respond, affect, emphasize, perceive.*

Meet the Authors

Robert **Frost** (1874–1963)

Born on the West Coast in California, Robert Frost and his poetry are often associated with New England. His family moved to Massachusetts when he was eleven, and he spent most of his life in the Northeast.

Slow Path to Fame Frost began writing poetry in high school. He kept writing while he worked as a farmer, mill worker, newspaper reporter, and teacher. After his book *North of Boston* became a bestseller in 1914, he went on to win four Pulitzer Prizes.

E.E. **Cummings** (1894–1962)

As a poet, E.E. Cummings experimented with punctuation, spelling, capitalization, and the arrangement of words on the page. For example, he liked to use lowercase words in his poems and even in his name. His words in many poems seem to be scattered aimlessly across the page. However, especially when the poems are read aloud, the "scattered" words create the effects Cummings wanted to achieve.

Painting Poems Edward Estlin Cummings was born in Cambridge, Massachusetts. During World War I, he drove an ambulance in France. After the war, Cummings studied painting, which perhaps explains why he became so interested in the visual effect of his poems.

Go **Online**
Author Link

For: More about the authors
Visit: www.PHSchool.com
Web Code: ele-9406

Dust of Snow

Robert Frost

The way a crow
Shook down on me
The dust of snow
From a hemlock[1] tree

5 Has given my heart
A change of mood
And saved some part
Of a day I had <u>rued</u>.

---

1. **hemlock** (hem′ läk′) *n.* evergreen tree; member of the pine family.

Literary Analysis
Imagery To which sense or senses does the image of a dust of snow appeal?

Vocabulary Builder
rued (rōōd) *v.* regretted

Thinking About the Selection

1. **(a) Recall:** What is the action that changes the speaker's mood? **(b) Classify:** Would you describe this action as being planned or occurring by chance? Explain.

2. **(a) Recall:** Describe the change that the action brings about in the speaker. **(b) Analyze:** Why do you think the action has this effect? **(c) Generalize:** What lesson do you think the speaker learns from this experience?

3. **Extend:** If such small, unexpected natural events happened every day, do you think they would have the same impact on a person? Why or why not?

who knows if the moon's   E.E. CUMMINGS

who knows if the moon's
a balloon, coming out of a keen[1] city
in the sky—filled with pretty people?
(and if you and i should

5   get into it, if they
should take me and take you into their balloon,
why then
we'd go up higher with all the pretty people

than houses and <u>steeples</u> and clouds:
10 go sailing
away and away sailing into a keen
city which nobody's ever visited, where

always
        it's
15   Spring) and everyone's
in love and flowers pick themselves

Literary Analysis
Imagery What kind of movement does the balloon image suggest to you?

Vocabulary Builder
steeples (stē´ pəls)
n. towers rising above churches or other structures

---

1. **keen** (kēn) *adj.* slang for *good, fine*.

Thinking About the Selection

1. (a) **Recall:** If the moon were a balloon, where might it take the speaker and "you," according to this poem?
   (b) **Interpret:** Describe the "keen city."
2. (a) **Speculate:** Why do you think lines 13–15 are arranged differently from the other lines in the poem?
   (b) **Extend:** Why might a place where everything is perfect appeal to a person?

Apply the Skills

Dust of Snow • who knows if the moon's

Comparing Imagery

1. **(a)** For each poem, choose an image and explain which senses the words appeal to. **(b)** Complete a graphic organizer like the one shown for each poem to analyze the poem's mood. In the center, write a word that describes the mood. Then, in the outer circles, list images, words, or phrases in the poem that help develop the mood.

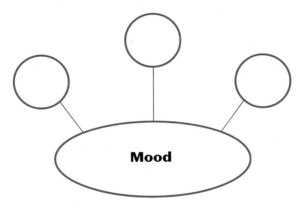

2. In "who knows if the moon's," how does the imagery create a feeling of floating or weightlessness? List details that suggest this movement.

Writing to Compare Literary Works

Write an essay in which you compare the role nature plays in each poem. Use these questions to get started:
- In each poem, is the image of nature positive or negative? What words or phrases suggest this?
- Does nature play a central role, or is it part of the background for the action?
- What words or phrases contribute to the image of nature?

Vocabulary Builder

Practice Answer each question and explain your answer.

1. Is it likely that you will find steeples in a city that limits the height of buildings to one floor?
2. If you rued an action, would you feel good about it?

QuickReview

Image: word or phrase that appeals to one or more of the five senses

Imagery: language that uses images to create word pictures

Mood: the feeling that a poem creates in a reader

Assessment
For: Self-test
Visit: www.PHSchool.com
Web Code: ela-6406

Reading

Directions: *Questions 1–5 are based on the following selection.*

It is fascinating to <u>contemplate</u>, or think about, how communication has improved over time. A thousand years ago, explorers brought news from country to country. It could take months or years for information to reach a <u>remote</u> land. In the 1800s, America introduced the Pony Express. Letters traveled across the country in "just" a week or so. The invention of the telephone <u>enabled</u> news to travel much faster by wire. Today, we communicate even faster with the Internet. This amazing invention makes it possible to spread news <u>internationally</u> in an instant. We share conversations, mail, and information electronically almost as rapidly as we change the channels on the television.

1. **What phrase in the first sentence states the meaning of *contemplate*?**
   A   It is fascinating
   B   or think about
   C   how communication has improved
   D   over time

2. **What word makes the most sense as a replacement for *enabled*?**
   A   stopped
   B   confused
   C   allowed
   D   invented

3. **What is the meaning of *rapidly*?**
   A   believably
   B   electronically
   C   remotely
   D   quickly

4. **What word best replaces the word *remote* in the third sentence?**
   A   hot
   B   freezing
   C   nearby
   D   faraway

5. **What detail in the passage suggests what a *remote* land is?**
   A   It could take many months for information to reach it.
   B   The Pony Express started in the 1800s.
   C   Communication has improved over time.
   D   We communicate faster with the Internet.

Assessment Practice

Vocabulary

Directions *Choose the word that best completes the sentence.*

6. **When a word has multiple meanings, the reader has to look at the _____ clues to decide how it is being used.**
   A restated
   B defined
   C context
   D explain

7. **If you cannot _____ a word, you should look it up in a dictionary.**
   A restate
   B define
   C context
   D preview

8. **To _____ a chapter in a textbook, you first read the section headings.**
   A restate
   B define
   C preview
   D explain

9. **When you paraphrase a line, you _____ it.**
   A restate
   B define
   C preview
   D explain

10. **The teacher _____ how the poet started his writing career.**
    A restated
    B defined
    C previewed
    D explained

Directions *Choose the correct definition for each word.*

11. **restate**
    A state before
    B state in order
    C state again
    D state for the first time

12. **preview**
    A view before
    B view correctly
    C view again
    D view once

13. **redo**
    A do after
    B do incorrectly
    C do prior to
    D do again

14. **prejudge**
    A judge fairly
    B judge again
    C judge after
    D judge before

15. **return**
    A turn back
    B turn down
    C turn forward
    D turn up

Writing for Assessment

Teachers use **writing for assessment** to measure how much you have learned or how well your writing skills have progressed. Follow the steps in this workshop to practice writing for assessment.

Assignment Write an answer to this **writing prompt** or one your teacher provides:

Description of Jobs of the Future Write an essay to describe three jobs you think will be important ten years from now. For each job, tell what skills or knowledge workers will need.

What to Include To succeed, your writing for assessment should feature the following elements:

- a response to the prompt, tailored to a specific audience
- a thesis statement or main idea that is clearly worded and supported
- an appropriate organizational pattern
- a complete response written within a limited time

To preview the criteria on which your assessment writing may be judged, see the rubric on page 570.

Using the Form

You may use this form in these situations:

- essay tests
- chapter or unit tests
- end of year exams

Prewriting

Spend about a quarter of your time prewriting.

Identify Your Purpose

Decide what the writing prompt asks you to do. Look for **key words** and terms that signal the exact task. The chart shown here identifies common key words and explains what you should do.

Gathering Details

Because there is a time limit, you need to generate notes quickly and efficiently. Take a few minutes to jot down as many ideas and details as you can.

KEY WORDS	
Key Words	**What You Will Do**
explain	Give a clear, complete account of an event or a process.
compare and contrast	Provide details about how two or more things are alike and how they are different.
describe	Provide vivid sensory details to paint a word picture of a person, place, or thing.
argue, convince	Take a position on an issue and present strong reasons to support your side.

Drafting

Spend about half your time drafting.

Shaping Your Writing

Write a thesis statement. It is essential that you have a thesis statement that clearly states your main idea. Review both the prompt and the details you have gathered, and write a single sentence that presents your main point.

Plan your organization. Consider the clearest plan for organizing and presenting your details. The chart shown here provides suggestions for each type of writing.

Type of Essay	Method of Organization
story, summary, explanation	**Chronological Order:** Describe events in the order they happen.
persuasive or classification essay	**Order of Importance:** Begin with your weakest reason and build to your most important.
description	**Spatial Order:** Present details from top to bottom, left to right, or front to back.

Providing Elaboration

Support your ideas with facts and details. While you cannot use your notebook or other reference sources, you should include as much specific information as possible. Include examples to defend your ideas.

Revising

Spend about one quarter of your time revising and editing.

Check your tone and word choice. Your test essay should have a formal tone, avoiding words that are slang or vague. Revise your essay, focusing on your tone and word choice.

> **Informal and Vague:** Years from now, scientists will need to know much more technical stuff than they do now.
>
> **Formal and Precise:** In ten years, biologists will need to grasp new technical data and advancements.

Integrating Grammar Skills

Revising for Strong, Functional Sentences

Make sure that each sentence in your essay serves the function it should and that each one has the correct end punctuation.

Identifying Errors in Sentence Functions and Punctuation

There are four types of sentences. Each type uses a specific punctuation mark. This chart provides a quick review.

Prentice Hall Writing and Grammar Connection: Chapter 21, Section 1

Type of Sentence	Function	End Punctuation	Example(s)
declarative	makes a statement	period	Space travel may be available some day.
interrogative	asks a question	question mark	Would you like a vacation on Mars?
exclamatory	shows strong feelings	exclamation point	What a thrilling trip that would be!
imperative	gives an order or a direction	period or exclamation point	Please fasten your seat belt. Watch out!

Fixing Errors To find and fix errors related to sentence function and end punctuation, follow these steps:

1. **Read each sentence that you have written.**
2. **Think about the function, or job, you wanted it to do.**
3. **Use the appropriate punctuation mark at the end of the sentence.**

Apply It to Your Editing

Reread the draft of your essay. Carefully think about the function, or job, of each sentence. Then use the rules and examples above to make sure that you have used the correct end punctuation.

Student Model: Liz Dzialo
Tiverton, RI

Writing Prompt: Write an essay about local or national news. In your essay, divide the news into "cheers" or "jeers," depending on whether you like the news or not—whether you cheer it or jeer it!

Cheers and Jeers

At my school and in my community, there are some things that make me happy and some things that make me unhappy. Here are some of my opinions on local issues—a list of cheers for the things I like and jeers for things I do not like.

In the first paragraph, Liz clearly outlines the topic of her essay.

Cheers to my school for holding a successful charity supper. They made over $1,000, and a local family in need is getting the majority of it. I am really glad that so many people came and I am sure that the family was also very grateful.

Jeers to my school for making students wait outside before school. It is not fair that the students have to stand outside and freeze. It has been really cold lately, and we should be allowed to go inside to get warm. There is enough room inside the building, so what is the point of making us stand outside? I think they should consider letting us in before the weather gets even colder.

By discussing both positive and negative news events, Liz addresses all aspects of the prompt.

Cheers to the town of Tiverton for building the Muddy Moose! It's a great little place to get ice cream, coffee, pastries, and other food. Even though they only serve one type of ice cream—soft-serve— the food is very good. I think it is a nice place to sit, relax, and have a cup of coffee or ice cream. It is bad that they put Dairy Dip out of business, but you have to admit Muddy Moose is better.

Jeers to Tiverton for building a new bank. They demolished Guimonds to make a bank. Even though it will be good to have a bank nearby, it will bring much more traffic. There is already enough traffic at the four-way intersection where it is being built. In the morning, on the way to school it will be horrible. We do not need any more new buildings in Tiverton. Soon Tiverton will start looking like a big city!

Liz follows a logical organization by alternating "cheers" with "jeers." She also supports ideas with evidence.

On reviewing these local news events, it seems Tiverton has a balance of good and bad news—at least there is enough good news for it to remain a good place to live.

Editing and Proofreading

Because such essays are written under a time limit, errors in capitalization, punctuation, and spelling can easily occur.
Focus on Punctuation: Look at every sentence in your essay. Check to make sure that each one starts with a capital letter and ends with the correct punctuation mark.

Publishing and Presenting

Consider one of the following ways to share your writing:
Discuss it. Compare your work with your classmates who have responded to the same writing prompt. Discuss any difficulties you may have encountered in completing the practice test, and share tips concerning how to solve such problems.
Prepare for upcoming tests. Put your completed essay in your portfolio. As an essay test approaches, take your practice test out and review the steps you took to complete it successfully. Share your tips and suggestions with classmates.

Reflecting on Your Writing

Writer's Journal Jot down your thoughts on writing for assessment. Begin by answering these questions:
- What do you usually do to prepare for an essay test?
- What did this practice activity teach you about preparing more fully or effectively?

> *Prentice Hall Writing and Grammar Connection: Chapter 13*

Rubric for Self-Assessment

To assess your essay, use this rubric:

Criteria	Rating Scale				
	not very				*very*
Focus: How clearly stated is the thesis statement or main idea?	1	2	3	4	5
Organization: How well does your organization suit your answer to the writing prompt?	1	2	3	4	5
Support/Elaboration: How well did you use details, facts, and reasons for support?	1	2	3	4	5
Style: How well did you use language that directly answers the question?	1	2	3	4	5
Conventions: How correct is your grammar, especially your use of punctuation?	1	2	3	4	5

Unit 4
Part 2

Paraphrase

Skills You Will Learn

Reading Skill: *Reread to Paraphrase*
Literary Analysis: *Forms of Poetry: Haiku, Limerick, Concrete*

Reading Skill: *Read Aloud According to Punctuation*
Literary Analysis: *Sound Devices: Alliteration, Repetition, Onomatopoeia*

Reading Skill: *Reading to Perform a Task*

Literary Analysis: *Comparing Sensory Language*

Literature You Will Read

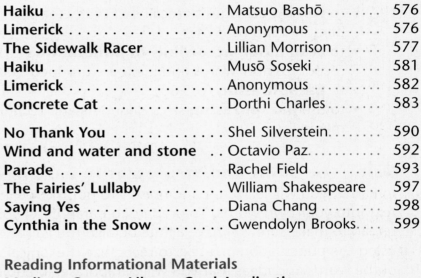

Reading: Paraphrasing

▶ **Paraphrasing** is restating an author's words in your own words.

Skills and Strategies you will learn in Part 2

In Part 2 you will learn

- to **reread** passages to recall and clarify for paraphrasing (p. 574)
- to **read aloud according to punctuation** to recognize how words and ideas are grouped as an aid to **paraphrasing** (p. 588)
- to use **paraphrasing** skills to understand technical manuals (p. 604)

Using the Skills and Strategies in Part 2

In Part 2, you will learn to paraphrase—to put the meaning of a text into your own words. To prepare to paraphrase, you will reread to make sure you have all the details. You will also practice using the punctuation in a text to recognize the logical grouping of the words and ideas that you will paraphrase. In addition, you will practice using paraphrasing to check your own understanding of a text.

Original Text	Paraphrase
At first, it is true, I thought There were only Peaches & wild grapes. That watermelon Lush, refreshing Completed my range. 　　　　*–Alice Walker*	Yes, when I was young I believed that peaches, wild grapes, and wonderful, tasty watermelon were all there was.

Academic Vocabulary: Words for Discussing Paraphrasing

The following words will help you write and talk about paraphrasing the selections in this unit.

Word	Definition	Sample Sentence
convey *v.*	communicate; carry from place to place	*Convey* the idea in your own words.
explain *v.*	make clear or understandable	Can you *explain* the idea more simply?
paraphrase *v.*	restate in your own words	Please *paraphrase* the quotation.
passage *n.*	a body of text	The *passage* he read was long.
represent *v.*	stand for	Clocks *represent* time.

Vocabulary Skill: Idioms

▶ An **idiom** is an expression or phrase from a particular language or region that is not meant to be understood literally.

Some idioms are common, and you recognize what they mean. However, because others may have come from a specific language, region, or culture, they may seem strange when you first hear or read them. Often the context or situation in which the idiom is used can give a hint to its meaning.

In Part 2, you will learn
  • to recognize idioms   • to restate idioms in your own words

▶ **Example:**
Idiom: We *called on* Aunt Sarah.
Restatement: We *visited* Aunt Sarah.

Activity With a partner, list five idioms. Then, share your list with other pairs. Working together, come up with fifteen idioms and explain them.

You can apply the instructions on this page to these poems.

Poetry Collection 1	Poetry Collection 2
Haiku, page 576	*Haiku,* page 581
Limerick, page 576	*Limerick,* page 582
The Sidewalk Racer, page 577	*Concrete Cat,* page 583

Reading Skill

Paraphrasing is restating an author's words in your own words. Paraphrasing difficult or confusing passages in a poem helps you clarify the meaning. Use these steps to help you:

- Stop and **reread** any difficult lines or passages.
- Identify unfamiliar words, find their meaning, and replace them with words that mean nearly the same thing.
- Restate the lines in your own words.
- Reread to see whether your paraphrase makes sense.

As you read the following poems, use a chart like the one shown to help you paraphrase difficult lines.

Line
Afoot and lighthearted, I take to the open road.
Unfamiliar Word(s)
afoot = on foot lighthearted = happy take to = start out on
Paraphrase
On foot and happy, I start out on the road.

Literary Analysis

Poets use different **forms of poetry** suited to the ideas, images, and feelings they want to express. Here are three poetic forms:

- In a **concrete poem**, words are arranged in a shape that reflects the subject of the poem.
- A **haiku** is a Japanese verse form with three lines. Line 1 has five syllables, line 2 has seven, and line 3 has five.
- A **limerick** is a funny poem of five lines. Lines 1, 2, and 5 rhyme and have three beats, or stressed syllables. Lines 3 and 4 rhyme and have two beats.

Vocabulary Builder

Poetry Collection 1

- **flaw** (flô) *n.* break; crack (p. 576) *Water leaked in through a flaw in the roof.*

- **skimming** (skim´ iŋ) *adj.* gliding; moving swiftly and lightly over a surface (p. 577) *He saw the boat skimming along the water.*

Poetry Collection 2

- **howl** (houl) *v.* make a loud, sorrowful sound (p. 581) *Coyotes howl at night.*

- **rage** (rāj) *n.* very strong anger (p. 581) *The branches whipped about in a rage.*

- **fellow** (fel´ ō) *n.* man or boy (p. 582) *The visitor was a fellow named Arthur.*

Build Understanding • *Poetry Collection 1*

Connecting to the Literature

Reading/Writing Connection In poetry, everyday actions, scenes, and words are presented in a fresh, new way. Bashō's haiku brings one moment in nature into sharp focus. A limerick twists simple words into hilarious knots. "The Sidewalk Racer" captures the zest of skateboarding. Make a list of times when you found a whole new way of looking at something. Use at least three of the following words: *analyze, concentrate, display, link.*

Meet the Authors

Matsuo **Bashō** (1644–1694)
Haiku (p. 576)

Bashō was born into a family of Japanese landowners. When Bashō was twelve, his father died. Bashō then entered the service of a local lord and began to write poetry. He was an important developer of the haiku form and one of its greatest masters. Bashō wrote "An old silent pond" in the spring of 1686. He revised the poem several times, changing it from the past to the present tense, until he felt that it was right. The Japanese have built a monument near the place where Bashō is believed to have written this haiku.

Lillian **Morrison** (b. 1917)
The Sidewalk Racer (p. 577)

As a child growing up in Jersey City, New Jersey, Lillian Morrison played street games and sports. The rhymes and chants she heard on the playground inspired her love of poetry. As an adult, Morrison spent nearly forty years working in the New York Public Library. She has written several books of poetry, including *The Sidewalk Racer and Other Poems of Sports and Motion.* Morrison has said, "I love rhythms, the body movement implicit in poetry, explicit in sports." Many of her poems, such as "The Sidewalk Racer," celebrate the human body in motion.

Go **Online**
Author Link

For: More about the authors
Visit: www.PHSchool.com
Web Code: ele-9408

Haiku

Bashō

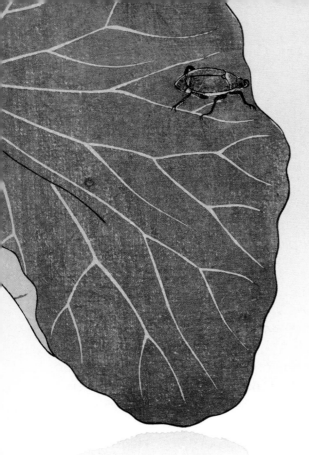

An old silent pond . . .
A frog jumps into the pond,
splash! Silence again.

Limerick Anonymous

A flea and a fly in a flue
Were caught, so what could they do?
Said the fly, "Let us flee."
"Let us fly," said the flea.
5 So they flew through a <u>flaw</u> in the flue.

Vocabulary Builder
flaw (flô) *n.* break;
crack

The Sidewalk Racer
or On the Skateboard

Lillian Morrison

Vocabulary Builder
skimming (skim´ iŋ)
adj. gliding; moving
swiftly and lightly
over a surface

Skimming
an asphalt sea
I swerve, I curve, I
sway; I speed to whirring
5   sound an inch above the
ground; I'm the sailor
and the sail, I'm the
driver and the wheel
I'm the one and only
10   single engine
human auto
mobile.

◄ **Critical Viewing**
What words might
describe the
spirit of both this
skateboarder and the
poem? **[Connect]**

Apply the Skills

Poetry Collection 1

Thinking About the Selections

1. **Respond:** Which poem expresses the most vivid images of movement? Explain.
2. **(a) Recall:** Describe the setting of the haiku. **(b) Generalize:** What overall feeling does the haiku create? Explain.
3. **(a) Recall:** What consonant sound is repeated in the limerick? **(b) Analyze:** How does this sound contribute to the humor in the poem?
4. **(a) Interpret:** Which words and phrases help show motion in "The Sidewalk Racer"? **(b) Analyze:** How can the speaker be both "the sailor / and the sail"? **(c) Draw Conclusions:** Which image do you think most successfully conveys the sense of being on a skateboard? Explain.
5. **(a) Infer:** How does the speaker feel about skateboarding? **(b) Support:** Which details support your answer? **(c) Extend:** Describe the speaker's personality.

Reading Skill

6. **(a) Paraphrase** the haiku by Bashō in your own words. **(b)** Why might rereading the haiku help you restate it?
7. How would you **paraphrase** lines 3–5 of the limerick?
8. Restate line 6 through the end of "The Sidewalk Racer" in your own words.

Literary Analysis

9. What image or word picture is presented in each line of the **haiku**? Use a web like this one to record your answer.

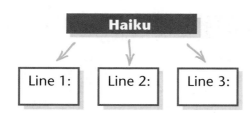

10. Would "The Sidewalk Racer" be more or less effective if it were written in a different shape? Explain.
11. Would it be possible to write a serious **limerick**? Explain.

QuickReview

Poems at a Glance

Haiku describes a peaceful scene in nature.

Limerick shows a funny scene between a fly and a flea.

The Sidewalk Racer re-creates a thrilling ride on a skateboard.

Go Online
Assessment
For: Self-test
Visit: www.PHSchool.com
Web Code: ela-6407

Paraphrase: to restate an author's words in your own words

Forms of Poetry: patterns or types of poetry, including *haiku, limericks,* and *concrete poetry*

Vocabulary Builder

Practice Match the situation in each item with a vocabulary word from the Poetry Collection 1 list on page 574.

1. Milk dripped from a crack in the glass.
2. Jay watched as the birds went gliding by.

Writing

Now that you have read an example of a haiku, a limerick, and a concrete poem, try writing your own **poem.**

- Review the forms of poetry on page 574 and choose one.
- Brainstorm for topics. If you are writing a limerick, think of rhyming words you might use.
- Follow the patterns of the poem form you chose.
- Read your poem aloud to a small group of classmates.

For *Grammar, Vocabulary,* and *Assessment,* see **Build Language Skills,** pages 586–587.

Extend Your Learning

Listening and Speaking Prepare and deliver an **oral response** to one of the poems in this collection.

- Give a clear oral reading of the poem.
- Provide your interpretation, or explanation, of the poem's meaning. Support your interpretation with examples.
- Share your evaluation of the success of the poem. Then, ask your classmates for feedback.

Research and Technology Using a computer, develop and design a **presentation of a poem** that you have chosen from this collection. Since lines of poetry must break as they are originally written, set wide enough margins. Next, choose a font, or style of type, that will be easy to read. Then, use tabs to set off indented lines, and put the title in large type. When the poem is set accurately, add pictures or designs to enhance the poem's appearance.

Connecting to the Literature

Reading/Writing Connection Poets paint word pictures that give you a new way to look at the world around you. They create meaning by using patterns of words, rhyme, and rhythm. In a few sentences, show how you might describe poetry to someone who has never experienced it before. Use at least three of these words: *motivate, illustrate, display, expand, modify.*

Review

For **Reading Skill, Literary Analysis,** and **Vocabulary Builder,** see page 574.

Meet the Authors

Musō **Soseki** (1275–1351)
Haiku (p. 581)

Musō Soseki made many important contributions to Japanese culture during his lifetime. He was a poet, scholar, and garden designer. He was also valued for his skills as an advisor to emperors and as a mediator during a period of civil wars in Japan. Soseki served as abbot, or head, of a Buddhist monastery. He was considered a great spiritual master and one of the most important religious leaders of his time. The haiku presented on the following page is one of a large body of poetry that Soseki wrote.

Haiku's Roots Haiku grew out of the "linked poem," or renga, tradition, which was popular in Japan in Soseki's day. Several poets would get together to compose a renga—short stanzas linked together to form one long poem. The renga eventually developed into the haiku form we know today, with its characteristic pattern of syllables and imagery.

Dorthi **Charles** (b. 1960)
Concrete Cat (p. 583)

Dorthi Charles was a student when she wrote "Concrete Cat." Readers especially enjoy the innovative way that Charles presents her subject.

Go Online
Author Link

For: More about the authors
Visit: www.PHSchool.com
Web Code: ele-9409

Haiku
Musō Soseki

Over the wintry
forest, winds <u>howl</u> in a <u>rage</u>
with no leaves to blow.

▲ Critical Viewing
What details in this
wintry scene are
similar to the scene
the poet describes?
[Compare]

Vocabulary Builder
howl (houl) *v.* make a
loud, sorrowful sound

rage (rāj) *n.* very
strong anger

Limerick

Anonymous

There was a young <u>fellow</u> named Hall,
Who fell in the spring in the fall;
    'Twould have been a sad thing
    If he'd died in the spring,
5   But he didn't—he died in the fall.

Concrete Cat

Dorthi Charles

```
   A         A
 e   r     e   r

  eYe    eYe        stripestripestripestripe  t
whisker        whisker   stripestripestripe  a
whisker   m   h  whisker  stripestripestripestripe  i  t  a  i  l
whisker   o   t  whisker   stripestripestripe
         U            stripestripestripestripe

      paw paw      paw paw                    ǝsnoɯ

  dishdish                        litterbox
                                  litterbox
```

Apply the Skills

Poetry Collection 2

Thinking About the Selections

1. **Respond:** Which poem expresses the most memorable ideas? Explain your answer.
2. **(a) Recall:** What action does the haiku describe?
   (b) Infer: Why are there no leaves for the winds to blow?
3. **(a) Recall:** In the haiku, what emotion does the poet assign to the winds? **(b) Infer:** Why do you think the poet chose this emotion? **(c) Interpret:** What human character trait might the haiku be describing? Explain.
4. **(a) Recall:** What incident is described in the limerick? **(b) Interpret:** What are the double meanings of *spring* and *fall* in the limerick? **(c) Analyze:** How do both meanings contribute to the humor in the limerick?
5. **Evaluate:** Do you think that "Concrete Cat" is a work of art, a poem, or both? Explain.

Reading Skill

6. **(a) Paraphrase** the haiku by Soseki in your own words. **(b)** Why might rereading the haiku several times help you restate it?
7. How would you **paraphrase** lines 1 and 2 of the limerick?
8. Review "Concrete Cat." In your own words, restate the meaning of the words that form the cat's head.

Literary Analysis

9. What image or word picture is presented in each line of the **haiku**? Use a web like this one to record your answer.

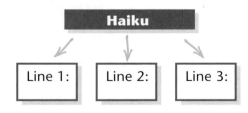

10. Would "Concrete Cat" be more or less effective if it were written in a different shape? Explain.
11. Would it be possible to write a serious **limerick**? Explain.

QuickReview

Poems at a Glance

Haiku describes a chilling winter scene.

Limerick presents wordplay to describe an unfortunate accident.

Concrete Cat provides a word picture of a cat.

Go Online
Assessment
For: Self-test
Visit: www.PHSchool.com
Web Code: ela-6408

Paraphrase: to restate an author's words in your own words

Forms of Poetry: patterns or types of poetry, including *haiku, limericks,* and *concrete poetry*

Vocabulary Builder

Practice Match the situation in each item with a vocabulary word from the Poetry Collection 2 list on page 574.

1. a young man walking to school
2. a woman who is angry about missing the bus
3. wolves communicating with each other

Writing

Now that you have read an example of a haiku, a limerick, and a concrete poem, try writing your own **poem.**

- Review the forms of poetry on page 574 and choose one.
- Brainstorm for topics. If you are writing a limerick, think of rhyming words you might use.
- Follow the patterns of the poem form you chose.
- Read your poem aloud to a small group.

For *Grammar, Vocabulary,* and *Assessment,* see **Build Language Skills,** pages 586–587.

Extend Your Learning

Listening and Speaking Prepare and deliver an **oral response** to one of the poems in this collection.

- Give a clear oral reading of the poem.
- Provide your interpretation, or explanation, of the poem's meaning. Support your interpretation with examples.
- Share your evaluation of the success of the poem. Then, ask your classmates for feedback.

Research and Technology Using a computer, develop and design a **presentation of a poem** that you have chosen from this collection. Since lines of poetry must break as they are originally written, set wide enough margins. Next, choose a font, or style of type, that will be easy to read. Then, use tabs to set off indented lines, and put the title in large type. When the poem is set accurately, add pictures or designs to enhance the poem's appearance.

Build Language Skills

Poetry Collection 1 • Poetry Collection 2

Vocabulary Skill

Idioms **Idioms** are expressions that convey a meaning that is different from the literal meaning of the words. For example, "I ran into Mike at the mall," means you met him unexpectedly, not that you literally ran until you bumped into Mike.

Restate idioms in your own words to understand the meaning.

Example: By the end of class **her head was spinning.**
Restatement: By the end of class she was **overwhelmed and confused.**

Practice Rewrite each sentence, restating the idioms in your own words. Then, use each idiom in a new sentence.

1. He <u>dropped the ball</u> on this assignment.
2. I can't seem to get that idea <u>through my head</u>.
3. Before wrestling season, the boys <u>cut down</u> on snacks.

Grammar Lesson

Subject Complements: Direct and Indirect Objects

A **direct object** is a noun or pronoun that receives the action of the verb and answers the question *Who?* or *What?* An **indirect object** names the person or thing to whom or for whom an action is done and answers the question *To or for whom?* or *To or for what?*

MorePractice

For more practice with direct and indirect objects, see the Grammar Handbook, p. 34.

Sentence	Question	Answer	Direct Object/ Indirect Object
Elsa baked bread.	Baked *what?*	*bread*	bread (direct object)
Mimi brought us a surprise.	Brought *what?*	*surprise*	surprise (direct object)
	Brought *to whom?*	*us*	us (indirect object)

Practice Identify the direct object in each sentence. Then, rewrite the sentence with a different direct object. If the sentence contains an indirect object, circle it.

1. Carlos enjoys football.
2. The two girls shared a locker.
3. Dad sent Gail a letter.
4. She ordered a bouquet.

𝒲𝒢 *Prentice Hall Writing and Grammar Connection: Chapter 19, Section 5*

Reading: Paraphrasing

Directions: *Read the selection. Then answer the questions.*

(1) Rhythm and sound are important in poetry. (2) These two elements give the poem its beat and musical quality. (3) They are like the musical background of a song with lyrics. (4) If the poem is a good one, the sounds and rhythm also add to the poem's meaning. (5) For example, a poem about spring would probably not have a slow, mournful rhythm.

1. Which of these is the best paraphrase of sentence 2 in this selection?

   A Poems are musical.

   B Rhythm and sound give a poem its musical quality.

   C Two elements of a poem are its beat and quality.

   D Each poem has its own beat.

2. If you were reading sentence 5 aloud, how many slight pauses would there be?

   A none

   B one

   C two

   D three

3. What does the pronoun "they" in sentence 3 refer to?

   A musical quality

   B rhythm and sound

   C beat and music

   D sound and music

4. Which is a good paraphrase of the words "slow, mournful rhythm"?

   A a beat that is not quick

   B a beat that is not fast

   C a beat that is drawn out and gives the impression of sadness

   D a beat that is like a funeral dirge

Timed Writing: Comparison [Critical Stance]

Review *Poetry Collection 1* or *Poetry Collection 2*. Compare and contrast the poems in the collection. In your comparison, discuss similarities and differences in the structures, topics, and the feelings conveyed in the poems. **(25 minutes)**

 Writing Workshop: *Work in Progress*

Comparison-and-Contrast

For a comparison-and-contrast essay you may write, choose two inanimate objects that you can see. For example, you might list two different shoes or two books. For each, describe the object's use and style. Save this work in your writing portfolio.

You can apply the instructions on this page to these poems.

Poetry Collection 1
No Thank You, page 590
Wind and water and stone,
page 592
Parade, page 593

Poetry Collection 2
The Fairies' Lullaby, page 597
Saying Yes, page 598
Cynthia in the Snow, page 599

Reading Skill

Paraphrasing is restating something in your own words. To paraphrase a poem, you must first understand it. Then, use simpler language to restate its meaning. **Reading aloud fluently according to punctuation** will help you group words for meaning.

- When you read a poem aloud, do not automatically stop at the end of each line.
- Use the chart shown here to decide where to pause.

Literary Analysis

Sound devices are a writer's tools for bringing out the music in words and for expressing feelings. Sound devices commonly used in poetry include the following:

- **Repetition:** the use, more than once, of any element of language—a sound, word, phrase, clause, or sentence—as in *of the people, by the people, and for the people*
- **Alliteration:** the repetition of initial consonant sounds, such as the *b* sound in *big bad wolf*
- **Onomatopoeia:** the use of a word that sounds like what it means, such as *roar* and *buzz*

Poetry Reading Guide	
Punctuation	**How to Read**
no punctuation	Do not pause. Keep reading.
comma (,)	slight pause
colon (:) semicolon (;) dash (—)	longer pause
period (.) question mark (?) exclamation point (!)	longest pause

Vocabulary Builder

Poetry Collection 1

- **dispersed** (di spurst´) *v.* distributed in many directions (p. 592) *The children dispersed bread crumbs for the pigeons.*
- **leisurely** (lē´ zhər lē) *adv.* in an unhurried way (p. 593) *I had time to stroll leisurely.*

Poetry Collection 2

- **nigh** (nī) *adv.* near (p. 597) *A chorus of birds signaled that dawn was nigh.*
- **offense** (ə fens´) *n.* harmful act (p. 597) *I did not mean my joke to be an offense.*

Connecting to the Literature

Reading/Writing Connection These poems contain vivid pictures of ordinary things—kittens, a landscape, and a circus parade. Write a few sentences to explain why a poet might choose such common topics. Use at least three of the following words: *adjust, clarify, communicate, interpret.*

Meet the Authors

Shel **Silverstein** (1932–1999)
No Thank You (p. 590)

Chicago-born Shel Silverstein was a talented poet, cartoonist, playwright, and songwriter. His popular poetry collections—*Where the Sidewalk Ends* and *A Light in the Attic*—show his imaginative sense of humor, which both children and adults enjoy. Silverstein also wrote the classic children's book *The Giving Tree*.

Octavio **Paz** (1914–1998)
Wind and water and stone (p. 592)

Although Mexican poet Octavio Paz (ok täv´ yō päs) lived in and visited many countries, he remained deeply committed to his Mexican heritage. In "Wind and water and stone," he captures a Mexican landscape and uses it to suggest how a culture changes and yet stays the same. In 1990, Paz received the Nobel Prize in Literature.

Rachel **Field** (1894–1942)
Parade (p. 593)

Rachel Field could not read until she was ten. This late reader, however, became a well-known writer of books for adults and children. She also became the first woman to receive a Newbery award for children's literature. One reason for her success as a writer was her "camera memory," which stored details such as those described in "Parade."

Go **Online**
Author Link
For: More about the authors
Visit: www.PHSchool.com
Web Code: ele-9410

No Thank You

SHEL SILVERSTEIN

No I do not want a kitten,
No cute, cuddly kitty-poo,
No more long hair in my cornflakes,
No more midnight meowing mews.

5 No more scratchin', snarlin', spitters,
No more sofas clawed to shreds,
No more smell of kitty litter,
No more mousies in my bed.

No I will not take that kitten—
10 I've had lice and I've had fleas,
I've been scratched and sprayed and bitten,
I've developed allergies.

If you've got an ape, I'll take him,
If you have a lion, that's fine,
15 If you brought some walking bacon,
Leave him here, I'll treat him kind.

I have room for mice and gerbils,
I have beds for boars and bats,
But please, *please* take away that kitten—
20 Quick—'fore it becomes a cat.
Well . . . it is kind of cute at that.

Literary Analysis
Sound Devices What sound device is used in lines 5 and 6?

Reading Skill
Paraphrasing How do the ellipsis points (. . .) help you understand the poet's meaning?

Wind and water and stone

Octavio Paz

The water hollowed the stone,
the wind <u>dispersed</u> the water,
the stone stopped the wind.
Water and wind and stone.

5   The wind sculpted the stone,
the stone is a cup of water,
the water runs off and is wind.
Stone and wind and water.

The wind sings in its turnings,
10   the water murmurs as it goes,
the motionless stone is quiet.
Wind and water and stone.

One is the other, and is neither:
among their empty names
15   they pass and disappear,
water and stone and wind.

Vocabulary Builder
dispersed (di spʉrst′)
v. distributed in
many directions

Literary Analysis
Sound Devices What
effect is created by
the repetition of the
words in the fourth
line of each stanza?

PARADE
Rachel Field

Background "Parade" describes an old tradition—the circus parade. Before television and radio, the best way to advertise coming attractions was a march down Main Street featuring clowns, wild animals in cages, and a giant musical instrument called a calliope.

This is the day the circus comes
With blare of brass, with beating drums,
And clashing cymbals, and with roar
Of wild beasts never heard before
5 Within town limits. Spick and span
Will shine each gilded cage and van;
Cockades at every horse's head
Will nod, and riders dressed in red
Or blue trot by. There will be floats
10 In shapes like dragons, thrones and boats,
And clowns on stilts; freaks big and small,
Till <u>leisurely</u> and last of all
Camels and elephants will pass
Beneath our elms, along our grass.

Reading Skill
Paraphrasing In reading this poem aloud, would you stop or keep reading at the end of line 3? Explain.

Vocabulary Builder
leisurely (lē´ zhər lē) *adv.* in an unhurried way

Apply the Skills

Poetry Collection 1

Thinking About the Selections

1. **Respond:** Did any of these poems end in a way that surprised you? Explain your answer.
2. **(a) Recall:** In "No Thank You," what are three reasons the speaker gives for not wanting another kitten?
   (b) Speculate: Why do you think the poet says that he would prefer an ape, lion, pig, or boar to a cat?
3. **(a) Recall:** According to "Wind and water and stone," what does each of the three natural elements do? **(b) Connect:** Why is it appropriate to say that the three natural elements depend on one another?
4. **(a) Recall:** What details in "Parade" describe the town?
   (b) Infer: What do these details suggest about the town?

Reading Skill

5. Read "No Thank You" aloud. **(a)** How does the punctuation—especially the commas—help you understand the poem? **(b) Paraphrase** the poem.
6. **(a)** When you read the final stanza of "Wind and water and stone" aloud, what do you do because of the colon?
   (b) Paraphrase the stanza.
7. How does the punctuation affect the pace of "Parade"?

Literary Analysis

8. Complete a chart like the one shown by listing examples of **sound devices** in each poem.

	"Wind and water and stone"	"Parade"	"No Thank You"
repetition			
alliteration			
onomatopoeia			

9. How do the sound devices add to the poems? Jot down a few ideas. Then, discuss your answers with a partner and choose one idea to share with the class.

QuickReview

Poems at a Glance

No Thank You presents the irresistible attraction of cats.

Wind and water and stone describes the interaction of natural elements.

Parade describes the excitement of a circus arrival.

Go Online
Assessment
For: Self-test
Visit: www.PHSchool.com
Web Code: ela-6409

Paraphrasing: restating something in your own words

Sound Devices: techniques, such as *repetition, alliteration,* and *onomatopoeia,* that bring out the music of language

Vocabulary Builder

Practice Answer each question based on the meaning of the underlined word.

1. Where might you find people walking <u>leisurely</u>?
2. Why might a crowd have suddenly <u>dispersed</u>?

Writing

Write a **prose description** of the scene suggested by one of the poems in this collection.

- Reread all the poems and select one poem as your subject.
- In your own words, create a list to capture the details and emotion in the scene. Make sure the words you use appeal to the senses. For example, jot down details such as *scratchy kitten, whispery wind,* and *thumping drum*. Write a paragraph using your list to re-create the picture that the poet painted.

For *Grammar, Vocabulary,* and *Assessment,* see **Build Language Skills,** pages 602–603.

Extend Your Learning

Listening and Speaking Present a **dramatic reading** of one of the poems in this collection.

- Rehearse your reading of the poem. Pay particular attention to punctuation and pauses.
- Vary the volume and tone of your voice to show emotions.
- After your reading, invite feedback from classmates.

Research and Technology A résumé is a specially formatted summary of important information about a person's career and education. Prepare a résumé for a poet whose work appears here. First, search online for information about the poet, including schools attended, titles of books, and awards. Then, find examples of common résumé formats. Choose one and write a résumé to showcase what you have learned about the poet.

Connecting to the Literature

Reading/Writing Connection At first, each of these poems seems to be about one person. Yet any reader can find in the poem a message for himself or herself. Jot down your ideas about how poetry, stories, and songs can teach you about life. Use three of the following words: *adapt, capture, confirm, contrast.*

Review

For **Reading Skill, Literary Analysis,** and **Vocabulary Builder,** see page 588.

Meet the Authors

William **Shakespeare** (1564–1616)
The Fairies' Lullaby (p. 597)

   William Shakespeare is the most highly regarded writer in the English language. Born in the English town of Stratford-upon-Avon, Shakespeare went to London as a young man. There he began writing and acting in plays. He wrote at least 37 plays and more than 150 poems. "The Fairies' Lullaby" is from the play *A Midsummer Night's Dream.*

Diana **Chang** (b. 1934)
Saying Yes (p. 598)

   Diana Chang admits that she is "preoccupied" with identity and the way people search to understand who they are. She explores her Chinese American identity in her novels and poems. Chang's self-expression does not stop with her writing. She also paints and has exhibited her paintings in art galleries.

Gwendolyn **Brooks** (1917–2000)
Cynthia in the Snow (p. 599)

   Gwendolyn Brooks wrote many poems about her neighbors in Chicago, the city she lived in most of her life. She started writing when she was seven and published her work in a well-known magazine as a teenager. In 1950, Brooks became the first African American writer to win a Pulitzer Prize.

Go Online
Author Link

For: More about the authors
Visit: www.PHSchool.com
Web Code: ele-9411

The Fairies' Lullaby

from A Midsummer Night's Dream

William Shakespeare

Fairies. You spotted snakes with double tongue,
    Thorny hedgehogs, be not seen.
Newts and blindworms,[1] do no wrong,
    Come not near our fairy Queen.

5 **Chorus.** Philomel,[2] with melody
    Sing in our sweet lullaby;
Lulla, lulla, lullaby, lulla, lulla, lullaby.
    Never harm,
    Nor spell, nor charm,
10   Come our lovely lady <u>nigh</u>.
    So, good night, with lullaby.

Fairies. Weaving spiders, come not here.
    Hence, you long-legged spinners, hence!
Beetles black, approach not near.
15   Worm nor snail do no <u>offense</u>.

Chorus. Philomel, with melody
    Sing in our sweet lullaby;
Lulla, lulla, lullaby, lulla, lulla, lullaby.
    Never harm,
20   Nor spell, nor charm,
    Come our lovely lady nigh.
    So, good night, with lullaby.

Reading Skill
Paraphrasing In reading aloud, why would you keep reading at the end of line 5? How would you paraphrase lines 5 and 6?

Vocabulary Builder
nigh (nī) *adv.* near

offense (ə fens´) *n.* harmful act

Literary Analysis
Sound Devices What effect does the repetition of the word *nor* have in line 9 and line 20?

---

1. newts (nōōts) **and blindworms** *n.* newts are salamanders, which look like lizards but are related to frogs. Blindworms are legless lizards.
2. Philomel (fil´ ə mel´) *n.* nightingale.

Saying Yes

Diana Chang

"Are you Chinese?"
"Yes."

"American?"
"Yes."

5　"*Really* Chinese?"
"No . . . not quite."

"*Really* American?"
"Well, actually, you see . . ."

But I would rather say
10　yes.
Not neither-nor,
not maybe,
but both, and not only

The homes I've had,
15　the ways I am

I'd rather say it
twice,
yes.

▲ Critical Viewing
Do you think the poet, pictured here, likes what she sees in the mirror? Explain. [Infer]

Reading Skill
Paraphrasing How does the period after each use of the word *yes* help you understand the poem's meaning?

Cynthia in the Snow
Gwendolyn Brooks

It SUSHES.
It hushes
The loudness in the road.
It flitter-twitters,
5 And laughs away from me.
It laughs a lovely whiteness,
And whitely whirs away,
To be
Some otherwhere,
10 Still white as milk or shirts.
So beautiful it hurts.

Literary Analysis
Sound Devices What sound device is at work in the words *SUSHES, hushes,* and *flitter-twitters*? What do these words express?

Apply the Skills

Thinking About the Selections

1. **Respond:** Which poem appeals to you the most? Explain.
2. **(a) Recall:** Name all the creatures the fairies address in "The Fairies' Lullaby." **(b) Classify:** What do all these creatures have in common?
3. **(a) Recall:** What questions are being asked of the speaker in "Saying Yes"? **(b) Infer:** Why might these questions make the speaker feel uncomfortable? **(c) Evaluate:** Do you feel that the speaker in "Saying Yes" has a good attitude toward her identity? Why or why not?
4. **(a) Recall:** In "Cynthia in the Snow," what five things does the snow do? **(b) Analyze:** What is the speaker's overall reaction to the snow?

Reading Skill

5. Read "Saying Yes" aloud. **(a)** How does the punctuation—especially the question marks—help you understand the poem? **(b)** Paraphrase the poem.
6. **(a)** In "The Fairies' Lullaby," after which words should the chorus pause? **(b) Paraphrase** the chorus's lines.
7. How does the punctuation affect the pace, or timing, of the words in "Cynthia in the Snow"?

Literary Analysis

8. Complete a chart like the one shown by listing examples of **sound devices** in each poem.

	"The Fairies' Lullaby"	"Cynthia in the Snow"	"Saying Yes"
repetition			
alliteration			
onomatopoeia			

9. How do the sound devices in these poems add to the poems? Jot down a few ideas. Then, discuss your answers with a partner and choose one idea to share with the class.

QuickReview

Poems at a Glance

The Fairies' Lullaby presents a plea to make unpleasantness go away.

Saying Yes provides an exploration of one's identity.

Cynthia in the Snow shows one person's appreciation of nature.

Go **Online**
 Assessment

For: Self-test
Visit: www.PHSchool.com
Web Code: ela-6410

Paraphrasing: restating something in your own words

Sound Devices: techniques, such as *repetition, alliteration,* and *onomatopoeia,* that bring out the music of language

Vocabulary Builder

Practice Answer each question based on the meaning of the underlined word.

1. What is an example of a child's minor <u>offense</u>?
2. Why would you say that something is <u>nigh</u>?

Writing

Write a **prose description** of the scene suggested by one of the poems in this collection.

- Reread all the poems and select one poem as your subject.
- In your own words, create a list to capture the details and emotion in the scene. Make sure the words you use appeal to the senses. For example, create details such as *slithery snakes, questions tossed like balls,* or *dancing snow.* Write a paragraph using your list to re-create the picture that the poet painted.

For *Grammar, Vocabulary,* and *Assessment,* see **Build Language Skills,** pages 602–603.

Extend Your Learning

Listening and Speaking Present a **dramatic reading** of one of the poems in this collection.

- Rehearse your reading of the poem. Pay particular attention to punctuation and pauses.
- Vary the volume and tone of your voice to show different emotions as you move through the poem.
- After your reading, invite feedback from classmates.

Research and Technology A **résumé** is a specially formatted summary of important information about a person's career and education. Prepare a résumé for a poet whose work appears here. First, search online for information about the poet, including schools attended, titles of books, and awards. Then, find examples of common résumé formats. Choose one and write a résumé to showcase what you have learned about the poet.

Build Language Skills

Poetry Collection 1 • Poetry Collection 2

Vocabulary Skill

Idioms **Idioms** are expressions that are not intended to be understood literally. In fact, some idioms in English would result in surprising effects if they conveyed literal meaning.

▶ **Example:** It's raining cats and dogs.

Often the context, or situation in which the idiom is used, gives you an idea of its meaning. In addition, dictionaries often list the meaning at the end of the entry for the first word, or a significant word, of the idiom. For example, *raining cats and dogs* would be listed at the end of the entry for *rain.*

Practice Tell what you think each idiom means. Check your answer in a dictionary. Then, use the idiom in a sentence.

1. coming down with
2. face the music

3. pick up the pieces
4. need a hand

Grammar Lesson

Predicate Nouns and Predicate Adjectives A **subject complement** is a noun, a pronoun, or an adjective that appears with a linking verb and tells something about the subject of the sentence. A **predicate noun** renames or identifies the subject of a sentence. A **predicate adjective** describes the subject of a sentence.

> **Predicate noun** Lucy is an excellent *doctor.*
> **Predicate adjective** Marc is very *happy* with his classes.

Practice Identify the predicate noun or the predicate adjectives in each sentence. Then, rewrite each sentence, replacing each predicate noun and each predicate adjective with a different one.

1. The sculpture is beautiful.
2. Glacier National Park is a huge area.
3. A brisk walk is good exercise.
4. The laundry was clean.
5. Tran is a musician.

MorePractice

For more on predicate nouns and predicate adjectives, see the Grammar Handbook, p. R34.

W̶G Prentice Hall Writing and Grammar Connection: Chapter 19, Section 6

Assessment Practice

Reading: Paraphrasing

Directions: *Read the selection. Then, answer the questions.*

(1) On my visit with Aunt Lilly, she took me to Wilkey Park. (2) She suggested that we ride the giant Ferris wheel. (3) Initially, I enjoyed looking down and seeing the park spread out below us. (4) We kept going up, higher and higher. (5) By the time we reached the top of the ride, I had shut my eyes and refused to open them until my feet touched the ground again.

1. Which is the best paraphrase of sentence 3?
   A The narrator likes the first part of the ride.
   B The park is all around them.
   C The ride is exciting.
   D The narrator enjoys her aunt.

2. In a paraphrase of sentences 4 and 5, what information is necessary?
   A the name of the narrator's aunt
   B how the people looked
   C the fact that the narrator is afraid
   D the exact height of the Ferris wheel

3. Which best completes the chart?

At first, I liked the Ferris wheel.		Then I was frightened.

   A The people seemed very small.
   B We went to Wilkey Park.
   C The ride took us higher.
   D Aunt Lilly was not scared.

4. Which of these is the best paraphrase of sentence 5?
   A The narrator is frightened for the rest of the ride.
   B Aunt Lilly changes her mind about the Ferris wheel.
   C The narrator likes the top of the Ferris wheel.
   D Aunt Lilly and the narrator reach the top of the ride.

Timed Writing: Comparison [Critical Stance]

Review *Poetry Collection 1* or *Poetry Collection 2*. Compare and contrast the poet's use of sound. Discuss how each poem's sound devices contribute to similarities and differences in the moods, or feelings, of the poems. **(20 minutes)**

 Writing Workshop: *Work in Progress*

In the outer circles of a Venn diagram, jot down notes about the differences you see between the objects you have chosen. In the overlapping middle section, write details about how the subjects are alike. Save this Venn diagram in your writing portfolio.

Applications

In Part 2, you are learning about paraphrasing texts. Paraphrasing is also useful for restating directions on forms and applications, such as the application on page 606 to enter a poetry contest. If you would rather read poetry than write it, a library card application can open the door to a world of poetry.

About Applications

When you fill out an **application,** you provide information to an individual or a group that will make a decision based on that information. Here are some reasons that people fill out applications:

- to get a library card
- to get a job
- to be admitted to a school
- to open a savings account
- to join a club
- to get a driver's license

When completing an application, read each part carefully. Note when and where it should be turned in and whether any payments or other paperwork should be included.

Reading Skill

When you fill out an application, you are **reading to perform a task.** The task is to provide accurate, complete information. On some applications, the directions are numbered and written in sentences. On others, brief labels tell what information should be provided in each section. To successfully complete an application, preview and review the text.

- **Preview** First, look over the directions and questions. Mentally **paraphrase** the directions to make sure that you can answer the questions listed in the chart shown.

- **Review** After you have filled out the application, review it. Make sure that you have completed all the necessary sections and that the information is legible, or readable.

Previewing an Application

1. What information is being asked for?
2. On which line should the information be placed?
3. Must the information be typed, printed, or keyed?
4. What other documents or items should be included?
5. Which information is optional and which is required?
6. When is the application due? To whom should it be sent?

Madison County Public Library Card Application Form

The library requires I.D. and written proof of current address. All library transactions and information are strictly confidential.
Please print:

These lines tell you what else you need to supply when you submit your application.

Today's Date _____ **Staff Use** Card # _____

Mr. _____ Mrs. _____ Miss _____ Ms. _____ Dr. _____

Name _____
                        Last   First   Middle

Current Address _____
                       Street (including house number) or PO box

City _____ State _____ Zip Code _____

Date of Birth _____

Home Telephone _____ Work Telephone _____

Patron Type—Circle One

    A—Adult (age 18 & over)   YA—Young Adult (age 14–17)
    J—Juvenile (age 0–13)   CS—College Student (any age)

_____

Permanent Address (if different from current address):

_____

Street (including house number) or PO box

City _____ State _____ Zip Code _____

Parent/Legal Guardian's Name (if under age 14) _____

Driver's License or Social Security Number _____

E-mail Address (optional)_____

The word *optional* next to an item in an application means that the information is not required. You can decide whether to provide this information.

    I understand that by signing this form and accepting this library card I am responsible for all materials checked out using this card and for charges that may be assessed to me. I agree to give prompt notice to the library of any address change.

    If I am signing as a parent or legal guardian, I accept responsibility for my child's use of the card and agree to pay any fines or other charges incurred by my child. As a parent, I am aware that the library permits children to have access to all materials and is not responsible for restricting or censoring the materials which children may select.

Cardholder Signature _____

Parent / Legal Guardian Signature _____

Reading Informational Materials

STUDENT POETRY CONTEST
North Carolina Poetry Society

Prizes to Be Awarded
All winning poems will also be published!
- **First Place: Trophy + Certificate + $25.00**
  - **Second Place: Certificate + $15.00**
  - **Third Place: Certificate + $10.00**
  - **Honorable Mention: Certificate**

For Students of North Carolina Schools

Because this is a contest, the application describes the awards.

Who may enter this contest?
Students in grades 3–12 and college undergraduates.

This question format highlights specific information and anticipates an applicant's questions.

What are the types of entries and awards?
- The Travis Tuck Jordan Award is for students in grades 3–5.
- The Frances W. Phillips Award is for poems about the environment and is for students in grades 3–8.
- The Mary Chilton Award is for students in grades 6–8.
- The Marie Barringer Rogers Award is for students in grades 9–undergraduate.
- The Lyman Haiku Award is for students in grades 9–undergraduate.

Note: All poems except the Lyman Haiku entries may be in any form but must have no more than 32 lines per poem.

What are the rules and how do I enter the contest?
1. You may submit one poem for each category.
2. Send two typed copies of each poem on 8½ X 11 paper.
3. In the upper left corner of each copy, type the name of the award category you are entering. Do not put your name or address on these copies.
4. On a separate piece of paper, type or print
  - the name of the category and the title of the poem you are entering
  - your name, your home address and zip code, and your phone number
  - the name of your school, your grade, your school address and telephone number, and the name of your teacher
5. Your teacher must sign the paper (see item 4 above).
6. You must also sign the paper and write: I pledge that this is my original poem.

You should follow these numbered steps carefully to make sure your entry is submitted correctly.

Note: The copies of your poems that you submit to this contest will not be returned to you, so please be sure to keep copies of your poems for yourself.

Reading: Reading to Perform a Task

Directions: *Choose the best answer to each question.*

1. Which of these is required in order to complete the library application?
   A proof of current address
   B an e-mail address
   C a permanent job
   D a fee of five dollars

2. According to the application for the poetry contest, in which form must the poems be submitted?
   A professionally printed
   B electronically produced
   C handwritten
   D typed

3. Which group is *not* eligible to enter the poetry contest?
   A students in grades 3–5
   B students in grades 6–8
   C college graduates
   D college students

Reading: Comprehension and Interpretation

Directions: *Write your answers on a separate piece of paper.*

4. **(a)** On the library application, which patron type requires the signature of a parent or guardian? **(b)** What ages does this group include? **[Knowledge]**

5. Why does the poetry contest require entrants to sign a pledge stating that their poems are original? **[Generating]**

Timed Writing: Explanation [Connections]

Applications ask for information, but they often *provide* information as well. Paraphrase the information on the library application to explain the privileges and responsibilities that come with having a library card. **(15 minutes)**

Sensory Language

Sensory language is writing or speech that appeals to one or more of the five senses—sight, hearing, touch, taste, and smell. The use of sensory language creates clear word pictures, or **images,** for the reading or listening audience. Look at these examples:

- *An icy wind blew in with an eerie moan.* (appeals to touch and hearing)
- *She sank her teeth into a juicy, sweet peach.* (appeals to taste and touch)
- *The fragrance of the fresh pink roses filled the room.* (appeals to smell and sight)

Comparing Sensory Language

Writers often use sensory language to stir up memories and associations in a reader's mind. As you read the following poems, use a chart like the one shown to record sensory details and the sense or senses to which each detail appeals. Think about the following questions for each poem:

- What ideas do the details help convey?
- What feelings do the details evoke in you?

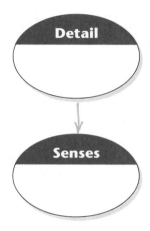

Vocabulary Builder

At First, It Is True, I Thought There Were Only Peaches & Wild Grapes

- **sole** (sōl) *adj.* single; only (p. 612) *As the sole owner, he received the entire profit.*
- **naïve** (nä ēv´) *adj.* innocent; not worldly (p. 612) *New to the city, she was trusting and naïve.*
- **savoring** (sā´ vər iŋ) *v.* tasting with delight (p. 612) *The cat licked its bowl, savoring every crumb.*

Alphabet

- **glisten** (glis´ ən) *v.* shine or sparkle (p. 613) *New bicycles glisten in the bright lights of the store.*
- **phrasings** (frāz´ iŋs) *n.* ways of speaking (p. 614) *We were amused by the little girl's childish phrasings.*

Build Understanding

Connecting to the Literature

Reading/Writing Connection Each of these poems describes a place that is important to the speaker. Jot down a short description of a place that is important to you and explain what makes it special. Use at least three of these words: *appreciate, maintain, equate, focus, identify.*

Meet the Authors

Alice **Walker** (b. 1944)

As the youngest of eight children of Georgia sharecroppers, Alice Walker did not seem bound for college. Yet she graduated from high school at the top of her class and went on scholarship to Spelman College in Atlanta and then Sarah Lawrence College in New York.

A Storytelling Tradition Both of Walker's parents were storytellers. Her own storytelling earned her a Pulitzer Prize in 1983 for the novel *The Color Purple.* Her other works include poetry, novels, short stories, and essays.

Naomi Shihab **Nye** (b. 1952)

Naomi Shihab Nye was born to a Palestinian father and an American mother. She has lived in the United States and in the Middle East. In her writing—poems, short stories, and children's books—she draws on her heritage and world travel.

History and Home Nye has said she enjoys traveling because of "that luminous sense of being invisible . . . having no long, historical ties, simply being a drifting eye." Still, she says, ". . . after a while, I grow tired of that feeling and want to be somewhere where the trees are my personal friends again." Nye explores history and home in her poem "Alphabet."

Go Online
Author Link

For: More about the authors
Visit: www.PHSchool.com
Web Code: ele-9412

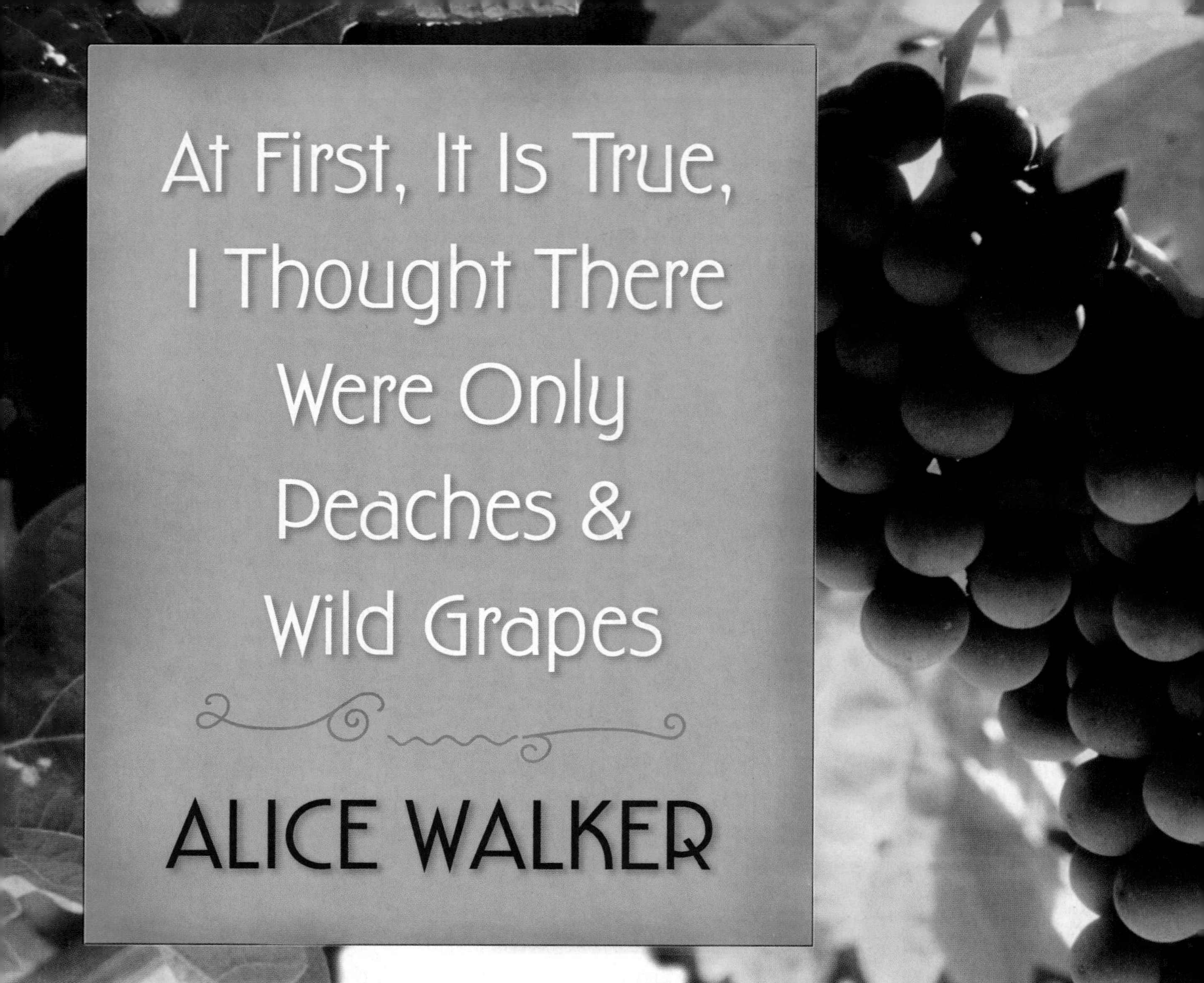

At First, It Is True, I Thought There Were Only Peaches & Wild Grapes

ALICE WALKER

To my delight
I have found myself
Born
Into a garden
5   Of many fruits.

At first, it is true,
I thought
There were only
Peaches & wild grapes.
10   That watermelon
Lush, refreshing
Completed my range.

Literary Analysis
Sensory Language
To what senses do
lines 4–5 appeal?

But now, Child,
I can tell you
15 There is such
A creature
As the wavy green
Cherimoya[1]
The black loudsmelling
20 & delicious
Durian[2]
The fleshy orange mango
And the spiky, whitehearted
Soursop.[3]

Literary Analysis
Sensory Language
Which words in this stanza appeal to the sense of touch?

---

1. cherimoya (cher´ ə moī´ ə) *n.* large tropical fruit with leathery skin and soft pulp.
2. durian (dŏŏ´ rē ən) *n.* huge fruit (native to Southeast Asia) with strong smell and taste.
3. soursop (sour´ säp´) *n.* guanabana; large spiny tropical fruit with an acidy taste.

25   In my garden
Imagine!
At first I thought
I could live
On blue plums
30 That fresh yellow pears
Might become
My <u>sole</u> delight.

I was <u>naïve</u>, Child.

Infinite is
35   The garden
Of many fruits.
Tasting them
I myself
Spread out
40   To cover
The earth.

<u>Savoring</u> each &
Every
One—date, fig, persimmon,
45   passion fruit—
I am everywhere
At home.

Thinking About the Selection

1. **Respond:** What fruit from the speaker's garden would you most like to try? Why?

2. **(a) Recall:** According to lines 6–12 and 27–32, what did the speaker at first think she would find in her garden?
   (b) Interpret: Why might she have had those limited expectations at first?

3. **(a) Recall:** What four "creatures" is the speaker amazed to find in her garden? **(b) Infer:** Why do these items surprise the speaker?

4. **(a) Interpret:** Describe the change in the speaker through the poem. **(b) Generalize:** What message about life does this change illustrate?

Alphabet

Naomi Shihab Nye

One by one
the old people
of our neighborhood
are going up
5 into the air

their yards
still wear
small white narcissus[1]
sweetening winter

10 their stones
<u>glisten</u>
under the sun
but one by one

Vocabulary Builder
glisten (glis´ ən) *v.*
shine or sparkle

---

1. narcissus (när sis´ əs) *n.* heavily scented bulb plant with white or yellow flowers.

15   we are losing
      their housecoats
      their formal <u>phrasings</u>
      their cupcakes

      When I string their names
      on the long cord

20   when I think how
      there is almost no one left
      who remembers
      what stood in that
      brushy spot
25   ninety years ago

      when I pass their yards
      and the bare peach tree
      bends a little
      when I see their rusted chairs
30   sitting in the same spots

      what will be forgotten
      falls over me
      like the sky
      over our whole neighborhood

35   or the time my plane
      circled high above our street
      the roof of our house
      dotting the tiniest
      "i"

Vocabulary Builder
phrasings (frāz´ iŋs) *n.*
ways of speaking

Literary Analysis
Sensory Language
To what senses do
the words *rusted
chairs* appeal?

Thinking About the Selection

1. **(a) Recall:** What three things belonging to the old people does the speaker say "we are losing"? **(b) Infer:** Why might these three things hold special meaning for the speaker? **(c) Distinguish:** Why can't these people or things be replaced?

2. **(a) Recall:** Which words describe the tree that stands in the yards of the old people? **(b) Interpret:** Why do you think the author chose these words to describe the tree?

Apply the Skills

At First, It Is True, I Thought There Were Only Peaches & Wild Grapes • Alphabet

Comparing Sensory Language

1. On a chart like the one shown, record the different types of sensory images from each of the poems.

	Sight	Hearing	Touch	Taste	Smell
At First, It Is . . .					
Alphabet					

2. **(a)** Which poem includes more images that relate to touch and taste? **(b)** Why are these types of images well suited to the subject of this poem?

3. **(a)** Which poem includes more images that relate to sight? **(b)** How do these images help you understand this poem's message?

Writing to Compare Literary Works

In an essay, compare and contrast the use of sensory language in the two poems. Consider these questions to get started:
- Which images in the two poems are the clearest to you? Why?
- How does the sensory language in each poem help you understand what the poet wishes to express?
- Which poem uses sensory language more vividly?

Vocabulary Builder

Practice Use each pair of words correctly in a sentence.

1. savoring; dessert
2. sole; possession
3. naïve; child
4. glisten; sunshine
5. phrasings; speech

Go Online
—Assessment
For: Self-test
Visit: www.PHSchool.com
Web Code: ela-6411

Reading

Directions: *Read the selection. Then answer the questions.*

1 Under a spreading chestnut tree
2   The village smithy stands;
3 The smith, a mighty man is he,
4   With large and sinewy hands;
5 And the muscles of his brawny arms
6 Are strong as iron bands.

—from "The Village Blacksmith" by Henry Wadsworth Longfellow

1. What is the best paraphrase of the first two lines?
A The blacksmith of the village works in the shade.
B The village blacksmith is standing under the tree looking around.
C The village blacksmith has been struck by a falling tree.
D The blacksmith's shop is next to a large chestnut tree.

2. What is another way to say "a mighty man is he"?
A He is a strong man.
B He is a politically powerful person.
C He is famous.
D He is a legend in the town.

3. How many sentences are in this selection?
A one
B three
C four
D six

4. If you read this aloud you would group the words into
A six groups.
B five groups.
C three groups.
D one group.

5. Which is the best paraphrase of "large and sinewy hands"?
A strong hands
B hands that are a working man's hands
C hands that have worked with iron
D big and muscular hands

Assessment Practice

Vocabulary

Directions: *Choose the best word to complete each sentence.*

6. The Student Council's job is to _____ all of the students.
- **A** convey
- **B** examine
- **C** paraphrase
- **D** represent

7. I tried to _____ the directions for the chemistry lab so that they were clearer to me.
- **A** convey
- **B** examine
- **C** paraphrase
- **D** represent

8. We _____ the text carefully but couldn't find clues that were concealed in the characters' dialogue.
- **A** conveyed
- **B** examined
- **C** paraphrased
- **D** represented

9. The _____ included details of the exploration of the Arctic Circle.
- **A** conveyance
- **B** examination
- **C** representation
- **D** passage

10. A good poet can _____ the emotion of an event.
- **A** convey
- **B** examine
- **C** pass
- **D** paraphrase

Directions: *Read the italicized idiom, and choose the sentence that best restates the meaning of the given sentence.*

11. The frog *turned into* a prince.
- **A** It bumped a prince.
- **B** It moved around a prince.
- **C** It became a prince.
- **D** It folded a prince.

12. We knew there would be *a showdown.*
- **A** We could tell there would be a fight.
- **B** We were sure they would arrive.
- **C** We believed the play would begin.
- **D** We understood that the curtain would fall.

13. I would like to give that rude clerk *a piece of my mind.*
- **A** I want to share.
- **B** I wish I could remember her.
- **C** I want to tell her I am angry.
- **D** I will listen to what she has to say.

14. She will have to *take her turn* like everyone else.
- **A** She will have to go in order.
- **B** She will have to spin around.
- **C** She will have to buy something.
- **D** She will have to carry her own things.

15. You can't *teach an old dog new tricks.*
- **A** People shouldn't train animals.
- **B** Dogs don't learn well.
- **C** People enjoy watching animals perform.
- **D** It is difficult for some people to change their ways.

Words With Prefixes and Suffixes

Prefixes are word parts added to the beginning of base words.

Suffixes are word parts added to the ends of words.

Master the Basics The following information will help you spell many words with prefixes and suffixes correctly.
- The spelling of a base word does not change when a prefix is added.
- To add a suffix beginning with a consonant (-*ful, -tion, -ly*):
  - Change *y* to *i* in the base word, unless a consonant precedes the *y*.
  - Most other times, do not change the base word.
- To add suffixes beginning with a vowel (-*ion, -al, -able*):
  - Change *y* to *i* in the base word, unless a consonant precedes the *y*.
  - Usually, drop the final *e* in the base word.
  - Most other times, do not change the base word.

" . . . and if you reelect me I promise to double the length of recess! "

CLASS PRESIDENTIAL DEBATE

Word List
disappoint
misspent
reelect
argument
announcement
joyous
stubbornness
pitiful
irritation
burial

Practice *Look at the Word List. Then, follow the directions.*

1. Write three words with prefixes. Underline each prefix.

2. Write three words that have suffixes starting with vowels. Circle the word in which the spelling of the base word does *not* change.

3. Write four words that have suffixes starting with consonants. Circle the word that does *not* follow the guidelines.

A. Directions: *Write the letter of the sentence in which the underlined word is spelled correctly.*

1. **A** We heard the <u>announcment</u> that Terry had won a scholarship.
    B This was a <u>joyous</u> day for his parents.
    C They always tried to help Terry, and he did not want to <u>dissappoint</u> them.
    D Hard work and <u>stubborness</u> helped him succeed.

2. **A** Grandpa witnessed the <u>burial</u> of a time capsule under City Hall.
    B He and his friend had an <u>arguement</u> about the exact date of the event.
    C This became a source of great <u>irritateion</u> between them.
    D Grandma thinks it is <u>pitifull</u>.

3. **A** We do not want to <u>relect</u> him.
    B He has <u>mispent</u> our money.
    C His <u>stubornness</u> is a problem.
    D We are hoping for an <u>announcement</u>.

4. **A** I don't want to <u>disapoint</u> you, but your report is not very good.
    B In fact, it is rather <u>pityful</u>.
    C Don't start an <u>argument</u> about it.
    D You completely forgot to tell about the <u>buryial</u> of the treasure chest.

B. Directions: *Choose the correct spelling for each word.*

1. A good _____ is important for success.
    A educateion
    B education
    C educattion
    D educatetion

2. _____ can get you in trouble.
    A Lazyness
    B Lazyiness
    C Lazinness
    D Laziness

3. Please don't _____ your friends.
    A mistreat
    B misstreat
    C misttreat
    D misreat

4. That kitten is very _____.
    A playiful
    B plaiful
    C playful
    D playfful

5. An _____ artist did this painting.
    A unknown
    B unnknown
    C unkknown
    D unown

Exposition: Comparison-Contrast Essay

A **comparison-and-contrast essay** uses factual details to analyze similarities and differences between two or more subjects. Whether it's a comparison of two candidates or two tomato soups, a well-written comparison shows the importance of the analysis. Follow the steps in this workshop to write a comparison-and-contrast essay.

Assignment Write a comparison-and-contrast essay in which you examine the similarities and differences between two subjects.

What to Include Your comparison-and-contrast essay should feature the following elements:

- a topic involving two or more subjects that are alike and different in notable ways
- an organizational pattern that illustrates similarities and differences
- a strong opening paragraph that grabs readers' interest
- facts, descriptions, and examples that show how the two subjects are alike and different

To preview the criteria on which your comparison-and-contrast essay may be judged, see the rubric on page 627.

Using the Form
You may use elements of this form in these writing situations:

- literary reviews
- movie reviews
- product comparisons

 Writing Workshop: *Work in Progress*

If you have completed the Work-in-Progress assignments, you have in your portfolio several ideas you can use in your comparison-and-contrast essay. Continue to develop these ideas, or explore a new idea as you complete the Writing Workshop.

Reading Writing
Connection

To get the feel for comparison-and-contrast, read "Race to the End of the Earth," by William G. Scheller on page 309.

Prewriting

Choosing Your Topic

Choose subjects that are similar and different in important ways. Use one of these strategies to find a topic:

- **Quicklist** Make a three-column chart. In the first column, jot down people, places, and things that are interesting to you. In the second column, list an adjective to describe each one. Then, in the third column, provide a detail about each one. Review your list, looking for ideas that it suggests, such as two brands of frozen pizza or two sports you enjoy. Choose a pair of such ideas as your topic.

- **Media Flip-Through** As you read a magazine or watch television, jot down pairs of related subjects such as issues in the news, television programs, or films. Review your notes, and choose the most interesting topic.

Narrowing Your Topic

You could probably write an entire book comparing and contrasting Mexico and Spain. To make your broad topic more manageable, divide it into smaller subtopics. Then choose one, such as Mexican and Spanish food, as the focus of your essay.

Gathering Details

Use a Venn diagram. Gather facts, descriptions, and examples that you can use to make comparisons and contrasts. Organize your details in a Venn diagram like the one shown. In the two outside sections, record details about how each subject is different. In the overlapping area, record similarities.

Rap   **Rock**

- spoken
- melodies not important
- kids like

- drumbeats
- lyrics
- rhymes

- sung
- melodies important
- parents like

Work in Progress
Review the work you did on pages 587 and 603.

Writing Workshop

Drafting

Shaping Your Writing

Follow an appropriate organizational pattern. Decide how you will organize your essay. Choose one of these plans:

- **Block Method:** Present all the details about one subject first. Then present all the details about the second subject. This method works well when you are writing about more than two things or are covering many different types of details.

Block	Point by Point
1. Introduction	1. Introduction
2. Tyrannosaurus: diet, size, and mobility	2. Diet of tyrannosaurus vs. velociraptor
3. Velociraptor: diet, size, and mobility	3. Size and mobility of tyrannosaurus vs. velociraptor
4. Conclusion	4. Conclusion

- **Point-by-Point Method:** Discuss each aspect of your subjects in turn. For example, if you are comparing two types of dinosaurs, you could first discuss the diets of each one, then the size and mobility, and so on.

Plan your introduction. Begin your essay with a strong introductory paragraph that does the following:
- introduces the subjects you are comparing and contrasting
- identifies the features or aspects you will discuss
- states a main idea about your subjects

Providing Elaboration

Use specific details. The more you can pinpoint the similarities and differences, the more interesting and vibrant your essay will be. Compare the following examples.

    General: holiday meal

    Concrete: holiday breakfast of omelettes and cinnamon rolls

Use transitions. Use transitional words and phrases to signal that you are discussing either a similarity or a difference. Transitions that show similarity include *similarly, also, both,* and *like.* Transitions that show difference include *by contrast, unlike, on the other hand, but,* and *however.*

From the Author's Desk

Gary Soto

Gary Soto

On Revising a Comparison

The type of writing known as comparison and contrast relates to something that we sometimes do naturally: look at others and compare them to ourselves. Perhaps the earliest example of that kind of comparison occurs between two siblings. In this paragraph, for instance, I compare myself with my older brother, Rick, and come up short as usual. Below is the first draft with small revisions. I learned to write quickly and then go back to polish the writing.

"The first sentence is always the scariest for me."
——————Gary Soto

Professional Model:
from *"My Brother and Me"*

    My brother Rick is thirteen months older than I am and has always been at least a head taller. ~~Thus,~~ When we were kids, ~~there-fore,~~ he cast a much larger shadow in the world. I was the tag-along kid who followed Rick because where he went was always cool. He seemed to be a lot stronger. When he shouldered a baseball bat, his swing was smooth. When I tried to do the same thing, I grunted through a strike. ~~Or if~~ The few times I did connect, the ball would dribble toward second base for an easy out. When ~~he~~ Rick went out for a pass during our front yard football games, the ball dropped sweetly into his outstretched arms. And me? With my mouth open, I juggled the ball ~~like~~ as if it ~~was~~ were three oranges tossed at me, concentrating intently before I dropped it.

I added much to subtly emphasize Rick's literal height advantage and the significant feeling of inferiority that I harbored.

The few times better indicates how poorly I played compared to Rick. I didn't scream, "Man, I was lousy all the time!"—which would have been an overstatement.

Naming my brother reminds the reader that I'm comparing Rick to Gary.

Revising

Revising Your Overall Structure

Check organization and balance. Your essay should give equal space to each subject and should be organized consistently. Reread your essay. Use a red marker to underline or highlight all the features and details related to one subject. Use a yellow marker for the other subject.

- If one color dominates, add more features and details related to the other subject.
- If one color appears in large chunks, followed by other places where the colors seem to alternate, revise your organizational plan. For example, you may have made the mistake of starting with block organization and then switching to point-by-point.

Peer Review: Have a classmate read your draft. Ask your reader to give you feedback about the organization and balance and to show you places where more information would improve your essay.

To read the complete student model, see page 626.

Student Model: Coding for Organization and Balance

For one thing, letters are used to spell words, <u>and numbers are used to, well, write numbers!</u> Also, numbers go on forever, while letters stop at z, the 26th letter. No matter how many letters you have in your alphabet, whether it's Hebrew, Spanish, Greek, or anything else, it will always end somewhere. But numbers just keep right on going.

> Jessica realized that she had included more details about letters than numbers, so she added this sentence about numbers.

Revising Your Word Choice

Check subject-verb agreement. Check your draft for subject-verb agreement. Make sure that sentences with singular subjects have singular verbs and that sentences with plural subjects have plural verbs.

➤ **Example:** Unlike football, hockey **is** played on ice. (singular subject, singular verb)
Both football and hockey **are** fast-paced games. (plural subject, plural verb)

Integrating Grammar Skills

Revising Choppy Sentences

You can combine choppy sentences in your writing by using **compound complements**.

Understanding Complements Some sentences need **complements,** which are additional words that complete their meaning. These complements are dependent on the type of verb in the sentence. **Action verbs** take direct and indirect objects. **Linking verbs** take predicate adjectives and predicate nouns. (For more on complements, see pages 586 and 602.)

Prentice Hall Writing and Grammar Connection: Chapter 19, Sections 5 and 6

Sentence Combining Using Complements This chart shows how combining complements can eliminate choppy sentences.

Complement	Choppy Sentences	Compound Complements
predicate adjective	Tennis is **fast-paced**. It is **fun**.	Tennis is fast-paced and fun.
predicate noun	One great sport is **tennis**. Another is **badminton**.	Two great sports are tennis and badminton.
direct object	Playing tennis well requires **equipment**. It requires **practice**.	Playing tennis well requires equipment and practice.
indirect object	Tennis gives **me** great exercise. It gives **Ed** exercise.	Tennis gives Ed and me exercise.

Fixing Choppy Sentences Follow these steps to find and fix choppy sentences by combining them with compound complements:

1. **Look for pairs of short, choppy sentences.**
2. **For each sentence pair, look at the complements that follow each verb.**

Apply It to Your Editing

Reread the draft of your essay aloud. Listen for pairs of choppy sentences that compare or contrast your subjects. Then, use the rules and examples above to make all necessary corrections.

Writing Workshop

Student Model: Jessica Kursan
Franklin Lakes, NJ

Letters . . . Or Numbers?

Have you ever heard the saying, "You can't compare apples and oranges"? Well, I've done it, so I know it's possible. But I'm not here to compare apples and oranges. I'm here to compare something else: numbers and letters. Numbers and letters have so many unusual properties about them. They are probably two of the most difficult things to compare, but I'll tackle them anyway.

We'll start off with their differences. Numbers and letters have a lot of differences, obviously, but I'm only going to name a few. For one thing, letters are used to spell words, and numbers are used to, well, write numbers! Also, numbers go on forever, while letters stop at *z*, the twenty-sixth letter. No matter how many letters you have in your alphabet, whether it's Hebrew, Spanish, Greek, or anything else, it will always end somewhere. But numbers just keep right on going.

Also, letters can represent numbers, but not the other way around, unless you're a computer programmer. For example, you could have a list of instructions, and the steps could be labeled A, B, C, instead of 1, 2, 3. But you can't say that 586 spells *car*.

Numbers and letters have about as many similarities as they do differences, and they are just as simple. For one thing, words and numbers are both used in everyday speech. For example, you could say, "Mr. Johnson, may I walk your dog?" "But I have two dogs." Just the words themselves that you speak are made up of letters and numbers.

In addition, letters and numbers must be precise. This is tough to explain. Letters cannot just be arranged into any order. They have to spell out a real word. For example, you can't just grab a bunch of letters and stick them together because they look pretty. If you had a word like *sdlkhjiower*, what would it mean? Where would you use it? How would you pronounce it? None of these questions has a real answer because *sdlkhjiower* is not a real word.

It's the same with numbers. You need to make sure your answer is precise. Also, you can't just say, "Well, I like 14, so I'm going to make 93 and 27 equal 14." That's not how it works. As with letters, you can't put numbers together just because they look good.

As you see, numbers and letters have many differences, but also many similarities. If you take the time, I'm sure you can find even more on your own.

Jessica's introduction grabs the reader's attention and names her topics for comparison.

The essay uses a point-by-point organization, first addressing differences and then similarities.

Jessica uses examples to explain each point she presents.

A conclusion sums up Jessica's ideas and invites the reader to consider the topic further.

Editing and Proofreading

Correct errors in spelling, grammar, and punctuation.
Focus on Double Comparisons: Comparison-and-contrast essays often contain comparative adjectives. Avoid using double comparisons. Never use *-er* or *-est* and *more* or *most* to form the comparative and superlative degrees in the same sentence.

>   **Incorrect:** The great dane was the *most biggest* dog in the show.

>   **Correct:** The great dane was the *biggest* dog in the show.

Publishing and Presenting

Consider one of the following ways to share your writing:
Create a picture essay. Find photographs to illustrate the similarities and differences you have discussed. Then, share your illustrated essay with classmates.
Create an audiotape. Practice reading your essay aloud a few times. Read slowly and clearly, emphasizing the strongest points. Then, record it and share it with a group of classmates.

Reflecting on Your Writing

Writer's Journal Jot down your ideas on writing a comparison-and-contrast essay. Begin by answering these questions:

- Do you view your topic differently now that you have analyzed it thoroughly? Explain.
- What prewriting strategy would you use again? Why?

> *Prentice Hall Writing and Grammar Connection: Chapter 8*

Rubric for Self-Assessment

To assess your comparison-and-contrast essay, use this rubric:

Criteria	Rating Scale
	not very very
Focus: How clearly does the topic state how two or more subjects are alike and different?	1 2 3 4 5
Organization: How effectively are points of comparison organized?	1 2 3 4 5
Support/Elaboration: How well do you use facts, descriptions, and examples to describe similarities and differences?	1 2 3 4 5
Style: How effective is your language in grabbing the reader's interest?	1 2 3 4 5
Conventions: How correct is your grammar, especially your use of the compound complements?	1 2 3 4 5

Delivering a Persuasive Speech

A **persuasive speech** shares many of the characteristics of a persuasive composition. The following speaking strategies will help you engage and convince your listeners.

Engage Listeners

Like compositions, persuasive speeches provide clear position statements and include supporting evidence in logical order. Follow these guidelines to plan and deliver a persuasive speech.

Start strong. Begin with a startling comparison or an anecdote that will capture your audience's attention.

Make contact. Your audience will hear your presentation only once—make sure they hear each and every word.

- Speak loudly and slowly enough to be heard and understood.
- Make eye contact.
- Move around the room as you speak.
- Pause after key points.

Convince Listeners

To convince an audience of listeners, use speaking strategies that will highlight your strongest support.

Repeat key points. As a speaker, make sure your audience does not miss your most important evidence and support. After explaining a key point, repeat it in a single sentence. After explaining several points, pause and restate the points in order.

Use visuals. A picture or chart can be a dramatic illustration of a point you are making. If you say that accidents are increasing, use a bar graph or a line graph to show the increase.

Feedback Form for Persuasive Presentation
Rating System
+ = Excellent ✓= average – = weak
Content
Clear position _____
Clear attitude _____
Logical organization _____
Amount of strong evidence_____
Respond honestly to these questions:
What impact did the presentation have on you?
What question does the presentation raise for you?
On what point would you challenge the speaker?
How can you affirm something the speaker has said?

Activity ⟩ *Plan a Persuasive Speech*

Plan and deliver your speech to the class. Ask for feedback on how you can improve your delivery. Use a feedback form like the one shown.

Appreciating Poetry

Prentice Hall Anthology

Prentice Hall, 2000

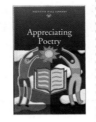

Anthology This collection of poems ranging from serious to silly celebrates changes in nature and in life. The poets' subjects cover baseball, dead bugs, goats, and poems themselves. This is an anthology in which everyone will find a poem to remember.

Secret of the Andes

Ann Nolan Clark

Puffin, 1976

Novel Cusi, a modern Inca boy, lives high up in the Andes mountains of Peru. He is an Inca Indian whose ancestors founded the great Incan Empire. Cusi leaves his mountain home to learn the mysterious secrets of his ancient ancestors. He slowly discovers the truth about his birth and his people's ancient glory, and then must prove himself worthy of a fabulous secret from the past.

Lyddie

Katherine Paterson

Puffin Books, 1991

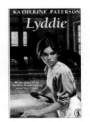

Novel *Lyddie* is set in the mid-1800s, a time when much of America was undergoing tremendous change. The character of Lyddie is a victim of this change. Lyddie's parents are gone and her brother and sisters are sent to live with other people. Determined to reunite her family, Lyddie works from dawn to dusk running a weaving loom in a murky factory. But when working conditions affect her friend's health, she must make some difficult and heart-wrenching choices.

Rascal

Sterling North

Puffin Books, 1990

Novel Rascal is only a baby when Sterling brings him home. But the mischievous raccoon is ready to join Sterling in swimming, fishing, and camping excursions. They are partners and best friends, until the spring day when suddenly everything changes.

These titles are available in the Penguin/Prentice Hall Literature Library.
Consult your teacher before you choose one.

Think About It Fairy tales, in their many forms, have been passed down through generations. Many are told to teach a moral lesson or warn against certain attitudes or practices. Sometimes they are simply tales for children of all ages to read and enjoy. In this adaptation of "The Princess and the Pea," Barbara McClintock retells the timeless tale in the popular format of a comic book.

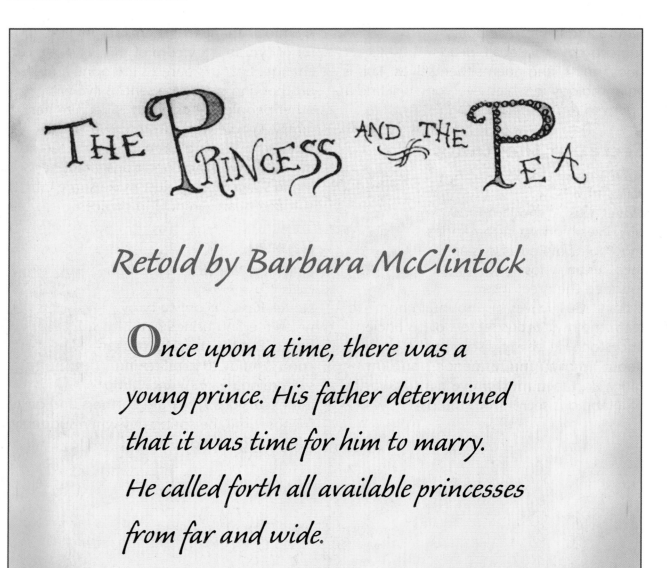

The Princess and the Pea

Retold by Barbara McClintock

Once upon a time, there was a young prince. His father determined that it was time for him to marry. He called forth all available princesses from far and wide.

The Next Morning.

Leotine and Lionel were married the very next day.

More to Explore
Art Spiegelman and Françoise Mouly included McClintock's adaptation in their collection *Little Lit: Folklore & Fairy Tale Funnies*. Spiegelman says of the growing popularity of graphic literature, "People think in . . . images . . . and . . . in bursts of language, not in paragraphs."

Readings in Classic Stories
Talk About It

Use these questions to guide a discussion.

1. **(a)** What kind of animals represent the royal family? **(b)** Why do you think the artist chose these animals?

2. **(a)** Why do Prince Lionel's parents construct such a strange bed for Leotine? **(b)** Does their plan work? Why or why not?

3. In small groups, discuss the strengths and weaknesses of the comic book format. Use these questions to get started:
   • What do you think of the comic book style of storytelling?
   • What do the illustrations add to the tale? What is lost?

Choose a point-person to share your group's ideas with the class.

Unit
5

Drama

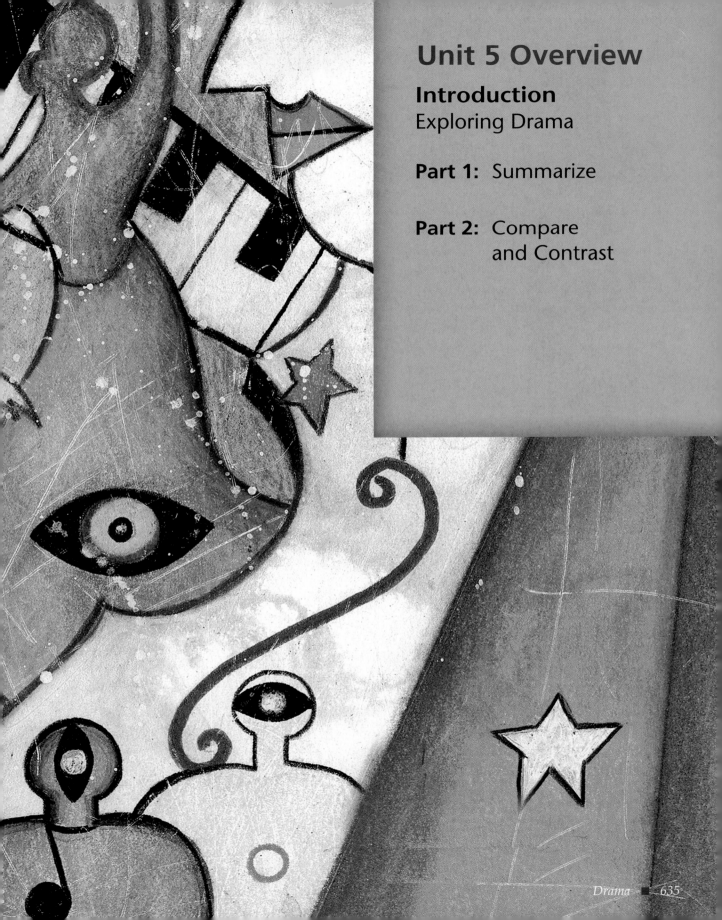

Unit 5 Overview

Introduction
Exploring Drama

Part 1: Summarize

Part 2: Compare
and Contrast

Introduction:
Drama

Joseph
Bruchac

Joseph Bruchac
Talks About the Form

Plays are meant to be played. **Drama** is not quiet and solitary like the other literary forms. You can read a poem or story aloud, but it isn't required. Reading drama to yourself can be rewarding, but it is even better when read aloud or acted. With drama, you must use your voice, body, emotions, and imagination.

▲ Joseph Bruchac
has written plays,
stories, poems, and
songs that draw on
his Native American
heritage.

Entering a Different World

Drama, you see, doesn't just ask you to identify with a character, it requires you to BE that person for a while. When you act in a play, you stop being yourself. You enter a world different from your everyday existence.

Drama Has a Long History

Thousands of years ago, plays were staged in ancient Greece. Those Greek comedies and tragedies are still enjoyed and understood by audiences today. The three major elements of plays have not changed since then. The first is **dialogue:** characters talking to each other and to the audience. The second is **action:** the physical things that people do in the play, including facial expressions. The third is **setting:** the stage, lighting, and scenery.

▶ Critical Viewing Which details in this picture suggest the importance of reading drama actively? [**Connect**]

Putting on Plays in West Africa

I read plays when I was in school. But I didn't really understand drama until after I graduated from college and became a volunteer teacher in Ghana, West Africa.

One of my jobs was to put on school plays—written by dramatists from Shakespeare to such modern African playwrights as Wole Soyinka (wō´ lā shō yiŋ´ kə) of Nigeria, winner of the Nobel Prize for Literature. I directed plays and acted in them with my African students. I adapted traditional Ghanaian stories as short plays for them to perform. I learned by doing.

Life is action; that is why our lively art, which stems from life, is . . . active. It is not without reason that our word "drama" is derived from the Greek word which means "I do." In Greek, this is related to literature, to playwriting, to poetry. . .

from *Creating a Role*
—**Constantin Stanislavski**

The passage shown here was written by a man who also learned by doing. He has been called the greatest of all acting teachers. What he says is not just advice for actors, but an important insight into the nature of drama as a whole.

More About the Author

Joseph **Bruchac** (b. 1942)

As a professional storyteller, **Joseph Bruchac** has performed at storytelling festivals in Europe and the United States. In his writings, Bruchac attempts to give an honest picture of Native American people and culture, free of inaccuracies and stereotypes. He draws upon storytelling traditions of the Abenaki (ab´ ə nak´ ē) people, his ancestors. For many years he has worked with the Poetry in Schools Program to encourage young people to express themselves through poetry.

Fast Facts

▶ Bruchac spent eight years teaching creative writing to prison inmates.
▶ To write *Sacajawea* (2000), he read the journals of Lewis and Clark and traveled the actual route that they took.

Learning About Drama

Elements of Drama

Drama is different from other forms of literature because it is written to be performed. When you read a drama, you should imagine that you see and hear the action of the performance. However, like other forms of literature, drama includes **characters**—people who take part in the action. It often also includes a **conflict,** or a problem between two characters or forces. Like other forms of literature, drama illustrates a **theme**, a message or insight about life.

ZIGGY©1998 ZIGGY AND FRIENDS, INC. Reprinted with permission of UNIVERSAL PRESS SYNDICATE. All rights reserved.

The following elements help readers and performers create the magic of drama:

- **Acts** are the units of the action in a drama. Acts are often divided into parts called **scenes**.
- **Dialogue** is the term given to the words characters say. Quotation marks are not used in a **script,** which is a printed form of the play. Instead, the words of each character appear next to the character's name.
- **Stage directions** are sets of bracketed information that tell what the stage looks like and how the characters should move and speak.
- The **set** is the construction on stage that suggests the time and place of the action.
- **Props** are the movable items—objects like a book, a suitcase, or a flashlight—that the actors use to make their actions look realistic.

Types of Drama

Drama is a word often used to describe plays that address a serious subject.

Comedy is a form of drama that has a happy ending. The humor often comes out of the characters' dialogue and situation. Comedies can be written purely for entertainment but can also be used to address serious issues.

Tragedy is a form of drama in which events lead to the downfall of the main character. This character is often a person of great significance, like a king or a heroic figure.

Drama is often written for stage performance. However, the dramatic format is used to present scripts for other types of performances:

- **Screenplays** are scripts from which movies are produced. **Teleplays** are types of screenplays written for television. Each of these includes camera angles and can require more variety of scene changes than a stage play.
- **Radio plays** are the written format of radio broadcasts. They can include sound effects, but not lighting or staging instructions.

▼ **Critical Viewing**
How do these masks effectively convey the art of drama? **[Analyze]**

Check Your Understanding

Identify *character, dialogue, stage directions,* and *props* in the following excerpt from *The Phantom Tollbooth,* by Susan Nanus. Discuss your responses with a partner.

ACT I, SCENE ii The Road to Dictionopolis
[ENTER MILO *in his car.*]
MILO. This is weird! I don't recognize any of this scenery at all. [A SIGN *is held up before* MILO, *startling him.*]
Huh? . . .

From the Author's Desk
Joseph Bruchac Introduces "Gluskabe and Old Man Winter"

Traditional stories are an important part of all American Indian cultures, including that of my own Abenaki people. Much of what I know about Abenaki culture, history, and philosophy of life I've learned from such stories.

To this day, traditional tales are still being told by Native Americans because, as an elder once explained to me, "our stories remember when people forget."

Dramatizing Folk Tales

Traditional Native American stories are told aloud by one person. Although they are not acted out on a stage, they are very theatrical. Storytellers change their voices, their facial expressions, and their body movements to express different **characters.**

When you hear a well-told story, you enter the world of the story. You can see it and feel it happening around you. Thus it is often not that hard to adapt such a story with many characters into a play.

Dramas and Folk Tales: Entertaining and Teaching

I love dramatizing folk tales because they are not just entertaining, but also full of useful lessons. That is true of much of drama also.

The great English playwright George Bernard Shaw began writing his plays to change society for the better. However, he soon learned that no one would listen to his **theme**, or message, unless his plays were also fun to experience.

Gluskabe (glōō skä´ bā) and his wise grandmother are central characters in many of our Abenaki tales. They live at a time long ago, either just before or soon after the arrival of the human beings. His power and her wisdom are used to help the people and keep things in balance. As you read this play, think about how it entertains while conveying a message about keeping things in balance.

GLUSKABE ✦ AND ✦ OLD MAN WINTER

Joseph Bruchac

▲ **Critical Viewing**
What is Gluskabe's attitude toward Old Man Winter in this picture? **[Interpret]**

CHARACTERS

Speaking Roles

NARRATOR

GLUSKABE

GRANDMOTHER WOODCHUCK

HUMAN BEING

OLD MAN WINTER

FOUR OR MORE SUMMER LAND PEOPLE including the leader

FOUR CROWS

Non-speaking Roles

SUN

FLOWERS

PLANTS

Scene I: *Gluskabe and Grandmother Woodchuck's Wigwam*

GLUSKABE *and* GRANDMOTHER WOODCHUCK *sit inside with their blankets over their shoulders.*

NARRATOR: Long ago Gluskabe (gloo-SKAH-bey) lived with his grandmother, Woodchuck, who was old and very wise. Gluskabe's job was to help the people.

GLUSKABE: It is very cold this winter, Grandmother.

GRANDMOTHER WOODCHUCK: *Ni ya yo* (nee yah yo), Grandson. You are right!

GLUSKABE: The snow is very deep, Grandmother.

GRANDMOTHER WOODCHUCK: *Ni ya yo*, Grandson.

GLUSKABE: It has been winter for a very long time, Grandmother.

GRANDMOTHER WOODCHUCK: *Ni ya yo*, Grandson. But look, here comes one of those human beings who are our friends.

HUMAN BEING: *Kwai, Kwai, nidobak* (kwy kwy nee-DOH-bahk). Hello, my friends.

GLUSKABE AND GRANDMOTHER WOODCHUCK: *Kwai, kwai, nidoba* (kwy kwy nee-DOH-bah).

HUMAN BEING: Gluskabe, I have been sent by the other human beings to ask you for help. This winter has been too long. If it does not end soon, we will all die.

GLUSKABE: I will do what I can. I will go to the wigwam of Old Man Winter. He has stayed here too long. I will ask him to go back to his home in the Winter Land to the north.

GRANDMOTHER WOODCHUCK: Be careful, Gluskabe.

GLUSKABE: Don't worry, Grandmother. Winter cannot beat me.

Scene II: *The Wigwam of Old Man Winter*

OLD MAN WINTER *sits in his wigwam, "warming" his hands over his fire made of ice. The four balls of summer are on one side of the stage.* GLUSKABE *enters stage carrying his bag*

Drama Characters The narrator introduces and describes the play's two main characters, Gluskabe and his grandmother.

Joseph Bruchac
Author's Insight
The Abenakis call the four directions by the names of Dawn Land, Summer Land, Sunset Land, and Winter Land.

and stands to the side of the wig-wam door. He taps on the wig-wam.

OLD MAN WINTER: Who is there!

GLUSKABE: It is Gluskabe.

OLD MAN WINTER: Ah, come inside and sit by my fire.

GLUSKABE *enters the wigwam.*

GLUSKABE: The people are suffering. You must go back to your home in the Winter Land.

OLD MAN WINTER: Oh, I must, eh? But tell me, do you like my fire?

GLUSKABE: I do not like your fire. Your fire is not warm. It is cold.

OLD MAN WINTER: Yes, my fire is made of ice. And so are you!

OLD MAN WINTER *throws his white sheet over* GLUSKABE. GLUSKABE *falls down.* OLD MAN WINTER *stands up.*

OLD MAN WINTER: No one can defeat me!

OLD MAN WINTER *pulls* GLUSKABE *out of the lodge. Then he goes back inside and closes the door flap. The Sun comes out and shines on* GLUSKABE. GLUSKABE *sits up and looks at the Sun.*

GLUSKABE: Ah, that was a good nap! But I am not going into Old Man Winter's lodge again until I talk with my grandmother.

Gluskabe begins walking across the stage toward the four balls. GRANDMOTHER WOODCHUCK *enters.*

GRANDMOTHER WOODCHUCK: It is still winter, Gluskabe! Did Old Man Winter refuse to speak to you?

GLUSKABE: We spoke, but he did not listen. I will speak to him again; and I will make him listen. But tell me, Grandmother, where does the warm weather come from?

▲ **Critical Viewing**
Why is Gluskabe wearing a patch over one eye? **[Connect]**

Joseph Bruchac
Author's Insight
Abenaki elders are valued for their wisdom. This dialogue reveals how Gluskabe needs his grandmother's knowledge to succeed.

☑ **Reading Check**

What has Gluskabe learned about Old Man Winter?

GRANDMOTHER WOODCHUCK: It is kept in the Summer Land.

GLUSKABE: I will go there and bring summer back here.

GRANDMOTHER WOODCHUCK: Grandson, the Summer Land people are strange people. Each of them has one eye. They are also greedy. They do not want to share the warm weather. It will be dangerous.

GLUSKABE: Why will it be dangerous?

GRANDMOTHER WOODCHUCK: The Summer Land people keep the summer in a big pot. They dance around it. Four giant crows guard the pot full of summer. Whenever a stranger tries to steal summer, those crows fly down and pull off his head!

GLUSKABE: Grandmother, I will go to the Summer Land. I will cover up one eye and look like the people there. And I will take these four balls of <u>sinew</u> with me.

Gluskabe *picks up the four balls, places them in his bag, and puts the bag over his shoulder.*

Scene III: *The Summer Land Village*

The SUMMER LAND PEOPLE *are dancing around the pot full of summer. They are singing a snake dance song, following their leader, who shakes a rattle in one hand. Four Crows stand guard around the pot as the people dance.*

SUMMER LAND PEOPLE: *Wee gai wah neh* (wee guy wah ney),
Wee gai wah neh,
Wee gai wah neh, wee gai wah neh,
Wee gai wah neh, wee gai wah neh,
Wee gai wah neh.

Gluskabe enters, wearing an eye patch and carrying his bag with the balls in it.

GLUSKABE: *Kwai, kwai, nidobak!* Hello, my friends.

Everyone stops dancing. They gather around GLUSKABE.

LEADER OF THE SUMMER LAND PEOPLE: Who are you?

GLUSKABE: I am not a stranger. I am one of you. See, I have one eye.

SECOND SUMMER LAND PERSON: I do not remember you.

GLUSKABE: I have been gone a long time.

THIRD SUMMER LAND PERSON: He does have only one eye.

FOURTH SUMMER LAND PERSON: Let's welcome him back. Come join in our snake dance.

The singing and dancing begin again: "Wee gai wah neh," etc. Gluskabe is at the end of the line as the dancers circle the pot full of summer. When Gluskabe is close enough, he reaches in, grabs one of the summersticks, and breaks away, running back and forth.

LEADER OF THE SUMMER LAND PEOPLE: He has taken one of our summersticks!

SECOND SUMMER LAND PERSON: Someone stop him!

THIRD SUMMER LAND PERSON: Crows, catch him!

FOURTH SUMMER LAND PERSON: Pull off his head!

The Crows swoop after Gluskabe. He reaches into his pouch and pulls out one of the balls. As each Crow comes up to him, he ducks his head down and holds up the ball. The Crow grabs the ball. Gluskabe keeps running, and pulls out another ball, repeating his actions until each of the Crows has grabbed a ball.

FIRST CROW: *Gah-gah!* I have his head.

SECOND CROW: *Gah-gah!* No, I have his head!

THIRD CROW: *Gah-gah!* Look, I have his head!

FOURTH CROW: *Gah-gah!* No, look—I have it too!

LEADER OF THE SUMMER LAND PEOPLE: How many heads did that stranger have?

SECOND SUMMER LAND PERSON: He has tricked us. He got away.

Joseph Bruchac
Author's Insight
In drama, audiences know more than certain characters. Thus, we are "in on the joke" when Gluskabe tricks the Summer Land People.

Joseph Bruchac
Author's Insight
"Gah-gah" is both the Abenaki name for "crow" and the sound crows make. So I have every crow saying "Gah-gah" first.

Reading Check

Why are the Summer Land People angry with Gluskabe?

Scene IV: *The Wigwam of Old Man Winter*

Gluskabe walks up to Old Man Winter's wigwam. He holds the summerstick in his hand and taps on the door.

OLD MAN WINTER: Who is there!

GLUSKABE: It is Gluskabe.

OLD MAN WINTER: Ah, come inside and sit by my fire.

Gluskabe enters, sits down, and places the summerstick in front of Old Man Winter.

GLUSKABE: You must go back to your home in the Winter Land.

OLD MAN WINTER: Oh, I must, eh? But tell me, do you like my fire?

GLUSKABE: Your fire is no longer cold. It is getting warmer. Your wigwam is melting away. You are getting weaker.

OLD MAN WINTER: No one can defeat me!

GLUSKABE: Old Man, you are defeated. Warm weather has returned. Go back to your home in the north.

The blanket walls of Old Man Winter's wigwam collapse. Old Man Winter stands up and walks away as swiftly as he can, crouching down as if getting smaller. People carrying the cutouts of the Sun, Flowers, and Plants come out and surround Gluskabe as he sits there, smiling.

NARRATOR: So Gluskabe defeated Old Man Winter. Because he brought only one small piece of summer, winter still returns each year. But, thanks to Gluskabe, spring always comes back again.

Q. Did you change the folk tale when you made it a play?

A. A folk tale is told by a storyteller and a play is acted out by a group of people. Giving speaking parts to a number of characters is my biggest change. I also had to insert stage directions to be used if this is actually put on as a play. However, the events of the story are still the same.

Q. In addition to telling stories, did the Abenaki put on plays?

A. Although our storytellers were good actors, changing their voices for different characters, the Abenaki people did not put on plays until after the arrival of the Europeans. However, our traditional stories are dramatic and easy to adapt as plays.

Q. Why are there four crows in this story? Why not two?

A. Four is a very powerful number for American Indians. Just as European stories have things in threes, our Abenaki stories have multiples of four. We believe that reflects nature, where there are four seasons, four directions, and so on.

StudentCorner

Q. What lesson does this play teach?
—J. J. Walker, Phoenix, Arizona

A. There are several lessons in this play. One of them is that it is better to be generous than to be selfish. Certain things, like water and air and summer, are gifts that are meant to be shared. It also teaches that we should listen to the advice of our elders, as Gluskabe does after being defeated the first time.

 Writing Workshop: *Work in Progress*

Response to Literature: Letter

For a letter to an author you may write, make a list of the five books you like best. Save this Book List in your writing portfolio.

Apply the Skills

Drama

Thinking About the Selection

1. **Respond:** Do you admire heroes like Gluskabe, who use cleverness or deception to fool others? Why or why not?
2. **(a) Recall:** What happens when Gluskabe first asks for Old Man Winter's help? **(b) Infer:** Why does Gluskabe need Grandmother Woodchuck's advice before he can defeat Old Man Winter? **(c) Analyze:** What is Gluskabe's plan?

Drama Review

3. What is the main **conflict** in this **drama**?
4. **(a)** In a chart like the one shown, list actions taken by Old Man Winter and the Summer Land People. Then identify and list **dialogue** about Old Man Winter and the Summer Land People. **(b)** Share your chart with a partner. How has your understanding of the characters changed?

Character	Action of the Character	Dialogue About the Character
Old Man Winter	warms his hands over fire made of ice	**Grandmother Woodchuck:** "Be careful, Gluskabe."
Summer Land People	dance around the pot full of summer	**Grandmother Woodchuck:** "The Summer Land People are strange people."

Research the Author

Plan a **storytelling program** featuring traditional tales by Joseph Bruchac. Follow these steps:
- Using the Internet and library resources, identify several Native American stories Bruchac has written.
- Choose two classmates to be your performance partners, with each person reading a different part.
- Ask your audience what the tales convey.

QuickReview

Selection at a Glance
In this traditional Native American tale, Gluskabe, a young Abenaki, outsmarts Old Man Winter, with help from his wise grandmother.

For: Self-test
Visit: www.PHSchool.com
Web Code: ela-6501

Drama: literature that is written to be performed before an audience

Conflict: a problem between two characters or forces

Dialogue: words spoken by the characters

Characters: people who take part in the action

Skills You Will Learn

Reading Skill: *Reread to Identify Main Events*
Literary Analysis: *Dialogue*

Literary Analysis: *Comparing a Novel to Its Dramatization*

Reading Skill: *Outlining*

Literature You Will Read

Reading and Vocabulary Skills Preview

Reading: Summarizing

▶ A **summary** is a brief statement that presents the main ideas of a longer piece of writing.

Skills and Strategies You Will Learn in Part 1

In Part 1 you will learn:

- to **reread to identify main events** to **summarize** (p. 652)
- to **organize events** to **summarize** (p. 652)
- to **outline main events** according to **organizational structure** to **summarize** (p. 690)

Using the Skills and Strategies in Part 1

In Part 1, you will learn to **summarize**. You will practice reviewing the text to recall its most important events. In addition, you will learn to organize the main ideas and events and to create outlines.

Original Text: When Nikolas Tesla came to the United States in 1884, he began working for Thomas Edison. He worked with Edison on problems with the direct current system of transmitting electricity. After the problem was solved, the two inventors disagreed about who deserved more of the credit. Tesla quit and went on to develop his own system for electronic transmission—alternating current. Today, most homes use alternating current, the system that Tesla perfected.

Summary Tesla worked for Thomas Edison when he first arrived in the United States. After a disagreement over who really solved the problems with direct current, Tesla stopped working for Edison. On his own, he made possible the use of alternating current, which is the system we use today.

Outline
I. Tesla worked for Edison
  A. Tesla helped Edison with direct current problem.
  B. They solved the problem
  C. They disagreed about who should get credit.

II. Tesla worked on his own
  A. Quit working for Edison
  B. Developed his own system of delivering current.
  C. More people use his system today.

Academic Vocabulary: Words for Discussing Summarizing

The following words will help you write and talk about summarizing as you read the selections in this unit.

Word	Definition	Sample Sentence
brief *adj.*	short	A *brief* essay has few paragraphs.
describe *v.*	tell or write about	*Describe* the details of the scene.
recall *v.*	remember	A summary helps the reader *recall* important details.
review *v.*	look at again	*Review* your work for errors.
summary *n.*	the main ideas in brief form	Write a *summary* of the story.

Vocabulary Skill: Roots

▶ A **root** is the basic unit of meaning in a word.

In Part 1, you will learn
- the root *-brev-*
- the root *-scrib-*

Many words come into English through a series of other languages. For this reason, words that share the same root may have variations in spelling.

▶ **Example:** brev-   brief   brevity

Activity Group these words according to the root you think they share. Then add one more word to each root list. Check your answers in a dictionary.

1. brief
2. inscription
3. prescribe
4. abbreviate
5. describe

These skills will help you become a better reader. Practice them with Act I of *The Phantom Tollbooth* (p. 654).

Reading Skill

A **summary** of a piece of writing is a short statement that presents the main ideas and most important points. To summarize a drama, first **reread to identify main events**. Include only major events that move the story forward. Then, organize events in the order in which they happen. As you read, use a chart like the one shown to record the major events in Act I. Refer to your chart when you write a summary.

Event 1

↓

Event 2

↓

Event 3

Literary Analysis

A **drama** is a story that is written to be performed. Like short stories, dramas have characters, a setting, and a plot. In dramas, however, these elements are developed mainly through **dialogue**, the words spoken by the characters. In the **script,** or written form, of a drama, the characters' names appear before their dialogue. Look at this example:

> **Katrina.** I can't believe you said that!
> **Wallace.** I was only kidding.

Paying attention to what the characters say will help you understand and enjoy the script of a drama.

Vocabulary Builder

The Phantom Tollbooth, Act I

- **ignorance** (ig´ nə rəns) *n.* lack of knowledge, education, or experience (p. 654) *Babies are born in a state of ignorance.*

- **precautionary** (pri kô´ shə ner´ ē) *adj.* done to prevent harm or danger (p. 656) *Locking the door is a precautionary step against theft.*

- **consideration** (kən sid´ ər ā´ shən) *n.* careful thought or attention (p. 664) *After much consideration, they bought the house.*

- **ferocious** (fə rō´ shəs) *adj.* wild and dangerous (p. 665) *Cats may be gentle, but lions are ferocious.*

- **misapprehension** (mis´ ap rē hen´ shən) *n.* misunderstanding (p. 667) *She was under the misapprehension that snakes are slimy.*

- **unabridged** (un´ ə brijd´) *adj.* complete; not shortened (p. 670) *He read the unabridged book because he wanted all the details.*

Background

Descriptive Names The names of these characters and places in *The Phantom Tollbooth* describe their qualities:

- The **Lethargarians** are sleepy characters who spend their days lounging around. Their name comes from the word *lethargy,* which means "sluggishness" or "lack of energy."
- **Digitopolis** is the place where all numbers come from. Its name is a combination of the word *digit,* which means "number," and the Greek root *-polis,* which means "city."
- **Dictionopolis** is the place where all words are born. Its name combines *diction,* which means "speech" or "language," with *-polis.*

Connecting to the Literature

Reading/Writing Connection Milo, the main character in *The Phantom Tollbooth,* suffers from boredom. To cure it, he sets out on a wonderful adventure. Make a list of possible reasons why students your age might be bored. Then, add possible cures for boredom. Use three of the following words: *involve, motivate, participate, bore, require.*

Meet the Author

Susan **Nanus**

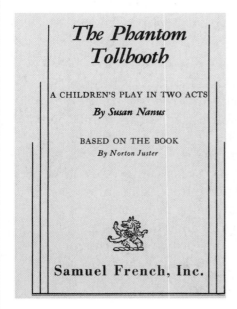

The Phantom Tollbooth

A CHILDREN'S PLAY IN TWO ACTS

By Susan Nanus

BASED ON THE BOOK
By Norton Juster

Samuel French, Inc.

Susan Nanus has written many award-winning scripts for dramas, television miniseries, and movies. In 1997, she won the Writers Guild Award for best original script for the television drama *Harvest of Fire.*

Writing Adaptations Like other screenwriters, Nanus sometimes adapts, or reworks, novels to create screenplays for movies and scripts for stage plays. Her script for *The Phantom Tollbooth* was adapted from a novel by Norton Juster. Nanus lives in Los Angeles, where she writes scripts for television and movies.

For: More about the author
Visit: www.PHSchool.com
Web Code: ele-9502

The Phantom Tollbooth

Susan Nanus

Based on the book by Norton Juster

CAST (in order of appearance)

* THE CLOCK
* MILO, a boy
* THE WHETHER MAN
* SIX LETHARGARIANS
* TOCK, THE WATCHDOG (same as the clock)
* AZAZ THE UNABRIDGED, KING OF DICTIONOPOLIS
* THE MATHEMAGICIAN, KING OF DIGITOPOLIS
* PRINCESS SWEET RHYME
* PRINCESS PURE REASON
* GATEKEEPER OF DICTIONOPOLIS

* THREE WORD MERCHANTS
* THE LETTERMAN (fourth word merchant)
* SPELLING BEE
* THE HUMBUG
* THE DUKE OF DEFINITION
* THE MINISTER OF MEANING
* THE EARL OF ESSENCE
* THE COUNT OF CONNOTATION
* THE UNDERSECRETARY OF UNDERSTANDING

* A PAGE
* KAKAFONOUS A. DISCHORD, DOCTOR OF DISSONANCE
* THE AWFUL DYNNE
* THE DODECAHEDRON
* MINERS OF THE NUMBERS MINE
* THE EVERPRESENT WORDSNATCHER
* THE TERRIBLE TRIVIUM
* THE DEMON OF INSINCERITY
* SENSES TAKER

The SETS

1. MILO'S BEDROOM—with shelves, pennants, pictures on the wall, as well as suggestions of the characters of the Land of Wisdom.
2. THE ROAD TO THE LAND OF WISDOM—a forest, from which the Whether Man and the Lethargarians emerge.
3. DICTIONOPOLIS—a marketplace full of open air stalls as well as little shops. Letters and signs should abound.
4. DIGITOPOLIS—a dark, glittering place without trees or greenery, but full of shining rocks and cliffs, with hundreds of numbers shining everywhere.
5. THE LAND OF <u>IGNORANCE</u>—a gray, gloomy place full of cliffs and caves, with frightening faces. Different levels and heights should be suggested through one or two platforms or risers, with a set of stairs that lead to the castle in the air.

Act I Scene i

[*The stage is completely dark and silent. Suddenly the sound of someone winding an alarm clock is heard, and after that, the sound of loud ticking is heard.*]

[*LIGHTS UP on the* CLOCK, *a huge alarm clock. The* CLOCK *reads 4:00. The lighting should make it appear that the* CLOCK *is suspended in mid-air (if possible). The* CLOCK *ticks for 30 seconds.*]

CLOCK. See that! Half a minute gone by. Seems like a long time when you're waiting for something to happen, doesn't it? Funny thing is, time can pass very slowly or very fast, and sometimes even both at once. The time now? Oh, a little after four, but what that means should depend on you. Too often, we do something simply because time tells us to. Time for school, time for bed, whoops, 12:00, time to be hungry. It can get a little silly, don't you think? Time is important, but it's what you do with it that makes it so. So my advice to you is to use it. Keep your eyes open and your ears perked. Otherwise it will pass before you know it, and you'll certainly have missed something!

Things have a habit of doing that, you know. Being here one minute and gone the next.

In the twinkling of an eye.

In a jiffy.

In a flash!

I know a girl who yawned and missed a whole summer vacation. And what about that caveman who took a nap one afternoon, and woke up to find himself completely alone. You see, while he was sleeping, someone had invented the wheel and everyone had moved to the suburbs. And then of course, there is Milo. [*LIGHTS UP to reveal* MILO's *Bedroom. The* CLOCK *appears to be on a shelf in the room of a young boy—a room filled with books, toys, games, maps, papers, pencils, a bed, a desk. There is a dartboard with numbers and the face of the* MATHEMAGICIAN, *a bedspread made from* KING AZAZ's *cloak, a kite looking like the spelling bee, a punching bag with the* HUMBUG's *face, as well as records, a television, a toy car, and a large box that is wrapped and has an envelope taped to the top. The sound of* FOOTSTEPS *is heard, and then enter* MILO *dejectedly. He*

The Phantom Tollbooth, Act I ■ 655

Vocabulary Builder
ignorance (ig´ nə rəns)
n. lack of knowledge, education, or experience

Reading Skill
Summary How would you summarize the point Clock is making?

Reading Check

How do you know what characters and sets are in this play?

throws down his books and coat, flops into a chair, and sighs loudly.] Who never knows what to do with himself—not just sometimes, but always. When he's in school, he wants to be out, and when he's out, he wants to be in. [*During the following speech,* MILO *examines the various toys, tools, and other possessions in the room, trying them out and rejecting them.*] Wherever he is, he wants to be somewhere else—and when he gets there, so what. Everything is too much trouble or a waste of time. Books—he's already read them. Games—boring. T.V.— dumb. So what's left? Another long, boring afternoon. Unless he bothers to notice a very large package that happened to arrive today.

MILO. [*Suddenly notices the package. He drags himself over to it, and disinterestedly reads the label.*] "For Milo, who has plenty of time." Well, that's true. [*Sighs and looks at it.*] No. [*Walks away.*] Well . . . [*Comes back. Rips open envelope and reads.*]

A VOICE. "One genuine turnpike tollbooth, easily assembled at home for use by those who have never traveled in lands beyond."

MILO. Beyond what? [*Continues reading.*]

A VOICE. "This package contains the following items:" [MILO *pulls the items out of the box and sets them up as they are mentioned.*] "One (1) genuine turnpike tollbooth to be erected according to directions. Three (3) <u>precautionary</u> signs to be used in a precautionary fashion. Assorted coins for paying tolls. One (1) map, strictly up to date, showing how to get from here to there. One (1) book of rules and traffic regulations which may not be bent or broken. Warning! Results are not guaranteed. If not perfectly satisfied, your wasted time will be refunded."

MILO. [*Skeptically.*] Come off it, who do you think you're kidding? [*Walks around and examines tollbooth.*] What am I

Literature in Context

Culture Connection

Turnpike Tollbooth A turnpike is a road that people pay a fee, or toll, to use. Long ago, long spears called pikes barred the road. The pikes were turned aside only after travelers paid the toll to use the road. A tollbooth is the booth or gate at which tolls are collected. The first record of tolls being collected dates from about 2000 B.C., when tolls were collected on a Persian military road between Babylon and Syria.

Connect to the Literature

How might the tollbooth—an unusual gift—affect Milo's bored state of mind?

Vocabulary Builder
precautionary (pri kô´ shə ner´ ē) *adj.* done to prevent harm or danger

supposed to do with this? [*The ticking of the* CLOCK *grows loud and impatient.*] Well . . . what else do I have to do. [MILO *gets into his toy car and drives up to the first sign.*]

VOICE. "HAVE YOUR DESTINATION IN MIND."

MILO. [*Pulls out the map.*] Now, let's see. That's funny. I never heard of any of these places. Well, it doesn't matter anyway. Dictionopolis. That's a weird name. I might as well go there. [*Begins to move, following map. Drives off.*]

CLOCK. See what I mean? You never know how things are going to get started. But when you're bored, what you need more than anything is a rude awakening.

[*The* ALARM *goes off very loudly as the stage darkens. The sound of the alarm is transformed into the honking of a car horn, and is then joined by the blasts, bleeps, roars and growls of heavy highway traffic. When the lights come up,* MILO's *bedroom is gone and we see a lonely road in the middle of nowhere.*]

Scene ii The Road to Dictionopolis

Reading Skill
Summary Reread Scene i to identify and summarize the key events.

[*ENTER* MILO *in his car.*]

MILO. This is weird! I don't recognize any of this scenery at all. [*A* SIGN *is held up before* MILO, *startling him.*] Huh? [*Reads.*] WELCOME TO EXPECTATIONS. INFORMATION, PREDICTIONS AND ADVICE CHEERFULLY OFFERED. PARK HERE AND BLOW HORN. [MILO *blows horn.*]

WHETHER MAN. [*A little man wearing a long coat and carrying an umbrella pops up from behind the sign that he was holding. He speaks very fast and excitedly.*] My, my, my, my, my, welcome, welcome, welcome, welcome to the Land of Expectations, Expectations, Expectations! We don't get many travelers these days; we certainly don't get many travelers. Now what can I do for you? I'm the Whether Man.

MILO. [*Referring to map.*] Uh . . . is this the right road to Dictionopolis?

WHETHER MAN. Well now, well now, well now, I don't know of any wrong road to Dictionopolis, so if this road goes to

Literary Analysis
Dialogue in Drama What do you learn about the Whether Man from his first speech?

Reading Check

What is in the package Milo opens?

The Phantom Tollbooth, Act I ■ *657*

Dictionopolis at all, it must be the right road, and if it doesn't, it must be the right road to somewhere else, because there are no wrong roads to anywhere. Do you think it will rain?

MILO. I thought you were the Weather Man.

WHETHER MAN. Oh, no, I'm the Whether Man, not the weather man. [*Pulls out a SIGN or opens a FLAP of his coat, which reads: "WHETHER."*] After all, it's more important to know whether there will be weather than what the weather will be.

MILO. What kind of place is Expectations?

WHETHER MAN. Good question, good question! Expectations is the place you must always go to before you get to where you are going. Of course, some people never go beyond Expectations, but my job is to hurry them along whether they like it or not. Now what else can I do for you? [*Opens his umbrella.*]

MILO. I think I can find my own way.

WHETHER MAN. Splendid, splendid, splendid! Whether or not you find your own way, you're bound to find some way. If you happen to find my way, please return it. I lost it years ago. I imagine by now it must be quite rusty. You did say it was going to rain, didn't you? [*Escorts MILO to the car under the open umbrella.*] I'm glad you made your own decision. I do so hate to make up my mind about anything, whether it's good or bad, up or down, rain or shine. Expect everything, I always say, and the unexpected never happens. Goodbye, goodbye, goodbye, good . . .

[*A loud CLAP of THUNDER is heard.*] Oh dear! [*He looks up at the sky, puts out his hand to feel for rain, and RUNS AWAY. MILO watches puzzledly and drives on.*]

MILO. I'd better get out of Expectations, but fast. Talking to a guy like that all day would get me nowhere for sure. [*He tries to speed up, but finds instead that he is moving slower and slower.*] Oh, oh, now what? [*He can barely move. Behind MILO, the LETHARGARIANS begin to enter from all parts of the*

Literary Analysis
Dialogue in Drama
What do you learn about the action from this dialogue between Milo and Whether Man?

Literary Analysis
Dialogue in Drama
How do Milo's words here move the plot along?

stage. They are dressed to blend in with the scenery and carry small pillows that look like rocks. Whenever they fall asleep, they rest on the pillows.] Now I really am getting nowhere. I hope I didn't take a wrong turn. [*The car stops. He tries to start it. It won't move. He gets out and begins to tinker with it.*] I wonder where I am.

▼ **Critical Viewing**
Which details here give clues to what the Lethargarians are like? **[Analyze]**

LETHARGARIAN 1. You're . . . in . . . the . . . Dol . . . drums . . . [MILO *looks around.*]

LETHARGARIAN 2. Yes . . . the . . . Dol . . . drums . . . [*A YAWN is heard.*]

MILO. [*Yelling.*] WHAT ARE THE -DOL-DRUMS?

LETHARGARIAN 3. The Doldrums, my friend, are where nothing ever happens and nothing ever changes. [*Parts of the Scenery stand up or Six People come out of the scenery colored in the same colors of the trees or the road. They move very slowly and as soon as they move, they stop to rest again.*] Allow me to introduce all of us. We are the Lethargarians at your service.

MILO. [*Uncertainly.*] Very pleased to meet you. I think I'm lost. Can you help me?

LETHARGARIAN 4. Don't say think. [*He yawns.*] It's against the law.

LETHARGARIAN 1. No one's allowed to think in the Doldrums. [*He falls asleep.*]

LETHARGARIAN 2. Don't you have a rule book? It's local ordinance 175389-J. [*He falls asleep.*]

MILO. [*Pulls out rule book and reads.*] Ordinance 175389-J: "It shall be unlawful, illegal and unethical to think, think of thinking, surmise, presume, reason, meditate or speculate while in the Doldrums. Anyone breaking this law shall be severely punished." That's a ridiculous law! Everybody thinks.

✓**Reading Check**

What are the Doldrums?

ALL THE LETHARGARIANS. We don't!

LETHARGARIAN 2. And most of the time, you don't, that's why you're here. You weren't thinking and you weren't paying attention either. People who don't pay attention often get stuck in the Doldrums. Face it, most of the time, you're just like us. [*Falls, snoring, to the ground.* MILO *laughs.*]

LETHARGARIAN 5. Stop that at once. Laughing is against the law. Don't you have a rule book? It's local ordinance 574381-W.

MILO. [*Opens rule book and reads.*] "In the Doldrums, laughter is frowned upon and smiling is permitted only on alternate Thursdays." Well, if you can't laugh or think, what can you do?

LETHARGARIAN 6. Anything as long as it's nothing, and everything as long as it isn't anything. There's lots to do. We have a very busy schedule . . .

LETHARGARIAN 1. At 8:00 we get up and then we spend from 8 to 9 daydreaming.

LETHARGARIAN 2. From 9:00 to 9:30 we take our early mid-morning nap . . .

LETHARGARIAN 3. From 9:30 to 10:30 we dawdle and delay . . .

LETHARGARIAN 4. From 10:30 to 11:30 we take our late early morning nap . . .

LETHARGARIAN 5. From 11:30 to 12:00 we bide our time and then we eat our lunch.

LETHARGARIAN 6. From 1:00 to 2:00 we linger and loiter . . .

LETHARGARIAN 1. From 2:00 to 2:30 we take our early afternoon nap . . .

LETHARGARIAN 2. From 2:30 to 3:30 we put off for tomorrow what we could have done today . . .

LETHARGARIAN 3. From 3:30 to 4:00 we take our early late afternoon nap . . .

LETHARGARIAN 4. From 4:00 to 5:00 we loaf and lounge until dinner . . .

Literary Analysis
Dialogue in Drama
What does this dialogue reveal about the Doldrums?

Literary Analysis
Dialogue in Drama
Ellipsis points—three spaced periods—often indicate a pause or an unfinished thought. How does this punctuation help you understand the way the dialogue should be read?

Measuring Time

The Latin poet Ovid coined the phrase "Time flies." Through the ages, telling time has advanced from tracking shadows to measuring vibrations.

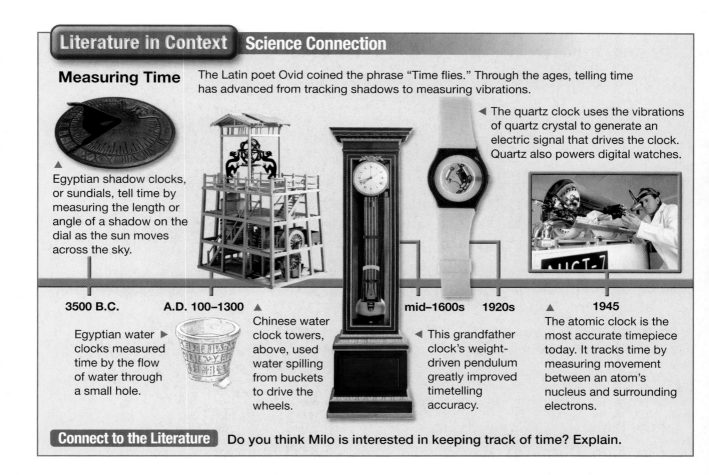

Egyptian shadow clocks, or sundials, tell time by measuring the length or angle of a shadow on the dial as the sun moves across the sky.

◄ The quartz clock uses the vibrations of quartz crystal to generate an electric signal that drives the clock. Quartz also powers digital watches.

3500 B.C.

Egyptian water ► clocks measured time by the flow of water through a small hole.

A.D. 100–1300 ▲

Chinese water clock towers, above, used water spilling from buckets to drive the wheels.

mid–1600s

◄ This grandfather clock's weight-driven pendulum greatly improved timetelling accuracy.

1920s

1945

The atomic clock is the most accurate timepiece today. It tracks time by measuring movement between an atom's nucleus and surrounding electrons.

Connect to the Literature Do you think Milo is interested in keeping track of time? Explain.

LETHARGARIAN 5. From 6:00 to 7:00 we dilly-dally . . .

LETHARGARIAN 6. From 7:00 to 8:00 we take our early evening nap and then for an hour before we go to bed, we waste time.

LETHARGARIAN 1. [*Yawning.*] You see, it's really quite strenuous doing nothing all day long, and so once a week, we take a holiday and go nowhere.

LETHARGARIAN 5. Which is just where we were going when you came along. Would you care to join us?

MILO. [*Yawning.*] That's where I seem to be going, anyway. [*Stretching.*] Tell me, does everyone here do nothing?

LETHARGARIAN 3. Everyone but the terrible watchdog. He's always sniffing around to see that nobody wastes time. A most unpleasant character.

MILO. The Watchdog?

LETHARGARIAN 6. THE WATCHDOG!

Reading Check

Basically, what do the Lethargarians do all day?

ALL THE LETHARGARIANS. [*Yelling at once.*] RUN! WAKE UP! RUN! HERE HE COMES! THE WATCHDOG! [*They all run off and ENTER a large dog with the head, feet, and tail of a dog, and the body of a clock, having the same face as the character THE CLOCK.*]

WATCHDOG. What are you doing here?

MILO. Nothing much. Just killing time. You see . . .

WATCHDOG. KILLING TIME! [*His ALARM RINGS in fury.*] It's bad enough wasting time without killing it. What are you doing in the Doldrums, anyway? Don't you have anywhere to go?

MILO. I think I was on my way to Dictionopolis when I got stuck here. Can you help me?

WATCHDOG. Help you! You've got to help yourself. I suppose you know why you got stuck.

MILO. I guess I just wasn't thinking.

WATCHDOG. Precisely. Now you're on your way.

MILO. I am?

WATCHDOG. Of course. Since you got here by not thinking, it seems reasonable that in order to get out, you must start thinking. Do you mind if I get in? I love automobile rides. [*He gets in. They wait.*] Well?

MILO. All right. I'll try. [*Screws up his face and thinks.*] Are we moving?

WATCHDOG. Not yet. Think harder.

MILO. I'm thinking as hard as I can.

WATCHDOG. Well, think just a little harder than that. Come on, you can do it.

MILO. All right, all right. . . . I'm thinking of all the planets in the solar system, and why water expands when it turns to ice, and all the words that begin with "q," and . . . [*The wheels begin to move.*] We're moving! We're moving!

WATCHDOG. Keep thinking.

MILO. [*Thinking.*] How a steam engine works and how to bake a pie and the difference between Fahrenheit and Centigrade . . .

Reading Skill
Summary Would you include the arrival of the Watchdog in a summary of this scene? Why or why not?

Literary Analysis
Dialogue in Drama How does Milo and the Watchdog's dialogue help you understand the problem here?

◀ **Critical Viewing**
Why is a clock part of this character's body?
[Connect]

WATCHDOG. Dictionopolis, here we come.

MILO. Hey, Watchdog, are you coming along?

TOCK. You can call me Tock, and keep your eyes on the road.

MILO. What kind of place is Dictionopolis, anyway?

TOCK. It's where all the words in the world come from. It used to be a marvelous place, but ever since Rhyme and Reason left, it hasn't been the same.

MILO. Rhyme and Reason?

TOCK. The two princesses. They used to settle all the arguments between their two brothers who rule over the Land of Wisdom. You see, Azaz is the king of Dictionopolis and the Mathemagician is the king of Digitopolis and they almost never see eye to eye on anything. It was the job of the Princesses Sweet Rhyme and Pure Reason to solve the differences between the two kings, and they always did so well that both sides usually went home feeling very satisfied. But then, one day, the kings had an argument to end all arguments. . . .

[*The LIGHTS DIM on* TOCK *and* MILO, *and come up on* KING AZAZ *of Dictionopolis on another part of the stage.* AZAZ *has a great stomach, a grey beard reaching to his waist, a small crown and a long robe with the letters of the alphabet written all over it.*]

Reading Check

What does Milo think about to get his car to move?

AZAZ. Of course, I'll abide by the decision of Rhyme and Reason, though I have no doubt as to what it will be. They will choose words, of course. Everyone knows that words are more important than numbers any day of the week.

[*The* MATHEMAGICIAN *appears opposite* AZAZ. *The* MATHEMAGICIAN *wears a long flowing robe covered entirely with complex mathematical equations, and a tall pointed hat. He carries a long staff with a pencil point at one end and a large rubber eraser at the other.*]

MATHEMAGICIAN. That's what you think, Azaz. People wouldn't even know what day of the week it is without numbers. Haven't you ever looked at a calendar? Face it, Azaz. It's numbers that count.

AZAZ. Don't be ridiculous. [*To audience, as if leading a cheer.*] Let's hear it for WORDS!

MATHEMAGICIAN. [*To audience, in the same manner.*] Cast your vote for NUMBERS!

AZAZ. A, B, C's!

MATHEMAGICIAN. 1, 2, 3's! [*A FANFARE is heard.*]

AZAZ AND MATHEMAGICIAN. [*To each other.*] Quiet! Rhyme and Reason are about to announce their decision.

[RHYME *and* REASON *appear.*]

RHYME. Ladies and gentlemen, letters and numerals, fractions and punctuation marks—may we have your attention, please. After careful <u>consideration</u> of the problem set before us by King Azaz of Dictionopolis [AZAZ *bows.*]

and the Mathemagician of Digitopolis [MATHEMAGICIAN *raises his hands in a victory salute.*] we have come to the following conclusion:

REASON. Words and numbers are of equal value, for in the cloak of knowledge, one is the warp and the other is the woof.

RHYME. It is no more important to count the sands than it is to name the stars.

Reading Skill
Summary Briefly explain the argument between Azaz and the Mathemagician.

Vocabulary Builder
consideration (kən sid′ ər ā′ shən) *n.* careful thought or attention

RHYME AND REASON. Therefore, let both kingdoms, Diction-opolis and Digitopolis, live in peace.

[*The sound of CHEERING is heard.*]

AZAZ. Boo! is what I say. Boo and Bah and Hiss!

MATHEMAGICIAN. What good are these girls if they can't even settle an argument in anyone's favor? I think I have come to a decision of my own.

AZAZ. So have I.

AZAZ AND MATHEMAGICIAN. [*To the* PRINCESSES.] You are hereby banished from this land to the Castle-in-the-Air. [*To each other.*] *And as for you, KEEP OUT OF MY WAY!* [*They stalk off in opposite directions.*]

[*During this time, the set has been changed to the Market Square of Dictionopolis. LIGHTS come UP on the deserted square.*]

TOCK. And ever since then, there has been neither Rhyme nor Reason in this kingdom. Words are misused and numbers are mismanaged. The argument between the two kings has divided everyone and the real value of both words and numbers has been forgotten. What a waste!

MILO. Why doesn't somebody rescue the Princesses and set everything straight again?

TOCK. That is easier said than done. The Castle-in-the-Air is very far from here, and the one path which leads to it is guarded by <u>ferocious</u> demons. But hold on, here we are. [*A Man appears, carrying a Gate and a small Toll-booth.*]

GATEKEEPER. AHHHHREMMMM! This is Dictionopolis, a happy kingdom, advantageously located in the foothills of Confusion and caressed by gentle breezes from the Sea of Knowledge. Today, by royal proclamation, is Market Day. Have you come to buy or sell?

MILO. I beg your pardon?

GATEKEEPER. Buy or sell, buy or sell. Which is it? You must have come here for a reason.

MILO. Well, I . . .

GATEKEEPER. Come now, if you don't have a reason, you must at least have an explanation or certainly an excuse.

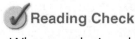

MILO. [*Meekly.*] Uh . . . no.

GATEKEEPER. [*Shaking his head.*] Very serious. You can't get in without a reason. [*Thoughtfully.*] Wait a minute. Maybe I have an old one you can use. [*Pulls out an old suitcase from the tollbooth and rummages through it.*] No . . . no . . . no . . . this won't do . . . hmmm . . .

MILO. [*To* TOCK.] What's he looking for? [TOCK *shrugs.*]

GATEKEEPER. Ah! This is fine. [*Pulls out a Medallion on a chain. Engraved in the Medallion is: "WHY NOT?"*] Why not. That's a good reason for almost anything . . . a bit used, perhaps, but still quite serviceable. There you are, sir. Now I can truly say: Welcome to Dictionopolis.

[*He opens the Gate and walks off.* CITIZENS *and* MERCHANTS *appear on all levels of the stage, and* MILO *and* TOCK *find themselves in the middle of a noisy marketplace. As some people buy and sell their wares, others hang a large banner which reads:* WELCOME TO THE WORD MARKET.]

MILO. Tock! Look!

MERCHANT 1. Hey-ya, hey-ya, hey-ya, step right up and take your pick. Juicy tempting words for sale. Get your fresh-picked "if 's," "and's" and "but's"! Just take a look at these nice ripe "where's" and "when's."

MERCHANT 2. Step right up, step right up, fancy, best-quality words here for sale. Enrich your vocabulary and expand your speech with such elegant items as "quagmire," "flabbergast," or "upholstery."

MERCHANT 3. Words by the bag, buy them over here. Words by the bag for the more talkative customer. A pound of "happy's" at a very reasonable price . . . very useful for "Happy Birthday," "Happy New Year," "happy days," or "happy-go-lucky." Or how about a package of "good's," always handy for "good morning," "good afternoon," "good evening," and "goodbye."

MILO. I can't believe it. Did you ever see so many words?

TOCK. They're fine if you have something to say. [*They come to a Do-It-Yourself Bin.*]

Step right up, step right up, fancy, best-quality words here for sale.

MILO. [*To* MERCHANT 4 *at the bin.*] Excuse me, but what are these?

MERCHANT 4. These are for people who like to make up their own words. You can pick any assortment you like or buy a special box complete with all the letters and a book of instructions. Here, taste an "A." They're very good. [*He pops one into* MILO's *mouth.*]

MILO. [*Tastes it hesitantly.*] It's sweet! [*He eats it.*]

MERCHANT 4. I knew you'd like it. "A" is one of our best-sellers. All of them aren't that good, you know. The "Z," for instance—very dry and sawdusty. And the "X"? Tastes like a trunkful of stale air. But most of the others aren't bad at all. Here, try the "I."

MILO. [*Tasting.*] Cool! It tastes icy.

MERCHANT 4. [*To* TOCK.] How about the "C" for you? It's as crunchy as a bone. Most people are just too lazy to make their own words, but take it from me, not only is it more fun, but it's also *de*-lightful, [*Holds up a "D."*] *e*-lating, [*Holds up an "E."*] and extremely *u*seful! [*Holds up a "U."*]

MILO. But isn't it difficult? I'm not very good at making words.

[*The* SPELLING BEE, *a large colorful bee, comes up from behind.*]

SPELLING BEE. Perhaps I can be of some assistance . . . a-s-s-i-s-t-a-n-c-e. [*The Three turn around and see him.*] Don't be alarmed . . . a-l-a-r-m-e-d. I am the Spelling Bee. I can spell anything. Anything. A-n-y-t-h-i-n-g. Try me. Try me.

MILO. [*Backing off,* TOCK *on his guard.*] Can you spell good-bye?

SPELLING BEE. Perhaps you are under the <u>misapprehension</u> . . . m-i-s-a-p-p-r-e-h-e-n-s-i-o-n that I am dangerous. Let me assure you that I am quite peaceful. Now, think of the most difficult word you can, and I'll spell it.

MILO. Uh . . . o.k. [*At this point,* MILO *may turn to the audience and ask them to help him choose a word or he may think of one on his own.*] How about . . . "Curiosity"?

Reading Skill
Summary Would you include the scene in the Word Market in a summary of Scene ii? Why or why not?

Vocabulary Builder
misapprehension
(mis´ ap rē hen´ shən)
n. misunderstanding

Reading Check

What is sold in the Dictionopolis marketplace?

SPELLING BEE. [*Winking.*] Let's see now . . . uh . . . how much time do I have?

MILO. Just ten seconds. Count them off, Tock.

SPELLING BEE. [*As* TOCK *counts.*] Oh dear, oh dear. [*Just at the last moment, quickly.*] C-u-r-i-o-s-i-t-y.

MERCHANT 4. Correct! [ALL *Cheer.*]

MILO. Can you spell anything?

SPELLING BEE. [*Proudly.*] Just about. You see, years ago, I was an ordinary bee minding my own business, smelling flowers all day, occasionally picking up part-time work in people's bonnets. Then one day, I realized that I'd never amount to anything without an education, so I decided that . . .

HUMBUG. [*Coming up in a booming voice.*] BALDERDASH! [*He wears a lavish coat, striped pants, checked vest, spats and a derby hat.*] Let me repeat . . . BALDERDASH! [*Swings his cane and clicks his heels in the air.*] Well, well, what have we here? Isn't someone going to introduce me to the little boy?

SPELLING BEE. [*Disdainfully.*] This is the Humbug. You can't trust a word he says.

HUMBUG. NONSENSE! Everyone can trust a Humbug. As I was saying to the king just the other day . . .

SPELLING BEE. You've never met the king. [*To* MILO.] Don't believe a thing he tells you.

HUMBUG. Bosh, my boy, pure bosh. The Humbugs are an old and noble family, honorable to the core. Why, we fought in the Crusades with Richard the Lionhearted, crossed the Atlantic with Columbus, blazed trails with the pioneers. History is full of Humbugs.

▲ **Critical Viewing**
How does this picture of Spelling Bee compare with his description in the play? [**Compare**]

Literary Analysis
Dialogue in Drama
The word *humbug* means "nonsense" or "trickery." How do Humbug's words relate to his name?

SPELLING BEE. A very pretty speech . . . s-p-e-e-c-h. Now, why don't you go away? I was just advising the lad of the importance of proper spelling.

HUMBUG. BAH! As soon as you learn to spell one word, they ask you to spell another. You can never catch up, so why bother? [*Puts his arm around* MILO.] Take my advice, boy, and forget about it. As my great-great-great-grandfather George Washington Humbug used to say . . .

SPELLING BEE. You, sir, are an impostor i-m-p-o-s-t-o-r who can't even spell his own name!

HUMBUG. What? You dare to doubt my word? The word of a Humbug? The word of a Humbug who has direct access to the ear of a King? And the king shall hear of this, I promise you . . .

VOICE 1. Did someone call for the King?

VOICE 2. Did you mention the monarch?

VOICE 3. Speak of the sovereign?

VOICE 4. Entreat the Emperor?

VOICE 5. Hail his highness?

[*Five tall, thin gentlemen regally dressed in silks and satins, plumed hats and buckled shoes appear as they speak.*]

MILO. Who are they?

SPELLING BEE. The King's advisors. Or in more formal terms, his cabinet.

MINISTER 1. Greetings!

MINISTER 2. Salutations!

MINISTER 3. Welcome!

MINISTER 4. Good Afternoon!

MINISTER 5. Hello!

MILO. Uh . . . Hi.

[*All the* MINISTERS, *from here on called by their numbers, unfold their scrolls and read in order.*]

Literary Analysis
Dialogue in Drama
What does the dialogue between Humbug and Spelling Bee show about their relationship?

Reading Check

What advice does Spelling Bee give Milo?

MINISTER 1. By the order of Azaz the <u>Unabridged</u> . . .

MINISTER 2. King of Dictionopolis . . .

MINISTER 3. Monarch of letters . . .

MINISTER 4. Emperor of phrases, sentences, and miscellaneous figures of speech . . .

MINISTER 5. We offer you the hospitality of our kingdom . . .

MINISTER 1. Country

MINISTER 2. Nation

MINISTER 3. State

MINISTER 4. Commonwealth

MINISTER 5. Realm

MINISTER 1. Empire

MINISTER 2. Palatinate

MINISTER 3. Principality.

MILO. Do all those words mean the same thing?

MINISTER 1. Of course.

MINISTER 2. Certainly.

MINISTER 3. Precisely.

MINISTER 4. Exactly.

MINISTER 5. Yes.

MILO. Then why don't you use just one? Wouldn't that make a lot more sense?

MINISTER 1. Nonsense!

MINISTER 2. Ridiculous!

MINISTER 3. Fantastic!

MINISTER 4. Absurd!

MINISTER 5. Bosh!

MINISTER 1. We're not interested in making sense. It's not our job.

MINISTER 2. Besides, one word is as good as another, so why not use them all?

MINISTER 3. Then you don't have to choose which one is right.

Vocabulary Builder
unabridged (un´ ə brijd´) *adj.* complete; not shortened

Literary Analysis
Dialogue in Drama
How does the dialogue of the five ministers show the importance of words in Dictionopolis?

MINISTER 4. Besides, if one is right, then ten are ten times as right.

MINISTER 5. Obviously, you don't know who we are.

[*Each presents himself and* MILO *acknowledges the introduction.*]

MINISTER 1. The Duke of Definition.

MINISTER 2. The Minister of Meaning.

MINISTER 3. The Earl of Essence.

MINISTER 4. The Count of Connotation.

MINISTER 5. The Undersecretary of Understanding.

ALL FIVE. And we have come to invite you to the Royal Banquet.

SPELLING BEE. The banquet! That's quite an honor, my boy. A real h-o-n-o-r.

HUMBUG. DON'T BE RIDICULOUS! Everybody goes to the Royal Banquet these days.

SPELLING BEE. [*To the* HUMBUG.] True, everybody does go. But some people are invited and others simply push their way in where they aren't wanted.

HUMBUG. HOW DARE YOU? You buzzing little upstart, I'll show you who's not wanted . . . [*Raises his cane threateningly.*]

SPELLING BEE. You just watch it! I'm warning w-a-r-n-i-n-g you! [*At that moment, an ear-shattering blast of* TRUMPETS, *entirely off-key, is heard, and a* PAGE *appears.*]

PAGE. King Azaz the Unabridged is about to begin the Royal banquet. All guests who do not appear promptly at the table will automatically lose their place. [*A huge Table is carried out with* KING AZAZ *sitting in a large chair, carried out at the head of the table.*]

AZAZ. Places. Everyone take your places. [*All the characters, including the* HUMBUG *and the* SPELLING BEE, *who forget their quarrel, rush to take their places at the table.* MILO *and* TOCK *sit near the king.* AZAZ *looks at* MILO.] And just who is this?

MILO. Your Highness, my name is Milo and this is Tock. Thank you very much for inviting us to your banquet, and I think your palace is beautiful!

Reading Skill
Summary Briefly restate two ideas included in the ministers' welcome.

Literary Analysis
Dialogue in Drama How do these stage directions reinforce Azaz's words?

Reading Check

What is the main responsibility of the ministers?

MINISTER 1. Exquisite.

MINISTER 2. Lovely.

MINISTER 3. Handsome.

MINISTER 4. Pretty.

MINISTER 5. Charming.

AZAZ. SILENCE! Now tell me, young man, what can you do to entertain us? Sing songs? Tell stories? Juggle plates? Do tumbling tricks? Which is it?

MILO. I can't do any of those things.

AZAZ. What an ordinary little boy. Can't you do anything at all?

MILO. Well . . . I can count to a thousand.

AZAZ. AARGH, numbers! Never mention numbers here. Only use them when we absolutely have to. Now, why don't we change the subject and have some dinner? Since you are the guest of honor, you may pick the menu.

MILO. Me? Well, uh . . . I'm not very hungry. Can we just have a light snack?

AZAZ. A light snack it shall be!

[AZAZ *claps his hands. Waiters rush in with covered trays. When they are uncovered, Shafts of Light pour out. The light may be created through the use of battery-operated flashlights which are secured in the trays and covered with a false bottom. The Guests help themselves.*]

HUMBUG. Not a very substantial meal. Maybe you can suggest something a little more filling.

MILO. Well, in that case, I think we ought to have a square meal . . .

AZAZ. [*Claps his hands.*] A square meal it is! [*Waiters serve trays of Colored Squares of all sizes. People serve themselves.*]

SPELLING BEE. These are awful. [HUMBUG *coughs and all the Guests do not care for the food.*]

Literary Analysis
Dialogue in Drama
How do the dialogue and stage directions show that "a light snack" has different meanings for Milo and Azaz?

AZAZ. [*Claps his hands and the trays are removed.*] Time for speeches. [*To* MILO.] You first.

MILO. [*Hesitantly.*] Your Majesty, ladies and gentlemen, I would like to take this opportunity to say that . . .

AZAZ. That's quite enough. Mustn't talk all day.

MILO. But I just started to . . .

AZAZ. NEXT!

HUMBUG. [*Quickly.*] Roast turkey, mashed potatoes, vanilla ice cream.

SPELLING BEE. Hamburgers, corn on the cob, chocolate pudding p-u-d-d-i-n-g. [*Each Guest names two dishes and a dessert.*]

AZAZ. [*The last.*] Pâté de foie gras, soupe à l'oignon, salade endives, fromage et fruits et demi-tasse. [*He claps his hands. Waiters serve each Guest his Words.*] Dig in. [*To* MILO.] Though I can't say I think much of your choice.

MILO. I didn't know I was going to have to eat my words.

AZAZ. Of course, of course, everybody here does. Your speech should have been in better taste.

MINISTER 1. Here, try some somersault. It improves the flavor.

MINISTER 2. Have a rigamarole. [*Offers breadbasket.*]

MINISTER 3. Or a ragamuffin.

MINISTER 4. Perhaps you'd care for a synonym bun.

MINISTER 5. Why not wait for your just desserts?

AZAZ. Ah yes, the dessert. We're having a special treat today . . . freshly made at the half-bakery.

MILO. The half-bakery?

AZAZ. Of course, the half-bakery! Where do you think half-baked ideas come from? Now, please don't interrupt. By royal command, the pastry chefs have . . .

MILO. What's a half-baked idea?

Aargh,
Numbers! Never mention numbers here.

Literary Analysis
Dialogue in Drama
Identify one pun, or play on words, that adds humor to this dialogue.

✔ **Reading Check**

What does Azaz forbid Milo to discuss?

[AZAZ *gives up the idea of speaking as a cart is wheeled in and the Guests help themselves.*]

HUMBUG. They're very tasty, but they don't always agree with you. Here's a good one. [HUMBUG *hands one to* MILO.]

MILO. [*Reads.*] "The earth is flat."

SPELLING BEE. People swallowed that one for years. [*Picks up one and reads.*] "The moon is made of green cheese." Now, there's a half-baked idea.

[*Everyone chooses one and eats. They include: "It Never Rains But Pours," "Night Air Is Bad Air," "Everything Happens for the Best," "Coffee Stunts Your Growth."*]

AZAZ. And now for a few closing words. Attention! Let me have your attention! [*Everyone leaps up and Exits, except for* MILO, TOCK, *and the* HUMBUG.] Loyal subjects and friends, once again on this gala occasion, we have . . .

MILO. Excuse me, but everybody left.

AZAZ. [*Sadly.*] I was hoping no one would notice. It happens every time.

HUMBUG. They're gone to dinner, and as soon as I finish this last bite, I shall join them.

MILO. That's ridiculous. How can they eat dinner right after a banquet?

AZAZ. SCANDALOUS! We'll put a stop to it at once. From now on, by royal command, everyone must eat dinner before the banquet.

MILO. But that's just as bad.

HUMBUG. Or just as good. Things which are equally bad are also equally good. Try to look at the bright side of things.

MILO. I don't know which side of anything to look at. Everything is so confusing, and all your words only make things worse.

AZAZ. How true. There must be something we can do about it.

Reading Skill
Summary Briefly summarize the events at the banquet.

HUMBUG. Pass a law.

AZAZ. We have almost as many laws as words.

HUMBUG. Offer a reward. [AZAZ *shakes his head and looks madder at each suggestion.*] Send for help? Drive a bargain? Pull the switch? Lower the boom? Toe the line?

[*As AZAZ continues to scowl, the HUMBUG loses confidence and finally gives up.*]

MILO. Maybe you should let Rhyme and Reason return.

AZAZ. How nice that would be. Even if they were a bother at times, things always went so well when they were here. But I'm afraid it can't be done.

HUMBUG. Certainly not. Can't be done.

MILO. Why not?

HUMBUG. [*Now siding with* MILO.] Why not, indeed?

AZAZ. Much too difficult.

HUMBUG. Of course, much too difficult.

MILO. You could, if you really wanted to.

HUMBUG. By all means, if you really wanted to, you could.

AZAZ. [*To* HUMBUG.] How?

MILO. [*Also to* HUMBUG.] Yeah, how?

HUMBUG. Why . . . uh, it's a simple task for a brave boy with a stout heart, a steadfast dog and a serviceable small automobile.

AZAZ. Go on.

HUMBUG. Well, all that he would have to do is cross the dangerous, unknown countryside between here and Digitopolis, where he would have to persuade the Mathemagician to release the Princesses, which we know to be impossible because the Mathemagician will never agree with Azaz about anything. Once achieving that, it's a simple matter of entering the Mountains of Ignorance

> Things which are equally bad are also equally good.

Literary Analysis
Dialogue in Drama
What major problem do Milo and Azaz discuss here?

✓ **Reading Check**

Why has everyone left the banquet?

from where no one has ever returned alive, an effortless climb up a two thousand foot stairway without railings in a high wind at night to the Castle-in-the-Air. After a pleasant chat with the Princesses, all that remains is a leisurely ride back through those chaotic crags where the frightening fiends have sworn to tear any intruder limb from limb and devour him down to his belt buckle. And finally after doing all that, a triumphal parade! If, of course, there is anything left to parade . . . followed by hot chocolate and cookies for everyone.

AZAZ. I never realized it would be so simple.

MILO. It sounds dangerous to me.

TOCK. And just who is supposed to make that journey?

AZAZ. A very good question. But there is one far more serious problem.

MILO. What's that?

AZAZ. I'm afraid I can't tell you that until you return.

MILO. But wait a minute, I didn't . . .

AZAZ. Dictionopolis will always be grateful to you, my boy, and your dog. [AZAZ *pats* TOCK *and* MILO.]

TOCK. Now, just one moment, sire . . .

AZAZ. You will face many dangers on your journey, but fear not, for I can give you something for your protection. [AZAZ *gives* MILO *a box.*] In this box are the letters of the alphabet. With them you can form all the words you will ever need to help you overcome the obstacles that may stand in your path. All you must do is use them well and in the right places.

MILO. [*Miserably.*] Thanks a lot.

AZAZ. You will need a guide, of course, and since he knows the obstacles so well, the Humbug has cheerfully volunteered to accompany you.

HUMBUG. Now, see here . . . !

AZAZ. You will find him dependable, brave, resourceful and loyal.

HUMBUG. [*Flattered.*] Oh, your Majesty.

Literary Analysis
Dialogue in Drama What function does this speech serve in the play's action?

Literary Analysis
Dialogue in Drama Based on these lines, how does Azaz feel about the power of words?

Reading Skill
Summary Reread Scene ii and summarize the main events.

MILO. I'm sure he'll be a great help. [*They approach the car.*]

TOCK. I hope so. It looks like we're going to need it.

[*The lights darken and the* KING *fades from view.*]

AZAZ. Good luck! Drive carefully! [*The three get into the car and begin to move. Suddenly a thunderously loud NOISE is heard. They slow down the car.*]

MILO. What was that?

TOCK. It came from up ahead.

HUMBUG. It's something terrible, I just know it. Oh, no. Something dreadful is going to happen to us. I can feel it in my bones. [*The NOISE is repeated. They all look at each other fearfully as the lights fade.*]

Apply the Skills

The Phantom Tollbooth, Act I

Thinking About the Selection

1. **Respond:** Which character would you most like to meet? Explain.
2. **(a) Recall:** Who are Rhyme and Reason? **(b) Identify Cause and Effect:** What effect does their absence have on Dictionopolis?
3. **(a) Recall:** How does Humbug describe the journey that Milo must make? **(b) Predict:** In Act II, Milo will start his journey. What do you think it will be like? Give three details from Act I to support your answer.
4. **(a) Recall:** What does King Azaz give Milo? **(b) Hypothesize:** Describe a situation in which the gift might help Milo.

Reading Skill

5. **(a)** What events would you include in a **summary** of Act I? **(b)** Explain why they are the most important events.

Literary Analysis

6. Copy and complete the chart to explain how the **dialogue** shows something about a character's personality, the setting, and an action. An example has been provided.

Dialogue	What It Suggests
MILO. Well, it doesn't matter anyway. Dictionopolis. That's a weird name. I might as well go there.	*Character:* Milo is bored. He doesn't care about anything.
GATEKEEPER. This is Dictionopolis, a happy kingdom, advantageously located in the foothills of Confusion and caressed by gentle breezes from the Sea of Knowledge.	*Setting:*
WATCHDOG. Do you mind if I get in? I love automobile rides.	*Action:*

Vocabulary Builder

Practice Each of the following word groups contains words or phrases that have related meanings. Write a vocabulary word from page 652 that fits with each group. Explain your answers.

1. growling, dangerous, _____
2. confusion, disagreement, _____
3. dullness, no idea, _____
4. study, decision making, _____
5. carefully planned, safe, _____
6. complete, full, _____

Writing

Write a **summary** of Act I using the chart from page 652 as a reference. Be sure to do the following:

- Include only important events, characters, and ideas.
- Present events in the order in which they occur.
- Eliminate unimportant details to keep your summary brief.

For *Grammar, Vocabulary,* and *Assessment,* see **Build Language Skills,** pages 680–681.

Extend Your Learning

Listening and Speaking Write and deliver a brief **speech** that Milo might have given at the banquet about his experiences so far. Rehearse the speech before presenting it, using gestures and the tone of your voice to reinforce your words.

Research and Technology Working with a small group, conduct Internet research to prepare a **multimedia presentation** on a topic related to the history of drama. Include the following:

- Facts about the history of drama
- Printouts, slides, photos, or drawings
- Diagrams, time lines, or other graphics

Let each group member deliver part of the presentation.

Build Language Skills

The Phantom Tollbooth

Vocabulary Skill

Roots A **word root** is the basic unit of meaning in a word. For example, the **Latin root** *-brev-* means "short." This root is part of the English words *brief,* an adjective meaning "short" or "quick," and *brevity,* a noun that names the quality of being short or brief. In the same way, the **Latin root** *-scrib-,* meaning "write," is part of the English words *script* and *scribble.*

Practice Explain how the meaning of *-brev-* or *-scrib-* contributes to the meaning of each italicized word. Then, answer the questions, using the italicized words.

1. Why is *brevity* important in a summary?

2. What do you write in a *description*?

3. What is written in a *script* for a play?

Grammar Lesson

Prepositions and Prepositional Phrases A **preposition** is a word that relates a noun or pronoun to another word in the sentence. Common prepositions include *on, between, by, from, on, with, at, for.*

A **prepositional phrase** is a group of words that begins with a preposition and includes a noun or pronoun. The noun or pronoun that is being related to another word in the sentence is called the **object of the preposition.**

More Practice

For more practice with prepositions and prepositional phrases, see the Grammar Handbook, p. R32.

Practice Complete this chart by filling in the missing information.

Sentence	Prepositional Phrase	Preposition	Object of the Preposition
1. The dog is on the couch.			couch
2. After the game, let's have lunch.	after the game		
3. We had fun at the party.		at	

Reading: Summarizing

Directions: *Read the selection. Then, answer the questions.*

Joan has always dreamed of visiting the Grand Canyon. Now her dream is about to come true. She just won the grand prize in a contest: a trip for four to the Grand Canyon. The prize also includes round-trip airfare and four nights in a luxury hotel. Jane and her family are all very excited that they are going to see one of the most spectacular places on Earth.

1. What is the paragraph's main idea?
   A Jane dreamed of visiting the Grand Canyon.
   B She can stay at a hotel.
   C Jane won a trip to the Grand Canyon.
   D Jane and her family are excited.

2. Which of the following details could be left out of the summary?
   A Jane won the prize in a contest.
   B The prize is for four people.
   C The Grand Canyon is spectacular.
   D Jane's family has always dreamed of visiting the Grand Canyon.

3. Which of the following best summarizes the paragraph?
   A Jane and her family are excited about winning.
   B The Grand Canyon is one of the most spectacular places on Earth.
   C Jane's dream of visiting the Grand Canyon will come true because she won a contest.
   D The prize in a contest includes round-trip airfare and four nights in a luxury hotel for four people.

Timed Writing: Persuasion [Critical Stance]

In Act 1 of *The Phantom Tollbooth,* Rhyme and Reason are banished because they say that words and numbers are equal in value. Write a persuasive essay stating whether you agree or disagree with that statement. Support your opinion. **(30 minutes)**

 Writing Workshop: *Work in Progress*

Response to Literature: Letter
Choose one of the literary works that you had the strongest reaction to. Write a sentence or two that identifies the work and summarizes your overall reaction. Save this Reaction List in your writing portfolio.

Novels and Dramatizations

A novel and its dramatization feature the same story, characters, and conflict. However, there are some basic differences between the two presentations.

- A **novel** is written in prose. It is divided into chapters, and the chapters are presented in paragraphs. Words the characters say are set inside quotation marks. The story is told by a narrator, who is either a character in the story or an outside storyteller. Novels vary in length and can be more than 500 pages long.
- A **drama** is written in a script format, divided into acts and scenes. Words the characters say are called lines or speeches. The story is told through the words and actions of the characters and through stage directions. Most plays take between ninety minutes and three hours to perform.

Comparing a Novel to Its Dramatization

The drama *The Phantom Tollbooth*, written by Susan Nanus, is based on the novel of the same name, written by Norton Juster. To find the differences between the formats, note the changes you see. As you read this chapter from the novel *The Phantom Tollbooth,* use a Venn diagram to compare and contrast it with Act I, Scene i, of the play, which begins on page 654.

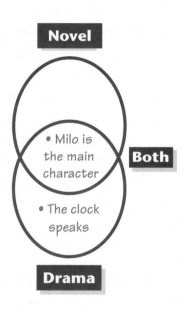

Vocabulary Builder

The Phantom Tollbooth, Chapter 1

- **dejectedly** (dē jek´ tid lē) *adv.* sadly; with low spirits (p. 684) *The losing team walked* <u>dejectedly</u> *off the field.*

- **glumly** (glum´ lē) *adv.* in a gloomy or sullen way (p. 684) *I went to the theater to cheer up instead of sitting* <u>glumly</u> *at home.*

- **impractical** (im prak´ ti kəl) *adj.* not workable or particularly useful (p. 687) *Dull scissors are* <u>impractical</u> *for cutting cardboard.*

- **wistfully** (wist´ fə lē) *adv.* in a hopeful, yearning way (p. 688) *The children stared* <u>wistfully</u> *at the toys in the shop window.*

"Illustrations" by Jules Feiffer, copyright ©1961 by Jules Feiffer. Copyright renewed 1989 by Jules Feiffer, from THE PHANTOM TOLLBOOTH by Norton Juster, illustrated by Jules Feiffer. Used with permission of Random House Children's Books, a division of Random House, Inc.

from
The Phantom Tollbooth

Milo
Norton Juster

◄ **Critical Viewing**
Based on the expression on Milo's face, how would you describe his feelings here? **[Analyze]**

There was once a boy named Milo who didn't know what to do with himself—not just sometimes, but always.

When he was in school he longed to be out, and when he was out he longed to be in. On the way he thought about coming home, and coming home he thought about going. Wherever he was he wished he were somewhere else, and when he got there he wondered why he'd bothered. Nothing really interested him—least of all the things that should have.

"It seems to me that almost everything is a waste of time," he remarked one day as he walked <u>dejectedly</u> home from school. "I can't see the point in learning to solve useless problems, or subtracting turnips from turnips, or knowing where Ethiopia is or how to spell February." And, since no one bothered to explain otherwise, he regarded the process of seeking knowledge as the greatest waste of time of all.

As he and his unhappy thoughts hurried along (for while he was never anxious to be where he was going, he liked to get there as quickly as possible) it seemed a great wonder that the world, which was so large, could sometimes feel so small and empty.

"And worst of all," he continued sadly, "there's nothing for me to do, nowhere I'd care to go, and hardly anything worth seeing." He punctuated this last thought with such a deep sigh that a house sparrow singing nearby stopped and rushed home to be with his family.

Without stopping or looking up, Milo dashed past the buildings and busy shops that lined the street and in a few minutes reached home—dashed through the lobby— hopped onto the elevator—two, three, four, five, six, seven, eight, and off again—opened the apartment door—rushed into his room—flopped dejectedly into a chair, and grumbled softly, "Another long afternoon."

He looked <u>glumly</u> at all the things he owned. The books that were too much trouble to read, the tools he'd never learned to use, the small electric automobile he hadn't driven in months—or was it years?—and the hundreds of other games and toys, and bats and balls, and bits and pieces scattered around him. And then, to one side of the room, just next to the phonograph,[1] he noticed something he had certainly never seen before.

---

1. phonograph (fō´ nə graf) *n.* a machine that plays vinyl sound recordings, or records.

Who could possibly have left such an enormous package and such a strange one? For, while it was not quite square, it was definitely not round, and for its size it was larger than almost any other big package of smaller dimension that he'd ever seen.

Attached to one side was a bright-blue envelope which said simply: "FOR MILO, WHO HAS PLENTY OF TIME."

Of course, if you've ever gotten a surprise package, you can imagine how puzzled and excited Milo was; and if you've never gotten one, pay close attention, because some-day you might.

"I don't think it's my birthday," he puzzled, "and Christmas must be months away, and I haven't been outstandingly good, or even good at all." (He had to admit this even to himself.) "Most probably I won't like it anyway, but since I don't know where it came from, I can't possibly send it back." He thought about it for quite a while and then opened the envelope, but just to be polite.

"ONE GENUINE TURNPIKE TOLLBOOTH," it stated—and then it went on:

"EASILY ASSEMBLED AT HOME, AND FOR USE BY THOSE WHO HAVE NEVER TRAVELED IN LANDS BEYOND."

"Beyond what?" thought Milo as he continued to read.

"THIS PACKAGE CONTAINS THE FOLLOWING ITEMS:

"One (1) genuine turnpike tollbooth to be erected according to directions.

"Three (3) precautionary signs to be used in a precautionary fashion.

"Assorted coins for use in paying tolls.

"One (1) map, up to date and carefully drawn by master cartographers,[2] depicting natural and man-made features.

"One (1) book of rules and traffic regulations, which may not be bent or broken."

And in smaller letters at the bottom it concluded:

"RESULTS ARE NOT GUARANTEED, BUT IF NOT PERFECTLY SATISFIED, YOUR WASTED TIME WILL BE REFUNDED."

Following the instructions, which told him to cut here, lift there, and fold back all around, he soon had the tollbooth

---

2. **cartographers** (kär täg´ rə fərz) *n.* people who make maps.

Literary Analysis
Novel and Drama
What elements of the drama's storyline do you recognize here?

Literary Analysis
Novel and Drama
How are the contents of the letter revealed in the novel? How does the drama differ?

 Reading Check

Why is Milo puzzled about receiving a surprise package?

unpacked and set up on its stand. He fitted the windows in place and attached the roof, which extended out on both sides, and fastened on the coin box. It was very much like the tollbooths he'd seen many times on family trips, except of course it was much smaller and purple.

"What a strange present," he thought to himself. "The least they could have done was to send a highway with it, for it's terribly <u>impractical</u> without one." But since, at the time, there was nothing else he wanted to play with, he set up the three signs,

> SLOW DOWN APPROACHING TOLLBOOTH
>
> PLEASE HAVE YOUR FARE[3] READY
>
> HAVE YOUR DESTINATION IN MIND

and slowly unfolded the map.

As the announcement stated, it was a beautiful map, in many colors, showing principal roads, rivers and seas, towns and cities, mountains and valleys, intersections and detours, and sites of outstanding interest both beautiful and historic.

The only trouble was that Milo had never heard of any of the places it indicated, and even the names sounded most peculiar.

"I don't think there really is such a country," he concluded after studying it carefully. "Well, it doesn't matter anyway." And he closed his eyes and poked a finger at the map.

"Dictionopolis," read Milo slowly when he saw what his finger had chosen. "Oh, well, I might as well go there as anywhere."

He walked across the room and dusted the car off carefully. Then, taking the map and rule book with him, he

---

3. fare (fer) *n.* a toll, or fee, that motorists pay at a tollbooth for the right to use certain highways, tunnels, and bridges.

◀ **Critical Viewing**
How does this picture compare with the author's description of Milo's room and the tollbooth? **[Compare and Contrast]**

Vocabulary Builder
impractical (im prak´ ti kəl) *adj.* not workable or particularly useful

Literary Analysis
Novel and Drama
What clues tell you whether the narrator is inside or outside the story?

 **Reading Check**

What is so strange about the map Milo receives?

hopped in and, for lack of anything better to do, drove slowly up to the tollbooth. As he deposited his coin and rolled past he remarked <u>wistfully</u>, "I do hope this is an interesting game, otherwise the afternoon will be so terribly dull."

Vocabulary Builder
wistfully (wist′ fə lē) *adv.* in a hopeful, yearning way

"illustrations" by Jules Feiffer, copyright ©1961 by Jules Feiffer. Copyright renewed 1989 by Jules Feiffer, from THE PHANTOM TOLLBOOTH by Norton Juster, illustrated by Jules Feiffer. Used with permission of Random House Children's Books, a division of Random House, Inc.

Thinking About the Selection

1. **Respond:** Can you relate to the way Milo feels in this excerpt? Why or why not?

2. **(a) Recall:** What does Milo discover in his room?
   (b) Deduce: What is so interesting about the mysterious arrival?

3. **(a) Summarize:** What are the contents of the package?
   (b) Draw Conclusions: Why does Milo decide to assemble the tollbooth?

4. **(a) Recall:** What does Milo say aloud at the end of the chapter? **(b) Speculate:** Why do you think the author has Milo speak, even though he is alone?

Apply the Skills

The Phantom Tollbooth, Act I, Scene i
• *The Phantom Tollbooth, Chapter 1*

Comparing a Novel to Its Dramatization

1. In a chart like the one shown, explain how readers learn the answer to each question. One example has been done.

Question	Novel Format	Drama Format
How does Milo feel?	The narrator's and Milo's words tell readers he is bored.	The CLOCK tells readers. The stage directions describe his actions.
What is in Milo's room?		
What is in the package?		

2. **(a)** What kinds of details are given in the play's stage directions? **(b)** How are these details revealed in the novel?

Writing to Compare Literary Works

In a brief essay, compare and contrast your experience of reading a novel and its dramatization. Use the following questions to get started:

- What features in a novel help you see and hear the characters, settings, and actions?
- What features in a drama script help you see and hear the characters, settings, and actions?
- How does your imagination help you read each format?
- Which format do you prefer? Why?

Vocabulary Builder

Practice Answer each question. Explain your answer.

1. If you got a present you liked, would you react *glumly*?
2. Would you sit *dejectedly* if you won a contest?
3. If your best friend moved away, would you think of him or her *wistfully*?
4. Would markers be *impractical* tools for making a poster?

QuickReview

Novel: a long work of fiction
Drama: a story written to be performed by actors

Go Online
—Assessment
For: Self-test
Visit: www.PHSchool.com
Web Code: ela-6503

Reading Informational Materials

Problem-and-Solution Essays

In Part 1, you are learning how to summarize literature. Summarizing is also helpful in reading informational materials such as problem-and-solution essays. In *The Phantom Tollbooth*, Act I, a boy takes a trip to overcome boredom. This essay gives ideas for preventing boredom—in dogs.

About Problem-and-Solution Essays

A **problem-and-solution essay** explains a problem to readers. Then, it offers solutions, supported by facts or examples. The problem might be personal, local, or universal. For example, a student might write about improving school lunches. An effective problem-and-solution essay has these features:

- It clearly explains the problem and the situation surrounding it.
- It explains and defends proposed solutions.
- It uses details to support important points.
- It has consistent, logical organization.

Reading Skill

An outline is an organized list of main ideas and significant details. **Outlining** can help you summarize the information in a text because it draws your attention to the most important ideas and supporting details in the essay. To create an outline, first identify the main ideas in the essay. Then, list subtopics for each main idea, and finally, list details. The example shows a formal outline structure you can use to take notes as you read.

I. First Main Idea
    A. First subtopic
        1. supporting detail
        2. supporting detail
    B. Second subtopic
        1. supporting detail
        2. supporting detail

BOREDOM **BLUES** BEGONE

Sherri Regalbuto

The first paragraph introduces the problem.

IF you've ever watched a documentary on zoo animals, you will have noticed that a great deal of time is spent on making sure the zoo animals do not become bored. An animal that lives in the same surroundings and is fed in the same manner and at the same time every day can become bored and depressed.

The writer provides supporting details about the problem, then proposes a solution.

Keeping our dogs from becoming bored is just as important. Bored dogs can get into all sorts of trouble if left to entertain themselves. You can entertain, educate, and enrich the life of your canine with these simple activities:

• Take some small dry treats and hide them around the house while your dogs are in another room. Make sure they are easily accessible for your dogs so they don't have to scratch anything up to get them. Let your dogs out and tell them to find the treats. Help with the first couple if you need to.

The writer gives more specific examples of ways to solve the problem.

• Take a big old pile of blankets and hide treats in the blankets. Set your dogs loose on the pile and tell them to "find" the treats.

• Bobbing is another fun activity, especially on a summer day that is too hot to venture out. Fill a kiddy pool, large pot or pail with a couple of inches of water. Throw your dogs' favorite waterproof toys or water-tough treats (meaty type) into the water and let them figure out how to get them out. Some dogs are naturals at this, but some can take a while to figure out how to get the toy without getting water up their noses. Don't push: Let them figure it out on their own time. Many dogs will learn how to retrieve items from underwater once they learn the "don't sniff under water" rule.

- Got a digger demolishing your backyard? Build a sandbox for your digger and hide treats (dry cracker type) under the sand. Once dogs are rewarded for digging in this area, they are sure to adopt the new digs!

- When you purchase new toys, keep some put away. Bring a new one out each week and put an old one away. Just like kids, dogs like to get a new toy and the new toy is always the favorite of the week.

- Plan a play date. Play dates are a wonderful activity for you and your dog. If you know of someone with a friendly dog, invite them over to play in your backyard. Not only will your dog have a new playmate, you will have fun discussing your dogs having so much fun.

- Mealtime can be very boring for dogs. Take their regular ration of food and stuff it into an indestructible toy and let them scavenge it out. Hide dry dog food around the house or use it for your obedience and trick training. Dogs do not have to eat their meal out of a bowl.

- Give your dog a new toy each week. You can have half a dozen toys and each week bring out a new one and put the old one back in storage — that way there is always something new for the dog to enjoy.

- Obedience and trick training is a wonderful activity. Done in a fun and positive method, your dog will love school time.

Use your imagination and introduce your dog to some new, fun, and different ways for the two of you to spend your time together.

Bulleted items offer methods and instructions in an organized way.

The closing sentence summarizes the solution to the problem.

Reading: Outlining

Directions: *Choose the letter of the best answer to each question.*

1. Which of the following might you use as a main heading?
   A Walking your dog is important.
   B Animals in the wild do not get bored.
   C Changing mealtimes is one solution.
   D Boredom can lead to problems for dogs.

2. Which detail supports the idea that "a busy dog is a happy dog"?
   A Dogs like a variety of activities.
   B Some dogs have behavior problems.
   C Dogs get information from sniffing.
   D Mealtime can be boring for a dog.

3. Which detail supports the problem presented in the essay?
   A Animals in the wild deal with different daily problems.
   B Dogs can become depressed when they are bored.
   C Most dogs enjoy getting new toys.
   D Vary your dog's regular walk.

Reading: Comprehension and Interpretation

Directions: *Write your answers on a separate sheet of paper.*

4. Describe ways that animals in the wild avoid becoming bored. **[Knowledge]**

5. Propose an idea for varying a dog's routine. **[Integrating]**

6. Describe surroundings that would provide activities for dogs. **[Applying]**

Timed Writing: Summary [Cognition]

Create an informal outline of the information in "Boredom Blues Begone." Then, use the outline to write a brief summary of the essay. Use your own words to explain the problem and solutions presented in the essay. **(20 minutes)**

Reading

Directions: *Questions 1–4 are based on the following selection.*

Drama has its roots in Ancient Greece. Tragedies were performed during religious festivals. Later, contests were held during festivals. Comedies were also performed in these competitions. Aristophanes is probably the best known Greek comic playwright. His plays are still performed and studied today.

1. **What is the topic of the selection?**
   A origins of drama
   B types of drama
   C writers of drama
   D characteristics of drama

2. **What would be the best summary of the last two sentences?**
   A Festivals included comedies. Aristophanes' comedies are famous.
   B Competition included drama. Aristophanes was a playwright.
   C Aristophanes, a famous Greek playwright, wrote plays performed at religious festivals.
   D The comedies of Aristophanes, a famous Greek playwright, have withstood the test of time.

3. **Which sentence best expresses the** main idea that should be included in a summary?
   A Greek religious festivals were competitions for playwrights.
   B Drama competitions had both tragedy and comedy.
   C Drama and comedy were written for drama competitions.
   D Plays were originally performed as part of Greek religious festivals.

4. **Which detail best completes the outline?**

   > I. Roots of Drama
   >   A _____
   >   1. Festivals
   >   2. Contests
   >   B Types
   >   1. Drama
   >   2. Comedy

   A First Playwrights
   B Aristophanes
   C First Performances
   D Tragedies

Vocabulary

Directions *Choose the word that best completes each of the following sentences.*

5. The word *shady* could _____ a tree or a dishonest person.
   - A brief
   - B describe
   - C summary
   - D review

6. Write a _____ of the entire story in ten sentences.
   - A describe
   - B recall
   - C brief
   - D summary

7. I was unable to _____ the name of the main character's son in the play.
   - A brief
   - B summary
   - C describe
   - D recall

8. Good writing should be _____ and to the point.
   - A brief
   - B review
   - C summary
   - D recall

9. I want to be a critic and _____ plays.
   - A recall
   - B review
   - C brief
   - D recall

Directions *Choose the word that does* not *fit the description.*

10. having a meaning related to "short"
    - A briefly
    - B brevity
    - C bravely
    - D briefness

11. having a meaning related to "writing"
    - A scraping
    - B description
    - C scripture
    - D scripts

12. having a meaning related to "writing"
    - A scrip
    - B scriptograph
    - C scrap
    - D script

13. having a meaning related to "writing"
    - A scriptorium
    - B scribe
    - C scrivener
    - D scrimp

14. having a meaning related to "short"
    - A briefing
    - B bravado
    - C briefer
    - D briefest

Response to Literature: Letter

A **response to literature** discusses what is of value in a book, short story, essay, article, or poem. One excellent way to respond to literature is to write a letter to an author. Follow the steps outlined in this workshop to write your own letter to an author.

Assignment Write a letter to a favorite author to share your response to his or her work.

What to Include Your letter should feature these elements:
- an introduction that identifies the work(s) and summarizes your overall reaction
- examples from the author's work to support your ideas
- a clear organizational format
- elements of formal business letters
- a respectful tone
- error-free writing, including correct use of participial phrases

To preview the criteria on which your letter may be judged, see the rubric on page 700.

Prewriting

Choosing Your Topic

Self-interview Write answers to these questions:
- What is my favorite type of reading?
- Which character from my reading would I like to be?
- What is the scariest/funniest/best book I have read?

Choose a work from among your answers as your topic.

Narrowing Your Topic and Gathering Details

Use a hexagon. To focus your letter, review the work of literature you will discuss. Using the six headings of a hexagon like the one shown, gather details about the work. Then review your ideas and choose one to present in a letter.

Using the Form

You might use elements of this form in these types of writing:
- movie reviews
- book reviews
- critical responses
- book reports

Work in Progress

Review the work you did on pages 647 and 681.

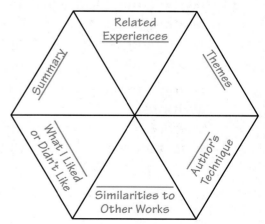

Drafting

Shaping Your Writing

Use business letter standard format. Include these elements:
- **Heading:** your address and the date of the letter
- **Inside address:** the name and address that show where the letter will be sent
- **Greeting:** an opening, including the recipient's name if known, followed by a colon
- **Body:** text that explains and develops your message
- **Closing:** *Sincerely* or *Respectfully,* followed by a comma
- **Signature:** your full name—printed or typed—and your handwritten signature above it

In **block format,** each part of the letter begins at the left margin. In **modified block format,** the heading, the closing, and the signature are indented to the center of the page.

Providing Elaboration

Justify your response. Elaborate on your general ideas and reactions with details from the literature.

Revising

Revising Your Overall Structure

Balance your introduction and conclusion. The ideas in your first and last paragraphs should balance. If the statements do not match, revise to improve your writing.

Block Format

Modified Block Format

To read the complete student model, see page 699.

Student Model: Balancing Introduction and Conclusion

I absolutely marvel at the simple words you can pull together to create the greatest adventure of all time. I love the impossible paths you lead me through. Your stories have no boundaries. . . .

Thank you for putting everything into creating numerous novels that have expanded imagination beyond the outside world.

Jennifer's first paragraph describes why the author's writing is so enjoyable to her.

Jennifer's last paragraph matches the idea she stated in the first paragraph for balance.

Revising Your Paragraphs

Add a quotation. Review the literature to find quotations that support the ideas in your letter.

Integrating Grammar Skills

Revising Choppy Sentences With Participial Phrases

Prentice Hall Writing and Grammar Connection: Chapter 22, Section 1

A **participle** is a form of a verb that acts as an adjective. A **present participle** is the *-ing* form of a verb: *relaxing* or *catching.* A **past participle** is the past form of the verb: *relaxed* or *caught.*

A **participial phrase** combines a present or past participle with other words to make a phrase. The entire phrase acts as an adjective.

▶ **Example:** *Catching the ball,* Damon threw it to home plate.
> *Relaxing after the game,* Bill listened to music.
> *Caught in the rain,* we got soaking wet.
> *Relaxed and happy,* the children played quietly.

Using Participial Phrases Effectively You can often use a participial phrase to combine a pair of related sentences. Placing the participial phrase at the beginning of the new sentence will add variety to your sentence structure. Look at these examples:

Short sentences	Combined
The lizard crawled slowly. It vanished into its burrow.	*Crawling slowly,* the lizard vanished into its burrow.

Combining Sentences with Participial Phrases Follow these steps to combine sentences:

1. **Look for pairs of short, related sentences.**
2. **Find the verb in each sentence of the pair.** Determine whether you can use one of these verbs, plus other words in the sentence, to form a participial phrase.
3. **Follow the examples to rewrite the sentence pair,** creating a stronger single sentence.

Apply It to Your Editing

Look for pairs of short, related sentences in your letter. Use the rules and examples above to revise using participial phrases.

Student Model: Jennifer Miller
Boise, Idaho

Jennifer Miller
555 Any Street
Boise, Idaho 99009

October 4, 20–

Ms. Tamora Pierce
333 Any Avenue
New York, New York 10007

Dear Ms. Tamora Pierce:

In "The Circle Opens #2: Street Magic," I absolutely marvel at the simple words you can pull together to create the greatest adventure of all time. I love the impossible paths you lead me through. Your stories have no boundaries. You are able to think through the whole story and then add mysterious clues that lead up to the answer.

You've written so many books that follow into the next series. I enjoy how you build new characters and intermingle previous relationships to come up with an entirely new story line. Maybe your next series could be about Neal's second daughter who can foretell the future through drawing pictures. That would be exciting.

The passion and rhythm you put in your writing really sets the mood of the novel. Your characters turn into true living beings with feelings and emotions that are so deeply expressed that the reader feels them too. You have definitely captured the hearts of all who have read your books, including my 41-year-old dad. Thank you for putting everything into creating numerous novels that have expanded imagination beyond the outside world.

Sincerely,

Jennifer Miller

Jennifer Miller

Jennifer writes her letter in block format.

The introduction identifies the work and makes it clear what Jennifer's feelings are about the author's writing.

To support her ideas, Jennifer mentions a character from the book.

The conclusion balances the introduction.

Writing Workshop

Editing and Proofreading

Correct your letter to make it error-free.

Focus on Formatting Because formal letters must follow specific rules for formatting, make sure that such features as the heading, inside address, salutation, and closing follow the standard format. To learn more about business letter format, see page R23.

Publishing and Presenting

Consider one of the following ways to share your writing:

Make a bulletin board display. Create a poster or other graphic display item, featuring biographical information about the author, a copy of your letter, and related artwork to showcase.

Send your letter. If you have chosen a living author, mail your letter to the author, in care of the publisher. Share your letter, and any response you receive, with your classmates.

Reflecting on Your Writing

Writer's Journal Jot down your thoughts on writing a letter to an author. Begin by answering these questions:

- Which revision strategy was most useful?
- In the process of writing, what did you learn about the author you chose?

> *Prentice Hall Writing and Grammar Connection: Chapter 12*

Rubric for Self-Assessment

To assess your letter, use the following rubric:

Criteria	Rating Scale				
	not very				*very*
Focus: How clearly do you state your reaction to the author's work?	1	2	3	4	5
Organization: How well do you organize your letter using standard business format?	1	2	3	4	5
Support/Elaboration: How well do you use examples from the author's work to support your ideas?	1	2	3	4	5
Style: How formal and polite is the language?	1	2	3	4	5
Conventions: How correct is your grammar, especially your use of participial phrases?	1	2	3	4	5

Unit 5
Part 2

Compare and Contrast

Skills You Will Learn

Reading Skill: *Picture the Action to Compare and Contrast*
Literary Analysis: *Stage Directions*

Literature You Will Read

Reading: Compare and Contrast

> A **comparison** tells how two or more things are alike, or similar. A **contrast** tells how two or more things are different.

Skills and Strategies You Will Learn in Part 2

In Part 2 you will learn:

- to **picture the action** in a drama (p. 704)
- to **compare and contrast** characteristics and elements in a drama (p. 704)

Using the Skills and Strategies in Part 2

In Part 2 you will **compare and contrast** characters, situations, and events. You will learn to use dialogue and descriptions to help you picture the characters and the action. This strategy will help you compare and contrast characters, events, and other elements of drama.

This example shows how you will apply the skills and strategies you will learn in Part 2.

FIRST - picture the scene in your mind -

Milo (*suddenly notices the package. He drags himself over to it, and disinterestedly, reads the label*) "For Milo, who has plenty of time." Well, that's true.
Gatekeeper Buy or sell, buy or sell. Which is it? You must have come here for a reason.

ASK • Which character has more time?
• Which character's speech is hurried?
• What is different about the characters?

Academic Vocabulary: Words for Discussing Comparing and Contrasting

These words will help you write and talk about comparing and contrasting as you read the selections in Part 2.

Word	Definition	Sample Sentence
unique *adj.*	one of a kind	Poe's style is *unique*.
compare *v.*	show how things are alike	*Compare* the plays in an essay.
contrast *v.*	show how things are different	*Contrast* the characters' motives.
characteristic *n.*	quality or feature	Plot is a *characteristic* of a story.
element *n.*	part of the whole	The setting is a key *element*.

Vocabulary Skill: Borrowed and Foreign Words

In Part 2, you will learn about words that have been borrowed from a variety of languages. Many English words have their origins in Latin and Greek. The chart shows some reasons other languages have had an influence on English.

French	Spanish	Italian	Native American
In 1066, the French con- quered the area that is now England.	Spanish-speaking settlers lived alongside English- speaking people.	Immigrants brought with them words that described their unique culture.	Settlers borrowed many words from Native Americans.

Activity Organize the words into groups based on the language you think they came from—French, Spanish, Italian, or Native American. Check your answers in a dictionary, and revise your lists.

canyon	jeans	moccasin
noodle	taco	mosquito

These skills will help you become a better reader. Practice them with Act II of *The Phantom Tollbooth* (p. 706).

Reading Skill

When you **compare** two things, you tell how they are alike. When you **contrast** two things, you tell how they are different. As you read drama, **picture the action** to compare and contrast characters, situations, and events. To picture the action, pay attention to the dialogue and the descriptions of how characters speak and act.

Literary Analysis

Stage directions are the words in a drama that the characters do not say. They tell performers how to move and speak, and they help readers picture the action, sounds, and scenery. Stage directions are usually printed in italics and set between brackets, as in this example.

> **CARLOS.** [*To ISABEL.*] Remember, don't make a sound! [*He tiptoes offstage.*]

As you read, use a chart like the one shown to record stage directions that help you picture the action and understand what the characters are thinking and feeling.

Stage Direction
What It Shows About the Character or Action

Vocabulary Builder

The Phantom Tollbooth, Act II

- **dissonance** (dis´ ə nəns) *n.* harsh or unpleasant combination of sounds (p. 706) *Poorly tuned instruments create <u>dissonance</u> in an orchestra.*

- **deficiency** (dē fish´ ən sē) *n.* shortage or lack (p. 708) *Eat a well-balanced meal to protect against a vitamin <u>deficiency</u>.*

- **admonishing** (ad män´ ish iŋ) *adj.* disapproving (p. 712) *The librarian gave the noisy group an <u>admonishing</u> look.*

- **accurate** (ak´ yə rət) *adj.* exactly right; free from errors (p. 713) *My broken watch no longer gives the <u>accurate</u> time.*

- **iridescent** (ir´ i des´ ənt) *adj.* showing different colors when seen from different angles (p. 715) *The peacock's <u>iridescent</u> feathers can appear either blue or green.*

- **malicious** (mə lish´ əs) *adj.* having or showing evil intentions (p. 723) *There was no truth to the neighbors' <u>malicious</u> gossip.*

Background

Words Versus Numbers In *The Phantom Tollbooth,* Azaz and the Mathemagician cannot agree about which is more important—words or numbers. Without words, we would not be able to talk, read, write, or learn. Without numbers, on the other hand, we would not have money, maps, calendars, clocks, or schedules.

Connecting to the Literature

Reading/Writing Connection In Act II, Milo considers the importance of words and numbers. Think about how you use them; then, write two sentences about why words and numbers are important to you. Use at least three of these words: *clarify, compute, define, communicate.*

Meet the Author

Norton **Juster** (b. 1929)

Norton Juster's first career was as an architect, designing buildings and other structures. He took up creative writing in his spare time "as a relaxation" from architecture. When he began writing *The Phantom Tollbooth,* the novel on which this drama is based, he thought it was just a short story for his own pleasure. Yet before long, Juster says, "it had created its own life, and I was hooked." The novel has been translated into several foreign languages and adapted for an animated film. Juster has even rewritten it as an opera!

Fast Facts

▶ Although *The Phantom Tollbooth* was first published in 1961, Juster still gets fan mail from new readers. He tries to answer every letter.

▶ Juster described Tock as "the friend your mother wanted you to play with" and the Humbug as "the kind of kid your folks *didn't* want you to play with."

Go Online
Author Link

For: More about the author
Visit: www.PHSchool.com
Web Code: ele-9503

The Phantom Tollbooth

Susan Nanus

Based on the book by Norton Juster

Review and Anticipate

In Act I, Milo is lifted from his boredom into a strange king-dom that is in conflict over the importance of letters and numbers. After traveling through Dictionopolis, he agrees to rescue the princesses who can settle the conflict. As Act II opens, Milo enters Digitopolis with Tock and Humbug—characters who will help him rescue the princesses.

Act II Scene i

The set of Digitopolis glitters in the background, while Upstage Right near the road, a small colorful Wagon sits, looking quite deserted. On its side in large letters, a sign reads: "KAKAFONOUS A. DISCHORD Doctor of <u>Dissonance</u>." Enter MILO, TOCK, *and* HUMBUG, *fearfully. They look at the wagon.*

TOCK. There's no doubt about it. That's where the noise was coming from.

HUMBUG. [*To* MILO.] Well, go on.

MILO. Go on what?

HUMBUG. Go on and see who's making all that noise in there. We can't just ignore a creature like that.

MILO. Creature? What kind of creature? Do you think he's dangerous?

HUMBUG. Go on, Milo. Knock on the door. We'll be right behind you.

MILO. O.K. Maybe he can tell us how much further it is to Digitopolis.

Literary Analysis
Stage Directions
What information about setting do these stage directions provide?

Vocabulary Builder
dissonance (dis´ ə nəns) *n.* harsh or unpleasant combination of sounds

[MILO *tiptoes up to the wagon door and KNOCKS timidly. The moment he knocks, a terrible CRASH is heard inside the wagon, and* MILO *and the others jump back in fright. At the same time, the Door Flies Open, and from the dark interior, a Hoarse* VOICE *inquires.*]

VOICE. Have you ever heard a whole set of dishes dropped from the ceiling onto a hard stone floor? [*The Others are speechless with fright.* MILO *shakes his head.* VOICE *happily.*] Have you ever heard an ant wearing fur slippers walk across a thick wool carpet? [MILO *shakes his head again.*] Have you ever heard a blindfolded octopus unwrap a cellophane-covered bathtub? [MILO *shakes his head a third time.*] Ha! I knew it. [*He hops out, a little man, wearing a white coat, with a stethoscope around his neck, and a small mirror attached to his forehead, and with very huge ears, and a mortar and pestle in his hands. He stares at* MILO, TOCK *and* HUMBUG.] None of you looks well at all! Tsk, tsk, not at all. [*He opens the top or side of his Wagon, revealing a dusty interior resembling an old apothecary shop, with shelves lined with jars and boxes, a table, books, test tubes and bottles and measuring spoons.*]

MILO. [*Timidly.*] Are you a doctor?

DISCHORD. [VOICE.] I am KAKAFONOUS A. DISCHORD, DOCTOR OF DISSONANCE! [*Several small explosions and a grinding crash are heard.*]

HUMBUG. [*Stuttering with fear.*] What does the "A" stand for?

DISCHORD. AS LOUD AS POSSIBLE! [*Two screeches and a bump are heard.*] Now, step a little closer and stick out your tongues. [DISCHORD *examines them.*] Just as I expected. [*He opens a large dusty book and thumbs through the pages.*] You're all suffering from a severe lack of noise. [DISCHORD *begins running around, collecting bottles, reading the labels to himself as he goes along.*] "Loud Cries." "Soft Cries." "Bangs, Bongs, Swishes. Swooshes." "Snaps and Crackles." "Whistles and Gongs." "Squeeks, Squawks, and Miscellaneous Uproar." [*As he reads them off, he pours a little of each into a large glass beaker and stirs the mixture with a*

Literary Analysis
Stage Directions
What information about sound effects do you learn from these stage directions?

Reading Skill
Compare and Contrast Based on his actions so far, how is Dischord similar to and different from doctors in real life?

Reading Check

Why are Milo, Tock, and Humbug frightened?

wooden spoon. The concoction smokes and bubbles.] Be ready in just a moment.

MILO. [*Suspiciously.*] Just what kind of doctor are you?

DISCHORD. Well, you might say, I'm a specialist. I specialize in noises, from the loudest to the softest, and from the slightly annoying to the terribly unpleasant. For instance, have you ever heard a square-wheeled steamroller ride over a street full of hard-boiled eggs? [*Very loud CRUNCHING SOUNDS are heard.*]

MILO. [*Holding his ears.*] But who would want all those terrible noises?

DISCHORD. [*Surprised at the question.*] Everybody does. Why, I'm so busy I can hardly fill all the orders for noise pills, racket lotion, clamor salve and hubbub tonic. That's all people seem to want these days. Years ago, everyone wanted pleasant sounds and business was terrible. But then the cities were built and there was a great need for honking horns, screeching trains, clanging bells and all the rest of those wonderfully unpleasant sounds we use so much today. I've been working overtime ever since and my medicine here is in great demand. All you have to do is take one spoonful every day, and you'll never have to hear another beautiful sound again. Here, try some.

HUMBUG. [*Backing away.*] If it's all the same to you, I'd rather not.

MILO. I don't want to be cured of beautiful sounds.

TOCK. Besides, there's no such sickness as a lack of noise.

DISCHORD. How true. That's what makes it so difficult to cure. [*Takes a large glass bottle from the shelf.*] Very well, if you want to go all through life suffering from a noise <u>deficiency</u>, I'll just give this to Dynne for his lunch. [*Uncorks the bottle and pours the liquid into it. There is a rumbling and then a loud explosion accompanied by*

smoke, out of which DYNNE, *a smog-like creature with yellow eyes and a frowning mouth, appears.*]

DYNNE. [*Smacking his lips.*] Ahhh, that was good, Master. I thought you'd never let me out. It was really cramped in there.

DISCHORD. This is my assistant, the awful Dynne. You must forgive his appearance, for he really doesn't have any.

MILO. What is a Dynne?

DISCHORD. You mean you've never heard of the awful Dynne? When you're playing in your room and making a great amount of noise, what do they tell you to stop?

MILO. That awful din.

DISCHORD. When the neighbors are playing their radio too loud late at night, what do you wish they'd turn down?

TOCK. That awful din.

DISCHORD. And when the street on your block is being repaired and the drills are working all day, what does everyone complain of?

HUMBUG. [*Brightly.*] The dreadful row.

DYNNE. The Dreadful Rauw was my grandfather. He perished in the great silence epidemic of 1712. I certainly can't understand why you don't like noise. Why, I heard an explosion last week that was so lovely, I groaned with appreciation for two days. [*He gives a loud groan at the memory.*]

DISCHORD. He's right, you know! Noise is the most valuable thing in the world.

MILO. King Azaz says words are.

DISCHORD. NONSENSE! Why, when a baby wants food, how does he ask?

DYNNE. [*Happily.*] He screams!

DISCHORD. And when a racing car wants gas?

DYNNE. [*Jumping for joy.*] It chokes!

DISCHORD. And what happens to the dawn when a new day begins?

Literary Analysis
Stage Directions
How does this stage direction help you imagine what Dynne is like?

Reading Skill
Compare and Contrast How are Dischord's opinions different from most people's regarding sounds?

Reading Check

What caused people to want noise and hubbub rather than pleasant sounds?

DYNNE. [*Delighted.*] It breaks!

DISCHORD. You see how simple it is? [*To* DYNNE.] Isn't it time for us to go?

MILO. Where to? Maybe we're going the same way.

DYNNE. I doubt it. [*Picking up empty sacks from the table.*] We're going on our collection rounds. Once a day, I travel throughout the kingdom and collect all the wonderfully horrible and beautifully unpleasant sounds I can find and bring them back to the doctor to use in his medicine.

DISCHORD. Where are you going?

MILO. To Digitopolis.

DISCHORD. Oh, there are a number of ways to get to Digitopolis, if you know how to follow directions. Just take a look at the sign at the fork in the road. Though why you'd ever want to go there, I'll never know.

MILO. We want to talk to the Mathemagician.

HUMBUG. About the release of the Princesses Rhyme and Reason.

DISCHORD. Rhyme and Reason? I remember them. Very nice girls, but a little too quiet for my taste. In fact, I've been meaning to send them something that Dynne brought home by mistake and which I have absolutely no use for. [*He rummages through the wagon.*] Ah, here it is . . . or maybe you'd like it for yourself. [*Hands* MILO *a Package.*]

MILO. What is it?

DISCHORD. The sounds of laughter. They're so unpleasant to hear, it's almost unbearable. All those giggles and snickers and happy shouts of joy, I don't know what Dynne was thinking of when he collected them. Here, take them to the Princesses or keep them for yourselves, I don't care. Well, time to move on. Goodbye now and good luck! [*He has shut the wagon by now and gets in. LOUD NOISES begin to erupt as* DYNNE *pulls the wagon off-stage.*]

MILO. [*Calling after them.*] But wait! The fork in the road . . . you didn't tell us where it is . . .

TOCK. It's too late. He can't hear a thing.

Reading Skill
Compare and Contrast How are these rounds different from the daily rounds of people such as mail carriers?

Literary Analysis
Stage Directions How do these stage directions help you understand what Dischord is doing?

HUMBUG. I could use a fork of my own, at the moment. And a knife and a spoon to go with it. All of a sudden, I feel very hungry.

MILO. So do I, but it's no use thinking about it. There won't be anything to eat until we reach Digitopolis. [*They get into the car.*]

HUMBUG. [*Rubbing his stomach.*] Well, the sooner the better is what I say. [*A SIGN suddenly appears.*]

DIGITOPOLIS	5 Miles
	1,600 Rods
	8,800 Yards
	26,400 Feet
	316,800 Inches
	633,600 Half Inches **AND THEN SOME**

◀ **Critical Viewing**
How are the different measurements on this sign related? **[Analyze]**

VOICE. [*A strange voice from nowhere.*] But which way will get you there sooner? That is the question.

TOCK. Did you hear something?

MILO. Look! The fork in the road and a signpost to Digitopolis! [*They read the Sign.*]

HUMBUG. Let's travel by miles, it's shorter.

MILO. Let's travel by half inches. It's quicker.

TOCK. But which road should we take? It must make a difference.

MILO. Do you think so?

TOCK. Well, I'm not sure, but . . .

HUMBUG. He could be right. On the other hand, he could also be wrong. Does it make a difference or not?

VOICE. Yes, indeed, indeed it does, certainly, my yes, it does make a difference.

[*The* DODECAHEDRON *appears, a 12-sided figure with a different face on each side, and with all the edges labeled with a small letter and all the angles labeled with a large letter. He wears a beret and peers at the others with a serious face. He doffs his cap and recites:*]

✓ Reading Check

What does Dischord give to Milo, and why?

DODECAHEDRON. *My angles are many.*
My sides are not few.
I'm the Dodecahedron.
Who are you?

MILO. What's a Dodecahedron?

DODECAHEDRON. [*Turning around slowly.*] See for yourself. A Dodecahedron is a mathematical shape with 12 faces. [*All his faces appear as he turns, each face with a different expression. He points to them.*] I usually use one at a time. It saves wear and tear. What are you called?

MILO. Milo.

DODECAHEDRON. That's an odd name. [*Changing his smiling face to a frowning one.*] And you have only one face.

MILO. [*Making sure it is still there.*] Is that bad?

DODECAHEDRON. You'll soon wear it out using it for everything. Is everyone with one face called Milo?

MILO. Oh, no. Some are called Billy or Jeffery or Sally or Lisa or lots of other things.

DODECAHEDRON. How confusing. Here everything is called exactly what it is. The triangles are called triangles, the circles are called circles, and even the same numbers have the same name. Can you imagine what would happen if we named all the twos Billy or Jeffery or Sally or Lisa or lots of other things? You'd have to say Robert plus John equals four, and if the fours were named Albert, things would be hopeless.

MILO. I never thought of it that way.

DODECAHEDRON. [*With an <u>admonishing</u> face.*] Then I suggest you begin at once, for in Digitopolis, everything is quite precise.

MILO. Then perhaps you can help us decide which road we should take.

DODECAHEDRON. [*Happily.*] By all means. There's nothing to it. [*As he talks, the three others try to solve the problem on a Large Blackboard that is wheeled onstage for the occasion.*] Now, if a small car carrying three people at 30 miles an hour for 10 minutes along a road 5 miles long at 11:35 in the morning starts at the same time as

Literary Analysis
Stage Directions
Why would the information presented here be important to a group performing the play?

Vocabulary Builder
admonishing (ad män´ ish iŋ) *adj.* disapproving

3 people who have been traveling in a little automobile at 20 miles an hour for 15 minutes on another road exactly twice as long as half the distance of the other, while a dog, a bug, and a boy travel an equal distance in the same time or the same distance in an equal time along a third road in mid-October, then which one arrives first and which is the best way to go?

HUMBUG. Seventeen!

MILO. [*Still figuring frantically.*] I'm not sure, but . . .

DODECAHEDRON. You'll have to do better than that.

MILO. I'm not very good at problems.

DODECAHEDRON. What a shame. They're so very useful. Why, did you know that if a beaver 2 feet long with a tail a foot and a half long can build a dam 12 feet high and 6 feet wide in 2 days, all you would need to build Boulder Dam is a beaver 68 feet long with a 51 foot tail?

HUMBUG. [*Grumbling as his pencil snaps.*] Where would you find a beaver that big?

DODECAHEDRON. I don't know, but if you did, you'd certainly know what to do with him.

MILO. That's crazy.

DODECAHEDRON. That may be true, but it's completely <u>accurate</u>, and as long as the answer is right, who cares if the question is wrong?

TOCK. [*Who has been patiently doing the first problem.*] All three roads arrive at the same place at the same time.

DODECAHEDRON. Correct! And I'll take you there myself. [*The blackboard rolls off, and all four get into the car and drive off.*] Now you see how important problems are. If you hadn't done this one properly, you might have gone the wrong way.

MILO. But if all the roads arrive at the same place at the same time, then aren't they all the right road?

DODECAHEDRON. [*Glaring from his upset face.*] Certainly not! They're all the wrong way! Just because you have a choice, it doesn't mean that any of them has to be right.

Reading Skill
Compare and Contrast Based on his words and actions, how is Dodecahedron different from Milo and Humbug?

Vocabulary Builder
accurate (ak′ yə rət) *adj.* exactly right; free from errors

As long as the answer is right, who cares if the question is wrong?

✔**Reading Check**

Based on their responses to the problem Dodecahedron poses, who is best at mathematics: Milo, Tock, or Humbug?

The Phantom Tollbooth, Act II ■ 713

[*Pointing in another direction.*] That's the way to Digitopolis and we'll be there any moment. [*Suddenly the lighting grows dimmer.*] In fact, we're here. Welcome to the Land of Numbers.

HUMBUG. [*Looking around at the barren landscape.*] It doesn't look very inviting.

MILO. Is this the place where numbers are made?

DODECAHEDRON. They're not made. You have to dig for them. Don't you know anything at all about numbers?

MILO. Well, I never really thought they were very important.

DODECAHEDRON. NOT IMPORTANT! Could you have tea for two without the 2? Or three blind mice without the 3? And how would you sail the seven seas without the 7?

MILO. All I meant was . . .

DODECAHEDRON. [*Continues shouting angrily.*] If you had high hopes, how would you know how high they were? And did you know that narrow escapes come in different widths? Would you travel the whole world wide without ever knowing how wide it was? And how could you do anything at long last without knowing how long the last was? Why, numbers are the most beautiful and valuable things in the world. Just follow me and I'll show you. [*He motions to them and pantomimes walking through rocky terrain with the others in tow. A Doorway similar to the Tollbooth appears and the* DODECAHEDRON *opens it and motions the others to follow him through.*] Come along, come along. I can't wait for you all day. [*They enter the doorway and the lights are dimmed very low, as to simulate the interior of a cave. The SOUNDS of scrapings and tapping, scuffling and digging are heard all around them. He hands them Helmets with flashlights attached.*] Put these on.

MILO. [*Whispering.*] Where are we going?

▼ Critical Viewing
Which qualities of Dodecahedron are the most interesting to you? Why?
[Respond]

DODECAHEDRON. We're here. This is the numbers mine. [*LIGHTS UP A LITTLE, revealing Little Men digging and chopping, shoveling and scraping.*] Right this way and watch your step. [*His voice echoes and reverberates. Iridescent and glittery numbers seem to sparkle from everywhere.*]

MILO. [*Awed.*] Whose mine is it?

VOICE OF MATHEMAGICIAN. By the four million eight hundred and twenty-seven thousand six hundred and fifty-nine hairs on my head, it's mine, of course! [*ENTER the* MATHEMAGICIAN, *carrying his long staff which looks like a giant pencil.*]

HUMBUG. [*Already intimidated.*] It's a lovely mine, really it is.

MATHEMAGICIAN. [*Proudly.*] The biggest number mine in the kingdom.

MILO. [*Excitedly.*] Are there any precious stones in it?

MATHEMAGICIAN. Precious stones! [*Then softly.*] By the eight million two hundred and forty-seven thousand three hundred and twelve threads in my robe, I'll say there are. Look here. [*Reaches in a cart, pulls out a small object, polishes it vigorously and holds it to the light, where it sparkles.*]

MILO. But that's a five.

MATHEMAGICIAN. Exactly. As valuable a jewel as you'll find anywhere. Look at some of the others. [*Scoops up others and pours them into* MILO's *arms. They include all numbers from 1 to 9 and an assortment of zeros.*]

DODECAHEDRON. We dig them and polish them right here, and then send them all over the world. Marvelous, aren't they?

TOCK. They are beautiful. [*He holds them up to compare them to the numbers on his clock body.*]

MILO. So that's where they come from. [*Looks at them and carefully hands them back, but drops a few which smash and break in half.*] Oh, I'm sorry!

MATHEMAGICIAN. [*Scooping them up.*] Oh, don't worry about that. We use the broken ones for fractions. How about

Vocabulary Builder
iridescent (ir´ ə des´ ənt) *adj.* showing different colors when seen from different angles

Literary Analysis
Stage Directions
What information do these stage directions provide about the action?

Reading Check

What do Dodecahedron and Mathemagician find exciting and valuable?

some lunch? [*Takes out a little whistle and blows it. Two miners rush in carrying an immense cauldron which is bubbling and steaming. The workers put down their tools and gather around to eat.*]

HUMBUG. That looks delicious! [TOCK *and* MILO *also look hungrily at the pot.*]

MATHEMAGICIAN. Perhaps you'd care for something to eat?

MILO. Oh, yes, sir!

TOCK. Thank you.

HUMBUG. [*Already eating.*] Ummm . . . delicious! [*All finish their bowls immediately.*]

MATHEMAGICIAN. Please have another portion. [*They eat and finish.* MATHEMAGICIAN *serves them again.*] Don't stop now. [*They finish.*] Come on, no need to be bashful. [*Serves them again.*]

MILO. [*To* TOCK *and* HUMBUG *as he finishes again.*] Do you want to hear something strange? Each one I eat makes me a little hungrier than before.

MATHEMAGICIAN. Do have some more. [*He serves them again. They eat frantically, until the* MATHEMAGICIAN *blows his whistle again and the pot is removed.*]

HUMBUG. [*Holding his stomach.*] Uggghhh! I think I'm starving.

MILO. Me, too, and I ate so much.

DODECAHEDRON. [*Wiping the gravy from several of his mouths.*] Yes, it was delicious, wasn't it? It's the specialty of the kingdom . . . subtraction stew.

TOCK. [*Weak from hunger.*] I have more of an appetite than when I began.

MATHEMAGICIAN. Certainly, what did you expect? The more you eat, the hungrier you get, everyone knows that.

▲ **Critical Viewing**
Which details in the picture suggest that this is Mathemagician? **[Analyze]**

MILO. They do? Then how do you get enough?

MATHEMAGICIAN. Enough? Here in Digitopolis, we have our meals when we're full and eat until we're hungry. That way, when you don't have anything at all, you have more than enough. It's a very economical system. You must have been stuffed to have eaten so much.

DODECAHEDRON. It's completely logical. The more you want, the less you get, and the less you get, the more you have. Simple arithmetic, that's all. [TOCK, MILO *and* HUMBUG *look at him blankly.*] Now, look, suppose you had something and added nothing to it. What would you have?

MILO. The same.

DODECAHEDRON. Splendid! And suppose you had something and added less than nothing to it? What would you have then?

HUMBUG. Starvation! Oh, I'm so hungry.

DODECAHEDRON. Now, now, it's not as bad as all that. In a few hours, you'll be nice and full again . . . just in time for dinner.

MILO. But I only eat when I'm hungry.

MATHEMAGICIAN. [*Waving the eraser of his staff.*] What a curious idea. The next thing you'll have us believe is that you only sleep when you're tired.

[*The mine has disappeared as well as the Miners.*]

HUMBUG. Where did everyone go?

MATHEMAGICIAN. Oh, they're still in the mine. I often find that the best way to get from one place to another is to erase everything and start again. Please make yourself at home.

[*They find themselves in a unique room, in which all the walls, tables, chairs, desks, cabinets and blackboards are labeled to show their heights, widths, depths and distances to and from each other. To one side is a gigantic notepad on an artist's easel, and from hooks and strings hang a collection of rulers, measures, weights and tapes, and all other measuring devices.*]

MILO. Do you always travel that way? [*He looks around in wonder.*]

Reading Skill
Compare and Contrast How are the meals that characters eat in Digitopolis different from real-life meals?

**Reading Check**

What is the easiest way for Mathemagician to get from one place to another?

MATHEMAGICIAN. No, indeed! [*He pulls a plumb line from a hook and walks.*] Most of the time I take the shortest distance between any two points. And of course, when I have to be in several places at once . . . [*He writes 3 x 1 = 3 on the notepad with his staff.*] I simply multiply. [THREE FIGURES *looking like the* MATHEMAGICIAN *appear on a platform above.*]

MILO. How did you do that?

MATHEMAGICIAN AND THE THREE. There's nothing to it, if you have a magic staff. [THE THREE FIGURES *cancel themselves out and disappear.*]

HUMBUG. That's nothing but a big pencil.

MATHEMAGICIAN. True enough, but once you learn to use it, there's no end to what you can do.

MILO. Can you make things disappear?

MATHEMAGICIAN. Just step a little closer and watch this. [*Shows them that there is nothing up his sleeve or in his hat. He writes:*]

4 + 9 - 2 x 16 + 1 = 3 x 6 - 67 + 8 x 2 - 3 + 26 - 1 - 34 + 3 - 7 + 2 - 5 = [*He looks up expectantly.*]

HUMBUG. Seventeen?

MILO. It all comes to zero.

MATHEMAGICIAN. Precisely. [*Makes a theatrical bow and rips off paper from notepad.*] Now, is there anything else you'd like to see? [*At this point, an appeal to the audience to see if anyone would like a problem solved.*]

MILO. Well . . . can you show me the biggest number there is?

MATHEMAGICIAN. Why, I'd be delighted. [*Opening a closet door.*] We keep it right here. It took four miners to dig it out. [*He shows them a huge "3" twice as high as the* MATHEMAGICIAN.]

MILO. No, that's not what I mean. Can you show me the longest number there is?

MATHEMAGICIAN. Sure. [*Opens another door.*] Here it is. It took three carts to carry it here. [*Door reveals an "8" that is as wide as the "3" was high.*]

MILO. No, no, that's not what I meant either. [*Looks helplessly at* TOCK.]

TOCK. I think what you would like to see is the number of the greatest possible magnitude.

MATHEMAGICIAN. Well, why didn't you say so? [*He busily measures them and all other things as he speaks, and marks it down.*] What's the greatest number you can think of? [*Here, an appeal can also be made to the audience or* MILO *may think of his own answers.*]

MILO. Uh . . . nine trillion, nine hundred and ninety-nine billion, nine hundred ninety-nine million, nine-hundred ninety-nine thousand, nine hundred and ninety-nine [*He puffs.*]

MATHEMAGICIAN. [*Writes that on the pad.*] Very good. Now add one to it. [MILO *or audience does.*] Now add one again. [MILO *or audience does so.*] Now add one again. Now add one again. Now add . . .

MILO. But when can I stop?

MATHEMAGICIAN. Never. Because the number you want is always at least one more than the number you have, and it's so large that if you started saying it yesterday, you wouldn't finish tomorrow.

HUMBUG. Where could you ever find a number so big?

MATHEMAGICIAN. In the same place they have the smallest number there is, and you know what that is?

MILO. The smallest number . . . let's see . . . one one-millionth?

MATHEMAGICIAN. Almost. Now all you have to do is divide that in half and then divide that in half and then divide that in half and then divide that . . .

MILO. Doesn't that ever stop either?

MATHEMAGICIAN. How can it when you can always take half of what you have and divide it in half again? Look. [*Pointing offstage.*] You see that line?

Reading Skill

Compare and Contrast Based on Mathemagician's actions here, how does he see numbers differently from Milo?

Reading Check

What does Mathemagician teach Milo about numbers?

MILO. You mean that long one out there?

MATHEMAGICIAN. That's it. Now, if you just follow that line forever, and when you reach the end, turn left, you will find the Land of Infinity. That's where the tallest, the shortest, the biggest, the smallest and the most and the least of everything are kept.

MILO. But how can you follow anything forever? You know, I get the feeling that everything in Digitopolis is very difficult.

MATHEMAGICIAN. But on the other hand, I think you'll find that the only thing you can do easily is be wrong, and that's hardly worth the effort.

MILO. But . . . what bothers me is . . . well, why is it that even when things are correct, they don't really seem to be right?

MATHEMAGICIAN. [*Grows sad and quiet.*] How true. It's been that way ever since Rhyme and Reason were banished. [*Sadness turns to fury.*] And all because of that stubborn wretch Azaz! It's all his fault.

MILO. Maybe if you discussed it with him . . .

MATHEMAGICIAN. He's just too unreasonable! Why just last month, I sent him a very friendly letter, which he never had the courtesy to answer. See for yourself. [*Puts the letter on the easel. The letter reads:*]

4738 1919,

667 394107 5841 62589 85371 14

39588 7190434 203 27689 57131 481206.

5864 98053,

62179875073

MILO. But maybe he doesn't understand numbers.

MATHEMAGICIAN. Nonsense! Everybody understands numbers. No matter what language you speak, they always mean the same thing. A seven is a seven everywhere in the world.

MILO. [*To* TOCK *and* HUMBUG.] Everyone is so sensitive about what he knows best.

Reading Skill
Compare and Contrast Do real-life situations support Mathemagician's statement about being wrong? Explain.

A seven is a seven everywhere in the world.

TOCK. With your permission, sir, we'd like to rescue Rhyme and Reason.

MATHEMAGICIAN. Has Azaz agreed to it?

TOCK. Yes, sir.

MATHEMAGICIAN. THEN I DON'T! Ever since they've been banished, we've never agreed on anything, and we never will.

MILO. Never?

MATHEMAGICIAN. NEVER! And if you can prove otherwise, you have my permission to go.

MILO. Well then, with whatever Azaz agrees, you disagree.

MATHEMAGICIAN. Correct.

MILO. And with whatever Azaz disagrees, you agree.

MATHEMAGICIAN. [*Yawning, cleaning his nails.*] Also correct.

MILO. Then, each of you agrees that he will disagree with whatever each of you agrees with, and if you both disagree with the same thing, aren't you really in agreement?

MATHEMAGICIAN. I'VE BEEN TRICKED! [*Figures it over, but comes up with the same answer.*]

TOCK. And now may we go?

MATHEMAGICIAN. [*Nods weakly.*] It's a long and dangerous journey. Long before you find them, the demons will know you're there. Watch out for them, because if you ever come face to face, it will be too late. But there is one other obstacle even more serious than that.

MILO. [*Terrified.*] What is it?

MATHEMAGICIAN. I'm afraid I can't tell you until you return. But maybe I can give you something to help you out. [*Claps hands. ENTER the* DODECAHEDRON, *carrying something on a pillow. The* MATHEMAGICIAN *takes it.*] Here is your own magic staff. Use it well and there is nothing it can't do for you. [*Puts a small, gleaming pencil in* MILO's *breast pocket.*]

HUMBUG. Are you sure you can't tell about that serious obstacle?

Literary Analysis
Stage Directions
What does this stage direction suggest about Mathemagician's opinion of himself?

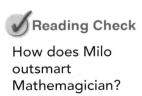

Reading Check

How does Milo outsmart Mathemagician?

MATHEMAGICIAN. Only when you return. And now the Dodecahedron will escort you to the road that leads to the Castle-in-the-Air. Farewell, my friends, and good luck to you. [*They shake hands, say goodbye, and the* DODECAHEDRON *leads them off.*] Good luck to you! [*To himself.*] Because you're sure going to need it. [*He watches them through a telescope and marks down the calculations.*]

DODECAHEDRON. [*He re-enters.*] Well, they're on their way.

MATHEMAGICIAN. So I see. . . [DODECAHEDRON *stands waiting.*] Well, what is it?

DODECAHEDRON. I was just wondering myself, your Number-ship. What actually is the serious obstacle you were talking about?

MATHEMAGICIAN. [*Looks at him in surprise.*] You mean you really don't know?

BLACKOUT

Scene ii The Land of Ignorance

LIGHTS UP on RHYME *and* REASON, *in their castle, looking out two windows.*

RHYME. *I'm worried sick, I must confess*
I wonder if they'll have success
All the others tried in vain,
And were never seen or heard again.

REASON. Now, Rhyme, there's no need to be so pessimistic. Milo, Tock, and Humbug have just as much chance of succeeding as they do of failing.

RHYME. *But the demons are so deadly smart*
They'll stuff your brain and fill your heart
With petty thoughts and selfish dreams
And trap you with their nasty schemes.

REASON. Now, Rhyme, be reasonable, won't you? And calm down, you always talk in couplets when you get nervous. Milo has learned a lot from his journey. I think he's a match for the demons and that he might soon be knocking at our door. Now come on, cheer up, won't you?

Literary Analysis
Stage Directions
BLACKOUT means that all the lights focused on the stage are turned off. How does this add suspense here?

Literary Analysis
Stage Directions
What effect does the stage direction *LIGHTS UP* have on the action?

RHYME. I'll try.

[*LIGHTS FADE on the* PRINCESSES *and COME UP on the little Car, traveling slowly.*]

MILO. So this is the Land of Ignorance. It's so dark. I can hardly see a thing. Maybe we should wait until morning.

VOICE. They'll be mourning for you soon enough. [*They look up and see a large, soiled, ugly bird with a dangerous beak and a* <u>malicious</u> *expression.*]

MILO. I don't think you understand. We're looking for a place to spend the night.

BIRD. [*Shrieking.*] It's not yours to spend!

MILO. That doesn't make any sense, you see . . .

BIRD. Dollars or cents, it's still not yours to spend.

MILO. But I don't mean . . .

BIRD. Of course you're mean. Anybody who'd spend a night that doesn't belong to him is very mean.

TOCK. Must you interrupt like that?

BIRD. Naturally, it's my job. I take the words right out of your mouth. Haven't we met before? I'm the Everpresent Wordsnatcher.

MILO. Are you a demon?

BIRD. I'm afraid not. I've tried, but the best I can manage to be is a nuisance. [*Suddenly gets nervous as he looks beyond the three.*] And I don't have time to waste with you. [*Starts to leave.*]

TOCK. What is it? What's the matter?

MILO. Hey, don't leave. I wanted to ask you some questions. . . . Wait!

BIRD. Weight? Twenty-seven pounds. Bye-bye. [*Disappears.*]

MILO. Well, he was no help.

MAN. Perhaps I can be of some assistance to you? [*There appears a beautifully dressed man, very polished and clean.*] Hello, little boy. [*Shakes* MILO's *hand.*] And how's the faithful dog? [*Pats* TOCK.] And who is this handsome creature? [*Tips his hat to* HUMBUG.]

Vocabulary Builder
malicious (mə lish′ əs) *adj.* having or showing evil intentions

Reading Skill
Compare and Contrast How is the bird like other characters Milo meets?

Reading Check

How does Reason reassure Rhyme?

HUMBUG. [*To others.*] What a pleasant surprise to meet someone so nice in a place like this.

MAN. But before I help you out, I wonder if first you could spare me a little of your time, and help me with a few small jobs?

HUMBUG. Why, certainly.

TOCK. Gladly.

MILO. Sure, we'd be happy to.

MAN. Splendid, for there are just three tasks. First, I would like to move this pile of sand from here to there. [*Indicates through pantomime a large pile of sand.*] But I'm afraid that all I have is this tiny tweezers. [*Hands it to* MILO, *who begins moving the sand one grain at a time.*] Second, I would like to empty this well and fill that other, but I have no bucket, so you'll have to use this eyedropper. [*Hands it to* TOCK, *who begins to work.*] And finally, I must have a hole in this cliff, and here is a needle to dig it. [HUMBUG *eagerly begins. The man leans against a tree and stares vacantly off into space. The LIGHTS indicate the passage of time.*]

MILO. You know something? I've been working steadily for a long time, now, and I don't feel the least bit tired or hungry. I could go right on the same way forever.

MAN. Maybe you will. [*He yawns.*]

MILO. [*Whispers to* TOCK.] Well, I wish I knew how long it was going to take.

TOCK. Why don't you use your magic staff and find out?

MILO. [*Takes out pencil and calculates. To* MAN.] Pardon me, sir, but it's going to take 837 years to finish these jobs.

MAN. Is that so? What a shame. Well then you'd better get on with them.

MILO. But . . . it hardly seems worthwhile.

MAN. WORTHWHILE! Of course they're not worthwhile. I wouldn't ask you to do anything that was worthwhile.

TOCK. Then why bother?

MAN. Because, my friends, what could be more important than doing unimportant things? If you stop to do enough of them, you'll never get where you are going. [*Laughs villainously.*]

MILO. [*Gasps.*] Oh, no, you must be . . .

MAN. Quite correct! I am the Terrible Trivium, demon of petty tasks and worthless jobs, ogre of wasted effort and monster of habit. [*They start to back away from him.*] Don't try to leave, there's so much to do, and you still have 837 years to go on the first job.

MILO. But why do unimportant things?

MAN. Think of all the trouble it saves. If you spend all your time doing only the easy and useless jobs, you'll never have time to worry about the important ones which are so difficult. [*Walks toward them whispering.*] Now do come and stay with me. We'll have such fun together. There are things to fill and things to empty, things to take away and things to bring back, things to pick up and things to put down . . . [*They are transfixed by his soothing voice. He is about to embrace them when a* VOICE *screams.*]

VOICE. Run! Run! [*They all wake up and run with the Trivium behind. As the voice continues to call out directions, they follow until they lose the Trivium.*] RUN! RUN! This way! This way! Over here! Over here! Up here! Down there! Quick, hurry up!

TOCK. [*Panting.*] I think we lost him.

VOICE. Keep going straight! Keep going straight! Now step up! Now step up!

MILO. Look out! [*They all fall into a Trap.*] But he said "up!"

VOICE. Well, I hope you didn't expect to get anywhere by listening to me.

HUMBUG. We're in a deep pit! We'll never get out of here.

VOICE. That is quite an accurate evaluation of the situation.

MILO. [*Shouting angrily.*] Then why did you help us at all?

VOICE. Oh, I'd do as much for anybody. Bad advice is my specialty. [*A Little Furry Creature appears.*] I'm the demon of Insincerity. I don't mean what I say; I don't mean what I do; and I don't mean what I am.

> **Reading Skill**
> **Compare and Contrast** How is Terrible Trivium similar to the Lethargarians, who appear in Act I?

Reading Check

Where are Milo, Humbug, and Tock stuck?

MILO. Then why don't you go away and leave us alone!

INSINCERITY. (VOICE) Now, there's no need to get angry. You're a very clever boy and I have complete confidence in you. You can certainly climb out of that pit . . . come on, try . . .

MILO. I'm not listening to one word you say! You're just telling me what you think I'd like to hear, and not what is important.

INSINCERITY. Well, if that's the way you feel about it . . .

MILO. That's the way I feel about it. We will manage by ourselves without any unnecessary advice from you.

INSINCERITY. [*Stamping his foot.*] Well, all right for you! Most people listen to what I say, but if that's the way you feel, then I'll just go home. [*Exits in a huff.*]

HUMBUG. [*Who has been quivering with fright.*] And don't you ever come back! Well, I guess we showed him, didn't we?

MILO. You know something? This place is a lot more dangerous than I ever imagined.

TOCK. [*Who's been surveying the situation.*] I think I figured a way to get out. Here, hop on my back. [MILO *does so.*] Now, you, Humbug, on top of Milo. [*He does so.*] Now hook your umbrella onto that tree and hold on. [*They climb over* HUMBUG, *then pull him up.*]

HUMBUG. [*As they climb.*] Watch it! Watch it, now. Ow, be careful of my back! My back! Easy, easy . . . oh, this is so difficult. Aren't you finished yet?

TOCK. [*As he pulls up* HUMBUG.] There. Now, I'll lead for a while. Follow me, and we'll stay out of trouble. [*They walk and climb higher and higher.*]

▲ **Critical Viewing**
How does this image show that Milo, Tock, and Humbug need one another in order to succeed?
[Connect]

726 ■ *Drama*

HUMBUG. Can't we slow down a little?

TOCK. Something tells me we better reach the Castle-in-the-Air as soon as possible, and not stop to rest for a single moment. [*They speed up.*]

MILO. What is it, Tock? Did you see something?

TOCK. Just keep walking and don't look back.

MILO. You *did* see something!

HUMBUG. What is it? Another demon?

TOCK. Not just one, I'm afraid. If you want to see what I'm talking about, then turn around. [*They turn around. The stage darkens and hundreds of Yellow Gleaming Eyes can be seen.*]

HUMBUG. Good grief! Do you see how many there are? Hundreds! The Overbearing Know-it-all, the Gross Exaggeration, the Horrible Hopping Hindsight, . . . and look over there! The Triple Demons of Compromise! Let's get out of here! [*Starts to scurry.*] Hurry up, you two! Must you be so slow about everything?

MILO. Look! There it is, up ahead! The Castle-in-the-Air! [*They all run.*]

HUMBUG. They're gaining!

MILO. But there it is!

HUMBUG. I see it! I see it!

[*They reach the first step and are stopped by a little man in a frock coat, sleeping on a worn ledger. He has a long quill pen and a bottle of ink at his side. He is covered with ink stains over his clothes and wears spectacles.*]

TOCK. Shh! Be very careful. [*They try to step over him, but he wakes up.*]

SENSES TAKER. [*From sleeping position.*] Names? [*He sits up.*]

HUMBUG. Well, I . . .

SENSES TAKER. *NAMES?* [*He opens book and begins to write, splattering himself with ink.*]

HUMBUG. Uh . . . Humbug, Tock and this is Milo.

SENSES TAKER. Splendid, splendid. I haven't had an "M" in ages.

Reading Skill
Compare and Contrast How is the way these new creatures make their entrance different from the way other characters appear onstage?

Reading Check

Why are Milo and the others running?

MILO. What do you want our names for? We're sort of in a hurry.

SENSES TAKER. Oh, this won't take long. I'm the official Senses Taker and I must have some information before I can take your sense. Now if you'll just tell me: [*Handing them a form to fill. Speaking slowly and deliberately.*] When you were born, where you were born, why you were born, how old you are now, how old you were then, how old you'll be in a little while . . .

MILO. I wish he'd hurry up. At this rate, the demons will be here before we know it!

▼ **Critical Viewing**
Does this picture of Senses Taker match the image you formed as you read his description in the stage directions? Explain. [**Compare and Contrast**]

SENSES TAKER. . . . Your mother's name, your father's name, where you live, how long you've lived there, the schools you've attended, the schools you haven't attended . . .

HUMBUG. I'm getting writer's cramp.

TOCK. I smell something very evil and it's getting stronger every second. [*To* SENSES TAKER.] May we go now?

SENSES TAKER. Just as soon as you tell me your height, your weight, the number of books you've read this year . . .

MILO. We have to go!

SENSES TAKER. All right, all right, I'll give you the short form. [*Pulls out a small piece of paper.*] Destination?

MILO. But we have to . . .

SENSES TAKER. *DESTINATION?*

MILO, TOCK AND HUMBUG. The Castle-in-the-Air! [*They throw down their papers and run past him up the first few stairs.*]

SENSES TAKER. Stop! I'm sure you'd rather see what I have to show you. [*Snaps his fingers; they freeze.*] A circus of your very own. [*CIRCUS MUSIC is heard.* MILO *seems to go into a trance.*] And wouldn't you enjoy this most wonderful smell? [TOCK *sniffs and goes into a trance.*] And here's something I know you'll enjoy hearing . . . [*To* HUMBUG. *The sound of CHEERS and APPLAUSE for* HUMBUG *is heard, and he goes into a trance.*] There we are. And now, I'll just sit back and let the demons catch up with you.

[MILO *accidentally drops his package of gifts. The Package of Laughter from* DR. DISCHORD *opens and the Sounds of Laughter are heard. After a moment,* MILO, TOCK *and* HUMBUG *join in laughing and the spells are broken.*]

MILO. There was no circus.

TOCK. There were no smells.

HUMBUG. The applause is gone.

SENSES TAKER. I warned you I was the Senses Taker. I'll steal your sense of Purpose, your sense of Duty, destroy your sense of Proportion—and but for one thing, you'd be helpless yet.

MILO. What's that?

SENSES TAKER. As long as you have the sound of laughter, I cannot take your sense of Humor. Agh! That horrible sense of humor.

HUMBUG. HERE THEY COME! LET'S GET OUT OF HERE!

[*The demons appear in nasty slithering hordes, running through the audience and up onto the stage, trying to attack* TOCK, MILO *and* HUMBUG. *The three heroes run past the* SENSES TAKER *up the stairs toward the Castle-in-the-Air with the demons snarling behind them.*]

MILO. Don't look back! Just keep going! [*They reach the castle. The two princesses appear in the windows.*]

PRINCESSES. Hurry! Hurry! We've been expecting you.

MILO. You must be the Princesses. We've come to rescue you.

HUMBUG. And the demons are close behind!

TOCK. We should leave right away.

Literary Analysis
Stage Directions
Without these stage directions, would you be able to picture the action here? Explain.

**Reading Check**

What happens to Senses Taker when Milo drops the Package of Laughter?

PRINCESSES. We're ready anytime you are.

MILO. Good, now if you'll just come out. But wait a minute— there's no door! How can we rescue you from the Castle-in-the-Air if there's no way to get in or out?

HUMBUG. Hurry, Milo! They're gaining on us.

REASON. Take your time, Milo, and think about it.

MILO. Ummm, all right . . . just give me a second or two. [*He thinks hard.*]

HUMBUG. I think I feel sick.

MILO. I've got it! Where's that package of presents? [*Opens the package of letters.*] Ah, here it is. [*Takes out the letters and sticks them on the door, spelling:*] E-N-T-R-A-N-C-E. Entrance. Now, let's see. [*Rummages through and spells in smaller letters:*] P-u-s-h. Push. [*He pushes and a door opens. The* PRINCESSES *come out of the castle. Slowly, the demons ascend the stairway.*]

HUMBUG. Oh, it's too late. They're coming up and there's no other way down!

MILO. Unless . . . [*Looks at* TOCK.] Well . . . Time flies, doesn't it?

TOCK. Quite often. Hold on, everyone, and I'll take you down.

HUMBUG. Can you carry us all?

TOCK. We'll soon find out. Ready or not, here we go! [*His alarm begins to ring. They jump off the platform and disappear. The demons, howling with rage, reach the top and find no one there. They see the* PRINCESSES *and the heroes running across the stage and bound down the stairs after them and into the audience. There is a mad chase scene until they reach the stage again.*]

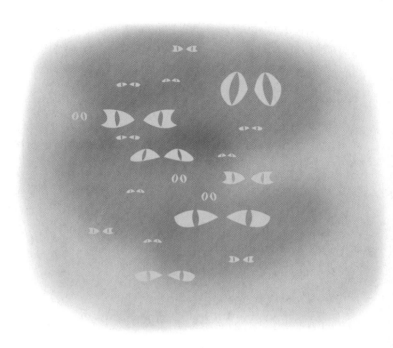

Reading Skill
Compare and Contrast Based on Milo's actions here, how has he changed since leaving his bedroom?

HUMBUG. I'm exhausted! I can't run another step.

MILO. We can't stop now . . .

TOCK. Milo! Look out there! [*The armies of* AZAZ *and* MATHE-MAGICIAN *appear at the back of the theater, with the Kings at their heads.*]

AZAZ. [*As they march toward the stage.*] Don't worry, Milo, we'll take over now.

MATHEMAGICIAN. Those demons may not know it, but their days are numbered!

SPELLING BEE. Charge! C-H-A-R-G-E! Charge! [*They rush at the demons and battle until the demons run off howling. Everyone cheers. The* FIVE MINISTERS OF AZAZ *appear and shake* MILO's *hand.*]

MINISTER 1. Well done.

MINISTER 2. Fine job.

MINISTER 3. Good work!

MINISTER 4. Congratulations!

MINISTER 5. CHEERS! [*Everyone cheers again. A fanfare interrupts. A* PAGE *steps forward and reads from a large scroll:*]

PAGE. *Henceforth, and forthwith,*
Let it be known by one and all,
That Rhyme and Reason
Reign once more in Wisdom.

[*The* PRINCESSES *bow gratefully and kiss their brothers, the Kings.*]

And furthermore,
The boy named Milo,
The dog known as Tock,
And the insect hereinafter referred to as the Humbug
Are hereby declared to be Heroes of the Realm.

[*All bow and salute the heroes.*]

MILO. But we never could have done it without a lot of help.

REASON. That may be true, but you had the courage to try, and what you can do is often a matter of what you *will* do.

Literary Analysis
Stage Directions
How do these stage directions help you know what the characters are feeling?

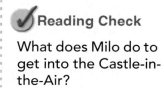

Reading Check

What does Milo do to get into the Castle-in-the-Air?

AZAZ. That's why there was one very important thing about your quest we couldn't discuss until you returned.

MILO. I remember. What was it?

AZAZ. Very simple. It was impossible!

MATHEMAGICIAN. *Completely* impossible!

HUMBUG. Do you mean . . . ? [*Feeling faint.*] Oh . . . I think I need to sit down.

AZAZ. Yes, indeed, but if we'd told you then, you might not have gone.

MATHEMAGICIAN. And, as you discovered, many things are possible just as long as you don't know they're impossible.

MILO. I think I understand.

RHYME. I'm afraid it's time to go now.

REASON. And you must say goodbye.

MILO. To everyone? [*Looks around at the crowd. To* TOCK *and* HUMBUG.] Can't you two come with me?

HUMBUG. I'm afraid not, old man. I'd like to, but I've arranged for a lecture tour which will keep me occupied for years.

TOCK. And they do need a watchdog here.

MILO. Well, O.K., then. [MILO *hugs the* HUMBUG.]

HUMBUG. [*Sadly.*] Oh, bah.

MILO. [*He hugs* TOCK, *and then faces everyone.*] Well, good-bye. We all spent so much time together, I know I'm going to miss you. [*To the* PRINCESSES.] I guess we would have reached you a lot sooner if I hadn't made so many mistakes.

REASON. You must never feel badly about making mistakes, Milo, as long as you take the trouble to learn from them. Very often you learn more by being wrong for the right reasons than you do by being right for the wrong ones.

MILO. But there's so much to learn.

RHYME. That's true, but it's not just learning that's important. It's learning what to do with what you learn and learning why you learn things that matters.

Reading Skill
Compare and Contrast Do you think there are real-life situations in which Mathemagician's statement might hold true? Explain.

Reading Skill
Compare and Contrast Which piece of advice—Reason's or Rhyme's—do you agree with more? Explain.

MILO. I think I know what you mean, Princess. At least, I hope I do. [*The car is rolled forward and* MILO *climbs in.*] Goodbye! Goodbye! I'll be back someday! I will! Anyway, I'll try. [*As* MILO *drives the set of the Land of Ignorance begins to move offstage.*]

AZAZ. Goodbye! Always remember. Words! Words! Words!

MATHEMAGICIAN. And numbers!

AZAZ. Now, don't tell me you think numbers are as important as words?

MATHEMAGICIAN. Is that so? Why I'll have you know . . . [*The set disappears, and* MILO*'s Room is seen onstage.*]

MILO. [*As he drives on.*] Oh, oh, I hope they don't start all over again. Because I don't think I'll have much time in the near future to help them out. [*The sound of loud ticking is heard.* MILO *finds himself in his room. He gets out of the car and looks around.*]

THE CLOCK. Did someone mention time?

MILO. Boy, I must have been gone for an awful long time. I wonder what time it is. [*Looks at clock.*] Five o'clock. I wonder what day it is. [*Looks at calendar.*] It's still today! I've only been gone for an hour! [*He continues to look at his calendar, and then begins to look at his books and toys and maps and chemistry set with great interest.*]

CLOCK. An hour. Sixty minutes. How long it really lasts depends on what you do with it. For some people, an hour seems to last forever. For others, just a moment, and so full of things to do.

MILO. [*Looks at clock.*] Six o'clock already?

CLOCK. In an instant. In a trice. Before you have time to blink. [*The stage goes black in less than no time at all.*]

Literary Analysis
Stage Directions
Based on these stage directions, how do you think Milo now feels about time?

Apply the Skills

The Phantom Tollbooth, **Act II**

Thinking About the Selection

1. **(a) Respond:** Of all the senses that the Senses Taker wants to steal, which do you think is most important? Why?
   (b) Discuss: Share your response with a partner. Discuss how someone else's response did or did not change your ideas.

2. **(a) Recall:** What does the Terrible Trivium want Milo, Tock, and Humbug to do? **(b) Deduce:** What will be the result if they follow his directions? **(c) Interpret:** What lesson does Milo learn through his experience with the Terrible Trivium?

3. **(a) Recall:** How is the Senses Taker's spell broken?
   (b) Draw Conclusions: What does Milo learn about humor from his encounter with the Senses Taker?

4. **Evaluate:** Do you agree that the speed of time depends on what you are doing? Support your answer.

Reading Skill

Create three Venn diagrams like the one shown. Then use details from Act II to **compare** and **contrast** these characters:

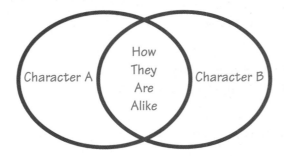

5. Rhyme and Reason
6. Senses Taker and Terrible Trivium
7. Humbug and Tock

Literary Analysis

8. **(a)** Describe one place in the play where **stage directions** are necessary for understanding the events. **(b)** Find one place in the play that has no stage directions. Using your imagination, write your own stage directions for that scene.

QuickReview

Act II at a Glance
In his attempt to rescue Rhyme and Reason, Milo learns important lessons about using time wisely, believing in himself, and thinking carefully.

For: Self-test
Visit: www.PHSchool.com
Web Code: ela-6504

Compare: show how two or more things are alike

Contrast: show how two or more things are different

Stage Directions: words in a drama that tell performers how to move and speak, and help readers picture the action, sounds, and scenery

Vocabulary Builder

Practice Write a sentence for each prompt. Use a vocabulary word from page 704 in each sentence.

1. a necktie that looks red or blue from different angles
2. the sounds that two yowling cats make
3. the correct answer to a word problem in math class
4. a look that a baby sitter might give a rude child
5. the act of spreading unkind gossip
6. a person's lack of enough vitamin C

Writing

Imagine you are a drama critic, and write a **review** of *The Phantom Tollbooth*. Review Act I and Act II. Note parts you enjoyed and parts you did not enjoy. Note characters you liked the most and least. Begin by writing your overall opinion of the play. Then, use your notes to support your opinion.

For *Grammar, Vocabulary,* and *Assessment,* see **Build Language Skills,** pages 736–737.

Extend Your Learning

Listening and Speaking With a group, hold a **debate** on this statement: *Numbers are more important and more fun than words.* Divide into two teams, one speaking for numbers and one speaking for words. Plan with your team how you will express your ideas and opinions. Support and prove your points with examples from the play and from your own knowledge and experiences.

Research and Technology Use reference materials to research and prepare a **math report** on the concept of infinity and what scientists believe to be the largest and smallest numbers. Display your findings in a chart, a diagram, or another useful graphic device. Prepare a written summary to accompany your visual.

Build Language Skills

Vocabulary Skill

Borrowed and Foreign Words Words that are "**borrowed**" from other languages often reflect cultural influences. For example, when Italian immigrants introduced an unusual pie with tomato sauce and cheese to the English-speaking world, they also introduced its name, *pizza*. The chart shows some of the cultural influences reflected in words borrowed from other languages.

French and Italian	Spanish	Native American
European culture, fashion, art, and food: *ballet, violin, pizza*	American Southwest, landscape, lifestyle: *ranch, tornado, balcony*	North American wildlife and culture: *maize, moccasin, raccoon*

Practice Explain which language you think each word is borrowed from. Then, check your answers in a dictionary.

1. fiesta   **2.** quiche   **3.** violin   **4.** pane   **5.** rodeo   **6.** piano

Grammar Lesson

Gerund and Gerund Phrases A gerund is a verb form that ends in *-ing* and is used as a noun. A gerund phrase is a group of words containing a gerund and any modifiers or other words that relate to it.

Gerund	*Singing* is fun. I enjoy *reading*.
Gerund Phrase	*Singing that song* was fun.
	I enjoy *reading about horses*.

Practice Create a gerund by adding *-ing* to each verb below. Then, write a sentence that includes a gerund phrase.

▶ **Example:** hike   *hiking*   They enjoyed *hiking in the woods*.

1. cook   **2.** make   **3.** answer   **4.** dance   **5.** send

MorePractice

For more practice with gerunds, see the Grammar Handbook, p. R36.

W͞G Prentice Hall Writing and Grammar Handbook.

Directions: *Read the selections. Then, answer the questions.*

Selection 1
Light from the Andromeda Galaxy has traveled for about 3 million years before reaching Earth. The light you see began its journey 3 million years ago.

Selection 2
Looking up, thousands of distant stars dance like fairies in the night sky. These tiny pinpoints of light twinkle happily along, not caring what is happening in our world.

1. Which would be the best visual to help you understand Selection 1?
   A a diagram
   B a chart
   C a flowchart
   D a drawing

2. How are the selections similar?
   A Both deal with the Andromeda Galaxy.
   B Both are factual.
   C Both deal with light from stars.
   D Both give technical information.

3. What does the first selection contain that the second selection does not?
   A a sensory impression of the star's light
   B a statement of how long the light traveled before reaching Earth
   C an explanation of how light travels through space
   D a description of how light appears to a person on Earth

Timed Writing: Explanation [Connections]

The Mathemagician says, "Many things are possible just as long as you don't know they're impossible." State whether you agree or disagree with him, and explain your answer. Use examples from the play and everyday life to support your view.
(30 minutes)

 Writing Workshop: *Work in Progress*

Cause-and-Effect Essay
For a cause-and-effect essay you may write, list five events from history. Write one cause, or reason, why each event occurred. Save this History List in your writing portfolio.

Reading: Compare and Contrast

Directions: *Questions 1–5 are based on the following selection.*

In the play *Two Brothers,* the title characters can be compared and contrasted in important ways. Frank is a good individual who helps other people in his community, even when it means making personal sacrifices to do so. His brother Hank, on the other hand, is willing to cheat and lie in order to make his business succeed, and his practices harm others in town. Both brothers are serious, hard workers, and each admired the other as a child. Yet as adults, they have chosen different paths and goals in life. Frank speaks gently, while Hank speaks roughly. Hank's ultimate downfall and unexpected death contrast sharply with Frank's long life and popularity.

1. **How does the author treat the title characters?**
   A She only compares them.
   B She only contrasts them.
   C She compares and contrasts them.
   D She doesn't compare or contrast them.

2. **In what way are the brothers alike?**
   A They are both honest.
   B They are both hard-working.
   C They both die unexpectedly.
   D They both live a long life.

3. **What is one characteristic the author contrasts?**
   A the brothers' childhoods
   B the brothers' manner of speech
   C the brothers' looks
   D She contrasts nothing.

4. **What is one characteristic the author compares?**
   A the childhood admiration of the brothers
   B the goodness of the brothers
   C the ultimate outcome for the brothers
   D She compares nothing.

5. **Which word best completes the Venn diagram?**
   A hard-working
   B gentle
   C successful
   D rough

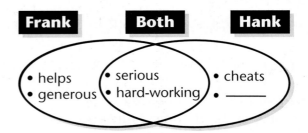

Assessment Practice

Directions *Choose the word that best completes each of the following sentences.*

6. **It is easy to _____ an elephant and an ant based on their looks.**
   A unique   **C** contrast
   B compare   **D** characteristic

7. **The way a person speaks can be a very revealing _____.**
   A unique   **C** compare
   B characteristic   **D** contrast

8. **Each main event in a play is an important _____ to be analyzed.**
   A compare
   B contrast
   C unique
   D element

9. **The character's _____ quality was not found in any other character in the story.**
   A compare   **C** unique
   B element   **D** characteristic

10. **You can _____ two events to show how they are alike.**
    A unique   **C** contrast
    B element   **D** compare

Directions *Answer the following questions based on the dictionary entry below.*

> **sombrero** *n.* [from Spanish *sombra*, shade] a hat with large brim worn in Mexico and the Southwest.

11. **From what foreign language does the word *sombrero* come?**
    A French   **C** Italian
    B Spanish   **D** Native American

12. **From what foreign word does the English word come?**
    A sombra   **C** hat
    B shade   **D** Mexico

13. **Where would you most likely see a sombrero?**
    A France   **C** Italy
    B Mexico   **D** Russia

Reading and Vocabulary Skills Review ■ 739

Syllables With No Sound Clues

All words contain one or more **syllables**—word parts that are pronounced as separate sounds. In multi-syllable words, an unstressed syllable vowel sound is pronounced as a schwa—an open neutral sound like the one you hear at the beginning of *ago.*

Sounds Like "Uh" to Me Particular letter combinations are used to spell most long and short vowel sounds. The schwa sound, however, can be spelled with almost any of the vowels. In a dictionary pronunciation, the schwa sound is represented with the symbol ə.

DICTIONARY SPELLING DEPARTMENT

a   i   e

An uh sound . . . hmm . . . make it an e this time

Practice Each word from the list is broken into syllables, but the syllables are out of order. Rearrange the syllables to spell each word correctly. Underline the unstressed syllable that contains the schwa sound.

1. ra cou geous
2. i cab net
3. gize a pol o
4. pi hos tal
5. ble la syl
6. po op site
7. rate sep a
8. en cal dar
9. gas o line
10. ve lope en

Word List
opposite
separate
cabinet
envelope
apologize
calendar
hospital
gasoline
courageous
syllable

Monitor Your Progress

Assessment Practice

A. Directions: *Write the letter of the sentence in which the underlined word is spelled correctly.*

1. **A** The two tickets came in the same <u>envalope</u>.
   B We put them in the <u>cabenet</u>.
   C Unfortunately, we put them in <u>seperate</u> drawers.
   D It's not <u>surprising</u> that we could find only one of them.

2. **A** The company developed a new and improved <u>tracter</u>.
   B It doesn't use a lot of <u>gasoline</u>.
   C This year, it pictured the new equipment on a <u>calender</u>.
   D Dad cut out the picture and hung it in the <u>gerage</u>.

3. **A** For every statement you made, I think the <u>opposite</u> is true.
   B This is not <u>suprising</u>, because we belong to different political parties.
   C I want to <u>apoligize</u> for criticizing you.
   D People are entitled to have <u>separite</u> and different opinions.

4. **A** Mr. Toomey has a <u>cabanet</u> filled with old nuts, bolts, and wires.
   B He keeps it in the back of his <u>cabinet</u>.
   C If he needs to repair his <u>tractir</u>, he has the parts he needs.
   D His <u>slogin</u> is "Waste not, want not."

B. Directions: *Write the letter of the word that is spelled correctly.*

1. Circle the date on your _____.
   A calendar
   B calender
   C calandar
   D calendir

2. You should _____ to your sister.
   A apoligize
   B epologize
   C apologize
   D apolojize

3. The book was sent in a padded _____.
   A envelop
   B anvelope
   C envalope
   D envelope

4. They live at _____ ends of the street.
   A opposite
   B oppisite
   C apposite
   D opposit

5. The hero was _____.
   A courageous
   B coragous
   C curageous
   D coregous

6. The socks are kept _____ from the shirts.
   A separate
   B seperate
   C separite
   D seperite

Exposition: Cause-and-Effect Essay

Almost anything that happens—from simple daily events to those that impact people worldwide—involves causes and effects. A **cause-and-effect essay** is a brief piece of expository writing that explains the reasons for something happening or the results of an event. Follow the steps outlined in this workshop to write your own cause-and-effect essay.

Assignment Write a cause-and-effect essay to explain the reasons leading to an event or situation and the results of the event or situation.

What to Include An effective cause-and-effect essay features the following elements:
- a thesis about the causes and effects of a situation
- facts and details that support the thesis statement
- an organizational pattern that emphasizes the cause-and-effect relationships
- transitions that make connections between ideas
- error-free writing, including a variety of sentence patterns

To preview the criteria on which your cause-and-effect essay may be judged, see the rubric on page 749.

 Writing Workshop: *Work in Progress*

If you have completed the Work-in-Progress assignments, you have in your portfolio several ideas you might want to use in your cause-and-effect essay. Continue developing these ideas, or explore a new idea as you complete the Writing Workshop.

Using the Form
You may use elements of this form in these types of writing:
- history, social studies, or geography reports
- scientific lab reports
- news reports

To get the feel for cause-and-effect writing, read "36 Beached Whales Die in St. Martin" on page 811.

Prewriting

Choosing Your Topic

To choose a topic for your essay, use the following strategies:

- **Brainstorming** In a group, discuss possible topics. You may wish to begin with a general idea such as "historical events" or a fill-in-the-blank exercise such as "What causes _____?" Review the results and choose an idea from the list as your topic.

- **Browsing** Look through the newspaper or a favorite magazine for topics that interest you. Circle key words or ideas and consider their causes or effects. Choose a topic based on what you find.

Narrowing Your Topic

Use a topic web. Create a topic web like the one shown here to help you evaluate and narrow your topic. First, write your topic inside a circle. Then, write connected ideas—subtopics—inside new circles around your topic. Label each idea "cause" or "effect." When you have finished, review your completed web. To narrow your topic, focus on a single one of your subtopics.

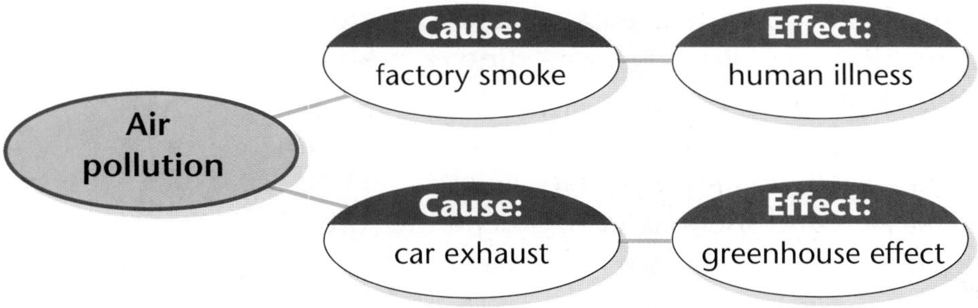

Work in Progress
Review the work you did on p. 737.

Gathering Details

Using a T-chart in research. To find facts and examples to explain the cause-and-effect relationship, you may need to conduct research. Use a T-chart to organize your ideas.

Drafting

Shaping Your Writing

Organize details. You may have identified a single cause and a single effect, or multiple causes for a single effect. This chart shows an example of a single cause with several effects. Select an organization for your essay from the following two common patterns.

- **Many Causes/Single Effect** If a number of unrelated events leads to a single result, focus one paragraph on each cause.

- **Single Cause/Many Effects** If one cause produces several effects, focus one paragraph on each effect.

Focus your writing with a strong thesis statement. Consider the cause-and-effect relationship you will discuss. Using your notes, craft one sentence that states your main idea.

Single Cause
You cleaned up your room.

Effect: You found the book you were looking for.

Effect: There's more room on your desk.

Effect: Your mother let you go out with your friends.

➤ **Example:** If the city builds a new sports stadium, local businesses will get the benefit of increased sales.

Providing Elaboration

Include enough information to build a link. Make sure that your sentences show the readers exactly how the events or situations are linked in cause-and-effect relationships. Provide supporting details that let you be precise rather than vague.

Vague: If your skin is damaged, you are at risk for illness.
Clear: If you are fair-skinned and spend a lot of time in the sun without wearing sunscreen, you are more likely to get skin cancer.

Connect with transitions. To show your readers the ideas you discuss, choose transitional words and phrases that make cause-and-effect relationships clear.

To show a cause: *Because* of the flood, many homes were damaged.
To show an effect: *As a result*, people will have to rebuild.

From the Author's Desk

Joseph Bruchac

Joseph Bruchac
On Showing Causes and Effects

This selection is from "Gluskabe and Dzidziz," my telling of a traditional Abenaki Indian tale. Gluskabe, a powerful hero, has just said that he can defeat anyone. But Dzidziz, the baby, turns out to be more than his match. By foolishly taking the baby's toy, Gluskabe causes several effects, including his own surrender. Cause-and-effect situations like this occur often in traditional tales, showing how our actions may have good—or bad—results.

"I'm a good writer but a great rewriter."

——Joseph Bruchac

Professional Model:
from *"Gluskabe and Dzidziz"*

Gluskabe bent closer. "Is that what gives you your power?" he said. ~~He decided to take it from the baby.~~ "Then I will take it from you." He ~~reached down and~~ pulled the leather turtle from the baby's hands. As soon as he did so the baby began to cry and scream. Gluskabe had never heard such a sound before. He ~~truly~~ thought it would break his ears and ~~so~~ he covered them with his hands.

~~Gluskabe told the baby to be silent.~~ "Be silent!" Gluskabe shouted, but Dzidziz did not stop screaming. Then Gluskabe tried singing to the baby. He sang a song ~~that was~~ powerful enough to calm the strong winds and quiet the most powerful storm. All around ˄the Place of White Stone the winds stopped blowing and the waters became calm. But within the wigwam Dzidziz still screamed.

"You have won," Gluskabe shouted. "Here." He gave the leather turtle back to the baby. But Dzidziz was not yet ready to stop crying. . . .

I shorten as I revise. Taking out unnecessary words makes the causes and effects stand out more clearly.

I turned some narrative into dialogue. Characters talking for themselves seem more real than those just talked about.

I added "the Place of White Stone" to give a better sense of place.

In my first draft, I only called Dzidziz "the baby." In my revision, I introduced the Abenaki word for baby, "Dzidziz." This makes it feel more like an Abenaki Indian story.

Writing Workshop

Revising

Revising Your Overall Structure

Test for logical organization. Examine the connections between your paragraphs. Follow these steps to be sure the topic sentences or main ideas in each paragraph support the thesis of your essay.

1. Highlight the topic sentence of each paragraph.
2. Read the topic sentences in the order in which they appear.
3. Label each connection to the topic as *cause* or *effect*.
4. Reorder sentences or paragraphs for clarity.

Reading → Writing Connection

To read the complete student model, see page 748.

Student Model: Checking Topic Sentences

<u>Cause</u> What you do to your skin as a child and as a young adult will affect your skin for your full life. . . . Doctors recommend that children apply sunscreen often. . . .

<u>Effect</u> Nobody's skin is immune to skin cancer. If your skin is damaged a lot by the sun during your childhood and adult years, your chances of getting skin cancer are greater. . . .

> These highlights show the order is logical—first presenting a cause, and then an effect.

Revising Your Sentences

Confirm the link. Be careful that your essay describes events that are connected by cause and effect, not just one event that happened after another.

Chronology:	We finished the test and the dismissal bell rang.
Cause and Effect:	When I finished the test, I turned in my paper.

Peer Review: Share your essay with a partner. Ask your reader to tell you whether all of your cause-and-effect relationships are accurate, logical, and clearly explained.

Confirm accuracy. Take another look at your research. Compare your notes against your draft to ensure that your writing correctly reflects the facts.

Integrating Grammar Skills

Combining Sentences for Variety

To add variety to your sentence patterns, include prepositional phrases, participial phrases, or gerund phrases.

Prentice Hall Writing and Grammar Connection: Chapter 21, Section 2

Type of Phrase	Its Use	Example
Prepositional phrase	• as an adjective • as an adverb	The boy **in the red jacket** is my brother. The book fell **off the table**.
Participial phrase	• as an adjective	**Nodding his head**, Jim agreed.
Gerund phrase	• as a noun	I enjoy **playing the guitar**.

Combining Short Sentences These examples show how to use phrases to pack information into your sentences.

• **Using a Prepositional Phrase**

Separate: The bus moved slowly. The road was wet.
Combined: The bus moved slowly *along the wet road.*

• **Using a Participial Phrase**

Separate: We enjoyed the show. We applauded wildly.
Combined: *Enjoying the show,* we applauded wildly.

• **Using a Gerund Phrase**

Separate: Don't order beef. It would be a mistake.
Combined: *Ordering beef* would be a mistake.

Fixing Choppy Sentences To improve a pattern of short sentences, follow these steps:

1. **Look for the relationship among ideas.** For example, one sentence might extend the idea of the other.
2. **Combine sentences to stress the connection among ideas.** Use prepositional, participial, or gerund phrases for variety.

Apply It to Your Editing

Read your essay looking for pairs of short, related sentences. Using the examples as a guide, combine some for variety.

Writing Workshop

Student Model: Bryson McCollum
Cumming, Georgia

Don't Get Burned

Sunscreen should always be worn when you are out in the sun because the sun can be very dangerous to your skin. If your skin is exposed to the sun's ultraviolet rays without sunscreen, it will turn red, burn, and hurt. Many people believe that burning their skin is one step closer to their desire of getting a tan. They do not realize that both burning and tanning your skin can damage it. Once you burn or tan and the redness or color begins to fade, the damaged skin may begin to peel, leaving a new, unhealthy, thin, and sensitive layer of skin.

What you do to your skin as a child and as a young adult will affect your skin for your full life. Sunscreen can help. Doctors recommend that children apply sunscreen often and at least 30 minutes before going out in the sun. Adults, children, and young adults will benefit from using sunscreens with sun protection factor (SPF) numbers 15 or more. The SPF numbers give some idea of how long you can stay out in the sun without burning. For example, an SPF of 15 should protect you for approximately 150 minutes—nearly two and a half hours—in the sun. While some sunscreens say they are waterproof, they do not give you total protection from water and sweat. As a result, it is also recommended that sunscreen be applied often.

Nobody's skin is immune to skin cancer. If your skin is damaged a lot by the sun during your childhood and adult years, your chances of getting skin cancer are greater than they are for people who have taken better steps toward protection. Some signs of skin cancer are leathery scab-like patches of skin that may be discolored, bleed, or burn. If you have been burned several times in a short period of time, you should be checked by a doctor because some forms of skin cancer cannot be detected.

So, think twice the next time you are at the beach or the pool without sunscreen, hoping to absorb the sun. Be careful and apply sunscreen to protect yourself from skin damage. Remember that even though a tan may look nice for a few days, it may cause you health problems and unhealthy-looking skin in the future.

Bryson begins by stating his thesis, the cause-and-effect relationship he will show.

Details about the sun's ability to damage the skin help support the writer's purpose.

The writer uses examples to make doctors' recommendations clear.

Each paragraph focuses on a cause or an effect related to Bryson's thesis.

Editing and Proofreading

Review your draft to fix errors.
Focus on Verb Tenses: Review your draft to be sure you have

written in a consistent verb tense—for example, using only the past tense (*I was*) or the present tense (*I am*). If you find a change in tense that you cannot justify, make the tense consistent with the rest of your draft.

Publishing and Presenting

Consider one of the following ways to share your writing:
Make a movie proposal. Treat your cause-and-effect essay like a script for a short film. Create a storyboard that shows the images that you would choose.
Make an oral presentation. Read your essay aloud to classmates or family members. Then invite questions and discussion.

Reflecting on Your Writing

Writer's Journal Jot down your thoughts on writing a cause-and-effect essay. Begin by answering these questions:
- Which strategies did you find particularly helpful for choosing a topic? Why?
- How do you view your topic differently now that you have analyzed its related causes and effects?

> *Prentice Hall Writing and Grammar: Chapter 9*

Rubric for Self-Assessment

To assess your cause-and-effect essay, use the following rubric:

Criteria	Rating Scale *not very* ... *very*				
Focus: How clearly is your thesis on cause and effect stated?	1	2	3	4	5
Organization: How effective is your organization?	1	2	3	4	5
Support/Elaboration: How convincing are the facts and details used for support?	1	2	3	4	5
Style: How well are transitions used to connect ideas?	1	2	3	4	5
Conventions: How correct is your use of grammar, especially your use of phrases?	1	2	3	4	5

Identifying Tone, Mood, and Emotion

Understanding oral communication involves being able to identify the speaker's tone, mood, and emotion.

- **Tone:** the speaker's attitude toward the subject
- **Mood:** the overall feeling of the presentation
- **Emotion:** the speaker's feelings

Using Verbal Clues

The words people choose are the spoken indications of tone, mood, and emotion.

Listen to tone of voice. In an oral presentation, a speaker conveys his or her attitude through tone of voice as well as through words. A serious speaker might speak slowly in a quiet voice. A speaker who is enthusiastically trying to persuade you might use a high-pitched voice and talk faster than in normal speech.

Consider content. The mood of a presentation is often a result of *what* is said in addition to *how* it is said. The feeling the audience gets from a presentation will be influenced by the subject.

Notice word choice. The specific words a speaker uses can indicate attitude and emotion. The intensity of a word is a clue to the speaker's emotion. The associations of a word can indicate attitude. Speakers also choose formal or informal language based on their audience and purpose.

Using Nonverbal Clues

Motion. A speaker who moves with energy and purpose creates a positive response toward his or her subject. Watch how a speaker stands, gestures, and leans to get a sense of the feelings they have and the feelings they want listeners to have.

Expression. Facial expressions are clues to emotions. Smiles and frowns are meant to communicate feelings. Watch expressions to connect the speaker's feelings with the words being spoken.

Checklist for Tone/ Mood/Emotion

Tone of voice
____ Energetic
____ Flat
____ Serious

Word Choice
____ intensity
____ positive words
____ negative words

Motion
____ Energetic
____ Static

Expression
____ Engaged
____ Intense
____ Bland

Activity › *Evaluating a Speech* › Watch a news interview program in which one or two people speak for at least five minutes. Keep a chart like the one shown to record verbal and nonverbal clues to the speakers' tone, mood, and emotion.

The War of the Worlds

H. G. Wells

Pacemaker Classics, 1993

Novel In 1877, an Italian astronomer reported seeing channels on Mars. The word *channels* was poorly translated into English as *canals.* As a result, many people thought that the astronomer had discovered water on Mars. This mistake made people wonder whether there was life on Mars. Inspired by this possibility, in 1898, H. G. Wells wrote *The War of the Worlds,* which was one of the first science-fiction novels to describe a Martian invasion of Earth. Although he was writing more than a hundred years ago, Wells had an amazing ability to predict the future. Many of the inventions he described later became reality.

Nerdlandia

Gary Soto

PaperStar, 1999

Drama In this play, Martin is a Chicano nerd who is in love with Ceci, the coolest girl in school. Ceci, in turn, has developed her own secret crush on this geeky guy. Helped by their bumbling but well-meaning friends, both Martin and Ceci transform themselves in the name of love; Martin becomes cool and Ceci becomes a nerdish beauty.

Eagle Song

Joseph Bruchac

Puffin, 1997

Novel Danny Bigtree's family has moved to New York City, and no matter how hard he tries, Danny cannot seem to fit in. He is homesick for the Mohawk reservation where he used to live. The kids in his class call him "Chief" and tease him about being an Indian. This bothers him until he learns a valuable lesson about pride, bravery, and Native American culture from his father.

Short Dramas and Teleplays

Prentice Hall Literature Library

Prentice Hall, 2000

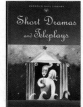

Anthology This collection of scenes and one-act plays opens the door to classic and contemporary drama. Well-known stories such as **"The Prince and the Pauper"** come to life on the page. Whether for performing or reading, this drama collection has something for everyone.

These titles are available in the Penguin/Prentice Hall Literature Library.
Consult your teacher before choosing one.

Think About It *You're a Good Man, Charlie Brown* is a musical based on Charles Schulz's popular comic strip *Peanuts*. The show is about events in the lives of Schulz's lovable characters. The musical first opened in New York in 1967, and a production toured the country until 1971. In 1999 the show had a successful Broadway revival, winning two Tony Awards. The following scene features Lucy, Schroeder, Linus, Patty, Snoopy, and everyone's favorite underdog—Charlie Brown.

from You're a Good Man, Charlie Brown

Clark Gesner

Based on the comic strip *Peanuts* by Charles M. Schulz

SCHROEDER. I'm sorry to have to say it right to your face, Lucy, but it's true. You're a very crabby person. I know your crabbiness has probably become so natural to you now that you're not even aware when you're being crabby, but it's true just the same. You're a very crabby person and you're crabby to just about everyone you meet. (LUCY *remains silent—just barely*) Now I hope you don't mind my saying this, Lucy, and I hope you'll take it in the spirit that it's meant. I think we should all be open to any opportunity to learn more about ourselves. I think Socrates was very right when he said that one of the first rules for anyone in life is "Know thyself." (LUCY *has begun whistling quietly to herself*) Well, I guess I've said about enough. I hope I haven't offended you or anything. (*He makes an awkward exit*)

LUCY. (*Sits in silence, then shouts offstage* at Schroeder) Well, what's Socrates got to do with it anyway, huh? Who was *he* anyway? Did he ever get to be king, huh! Answer me that, did he ever get to be king! (*Suddenly to herself, a real question*) *Did* he ever get to be king? (*She shouts offstage, now a question*) Who was Socrates, anyway? (*She gives up the rampage and plunks herself down*) "Know thyself," hmph. (*She thinks a moment, then makes a silent resolution to herself, exits and quickly returns with a clipboard and pencil.* CHARLIE BROWN *and* SNOOPY *have entered, still with baseball equipment*)

CHARLIE BROWN. Hey, Snoopy, you want to help me get my arm back in shape? Watch out for this one, it's a new fastball.

LUCY. Excuse me a moment, Charlie Brown, but I was wondering if you'd mind answering a few questions.

CHARLIE BROWN. Not at all, Lucy. What kind of questions are they?

LUCY. Well, I'm conducting a survey to enable me to know myself better, and first of all I'd like to ask: on a scale of zero to one hundred, using a standard of fifty as average, seventy-five as above average and ninety as exceptional, where would you rate me with regards to crabbiness?

CHARLIE BROWN. (*Stands in silence for a moment, hesitating*) Well, Lucy, I . . .

LUCY. Your ballots need not be signed and all answers will be held in strictest confidence.

CHARLIE BROWN. Well still, Lucy, that's a very hard question to answer.

LUCY. You may have a few moments to think it over if you want, or we can come back to that question later.

CHARLIE BROWN. I think I'd like to come back to it, if you don't mind.

> You're a very crabby person and you're crabby to just about everyone you meet.

LUCY. Certainly. This next question deals with certain character traits you may have observed. Regarding personality, would you say that mine is *A* forceful, *B* pleasing, or *C* objectionable? Would that be *A, B,* or *C*? What would your answer be to that, Charlie Brown, forceful, pleasing or objectionable, which one would you say, hmm? Charlie Brown, hmm?

CHARLIE BROWN. Well, I guess I'd have to say forceful, Lucy, but . . .

LUCY. "Forceful." Well, we'll make a check mark at the letter *A* then. Now, would you rate my ability to get along with other people as poor, fair, good or excellent?

CHARLIE BROWN. I think that depends a lot on what you mean by "get along with other people."

LUCY. You know, make friends, sparkle in a crowd, that sort of thing.

CHARLIE BROWN. Do you have a place for abstention?

LUCY. Certainly, I'll just put a check mark at "None of the above." The next question deals with physical appearance. In referring to my beauty, would you say that I was "stunning," "mysterious," or "intoxicating"?

CHARLIE BROWN. (*Squirming*) Well, gee, I don't know, Lucy. You look just fine to me.

LUCY. (*Making a check on the page*) "Stunning." All right, Charlie Brown, I think we should get back to that first question. On a scale of zero to one hundred, using a standard of fifty as average, seventy-five as . . .

CHARLIE BROWN. (*Loud interruption*) I . . . (*quieter*) . . . remember the question, Lucy.

LUCY. Well?

CHARLIE BROWN. (*Tentatively*) Fifty-one?

LUCY. (*Noting it down*) Fifty-one is your crabbiness rating for me. Very well then, that about does it. Thank you very much for helping with this survey, Charlie Brown. Your cooperation has been greatly appreciated. (*She shakes hands with* CHARLIE BROWN)

CHARLIE BROWN. (*Flustered*) It was a pleasure, Lucy, any time. Come on, Snoopy.

In referring to my beauty, would you say that I was "stunning," "mysterious," or "intoxicating"?

LUCY. Oh, just a minute, there is one more question. Would you answer "Yes" or "No" to the question: "Is Lucy Van Pelt the sort of person that you would like to have as president of your club or civic organization?"

CHARLIE BROWN. Oh, yes, by all means, Lucy.

LUCY. (*Making note*) Yes. Well, thank you very much. That about does it, I think. (CHARLIE BROWN exits, *but* SNOOPY *pauses, turns, and strikes a dramatic "thumbs down" pose to* LUCY) WELL, WHO ASKED YOU! (SNOOPY *makes a hasty exit.* LUCY *stands center stage, figuring to herself on the clipboard and mumbling*) Now let's see. That's a fifty-one, "None of the above," and . . . (*She looks up*) Schroeder was right. I can already feel myself being filled with the glow of self-awareness. (PATTY *enters. She is heading for the other side of the stage, when* LUCY *stops her*) Oh, Patty, I'm conducting a survey and I wonder if . . .

PATTY. A hundred and ten, C, "Poor," "None of the above," "No," and what are you going to do about the dent you made in my bicycle! (PATTY *storms off.* LUCY *watches her go, then looks at the audience*)

LUCY. It's amazing how fast word of these surveys gets around. (LINUS *wanders in and plunks himself down in front of the TV.* LUCY *crosses to him, still figuring*)

LUCY. Oh, Linus, I'm glad you're here. I'm conducting a survey and there are a few questions I'd like to ask you.

LINUS. Sure, go ahead.

LUCY. The first question is: on a scale of zero to one hundred, with a standard of fifty as average, seventy-five as above average and ninety as exceptional, where would you rate me with regards to crabbiness?

LINUS. (*Slowly turns his head to look at her, then turns back to the TV*) You're my big sister.

LUCY. That's not the question.

LINUS. No, but that's the answer.

LUCY. Come on, Linus, answer the question.

LINUS. (*Getting up and facing* LUCY) Look, Lucy, I know very well that if I give any sort of honest answer to that question you're going to slug me.

LUCY. Linus. A survey that is not based on honest answers is like a house that is built on a foundation of sand. Would I be spending my time to conduct this survey if I didn't expect complete candor in all the responses? I promise not to slug you. Now what number would you give me as your crabbiness rating?

LINUS. (*After a few moments of interior struggle*) Ninety-five. (LUCY *sends a straight jab to his jaw which lays him out flat*)

LUCY. No decent person could be expected to keep her word with a rating over ninety. (*She stalks off, busily figuring away on her clipboard*) Now, I add these two columns and that gives me my answer. (*She figures energetically, then finally sits up with satisfaction*) There, it's all done. Now, let's see what we've got. (*She begins to scan the page. A look of trouble skims over her face. She rechecks the figures. Her eternal look of self-confidence wavers, then crumbles*) It's true. I'm a crabby person. I'm a very crabby person and everybody knows it. I've been spreading crabbiness wherever I go. I'm a supercrab. It's a wonder anyone will still talk to me. It's a wonder I have any friends at all—(*She looks at the figures on the paper*) or even associates. I've done nothing but make life miserable for everyone. I've done nothing but breed unhappiness and resentment. Where did I go wrong? How could I be so selfish? How could . . . (LINUS *has been listening. He comes and sits near her*)

LINUS. What's wrong, Lucy?

LUCY. Don't talk to me, Linus. I don't deserve to be spoken to. I don't deserve to breathe the air I breathe. I'm no good, Linus. I'm no good.

LINUS. That's not true, Lucy.

LUCY. Yes it is. I'm no good, and there's no reason at all why I should go on living on the face of this earth.

LINUS. Yes there is.

LUCY. Name one. Just tell me one single reason why I should still deserve to go on living on this planet.

LINUS. Well, for one thing, you have a little brother who loves you. (LUCY *looks at him. She is silent. Then she breaks into a great, sobbing "Wah!"*) Every now and then I say the right thing.

(LUCY *continues sobbing as she and* LINUS *exit. A brief musical interlude, a change of light, and* SCHROEDER *and* SALLY *come onstage*)

No decent person could be expected to keep her word with a rating over ninety.

Meet the Artist

Charles M. Schulz (1922–2000) grew up a shy but intelligent boy. In 1950 his legendary comic strip—originally named *Li'l Folks*—was renamed *Peanuts* and made its debut in seven newspapers. It remains the most successful comic strip of all time.

Readings in Drama
Talk About It

Use the following questions to guide a discussion of the scene.

1. **(a)** Why do you think Lucy takes a survey? **(b)** Which characters respond to the survey honestly?

2. In small groups, consider the following questions:
   • Will the results of the survey make Lucy change? Explain.
   • What do you think this scene teaches audiences about life?

Choose a point-person to share your group's ideas with the class.

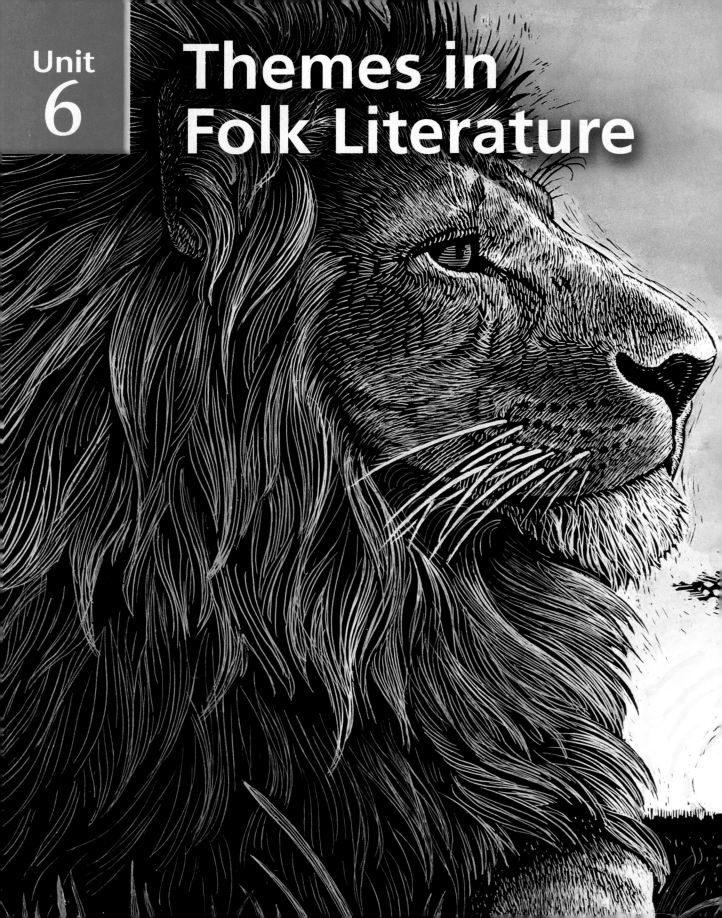

Unit 6

Themes in Folk Literature

Unit 6 Overview

Introduction
Exploring Themes
in Folk Literature

Part 1: Cause and Effect

Part 2: Purpose for Reading

Introduction:
Themes in Folk Literature

Julius Lester

▲ Julius Lester has written many works that explore the heritage of African Americans and that bring the past alive.

From the Author's Desk

Julius Lester
Talks About the Oral Tradition

Story is to our souls what blood is to our bodies. All of us love stories because we ourselves are stories. When we come home after a day at school or work, one of the first things we are asked is: "How was your day?" Our answer is almost invariably a story about what happened to us, or something we or someone else did.

Stories Passed on by Word of Mouth

A story does not have to be written by someone called a writer to be a story. In fact, most stories are not written. They belong to a genre of literature called the **oral tradition,** which includes tales and wise sayings passed on by word of mouth.

I imagine that the first stories in this tradition were told in caves or sitting around campfires. They probably began with someone saying excitedly, "Guess what happened to me today . . ."

Even as a child I was interested in stories. I loved listening to my father and my mother's mother tell stories about people they had known and what their lives had been like.

▶ Critical Viewing What does this picture "say" about stories and storytelling? **[Interpret]**

Storytelling: One Soul Trying to Touch Another

In everyone's family there is a similar oral tradition, stories passed down from generation to generation.

My father not only told me stories about what it was like when he was growing up in Arkansas, but he told stories about a very clever rabbit named Brer Rabbit and all the ways he played tricks on Brer Fox and Brer Wolf.

Stories from the oral tradition are important because they contain truths which have their source in the emotions of the person telling the story. The facts of the stories may or may not be true, but factual truth is only one kind of truth.

There is another kind. That is the truth residing in the effort of one soul to touch another soul by telling a story. And that kind of truth came first, as Kipling says in the passage shown here.

Each of us is a story seeking to be heard.

Fiction is Truth's elder Sister. Obviously. No one in the world knew what truth was until someone had told a story.

from "Fiction"
—Rudyard Kipling

More About the Author

Julius **Lester** (b. 1939)

When he was not yet ten, Julius Lester learned that members of his family had been slaves. He felt that he had to go back through time "to hear stories about those whose existence had made mine possible." For Lester, writing is a way of honoring the dead whose stories he has chosen to tell. He also draws on folklore, retelling old tales and enlivening them with "fresh street-talk language."

Fast Facts

▶ Lester's photographs of the civil rights movement have been exhibited in Washington, D.C.
▶ A singer, Lester has recorded two albums and performed with folk singers Pete Seeger and Judy Collins.

From the Author's Desk: Julius Lester ■ 761

Characteristics of Folk Literature

Long before there were books, there were stories. These stories were passed along by word of mouth from one generation to the next. The passing along of stories in this way is called the **oral tradition.** Folk literature—including folk tales, fables, myths, legends, folk songs, and fairy tales—originated in the oral tradition. As you study the oral tradition, you will encounter these common characteristics:

- **A universal theme** is a message about life that can be understood by people of most cultures.
- **Fantasy** is a type of writing that is highly imaginative and contains elements that are not found in real life.
- **Personification** is a type of figurative language in which a nonhuman subject is given human characteristics.
- **Irony** involves surprising, interesting, or amusing contradictions. Some folk tales and fables have surprise, or **ironic** endings because they do not turn out as you expect.

- **Hyperbole** is an exaggeration or an overstatement. It is often used in the oral tradition to create a comic effect and is not meant to be taken literally.
- **Dialect** is the form of a language spoken by people of a particular region or group. Storytellers often use dialect to add a realistic quality to the **characters,** or the people in a folktale.
- **Local customs** are the unique traditions or ways of life of a particular group. Details of local color help build the **setting**— the time and place of a story's action.

The Oral Tradition in Print

Folk tales were told not only to entertain, but also to communicate the shared ideas of a culture. They often deal with heroes, adventure, magic, or romance. These stories were told over generations and the details changed with each retelling. Eventually, these stories were compiled and written down.

Fables are brief stories or poems, usually with animal characters, that teach a lesson or moral that is stated directly at the end.

Myths are fictional tales that explain the actions of gods and heroes or explain natural phenomena. Like folk tales, myths were composed orally and passed down through generations. Every ancient culture has its own **mythology,** or collection of myths.

Legends are stories often based on fact. However, over time, details in legends move further away from factual events to describe people and actions that are more fictional than real. Legends are a culture's familiar and traditional stories. Sometimes a legend becomes the subject of an **allusion,** or reference to a well-known person, place, event, or literary work. For example, a modern novel might be referred to as a "Cinderella Story."

Check Your Understanding

For each item, indicate whether the work being described is a *legend,* a *myth,* a *folk tale,* or a *fable.* Compare your answers with a partner.

1. a story describing the enormous Paul Bunyan and the footprints he made to create 10,000 lakes
2. a story about the Roman god Apollo
3. a story in which a turtle beats a rabbit in a race, laughing all the way
4. a story in which a baker becomes a town's hero

From the Author's Desk
Julius Lester Introduces *Black Cowboy, Wild Horses*

My seventh grade history teacher at Northeast Junior High School in Kansas City, Kansas, was Ms. Rozetta K. Caldwell. She started me thinking about history, not only as the stories of great men and women, but also as the stories of ordinary people whose names and deeds go unrecorded.

The Story That Inspired My Book
Because three of my great-grandparents were slaves, I was especially interested in stories about people who had been slaves. One day I was reading a book and came across a story about an ex-slave named Bob Lemmons.

After slavery ended, he went to work as a cowboy on a ranch. There, Bob did what no one else was able to do. He captured herds of horses all by himself by making the horses believe he was a horse.

Historical Fiction: Research Sparks Imagination
Writing **historical fiction** requires the combining of two elements: research and the imagination. In order to tell Bob's story, I had to do research on black cowboys as well as research about the lives and habits of wild horses.

I did not put into the story all the **facts** I learned about black cowboys and wild horses. Yet my research gave me a feeling for the **setting** and **characters** about whom I would be writing. The research helped me to imagine what it may have felt like to be Bob Lemmons and what it might feel like to be a horse!

Living in Another Time and Place
So much of historical writing comes out of wondering, "What was it like when. . . .?" Imaginative historical writing enables us to live in another time and place, to be someone unlike ourselves. In the process, we learn a little more about what it means to be human.

BLACK COWBOY
WILD HORSES
a True Story

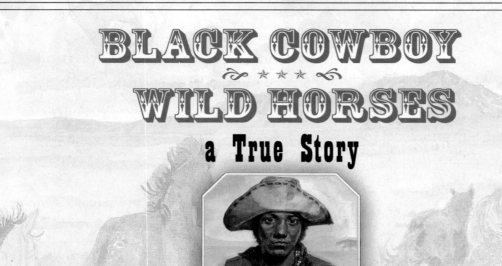

JULIUS LESTER

FIRST LIGHT. Bob Lemmons rode his horse slowly up the rise. When he reached the top, he stopped at the edge of the bluff. He looked down at the corral where the other cowboys were beginning the morning chores, then turned away and stared at the land stretching as wide as love in every direction. The sky was curved as if it were a lap on which the earth lay napping like a curled cat. High above, a hawk was suspended on cold threads of unseen winds. Far, far away, at what looked to be the edge of the world, land and sky kissed.

He guided Warrior, his black stallion, slowly down the bluff. When they reached the bottom, the horse reared, eager to run across the vastness of the plains until he reached forever. Bob smiled and patted him gently on the neck. "Easy. Easy," he whispered. "We'll have time for that. But not yet."

He let the horse trot for a while, then slowed him and began peering intently at the ground as if looking for the answer to a question he scarcely understood.

Julius Lester
Author's Insight In earlier drafts, I had Bob Lemmons walking his horse to the top of the hill. It wasn't until the third draft that I had him riding up the hill. To have him walk the horse up, then get on, is not as direct as him riding up the hill.

It was late afternoon when he saw them—the hoofprints of mustangs, the wild horses that lived on the plains. He stopped, dismounted, and walked around carefully until he had seen all the prints. Then he got down on his hands and knees to examine them more closely.

Some people learned from books. Bob had been a slave and never learned to read words. But he could look at the ground and read what animals had walked on it, their size and weight, when they had passed by, and where they were going. No one he knew could bring in mustangs by themselves, but Bob could make horses think he was one of them—because he was.

He stood, reached into his saddlebag, took out an apple, and gave it to Warrior, who chewed with noisy enthusiasm. It was a herd of eight mares, a colt, and a stallion. They had passed there two days ago. He would see them soon. But he needed to smell of sun, moon, stars, and wind before the mustangs would accept him.

The sun went down and the chilly night air came quickly. Bob took the saddle, saddlebag, and blanket off Warrior. He was cold, but could not make a fire. The mustangs would smell the smoke in his clothes from miles away. He draped a thick blanket around himself, then took the cotton sack of dried fruit, beef jerky, and nuts from his saddlebag and ate.

Oral Tradition
Legends Bob may have been a real cowboy but, in this story, his ability with horses is probably exaggerated.

▼ **Critical Viewing** What kind of relationship does Bob have with Warrior? **[Connect]**

When he was done, he lay his head on his saddle and was quickly asleep. Warrior grazed in the tall, sweet grasses.

As soon as the sun's round shoulders came over the horizon, Bob awoke. He ate, filled his canteen, and saddling Warrior, rode away. All day he followed the tracks without hurrying.

Near dusk, clouds appeared, piled atop each other like mountains made of fear. Lightning flickered from within them like candle flames shivering in a breeze. Bob heard the faint but distinct rumbling of thunder. Suddenly lightning vaulted from cloud to cloud across the curved heavens.

Warrior reared, his front hooves pawing as if trying to knock the white streaks of fire from the night sky. Bob raced Warrior to a nearby <u>ravine</u> as the sky exploded sheets of light. And there, in the distance, beneath the ghostly light, Bob saw the herd of mustangs. As if sensing their presence, Warrior rose into the air once again, this time not challenging the heavens but almost in greeting. Bob thought he saw the mustang stallion rise in response as the earth shuddered from the sound of thunder.

Then the rain came as hard and stinging as <u>remorse</u>. Quickly Bob put on his poncho, and turning Warrior away from the wind and the rain, waited. The storm would pass soon. Or it wouldn't. There was nothing to do but wait.

Finally the rain slowed and then stopped. The clouds thinned, and there, high in the sky, the moon appeared as white as grief. Bob slept in the saddle while Warrior grazed on the wet grasses.

The sun rose into a clear sky and Bob was awake immediately. The storm would have washed away the tracks, but they had been going toward the big river. He would go there and wait.

By mid-afternoon he could see the ribbon of river shining in the distance. He stopped, needing only to be close enough to see the horses when they came to drink. Toward evening he saw a trail of rolling, dusty clouds.

In front was the mustang herd. As it reached the water, the stallion slowed and stopped. He looked around, his head raised, nostrils flared, smelling the air. He turned in Bob's direction and sniffed the air again.

MODEL SELECTION

Julius Lester
Author's Insight
Descriptions must be vivid. The reader must not only see what is being described, but feel it also.

Vocabulary Builder
ravine (rə vēn´) *n.* a long, deep hollow in the earth's surface

remorse (re môrs´) *n.* guilt over a wrong one has done

Reading Check

What clues tell Bob he is near the mustang herd? **[Generalize]**

Bob tensed. Had he come too close too soon? If the stallion smelled anything new, he and the herd would be gone and Bob would never find them again. The stallion seemed to be looking directly at him. Bob was too far away to be seen, but he did not even blink his eyes, afraid the stallion would hear the sound. Finally the stallion began drinking and the other horses followed. Bob let his breath out slowly. He had been accepted.

Literature in Context | History Connection

Trail Riders

It was the job of many cowboys to herd cattle across great distances. For each trip a cowboy needed ten to twelve horses. The horses they chose were mustangs or broncos—swift, wild horses that first had to be tamed. Cowboys who tamed their own horses were called "broncobusters."

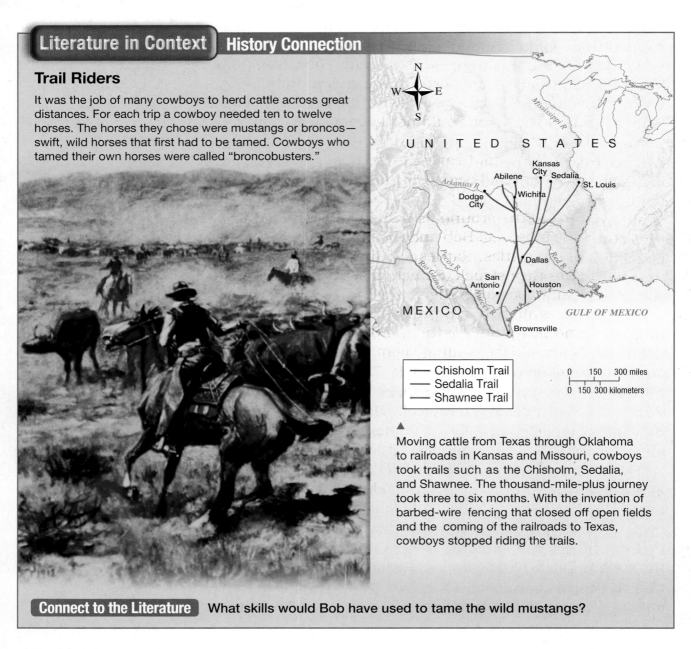

— Chisholm Trail
— Sedalia Trail
— Shawnee Trail

0   150   300 miles
0 150 300 kilometers

▲
Moving cattle from Texas through Oklahoma to railroads in Kansas and Missouri, cowboys took trails such as the Chisholm, Sedalia, and Shawnee. The thousand-mile-plus journey took three to six months. With the invention of barbed-wire fencing that closed off open fields and the coming of the railroads to Texas, cowboys stopped riding the trails.

Connect to the Literature   What skills would Bob have used to tame the wild mustangs?

The next morning he crossed the river and picked up the herd's trail. He moved Warrior slowly, without sound, without dust. Soon he saw them grazing. He stopped. The horses did not notice him. After a while he moved forward, slowly, quietly. The stallion raised his head. Bob stopped.

When the stallion went back to grazing, Bob moved forward again. All day Bob watched the herd, moving only when it moved but always coming closer. The mustangs sensed his presence. They thought he was a horse.

So did he.

The following morning Bob and Warrior walked into the herd. The stallion eyed them for a moment. Then, as if to test this newcomer, he led the herd off in a gallop. Bob lay flat across Warrior's back and moved with the herd. If anyone had been watching, they would not have noticed a man among the horses.

When the herd set out early the next day, it was moving slowly. If the horses had been going faster, it would not have happened.

The colt fell to the ground as if she had stepped into a hole and broken her leg. Bob and the horses heard the chilling sound of the rattles. Rattlesnakes didn't always give a warning before they struck. Sometimes, when someone or something came too close, they bit with the fury of fear.

The horses whinnied and pranced nervously, smelling the snake and death among them. Bob saw the rattler, as beautiful as a necklace, sliding silently through the tall grasses. He made no move to kill it. Everything in nature had the right to protect itself, especially when it was afraid.

The stallion galloped to the colt. He pushed at her. The colt struggled to get up, but fell to her side, shivering and kicking feebly with her thin legs. Quickly she was dead.

Already vultures circled high in the sky. The mustangs milled aimlessly. The colt's mother whinnied, refusing to leave the side of her colt. The stallion wanted to move the herd from there, and pushed the mare with his head. She refused to budge, and he nipped her on the rump. She skittered away. Before she could return to the colt, the stallion bit her again, this time harder. She ran toward the herd. He bit her a third time, and the herd was off. As they galloped

Oral Tradition
Personification Bob tracks the horses successfully because he moves and thinks like the animals. By indicating the horse's thoughts, the writer personifies the animals.

Julius Lester
Author's Insight
I am afraid of snakes. But Bob Lemmons would not be. I asked myself, "How would Bob have seen a snake?" To him, perhaps it was "as beautiful as a necklace."

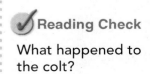 **Reading Check**

What happened to the colt?

away, Bob looked back. The vultures were descending from the sky as gracefully as dusk.

It was time to take over the herd. The stallion would not have the heart to fight fiercely so soon after the death of the colt. Bob galloped Warrior to the front and wheeled around, forcing the stallion to stop quickly. The herd, confused, slowed and stopped also.

Bob raised Warrior to stand high on his back legs, fetlocks pawing and kicking the air. The stallion's eyes widened. He snorted and pawed the ground, surprised and uncertain. Bob charged at the stallion.

Both horses rose on hind legs, teeth bared as they kicked at each other. When they came down, Bob charged Warrior at the stallion again, pushing him backward. Bob rushed yet again.

The stallion neighed loudly, and nipped Warrior on the neck. Warrior snorted angrily, reared, and kicked out with his forelegs, striking the stallion on the nose. Still

Oral Tradition
Conflict This pattern of animals clashing with humans is a common theme in the oral tradition.

▼ ▶ **Critical Viewing** These illustrations were created at the same time the story was written. What does their realistic style add to the story? **[Speculate]**

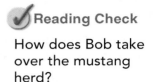

maintaining his balance, Warrior struck again and again. The mustang stallion cried out in pain. Warrior pushed hard against the stallion. The stallion lost his footing and fell to the earth. Warrior rose, neighing triumphantly, his front legs pawing as if seeking for the rungs on which he could climb a ladder into the sky.

The mustang scrambled to his feet, beaten. He snorted weakly. When Warrior made as if to attack again, the stallion turned, whinnied weakly, and trotted away.

✓ **Reading Check**

How does Bob take over the mustang herd?

Bob was now the herd's leader, but would they follow him? He rode slowly at first, then faster and faster. The mustangs followed as if being led on ropes.

Throughout that day and the next he rode with the horses. For Bob there was only the bulging of the horses' dark eyes, the quivering of their flesh, the rippling of muscles and bending of bones in their bodies. He was now sky and plains and grass and river and horse.

When his food was almost gone, Bob led the horses on one last ride, a dark surge of flesh flashing across the plains like black lightning. Toward evening he led the herd up the steep hillside, onto the bluff, and down the slope toward the big corral. The cowboys heard him coming and opened the corral gate. Bob led the herd, but at the last moment he swerved Warrior aside, and the mustangs flowed into the fenced enclosure. The cowboys leaped and shouted as they quickly closed the gate.

Bob rode away from them and back up to the bluff. He stopped and stared out onto the plains. Warrior reared and whinnied loudly.

"I know," Bob whispered. "I know. Maybe someday."

Maybe someday they would ride with the mustangs, ride to that forever place where land and sky kissed, and then ride on. Maybe someday.

Julius Lester
Author's Insight
What would it feel like to feel free, really free? For Bob and his horse, Warrior, it meant being as free as the mustang horses he had just captured.

▶ Critical Viewing How has artist Jerry Pinkney shown the strong emotional connection between Bob and Warrior? **[Draw Conclusions]**

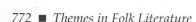

Q. Were there other black cowboys besides Bob Lemmons?

A. Scholars estimate there were between five thousand and nine thousand black cowboys out of some thirty-five thousand cowboys who worked in the West after the Civil War. Black cowboys worked on ranches and cattle drives, like other cowboys. Some were outlaws like Ben Hodges. There are black cowboys today. I wear a black cowboy hat.

Student Corner

Q. Do you like to write about characters that you feel you can relate to or characters that are not like you at all?
—**Kaitlyn Johnson, Somerset, Kentucky**

A. Good question, Kaitlyn. I would say that I write about both, meaning that just because somebody is not like me doesn't mean that I can't relate to him or her. About the only thing I share with Bob Lemmons is that we are both black. The few times I've been on a horse I've been terrified. The challenge of writing the story was to imagine myself into someone else's life to see if I could understand how he could capture mustang horses. And I wonder if the challenge for us as human beings is to try and imagine what it is like to be someone who is totally unlike us. We might understand and get along with each other better if we took the time and made the effort to imagine what it is like to be someone else.

 Writing Workshop: *Work in Progress*

Multimedia Presentation

For a multimedia presentation you may develop, look through your portfolio for a work to share. Make a list of media that could illustrate this work. Save the Media List in your writing portfolio.

Apply the Skills

Oral Tradition

Thinking About the Selection

1. **Respond:** Would this story have made a good tale to tell around a campfire in the Old West? Why or why not?

2. **(a) Recall:** What examples does the story provide about Bob Lemmons's legendary ability? **(b) Infer:** What danger does Bob face in approaching the mustangs too soon? **(c) Summarize:** What actions must Bob take to win over the herd?

3. **(a) Describe:** How does Bob depend on Warrior? **(b) Compare:** Why does it seem that Warrior's goals or dreams are the same as Bob's?

Oral Tradition Review

4. **(a)** Complete a diagram like the one shown by listing qualities about cowboy Bob that make him seem real and ones that exaggerate his abilities to make him seem like a **legend. (b)** Share your diagram with a partner. How has your understanding of Bob grown or changed?

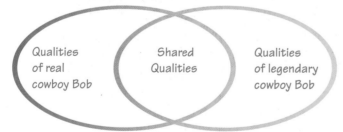

Qualities of real cowboy Bob

Shared Qualities

Qualities of legendary cowboy Bob

5. What is the **universal theme** in this **folk tale**?

Research the Author

Working with a group, plan a **reading** of passages from some of Julius Lester's books. Follow these steps:

- Have each person select one book by Lester, and identify a key passage to read. Ask your teacher to preview your selections.
- Before each student reads, present a short introduction to set the background and context of each excerpt.
- After the readings, invite class members to ask questions.

QuickReview

Selection at a Glance
A cowboy tracks a herd of wild horses he admires, becomes their leader, and guides them into a corral and captivity.

Go Online
Assessment
For: Self-test
Visit: www.PHSchool.com
Web Code: ela-6601

Oral tradition: passing stories from one generation to the next by word of mouth

Folk tales: stories that have been told, compiled over time, and eventually written

Legends: a culture's familiar stories about the past, based in fact but exaggerated in retelling

Universal theme: a message about life that can be understood by people of most cultures

Skills You Will Learn

Reading Skill: *Reread to Find Cause-and-Effect Relationships*
Literary Analysis: *Oral Tradition*

Reading Skill: *Ask Questions to Analyze Cause-and-Effect Relationships*
Literary Analysis: *Myths*

Reading Skill: *Identify Organizational Structure*

Literary Analysis: *Comparing Elements of Fantasy*

Literature You Will Read

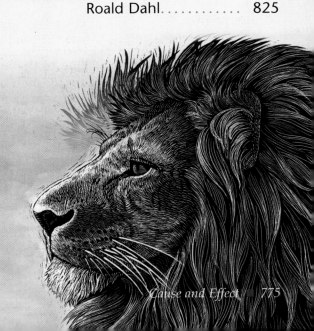

Reading: Cause and Effect

> A **cause** is the reason something happens. An **effect** is what
> happens as a result.

Skills and Strategies You Will Learn in Part 1

In Part 1, you will learn

- to **reread important passages** to find **cause-and-effect** relationships (p. 778)
- to **look for clues** that **signal cause and effect** (p. 792)
- to **use organizational structure** to **find cause-and-effect relationships** (p. 810)

Using the Skills and Strategies in Part 1

In Part 1, you will learn to identify word clues that signal cause-and-effect relationships, and to reread to identify cause and effect. You will also learn to use the organizational structure of selections to find cause-and-effect relationships.

This example shows how you will apply the skills and strategies you will learn in Part 1.

Clues That Indicate Cause and Effect

So	We were out of bread **so** we went to the store.
Consequently	The city is preserved by lava; **consequently**, scientists are able to recover many artifacts.
Due to	**Due to** the number of responses, we have not finished counting.
Present Participles (verbs ending in *-ing* used as modifiers)	The rain fell for days, **flooding** the streets.
Past Participles (verbs ending in *-ed* used as modifiers)	The trees were bare, **picked** clean by the locusts.

Academic Vocabulary: Words for Discussing Cause and Effect

The following words will help you write and talk about cause-and-effect relationships as you read the selections in this unit:

Word	Meaning	Sample Sentence
cause *n.*	why something happens	A motive is the *cause* of an action.
reason *n.*	why something happens	It is important to know the *reason* an author wrote a work.
effect *n.*	the consequence of	The *effect* of practice is that you become a better writer.
result *n.*	the consequence of	The *result* of reading is that you become a better reader.
relationship *n.*	the connection between two things	The connection between a cause and its effect is their *relationship*.

Vocabulary Skill: Synonyms

► A **synonym** is a word that means the same or nearly the same thing as another word.

Synonyms let you vary your writing so you keep the reader interested. You can say a *cause* is the *reason* something happens. The words *cause* and *reason* are synonyms.

Synonyms	Meaning
cause, reason, motive, basis, intent	why something happens
effect, result, outcome, aftermath, conclusion	the consequence

Activity Use a dictionary to look up the meaning of each word below. Then, write a synonym for the word. Explain any slight differences in the meanings of the words.

1. event   **2.** produce   **3.** emotion   **4.** relate

These skills will help you become a better reader. Practice them with either "The Tiger Who Would Be King" and "The Ant and the Dove" (p. 780) or "The Lion and the Bulls" and "A Crippled Boy" (p. 785).

Reading Skill

A **cause** is an event, action, or feeling that produces a result. The result is called an **effect**. Sometimes an effect is the result of a number of causes. To help you identify the relationship between an event and its causes, **reread** important passages in the work, looking for connections. Use a chart like the one shown to record the events and actions that produce an effect.

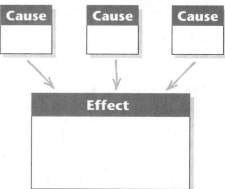

Literary Analysis

Fables and folk tales are part of the oral tradition of passing songs, stories, and poems from generation to generation by word of mouth.

- **Fables** are brief stories that teach a lesson or moral. They often feature animal characters.
- **Folk tales** feature heroes, adventure, magic, and romance. These stories often entertain while teaching a lesson.

Some fables and folk tales have **ironic**, or surprising, endings because they do not turn out as you expect.

Vocabulary Builder

The Tiger Who Would Be King

- **prowled** (prould) *v.* moved around quietly and secretly (p. 780) *The coyote prowled the field in search of mice.*
- **repulse** (ri puls´) *v.* drive back; repel an attack (p. 780) *A skunk sprays its scent to repulse attackers.*

The Ant and the Dove

- **startled** (stärt´ əld) *adj.* surprised (p. 781) *The balloon popped, and the startled baby cried.*

The Lion and the Bulls

- **slanderous** (slan´ dər əs) *adj.* including untrue and damaging statements (p. 785) *The candidate made slanderous comments about his opponent.*

A Crippled Boy

- **provided** (prə vīd´ id) *v.* supplied; furnished (p. 786) *Food will be provided.*
- **demonstrate** (dem´ ən strāt´) *v.* show clearly; prove (p. 787) *Let me demonstrate how the motor works.*

Connecting to the Literature

Reading/Writing Connection Both "The Tiger Who Would Be King" and "The Ant and the Dove" are stories that teach a lesson. Write a short description of a story you have read that taught a lesson. Use at least three of the following words: *achieve, react, adapt, demonstrate, minimize.*

Meet the Authors

James **Thurber** (1894–1961)

James Thurber wrote for his high-school and college newspapers in his home state of Ohio. He also wrote plays and songs for Ohio State University's drama club and columns for his hometown newspaper, *The Columbus Dispatch.*

Amusing His Readers During World War I, Thurber left college to join the U.S. military. He soon left this serious position to pursue his love of laughter through writing and cartooning. Much of his early work appeared in *The New Yorker* magazine. Although failing eyesight forced him to give up drawing, Thurber kept making people laugh with his writing.

Leo **Tolstoy** (1828–1910)

Born into a wealthy family in Russia, Leo Tolstoy inherited his family estate at age nineteen. By the time he was fifty, he had written some of the world's most famous novels, including *Anna Karenina* and *War and Peace.*

Famous, Yet Alone In midlife, Tolstoy began to reject his life of luxury. He surrendered the rights to many of his works and gave his property to his family. This world-famous writer died alone in a remote train station in Russia.

Go **Online**
Author Link
For: More about the authors
Visit: www.PHSchool.com
Web Code: ele-9602

The Tiger Who Would Be King

JAMES THURBER

One morning the tiger woke up in the jungle and told his mate that he was king of beasts.

"Leo, the lion, is king of beasts," she said.

"We need a change," said the tiger. "The creatures are crying for a change."

The tigress listened but she could hear no crying, except that of her cubs.

"I'll be king of beasts by the time the moon rises," said the tiger. "It will be a yellow moon with black stripes, in my honor."

"Oh, sure," said the tigress as she went to look after her young, one of whom, a male, very like his father, had got an imaginary thorn in his paw.

The tiger <u>prowled</u> through the jungle till he came to the lion's den. "Come out," he roared, "and greet the king of beasts! The king is dead, long live the king!"

Inside the den, the lioness woke her mate. "The king is here to see you," she said.

"What king?" he inquired, sleepily.

"The king of beasts," she said.

"I am the king of beasts," roared Leo, and he charged out of the den to defend his crown against the pretender.

It was a terrible fight, and it lasted until the setting of the sun. All the animals of the jungle joined in, some taking the side of the tiger and others the side of the lion. Every creature from the aardvark to the zebra took part in the struggle to overthrow the lion or to <u>repulse</u> the tiger, and some did not know which they were fighting for, and some fought for both, and some fought whoever was nearest, and some fought for the sake of fighting.

"What are we fighting for?" someone asked the aardvark.

"The old order," said the aardvark.

"What are we dying for?" someone asked the zebra.

"The new order," said the zebra.

When the moon rose, fevered and gibbous,[1] it shone upon a jungle in which nothing stirred except a macaw[2] and a cockatoo,[3] screaming in horror. All the beasts were dead except the tiger, and his days were numbered and his time was ticking away. He was monarch of all he surveyed, but it didn't seem to mean anything.

MORAL: You can't very well be king of beasts if there aren't any.

1. **gibbous** (gib´ əs) *adj.* more than half but less than completely illuminated.
2. **macaw** (mə kô´) *n.* bright-colored, harsh-voiced parrot of Central or South America.
3. **cockatoo** (kok´ ə tü´) *n.* crested parrot with white plumage tinged with yellow or pink.

Literary Analysis
Fables What conflict or problem does this fable address?

The Ant and the Dove

RUSSIAN FOLK TALE

LEO TOLSTOY

A thirsty ant went to the stream to drink. Suddenly it got caught in a whirlpool and was almost carried away.

At that moment a dove was passing by with a twig in its beak. The dove dropped the twig for the tiny insect to grab hold of. So it was that the ant was saved.

A few days later a hunter was about to catch the dove in his net. When the ant saw what was happening, it walked right up to the man and bit him on the foot. Startled, the man dropped the net. And the dove, thinking that you never can tell how or when a kindness may be repaid, flew away.

Vocabulary Builder
startled (stärt´ əld)
adj. surprised

The Ant and the Dove ■ 781

Apply the Skills

The Tiger Who Would Be King •
The Ant and the Dove

Thinking About the Selection

1. **Respond:** Do you find any parts of these two stories humorous? Explain.
2. **(a) Recall:** Which two animals fight to rule in "The Tiger Who Would Be King"? **(b) Infer:** Some of the animals join the fight for the sake of fighting. What does this suggest about them? **(c) Apply:** What human qualities does Thurber show in these animals?
3. **(a) Recall:** What does the dove in "The Ant and the Dove" do for the ant? **(b) Infer:** How does this action save the ant?
4. **Connect:** Does "The Ant and the Dove" remind you of any other story or stories? Explain.

Reading Skill

5. **(a)** In "The Tiger Who Would Be King," identify several **causes** of the fight in the jungle. **(b)** What is the **effect** of the fight?
6. What is the end **effect** of the dove's action in "The Ant and the Dove"?

Literary Analysis

7. Make a chart like the one shown to identify the elements of **fables** and **folk tales** in the two stories.

Title	Characters	Moral or Lesson

8. What is **ironic**, or surprising, about the ending of "The Tiger Who Would Be King"?

QuickReview

Stories at a Glance

"The Tiger Who Would Be King": A tiger takes on the king of the jungle, with unintended results.

"The Ant and the Dove": After a dove saves an ant from drowning, her kindness is repaid.

For: Self-test
Visit: www.PHSchool.com
Web Code: ela-6602

Cause: an event, an action, or a feeling that produces a result

Effect: the result

Fables and Folk Tales: brief stories in the oral tradition that often entertain and teach a lesson

Vocabulary Builder

Practice Respond to each item based on your knowledge of the italicized words. Explain your answers.

1. Explain why a wolf might have *prowled* near a river.
2. Provide two reasons why day-old garbage might *repulse* some people.
3. Identify three things that *startled* people might do.

Writing

Write a **fable** that teaches the same lesson as either "The Tiger Who Would Be King" or "The Ant and the Dove." For your fable, create different characters and change the plot.

- Brainstorm for a list of situations that illustrate the lesson you have chosen. Choose the idea you like best.
- Build up to the lesson by showing the causes and effects of each event. The action of the story should lead to the lesson at the end.
- Ask a partner whether the events you describe support the lesson. Use his or her suggestions when you revise.

For *Grammar, Vocabulary,* and *Assessment,* see **Build Language Skills,** pages 790–791.

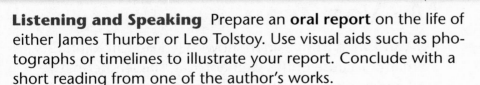

Extend Your Learning

Listening and Speaking Prepare an **oral report** on the life of either James Thurber or Leo Tolstoy. Use visual aids such as photographs or timelines to illustrate your report. Conclude with a short reading from one of the author's works.

Research and Technology Use electronic resources to conduct author, subject, and title searches to find retellings of "The Tiger Who Would Be King" and "The Ant and the Dove." Prepare an **annotated list**—a list with your notes—of the stories, including the following:

- the search engines and keywords you used to find the other versions
- a comparison of those versions to the stories you read

Fable and Folk Tale

Connecting to the Literature

Reading/Writing Connection In both of these tales, characters look for ways to achieve a goal. In real life, too, there are different paths to success. For example, we can depend on ourselves, or we can take advantage of others. Think of a goal you would like to achieve and jot down two ways to achieve it. Use at least three of these words: *rely, analyze, focus, isolate, cooperate.*

Review

For **Reading Skill, Literary Analysis,** and **Vocabulary Builder,** see page 778.

Meet the Authors

ESOPO

Aesop (ca. 620–560 B.C.)

Aesop's fables have been enjoyed for centuries. However, very little is known about the origin of these stories, including who actually wrote them.

A Man of Mystery According to tradition, Aesop was a Greek slave who lived on the island of Samos during the sixth century B.C. Some people believe that he defended criminals in court. Others believe that he was either an advisor or a riddle solver for one of the Greek kings. The most widely held theory, however, is that Aesop was not an actual person. Because certain stories in ancient Greece were told over and over, people may have invented an imaginary author for them.

My-Van Tran (b. 1947)

My-Van Tran is from Saigon, now called Ho Chi Minh City, in Vietnam. Because of the Vietnam War, she left her native land and moved to Australia. However, she never abandoned her cultural heritage.

Supporting International Ties She received a medal from the Australian government for fostering Australian-Asian relations. Now at the University of South Australia, My-Van Tran teaches Asian studies and the history and politics of Asia.

Go Online **Author Link**

For: More about the authors
Visit: www.PHSchool.com
Web Code: ele-9603

The LION and the BULLS
❋ ❋ ❋ Aesop ❋ ❋ ❋

A lion often prowled about a pasture where three bulls grazed together. He had tried without success to lure one or the other of them to the edge of the pasture. He had even attempted a direct attack, only to see them form a ring so that from whatever direction he approached he was met by the horns of one of them.

Then a plan began to form in the lion's mind. Secretly he started spreading evil and <u>slanderous</u> reports of one bull against the other. The three bulls, distrustingly, began to avoid one another, and each withdrew to a different part of the pasture to graze. Of course, this was exactly what the lion wanted. One by one he fell upon the bulls, and so made easy prey of them all.

MORAL: United we stand; divided we fall.

Vocabulary Builder
slanderous (slan´ dər əs) *adj.* including untrue and damaging statements

▼ **Critical Viewing**
Why might a lion be more successful sneaking up on its prey than attacking directly? **[Analyze]**

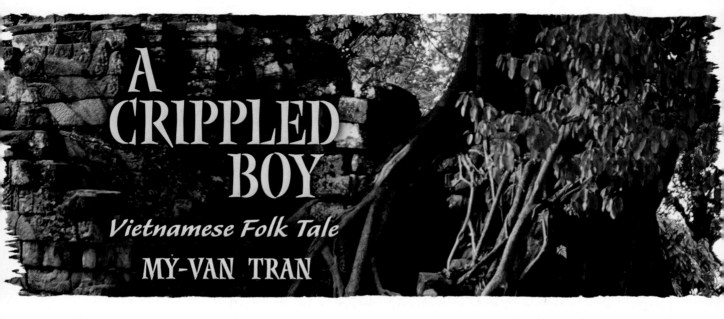

A CRIPPLED BOY

Vietnamese Folk Tale

MY-VAN TRAN

*L*ong, long ago there was a boy called Theo. He was crippled in both legs and could hardly walk. Since he could not work, he had no choice but to live on rice and vegetables which kind people gave him.

Often he sat watching other children play and run about. Unable to join them, he felt very miserable. To amuse himself Theo practiced throwing pebbles at targets. Hour after hour he would spend practicing his aim. Having nothing else to do he soon learned to hit all his targets. Other children took pity on him and gave him more pebbles to throw. Besides this, Theo could also make all sorts of shapes with stones on the ground.

One hot day Theo sat under a big banyan tree[1] which <u>provided</u> him with a delightful, cool shade under its thick leaves. He aimed stones at the thick foliage and managed to cut it into the outlines of animal forms. He was very pleased at what he could do and soon forgot his loneliness.

One day Theo was under his favorite banyan tree. To his surprise, he heard a drumbeat. Soon he saw many men in official clothes. It happened that the King was out for a country walk with some of his officials and was passing by Theo's tree.

---

1. banyan (ban´ yən) **tree** tropical fig tree.

Vocabulary Builder
provided (prə vīd´ id)
v. supplied; furnished

The King's attention was caught by the unusual shadow of the tree. He stopped and was very surprised to see little crippled Theo sitting there all alone.

Theo was very frightened and tried to get away; but he could not crawl very far. The King asked Theo what he had been doing. Theo told the King his story.

Then the King asked Theo to <u>demonstrate</u> his skill at pebble throwing. Theo was happy to do so. The King was impressed and asked Theo to return with him to the palace where the King said:

"I have a little job for you to do."

The following day, before the King had a meeting with his mandarins,[2] he ordered Theo to sit quietly behind a curtain. The King had ordered a few holes to be made in the curtain so that Theo could see what was going on.

"Most of my mandarins talk too much," the King explained. "They never bother to listen to me or let me finish my sentence. So if anybody opens his mouth to speak while I am talking, just throw a pebble into his mouth. This will teach him to shut up."

Sure enough, just as the meeting was about to start one mandarin opened his big mouth, ready to speak.

Oops! Something got into his mouth and he quickly closed it.

Another mandarin opened his mouth to speak but strangely enough he, too, shut his mouth without saying a word.

A miracle had happened. Throughout the whole meeting all the mandarins kept their silence.

For once the King could speak as much as he wanted without being interrupted. The King was extremely pleased with his success and the help that Theo had given him.

After that he always treasured Theo's presence and service. So Theo remained happily at the palace, no longer needing to beg for food and no longer always sitting alone under the banyan tree.

Vocabulary Builder
demonstrate (dem´ ən strāt) *v.* show clearly; prove

Reading Skill
Cause and Effect
Reread to find out what effect the King hopes that Theo's skill will have.

Literary Analysis
Folk Tales What conflict or problem does this folk tale develop and resolve?

---

2. **mandarins** (man´ də rinz) *n.* high-ranking officials and counselors.

Apply the Skills

The Lion and the Bulls • A Crippled Boy

Thinking About the Selection

1. **Respond:** What do you think of the solutions in both of these stories?
2. **(a) Speculate:** In "The Lion and the Bulls," what kinds of lies do you think the lion tells the bulls? **(b) Infer:** Why are the bulls willing to believe the lion?
3. **(a) Infer:** What human qualities does Aesop show in the animals? **(b) Assess:** Is an animal fable more or less effective than one with human characters? Explain.
4. **(a) Recall:** In "A Crippled Boy," why does Theo begin to throw stones? **(b) Analyze:** Name two ways in which Theo benefits from developing his talent.

Reading Skill

5. **(a)** In "The Lion and the Bulls," what **causes** the bulls to move away from one another? **(b)** What is the **effect** of this movement?
6. **(a) Recall:** What events cause the King to invite Theo to live at the palace? **(b)** What effect does living at the palace have on Theo?

Literary Analysis

7. Make a chart like the one shown to identify the elements of **fables and folk tales** in the two stories.

Title	Characters	Moral or Lesson

8. What is **ironic**, or surprising, about the ending of "A Crippled Boy"?

QuickReview

Stories at a Glance
"The Lion and the Bulls": A crafty lion catches three bulls.
"A Crippled Boy": A boy's skill at pebble throwing earns him a place in the king's palace.

For: Self-test
Visit: www.PHSchool.com
Web Code: ela-6603

Cause: an event, an action, or a feeling that produces a result
Effect: the result

Fables and Folk Tales: brief stories in the oral tradition that entertain and often teach a lesson

Vocabulary Builder

Practice Respond to each item based on your knowledge of the italicized words. Explain your responses.

1. Why do salespeople try to *demonstrate* their products?
2. Why is lunch sometimes *provided* on field trips?
3. Why are *slanderous* comments considered bad?

Writing

Write a **fable** that teaches the same lesson as either "The Lion and the Bulls" or "A Crippled Boy." For your fable, create different characters and change the plot.

- Brainstorm for a list of situations that illustrate the lesson you have chosen. Choose the idea you like best.
- Build up to the lesson by showing the causes and effects of each event. The action of the story should lead to the lesson at the end.
- Ask a partner whether the events you describe support the lesson. Use his or her suggestions when you revise.

For *Grammar, Vocabulary,* and *Assessment,* see **Build Language Skills,** pages 790–791.

Extend Your Learning

Listening and Speaking Prepare an **oral report** on either Aesop or My-Van Tran. Use visual aids such as photographs or timelines to illustrate your report. Conclude with a short reading from one of the author's works.

Research and Technology Use electronic resources to conduct author, subject, and title searches to find retellings of "The Lion and the Bulls" and "A Crippled Boy." Prepare an **annotated list**—a list with your notes—of the stories, including the following:

- the search engines and keywords you used to find the other versions
- a comparison of those versions to the stories you read

Build Language Skills

The Tiger Who Would Be King • The Ant and the Dove • The Lion and the Bulls • A Crippled Boy

Vocabulary Skill

Synonyms The words *cause* and *reason* are **synonyms**. They have the same basic meaning. Generally, you can use either word in a sentence without changing the meaning of the sentence. For example:

The *cause* of our late arrival was heavy traffic.
The *reason* for our late arrival was heavy traffic.

Practice Answer each of the following questions. Use a different synonym for the word in italics in each answer. You may need to change or rearrange other words in the sentence. Explain why you choose the synonym you do.

1. What is the *cause* of ants appearing at a picnic?
2. What might be a *reason* for having a party?
3. The explosion was the *result* of a chemistry experiment.
4. The *effect* of combining the paints was not pleasant.
5. Write down the *reasons* you solved the problem that way.

Grammar Lesson

Clauses: Independent and Subordinate A **clause** is a group of words with its own subject and verb. An **independent clause** has a subject and a verb and can stand by itself as a complete sentence. A **subordinate clause** has a subject and a verb but cannot stand by itself as a complete sentence.

Independent clause: Each year we climb to the top.
Subordinate clause: Before we climb to the top

Practice Add to the subordinate clauses to make complete sentences.

1. in case it begins to rain
2. because the boys arrive tomorrow
3. after you turn the corner
4. the bridge will be
5. when clouds cover the summit

More Practice

For more practice with Independent and Subordinate Clauses, see the Grammar Handbook, p. R36.

W̶G̶ Prentice Hall Writing and Grammar Connection: Chapter 20, Section 2

Monitor Your Progress

Reading: Cause and Effect

Directions: *Read the selection. Then, answer the questions.*

(1) The sun has a lot to do with wind. (2) The sun warms the surface of our planet. (3) The land warms up faster than water does. (4) For example, a forest warms up more quickly than a lake. (5) The warmed land and water give off heat at different rates. (6) As a result, when warm air rises, cooler air moves in to replace it. (7) This moving air is wind.

1. According to the passage, which cause-and-effect statement is true?
   A Our planet's warm air causes the sun's heat.
   B Wind is caused by the difference in water temperature.
   C Wind is caused by cooler air moving in to replace warm, rising air.
   D Wind is caused by forests.

2. Which of the following is a cause/effect relationship in the passage?
   A sun/forest
   B sun/wind
   C warm land/cool water
   D land warms/warm air rises

3. Which is the effect in the following statement? As warm air rises, cooler air moves in to replace it.
   A warm air rises
   B cooler air moves in
   C warm air
   D cool air

4. Which clue words signal a cause-and-effect relationship in sentence 6?
   A As a result
   B warm air rises
   C cooler air moves in
   D to replace it

Timed Writing: Persuasion [Critical Stance]

Review "The Tiger Who Would Be King," or "The Ant and the Dove." Choose one selection that you think has an important lesson. Write a persuasive essay that explains why the lesson is a good one. Use quotations from the text to support your view. **(30 minutes)**

 ## Writing Workshop: *Work in Progress*

Multimedia Presentation

From the work in your writing portfolio, choose an idea to illustrate in a multimedia presentation. Note the details you could illustrate using media. Save this work in your portfolio.

These skills will help you become a better reader. Practice them with either the Prologue from *The Whale Rider* (p. 794) or "Arachne" (p. 801).

Reading Skill

A **cause** is an event, action, or feeling that makes something happen. An **effect** is what happens. Sometimes an effect can become the cause of another event. For example, seeing someone lift a heavy object can cause you to offer help. Your help can then cause that person to feel good.

As you read, look for clue words such as *because, so,* and *as a result* that signal a cause-and-effect relationship. **Ask questions** such as "What happened?" and "Why did this happen?" to help you follow the cause-and-effect relationships.

Literary Analysis

Myths are fictional tales that describe the actions of gods or heroes. Every culture has its own myths. A myth can do one or more of the following:

- tell how the universe or a culture began
- explain something in nature, such as thunder
- teach a lesson
- express a value, such as courage

As you read, use a chart like the one shown to analyze the characteristics of myths.

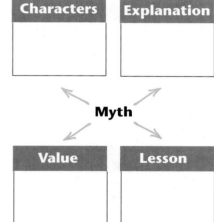

Vocabulary Builder

Prologue from *The Whale Rider*

- **clatter** (klat´ ər) *n.* rattling sound (p. 794) *The plastic plates fell to the floor with a loud* clatter.

- **reluctant** (ri luk´ tənt) *adj.* showing doubt or unwillingness (p. 796) *A picky eater is* reluctant *to try new foods.*

- **splendor** (splen´ dər) *n.* great brightness (p. 797) *We admired the* splendor *of the setting sun.*

Arachne

- **obscure** (əb skyoor´) *adj.* not well known (p. 801) *I have never heard of that* obscure *artist.*

- **mortal** (môr´ təl) *adj.* referring to humans, who eventually die (p. 803) *Mortal men cannot move mountains.*

- **obstinacy** (äb´ stə nə sē) *n.* stubbornness (p. 804) *The willful child was punished for her* obstinacy.

Build Understanding • Prologue from *The Whale Rider*

Background

Paikea The prologue to *The Whale Rider* introduces a story based on the legend of Paikea. This legend comes from the Maori people of New Zealand. In the story, Kahutia Te Rangi is carried on the back of the whale Paikea to the shores of what is now called New Zealand's North Island. Kahutia Te Rangi then assumes the name of the whale and makes his home on the island.

Connecting to the Literature

Reading/Writing Connection Among the Maori, whales were considered chiefs. In this selection, the whale is a symbol of power and nobility. Write sentences in which you name other animals that you associate with strength and greatness. Use at least three of these words: *project, assign, display, demonstrate.*

Myth

Meet the Author

Witi **Ihimaera** (b. 1944)

Witi Ihimaera was raised in the Maori culture of New Zealand. He became interested in writing at an early age and recalls scribbling stories across a wall of his room at his family farm. After publishing his first book in 1972, Ihimaera served his country in the Ministry of Foreign Affairs in Australia, New York, and Washington, D.C.

Being a Maori Ihimaera is the first Maori to publish both a novel and a collection of short stories. He says that he sees writing as a way to express his experience of being a Maori. He continues to write and also lectures in the English department at Auckland University in New Zealand.

Fast Facts

▶ Ihimaera wrote *The Whale Rider* in three weeks during 1978.

▶ Ihimaera says that *The Whale Rider* is the work of his "that the Maori community accepts best."

▶ The story inspired a 2003 movie that was successful in many countries.

Go **Online**
Author Link

For: More about the author
Visit: www.PHSchool.com
Web Code: ele-9604

Prologue from
The Whale Rider

Witi Ihimaera

In the old days, in the years that have gone before us, the land and sea felt a great emptiness, a yearning. The mountains were like a stairway to heaven, and the lush green rainforest was a rippling cloak of many colors. The sky was iridescent, swirling with the patterns of wind and clouds; sometimes it reflected the prisms of rainbow or southern aurora.[1] The sea was ever-changing, shimmering and seamless to the sky. This was the well at the bottom of the world, and when you looked into it you felt you could see to the end of forever.

This is not to say that the land and sea were without life, without vivacity. The tuatara, the ancient lizard with its third eye, was sentinel here, unblinking in the hot sun, watching and waiting to the east. The moa browsed in giant wingless herds across the southern island. Within the warm stomach of the rainforests, kiwi,[2] weka,[3] and the other birds foraged for *huhu* and similar succulent insects. The forests were loud with the <u>clatter</u> of tree bark, chatter of cicada, and murmur of fish-laden streams. Sometimes the forest grew suddenly quiet, and in wet bush could be heard the filigree of fairy laughter like a sparkling glissando.[4]

---

1. **southern aurora** (ô rôr´ ə) *n.* streamers or arches of light appearing above Earth in the Southern Hemisphere.
2. **kiwi** (kē´ wē) *n.* small, flightless New Zealand bird.
3. **weka** (wā´ kä) *n.* flightless New Zealand wading bird.
4. **glissando** (gli sän´ dō) *n.* quick sliding up or down the musical scale.

The sea, too, teemed with fish, but they also seemed to be waiting. They swam in brilliant shoals, like rains of glittering dust, throughout the greenstone depths—*hapuku, manga, kahawai, tamure, moki,* and *warehou*—herded by shark or *mango ururoa.* Sometimes from far off a white shape would be seen flying through the sea, but it would only be the serene flight of the *tarawhai,* the stingray with the spike on its tail.

Waiting. Waiting for the seeding. Waiting for the gifting. Waiting for the blessing to come.

Suddenly, looking up at the surface, the fish began to see the dark bellies of the canoes from the east. The first of the Ancients were coming, journeying from their island kingdom beyond the horizon. Then, after a period, canoes were seen to be returning to the east, making long cracks on the surface sheen. The land and the sea sighed with gladness:

We have been found.

The news is being taken back to the place of the Ancients.

Our blessing will come soon.

In that waiting time, earth and sea began to feel the sharp pangs of need, for an end to the yearning. The forests sent sweet perfumes upon the eastern winds and garlands of *pohutukawa* upon the eastern tides. The sea flashed continuously with flying fish, leaping high to look beyond the horizon and to be the first to announce the coming; in the

▲ **Critical Viewing**
What details in this picture capture the mood of the story? **[Connect]**

Reading Skill
Cause and Effect
What effect does the arrival and departure of the Ancients have on the land and the sea?

✓ **Reading Check**
What feeling did the land and sea have in the old days?

shallows, the chameleon sea horses pranced at attention. The only <u>reluctant</u> ones were the fairy people, who retreated with their silver laughter to caves in glistening waterfalls.

The sun rose and set, rose and set. Then one day, at its noon apex, the first sighting was made. A spume on the horizon. A dark shape rising from the greenstone depths of the ocean, awesome, leviathan, breaching through the surface and hurling itself skyward before falling seaward again. Underwater the muted thunder boomed like a great door opening far away, and both sea and land trembled from the impact of that downward plunging.

Suddenly the sea was filled with awesome singing, a song with eternity in it, a song to the land:

You have called and I have come,
bearing the gift of the Gods.

The dark shape rising, rising again. A whale, gigantic. A sea monster. Just as it burst through the sea, a flying fish leaping high in its ecstasy saw water and air streaming like thunderous foam from that noble beast and knew, ah yes,

▼ **Critical Viewing** What characteristics of whales, such as this one, might inspire people to develop myths about them? **[Speculate]**

that the time had come. For the sacred sign was on the monster, a swirling tattoo imprinted on the forehead.

Then the flying fish saw that astride the head, as it broke skyward, was a man. He was wondrous to look upon, the whale rider. The water streamed away from him and he opened his mouth to gasp in the cold air. His eyes were shining with <u>splendor</u>. His body dazzled with diamond spray. Upon that beast he looked like a small tattooed figurine, dark brown, glistening, and erect. He seemed, with all his strength, to be pulling the whale into the sky.

Rising, rising. And the man felt the power of the whale as it propelled itself from the sea. He saw far off the land long sought and now found, and he began to fling small spears seaward and landward on his magnificent journey toward the land.

Some of the spears in midflight turned into pigeons, which flew into the forests. Others, on landing in the sea, changed into eels. And the song in the sea drenched the air with ageless music, and land and sea opened themselves to him, the gift long waited for: *tangata*, man. With great gladness and thanksgiving, the man cried out to the land,
     Karanga mai, karanga mai, karanga mai.
Call me. But there was one spear, so it is told, the last, that, when the whale rider tried to throw it, refused to leave his hand. Try as he might, the spear would not fly.

So the whale rider uttered a prayer over the wooden spear, saying, "Let this spear be planted in the years to come, for there are sufficient spear already implanted. Let this be the one to flower when the people are troubled and it is most needed."

And the spear then leaped from his hands with gladness and soared through the sky. It flew across a thousand years. When it hit the earth, it did not change but waited for another hundred and fifty years to pass until it was needed.

The flukes of the whale stroked majestically at the sky.
Hui e, haumi e, taiki e.
Let it be done.

Vocabulary Builder
splendor (splen′ dər) *n.* great brightness

Literary Analysis
Myths Do you think the whale rider is a mortal or a god? Explain.

Literary Analysis
Myths What does this myth explain?

Apply the Skills

Prologue from *The Whale Rider*

Thinking About the Selection

1. **Respond:** What questions do you have about the whale rider?
2. **(a) Recall:** What emotions does the author give to the land and sea? **(b) Analyze:** What effect is created by giving human feelings to these nonhuman subjects?
3. **(a) Recall:** What are the canoes described as doing? **(b) Infer:** Why are the land and sea excited about the arrival of the Ancients?
4. **(a) Recall:** What happens to the spears that the whale rider throws? **(b) Speculate:** How might the last spear be important to future generations?
5. **(a) Speculate:** Based on the prologue to the book, what do you think *The Whale Rider* will be about? **(b) Support:** What details support your response? **(c) Discuss:** Share your ideas with a partner and decide together on a single answer to share with the class.

Reading Skill

6. What **causes** the land and sea to sigh with gladness?
7. What is the **effect** of the whale's jumping and plunging back into the sea?
8. Complete the chart to show causes and effects in the *Whale Rider* prologue.

Causes	Effects
The land and sea feel a great emptiness.	
	Flying fish leap to look beyond the horizon.
The whale rider says a prayer over the last spear.	

Literary Analysis

9. What does this **myth** explain in nature?
10. What values are taught in this myth?

QuickReview

Story at a Glance
The land and sea awaken to the long-awaited arrival of the whale rider, who will bear gifts from the gods.

Go Online
Assessment
For: Self-test
Visit: www.PHSchool.com
Web Code: ela-6604

Cause: an event, action, or feeling that makes something happen
Effect: what happens

Myths: tales that explain the natural world, teach a lesson, or express a value

Vocabulary Builder

Practice Match each situation below with the related vocabulary word from the list on page 792.

1. not wanting to jump into water
2. the brightness of a chest of gold coins
3. the noise of hoofs on the street

Writing

Write a brief **essay** in which you compare the sense of yearning, anticipation, and joy expressed in the selection with your own experience of waiting for something exciting to happen.

- Make notes about the feelings expressed in the prologue.
- Jot down notes about times when you have looked forward to an exciting event.
- As you draft, include ideas about the lessons that can be learned from waiting for an exciting event.
- Tell whether the story effectively conveys excitement.

Use your essay in a group discussion about how myths are related to real life.

For *Grammar, Vocabulary,* and *Assessment,* see **Build Language Skills,** pages 808–809.

Extend Your Learning

Listening and Speaking With a small group, prepare an **oral report** about the types of whales found near the coastline of New Zealand. Include photographs or drawings of one or more types of whales in your report. Present your report to the class, with each group member contributing to the oral presentation.

Research and Technology Use the Internet, CD-ROMs, and other library resources to prepare a written **report** about the central gods and goddesses in Polynesian or Maori mythology. For the characters you find, identify their powers and functions. Display your report in a classroom reading center or another location where your classmates can read it.

Build Understanding • *Arachne*

Background

Spiders Arachne is the name of the main character in this myth. *Arachnida* is the name of the class of creatures that includes spiders. Spiders live almost everywhere on the planet and are useful because they eat insect pests. The smallest spiders are the anapids, which are the size of the head of a pin. The largest are the tarantulas, some of which are as large as a dinner plate. Few spiders are harmful.

Connecting to the Literature

Reading/Writing Connection In "Arachne," a young woman learns a lesson about the dangers of being conceited. Life lessons—those learned from experience rather than from a book or a teacher—can be important in helping someone mature. In your notebook, list two or three life lessons you have learned. Use at least three of these words: *challenge, convince, protest, select, transfer.*

Review

For **Reading Skill, Literary Analysis,** and **Vocabulary Builder,** see page 792.

Meet the Author

Olivia E. **Coolidge** (b. 1908)

Olivia Ensor Coolidge was born and educated in England and has lived in both Europe and the United States. She has taught English, Latin, and Greek but is best known as a writer.

Accuracy and Detail In addition to writing about subjects from classical mythology, such as the Trojan War, she has written about colonial times in American history. Coolidge is known for the accuracy of her historical fiction and for her attention to detail.

Fast Facts

▶ Coolidge's first book for children and young adults was *Greek Myths,* published in 1949.
▶ Coolidge says she enjoys writing about legends and myths because she feels they express values that are still important today.

Go **O**nline
Author Link

For: More about the author
Visit: www.PHSchool.com
Web Code: ele-9605

A·r·a·c·h·n·e

Greek Myth

OLIVIA E. COOLIDGE

Arachne (detail), Arvis Stewart, Reprinted with the permission of Macmillian Publishing Company from the Macmillian Book of Greek Gods and Heros by Alice Low, illustrated by Arvis Stewart, Copyright © 1985 by Macmillian Publishing Company.

◄ **Critical Viewing**
What details show that the people in this picture are arguing? **[Analyze]**

Arachne [ə rak´ nē] was a maiden who became famous throughout Greece, though she was neither wellborn nor beautiful and came from no great city. She lived in an <u>obscure</u> little village, and her father was a humble dyer of wool. In this he was very skillful, producing many varied

Vocabulary Builder
obscure (əb skyoor´)
adj. not well known

shades, while above all he was famous for the clear, bright scarlet which is made from shellfish, and which was the most glorious of all the colors used in ancient Greece. Even more skillful than her father was Arachne. It was her task to spin the fleecy wool into a fine, soft thread and to weave it into cloth on the high, standing loom within the cottage. Arachne was small and pale from much working. Her eyes were light and her hair was a dusty brown, yet she was quick and graceful, and her fingers, roughened as they were, went so fast that it was hard to follow their flickering movements. So soft and even was her thread, so fine her cloth, so gorgeous her embroidery, that soon her products were known all over Greece. No one had ever seen the like of them before.

At last Arachne's fame became so great that people used to come from far and wide to watch her working. Even the graceful nymphs[1] would steal in from stream or forest and peep shyly through the dark doorway, watching in wonder the white arms of Arachne as she stood at the loom and threw the shuttle from hand to hand between the hanging threads, or drew out the long wool, fine as a hair, from the distaff[2] as she sat spinning. "Surely Athene[3] herself must have taught her," people would murmur to one another. "Who else could know the secret of such marvelous skill?"

Arachne was used to being wondered at, and she was immensely proud of the skill that had brought so many to look on her. Praise was all she lived for, and it displeased her greatly that people should think anyone, even a goddess, could teach her anything. There- fore when she heard them murmur, she would stop her work and turn round indig- nantly to say, "With my own ten fingers I gained this skill, and by hard practice from early morning till night. I never had time to

Reading Skill
Cause and Effect
What causes Arachne's work to be known all over Greece?

---

1. nymphs (nimfz) *n.* minor nature goddesses, represented as beautiful maidens living in rivers, trees, and mountains.
2. distaff (dis´ taf) *n.* stick on which flax or wool is wound for spinning.
3. Athene (ə thē´ nə) *n.* Greek goddess of wisdom, skills, and warfare.

stand looking as you people do while another maiden worked. Nor if I had, would I give Athene credit because the girl was more skillful than I. As for Athene's weaving, how could there be finer cloth or more beautiful embroidery than mine? If Athene herself were to come down and compete with me, she could do no better than I."

One day when Arachne turned round with such words, an old woman answered her, a gray old woman, bent and very poor, who stood leaning on a staff and peering at Arachne amid the crowd of onlookers. "Reckless girl," she said, "how dare you claim to be equal to the immortal gods themselves? I am an old woman and have seen much. Take my advice and ask pardon of Athene for your words. Rest content with your fame of being the best spinner and weaver that <u>mortal</u> eyes have ever beheld."

"Stupid old woman," said Arachne indignantly, "who gave you a right to speak in this way to me? It is easy to see that you were never good for anything in your day, or you would not come here in poverty and rags to gaze at my skill. If Athene resents my words, let her answer them herself. I have challenged her to a contest, but she, of course, will not come. It is easy for the gods to avoid matching their skill with that of men."

At these words the old woman threw down her staff and stood erect. The wondering onlookers saw her grow tall and fair and stand clad in long robes of dazzling white. They were terribly afraid as they realized that they stood in the presence of Athene. Arachne herself flushed red for a moment, for she had never really believed that the goddess would hear her. Before the group that was gathered there she would not give in; so pressing her pale lips together in <u>obstinacy</u> and pride, she led the goddess to one of the great looms and set herself before the other. Without a word both began to thread the long woolen strands that hang from the rollers, and between which the shuttle[4] moves back and forth. Many skeins lay heaped beside them to use, bleached white, and gold, and scarlet, and other shades, varied as the rainbow. Arachne had never thought of giving credit for her success to her father's skill in dyeing, though in actual truth the colors were as remarkable as the cloth itself.

Soon there was no sound in the room but the breathing of the onlookers, the whirring of the shuttles, and the creaking of the wooden frames as each pressed the thread up into place or tightened the pegs by which the whole was held straight. The excited crowd in the doorway began to see that the skill of both in truth was very nearly equal, but that, however the cloth might turn out, the goddess was the quicker of the two. A pattern of many pictures was growing on her loom. There was a border of twined branches of the olive, Athene's favorite tree, while in the middle, figures began to appear. As they looked at the glowing colors, the spectators realized that Athene was weaving into her pattern a last

Literature in Context

Culture Connection

Athene As goddess of wisdom and warfare, Athene was a key figure in Greek mythology. Athene protected her favorites, such as Odysseus and Heracles (or Hercules), and punished those who displeased her, including Arachne and Ajax, a famous Greek warrior. According to one story, the people of a major Greek city wanted to name their city after either Poseidon, the sea god, or Athene, depending on who gave them the more useful gift. Poseidon created horses, and Athene created olive trees. The gods judged Athene's gift more useful, so Athens was named for her. To honor Athene, the city built a great temple, called the Parthenon.

Connect to the Literature

Which of Athene's character traits does the story illustrate?

---

4. **shuttle** (shut´ əl) *n.* instrument used in weaving to carry thread back and forth.

Vocabulary Builder
obstinacy (äb´ stə nə sē) *n.* stubbornness

warning to Arachne. The central figure was the goddess herself competing with Poseidon for possession of the city of Athens; but in the four corners were mortals who had tried to strive with gods and pictures of the awful fate that had overtaken them. The goddess ended a little before Arachne and stood back from her marvelous work to see what the maiden was doing.

Never before had Arachne been matched against anyone whose skill was equal, or even nearly equal to her own. As she stole glances from time to time at Athene and saw the goddess working swiftly, calmly, and always a little faster than herself, she became angry instead of frightened, and an evil thought came into her head. Thus as Athene stepped back a pace to watch Arachne finishing her work, she saw that the maiden had taken for her design a pattern of scenes which showed evil or unworthy actions of the gods, how they had deceived fair maidens, resorted to trickery, and appeared on earth from time to time in the form of poor and humble people. When the goddess saw this insult glowing in bright colors on Arachne's loom, she did not wait while the cloth was judged, but stepped forward, her gray eyes blazing with anger, and tore Arachne's work across. Then she struck Arachne across the face. Arachne stood there a moment, struggling with anger, fear, and pride. "I will not live under this insult," she cried, and seizing a rope from the wall, she made a noose and would have hanged herself.

The goddess touched the rope and touched the maiden. "Live on, wicked girl," she said. "Live on and spin, both you and your descendants. When men look at you they may remember that it is not wise to strive with Athene." At that the body of Arachne shriveled up, and her legs grew tiny, spindly, and distorted. There before the eyes of the spectators hung a little dusty brown spider on a slender thread.

All spiders descend from Arachne, and as the Greeks watched them spinning their thread wonderfully fine, they remembered the contest with Athene and thought that it was not right for even the best of men to claim equality with the gods.

Literary Analysis
Myths Why is Arachne's design disrespectful to the gods?

Literary Analysis
Myths What traits of spiders does this myth explain?

Apply the Skills

Arachne

Thinking About the Selection

1. **Respond:** If you were Arachne, would you have challenged the goddess Athene? Why or why not?
2. **(a) Recall:** What does Arachne value more than anything else? **(b) Interpret:** Why does Arachne refuse to accept the advice of the old woman? **(c) Analyze:** What character traits does Arachne reveal through her behavior?
3. **(a) Recall:** What design does Athene weave? **(b) Infer:** What is Athene's original intention toward Arachne? **(c) Deduce:** What makes Athene angry?
4. **(a) Recall:** What does Athene do to Arachne? **(b) Speculate:** In ancient times, what lessons might this myth have taught its audiences?
5. **(a) Take a Position:** Do you think that it was fair of Athene to turn Arachne into a spider? Explain. **(b) Discuss:** Share your response with a partner and decide together on a single answer to share with the class.

Reading Skill

6. What is the **effect** of Arachne's skill as a weaver?
7. What **causes** Athene to visit Arachne?
8. Complete the chart to show causes and effects in "Arachne."

Causes	Effects
Arachne challenges Athene.	
	Arachne's design shows unworthy actions of the gods.
Athene touches the rope and touches Arachne.	

Literary Analysis

9. What does this **myth** explain about spiders?
10. What beliefs and values are taught in this myth?

QuickReview

Who's Who in the Story

Arachne: a young woman with great skill in weaving

Athene: Greek goddess of wisdom

Go Online
Assessment
For: Self-test
Visit: www.PHSchool.com
Web Code: ela-6605

Cause: an event, action, or feeling that makes something happen

Effect: what happens

Myths: tales that explain the natural world, teach a lesson, or express a value

Vocabulary Builder

Practice Use a vocabulary word from page 792 to rewrite each sentence so that it has the opposite meaning.

1. The movie's main character had superhuman qualities.
2. Everyone in the class had heard of the famous novel.
3. Her agreeable nature makes her easy to get along with.

Writing

Write a brief **essay** in which you consider the difference between learning lessons from stories and from your own experience.

- Make notes about the main lesson of "Arachne" and your response to learning this lesson through the myth.
- Jot down notes about lessons you have learned from your own experience.
- Think about these two ways of learning lessons. As you draft, identify the method you prefer and tell why.

Use your essay in a group discussion about how myths can relate to our lives.

For *Grammar, Vocabulary,* and *Assessment,* see **Build Language Skills,** pages 808–809.

Extend Your Learning

Listening and Speaking In a group, prepare an **oral report** of scientific information about spiders. Research their appearance, habitat, diet, and any other interesting aspects. Include photographs or drawings. Present your report to the class, with each group member contributing to the oral presentation.

Research and Technology Use the Internet, CD-ROMs, and other library resources to prepare a written **report** about one or more of the ancient Greek gods and goddesses, including Athene. As you research, find out whether the name of the god or goddess has become part of our language. Display your report in a location where your classmates can read it.

Build Language Skills

Arachne • Prologue from *The Whale Rider*

Vocabulary Skill

Synonyms The words *effect* and *result* are **synonyms**. They have the same basic meaning. Synonyms sometimes have slightly different shades of meaning.

➤ **Example:** The *effect* of getting too much sun can be a sunburn.
   The *result* of getting too much sun can be a sunburn.

Practice Answer each of the following questions. Use a different synonym for the word in italics in each answer. Explain the reasons for the synonym you choose.

1. What can be the *effect* of a heavy rainfall on a highway?
2. What may be the *effect* of losing a night's sleep?
3. What is the *effect* of the character's actions?
4. What is the *effect* of a long, dry summer?

Grammar Lesson

Simple, Compound, and Complex Sentences Sentences can be classified according to the number and kinds of their **clauses**—groups of words with their own subjects and verbs. This chart shows the three types of sentence structures.

MorePractice

For more practice with Sentence Structure see the Grammar Handbook, pp. R33-35.

Simple Sentence	Compound Sentence	Complex Sentence
A single independent clause	Two or more independent clauses	One independent clause and one or more subordinate clauses
The dog barked. He and I walked home.	Brad cooked the meal, Kai set the table, and I washed dishes.	Because the storm came, our game was postponed.

Practice Add to each group of words to make the kind of sentence shown in parentheses.

1. Lexi left on time, but (complex)
2. The barber gave Will (simple)
3. Latrice made a cake and (compound)
4. The whistle blew, the runners took off, and (complex)

W̶G Prentice Hall Writing and Grammar Connection: Chapter 20, Section 2

Reading: Cause and Effect

Directions: *Read the selection. Then, answer the questions.*

The auditorium was crowded. Paolo sat with his parents and his friend James near the stage. He tried to listen, but he was too nervous to really hear the music. He tried to think calming thoughts. Whatever happened today, his parents would still be proud of him. Then he imagined how it might feel to win the piano competition. He began to relax. Suddenly, Paolo heard his name called. His mother smiled and squeezed his hand. Paolo took a deep breath and walked confidently to the stage.

1. Why is the auditorium crowded?
   A There is a sports event.
   B There is a band concert.
   C There is a music contest.
   D There is an award ceremony.

2. Why is Paolo nervous?
   A His friend is playing piano in a contest.
   B His parents are disappointed in him.
   C He has just won an award.
   D He is about to compete in a piano contest.

3. What happens when Paolo imagines winning the contest?
   A He becomes nervous.
   B He begins to relax.
   C His heart rises to his throat.
   D He plays with confidence.

4. Which of these gives Paolo confidence just before he plays in the contest?
   A His mother squeezes his hand.
   B His friend wishes him good luck.
   C His father smiles at him.
   D His name is called.

Timed Writing: Explanation [Connections]

Review "The Lion and the Bulls" or "A Crippled Boy." Then, briefly explain how the lesson in one story applies to people living today.
(30 minutes)

 ## Writing Workshop: *Work in Progress*

Multimedia Presentation
Using the work in your writing portfolio, note how you would illustrate the main point of your presentation. Highlight the media that fits your topic. Write an explanation of why this media best fits the topic. Save this work in your writing portfolio.

Cause-and-Effect Articles

In Part 1, you are learning about cause and effect in literature. Understanding cause and effect is also important when reading informational materials such as textbooks, medical brochures, and articles that explain causes and effects. If you read the prologue to *The Whale Rider,* you may be interested in this article, because it explores an effect of whale behavior.

About Cause-and-Effect Articles

A **cause-and-effect article** identifies and explains connections between events and circumstances that bring about other events and circumstances. Such articles may be found in many newspapers and magazines and in your textbooks. Most cause-and-effect articles have the following characteristics:

- a clear explanation of one or more causes and/or effects
- facts, statistics, and other details to support an explanation
- a clear and consistent organization
- words that show connections among details

Reading Skill

To fully understand a text identify the **organizational structure,** or the way the writing is organized. Look for relationships among ideas. As you read, ask, *How are the ideas in this piece of writing connected to one another?* You might find that they are organized to show cause and effect. Cause is the reason behind an event. Effect is the result produced by the cause. Sometimes effects can become causes for new effects. As you read a cause-and-effect article, first identify the main event or effect. Then identify other causes and effects presented by the writer. Use a chart like the one shown to help you track causes and effects in the following article.

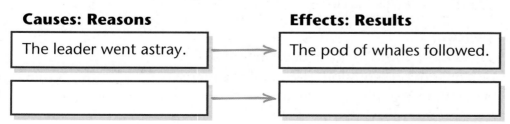

Causes: Reasons	Effects: Results
The leader went astray.	The pod of whales followed.

St. Martin, November 27, 2003

36 Beached Whales Die in St. Martin

By Marvin Hokstam, Associated Press

> The writer begins by stating the main cause-and-effect relationship in the article.

MARIGOT, St. Martin—Thirty-six whales beached themselves on the coast of this Caribbean island and died within hours despite the efforts of people who tried to push some back out to sea.

The short-finned pilot whales were believed to have beached themselves Monday night, and by noon Tuesday all were dead.

The animals were found before dawn by a man on his way to a dump in the French Caribbean territory, which shares an island with Dutch St. Maarten. Residents and tourists later gathered around the whales, which were up to 15 feet long.

> The writer presents supporting details about the whales' deaths.

Reading Informational Materials

People were able to push two whales back into the water, but they returned and beached themselves again, appearing exhausted, said Paul Ellinger, of the St. Maarten Nature Foundation. He said it seemed the whales had become disoriented.

"What's clear is that they got off course. What caused them to go off course? We'll have to check," Ellinger said. "It could be all kinds of reasons: the temperature of the water, their sonar system. It could have been anything."

Short-finned pilot whales usually swim in pods, and when a leader goes astray the entire pod often follows, Ellinger said.

Biologists were keeping three carcasses to investigate.

The whales covered the beach along the shallow Grand Cailles Bay, the mouth of which is fringed with coral reefs. The whales bore injuries apparently sustained when they ran aground.

French police arrived Tuesday morning and closed off the spot as workers dug beach-side graves to bury the remaining whales.

Sometimes the cause of an event is not known. In this case, the writer may present possible causes, based on the statements of experts.

The writer concludes with more details, which are themselves causes and effects.

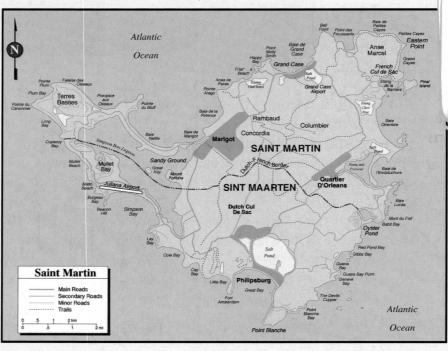

Reading: Cause and Effect

Directions: *Choose the letter of the best answer to each question about the cause-and-effect article.*

1. What happened when people pushed two of the whales back into the water?
    A The whales swam into the sea.
    B The whales returned to the beach.
    C The whales died in the water.
    D The whales dived to the ocean floor.

2. Which word in this sentence from the article identifies a cause-and-effect relationship? "It could be all kinds of reasons: the temperature of the water, their sonar system."
    A could
    B reasons
    C temperature
    D sonar

3. What is the apparent cause of the beached whales' injuries?
    A They were attacked by sharks.
    B They were harmed by people on the beach.
    C They were injured by other whales.
    D They swam over coral reefs and ran aground.

Reading: Comprehension and Interpretation

Directions: *Write your answers on a separate sheet of paper.*

4. What are some possible reasons that the whales went off course? **[Generating]**

5. What is one possible reason that two of the whales beached themselves again? **[Generating]**

6. Why do you think people want to understand the cause of the whales' death? **[Integrating]**

Timed Writing: Explanation [Connections]

Sometimes a single cause results in multiple effects. Write a brief explanation of how one cause presented in the article produced multiple effects. **(15 minutes)**

Elements of Fantasy

Fantasy is imaginative writing that contains elements not found in real life. Stories about a singing donkey, an undersea kingdom, or a magic skateboard are examples of fantasy.

Many fantastic stories contain **realistic elements**—characters, events, or situations that are true to life. Use questions like these to identify the fantastic and realistic elements in a story:

- Which elements of the story's setting could not exist in real life? Which elements could exist?
- Which elements of a character's behavior could not occur in real life? Which elements could occur?
- Which elements of the situation could not happen in real life? Which elements could happen?

Title:
Element
Fantastic or Realistic?
Why

Comparing Elements of Fantasy

Both "Mowgli's Brothers" and the passage from *James and the Giant Peach* are fantasies about animals and a boy. However, one contains more realistic elements than the other. Create a chart like the one shown for each story. Then, record fantastic and realistic elements as you read.

Vocabulary Builder

Mowgli's Brothers

- **quarry** (kwôr´ ē) *n.* prey; anything being hunted or pursued (p. 820) *The hunter spied his quarry near the top of a tree.*
- **fostering** (fôs´ tər iŋ) *n.* taking care of (p. 821) *Fostering the abandoned pups was a full-time job.*
- **monotonous** (mə nät´n əs) *adj.* unchanging; tiresome because it does not vary (p. 822) *Time passed slowly during the monotonous journey.*

- **dispute** (di spyo͞ot´) *n.* argument; debate; quarrel (p. 822) *There was a dispute over which driver had caused the accident.*

from James and the Giant Peach

- **intently** (in tent´ lē) *adv.* with great attention or determination (p. 827) *Hector stared intently at the strange blinking lights.*
- **colossal** (kə läs´ əl) *adj.* very large; huge (p. 830) *Ebony could barely lift the colossal trophy.*

Build Understanding

Connecting to the Literature

Reading/Writing Connection Think about which you like better—a fantasy or a story based on real life. Write a few sentences giving reasons for your preference. Use at least three of the following words: *appreciate, capture, emphasize, relax, perceive.*

Meet the Authors

Rudyard **Kipling** (1865–1936)

Rudyard Kipling was born in India to British parents. When he was very young, his Indian nurses told him folk tales that featured talking animals. These stories inspired the characters in many of Kipling's works, such as *The Jungle Book,* in which "Mowgli's Brothers" appears.

Award Winner As a young boy, Kipling was sent to school in England. At age sixteen, he returned to India as a journalist. His work as a reporter, fiction writer, and poet earned him the 1907 Nobel Prize in Literature.

Roald **Dahl** (1916–1990)

As a boy growing up in Wales, Roald Dahl loved books and stories. When he was eight years old, he began keeping a diary, carefully hiding it from his sisters in a tin box tied to a high tree branch. Years later, Dahl began his formal writing career by describing his experiences in the Royal Air Force during World War II.

Encouraging Young Readers Dahl became interested in writing stories for children while making up bedtime stories for his daughters. That is how *James and the Giant Peach* came to be written. He believed strongly in the importance of reading. "I have a passion for teaching kids to become readers," he once said.

Go **O**nline
Author Link

For: More about the authors
Visit: www.PHSchool.com
Web Code: ele-9606

MOWGLI'S BROTHERS
Rudyard Kipling

Now Chil the Kite[1] brings home the night
That Mang the Bat sets free—
The herds are shut in byre[2] and hut
For loosed till dawn are we.
This is the hour of pride and power,
Talon and tush[3] and claw.
Oh hear the call!—Good hunting all
That keep the Jungle Law!
—Night-Song in the Jungle

It was seven o'clock of a very warm evening in the Seeonee hills[4] when Father Wolf woke up from his day's rest, scratched himself, yawned, and spread out his paws one after the other to get rid of the sleepy feeling in their tips. Mother Wolf lay with her big gray nose dropped across her four tumbling, squealing cubs, and the moon shone into the mouth of the cave where they all lived. "Augrh!" said Father Wolf, "it is time to hunt again"; and he was going to spring downhill when a little shadow with a bushy tail crossed the threshold and whined: "Good luck go with you, O Chief of the Wolves; and good luck and strong white teeth go with the noble children, that they may never forget the hungry in this world."

It was the jackal—Tabaqui the Dishlicker—and the wolves of India despise Tabaqui because he runs about making mischief, and telling tales, and eating rags and pieces of leather from the village rubbish-heaps. But they

1. **Kite** (kīt) *n.* bird of the hawk family.
2. **byre** (bīr) *n.* cow barn.
3. **tush** (tush) *n.* tusk.
4. **Seeonee** (sē ō′ nē) **hills** hills in central India.

Literary Analysis
Elements of Fantasy
What element of fantasy is introduced in this paragraph? Explain.

are afraid of him too, because Tabaqui, more than anyone else in the jungle, is apt to go mad, and then he forgets that he was ever afraid of anyone, and runs through the forest biting everything in his way. Even the tiger runs and hides when little Tabaqui goes mad, for madness is the most disgraceful thing that can overtake a wild creature. We call it hydrophobia, but they call it *dewanee*—the madness—and run.

"Enter, then, and look," said Father Wolf, stiffly; "but there is no food here."

"For a wolf, no," said Tabaqui; "but for so mean a person as myself a dry bone is a good feast. Who are we, the Gidur log [the jackal-people], to pick and choose?" He scuttled to the back of the cave, where he found the bone of a buck with some meat on it, and sat cracking the end merrily.

"All thanks for this good meal," he said, licking his lips. "How beautiful are the noble children! How large are their eyes! And so young too! Indeed, indeed, I might have remembered that the children of Kings are men from the beginning."

Now, Tabaqui knew as well as anyone else that there is nothing so unlucky as to compliment children to their faces; and it pleases him to see Mother and Father Wolf look uncomfortable.

Tabaqui sat still, rejoicing in the mischief that he had made: then he said spitefully:

"Shere Khan, the Big One, has shifted his hunting-grounds. He will hunt among these hills for the next moon, so he has told me."

Shere Khan was the tiger who lived near the Waingunga River, twenty miles away.

"He has no right!" Father Wolf began angrily—"By the Law of the Jungle he has no right to change his quarters without due warning. He will frighten every head of game within ten miles, and I—I have to kill for two, these days."

"His mother did not call him Lungri [the Lame One] for nothing," said Mother Wolf, quietly. "He has been lame in one foot from his birth. That is why he has only killed cattle. Now the villagers of the Waingunga are angry with him, and he has come here to make our villagers angry. They will scour the Jungle for him when he is far away, and we

Literary Analysis
Elements of Fantasy
What is fantastic about Tabaqui's behavior? What is realistic about it?

✓ **Reading Check**

Why do the wolves despise Tabaqui?

and our children must run when the grass is set alight. Indeed, we are very grateful to Shere Khan!"

"Shall I tell him of your gratitude?" said Tabaqui.

"Out!" snapped Father Wolf. "Out and hunt with thy master. Thou hast done harm enough for one night."

"I go," said Tabaqui, quietly. "Ye can hear Shere Khan below in the thickets. I might have saved myself the message."

Father Wolf listened, and below in the valley that ran down to a little river, he heard the dry, angry, snarly, singsong whine of a tiger who has caught nothing and does not care if all the Jungle knows it.

"The fool!" said Father Wolf. "To begin a night's work with that noise! Does he think that our buck are like his fat Waingunga bullocks?"[5]

"H'sh! It is neither bullock nor buck he hunts tonight," said Mother Wolf. "It is Man." The whine had changed to a sort of humming purr that seemed to come from every quarter of the compass. It was the noise that bewilders woodcutters and gypsies sleeping in the open, and makes them run sometimes into the very mouth of the tiger.

"Man!" said Father Wolf, showing all his white teeth. "Faugh! Are there not enough beetles and frogs in the tanks that he must eat Man and on our ground too!"

The Law of the Jungle, which never orders anything without a reason, forbids every beast to eat Man except when he is killing to show his children how to kill, and then he must hunt outside the hunting-grounds of his pack or tribe. The real reason for this is that man-killing means, sooner or later, the arrival of white men on elephants, with guns, and hundreds of brown men with gongs and rockets and torches. Then everybody in the jungle suffers. The reason the beasts give among themselves is that Man is the weakest and most defenseless of all living things, and it is unsportsmanlike to touch him. They say too—and it is true—that man-eaters become mangy,[6] and lose their teeth.

The purr grew louder, and ended in the full-throated "Aaarh!" of the tiger's charge.

Literary Analysis
Elements of Fantasy
Do you think the behavior described in this paragraph is fantastic or realistic? Explain.

▼ **Critical Viewing**
What qualities of Mother Wolf do you see in this wolf?
[Connect]

---

5. **bullocks** (bŏŏl´ əks) *n.* steers.
6. **mangy** (mān´ jē) *adj.* having mange, a skin disease of mammals that causes sores and loss of hair.

Then there was a howl—an untigerish howl—from Shere Khan. "He has missed," said Mother Wolf. "What is it?"

Father Wolf ran out a few paces and heard Shere Khan muttering and mumbling savagely, as he tumbled about in the scrub.

"The fool has had no more sense than to jump at a wood-cutter's campfire, and has burned his feet," said Father Wolf, with a grunt. "Tabaqui is with him."

"Something is coming up hill," said Mother Wolf, twitching one ear. "Get ready."

The bushes rustled a little in the thicket, and Father Wolf dropped with his haunches under him, ready for his leap. Then, if you had been watching, you would have seen the most wonderful thing in the world—the wolf checked in mid-spring. He made his bound before he saw what it was he was jumping at, and then he tried to stop himself. The result was that he shot up straight into the air for four or five feet, landing almost where he left ground.

"Man!" he snapped. "A man's cub. Look!"

Directly in front of him, holding on by a low branch, stood a naked brown baby who could just walk—as soft and as dimpled a little atom[7] as ever came to a wolf's cave at night. He looked up into Father Wolf's face, and laughed.

"Is that a man's cub?" said Mother Wolf. "I have never seen one. Bring it here."

A wolf accustomed to moving his own cubs can, if necessary, mouth an egg without breaking it, and though Father Wolf's jaws closed right on the child's back not a tooth even scratched the skin, as he laid it down among the cubs.

"How little! How naked, and—how bold!" said Mother Wolf, softly. The baby was pushing his way between the cubs to get close to the warm hide. "Ahai! He is taking his meal with the others. And so this is a man's cub. Now, was there ever a wolf that could boast of a man's cub among her children?"

"I have heard now and again of such a thing, but never in our Pack or in my time," said Father Wolf. "He is altogether without hair, and I could kill him with a touch of my foot. But see, he looks up and is not afraid."

Literary Analysis
Elements of Fantasy
Do you think Father Wolf's behavior here could occur in real life? Why or why not?

Reading Check

Why does the Law of the Jungle generally forbid man-killing?

---

7. atom (atʹ əm) *n.* tiny piece of matter.

The moonlight was blocked out of the mouth of the cave, for Shere Khan's great square head and shoulders were thrust into the entrance. Tabaqui, behind him, was squeaking: "My lord, my lord, it went in here!"

"Shere Khan does us great honor," said Father Wolf, but his eyes were very angry. "What does Shere Khan need?"

"My quarry. A man's cub went this way," said Shere Khan. "Its parents have run off. Give it to me."

Shere Khan had jumped at a woodcutter's campfire, as Father Wolf had said, and was furious from the pain of his burned feet. But Father Wolf knew that the mouth of the cave was too narrow for a tiger to come in by. Even where he was, Shere Khan's shoulders and forepaws were cramped for want of room, as a man's would be if he tried to fight in a barrel.

"The Wolves are a free people," said Father Wolf. "They take orders from the Head of the Pack, and not from any striped cattle-killer. The man's cub is ours—to kill if we choose."

"Ye choose and ye do not choose! What talk is this of choosing? By the bull that I killed, am I to stand nosing into your dog's den for my fair dues? It is I, Shere Khan, who speak!"

The tiger's roar filled the cave with thunder. Mother Wolf shook herself clear of the cubs and sprang forward, her eyes, like two green moons in the darkness, facing the blazing eyes of Shere Khan.

"And it is I, Raksha [The Demon], who answer. The man's cub is mine, Lungri—mine to me! He shall not be killed. He shall live to run with the Pack and to hunt with the Pack; and in the end, look you, hunter of little naked cubs—frog-eater—fish-killer—he shall hunt thee! Now get hence, or by the Sambhur that I killed (I eat no starved cattle), back thou goest to thy mother, burned beast of the Jungle, lamer than ever thou camest into the world! Go!"

Father Wolf looked on amazed. He had almost forgotten the days when he won Mother Wolf in fair fight from five other wolves, when she ran in the Pack and was not called The Demon for compliment's sake. Shere Khan might have faced Father Wolf, but he could not stand up against Mother Wolf, for he knew that where he was she had all the

Vocabulary Builder
quarry (kwôr´ ē) *n.* prey; anything being hunted or pursued

▼ **Critical Viewing**
Do you think this tiger is friendly to humans? Why or why not? **[Speculate]**

advantage of the ground, and would fight to the death. So he backed out of the cave-mouth growling, and when he was clear he shouted:

"Each dog barks in his own yard! We will see what the Pack will say to this <u>fostering</u> of man-cubs. The cub is mine, and to my teeth he will come in the end, O bush-tailed thieves!"

Mother Wolf threw herself down panting among the cubs, and Father Wolf said to her gravely:

"Shere Khan speaks this much truth. The cub must be shown to the Pack. Wilt thou still keep him, Mother?"

"Keep him!" she gasped. "He came naked, by night, alone and very hungry; yet he was not afraid! Look, he has pushed one of my babies to one side already. And that lame butcher would have killed him and would have run off to the Waingunga while the villagers here hunted through all our lairs in revenge! Keep him? Assuredly I will keep him. Lie still, little frog. O thou Mowgli—for Mowgli the Frog I will call thee—the time will come when thou wilt hunt Shere Khan as he has hunted thee."

"But what will our Pack say?" said Father Wolf. The Law of the Jungle lays down very clearly that any wolf may, when he marries, withdraw from the Pack he belongs to; but as soon as his cubs are old enough to stand on their feet he must bring them to the Pack Council, which is generally held once a month at full moon, in order that the other wolves may identify them. After that inspection the cubs are free to run where they please, and until they have killed their first buck no excuse is accepted if a grown wolf of the Pack kills one of them. The punishment is death where the murderer can be found; and if you think for a minute you will see that this must be so.

Father Wolf waited till his cubs could run a little, and then on the night of the Pack Meeting took them and Mowgli and Mother Wolf to the Council Rock—a hilltop covered with stones and boulders where a hundred wolves could hide. Akela, the great gray Lone Wolf, who led all the Pack by strength and cunning, lay out at full length on his rock, and below him sat forty or more wolves of every size and color, from badger-colored veterans who could handle a buck alone, to young black three-year-olds who thought

Vocabulary Builder
fostering (fôs´ tər iŋ) *n.* taking care of

Reading Check

How does Mother Wolf respond to Shere Kahn's demands?

they could. The Lone Wolf had led them for a year now. He had fallen twice into a wolf-trap in his youth, and once he had been beaten and left for dead; so he knew the manners and customs of men. There was very little talking at the Rock. The cubs tumbled over each other in the center of the circle where their mothers and fathers sat, and now and again a senior wolf would go quietly up to a cub, look at him carefully, and return to his place on noiseless feet. Sometimes a mother would push her cub far out into the moonlight, to be sure that he had not been overlooked. Akela from his rock would cry: "Ye know the Law—ye know the Law. Look well, O Wolves!" and the anxious mothers would take up the call: "Look—look well, O Wolves!"

At last—and Mother Wolf's neck-bristles lifted as the time came—Father Wolf pushed "Mowgli the Frog," as they called him, into the center, where he sat laughing and playing with some pebbles that glistened in the moonlight.

Akela never raised his head from his paws, but went on with the <u>monotonous</u> cry: "Look well!" A muffled roar came up from behind the rocks—the voice of Shere Khan crying: "The cub is mine. Give him to me. What have the Free People to do with a man's cub?" Akela never even twitched his ears: all he said was: "Look well, O Wolves! What have the Free People to do with the orders of any save the Free People? Look well!"

There was a chorus of deep growls, and a young wolf in his fourth year flung back Shere Khan's question to Akela: "What have the Free People to do with the man's cub?" Now the Law of the Jungle lays down that if there is any <u>dispute</u> as to the right of a cub to be accepted by the Pack, he must be spoken for by at least two members of the Pack who are not his father and mother.

"Who speaks for this cub?" said Akela. "Among the Free People who speaks?" There was no answer, and Mother Wolf got ready for what she knew would be her last fight, if things came to fighting.

Then the only other creature who is allowed at the Pack Council—Baloo, the sleepy brown bear who teaches the wolf cubs the Law of the Jungle: old Baloo, who can come and go where he pleases because he eats only nuts and roots and honey—rose up on his hind quarters and grunted.

Literary Analysis
Elements of Fantasy
What details about this meeting at Council Rock are realistic? What details are fantastic?

Vocabulary Builder
monotonous (mə nät′n əs) *adj.* unchanging; tiresome because it does not vary

dispute (di spyo͞ot′) *n.* argument; debate; quarrel

▶ **Critical Viewing**
How do you think the other animals might behave toward a panther like the one shown? Explain. **[Speculate]**

"The man's cub—the man's cub?" he said. "I speak for the man's cub. There is no harm in a man's cub. I have no gift of words, but I speak the truth. Let him run with the Pack, and be entered with the others. I myself will teach him."

"We need yet another," said Akela. "Baloo has spoken, and he is our teacher for the young cubs. Who speaks besides Baloo?"

A black shadow dropped down into the circle. It was Bagheera the Black Panther, inky black all over, but with the panther marking showing up in certain lights like the pattern of watered silk. Everybody knew Bagheera, and nobody cared to cross his path; for he was as cunning as Tabaqui, as bold as the wild buffalo, and as reckless as the wounded elephant. But he had a voice as soft as wild honey dripping from a tree, and a skin softer than down.

"O Akela, and ye the Free People," he purred, "I have no right in your assembly; but the Law of the Jungle says that if there is a doubt which is not a killing matter in regard to a new cub, the life of that cub may be bought at a price. And the Law does not say who may or may not pay that price. Am I right?"

"Good! good!" said the young wolves, who are always hungry. "Listen to Bagheera. The cub can be bought for a price. It is the Law."

"Knowing that I have no right to speak here, I ask your leave."

"Speak then," cried twenty voices.

"To kill a naked cub is shame. Besides, he may make better sport for you when he is grown. Baloo has spoken in his behalf. Now to Baloo's word I will add one bull, and a fat one, newly killed, not half a mile from here, if ye will accept the man's cub according to the Law. Is it difficult?"

There was a clamor of scores of voices, saying: "What matter? He will die in the winter rains. He will scorch in the sun. What harm can a naked frog do us? Let him run with the Pack. Where is the bull, Bagheera? Let him

Literary Analysis
Elements of Fantasy
Does Baloo's speech in favor of keeping the child seem true to life or fantastic? Explain.

Reading Check

According to the Law of the Jungle, how must the Pack settle a dispute over accepting a cub?

be accepted." And then came Akela's deep bay, crying: "Look well—look well, O Wolves!"

Mowgli was still deeply interested in the pebbles, and he did not notice when the wolves came and looked at him one by one. At last they all went down the hill for the dead bull, and only Akela, Bagheera, Baloo, and Mowgli's own wolves were left. Shere Khan roared still in the night, for he was very angry that Mowgli had not been handed over to him.

"Ay, roar well," said Bagheera, under his whiskers; "for the time comes when this naked thing will make thee roar to another tune, or I know nothing of man."

"It was well done," said Akela. "Men and their cubs are very wise. He may be a help in time."

"Truly, a help in time of need; for none can hope to lead the Pack forever," said Bagheera.

Akela said nothing. He was thinking of the time that comes to every leader of every pack when his strength goes from him and he gets feebler and feebler till at last he is killed by the wolves and a new leader comes up—to be killed in his turn.

"Take him away," he said to Father Wolf, "and train him as befits one of the Free People."

And that is how Mowgli was entered into the Seeonee wolf-pack at the price of a bull and on Baloo's good word.

Literary Analysis
Elements of Fantasy
Which behavior described here is not likely to occur in real life?

Thinking About the Selection

1. **Respond:** If you were a member of the Council, would you want Mowgli in the pack? Why or why not?

2. **(a) Compare and Contrast:** How is Mowgli similar to the wolf cubs? How is he different? **(b) Analyze:** What qualities in Mowgli does Mother Wolf find appealing?

3. **(a) Recall:** Who pays for Mowgli's life? **(b) Evaluate:** Are his reasons based on his own self-interest or on what is good for the pack? **(c) Support:** What examples from the story support your answer?

4. **(a) Summarize:** Describe how the wolves in the pack make decisions. **(b) Take a Position:** Do you think this is an effective process? Explain.

from
James and the Giant Peach

Roald Dahl

I t was quite a large hole, the sort of thing an animal about the size of a fox might have made.

James knelt down in front of it and poked his head and shoulders inside.

He crawled in.

He kept on crawling.

▲ **Critical Viewing**
Which details of this picture are fantastic? Which are realistic? **[Analyze]**

This isn't just a hole, he thought excitedly. It's a tunnel!

The tunnel was damp and murky, and all around him there was the curious bitter-sweet smell of fresh peach. The floor was soggy under his knees, the walls were wet and sticky, and peach juice was dripping from the ceiling. James opened his mouth and caught some of it on his tongue. It tasted delicious.

He was crawling uphill now, as though the tunnel were leading straight toward the very center of the gigantic fruit. Every few seconds he paused and took a bite out of the wall. The peach flesh was sweet and juicy, and marvelously refreshing.

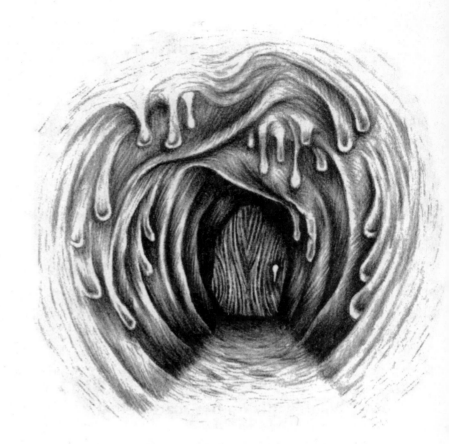

He crawled on for several more yards, and then suddenly—bang—the top of his head bumped into something extremely hard blocking his way. He glanced up. In front of him there was a solid wall that seemed at first as though it were made of wood. He touched it with his fingers. It certainly felt like wood, except that it was very jagged and full of deep grooves.

"Good heavens!" he said.

"I know what this is! I've come to the stone in the middle of the peach!"

Then he noticed that there was a small door cut into the face of the peach stone. He gave a push. It swung open. He crawled through it, and before he had time to glance up and see where he was, he heard a voice saying, "Look who's here!" And another one said, "We've been waiting for you!"

James stopped and stared at the speakers, his face white with horror.

▲ Critical Viewing
How does this picture of the tunnel compare with the description of it in the story? [Compare and Contrast]

Literary Analysis
Elements of Fantasy Identify one fantastic element and one realistic element in this paragraph.

He started to stand up, but his knees were shaking so much he had to sit down again on the floor. He glanced behind him, thinking he could bolt back into the tunnel the way he had come, but the doorway had disappeared. There was now only a solid brown wall behind him.

James's large frightened eyes traveled slowly around the room.

The creatures, some sitting on chairs, others reclining on a sofa, were all watching him <u>intently</u>.

Creatures?

Or were they insects?

An insect is usually something rather small, is it not? A grasshopper, for example, is an insect.

So what would you call it if you saw a grasshopper as large as a dog? As large as a large dog. You could hardly call that an insect, could you?

There was an Old-Green-Grasshopper as large as a large dog sitting on a stool directly across the room from James now.

And next to the Old-Green-Grasshopper, there was an enormous Spider.

And next to the Spider, there was a giant Ladybug with nine black spots on her scarlet shell.

Each of these three was squatting upon a magnificent chair.

On a sofa nearby, reclining comfortably in curled-up positions, there was a Centipede and an Earthworm.

On the floor over in the far corner, there was something thick and white that looked as though it might be a Silkworm. But it was sleeping soundly and nobody was paying any attention to it.

Every one of these "creatures" was at least as big as James himself, and in the strange greenish light that shone down from somewhere in the ceiling, they were absolutely terrifying to behold.

"I'm hungry!" the Spider announced suddenly, staring hard at James.

"I'm famished!" the Old-Green-Grasshopper said.

"So am I!" the Ladybug cried.

✓ **Reading Check**

What clues help James guess what the solid wall really is?

from *James and the Giant Peach* ■ 827

The Centipede sat up a little straighter on the sofa. "Everyone's famished!" he said. "We need food!"

Four pairs of round black glassy eyes were all fixed upon James.

The Centipede made a wriggling movement with his body as though he were about to glide off the sofa—but he didn't.

There was a long pause— and a long silence.

The Spider (who happened to be a female spider) opened her mouth and ran a long black tongue delicately over her lips. "Aren't you hungry?" she asked suddenly, leaning forward and addressing herself to James.

Poor James was backed up against the far wall, shivering with fright and much too terrified to answer.

"What's the matter with you?" the Old-Green-Grasshopper asked. "You look positively ill!"

"He looks as though he's going to faint any second," the Centipede said.

"Oh, my goodness, the poor thing!" the Ladybug cried. "I do believe he thinks it's him that we are wanting to eat!"

There was a roar of laughter from all sides.

"Oh dear, oh dear!" they said. "What an awful thought!"

"You mustn't be frightened," the Ladybug said kindly. "We wouldn't dream of hurting you. You are one of us now, didn't you know that? You are one of the crew. We're all in the same boat."

"We've been waiting for you all day long," the Old-Green-Grasshopper said. "We thought you were never going to turn up. I'm glad you made it."

"So cheer up, my boy, cheer up!" the Centipede said. "And meanwhile I wish you'd come over here and give me a hand with these boots. It takes me hours to get them all off by myself."

▲ Critical Viewing
Which detail of the illustration suggests that it is a spider? [Analyze]

Literary Analysis
Elements of Fantasy Identify one fantastic detail in this paragraph.

James decided that this was most certainly not a time to be disagreeable, so he crossed the room to where the Centipede was sitting and knelt down beside him.

"Thank you so much," the Centipede said. "You are very kind."

"You have a lot of boots," James murmured.

"I have a lot of legs," the Centipede answered proudly. "And a lot of feet. One hundred, to be exact."

"There he goes again!" the Earthworm cried, speaking for the first time. "He simply cannot stop telling lies about his legs! He doesn't have anything like a hundred of them! He's only got forty-two! The trouble is that most people don't bother to count them. They just take his word. And anyway, there is nothing marvelous, you know, Centipede, about having a lot of legs."

Literary Analysis
Elements of Fantasy
Could a conversation such as this one occur in real life? Explain.

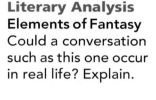

"Poor fellow," the Centipede said, whispering in James's ear. "He's blind. He can't see how splendid I look."

"In my opinion," the Earthworm said, "the really marvelous thing is to have no legs at all and to be able to walk just the same."

"You call that walking!" cried the Centipede. "You're a slitherer, that's all you are! You just slither along!"

"I glide," said the Earthworm primly.

"You are a slimy beast," answered the Centipede.

"I am not a slimy beast," the Earthworm said. "I am a useful and much loved creature. Ask any gardener you like. And as for you . . ."

"I am a pest!" the Centipede announced, grinning broadly and looking round the room for approval.

"He is so proud of that," the Ladybug said, smiling at James. "Though for the life of me I cannot understand why."

"I am the only pest in this room!" cried the Centipede, still grinning away. "Unless you count Old-Green-Grasshopper over there. But he is long past it now. He is too old to be a pest any more."

The Old-Green-Grasshopper turned his huge black eyes upon

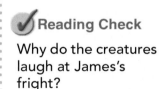

Reading Check

Why do the creatures laugh at James's fright?

"James," the Centipede said. "Your names is James, isn't it?"

"Yes."

"Well, James, have you ever in your life seen such a marvelous <u>colossal</u> Centipede as me?"

"I certainly haven't," James answered. "How on earth did you get to be like that?"

"Very peculiar," the Centipede said. "Very, very peculiar indeed. Let me tell you what happened. I was messing about in the garden under the old peach tree and suddenly a funny little green thing came wriggling past my nose. Bright green it was, and extraordinarily beautiful, and it looked like some kind of a tiny stone or crystal . . ."

"Oh, but I know what that was!" cried James.

"It happened to me, too!" said the Ladybug.

▲ **Critical Viewing**
What might the creatures be discussing in this picture? **[Speculate]**

Vocabulary Builder
colossal (kə läs´ əl)
adj. very large; huge

"And me!" Miss Spider said. "Suddenly there were little green things everywhere! The soil was full of them!"

"I actually swallowed one!" the Earthworm declared proudly.

"So did I!" the Ladybug said.

"I swallowed three!" the Centipede cried. "But who's telling this story anyway? Don't interrupt!"

"It's too late to tell stories now," the Old-Green-Grasshopper announced. "It's time to go to sleep."

"I refuse to sleep in my boots!" the Centipede cried. "How many more are there to come off, James?"

"I think I've done about twenty so far," James told him.

"Then that leaves eighty to go," the Centipede said.

"Twenty-two, not eighty!" shrieked the Earthworm. "He's lying again."

The Centipede roared with laughter.

"Stop pulling the Earthworm's leg," the Ladybug said.

This sent the Centipede into hysterics. "Pulling his leg!" he cried, wriggling with glee and pointing at the Earthworm.

"Which leg am I pulling? You tell me that?"

James decided that he rather liked the Centipede. He was obviously a rascal, but what a change it was to hear somebody laughing once in a while. He had never heard Aunt Sponge or Aunt Spiker laughing aloud in all the time he had been with them.

"We really must get some sleep," the Old-Green-Grasshopper said. "We've got a tough day ahead of us tomorrow. So would you be kind enough, Miss Spider, to make the beds?"

A few minutes later, Miss Spider had made the first bed. It was hanging from the ceiling, suspended by a rope of threads at either end so that actually it looked more like a hammock than a bed. But it was a magnificent affair, and the stuff that it was made of shimmered like silk in the pale light.

"I do hope you'll find it comfortable," Miss Spider said to the Old-Green-Grasshopper. "I made it as soft and silky as I possibly could. I spun it with gossamer. That's a much better quality thread than the one I use for my own web."

Literary Analysis
Elements of Fantasy
Which aspects of this good-natured teasing are realistic and which are fantastic?

**Reading Check**

How did the creatures get to be big?

"Thank you so much, my dear lady," the Old-Green-Grasshopper said, climbing into the hammock. "Ah, this is just what I needed. Good night, everybody. Good night."

Then Miss Spider spun the next hammock, and the Ladybug got in.

After that, she spun a long one for the Centipede, and an even longer one for the Earthworm.

"And how do you like your bed?" she said to James when it came to his turn. "Hard or soft?"

"I like it soft, thank you very much," James answered.

"For goodness' sake stop staring round the room and get on with my boots!" the Centipede said. "You and I are never going to get any sleep at this rate! And kindly line them up neatly in pairs as you take them off. Don't just throw them over your shoulder."

James worked away frantically on the Centipede's boots. Each one had laces that had to be untied and loosened before it could be pulled off, and to make matters worse, all the laces were tied up in the most complicated knots that had to be unpicked with fingernails. It was just awful. It took about two hours. And by the time James had pulled off the last boot of all and had lined them up in a row on the floor—twenty-one pairs altogether—the Centipede was fast asleep.

Literary Analysis
Elements of Fantasy
Is Miss Spider's bed-making behavior fantastic or realistic? Why?

Thinking About the Selection

1. **Respond:** As you read about James's experiences, did you want him to escape from the room? Why or why not?

2. **(a) Recall:** What is James's first reaction when he encounters the creatures? **(b) Infer:** How does he interpret their actions and words at first?

3. **(a) Recall:** What does the Centipede ask James to do? **(b) Infer:** What words would you use to describe the Centipede's personality? **(c) Analyze:** As a group, how do the creatures seem to get along? Give examples to support your answer.

4. **(a) Recall:** By bedtime, do you think James is beginning to like the creatures? Why or why not? **(b) Speculate:** What do you think will happen to James and his new friends? Why?

Apply the Skills

Mowgli's Brothers • from *James and the Giant Peach*

Comparing Elements of Fantasy

For each selection, complete a chart like the one shown to list the fantastic and realistic elements in each category.

Category	Fantastic Element	Realistic Element
Animals		
Human		
Setting		
Situation		

Writing to Compare Literary Works

In an essay, compare and contrast the use of fantastic and realistic elements in "Mowgli's Brothers" and in the excerpt from *James and the Giant Peach*. Tell which story contains more fantastic elements. Support your view with examples. Use the information in your charts and these questions to get started:

- In which story do the animals seem more realistic? Why?
- Is the boy in either story fantastic in some way—for example, is he able to do something he could not do in real life?
- Which story's setting seems more realistic?
- Could either situation happen in real life? Explain.

Vocabulary Builder

Practice Rewrite each sentence by replacing the italicized word with a word from the vocabulary list on page 814.

1. The teams settled the *disagreement* by sharing the gym.
2. An orange cat stared *without blinking* at a bird outside.
3. The hawk's *prey* was a field mouse.
4. Amy grew bored with the *dull* task.
5. Tran felt like an ant next to the *huge* sculpture.
6. *Taking care of* babies was done mainly by the males.

QuickReview

Fantasy: imaginative writing that contains elements not found in real life
Fantastic elements: details about characters, events, or situations that are not realistic
Realistic elements: details about characters, events, or situations that are true to life

Assessment
For: Self-test
Visit: www.PHSchool.com
Web Code: ela-6606

Reading

Directions: *Questions 1–5 are based on the following selection.*

I learned the hard way that telling a secret can lead to trouble. My friend Keisha told me about an after-school birthday party for Marta. Keisha asked me not to say anything to anyone *because* it was a surprise. Then, I saw Luis in the school cafeteria. I was sure he had been invited to the party, so I mentioned it to him. It turns out he hadn't been invited, and his feelings were hurt *as a result.* He told Keisha that he was upset, *and that* caused Keisha to get annoyed with me for saying something to him. Worst of all, because Keisha yelled at me *so* loudly, Marta overheard it and the whole *surprise* was spoiled!

1. **Keisha asked her friend not to say anything about the party. What was the cause of that?**
   A Her friend told Luis.
   B Luis was in the cafeteria.
   C The party was a surprise.
   D The party was for Marta.

2. **What was the result of Luis's finding out about the party?**
   A His feelings were hurt.
   B He came to the party.
   C He told Marta about the party.
   D He didn't talk to Keisha's friend.

3. **What clue word or phrase in the passage does *not* signal a cause/effect relationship?**
   A because
   B as a result
   C surprise
   D and that

4. **What was the cause of Keisha's yelling loudly at her friend?**
   A Marta heard about the party.
   B Keisha's friend got upset.
   C Keisha wanted Luis to hear her.
   D Keisha was annoyed.

5. **What was the result of Keisha's yelling?**
   A Keisha felt hurt.
   B Marta found out about the party.
   C Luis overheard news of the party.
   D Keisha's friend told Luis.

Assessment Practice

Vocabulary

Directions: *Choose the word that best completes each sentence.*

6. The two girls have a friendly _____.
   A cause
   B reason
   C result
   D relationship

7. Growth is the _____ of nutrition.
   A cause
   B reason
   C effect
   D relationship

8. The _____ for study is to learn.
   A reason
   B effect
   C result
   D relationship

9. The accident was the _____ of carelessness.
   A cause
   B reason
   C result
   D relationship

10. Studying harder _____ an improvement.
    A caused
    B effected
    C recalled
    D relationship

Directions: *Choose the word or phrase that could replace the italicized word.*

11. *revise*
    A predict
    B edit
    C change
    D support

12. *examine*
    A make a diagnosis
    B look at carefully
    C define in other words
    D answer questions

13. *significant*
    A defined
    B meaningless
    C important
    D textual

14. *convey*
    A caravan
    B transfer
    C plot
    D finish

15. *recall*
    A remember
    B demonstrate
    C determine
    D effect

Research: Multimedia Report

A **research report** presents detailed, factual information about a subject. A **multimedia report** is a special type of research report. It presents information through a variety of media, including text, slides, videos, music, maps, charts, and art. Follow the steps outlined in this workshop to create your own multimedia report.

Assignment Create a 15-minute multimedia report on a topic that you find particularly interesting.

What to Include Your multimedia report should have these features:
- a topic that can be thoroughly and effectively covered in the time and space that is allotted
- a clearly stated main idea
- supportive facts, details, examples, and explanations
- appropriate formatting
- appropriate and effective use of media elements
- error-free writing, including complete sentences

To preview the criteria on which your multimedia report may be judged, see the rubric on page 840.

Prewriting

Choosing Your Topic

Self Interview To find an interesting topic for your multimedia report, jot down your answers to these questions:
- What topics in my other classes interest me?
- What subjects do I know a lot about?
- What topic do I want to learn more about?

Gathering Details

Conduct research to find information on your topic and to identify different and new ways of presenting the information. For example, if you are researching a place, you might gather photos, maps, and video clips. If you are reporting on an activity, you might want to include a video demonstration.

Using the Form
You may use multimedia to enhance such writing projects as the following:
- speeches
- oral reports and presentations
- science fair projects

Work in Progress
Review the work you did on pages 773, 791, and 809.

Drafting

Shaping Your Writing

Write a script. Plan your presentation by writing a script. Include all words that you will speak and the directions that you will need to guide the media during your presentation. On the left side of a two-column chart, write the words of your script. On the right side, indicate sound effects, visuals, and other notes.

Providing Elaboration

Plan your media needs. Read your draft, making notes of media cited in the script. You will also need to complete these tasks:
- Draw pictures, make slides, or edit videos.
- Edit audio or other sound effects.
- Make charts and graphs.
- Copy or scan documents.

Revising

Revising Your Overall Structure

Evaluate media. Review your draft to find places where adding media will improve the audience's understanding and enjoyment. Review your script and the multimedia elements that you have included. Where workable, identify smoother transitions to link your script to your media.

To read the complete student model, see page 839.

Student Model: Revising to Evaluate Media

Script: A word of advice: Never go to a concert where the musicians can't add the fractions of the notes to get the correct beat count. If you do, though, you'd better have earplugs!

Sound: Music played off tempo

> The writers realized that sound effects would illustrate their point about the effect of math mistakes in music better than any description could.

Revising Your Procedure

Fine-tune your presentation. Rehearse your script until you are comfortable with the presentation. Be sure you can easily identify the controls on audio and video recorders.

Integrating Grammar Skills

Revising Sentence Fragments

Sentence fragments can make a multimedia presentation difficult for your listeners to understand. A **sentence fragment** is a group of words that does not express a complete thought. To fix fragments, add more information to complete the idea.

Prentice Hall Writing and Grammar Connection: Chapter 21, Section 4

Fragment: After I heard about the celebration.
Corrected: After I heard about the celebration, I started thinking about a gift.

Fragment: Although I got hurt when I fell.
Corrected: I really enjoyed the soccer game, although I got hurt when I fell.

Correcting Fragments Follow these steps to fix sentence errors in your writing.

1. **Consider the complete idea you mean to convey.**

2. **Eliminate the fragment by either adding it to a nearby sentence or adding the necessary words to turn the incomplete phrase into a sentence.** This chart shows several examples:

Changing Fragments Into Sentences	
Fragment	**Complete Sentence**
Near the old clown.	The silly puppy flopped down *near the old clown.*
Taking a bow.	*Taking a bow*, the ringmaster had tears in his eyes.
To ask nicely.	She planned *to ask nicely* to go to the circus.

Apply It to Your Editing

Choose three paragraphs in your draft. Read each set of words that is punctuated as a sentence. It may help to read these aloud, pausing after each period. Identify any sentence fragments and revise them by adding the necessary words and punctuation.

Student Model: David Papineau and Chris Casey
Indianapolis, IN

The Power of Numbers

Slide 1

Script: In this presentation, you will be shown the various uses of mathematics in a wide range of careers. You will also see some prime examples of what would happen if people did not know the fundamentals of mathematics in a real-life situation. So sit back and prepare to be amazed by . . . The Power of Numbers.

Visual: Blank screen (blues and greens). As the presentation begins, the following words appear letter by letter: The Power of Numbers

Sound: Typewriter

Sound: Explosion

> Math would be too broad a topic, but the writers have narrowed it to focus on how math is used in a variety of careers. Each slide will provide an example.

Slide 2

Script: A word of advice: Never go to a concert where the musicians can't add the fractions of the notes to get the correct beat count. If you do, though, you'd better have earplugs!

Visual: Violinist

Sound: Music played off tempo

> The best way to show the problems a "mathless musician" would have is to let the audience hear the results. The writers chose to include music that is played out of rhythm to support their point.

Slide 3

Script: The picture says it all. If you have a pilot who can't read graphs or make course calculations, you might find the plane way off course.

Visual: Snow-covered mountaintop with an airplane flying near it.

Sound: Airplane flying

> The use of a visual emphasizes the disastrous effects of a pilot's not knowing math.

[Slides 4–10 provide further examples developing the presentation's main idea.]

Slide 11

Script: So, now you've seen and heard a little bit about the power of numbers. Not only mathematicians need math in order to do a good job—musicians, pilots, store owners, and even chefs use some sort of math every day. A good grasp of math can help you in almost anything you choose to do!

Visual: Blank screens (reds and yellows). As the presentation closes, the following words appear letter by letter: The Power of Numbers

Sound: Explosion

Writing Workshop

Editing and Proofreading

Review your work to correct errors in spelling, grammar, and mechanics.

Focus on Presentation Materials: Mistakes look twice as bad when they are projected on a screen or printed on a handout. Check formatting and consistency and then, make revised copies before your presentation.

Publishing and Presenting

Consider these possibilities for sharing your multimedia report:
Report to a small audience. With a small group, take turns presenting your multimedia reports and offering feedback.
Take it on the road. Take your report to a site outside of your school. Contact a local library, club, or retirement community that might be interested in your report.

Reflecting on Your Writing

Writer's Journal Jot down your thoughts on writing a multimedia report. Begin by answering these questions:
- Which components of your multimedia report did you most enjoy creating?
- How might you use your skills in creating multimedia reports to enhance your participation in school clubs or after-school activities?

> *Prentice Hall Writing and Grammar Connection: Chapter 28, Section 2*

Rubric for Self-Assessment

To assess your multimedia report, use the following rubric:

Criteria	Rating Scale *not very* ... *very*
Focus: How clearly stated is your topic?	1 2 3 4 5
Organization: How clear is the method of organization?	1 2 3 4 5
Support/Elaboration: How well do you use a variety of media elements to provide support for the main ideas?	1 2 3 4 5
Style: How smooth are your transitions among media?	1 2 3 4 5
Conventions: How well have you corrected errors—including sentence fragments—in your material?	1 2 3 4 5

Skills You Will Learn

Reading Skill: *Preview the Text to Set a Purpose for Reading*
Literary Analysis: *Personification*

Reading Skill: *Adjust Your Reading Rate*

Reading Skill: *Make Connections*
Literary Analysis: *Universal Theme*

Literary Analysis: *Comparing Foreshadowing and Flashback*

Literature You Will Read

Reading and Vocabulary Skills Preview

Reading: Purpose for Reading

A **purpose for reading** is the reason you are reading a selection.

Skills and Strategies You Will Learn in Part 2

In Part 2 you will learn

- to **preview text** to **set a purpose** for your reading (p. 844)
- to **make connections** between literature and your own experience as your reading purpose (p. 864)
- to **skim and scan** to **match your purpose for reading** with appropriate texts (p. 860)

Using the Skills and Strategies in Part 2

In Part 2, you will learn to preview the text to get an idea of what you will find in it. Then, you can set a purpose or evaluate whether the text meets your purpose. You will also practice making connections between the text and what you know to meet your reading purpose. In addition, you will practice skimming and scanning as strategies for adjusting your reading rate for different purposes.

The chart shows some ways you might adjust your reading rate.

Before You Read	While You Read	After You Read
Preview to determine what purpose the text will help you achieve.	Read closely to learn facts and details and to understand connections between events.	Skim and scan to identify and relocate specific information that helps you achieve your purpose.

Academic Vocabulary: Words for Discussing a Purpose for Reading

The following words will help you write and talk about your purpose for reading.

Word	Meaning	Sample Sentence
purpose *n.*	intention; plan	When you read with a *purpose*, you read more effectively.
adapt *v.*	adjust	We will *adapt* our search to find more specific information.
establish *v.*	set up; cause to be	To help *establish* a purpose for reading, you preview the text.
enable *v.*	allow; assist	These details will *enable* you to support your theory.
focus *n.*	center of interest or attention	Knowing the *focus* of your reading makes it easier to concentrate.

Vocabulary Skill: Antonyms

▶ An **antonym** is a word that means the opposite of another word.

Knowing antonyms enriches your vocabulary and helps you recognize specific word meanings.

> **Example:** The clearly written text *enables* me to understand the ideas.
> The confusing text *interferes* with my understanding of the ideas.

Activity Provide an antonym for each word. Then, write a pair of sentences for each antonym pair to show how the words are opposite.

1. clear
2. accurate
3. brief

4. definite
5. include

These skills will help you become a better reader.
Practice them with either "He Lion, Bruh Bear, and
Bruh Rabbit" (p. 846) or "Why the Tortoise's Shell Is
Not Smooth" (p. 853).

Reading Skill

Your **purpose** for reading is the reason you read a
text. Sometimes you choose a text based on a purpose you already have. Other times you set a purpose
based on the kind of text you are about to read. **Setting a purpose** helps you focus your reading. You might set a purpose to
learn about a subject, to gain understanding, to take an action, or
simply to read for enjoyment.

Preview the text before you begin to read. Look at
the title, the pictures, and the beginnings of paragraphs to get an idea about the focus of the work. This
will help you set a purpose or decide whether the text
will fit a purpose you already have. Use a chart like the
one shown to record details as you preview the text.

Text Details	What the Details Suggest About the Text
Title	
Pictures	
Beginnings of paragraphs	

Literary Analysis

Personification is the representation of an animal or an object as
if it had a human personality, intelligence, or emotions. In folk
literature, personification is often used to give human qualities to
animal characters. Through the actions of these animal characters, human qualities, behavior, and problems can be illustrated in
a humorous way.

Vocabulary Builder

He Lion, Bruh Bear, and Bruh Rabbit

- **lair** (ler) *n.* den or resting place of a wild
  animal (p. 847) *The rabbit's lair was a hole
  in the ground.*
- **cordial** (kôr´ jəl) *adj.* warm and friendly
  (p. 847) *Our cordial neighbor welcomed us.*
- **thicket** (thik´ it) *n.* dense growth of
  shrubs or small trees (p. 849) *The gardener cut down the thicket to plant flowers.*

Why the Tortoise's Shell Is Not Smooth

- **famine** (fam´ in) *n.* shortage of food (p. 853)
  People died of starvation during the famine.
- **orator** (ôr´ ət ər) *n.* person who can speak
  well in public (p. 854) *The orator gave a
  powerful speech that excited the crowd.*
- **eloquent** (el´ ə kwənt) *adj.* persuasive and
  expressive (p. 854) *The senator's eloquent
  article is about ending world hunger.*

Background

Animal Characters When they came to North America, enslaved Africans brought folk tales that had been passed down from generation to generation. Many of the tales involve animals, such as rabbits, bears, or turtles, with human characteristics. One popular character in many of these folk tales is the clever rabbit known as Bruh Rabbit.

Connecting to the Literature

Reading/Writing Connection Like many folk tales, "He Lion, Bruh Bear, and Bruh Rabbit" uses animal characters that will remind you of real people and problems. Make a list of human qualities or problems that you could assign to a lion, a bear, and a rabbit. Use at least three of these words: *demonstrate, display, embody, exhibit.*

Meet the Author

Virginia **Hamilton** (1936–2002)

Virginia Hamilton came from Yellow Springs, Ohio, a town famous as a stop on the Underground Railroad before the Civil War. The Underground Railroad was a system set up to help slaves escape to free states and Canada.

Hamilton came from a family of storytellers, who passed along tales of their family experience and heritage. Although she focused her writing mainly on African American subjects and characters, the themes in her books are meaningful to all people.

First Novel and More In 1967, Hamilton published her first novel, *Zeely,* to wide acclaim. Her next novel, *The House of Dies Drear,* published in 1968, was a modern mystery about a house on the Underground Railroad. During her writing career Hamilton collected and retold tales she heard as a child. Some of her favorite stories are in *The People Could Fly: American Black Folktales.*

Go **Online**
Author Link

For: More about the author
Visit: www.PHSchool.com
Web Code: ele-9608

HE LION, BRUH BEAR, AND BRUH RABBIT

AFRICAN AMERICAN FOLK TALE

Virginia Hamilton

Say that he Lion would get up each and every mornin. Stretch and walk around. He'd roar, "ME AND MYSELF, ME AND MYSELF," like that. Scare all the little animals so they were afraid to come outside in the sunshine. Afraid to go huntin or fishin or whatever the little animals wanted to do.

"What we gone do about it?" they asked one another. Squirrel leapin from branch to branch, just scared. Possum[1] playin dead, couldn't hardly move him.

He Lion just went on, stickin out his chest and roarin, "ME AND MYSELF, ME AND MYSELF."

The little animals held a sit-down talk, and one by one and two by two and all by all, they decide to go see Bruh[2] Bear and Bruh Rabbit. For they know that Bruh Bear been around. And Bruh Rabbit say he has, too.

So they went to Bruh Bear and Bruh Rabbit. Said, "We have some trouble. Old he Lion, him scarin everybody, roarin every mornin and all day, "ME AND MYSELF, ME AND MYSELF," like that.

"Why he Lion want to do that?" Bruh Bear said.

"Is that all he Lion have to say?" Bruh Rabbit asked.

"We don't know why, but that's all he Lion can tell us and we didn't ask him to tell us that," said the little animals. "And him scarin the children with it. And we wish him to stop it."

Reading Skill
Purpose for Reading
Based on the title, what purpose might you set for reading this story?

▼ **Critical Viewing**
Why might a lion be used in a folk tale to represent someone with a high opinion of himself or herself? **[Draw Conclusions]**

---

1. **Possum** (päs´ əm) colloquial for "opossum," a small tree-dwelling mammal that pretends to be dead when it is trapped.
2. **Bruh** (bru) early African American dialect for "brother."

"Well, I'll go see him, talk to him. I've known he Lion a long kind of time," Bruh Bear said.

"I'll go with you," said Bruh Rabbit. "I've known he Lion most long as you."

That bear and that rabbit went off through the forest. They kept hearin somethin. Mumble, mumble. Couldn't make it out. They got farther in the forest. They heard it plain now. "ME AND MYSELF. ME AND MYSELF."

"Well, well, well," said Bruh Bear. He wasn't scared. He'd been around the whole forest, seen a lot.

"My, my, my," said Bruh Rabbit. He'd seen enough to know not to be afraid of an old he lion. Now old he lions could be dangerous, but you had to know how to handle them.

The bear and the rabbit climbed up and up the cliff where he Lion had his <u>lair</u>. They found him. Kept their distance. He watchin them and they watchin him. Everybody actin <u>cordial</u>.

"Hear tell you are scarin everybody, all the little animals, with your roarin all the time," Bruh Rabbit said.

"I roars when I pleases," he Lion said.

"Well, might could you leave off the noise first thing in the mornin, so the little animals can get what they want to eat and drink?" asked Bruh Bear.

"Listen," said he Lion, and then he roared: "ME AND MYSELF. ME AND MYSELF. Nobody tell me what not to do," he said. "I'm the king of the forest, *me and myself*."

"Better had let me tell you something," Bruh Rabbit said, "for I've seen Man, and I know him the real king of the forest."

He Lion was quiet awhile. He looked straight through that scrawny lil Rabbit like he was nothin atall. He looked at Bruh Bear and figured he'd talk to him.

"You, Bear, you been around," he Lion said.

"That's true," said old Bruh Bear. "I been about everywhere. I've been around the whole forest."

"Then you must know something," he Lion said.

"I know lots," said Bruh Bear, slow and quiet-like.

"Tell me what you know about Man," he Lion said. "He think him the king of the forest?"

Literary Analysis
Personification What human qualities does Bruh Rabbit have?

Vocabulary Builder
lair (ler) *n.* den or resting place of a wild animal

cordial (kôr´ jəl) *adj.* warm and friendly

Reading Check

Why are the little animals afraid of the lion?

"Well, now, I'll tell you," said Bruh Bear, "I been around, but I haven't ever come across Man that I know of. Couldn't tell you nothin about him."

So he Lion had to turn back to Bruh Rabbit. He didn't want to but he had to. "So what?" he said to that lil scrawny hare.

"Well, you got to come down from there if you want to see Man," Bruh Rabbit said. "Come down from there and I'll show you him."

He Lion thought a minute, an hour, and a whole day. Then, the next day, he came on down.

He roared just once, "ME AND MYSELF. ME AND MYSELF. Now," he said, "come show me Man."

So they set out. He Lion, Bruh Bear, and Bruh Rabbit. They go along and they go along, rangin the forest. Pretty soon, they come to a clearin. And playin in it is a little fellow about nine years old.

"Is that there Man?" asked he Lion.

"Why no, that one is called Will Be, but it sure is not Man," said Bruh Rabbit.

So they went along and they went along. Pretty soon, they come upon a shade tree. And sleepin under it is an old, olden fellow, about ninety years olden.

"There must lie Man," spoke he Lion. "I knew him wasn't gone be much."

"That's not Man," said Bruh Rabbit. "That fellow is Was Once. You'll know it when you see Man."

So they went on along. He Lion is gettin tired of strollin. So he roars, "ME AND MYSELF. ME AND MYSELF." Upsets Bear so that Bear doubles over and runs and climbs a tree.

"Come down from there," Bruh Rabbit tellin him. So after a while Bear comes down. He keepin his distance from he Lion, anyhow. And they set out some more. Goin along quiet and slow.

In a little while they come to a road. And comin on way down the road, Bruh

▼ Critical Viewing
How well does this bear fit your image of Bruh Bear? Explain. [Connect]

Rabbit sees Man comin. Man about twenty-one years old. Big and strong, with a big gun over his shoulder.

"There!" Bruh Rabbit says. "See there, he Lion? There's Man. You better go meet him."

"I will," says he Lion. And he sticks out his chest and he roars, "ME AND MYSELF. ME AND MYSELF." All the way to Man he's roarin proud, "ME AND MYSELF. ME AND MYSELF!"

"Come on, Bruh Bear, let's go!" Bruh Rabbit says.

"What for?" Bruh Bear wants to know.

"You better come on!" And Bruh Rabbit takes ahold of Bruh Bear and half drags him to a <u>thicket</u>. And there he makin the Bear hide with him.

For here comes Man. He sees old he Lion real good now. He drops to one knee and he takes aim with his big gun.

Old he Lion is roarin his head off: "ME AND MYSELF. ME AND MYSELF!"

The big gun goes off: PA-LOOOM!

He Lion falls back hard on his tail.

The gun goes off again. PA-LOOOM!

He Lion is flyin through the air. He lands in the thicket.

"Well, did you see Man?" asked Bruh Bear.

"I seen him," said he Lion. "Man spoken to me unkind, and got a great long stick him keepin on his shoulder. Then Man taken that stick down and him speakin real mean. Thunderin at me and lightnin comin from that stick, awful bad. Made me sick. I had to turn around. And Man pointin that stick again and thunderin at me some more. So I come in here, cause it seem like him throwed some stickers at me each time it thunder, too."

"So you've met Man, and you know zactly what that kind of him is," says Bruh Rabbit.

"I surely do know that," he Lion said back.

Awhile after he Lion met Man, things were some better in the forest. Bruh Bear knew what Man looked like so he could keep out of his way. That rabbit always did know to keep out of Man's way. The little animals could go out in the mornin because he Lion was more peaceable. He didn't walk around roarin at the top of his voice all the time. And when he Lion did lift that voice of his, it was like, "Me and Myself and Man. Me and Myself and Man." Like that.

Wasn't too loud at all.

Vocabulary Builder
thicket (thik´ it) *n.* dense growth of shrubs or small trees

Literary Analysis
Personification What human qualities does he Lion demonstrate here?

Reading Skill
Purpose for Reading Did you achieve your purpose for reading this folk tale? Why or why not?

Apply the Skills

He Lion, Bruh Bear, and Bruh Rabbit

Thinking About the Selection

1. **Respond:** Which character in "He Lion, Bruh Bear, and Bruh Rabbit" do you think is most amusing? Why?
2. **(a) Recall:** Why do the little animals seek help from Bruh Bear and Bruh Rabbit? **(b) Infer:** What do Bruh Bear and Bruh Rabbit think of he Lion? **(c) Analyze:** Why isn't Bruh Rabbit scared of he Lion?
3. **(a) Recall:** Why does he Lion want to see Man?
   (b) Compare and Contrast: Describe he Lion before and after he meets Man. **(c) Analyze Cause and Effect:** What causes the change in he Lion's attitude?
4. **(a) Draw Conclusions:** Based on he Lion's behavior, what lesson does this story appear to teach? **(b) Evaluate:** Does this lesson apply well to modern life? Explain.
5. **Take a Position:** What responsibility do individuals have to other members of a community?

Reading Skill

6. **(a)** What was your **purpose for reading** this folk tale?
   (b) How might your purpose be different if you were reading a nonfiction article about animals in the wild?
7. How well did the title and pictures give you a sense of what the folk tale would be about? Explain.

Literary Analysis

8. Complete a chart like the one shown to analyze one of the animal characters.

Character's Name:	
Animal Qualities:	Human Qualities:

9. Give three examples of **personification** in the description of Bruh Rabbit's character.

Vocabulary Builder

Practice In an **analogy,** the pairs of words or phrases have the same relationship. Use a vocabulary word from page 844 to complete each analogy.

1. *home* is to *dwelling* as *den* is to _____
2. *rude* is to *polite* as *ill-mannered* is to _____
3. *shrub* is to *bush* as *growth of small trees* is to _____

Writing

Use the details in "He Lion, Bruh Bear, and Bruh Rabbit" to write an **invitation** to the animals' "sit-down talk" in the beginning of the story.

- Begin your invitation with a paragraph that describes the purpose of the meeting.
- Be sure to include a date, time, and place for the meeting.

For *Grammar, Vocabulary,* and *Assessment,* see **Build Language Skills,** pages 858–859.

Extend Your Learning

Listening and Speaking In a group, present a **dramatic reading** of the scene in which he Lion, Bruh Bear, and Bruh Rabbit walk through the forest in search of Man. Act out the parts of the characters using exact words from the folk tale. Be sure to vary the volume and tone of your voice to show different levels of feeling, such as he Lion's questioning manner and Bruh Rabbit's impatience.

Research and Technology Use Internet and library resources to find folk tales that come from different countries. With a group, prepare a **presentation** of two folk tales with different origins. Group members can choose from the following tasks:
- Find variations of a folk tale using keyword searches.
- Use a word processing program to present two or more variations of the same folk tale.

Background

The Oral Tradition Folk tales are part of the oral tradition, which is the passing along of songs, stories, and poems by word of mouth. For example, "Why the Tortoise's Shell Is Not Smooth" was originally told orally. Many folk tales have now been preserved in written texts.

Connecting to the Literature

Reading/Writing Connection Stories from the oral tradition often illustrate a point or teach a lesson. The characters in "Why the Tortoise's Shell Is Not Smooth" become victims of faulty information. Their experiences illustrate the importance of having good information when making a decision. List two situations in which you think it is important to have complete, accurate information. Use at least three of these words: *evaluate, acquire, confirm, distort.*

Review

For **Reading Skill, Literary Analysis,** and **Vocabulary,** see page 844.

Meet the Author

Chinua **Achebe** (b. 1930)

Chinua Achebe likes to retell stories that originated in his native country of Nigeria many years ago. Achebe writes, "Our ancestors created their myths and legends and told their stories for a purpose. Any good story, any good novel, should have a message."

Achebe attended the local mission school where his father taught and then went to University College in Ibadan, Nigeria. He later studied in London.

Acclaim and Resettlement Achebe became a professional writer and won acclaim with *Things Fall Apart,* his 1958 novel about changing times in Africa. He later wrote poetry, essays, fiction, and nonfiction and started a literary magazine. Achebe left Nigeria when the political climate there made it too dangerous to stay. He now lives in the United States.

Go Online
Author Link

For: More about the author
Visit: www.PHSchool.com
Web Code: ele-9609

Why the Tortoise's Shell Is Not Smooth

Chinua Achebe

Low voices, broken now and again by singing, reached Okonkwo (ō kōn´ kwō) from his wives' huts as each woman and her children told folk stories. Ekwefi (e kwe´ fē) and her daughter, Ezinma (e zēn´ mä), sat on a mat on the floor. It was Ekwefi's turn to tell a story.

"Once upon a time," she began, "all the birds were invited to a feast in the sky. They were very happy and began to prepare themselves for the great day. They painted their bodies with red cam wood[1] and drew beautiful patterns on them with dye.

"Tortoise saw all these preparations and soon discovered what it all meant. Nothing that happened in the world of the animals ever escaped his notice; he was full of cunning. As soon as he heard of the great feast in the sky his throat began to itch at the very thought. There was a <u>famine</u> in those days and Tortoise had not eaten a good meal for two moons. His body rattled like a piece of dry stick in his empty shell. So he began to plan how he would go to the sky."

"But he had no wings," said Ezinma.

"Be patient," replied her mother. "That is the story. Tortoise had no wings, but he went to the birds and asked to be allowed to go with them.

" 'We know you too well,' said the birds when they had heard him. 'You are full of cunning and you are ungrateful. If we allow you to come with us you will soon begin your mischief.'

" 'You do not know me,' said Tortoise. 'I am a changed man. I have learned that a man who makes trouble for others is also making it for himself.'

Reading Skill
Purpose for Reading
What purpose for reading does this story's title present?

Vocabulary Builder
famine (fam´ in) *n.*
shortage of food

✓ Reading Check

Why is the tortoise hungry?

---

1. **red cam** (cam) **wood** hard West African wood that makes red dye.

"Tortoise had a sweet tongue, and within a short time all the birds agreed that he was a changed man, and they each gave him a feather, with which he made two wings.

"At last the great day came and Tortoise was the first to arrive at the meeting place. When all the birds had gathered together, they set off in a body. Tortoise was very happy as he flew among the birds, and he was soon chosen as the man to speak for the party because he was a great <u>orator</u>.

"'There is one important thing which we must not forget,' he said as they flew on their way. 'When people are invited to a great feast like this, they take new names for the occasion. Our hosts in the sky will expect us to honor this age-old custom.'

"None of the birds had heard of this custom but they knew that Tortoise, in spite of his failings in other directions, was a widely traveled man who knew the customs of different peoples. And so they each took a new name. When they had all taken, Tortoise also took one. He was to be called *All of you.*

"At last the party arrived in the sky and their hosts were very happy to see them. Tortoise stood up in his many-colored plumage and thanked them for their invitation. His speech was so <u>eloquent</u> that all the birds were glad they had brought him, and nodded their heads in approval of all he said. Their hosts took him as the king of the birds, especially as he looked somewhat different from the others.

"After kola nuts had been presented and eaten, the people of the sky set before their guests the most delectable dishes Tortoise had ever seen or dreamed of. The soup was brought out hot from the fire and in the very pot in which it had been cooked. It was full of meat and fish. Tortoise began to sniff aloud. There was pounded yam and also yam pottage[2] cooked with palm oil and fresh fish. There were also pots of palm wine. When everything had been set before the guests, one of the people of the sky came forward and tasted a little from each pot. He then invited the birds to eat. But Tortoise jumped to his feet and asked: 'For whom have you prepared this feast?'

"'For all of you,' replied the man.

"Tortoise turned to the birds and said: 'You remember that my name is *All of you.* The custom here is to serve the spokesman first and the others later. They will serve you when I have eaten.'

Vocabulary Builder
orator (ôr´ ət ər) *n.* person who can speak well in public

Vocabulary Builder
eloquent (el´ ə kwənt) *adj.* persuasive and expressive

Literary Analysis
Personification What human qualities does Tortoise have?

---

2. **yam** (yam) **pottage** (pät´ ij) *n.* thick stew made of sweet potatoes.

"He began to eat and the birds grumbled angrily. The people of the sky thought it must be their custom to leave all the food for their king. And so Tortoise ate the best part of the food and then drank two pots of palm wine, so that he was full of food and drink and his body grew fat enough to fill out his shell.

"The birds gathered round to eat what was left and to peck at the bones he had thrown all about the floor. Some of them were too angry to eat. They chose to fly home on an empty stomach. But before they left, each took back the feather he had lent to Tortoise. And there he stood in his hard shell full of food and wine but without any wings to fly home. He asked the birds to take a message for his wife, but they all refused. In the end Parrot, who had felt more angry than the others, suddenly changed his mind and agreed to take the message.

" 'Tell my wife,' said Tortoise, 'to bring out all the soft things in my house and cover the compound³ with them so that I can jump down from the sky without very great danger.'

"Parrot promised to deliver the message, and then flew away. But when he reached Tortoise's house he told his wife to bring out all the hard things in the house. And so she brought out her husband's hoes, machetes, spears, guns, and even his cannon. Tortoise looked down from the sky and saw his wife bringing things out, but it was too far to see what they were. When all seemed ready he let himself go. He fell and fell and fell until he began to fear that he would never stop falling. And then like the sound of his cannon he crashed on the compound."

"Did he die?" asked Ezinma.

"No," replied Ekwefi. "His shell broke into pieces. But there was a great medicine man in the neighborhood. Tortoise's wife sent for him and he gathered all the bits of shell and stuck them together. That is why Tortoise's shell is not smooth."

---

3. **compound** (käm´ pound) *n.* grounds surrounded by buildings.

Apply the Skills

Why the Tortoise's Shell Is Not Smooth

Thinking About the Selection

1. **Respond:** Do you think the tortoise got what he deserved? Why or why not?
2. **(a) Recall:** Why does Tortoise want to go to the great feast? **(b) Infer:** Why do the birds not want to take him?
3. **(a) Analyze:** Why do the birds decide to help Tortoise go to the feast? **(b) Deduce:** Why do they choose him to speak for the group? **(c) Assess:** How does Tortoise make use of this privilege?
4. **(a) Interpret:** Explain how Tortoise's new name allows him to eat before the birds eat. **(b) Apply:** What lesson have the birds learned about Tortoise?
5. **(a) Recall:** How does Tortoise get home?
   (b) Make a Judgment: Should the birds have helped Tortoise return home? Why or why not?

Reading Skill

6. **(a)** What was your **purpose for reading** this folk tale? **(b)** How might your purpose be different if you were reading a nonfiction article about tortoises?
7. How well did the title and pictures give you a sense of what the folk tale would be about? Explain.

Literary Analysis

8. Complete a chart like the one shown to analyze one of the animal characters.

Character's Name:	
Animal Qualities:	Human Qualities:

9. Give three examples of **personification** in the description of Tortoise's character.

QuickReview

Story at a Glance
Tortoise tricks the birds into taking him to a great feast in the sky.

Go Online
——Assessment
For: Self-test
Visit: www.PHSchool.com
Web Code: ela-6608

Purpose for Reading: your reason for reading a literary work

Personification: the representation of an animal or an object as if it had human qualities

Vocabulary Builder

Practice In an **analogy**, the pairs of words have the same relationship. Use a vocabulary word from page 844 to complete each analogy.

1. *speech* is to *speaker* as *oration* is to _____
2. *tiresome* is to *boring* as *persuasive* is to _____
3. *excess* is to *hunger* as *gluttony* is to _____

Writing

Use the details in "Why the Tortoise's Shell Is Not Smooth" to write an **invitation** to the feast in the sky.

- Begin your invitation with a paragraph that describes what will be served at the feast.
- Be sure to include the date, time, and place of the feast.

For *Grammar, Vocabulary,* and *Assessment,* see **Build Language Skills,** pages 858–859.

Extend Your Learning

Listening and Speaking In a group, present a **dramatic reading** of the scenes in which Tortoise asks the birds to take him to the feast in the sky and proposes taking a new name. Act out the parts of the characters using exact words from the text. Be sure to vary the volume and tone of your voice to show different levels of feeling, such as Tortoise's persuasive manner and the doubts the birds have.

Research and Technology Use Internet and library resources to find folk tales that originate in different countries. With a group, prepare a **presentation** of two folk tales with different origins. Group members can choose from the following tasks:

- Find variations of a folk tale using keyword searches.
- Use a word processing program to present two or more variations of the same folk tale.

Build Language Skills

Vocabulary Skill: Antonyms

An **antonym** is a word that is opposite in meaning to another word. Antonyms help you to distinguish qualities and characteristics and to show contrasts.

Practice Rewrite each sentence twice, using a different antonym for the italicized word. Explain how the meaning changes.

1. We liked our *initial* idea the best.
2. He forgot to include a *minor* detail.
3. We should not *reject* the suggestion without more information.

Grammar Lesson

Punctuation: Commas A **comma** is a punctuation mark used to separate words or groups of words. Commas signal readers to pause. They also help prevent confusion in meaning. This chart shows the correct use of commas for three or more words or phrases in a series.

For more practice with commas, see the Grammar Handbook, p. R31.

	Incorrect	Correct
Word in a Series	School supplies include pencils erasers notebooks and paper.	School supplies include pencils, erasers, notebooks, and paper.
Phrases in a Series	To find the library go up the stairs down the hallway and turn left at the double doors.	To find the library, go up the stairs, down the hallway, and turn left at the double doors.

Practice Rewrite the sentences to include the missing commas.

1. We will have a substitute teacher Tuesday Wednesday and Thursday.
2. Summer school is in session at the end of May all of June and the beginning of July.
3. Sue's favorite colors are red blue white and green.
4. England Mexico and Japan are labeled on the map.
5. Where are Bob's scarf Juan's coat and Tran's boots?

*W*G *Prentice Hall Writing and Grammar Connection, Chapter 26, Section 2.*

Reading: Purpose for Reading

Directions: *Read the selection. Then, answer the questions.*

Read, Enjoy, and Grow Wiser

Do you enjoy reading folk tales? These made-up stories are fiction. Even though they are made up, the good stories sound like they could be true. The plot, which is what happens in the story, should be believable. Usually there is a conflict in the story. By the end, the conflict is resolved. Often, the main character has learned something. The reader is left a little wiser, too.

1. Which of the following should you preview to set a purpose for reading?
   A the title
   B the first sentence
   C the writing style
   D all of the above

2. What is the best purpose for reading the passage?
   A to be entertained by a folk tale
   B a lesson with a character
   C to gain information about folk tales
   D to understand disagreements

3. Which detail best helps you achieve your purpose for reading the passage?
   A Do you enjoy reading folk tales?
   B Often, the main character has learned something.
   C Folk tales are good stories.
   D Plot is what happens in a story.

Timed Writing: Analysis [Interpretation]

Review "He Lion, Bruh Bear, and Bruh Rabbit" or "Why the Tortoise's Shell Is Not Smooth." Explain how the character of the lion or the tortoise changes during the story. Use examples from the story to illustrate the changes you describe. **(25 minutes)**

 ## Writing Workshop: *Work in Progress*

Research Paper

For a research paper, you can choose almost any topic that interests you, as long as you can locate information about it. Make a list of research topics you might write about. Save this Research List in your writing portfolio.

Reading Informational Materials

Editorials

In Part 2, you are learning about setting a purpose for reading. This skill is useful in reading informational materials such as editorials. One purpose you have for reading folk tales such as "Why the Tortoise's Shell Is Not Smooth" is to learn about what was important in ancient cultures. Editorials help you learn about issues that are important to people today.

About Editorials

An **editorial** is persuasive writing that offers the views of the editors or publishers of a newspaper, magazine, or other publication on an issue. The following are key characteristics of editorials:

- They state a viewpoint on an issue the editors or publishers believe is important.
- They try to get readers to believe something or take action.
- They use facts and reasons to support opinions.

Reading Skill

When you are studying, doing research, or trying to locate information in documents, **adjust your reading rate** to your **purpose for reading. Skim,** or glance quickly through a work to get a general idea of what it is about. **Scan,** or quickly read through a work to find specific information, to find key words or ideas, or to answer a question. For example, you might scan a chapter in a science book to find the definition of *igneous rock.* After locating the term, you would read closely to get the definition.

The chart will help you skim and scan for different purposes.

To determine overall topic and source of text	**Skim** title, first paragraph, and source of information
To answer questions about when something happened	**Scan** for mention of days, months, or years
To answer questions about a specific term	**Scan** for the term or related key words in the question
To answer questions about a person or group	**Scan** for the name of the person or group

PORTSMOUTH HERALD

This editorial appeared in the *Portsmouth Herald,* a New Hampshire newspaper.

Music for ALL

Traip music students' effort is commendable

The headline briefly identifies the issue that is the topic of the editorial.

And the band played on.

This past Tuesday night, Traip Academy students were eloquent when asking the School Committee not to bring the curtain down on the town's music program.

First, the students noted, a good high school education should go beyond reading, writing and arithmetic. We all

Reading Informational Materials

learn differently and for some, music will be the pied piper leading them on a path to higher learning.[1] The students also noted that the band is more than an academic endeavor, it is a part of town life that everyone can enjoy. Finally, the students pointed out that teenagers who are busy rehearsing and playing music are not out getting into trouble.

Clearly, the Kittery School Committee heard the message of these commendable students and decided to discuss the matter in greater detail at a public meeting on Feb. 26 with the goal of finding some other way to hold the line on education spending in town.

We understand that the Town Council does not have an endless pot of gold and cannot fund everything at the levels residents might desire. When money gets tight, tough choices have to be made.

But we would encourage the School Committee to look at the music program as essential, in many ways just as important as math, science and literature. Cuts to the program should be viewed with the same horror as we would view cuts to core curriculum.

Music is not a frill. It is one of mankind's greatest accomplishments and, at times, it can teach and inspire in a way that words and equations cannot.

We hope 2004 will not be the year the music dies in Kittery.

> **Facts and reasons support a particular viewpoint in the editorial.**

> **The writer clearly states the editor's or publisher's position in these two paragraphs. Additional reasons are presented.**

> **The editorial ends with a plea intended to influence the School Committee not to cut the music program.**

1. pied piper . . . learning an **allusion** to the folk tale about a musician who leads a town's children away.

Reading: Locating Information in Documents

Directions: *Choose the letter of the best answer to each question.*

1. What is the overall topic of the editorial?
   A the Kittery School Committee's Town Council
   B the math, science, and physical education programs in Portsmouth
   C the music program at Traip Academy in Portsmouth
   D something that is wrong

2. What is the editorial's opinion about the music program at Traip Academy?
   A The music program is not as essential as other subjects.
   B Interest in music should not go beyond the classroom.
   C Music is just as important as math, science, and literature.
   D Money can be better spent by the School Committee.

3. When will the Kittery School Committee meet again?
   A Tuesday
   B February 19
   C 2004
   D none of the above

Reading: Comprehension and Interpretation

Directions: *Write your answers on a separate sheet of paper.*

4. Would this article be useful to a reader whose purpose is to form an opinion on the value of music programs in schools? Explain your opinion. **[Evaluating]**

5. According to the Traip Academy students and the editorial writer, why is a music program important to learning? **[Analyzing]**

6. Explain how a school music program can benefit a town. **[Applying]**

Timed Writing: Persuasion [Connections]

Write a letter to the School Committee to try to persuade it either to keep or cut the music program. Use information from the editorial to support your arguments. **(20 minutes)**

The skills on this page will help you become a better reader. Practice them with either "The Stone" (p. 866) or "The Three Wishes" (p. 879).

Reading Skill

Setting a purpose for reading gives you a focus as you read. One general purpose you may set for all your reading is to **make connections.** Specifically, you can make connections between literature and your own experience by identifying the following:

- universal themes about big ideas such as friendship or courage
- details that give you glimpses into cultures other than your own
- ways the ideas in the text apply to your life

Literary Analysis

The theme of a literary work is its central idea or message about life and human nature. A **universal theme** is a message about life that is expressed regularly in many cultures and time periods. Examples of universal themes include the importance of courage, the power of love, and the danger of greed.

Character	
How character changes	
Meaning of change	
Universal theme	

Look for a universal theme in a literary work by focusing on the story's main character, conflicts the character faces, changes he or she undergoes, and the effects of these changes. As you read, use a chart like the one shown to help you determine the universal theme.

Vocabulary Builder

The Stone

- **plight** (plīt) *n.* awkward, sad, or dangerous situation (p. 869) *The shipwrecked sailors complained of their _plight_.*
- **jubilation** (joo´ bə lā´ shən) *n.* great joy; triumph (p. 871) *Soraya shouted with _jubilation_ when she won the medal.*

The Three Wishes

- **embraced** (em brāsd´) *v.* clasped in the arms, usually as an expression of affection (p. 880) *Kelly _embraced_ the girl who had rescued her kitten.*
- **greed** (grēd) *n.* a selfish desire for more than one's share of something (p. 881) *_Greed_ for money made him cheat customers.*

Build Understanding • *The Stone*

Background

Stories About Wishes For generations, stories about wishes—like "The Stone"—have been told all over the world. Many of these stories are about the problems that arise when a wish is granted. The moral of such stories is that people should be happy with their lives as they are. These stories are remembered and passed on because they teach about life.

Connecting to the Literature

Reading/Writing Connection Imagine yourself in the place of a character like the one in "The Stone" who is granted wishes. List three things you would request, and explain how your life might change if you received these things. Use at least three of these words: *acquire, obtain, enable, exceed, presume.*

Meet the Author

Lloyd **Alexander** (b. 1924)

Lloyd Alexander's parents were shocked when he told them that he wanted to become a writer. "My family pleaded with me to forget literature and do something sensible, such as find some sort of useful work," he recalls.

Home of the Imagination Alexander eventually became a famous author, after working for a bank, serving in World War II, and working for a magazine. He has written stories and novels about an imaginary kingdom called Prydain. "The Stone" takes place in Prydain, where fantastic happenings are a part of everyday life.

Fast Facts

▶ Alexander considers authors such as William Shakespeare, Charles Dickens, and Mark Twain his best writing teachers.

▶ Publishers turned down Alexander's novels for seven years before publishing one.

Go Online
Author Link

For: More about the author
Visit: www.PHSchool.com
Web Code: ele-9610

THE STONE

Lloyd Alexander

There was a cottager named Maibon, and one day he was driving down the road in his horse and cart when he saw an old man hobbling along, so frail and feeble he doubted the poor soul could go many more steps. Though Maibon offered to take him in the cart, the old man refused; and Maibon went his way home, shaking his

▲ Critical Viewing
What impression of old age is conveyed by this picture?
[Support]

head over such a pitiful sight, and said to his wife, Modrona:

"Ah, ah, what a sorry thing it is to have your bones creaking and cracking, and dim eyes, and dull wits. When I think this might come to me, too! A fine, strong-armed, sturdy-legged fellow like me? One day to go tottering, and have his teeth rattling in his head, and live on porridge, like a baby? There's no fate worse in all the world."

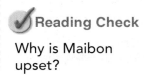

Reading Check

Why is Maibon upset?

"There is," answered Modrona, "and that would be to have neither teeth nor porridge. Get on with you, Maibon, and stop borrowing trouble. Hoe your field or you'll have no crop to harvest, and no food for you, nor me, nor the little ones."

Sighing and grumbling, Maibon did as his wife bade him. Although the day was fair and cloudless, he took no pleasure in it. His ax-blade was notched, the wooden handle splintery; his saw had lost its edge; and his hoe, once shining new, had begun to rust. None of his tools, it seemed to him, cut or chopped or delved[1] as well as they once had done.

"They're as worn out as that old codger I saw on the road," Maibon said to himself. He squinted up at the sky. "Even the sun isn't as bright as it used to be, and doesn't warm me half as well. It's gone threadbare as my cloak. And no wonder, for it's been there longer than I can remember. Come to think of it, the moon's been looking a little wilted around the edges, too.

"As for me," went on Maibon, in dismay, "I'm in even a worse state. My appetite's faded, especially after meals. Mornings, when I wake, I can hardly keep myself from yawning. And at night, when I go to bed, my eyes are so heavy I can't hold them open. If that's the way things are now, the older I grow, the worse it will be!"

In the midst of his complaining, Maibon glimpsed something bouncing and tossing back and forth beside a fallen tree in a corner of the field. Wondering if one of his piglets had squeezed out of the sty and gone rooting for acorns, Maibon hurried across the turf. Then he dropped his ax and gaped in astonishment.

There, struggling to free his leg which had been caught under the log, lay a short, thickset figure: a dwarf with red hair bristling in all directions beneath his round, close-fitting leather cap. At the sight of Maibon, the dwarf squeezed shut his bright red eyes and began holding his breath. After a moment, the dwarf's face went redder than his hair; his cheeks puffed out and soon turned

Reading Skill
Purpose for Reading
Based on your own experience, why do you think Maibon grumbles as he works?

---

1. **delved** (delvd) v. dug.

purple. Then he opened one eye and blinked rapidly at Maibon, who was staring at him, speechless.

"What," snapped the dwarf, "you can still see me?"

"That I can," replied Maibon, more than ever puzzled, "and I can see very well you've got yourself tight as a wedge under that log, and all your kicking only makes it worse."

At this, the dwarf blew out his breath and shook his fists. "I can't do it!" he shouted. "No matter how I try! I can't make myself invisible! Everyone in my family can disappear—Poof! Gone! Vanished! But not me! Not Doli! Believe me, if I could have done, you never would have found me in such a <u>plight</u>. Worse luck! Well, come on. Don't stand there goggling like an idiot. Help me get loose!"

At this sharp command, Maibon began tugging and heaving at the log. Then he stopped, wrinkled his brow, and scratched his head, saying:

"Well, now, just a moment, friend. The way you look, and all your talk about turning yourself invisible—I'm thinking you might be one of the Fair Folk."

"Oh, clever!" Doli retorted. "Oh, brilliant! Great clodhopper! Giant beanpole! Of course I am! What else! Enough gabbling. Get a move on. My leg's going to sleep."

"If a man does the Fair Folk a good turn," cried Maibon, his excitement growing, "it's told they must do one for him."

"I knew sooner or later you'd come round to that," grumbled the dwarf. "That's the way of it with you ham-handed, heavy-footed oafs. Time was, you humans got along well with us. But nowadays, you no sooner see a Fair Folk than it's grab, grab, grab! Gobble, gobble, gobble! Grant my wish! Give me this, give me that! As if we had nothing better to do!

"Yes, I'll give you a favor," Doli went on. "That's the rule, I'm obliged to. Now, get on with it."

Hearing this, Maibon pulled and pried and chopped away at the log as fast as he could, and soon freed the dwarf.

Doli heaved a sigh of relief, rubbed his shin, and cocked a red eye at Maibon, saying:

Vocabulary Builder
plight (plīt) *n.* awkward, sad, or dangerous situation

Literary Analysis
Universal Theme
What problem does Maibon face?

Reading Check

What is unusual about Doli?

"All right. You've done your work, you'll have your reward. What do you want? Gold, I suppose. That's the usual. Jewels? Fine clothes? Take my advice, go for something practical. A hazelwood twig to help you find water if your well ever goes dry? An ax that never needs sharpening? A cook pot always brimming with food?"

"None of those!" cried Maibon. He bent down to the dwarf and whispered eagerly, "But I've heard tell that you Fair Folk have magic stones that can keep a man young forever. That's what I want. I claim one for my reward."

Doli snorted. "I might have known you'd pick something like that. As to be expected, you humans have it all muddled. There's nothing can make a man young again. That's even beyond the best of our skills. Those stones you're babbling about? Well, yes, there are such things. But greatly overrated. All they'll do is keep you from growing any older."

"Just as good!" Maibon exclaimed. "I want no more than that!"

Doli hesitated and frowned. "Ah—between the two of us, take the cook pot. Better all around. Those stones—we'd sooner not give them away. There's a difficulty—"

"Because you'd rather keep them for yourselves," Maibon broke in. "No, no, you shan't cheat me of my due. Don't put me off with excuses. I told you what I want, and that's what I'll have. Come, hand it over and not another word."

Doli shrugged and opened a leather pouch that hung from his belt. He spilled a number of brightly colored pebbles into his palm, picked out one of the larger stones, and handed it to Maibon. The dwarf then jumped up, took to his heels, raced across the field, and disappeared into a thicket.

Laughing and crowing over his good fortune and his cleverness, Maibon hurried back to the cottage. There, he told his wife what had happened, and showed her the stone he had claimed from the Fair Folk.

"As I am now, so I'll always be!" Maibon declared, flexing his arms and thumping his chest. "A fine figure of a man! Oho, no gray beard and wrinkled brow for me!"

Literary Analysis
Universal Theme
Why is Doli frustrated by Maibon and other humans?

Instead of sharing her husband's <u>jubilation</u>, Modrona flung up her hands and burst out:

"Maibon, you're a greater fool than ever I supposed! And selfish into the bargain! You've turned down treasures! You didn't even ask that dwarf for so much as new jackets for the children! Nor a new apron for me! You could have had the roof mended. Or the walls plastered. No, a stone is what you ask for! A bit of rock no better than you'll dig up in the cow pasture!"

Crestfallen[2] and sheepish, Maibon began thinking his wife was right, and the dwarf had indeed given him no more than a common field stone.

"Eh, well, it's true," he stammered, "I feel no different than I did this morning, no better nor worse, but every way the same. That redheaded little wretch! He'll rue the day if I ever find him again!"

So saying, Maibon threw the stone into the fireplace. That night he grumbled his way to bed, dreaming revenge on the dishonest dwarf.

Next morning, after a restless night, he yawned, rubbed his eyes, and scratched his chin. Then he sat bolt upright in bed, patting his cheeks in amazement.

"My beard!" he cried, tumbling out and hurrying to tell his wife. "It hasn't grown! Not by a hair! Can it be the dwarf didn't cheat me after all?"

"Don't talk to me about beards," declared his wife as Maibon went to the fireplace, picked out the stone, and clutched it safely in both hands. "There's trouble enough in the chicken roost. Those eggs should have hatched by now, but the hen is still brooding on her nest."

"Let the chickens worry about that," answered Maibon. "Wife, don't you see what a grand thing's happened to me? I'm not a minute older than I was yesterday. Bless that generous-hearted dwarf!"

"Let me lay hands on him and I'll bless him," retorted Modrona. "That's all well and good for you. But what of me? You'll stay as you are, but I'll turn old and gray, and worn and wrinkled, and go doddering into my grave! And

---

2. **crestfallen** (krest´ fôl´ ən) *adj.* made sad or humble; disheartened.

The Stone ■ 871

Vocabulary Builder
jubilation (jōō´ bə lā´ shən) *n.* great joy; triumph

Reading Skill
Purpose for Reading
What big idea does Maibon's experience suggest to you?

Reading Check

What does Maibon realize when he wakes up in the morning?

what of our little ones? They'll grow up and have children of their own. And grandchildren, and great-grandchildren. And you, younger than any of them. What a foolish sight you'll be!"

But Maibon, gleeful over his good luck, paid his wife no heed, and only tucked the stone deeper into his pocket. Next day, however, the eggs had still not hatched.

"And the cow!" Modrona cried. "She's long past due to calve, and no sign of a young one ready to be born!"

"Don't bother me with cows and chickens," replied Maibon. "They'll all come right, in time. As for time, I've got all the time in the world!"

Having no appetite for breakfast, Maibon went out into the field. Of all the seeds he had sown there, however, he was surprised to see not one had sprouted. The field, which by now should have been covered with green shoots, lay bare and empty.

"Eh, things do seem a little late these days," Maibon said to himself. "Well, no hurry. It's that much less for me to do. The wheat isn't growing, but neither are the weeds."

Some days went by and still the eggs had not hatched, the cow had not calved, the wheat had not sprouted. And now Maibon saw that his apple tree showed no sign of even the smallest, greenest fruit.

"Maibon, it's the fault of that stone!" wailed his wife. "Get rid of the thing!"

"Nonsense," replied Maibon. "The season's slow, that's all."

Nevertheless, his wife kept at him and kept at him so much that Maibon at last, and very reluctantly, threw the stone out the cottage window. Not too far, though, for he had it in the back of his mind to go later and find it again.

Next morning he had no need to go looking for it, for there was the stone sitting on the window ledge.

"You see?" said Maibon to his wife. "Here it is back again. So, it's a gift meant for me to keep."

"Maibon!" cried his wife. "Will you get rid of it! We've had nothing but trouble since you brought it into the house. Now the baby's fretting and fuming. Teething, poor little thing. But not a tooth to

▼ **Critical Viewing** Find three details that suggest that the people in the painting lead a life similar to that of Maibon and his wife. **[Support]**

be seen! Maibon, that stone's bad luck and I want no part of it!"

Protesting it was none of his doing that the stone had come back, Maibon carried it into the vegetable patch. He dug a hole, not a very deep one, and put the stone into it.

Next day, there was the stone above ground, winking and glittering.

"Maibon!" cried his wife. "Once and for all, if you care for your family, get rid of that cursed thing!"

Seeing no other way to keep peace in the household, Maibon regretfully and unwillingly took the stone and threw it down the well, where it splashed into the water and sank from sight.

But that night, while he was trying vainly to sleep, there came such a rattling and clattering that Maibon clapped his hands over his ears, jumped out of bed, and went stumbling into the yard. At the well, the bucket was jiggling back and forth and up and down at the end of the rope; and in the bottom of the bucket was the stone.

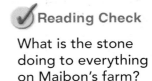

Reading Check

What is the stone doing to everything on Maibon's farm?

The Stone ■ 873

Now Maibon began to be truly distressed, not only for the toothless baby, the calfless cow, the fruitless tree, and the hen sitting desperately on her eggs, but for himself as well.

"Nothing's moving along as it should," he groaned. "I can't tell one day from another. Nothing changes, there's nothing to look forward to, nothing to show for my work. Why sow if the seeds don't sprout? Why plant if there's never a harvest? Why eat if I don't get hungry? Why go to bed at night, or get up in the morning, or do anything at all? And the way it looks, so it will stay for ever and ever! I'll shrivel from boredom if nothing else!"

"Maibon," pleaded his wife, "for all our sakes, destroy the dreadful thing!"

Maibon tried now to pound the stone to dust with his heaviest mallet; but he could not so much as knock a chip from it. He put it against his grindstone without so much as scratching it. He set it on his anvil and belabored it with hammer and tongs, all to no avail.

At last he decided to bury the stone again, this time deeper than before. Picking up his shovel, he hurried to the field. But he suddenly halted and the shovel dropped from his hands. There, sitting cross-legged on a stump, was the dwarf.

"You!" shouted Maibon, shaking his fist. "Cheat! Villain! Trickster! I did you a good turn, and see how you've repaid it!"

The dwarf blinked at the furious Maibon. "You mortals are an ungrateful crew. I gave you what you wanted."

"You should have warned me!" burst out Maibon.

"I did," Doli snapped back. "You wouldn't listen. No, you yapped and yammered, bound to have your way. I told you we didn't like to give away those stones. When you mortals get hold of one, you stay just as you are—but so does everything around you. Before you know it, you're mired in time

Literature in Context

Literature Connection

Rocks and Roles Stones play a role in many stories. For example, in Aesop's fable "The Crow and the Pitcher," a thirsty crow tries to drink from a pitcher, but the water is too far down for his beak to reach. After much thought, the crow solves his problem by dropping pebbles into the pitcher until the water rises enough that he can drink it. The moral: Necessity is the mother of invention.

In "The Stone," a rock causes problems rather than solving them when Maibon makes foolish choices.

Connect to the Literature

How might Maibon have used his stone wisely?

Reading Skill
Purpose for Reading
Based on your own experience, why is Doli angry with Maibon?

like a rock in the mud. You take my advice. Get rid of that stone as fast as you can."

"What do you think I've been trying to do?" blurted Maibon. "I've buried it, thrown it down the well, pounded it with a hammer—it keeps coming back to me!"

"That's because you really didn't want to give it up," Doli said. "In the back of your mind and the bottom of your heart, you didn't want to change along with the rest of the world. So long as you feel that way, the stone is yours."

"No, no!" cried Maibon. "I want no more of it. Whatever may happen, let it happen. That's better than nothing happening at all. I've had my share of being young, I'll take my share of being old. And when I come to the end of my days, at least I can say I've lived each one of them."

"If you mean that," answered Doli, "toss the stone onto the ground, right there at the stump. Then get home and be about your business."

Maibon flung down the stone, spun around, and set off as fast as he could. When he dared at last to glance back over his shoulder, fearful the stone might be bouncing along at his heels, he saw no sign of it, nor of the red-headed dwarf.

Maibon gave a joyful cry, for at that same instant the fallow field was covered with green blades of wheat, the branches of the apple tree bent to the ground, so laden they were with fruit. He ran to the cottage, threw his arms around his wife and children, and told them the good news. The hen hatched her chicks, the cow bore her calf. And Maibon laughed with glee when he saw the first tooth in the baby's mouth.

Never again did Maibon meet any of the Fair Folk, and he was just as glad of it. He and his wife and children and grandchildren lived many years, and Maibon was proud of his white hair and long beard as he had been of his sturdy arms and legs.

"Stones are all right, in their way," said Maibon. "But the trouble with them is, they don't grow."

Literary Analysis
Universal Theme
What message about change does Doli try to share with Maibon?

Apply the Skills

The Stone

Thinking About the Selection

1. **Respond:** Would you have given up the stone? Explain.
2. **(a) Recall:** How does Maibon get the stone? **(b) Infer:** Why does Maibon choose the stone over all the other gifts?
3. **(a) Recall:** How does the stone cause problems for Maibon, his family, and his farm? **(b) Analyze:** Why does Maibon say he will "shrivel from boredom"? **(c) Compare and Contrast:** How does this remark suggest that Maibon's opinion of the stone has changed?
4. **(a) Recall:** What happens when Maibon tries to throw away the stone? **(b) Interpret:** Why can't Maibon get rid of the stone? **(c) Analyze:** What new belief does Maibon have that finally allows him to rid himself of the stone?
5. **Take a Position:** Many messages in advertisements and on consumer products promote youthfulness. Do you think this is a good message? Why or why not?

Reading Skill

6. Use a chart like the one shown to note how details in the story helped you achieve the **purpose** of making connections.

Universal Theme	Cultural Details	Connections to Life

7. Use the details in your chart to explain how setting the purpose of making connections increased your understanding of the selection.

Literary Analysis

8. What lesson is Doli trying to teach Maibon when he says that the stones are greatly overrated?
9. What **universal theme** is revealed in the story, just after Doli explains to Maibon why the stone would not go away?

Vocabulary Builder

Practice Using your knowledge of the italicized words, answer each question. Write a sentence explaining your answer.

1. Could the situation of a family who lived through a terrible war be described as a *plight*?

2. Would you react with *jubilation* if your favorite team lost a championship game?

Writing

Write a **plot proposal**—a plan of story events—that illustrates a universal theme of "The Stone."

- Identify the universal theme.
- Brainstorm for a situation that demonstrates the theme.
- Write a brief description of the events that reveal the theme.

For *Grammar, Vocabulary,* and *Assessment,* see **Build Language Skills,** pages 884–885.

Extend Your Learning

Listening and Speaking Present an **oral response** to the theme of "The Stone." Follow these steps:

- Clearly state the story's theme.
- Use examples from other stories or your own experience to tell whether you agree or disagree with the message.
- Organize your ideas in a logical manner.

Rehearse your response after you have prepared it. Then, present it to a small group, making sure to speak slowly and clearly.

Research and Technology "The Stone" is about human aging. With a group, use technology resources to prepare a written and visual **report** on human growth. Find pictures and prepare diagrams that share facts, such as how often in a lifetime cells are replaced and what happens to skin as humans age. Compare facts and pictures you find with common beliefs about aging that may or may not be true.

Build Understanding • *The Three Wishes*

Background

Versions of Folk Tales Different versions of "The Three Wishes" exist in cultures around the world. Because folk tales are passed on orally, they can "migrate" from one place to another. Each storyteller adds details based on personal experience or culture. After a number of tellings, a new version of the tale emerges.

Connecting to the Literature

Reading/Writing Connection You may already know one or more versions of a "three wishes" tale. Think about the lessons you can learn from these stories by writing briefly about the positive and negative aspects of wishing for something. Use at least three of the following words: *acquire, obtain, enable, exceed, presume.*

Review

For **Reading Skill, Literary Analysis,** and **Vocabulary Builder,** see page 864.

Meet the Author

Ricardo E. **Alegría** (b. 1921)

Ricardo Alegría has been a leader in education, archaeology, and culture in his native Puerto Rico. Among other positions, Alegría served as the director of the Center for Advanced Studies of Puerto Rico and the Caribbean. On his 75th birthday, he was awarded the James Smithson Medal of the Smithsonian Institution for 50 years of contributions to arts and letters and to world culture.

Fast Facts

▶ Alegría is considered a major figure in preserving the culture, values, Spanish language, and history of Puerto Rico's native peoples.

▶ He has written nonfiction books on excavations of archaeological sites in Puerto Rico.

▶ "Culture is the way mankind expresses itself to live and live collectively," Alegría has said.

For: More about the author
Visit: www.PHSchool.com
Web Code: ele-9611

THE THREE WISHES
Puerto Rican Folk Tale
··· Ricardo E. Alegría ···

Many years ago, there lived a woodsman and his wife. They were very poor but very happy in their little house in the forest. Poor as they were, they were always ready to share what little they had with anyone who came to their door. They loved each other very much and were quite

▲ **Critical Viewing** What details in this image match the story's first sentences? **[Connect]**

content with their life together. Each evening, before eating, they gave thanks to God for their happiness.

One day, while the husband was working far off in the woods, an old man came to the little house and said that he had lost his way in the forest and had eaten nothing for many days. The woodsman's wife had little to eat herself, but, as was her custom, she gave a large portion of it to the old man. After he had eaten everything she gave him, he told the woman that he had been sent to test her and that, as a reward for the kindness she and her husband showed to all who came to their house, they would be granted a special grace. This pleased the woman, and she asked what the special grace was.

The old man answered, "Beginning immediately, any three wishes you or your husband may wish will come true."

When she heard these words, the woman was overjoyed and exclaimed, "Oh, if my husband were only here to hear what you say!"

The last word had scarcely left her lips when the woodsman appeared in the little house with the ax still in his hands. The first wish had come true.

The woodsman couldn't understand it at all. How did it happen that he, who had been cutting wood in the forest, found himself here in his house? His wife explained it all as she <u>embraced</u> him. The woodsman just stood there, thinking over what his wife had said. He looked at the old man who stood quietly, too, saying nothing.

Suddenly he realized that his wife, without stopping to think, had used one of the three wishes, and he became very annoyed when he remembered all of the useful things she might have asked for with the first wish. For the first time, he became angry with his wife. The desire for riches had turned his head, and he scolded his wife, shouting at her, among other things, "It doesn't seem possible that you could be so stupid! You've wasted one of our wishes, and now we have only two left! May you grow ears of a donkey!"

He had no sooner said the words than his wife's ears began to grow, and they continued to grow until they changed into the pointed, furry ears of a donkey.

Reading Skill
Purpose for Reading
To which details here can you most relate?

Vocabulary Builder
embraced (em brāsd´)
v. clasped in the arms, usually to express affection

Literary Analysis
Universal Theme
What conflict do the woodsman and his wife face?

When the woman put her hand up and felt them, she knew what had happened and began to cry. Her husband was very ashamed and sorry, indeed, for what he had done in his temper, and he went to his wife to comfort her.

The old man, who had stood by silently, now came to them and said, "Until now, you have known happiness together and have never quarreled with each other. Nevertheless, the mere knowledge that you could have riches and power has changed you both. Remember, you have only one wish left. What do you want? Riches? Beautiful clothes? Servants? Power?"

The woodsman tightened his arm about his wife, looked at the old man, and said, "We want only the happiness and joy we knew before my wife grew donkey's ears."

No sooner had he said these words than the donkey ears disappeared. The woodsman and his wife fell upon their knees to ask forgiveness for having acted, if only for a moment, out of covetousness[1] and <u>greed</u>. Then they gave thanks for all their happiness.

Vocabulary Builder
greed (grēd) *n.* a selfish desire for more than one's share of something

The old man left, but before going, he told them that they had undergone this test in order to learn that there can be happiness in poverty just as there can be unhappiness in riches. As a reward for their repentance, the old man said that he would bestow upon them the greatest happiness a married couple could know. Months later, a son was born to them. The family lived happily all the rest of their lives.

---

1. covetousness (kuv′ ət əs nes) *n.* envy; wanting what another person has.

Apply the Skills

The Three Wishes

Thinking About the Selection

1. **Respond:** Do you think the woodsman and his wife make a good third wish? Explain.
2. **(a) Recall:** Describe the life of the woodsman and his wife before they make the three wishes. **(b) Interpret:** How does the couple earn the chance to make three wishes? **(c) Draw Conclusions:** What does the old man's granting of a reward to the couple tell you about his values?
3. **(a) Recall:** How does the couple use the first two wishes? **(b) Compare and Contrast:** How does the behavior of the couple change after they are given the opportunity to make wishes? **(c) Analyze:** What does their changed behavior say about the consequences of greed?
4. **(a) Interpret:** How does the saying "Be careful what you wish for" apply to the couple? **(b) Speculate:** What lesson might the couple have learned from this experience?
5. **Take a Position:** Do you think that the couple deserved to be rewarded for their repentance? Why or why not?

Reading Skill

6. Use a chart like the one shown to note how details in the folk tale helped you achieve the **purpose** of making connections.

Universal Theme	Cultural Details	Connections to Life

7. Use the details in your chart to explain how setting the purpose of making connections increased your understanding of the selection.

Literary Analysis

8. What message about life does the author suggest in the first paragraph of the story?
9. What **universal theme** is revealed in the story, just after the wife's donkey ears disappear?

QuickReview

Story at a Glance
A poor but happy couple is granted three wishes.

Go Online
——Assessment
For: Self-test
Visit: www.PHSchool.com
Web Code: ela-6610

Purpose for Reading: your reason for reading a literary work

Universal Theme: a message about life that is expressed in many different cultures and time periods

Vocabulary Builder

Practice Using your knowledge of the italicized words, answer each question. Write a sentence explaining your answer.

1. Would *greed* motivate a person to donate a large sum of money to charity?
2. Would you *embrace* a relative whom you have not seen in a long time?

Writing

Write a **plot proposal**—a plan of story events—that illustrates a universal theme of "The Three Wishes."
- First, identify the universal theme.
- Then, brainstorm for a conflict or situation that could be used to demonstrate the theme.
- Write a brief description of the events that reveal the theme.

For *Grammar, Vocabulary,* and *Assessment,* see **Build Language Skills,** pages 884–885.

Extend Your Learning

Listening and Speaking Present an **oral response** to the theme of "The Three Wishes." Follow these steps:
- Clearly state the story's theme.
- Use examples from other stories or from your own experience to tell whether you agree or disagree with the story's message.
- Organize your ideas in a logical manner.

Rehearse your response after you have prepared it, to ensure that your message is clear. Then, present it to a small group, making sure to speak slowly and clearly.

Research and Technology With a group, use technology resources to prepare a written and visual **report** on the geographical aspects of Puerto Rico, the setting of this folk tale. Show drawings or photographs of various areas of the island, including any forests. Present your findings to the class.

Build Language Skills

The Stone • The Three Wishes

Vocabulary Skill

Antonyms Antonyms, words that have opposite meanings, are useful in your writing to show contrast. For example, the word *focused* describes something clear and definite. Its antonyms describe things that are not clear: *vague, unclear, indefinite.*

Practice Supply an antonym for each word. Then, use each word and antonym in a sentence.

1.compare   **2.**essential   **3.** enable

Grammar Lesson

Punctuation: Semicolons and Colons A **semicolon** connects two independent clauses that are closely connected in meaning. It also is used to separate items in a series if those items have commas within them. A **colon** is used after an independent clause to introduce a list of items, to show time, in the salutation of a business letter, and on warnings and labels.

Using Semicolons
I want to go to the Grand Canyon; my brother wants to see New York. The recipe calls for two eggs, lightly beaten; a cup of flour, sifted; and one stick of butter, melted.
Using Colons
You will need these items: a tent, boots, and a canteen. The train arrives at 4:55 P.M. Warning: No swimming in this lake.

Practice Rewrite each sentence, adding a semicolon or colon where needed.

1. The alarm clock woke us at 545 A.M.
2. Our guide showed us the following trees acacia, hackberry, and juniper.
3. Patrick enjoys reading mysteries I prefer reading biographies.
4. The sign said "Caution Watch for snakes on the trail."
5. Kyla has lived in Bangor, Maine Boise, Idaho and Dallas, Texas.

Reading: Purpose for Reading

Directions: *Read the selection. Then, answer the questions.*

Sultan and the Porcupine: A Sticky Situation

Tom and Sultan set out for the woods near Tom's cabin. Sultan is a big, curious dog. As Tom stopped to pick wild blackberries, Sultan trotted off. Suddenly, Tom heard a loud yelp. He found Sultan standing rigid, whimpering. Sultan's face was covered with porcupine quills. Tom picked up the dog and hurried back to the cabin. Luckily, Tom is a doctor. He gave Sultan a shot to relax him. Then, he carefully broke each barbed quill and gently pulled it out. Sultan recovered and never went near a porcupine again.

1. Which purpose for reading is suggested by the title?
   A to learn different sides of an issue
   B to be entertained
   C to gain insight into an issue
   D to learn a new skill

2. Which connection might you make in this passage?
   A having insight into another culture
   B relating to an unusual theme
   C undergoing a surprising event
   D learning a lesson in the wilderness

3. Which of these would *not* be helpful in setting a purpose for reading?
   A learning about the author's life
   B reading the first sentence
   C noting the writing style is formal or informal
   D reading the title of the passage

4. Which connection might you make based on your knowledge of porcupine quills?
   A Sultan is hurt.
   B Tom was careless.
   C Sultan should not hunt.
   D Tom should train Sultan better.

Timed Writing: Persuasion

[Connections]

Review "The Stone" or "The Three Wishes." Then, write an essay in which you convince readers of the dangers that can result from making wishes without considering the consequences. **(30 minutes)**

 Writing Workshop: *Work in Progress*

Research Paper

Choose a research topic from your list. Write a magnet word that represents the "big idea" of your topic. Then, list words, ideas, or details related to that topic. Save this work in your writing portfolio.

Foreshadowing and Flashback

To develop interesting and exciting stories, writers can use a range of **plot techniques** to help them tell the events in a story.

- **Foreshadowing** is the author's use of clues to hint at what might happen later in a story. For example, the description of a dark cloud in a story might foreshadow something bad that is about to happen. Foreshadowing helps build suspense, the quality that keeps you wondering what will happen next.
- A **flashback** is a scene that interrupts a story to describe an earlier event. Writers use flashback to show something about a character's past. For example, a flashback about a happy childhood journey might explain why an adult character loves to travel.

Comparing Foreshadowing and Flashback

Both of these plot techniques reveal important information and make readers want to keep reading. Foreshadowing takes readers into the future in a story. It can spark readers' curiosity without giving the plot away. Flashback takes readers into the past. It can satisfy readers' curiosity about a character or a situation.

Compare the use of foreshadowing and flashback in "Lob's Girl" and "Jeremiah's Song" by using a chart such as the one shown.

Lob's Girl
Foreshadowing
Flashback

Jeremiah's Song
Foreshadowing
Flashback

Vocabulary Builder

Lob's Girl

- **decisively** (dē sī′ siv lē′) *adv.* with determination (p. 888) *"I will win the race," Arin said decisively.*

- **resolutions** (rez′ə lōō′ shənz) *n.* intentions; things decided (p. 891) *At the new year, Tonia's resolutions were to eat more fruit and watch less television.*

- **melancholy** (mel′ən käl′ ē) *adj.* sad; gloomy (p. 891) *Hans recalled his old friend with a melancholy sigh.*

Jeremiah's Song

- **diagnosis** (dī əg nō′ sis) *n.* identification of a person's medical condition (p. 904) *The diagnosis was the baby had a cold.*

Build Understanding

Connecting to the Literature

Reading/Writing Connection Both "Lob's Girl" and "Jeremiah's Song" show the importance of personal connections—among people or even between people and their pets. In your notebook, jot down a few ideas to reflect on why making personal connections is important. Use at least three of these words: *appreciate, benefit, communicate, enrich, reinforce.*

Meet the Authors

Joan **Aiken** (1924–2004)

British author Joan Aiken began her writing career early—at the age of five! By her teens, she was a published author.

A Family of Writers Aiken's father was poet Conrad Aiken, and two of her sisters are professional writers. Fans of all ages enjoy reading her mysterious and unusual tales. Aiken once said, "Stories are like butterflies, which come fluttering out of nowhere, touch down for a brief instant, may be captured, may not, and then vanish into nowhere again."

Walter Dean **Myers** (b. 1937)

By age five, Walter Dean Myers was reading a newspaper every day. In spite of this impressive start with words, Myers did not think that writing would be his career.

Writing From Life Then, in his twenties, Myers won a writing contest. He has not stopped writing since—mostly about his heritage and his experiences growing up in Harlem, a part of New York City. Like the child in "Jeremiah's Song," Myers understands loss: He was three years old when his mother died.

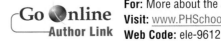

Go **Online**
Author Link

For: More about the authors
Visit: www.PHSchool.com
Web Code: ele-9612

Lob's Girl

Joan Aiken

Some people choose their dogs, and some dogs choose their people. The Pengelly family had no say in the choosing of Lob; he came to them in the second way, and very <u>decisively</u>.

It began on the beach, the summer when Sandy was five, Don, her older brother, twelve, and the twins were three. Sandy was really Alexandra, because her grandmother had a beautiful picture of a queen in a diamond tiara and high collar of pearls. It hung by Granny Pearce's kitchen sink and was as familiar as the doormat. When Sandy was born everyone agreed that she was the living spit of the picture, and so she was called Alexandra and Sandy for short.

On this summer day she was lying peacefully reading a comic and not keeping an eye on the twins, who didn't need it because they were occupied in seeing which of them could wrap the most seaweed around the other one's legs. Father—Bert Pengelly—and Don were up on the Hard painting the bottom boards of the boat in which Father went fishing for pilchards. And Mother—Jean Pengelly— was getting ahead with making the Christmas puddings because she never felt easy in her mind if they weren't made and safely put away by the end of August. As usual, each member of the family was happily getting on with his or her own affairs. Little did they guess how soon this state of things would be changed by the large new member who was going to erupt into their midst.

Sandy rolled onto her back to make sure that the twins were not climbing on slippery rocks or getting cut off by the tide. At the same moment a large body struck her forcibly in the midriff and she was covered by flying sand. Instinctively she shut her eyes and felt the sand being wiped off her face by something that seemed like a warm, rough, damp flannel. She opened her eyes and looked. It was a tongue. Its owner was a large and bouncy young Alsatian, or German shepherd, with topaz eyes, black-tipped prick ears, a thick, soft coat, and a bushy black-tipped tail.

"*Lob!*" shouted a man farther up the beach. "Lob, come here!"

But Lob, as if trying to atone[1] for the surprise he had given her, went on licking the sand off Sandy's face, wagging his tail so hard while he kept on knocking up more clouds of sand. His owner, a gray-haired man with a limp, walked over as quickly as he could and seized him by the collar.

"I hope he didn't give you a fright?" the man said to Sandy. "He meant it in play—he's only young."

"Oh, no, I think he's *beautiful*." said Sandy truly. She picked up a bit of driftwood and threw it. Lob, whisking easily out of his master's grip, was after it like a sand-colored bullet. He came back with the stick, beaming, and gave it to Sandy. At the same time he gave himself, though no one else was aware of this at the time. But with Sandy, too, it was love at first sight, and when, after a lot more stick-throwing, she and the twins joined Father and Don to go home for tea, they cast many a backward glance at Lob being led firmly away by his master.

1. **atone** (ə tōn´) *v.* make up for a wrong.

Literary Analysis
Foreshadowing and Flashback Based on this hint, what do you think is going to happen?

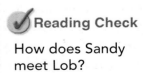

Reading Check

How does Sandy meet Lob?

"I wish we could play with him every day." Tess sighed.

"Why can't we?" said Tim.

Sandy explained. "Because Mr. Dodsworth, who owns him, is from Liverpool, and he is only staying at the Fisherman's Arms till Saturday."

"Is Liverpool a long way off?"

"Right at the other end of England from Cornwall, I'm afraid."

It was a Cornish fishing village where the Pengelly family lived, with rocks and cliffs and a strip of beach and a little round harbor, and palm trees growing in the gardens of the little whitewashed stone houses. The village was approached by a narrow, steep, twisting hill-road, and guarded by a notice that said LOW GEAR FOR 1 ½ MILES, DANGEROUS TO CYCLISTS.

The Pengelly children went home to scones with Cornish cream and jam, thinking they had seen the last of Lob. But they were much mistaken. The whole family was playing cards by the fire in the front room after supper when there was a loud thump and a crash of china in the kitchen.

"My Christmas puddings!" exclaimed Jean, and ran out.

"Did you put TNT in them, then?" her husband said.

But it was Lob, who, finding the front door shut, had gone around to the back and bounced in through the open kitchen window, where the puddings were cooling on the sill. Luckily only the smallest was knocked down and broken.

Lob stood on his hind legs and plastered Sandy's face with licks. Then he did the same for the twins, who shrieked with joy.

"Where does this friend of yours come from?" inquired Mr. Pengelly.

"He's staying at the Fisherman's Arms—I mean his owner is."

"Then he must go back there. Find a bit of string, Sandy, to tie to his collar."

"I wonder how he found his way here," Mrs. Pengelly said, when the reluctant Lob had been led whining away and Sandy had

Literary Analysis
Foreshadowing and Flashback What might this description of the road foreshadow?

▼ **Critical Viewing** What details here are like the village described in the story? **[Connect]**

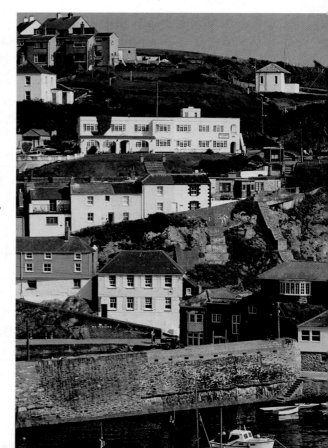

explained about their afternoon's game on the beach. "Fisherman's Arms is right around the other side of the harbor."

Lob's owner scolded him and thanked Mr. Pengelly for bringing him back. Jean Pengelly warned the children that they had better not encourage Lob any more if they met him on the beach, or it would only lead to more trouble. So they dutifully took no notice of him the next day until he spoiled their good <u>resolutions</u> by dashing up to them with joyful barks, wagging his tail so hard that he winded Tess and knocked Tim's legs from under him.

They had a happy day, playing on the sand.

The next day was Saturday. Sandy had found out that Mr. Dodsworth was to catch the half-past-nine train. She went out secretly, down to the station, nodded to Mr. Hoskins, the stationmaster, who wouldn't dream of charging any local for a platform ticket, and climbed up on the footbridge that led over the tracks. She didn't want to be seen, but she did want to see. She saw Mr. Dodsworth get on the train, accompanied by an unhappy-looking Lob with drooping ears and tail. Then she saw the train slide away out of sight around the next headland, with a <u>melancholy</u> wail that sounded like Lob's last good-bye.

Sandy wished she hadn't had the idea of coming to the station. She walked home miserably, with her shoulders hunched and her hands in her pockets. For the rest of the day she was so cross and unlike herself that Tess and Tim were quite surprised, and her mother gave her a dose of senna.

A week passed. Then, one evening, Mrs. Pengelly and the younger children were in the front room playing snakes and ladders. Mr. Pengelly and Don had gone fishing on the evening tide. If your father is a fisherman, he will never be home at the same time from one week to the next.

Suddenly, history repeating itself, there was a crash from the kitchen. Jean Pengelly leaped up, crying, "My blackberry jelly!" She and the children had spent the morning picking and the afternoon boiling fruit.

But Sandy was ahead of her mother. With flushed cheeks and eyes like stars she had darted into the kitchen, where she and Lob were hugging one another in a frenzy of joy.

Vocabulary Builder
resolutions (rez´ ə loo´shənz) *n.* intentions; things decided

Vocabulary Builder
melancholy (mel´ən käl´ ē) *adj.* sad; gloomy

Reading Check

What happens the week after Sandy watches the train leave the station?

About a yard of his tongue was out, and he was licking every part of her that he could reach.

"Good heavens!" exclaimed Jean. "How in the world did *he* get here?"

"He must have walked," said Sandy. "Look at his feet."

They were worn, dusty, and tarry. One had a cut on the pad.

"They ought to be bathed," said Jean Pengelly. "Sandy, run a bowl of warm water while I get disinfectant."

"What'll we do about him, Mother?" said Sandy anxiously.

Mrs. Pengelly looked at her daughter's pleading eyes and sighed.

"He must go back to his owner, of course," she said, making her voice firm. "Your dad can get the address from the Fisherman's tomorrow, and phone him or send a telegram. In the meantime he'd better have a long drink and a good meal."

Lob was very grateful for the drink and the meal, and made no objection to having his feet washed. Then he flopped down on the hearthrug and slept in front of the fire they had lit because it was a cold, wet evening, with his head on Sandy's feet. He was a very tired dog. He had walked all the way from Liverpool to Cornwall, which is more than four hundred miles.

The next day Mr. Pengelly phoned Lob's owner, and the following morning Mr. Dodsworth arrived off the night train, decidedly put out, to take his pet home. That parting was worse than the first. Lob whined, Don walked out of the house, the twins burst out crying, and Sandy crept up to her bedroom afterward and lay with her face pressed into the quilt, feeling as if she were bruised all over.

Jean Pengelly took them all into Plymouth to see the circus on the next day and the twins cheered up a little, but even the hour's ride in the train each way and the Liberty horses and performing seals could not cure Sandy's sore heart.

She need not have bothered, though. In ten days' time Lob was back—limping

▼ **Critical Viewing**
Which characteristics of this house would make it a nice home for Lob? **[Make a Judgment]**

this time, with a torn ear and a patch missing out of his furry coat, as if he had met and tangled with an enemy or two in the course of his four-hundred-mile walk.

Bert Pengelly rang up Liverpool again. Mr. Dodsworth, when he answered, sounded weary. He said, "That dog has already cost me two days that I can't spare away from my work—plus endless time in police stations and drafting newspaper advertisements. I'm too old for these ups and downs. I think we'd better face the fact, Mr. Pengelly, that it's your family he wants to stay with—that is, if you want to have him."

Bert Pengelly gulped. He was not a rich man; and Lob was a pedigreed dog. He said cautiously, "How much would you be asking for him?"

"Good heavens, man, I'm not suggesting I'd sell him to you. You must have him as a gift. Think of the train fares I'll be saving. You'll be doing me a good turn."

"Is he a big eater?" Bert asked doubtfully.

By this time the children, breathless in the background listening to one side of this conversation, had realized what was in the wind and were dancing up and down with their hands clasped beseechingly.

"Oh, not for his size," Lob's owner assured Bert. "Two or three pounds of meat a day and some vegetables and gravy and biscuits—he does very well on that."

Alexandra's father looked over the telephone at his daughter's swimming eyes and trembling lips. He reached a decision. "Well, then, Mr. Dodsworth," he said briskly, "we'll accept your offer and thank you very much. The children will be overjoyed and you can be sure Lob has come to a good home. They'll look after him and see he gets enough exercise. But I can tell you," he ended firmly, "if he wants to settle in with us he'll have to learn to eat a lot of fish."

So that was how Lob came to live with the Pengelly family. Everybody loved him and he loved them all. But there was never any question who came first with him. He was Sandy's dog. He slept by her bed and followed her everywhere he was allowed.

Nine years went by, and each summer Mr. Dodsworth came back to stay at the Fisherman's Arms and call on his erstwhile dog. Lob always met him with recognition and dignified pleasure, accompanied him for a walk or two—but

Reading Check

Why does Mr. Dodsworth give Lob to the Pengelly family?

showed no signs of wishing to return to Liverpool. His place, he intimated,[2] was definitely with the Pengellys.

In the course of nine years Lob changed less than Sandy. As she went into her teens he became a little slower, a little stiffer, there was a touch of gray on his nose, but he was still a handsome dog. He and Sandy still loved one another devotedly.

One evening in October all the summer visitors had left, and the little fishing town looked empty and secretive. It was a wet, windy dusk. When the children came home from school—even the twins were at high school now, and Don was a full-fledged fisherman—Jean Pengelly said, "Sandy, your Aunt Rebecca says she's lonesome because Uncle Will Hoskins has gone out trawling, and she wants one of you to go and spend the evening with her. You go, dear; you can take your homework with you."

Sandy looked far from enthusiastic.

"Can I take Lob with me?"

"You know Aunt Becky doesn't really like dogs—Oh, very well." Mrs. Pengelly sighed. "I suppose she'll have to put up with him as well as you."

Reluctantly Sandy tidied herself, took her schoolbag, put on the damp raincoat she had just taken off, fastened Lob's lead to his collar, and set off to walk through the dusk to Aunt Becky's cottage, which was five minutes' climb up the steep hill.

The wind was howling through the shrouds of boats drawn up on the Hard.

"Put some cheerful music on, do," said Jean Pengelly to the nearest twin. "Anything to drown that wretched sound while I make your dad's supper." So Don, who had just come in, put on some rock music, loud. Which was why the Pengellys did not hear the truck hurtle down the hill and crash against the post office wall a few minutes later.

Dr. Travers was driving through Cornwall with his wife, taking a late holiday before patients began coming down with winter colds and flu. He saw the sign that said STEEP HILL. LOW GEAR FOR 1 $\frac{1}{2}$ MILES. Dutifully he changed into second gear.

Literary Analysis
Foreshadowing and Flashback What do you think the descriptions in these paragraphs foreshadow?

---

2. **intimated** (in´ tə māt´əd) *v.* hinted; made known indirectly.

"We must be nearly there," said his wife, looking out of her window. "I noticed a sign on the coast road that said the Fisherman's Arms was two miles. What a narrow, dangerous hill! But the cottages are very pretty—Oh, Frank, stop, *stop*! There's a child, I'm sure it's a child—by the wall over there!"

Dr. Travers jammed on his brakes and brought the car to a stop. A little stream ran down by the road in a shallow stone culvert, and half in the water lay something that looked, in the dusk, like a pile of clothes—or was it the body of the child? Mrs. Travers was out of the car in a flash, but her husband was quicker.

"Don't touch her, Emily!" he said sharply. "She's been hit. Can't be more than a few minutes. Remember that truck that overtook us half a mile back, speeding like the devil? Here, quick, go into that cottage and phone for an ambulance. The girl's in a bad way. I'll stay here and do what I can to stop the bleeding. Don't waste a minute."

Doctors are expert at stopping dangerous bleeding, for they know the right places to press. This Dr. Travers was able to do, but he didn't dare do more; the girl was lying in a queerly crumpled heap, and he guessed she had a number of bones broken and that it would be highly dangerous to move her. He watched her with great concentration, wondering where the truck had got to and what other damage it had done.

Mrs. Travers was very quick. She had seen plenty of accident cases and knew the importance of speed. The first cottage she tried had a phone; in four minutes she was back, and in six an ambulance was wailing down the hill.

Its attendants lifted the child onto a stretcher as carefully as if she were made of fine thistledown. The ambulance

▲ **Critical Viewing**
What elements of danger do you see in this picture? **[Analyze]**

Reading Check

What happens on the hill-road?

sped off to Plymouth—for the local cottage hospital did not take serious accident cases—and Dr. Travers went down to the police station to report what he had done.

He found that the police already knew about the speeding truck—which had suffered from loss of brakes and ended up with its radiator halfway through the post-office wall. The driver was concussed and shocked, but the police thought he was the only person injured—until Dr. Travers told his tale.

At half-past nine that night Aunt Rebecca Hoskins was sitting by her fire thinking aggrieved[3] thoughts about the inconsiderateness of nieces who were asked to supper and never turned up, when she was startled by a neighbor, who burst in, exclaiming, "Have you heard about Sandy Pengelly, then, Mrs. Hoskins? Terrible thing, poor little soul, and they don't know if she's likely to live. Police have got the truck driver that hit her—ah, it didn't ought to be allowed, speeding through the place like that at umpty miles an hour, they ought to jail him for life—not that that'd be any comfort for poor Bert and Jean."

Horrified, Aunt Rebecca put on a coat and went down to her brother's house. She found the family with white shocked faces; Bert and Jean were about to drive off to the hospital where Sandy had been taken, and the twins were crying bitterly. Lob was nowhere to be seen. But Aunt Rebecca was not interested in dogs; she did not inquire about him.

"Thank the Lord you've come, Beck," said her brother. "Will you stay the night with Don and the twins? Don's out looking for Lob and heaven knows when we'll be back; we may get a bed with Jean's mother in Plymouth."

"Oh, if only I'd never invited the poor child," wailed Mrs. Hoskins. But Bert and Jean hardly heard her.

That night seemed to last forever. The twins cried themselves to sleep. Don came home very late and grim-faced. Bert and Jean sat in a waiting room of the Western Counties Hospital, but Sandy was unconscious, they were told, and she remained so. All that could be done for her was done. She was given transfusions to replace all the blood

3. aggrieved (ə grēvd´) adj. offended; wronged.

Literary Analysis
Foreshadowing and Flashback What hints does this paragraph contain about possible events to come?

Literary Analysis
Foreshadowing and Flashback What clues in these paragraphs suggest that Lob may not be safe?

she had lost. The broken bones were set and put in slings and cradles.

"Is she a healthy girl? Has she a good constitution?" the emergency doctor asked.

"Aye, doctor, she is that," Bert said hoarsely. The lump in Jean's throat prevented her from answering; she merely nodded.

"Then she ought to have a chance. But I won't conceal from you that her condition is very serious, unless she shows signs of coming out from this coma."

But as hour succeeded hour, Sandy showed no signs of recovering consciousness. Her parents sat in the waiting room with haggard faces; sometimes one of them would go to telephone the family at home, or to try to get a little sleep at the home of Granny Pearce, not far away.

At noon next day Dr. and Mrs. Travers went to the Pengelly cottage to inquire how Sandy was doing, but the report was gloomy: "Still in a very serious condition." The twins were miserably unhappy. They forgot that they had sometimes called their elder sister bossy and only remembered how often she had shared her pocket money with them, how she read to them and took them for picnics and helped with their homework. Now there was no Sandy, no Mother and Dad, Don went around with a gray, shuttered face, and worse still, there was no Lob.

The Western Counties Hospital is a large one, with dozens of different departments and five or six connected buildings, each with three or four entrances. By that afternoon it became noticeable that a dog seemed to have taken up position outside the hospital, with the fixed intention of getting in. Patiently he would try first one entrance and then another, all the way around, and then begin again. Sometimes he would get a little way inside, following a visitor, but animals were, of course, forbidden, and he was always kindly but firmly turned out again. Sometimes the guard at the main entrance gave him a pat or offered him a bit of sandwich—he looked so wet and beseeching and desperate. But he never ate the sandwich. No one seemed to own him or to know where he came from; Plymouth is a large city and he might have belonged to anybody.

At tea time Granny Pearce came through the pouring rain to bring a flask of hot tea with brandy in it to her daughter

Literary Analysis
Foreshadowing and Flashback What do you learn about Sandy from the flashback in this paragraph?

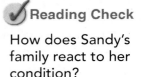

Reading Check

How does Sandy's family react to her condition?

and son-in-law. Just as she reached the main entrance the guard was gently but forcibly shoving out a large, agitated, soaking-wet Alsatian dog.

"No, old fellow, you can *not* come in. Hospitals are for people, not for dogs."

"Why, bless me," exclaimed old Mrs. Pearce. "That's Lob! Here, Lob, Lobby boy!"

Lob ran to her, whining. Mrs. Pearce walked up to the desk.

"I'm sorry, madam, you can't bring that dog in here," the guard said.

Mrs. Pearce was a very determined old lady. She looked the porter in the eye.

"Now, see here, young man. That dog has walked twenty miles from St. Killan to get to my granddaughter. Heaven knows how he knew she was here, but it's plain he knows. And he ought to have his rights! He ought to get to see her! Do you know," she went on, bristling, "that dog has walked the length of England—*twice*—to be with that girl? And you think you can keep him out with your fiddling rules and regulations?"

"I'll have to ask the medical officer," the guard said weakly.

"You do that, young man." Granny Pearce sat down in a determined manner, shutting her umbrella, and Lob sat patiently dripping at her feet. Every now and then he shook his head, as if to dislodge something heavy that was tied around his neck.

Presently a tired, thin, intelligent-looking man in a white coat came downstairs, with an impressive, silver-haired man in a dark suit, and there was a low-voiced discussion. Granny Pearce eyed them, biding her time.

"Frankly. . . not much to lose," said the older man. The man in the white coat approached Granny Pearce.

"It's strictly against every rule, but as it's such a serious case we are making an exception," he said to her quietly. "But only *outside* her bedroom door—and only for a moment or two."

Without a word, Granny Pearce rose and stumped upstairs. Lob followed close to her skirts, as if he knew his hope lay with her.

Literary Analysis
Foreshadowing and Flashback What do you think is foreshadowed when Granny Pearce recognizes the dog?

They waited in the green-floored corridor outside Sandy's room. The door was half shut. Bert and Jean were inside. Everything was terribly quiet. A nurse came out. The white-coated man asked her something and she shook her head. She had left the door ajar and through it could now be seen a high, narrow bed with a lot of gadgets around it. Sandy lay there, very flat under the covers, very still. Her head was turned away. All Lob's attention was riveted on the bed. He strained toward it, but Granny Pearce clasped his collar firmly.

"I've done a lot for you, my boy, now you behave yourself," she whispered grimly. Lob let out a faint whine, anxious and pleading.

At the sound of that whine Sandy stirred just a little. She sighed and moved her head the least fraction. Lob whined again. And then Sandy turned her head right over. Her eyes opened, looking at the door.

"Lob?" she murmured—no more than a breath of sound. "Lobby, boy?"

The doctor by Granny Pearce drew a quick, sharp breath. Sandy moved her left arm—the one that was not broken—from below the covers and let her hand dangle down, feeling, as she always did in the mornings, for Lob's furry head. The doctor nodded slowly.

"All right," he whispered. "Let him go to the bedside. But keep a hold of him."

Reading Check

How does Lob get into the hospital to see Sandy?

Granny Pearce and Lob moved to the bedside. Now she could see Bert and Jean, white-faced and shocked, on the far side of the bed. But she didn't look at them. She looked at the smile on her granddaughter's face as the groping fingers found Lob's wet ears and gently pulled them. "Good boy," whispered Sandy, and fell asleep again.

Granny Pearce led Lob out into the passage again. There she let go of him and he ran off swiftly down the stairs. She would have followed him, but Bert and Jean had come out into the passage, and she spoke to Bert fiercely.

"I don't know why you were so foolish as not to bring the dog before! Leaving him to find the way here himself—"

"But, Mother!" said Jean Pengelly. "That can't have been Lob. What a chance to take! Suppose Sandy hadn't—" She stopped, with her handkerchief pressed to her mouth.

"Not Lob? I've known that dog nine years! I suppose I ought to know my own granddaughter's dog?"

"Listen, Mother," said Bert. "Lob was killed by the same truck that hit Sandy. Don found him—when he went to look for Sandy's schoolbag. He was—he was dead. Ribs all smashed. No question of that. Don told me on the phone—he and Will Hoskins rowed a half mile out to sea and sank the dog with a lump of concrete tied to his collar. Poor old boy. Still—he was getting on. Couldn't have lasted forever."

"*Sank him at sea?* Then what—?"

Slowly old Mrs. Pearce, and then the other two, turned to look at the trail of dripping-wet footprints that led down the hospital stairs.

In the Pengellys' garden they have a stone, under the palm tree. It says: "Lob. Sandy's dog. Buried at sea."

Literary Analysis
Foreshadowing and Flashback Why does the author include this flashback to an earlier event?

Thinking About the Selection

1. **Respond:** Would a different ending for the story be more satisfying? Why or why not?

2. **(a) Recall:** How do Sandy and her family first meet Lob?
   (b) Speculate: Why does Lob travel more than 400 miles to the Pengellys' house? **(c) Analyze:** How does Sandy feel about Lob? Support your answer with evidence from the story.

3. **(a) Recall:** Why does Mr. Dodsworth give Lob to the Pengellys? **(b) Infer:** How do you think Mr. Dodsworth feels about giving the dog away?

4. **(a) Recall:** What happens when Sandy goes to visit her aunt? **(b) Interpret:** How does Lob help Sandy at the hospital? **(c) Speculate:** What does Lob's mysterious return at the end suggest about his bond with Sandy?

5. **(a) Evaluate:** Why do you think the author chose to end the story in such an unusual way? **(b) Take a Position:** How important is the relationship between people and animals? Explain.

Jeremiah's Song

Walter Dean Myers

I knowed my cousin Ellie was gonna be mad when Macon Smith come around to the house. She didn't have no use for Macon even when things was going right, and when Grandpa Jeremiah was fixing to die I just knowed she wasn't gonna be liking him hanging around. Grandpa Jeremiah raised Ellie after her folks died and they used to be real close. Then she got to go on to college and when she come back the first year she was different. She didn't want to hear all them stories he used to tell her anymore. Ellie said the stories wasn't true, and that's why she didn't want to hear them.

▲ **Critical Viewing**
What kind of song do you think this man is playing? **[Analyze]**

✓ **Reading Check**

Why does Grandpa Jeremiah raise Ellie?

I didn't know if they was true or not. Tell the truth I didn't think much on it either way, but I liked to hear them stories. Grandpa Jeremiah said they wasn't stories anyway, they was songs.

"They the songs of my people," he used to say.

I didn't see how they was songs, not regular songs anyway. Every little thing we did down in Curry seemed to matter to Ellie that first summer she come home from college. You couldn't do nothin' that was gonna please her. She didn't even come to church much. 'Course she come on Sunday or everybody would have had a regular fit, but she didn't come on Thursday nights and she didn't come on Saturday even though she used to sing in the gospel choir.

"I guess they teachin' her somethin' worthwhile up there at Greensboro," Grandpa Jeremiah said to Sister Todd. "I sure don't see what it is, though."

"You ain't never had no book learning, Jeremiah," Sister Todd shot back. She wiped at where a trickle of sweat made a little path through the white dusting powder she put on her chest to keep cool. "Them old ways you got ain't got nothing for these young folks."

"I guess you right," Grandpa Jeremiah said.

He said it but I could see he didn't like it none. He was a big man with a big head and had most all his hair even if it was white. All that summer, instead of sitting on the porch telling stories like he used to when I was real little, he would sit out there by himself while Ellie stayed in the house and watched the television or read a book. Sometimes I would think about asking him to tell me one of them stories he used to tell but they was too scary now that I didn't have nobody to sleep with but myself. I asked Ellie to sleep with me but she wouldn't.

"You're nine years old," she said, sounding real proper. "You're old enough to sleep alone."

I knew that. I just wanted her to sleep with me because I liked sleeping with her. Before she went off to college she used to put cocoa butter on her arms and face and it would smell real nice. When she come back from college she put something else on, but that smelled nice too.

It was right after Ellie went back to school that Grandpa Jeremiah had him a stroke and Macon started coming around. I think his mama probably made him come at first, but you could see he liked it. Macon had always been around, sitting over near the stuck window at church or going on the blueberry truck when we went picking down at Mister Gregory's place. For a long time he was just another kid, even though he was older'n me, but then, all of a sudden, he growed something fierce. I used to be up to his shoulder one time and

then, before I could turn around good, I was only up to his shirt pocket. He changed too. When he used to just hang around with the other boys and play ball or shoot at birds he would laugh a lot. He didn't laugh so much anymore and I figured he was just about grown. When Grandpa got sick he used to come around and help out with things around the house that was too hard for me to do. I mean, I could have done all the chores, but it would just take me longer.

When the work for the day was finished and the sows fed, Grandpa would kind of ease into one of his stories and Macon, he would sit and listen to them and be real interested. I didn't mind listening to the stories when Grandpa told them to Macon because he would be telling them in the middle of the afternoon and they would be past my mind by the time I had to go to bed.

Macon had an old guitar he used to mess with, too. He wasn't too bad on it, and sometimes Grandpa would tell him to play us a tune. He could play something he called "the Delta Blues" real good, but when Sister Todd or somebody from the church come around he'd play "Precious Lord" or "Just a Closer Walk With Thee."

Grandpa Jeremiah had been feeling poorly from that stroke, and one of his legs got a little drag to it. Just about

▲ **Critical Viewing**
Does this scene seem similar to the story's setting? Explain.
[Connect]

Literary Analysis
Foreshadowing and Flashback What clues here hint at a relationship developing between Macon and Grandpa Jeremiah?

 **Reading Check**

How does Macon help Grandpa Jeremiah?

real sick. He was breathing loud so you could hear it even in the next room and he would stay in bed a lot even when there was something that needed doing or fixing.

"I don't think he's going to make it much longer," Dr. Crawford said. "The only thing I can do is to give him something for the pain."

"Are you sure of your <u>diagnosis</u>?" Ellie asked. She was sitting around the table with Sister Todd, Deacon Turner, and his little skinny yellow wife.

Dr. Crawford looked at Ellie like he was surprised to hear her talking. "Yes, I'm sure," he said. "He had tests a few weeks ago and his condition was bad then."

"How much time he got?" Sister Todd asked.

"Maybe a week or two at best," Dr. Crawford said.

When he said that, Deacon Turner's wife started crying and goin' on and I give her a hard look but she just went on. I was the one who loved Grandpa Jeremiah the most and she didn't hardly even know him so I didn't see why she was crying.

Everybody started tiptoeing around the house after that. They would go in and ask Grandpa Jeremiah if he was comfortable and stuff like that or take him some food or a cold glass of lemonade. Sister Todd come over and stayed with us. Mostly what she did is make supper and do a lot of praying, which was good because I figured that maybe God would do something to make Grandpa Jeremiah well. When she wasn't doing that she was piecing on a fancy quilt she was making for some white people in Wilmington.

Ellie, she went around asking everybody how they felt about Dr. Crawford and then she went into town and asked about the tests and things. Sister Jenkins asked her if she thought she knowed more than Dr. Crawford, and Ellie rolled her eyes at her, but Sister Jenkins was reading out her Bible and didn't make no notice of it.

Harmonizing, 1979 Robert Gwathmey, Courtesy Terry Dintenfass Gallery, Estate of Robert Gwathmey/Licensed by VAGA, NewYork, NY

▲ **Critical Viewing**
What story characters might be presented in this picture? **[Connect]**

Vocabulary Builder
diagnosis (dī əg nō′sis) *n.* identification of a person's medical condition

rolled her eyes at her, but Sister Jenkins was reading out her Bible and didn't make no notice of it.

Then Macon come over.

He had been away on what he called "a little piece of a job" and hadn't heard how bad off Grandpa Jeremiah was. When he come over he talked to Ellie and she told him what was going on and then he got him a soft drink from the refrigerator and sat out on the porch and before you know it he was crying.

You could look at his face and tell the difference between him sweating and the tears. The sweat was close against his skin and shiny and the tears come down fatter and more sparkly.

Macon sat on the porch, without saying a word, until the sun went down and the crickets started chirping and carrying on. Then he went in to where Grandpa Jeremiah was and stayed in there for a long time.

Sister Todd was saying that Grandpa Jeremiah needed his rest and Ellie went in to see what Macon was doing. Then she come out real mad.

"He got Grandpa telling those old stories again," Ellie said. "I told him Grandpa needed his rest and for him not to be staying all night."

He did leave soon, but bright and early the next morning Macon was back again. This time he brought his guitar with him and he went on in to Grandpa Jeremiah's room. I went in, too.

Grandpa Jeremiah's room smelled terrible. It was all closed up so no drafts could get on him and the whole room was smelled down with disinfect[1] and medicine. Grandpa Jeremiah lay propped up on the bed and he was so gray he looked scary. His hair wasn't combed down and his head on the pillow with his white hair sticking out was enough to send me flying if Macon hadn't been there. He was skinny, too. He looked like his skin got loose on his bones, and when he lifted his arms, it hung down like he was just wearing it instead of it being a part of him.

---

1. **disinfect** (dis′ in fect′) *n.* dialect, or regional language, for disinfectant, a substance that kills germs.

Literary Analysis
Foreshadowing and Flashback What does the description of Grandpa Jeremiah suggest about events to come?

 Reading Check

How does Macon react to Grandpa Jeremiah's illness?

Macon sat slant-shouldered with his guitar across his lap. He was messin' with the guitar, not making any music, but just going over the strings as Grandpa talked.

"Old Carrie went around out back to where they kept the pigs penned up and she felt a cold wind across her face. . . ." Grandpa Jeremiah was telling the story about how a old woman out-tricked the Devil and got her son back. I had heard the story before, and I knew it was pretty scary. "When she felt the cold breeze she didn't blink nary an eye, but looked straight ahead. . . ."

All the time Grandpa Jeremiah was talking I could see Macon fingering his guitar. I tried to imagine what it would be like if he was actually plucking the strings. I tried to fix my mind on that because I didn't like the way the story went with the old woman wrestling with the Devil.

We sat there for nearly all the afternoon until Ellie and Sister Todd come in and said that supper was ready. Me and Macon went out and ate some collard greens, ham hocks, and rice. Then Macon he went back in and listened to some more of Grandpa's stories until it was time for him to go home. I wasn't about to go in there and listen to no stories at night.

Dr. Crawford come around a few days later and said that Grandpa Jeremiah was doing a little better.

"You think the Good Lord gonna pull him through?" Sister Todd asked.

"I don't tell the Good Lord what He should or should not be doing," Dr. Crawford said, looking over at Sister Todd and at Ellie. "I just said that my patient seems to be doing okay for his condition."

"He been telling Macon all his stories," I said.

"Macon doesn't seem to understand that Grandpa Jeremiah needs his strength," Ellie said. "Now that he's improving, we don't want him to have a set-back."

"No use in stopping him from telling his stories," Dr. Crawford said. "If it makes him feel good it's as good as any medicine I can give him."

I saw that this didn't set with Ellie, and when Dr. Crawford had left I asked her why.

Literary Analysis
Foreshadowing and Flashback What does Macon's behavior suggest about what he might do later?

"Dr. Crawford means well," she said, "but we have to get away from the kind of life that keeps us in the past."

She didn't say why we should be trying to get away from the stories and I really didn't care too much. All I knew was that when Macon was sitting in the room with Grandpa Jeremiah I wasn't nearly as scared as I used to be when it was just me and Ellie listening. I told that to Macon.

"You getting to be a big man, that's all," he said.

That was true. Me and Macon was getting to be good friends, too. I didn't even mind so much when he started being friends with Ellie later. It seemed kind of natural, almost like Macon was supposed to be there with us instead of just visiting.

Grandpa wasn't getting no better, but he wasn't getting no worse, either.

"You liking Macon now?" I asked Ellie when we got to the middle of July. She was dishing out a plate of smothered chops for him and I hadn't even heard him ask for anything to eat.

"Macon's funny," Ellie said, not answering my question. "He's in there listening to all of those old stories like he's really interested in them. It's almost as if he and Grandpa Jeremiah are talking about something more than the stories, a secret language."

I didn't think I was supposed to say anything about that to Macon, but once, when Ellie, Sister Todd, and Macon were out on the porch shelling butter beans after Grandpa got tired and was resting, I went into his room and told him what Ellie had said.

"She said that?" Grandpa Jeremiah's face was skinny and old looking but his eyes looked like a baby's, they was so bright.

"Right there in the kitchen is where she said it," I said. "And I don't know what it mean but I was wondering about it."

"I didn't think she had any feeling for them stories," Grandpa Jeremiah said. "If she think we talking secrets, maybe she don't."

"I think she getting a feeling for Macon," I said,

"That's okay, too," Grandpa Jeremiah said. "They both young."

Literary Analysis
Foreshadowing and Flashback What details here hint that something pleasant may lie ahead?

Reading Check

How do Ellie's feelings for Macon change?

"Yeah, but them stories you be telling, Grandpa, they about old people who lived a long time ago," I said.

"Well, those the folks you got to know about," Grandpa Jeremiah said. "You think on what those folks been through, and what they was feeling, and you add it up with what you been through and what you been feeling, then you got you something."

"What you got Grandpa?"

"You got you a bridge," Grandpa said. "And a meaning. Then when things get so hard you about to break, you can sneak across that bridge and see some folks who went before you and see how they didn't break. Some got bent and some got twisted and a few fell along the way, but they didn't break."

"Am I going to break, Grandpa?"

"You? As strong as you is?" Grandpa Jeremiah pushed himself up on his elbow and give me a look. "No way you going to break, boy. You gonna be strong as they come.

Literary Analysis
Foreshadowing and Flashback In what way are Grandpa Jeremiah's stories like flashbacks?

Literature in Context **Music Connection**

What Is the Delta Blues?

The hardships of plantation slaves were first told in song, though the words were more spoken than sung. These powerful songs were performed by wandering musicians who accompanied themselves on guitar or harmonica.

◀ The emotional and physical heart of this music was the Mississippi Delta, home to what is now known as the Delta blues.

Charley Patton is known as the father of the Delta blues.

◀ The great bluesman Muddy Waters was influenced by Son House and Robert Johnson. In the 1940s, Waters took the Delta blues north to Chicago.

Connect to the Literature In what ways do you think Grandpa Jeremiah's stories resemble the songs of the Delta blues?

One day you gonna tell all them stories I told you to your young'uns and they'll be as strong as you."

"Suppose I ain't got no stories, can I make some up?"

"Sure you can, boy. You make 'em up and twist 'em around. Don't make no mind. Long as you got 'em."

"Is that what Macon is doing?" I asked. "Making up stories to play on his guitar?"

"He'll do with 'em what he see fit, I suppose," Grandpa Jeremiah said. "Can't ask more than that from a man."

It rained the first three days of August. It wasn't a hard rain but it rained anyway. The mailman said it was good for the crops over East but I didn't care about that so I didn't pay him no mind. What I did mind was when it rain like that the field mice come in and get in things like the flour bin and I always got the blame for leaving it open.

When the rain stopped I was pretty glad. Macon come over and sat with Grandpa and had something to eat with us. Sister Todd come over, too.

"How Grandpa doing?" Sister Todd asked. "They been asking about him in the church."

"He's doing all right," Ellie said.

"He's kind of quiet today," Macon said. "He was just talking about how the hogs needed breeding."

"He must have run out of stories to tell," Sister Todd said. "He'll be repeating on himself like my father used to do. That's the way I hear old folks get."

Everybody laughed at that because Sister Todd was pretty old, too. Maybe we was all happy because the sun was out after so much rain. When Sister Todd went in to take Grandpa Jeremiah a plate of potato salad with no mayonnaise like he liked it, she told him about how people was asking for him and he told her to tell them he was doing okay and to remember him in their prayers.

Sister Todd came over the next afternoon, too, with some rhubarb pie with cheese on it, which is my favorite pie. When she took a piece into Grandpa Jeremiah's room she come right out again and told Ellie to go fetch the Bible.

It was a hot day when they had the funeral. Mostly everybody was there. The church was hot as anything, even though they had the window open. Some yellowjacks flew in and buzzed around Sister Todd's niece and then around

Literary Analysis
Foreshadowing and Flashback What event may be foreshadowed in Macon's description? Explain.

Reading Check

Why does Sister Todd ask Ellie to fetch the Bible?

Deacon Turner's wife and settled right on her hat and stayed there until we all stood and sang "Soon-a Will Be Done."

At the graveyard Macon played "Precious Lord" and I cried hard even though I told myself that I wasn't going to cry the way Ellie and Sister Todd was, but it was such a sad thing when we left and Grandpa Jeremiah was still out to the grave that I couldn't help it.

During the funeral and all, Macon kind of told everybody where to go and where to sit and which of the three cars to ride in. After it was over he come by the house and sat on the front porch and played on his guitar. Ellie was standing leaning against the rail and she was crying but it wasn't a hard crying. It was a soft crying, the kind that last inside of you for a long time.

Macon was playing a tune I hadn't heard before. I thought it might have been what he was working at when Grandpa Jeremiah was telling him those stories and I watched his fingers but I couldn't tell if it was or not. It wasn't nothing special, that tune Macon was playing, maybe halfway between them Delta blues he would do when Sister Todd wasn't around and something you would play at church. It was something different and something the same at the same time. I watched his fingers go over that guitar and figured I could learn that tune one day if I had a mind to.

Literary Analysis
Foreshadowing and Flashback What event might this last sentence foreshadow?

Thinking About the Selection

1. **Respond:** What might you say to the narrator to comfort him after his grandfather's death?

2. **(a) Recall:** What is Ellie's relationship to the narrator?
   (b) Interpret: Describe the narrator's feelings toward Ellie.

3. **(a) Recall:** Why does Ellie not want Macon around Grandpa Jeremiah's house at first? **(b) Draw Conclusions:** How does the narrator feel toward Macon?

4. **(a) Recall:** How does Macon feel about Grandpa?
   (b) Analyze: In what way or ways does Macon help Grandpa?

5. **(a) Interpret:** What are Grandpa Jeremiah's "songs"?
   (b) Take a Position: How important to future generations are songs and stories such as those Grandpa tells?

Apply the Skills

Lob's Girl • Jeremiah's Song

Comparing Foreshadowing and Flashback

1. Create a chart like the one shown for each story. (a) In the left two columns, list clues in the story and the events they foreshadow. (b) In the right two columns, list flashbacks in the story and tell what you learn from each one.

2. Based on your charts, which writer made more use of these plot devices? Explain.

Foreshadowing		Flashback	
Clues ⟶	Event	Detail ⟶	Reveals

Writing to Compare Literary Works

Compare and contrast the authors' use of foreshadowing and flashback in "Lob's Girl" and "Jeremiah's Song." In an essay, discuss the effects of the use of these plot techniques. Use these questions to get started:

- Which story has more suspense, based on the use of foreshadowing?
- Which story provides more background on the main characters through the use of flashback?
- What is the effect of the combination of foreshadowing and flashback in each story?
- Which story did you enjoy more? Explain.

Vocabulary Builder

Practice Choose the vocabulary word from page 886 that matches the description.

1. analysis of an illness
2. promises to yourself
3. how you might feel when a rainy day spoils your plans
4. how you might take charge of a situation

Go Online
Assessment

For: Self-test
Visit: www.PHSchool.com
Web Code: ela-6611

Reading

Directions: *Questions 1–5 are based on the following subtitles and first sentences:*

Culture: A Total Way of Life
Elements of Culture: Culture includes the work people do, their behaviors, their beliefs, and their ways of doing things.
  Some elements of a culture are easy to see.
People and Their Land: Geographers study culture, especially activities that relate to the environment. Geographers are interested in the effect people have on their environment.
  Natural changes and man-made changes have an impact on each other.

1. **After previewing, what would be a reading purpose?**
   A to be entertained
   B to be informed
   C to be persuaded
   D to be amused

2. **Which question helps you set a purpose for reading this passage?**
   A Was this assigned with related readings?
   B Was this assigned for tomorrow?
   C Was this assigned by a substitute?
   D Was this assigned to your friends?

3. **What will you learn from previewing?**
   A what a geographer is
   B how many pages are about beliefs
   C how often a cultural landscape changes
   D how culture relates to the environment

4. **What reading rate should you use?**
   A Skim the selection.
   B Scan the selection.
   C Read the selection carefully.
   D Read the selection quickly.

5. **What is indicated by a preview?**
   A The text will focus on cultural differences.
   B The text will focus on your own culture.
   C The text will focus on ancient cultures.
   D The text will focus on culture in general.

Assessment Practice

Vocabulary

Directions: *Choose the best definition of the italicized word.*

6. **It was difficult to *focus* on our work when it was so hot.**
   A concentrate
   B convene
   C detail
   D adjust

7. **To accommodate the new bus schedule, you may need to *adapt* your morning routine.**
   A become skilled at
   B repeat
   C become faster at
   D change

8. **In a good essay, the writer's *purpose* will be clear.**
   A plan
   B object
   C scheme
   D condition

9. **You need to *establish* your viewpoint in the first paragraph.**
   A break up
   B determine
   C make clear
   D hint at

10. **The lessons will *enable* her to improve more quickly than if she worked on her own.**
   A give power to
   B authorize
   C allow
   D motivate

Directions: *Choose the antonym of the italicized word.*

11. **Most writers *revise* their work several times.**
   A change
   B draft
   C work through once
   D see

12. **A research paper should include *facts*.**
   A proven ideas
   B research
   C opinions
   D events

13. **Please *review* the reading selection.**
   A reread
   B preview
   C delineate
   D detail

Word Families

Words that have the same root make up a **word family.** Many English word families are built around **Greek roots.** Often these roots keep the same spelling in all the words of the word family.

What Can You Learn From Ancient Greek? The words in this list are all part of very common word families built on Greek roots. The Greek root -*tele*- means "far," -*auto*- means "self," and -*cyc*- means "wheel" or "ring." The spelling of these forms does not change from word to word. If you keep this fact in mind, you will spell the list words and other words in the same word families correctly.

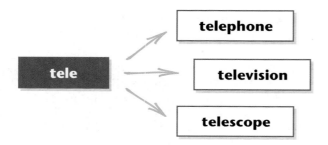

Practice Read the clues. Then, on your paper write the word from the Word List that matches each clue.

1. a two-wheeler
2. what you might want from a movie star
3. a program shown on a screen
4. the kind of screen you would show the program on
5. works by itself
6. hurricane
7. a way to talk to friends
8. four wheels and a gas pedal
9. reuse
10. a device for looking at the stars

Word List
telephone
television
telescope
telecast
automobile
automatic
autograph
bicycle
cyclone
recycle

A. Directions: *Write the letter of the sentence in which the underlined word is spelled correctly.*

1. **A** The politician spoke on the <u>telekast</u>.
    B He said it was important to <u>recycle</u> paper and aluminum.
    C "If you do it often enough, the procedure will become <u>automatick</u>," he said.
    D Maybe his advice could keep my room from looking like a <u>ciclone</u> hit it.

2. **A** The <u>autamobile</u> was invented about 100 years ago.
    B The <u>telefone</u> was invented even earlier.
    C I'd like to have the <u>autograf</u> of one of these inventors.
    D They made contact between people almost <u>automatic</u>.

3. **A** We entered a contest on <u>televishion</u>.
    B Two weeks later, we got a <u>telephone</u> call.
    C "You have won a <u>bycycle</u>!" the caller said.
    D "Or you may choose a <u>telascope</u> instead."

4. **A** A modern <u>automobeel</u> can be very fancy.
    B For example, it might even have a <u>telavision</u> in it.
    C Perhaps one day we will even be able to <u>recyckle</u> gasoline.
    D In the meantime, I prefer simple transportation like a <u>bicycle</u>.

B. Directions: *Write the letter of the word that would be the correct spelling to fill in the blank.*

1. They have set up a _____ on their roof.
    A telescope
    B telascope
    C telaskoap
    D telescoap

2. A _____ is a very powerful storm.
    A cycloan
    B ciclone
    C cyclone
    D cicloan

3. The World Series _____ was in October.
    A telakast
    B telecast
    C telicast
    D telekast

4. A famous _____ can be worth a lot of money.
    A autografph
    B autograf
    C autigraph
    D autograph

5. Our _____ is in the kitchen.
    A televishion
    B telavishion
    C television
    D telivision

6. This lamp has an _____ switch.
    A automatick
    B automatic
    C autamatick
    D autamatic

Research: Research Report

A **research report** presents facts and information gathered from several credible sources, including public records, reference books, informational Web sites, and periodicals. A research report includes a bibliography or a Works Cited list, which credits each source. Follow the steps outlined in this workshop to write your own research report.

Assignment Write a research report to gain more knowledge about a topic that interests you.

What to Include To succeed, your research report should feature the following elements:

- a topic that is narrow enough in scope to cover thoroughly
- a strong introduction that clearly defines the topic
- facts, details, examples, and explanations from a variety of credible sources to support the main ideas
- a clear method of organization
- a bibliography containing accurate and complete citations for all sources
- error-free grammar including proper punctuation of citations and titles of reference works

To preview the criteria on which your research report may be judged, see the rubric on page 925.

Using the Form

Research skills are useful in these writing situations:

- history and science reports
- newspaper or magazine articles
- informative essays and speeches

Writing Workshop: *Work in Progress*

If you have completed the Work-in-Progress assignments, you already have, in your portfolio, ideas to use in your research report. Continue to develop these ideas, or explore a new idea as you complete the Writing Workshop.

Prewriting

Choosing Your Topic

Browsing Browse through reference books at a library. For example, flip through an atlas, an almanac, or a volume of an encyclopedia. Jot down each person, place, object, or event that interests you. Then scan your notes and circle any words or phrases that suggest a good topic.

Category List For categories such as *people, historic events, inventions,* and *places,* jot down two or three examples of each. Then, choose a topic from this list.

Work in Progress
Review the work you did on pages 859 and 885.

Narrowing Your Topic

Use a topic web. Make sure that your topic isn't too broad to cover effectively. Narrow your topic by using a topic web. Each row should contain smaller and smaller aspects of your general topic. This topic web narrows the general topic "Ancient Rome" down to a specific building in ancient Rome.

Gathering Details

Take notes from a variety of sources. As part of your research, locate **primary sources**—firsthand or original accounts, such as interview transcripts and

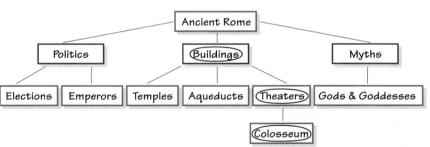

newspaper articles. In addition, use **secondary sources**—accounts that are not original, such as encyclopedia entries. As you gather facts, details, examples, and explanations, take careful notes, using source cards and note cards.

- On each **source card,** write down information about each source—title, author, publication date and place, and page numbers.
- On each **note card,** write down information to use in your report. Use quotation marks when you copy words exactly, and indicate the page number on which the quotation appears. In most cases, use your own words.

Drafting

Shaping Your Writing

Organize your research report. Group your notes by categories that break your topic into subtopics. For example, if you are writing about the Colosseum, you might use these topics in your outline:

- architecture
- construction
- events held
- spectators

Use Roman numerals (I, II, III) to number the subtopics and letters (A, B) to show details and facts related to each subtopic, as in the outline shown here.

Match your draft to your outline. A solid, detailed outline will serve as a map, guiding you through the writing of your draft. The headings with Roman numerals indicate main sections of your report. You may need to write several paragraphs to cover each Roman numeral topic fully. Organize your paragraphs around the topics with capital letters.

> **I. Introduction**
>
> **II. Architecture of Colosseum**
> **A.** measurements
> **B.** building material
>
> **III. Construction of Colosseum**
> **A.** beginning date
> **B.** workers
>
> **IV. Conclusion**

Providing Elaboration

Support main ideas with facts. Using your outline, write sentences to express each main idea in your report. Leave spaces between each line of your draft, and keep wide margins. Then, refer to your note cards and fill in these empty spaces with the supporting facts, details, examples, and explanations that you gathered through your research.

Prepare to cite sources. To avoid **plagiarism**—presenting another's work as your own—you must include documentation every time you use another writer's ideas. As you draft, circle ideas that come from your sources. At this stage, for each circled item, use parentheses to note the author's last name and the page numbers of the material used. You can use this information later to make a formal bibliography.

From the Author's Desk

Julius Lester
on Writing Vivid Descriptions

Julius
Lester

The writing of *Black Cowboy, Wild Horses* involved research. To make the story realistic and believable, I had to learn a lot about wild horses. How big was a herd? How was the herd organized? What did a herd do each day? Reading books about wild horses answered my questions. As you will see in the passage below, my research helped me write vivid descriptions.

―――――――――――

". . . describe, not explain."

―――――――――― —Julius Lester

Professional Model:
from *Black Cowboys, Wild Horses*

The ~~next~~ following morning Bob ∧and Warrior walked ~~his horse~~ into the herd. The stallion eyed ~~him~~ them for a moment. Then, as if to test this newcomer, ~~the stallion took~~ he led the herd off in a gallop. ~~Bob kicked his horse lightly and the romp was on.~~

~~He moved into the middle of the herd. He wanted to avoid the stallion's teeth. Stallions would sometimes gallop alongside a herd, biting a slow mare on the rump, ramming or bumping another who threatened to run separate from the group.~~

Bob lay flat across Warrior's back and moved with the herd. ∧If anyone had ∧been watching, ~~seen the herd~~ they would not have noticed ~~the~~ a man among the horses. ~~in its midst, lying almost flat across his horse's back as if he had caught the wind and was going to ride it to where land and sky became one.~~

In the first sentence I changed "next morning" to "following morning" because I had used the phrase "next morning" two paragraphs before. It is important to keep the writing fresh, and one way to do this is by not repeating key words and phrases.

I cut this paragraph because the explanation slows the action of the story and I am just showing off the research I did. I used this fact about the stallion biting mares later in the story, where it fit the action.

I also cut a large section from the last paragraph because there was too much description. I liked the figure of speech about riding the wind. But a writer must take out even those elements he likes, if they detract from the story.

Writing Workshop

Revising

Revising Your Paragraphs

Check for effective paragraph structure. In a research report, most body paragraphs should be built according to this plan:

- a **topic sentence (T)** stating the paragraph's main idea

- a **restatement (R)** or elaboration of the topic sentence

- strong **illustrations (I),** including facts, examples, or details about the main idea

Review your draft. Label each of your sentences a **T, R,** or **I.** If a paragraph contains a group of **I's,** make sure that you have a strong **T** that they support. If you find a **T** by itself, add **I's** to support it.

To read the complete student model, see page 922.

Student Model: Balancing Your Paragraphs

R *These people saw ice and snow all the time.* *R* *It was never warm enough for it to melt, so it piled up.*

T During the last ice age, or the Wisconsin Ice Age, people lived on the Earth. *I* In the summertime, women fished in chilly streams. The men hunted year-round.

The writer adds sentences that restate the topic sentence to achieve balance in the paragraph.

Revising Your Word Choice

Define technical terms and difficult words. While researching your report, you may have learned new words—either technical terms related to your topic or difficult words that were unfamiliar to you. Help your readers to understand and enjoy your report. Add context clues or definitions to make these words easier to understand.

Difficult: A popular show at the Roman Colosseum featured **gladiators.**

Defined: A popular show at the Roman Colosseum featured **gladiators,** trained fighters who often faced other men or even wild animals.

Peer Review: Work with a partner to identify words in your draft that should be defined. Your partner will be able to point out such words.

Integrating Grammar Skills

Punctuating Citations and Titles of Reference Works

When you cite sources, you must be sure to punctuate them correctly. Follow these guidelines for presenting the title of a work and the words of various sources in your research report:

- **Underlining and Italicizing** Underline or italicize the titles of long written works and the titles of periodicals to set them off.

- **Using Quotation Marks** Titles of short written works and Internet sites should be set off in quotation marks.

Prentice Hall Writing and Grammar Connection: Chapter 26, Section 4

Underlined / Italicized	Quotation Marks
Title of a Book	Title of a Short Story
Title of a Play	Chapter From a Book
Title of a Long Poem	Title of a Short Poem
Title of a Magazine	Title of an Article
Title of a Newspaper	Title of a Web Site

Including Direct Quotations A **direct quotation** conveys the exact words that another person wrote or said. These words must be set off with quotation marks within your research report.
- Introduce short quotations with a comma, and run them in with your own sentences, setting them off with quotation marks.
- Introduce quotations that are five lines or longer with a colon. Start a new line and indent the quotation. Do not use quotation marks.

Fixing Errors To find and fix errors involving quotation marks, underlining, and italics, follow these steps:

1. **Use your note cards and source cards to check the quoted material you have used.**

2. **Make sure that you have used the exact words that you found in your source.** Enclose these words in quotation marks.

3. **Check the source of each quotation.** Follow the punctuation rules above for the use of quotation marks and underlining or italicizing of titles.

Apply It to Your Editing

Reread the draft of your research report. Use the rules above to correct any mistakes in the punctuation of your citations.

Writing Workshop

Student Model: Elizabeth Cleary, Maplewood, NJ

Ice Ages

Ice ages occur every two hundred million years or so. An ice age is defined as a long period of cold where large amounts of water are trapped under ice. Although ice ages happened long ago, studying their causes and effects helps contemporary scientists understand geological conditions of the world today.

When an ice age does occur, ice covers much of the Earth. This ice forms when the climate changes. The polar regions become very cold and the temperatures drop everywhere else. The ice is trapped in enormous mountains of ice called glaciers. Glaciers can be as large as a continent in size. When the Earth's temperature warms up, the glaciers start to melt, forming rivers and lakes. Glaciers' tremendous weight and size can actually wear away mountains and valleys as the glaciers melt and move. The melting ice also raises ocean levels.

There are many different theories to explain why ice ages occur, but no one knows for sure. Many scientists agree that it is probably due to a combination of causes, including changes in the sun's intensity, the distance of the Earth from the sun, changes in ocean currents, the continental plates rubbing up against each other, and the varying amounts of carbon dioxide in the atmosphere (*PBS Nova* Web site "The Big Chill").

Map labels:
Southern extent of glacial ice 20,000 years ago

Landward limit of coastline in the past 5 million years

Location of coastline 20,000 years ago

Current location of coastline

300 MILES

400 KILOMETERS

Effects of Ice Age on Eastern Coastline of United States

The author defines her topic clearly in the highlighted sentence.

This map illustrates the writer's point that ice ages caused current conditions.

Here the author presents factual information related to the possible causes of ice ages.

During the last ice age, or the Wisconsin Ice Age, people lived on the Earth. These people saw ice and snow all the time. It was never warm enough for it to melt, so it piled up. In summertime, women fished in chilly streams. The men hunted year-round.

The skeleton of one person who lived and hunted during this time was found by some hikers in 1991 in the European Alps. He had been buried in the ice for nearly 5,000 years. Nicknamed the "Iceman," scientists believe that perhaps he was suddenly caught by a blizzard or that he possibly ran out of food, became weak, and died.

Scientists were able to learn a lot about this ancient period from the leather clothes and animal skins he was wearing and the tools he was carrying (Roberts, p. 38).

Ice ages also affect life today. The ice sheets that formed weighed a huge amount. When the ice retreated, it left behind large rocks and other debris which otherwise would not be there. Also, without ice ages, large bodies of water like the Great Lakes simply wouldn't exist. We depend on these bodies of water every day for fresh drinking water, recreation, and shipping large quantities of materials.

Scientists discovered ice ages because of Louis Agassiz, a nineteenth-century scientist who is sometimes called the "Father of Glaciology." In Switzerland, he saw boulders or granite far from where any granite should be. He also noticed scrapes and grooves, or striae. He theorized that glaciers had caused all of these geologic features (University of California Museum of Paleontology Web page).

Many animals that are extinct now lived during the Ice Age. The saber-toothed tiger and the mastodon, an elephant-like animal, formerly lived in North America. They became extinct because of climate change and hunting. Other animals became extinct as well because they could not adapt to the way the Earth was changing.

Baron Gerard de Geer, a Swedish geologist, did pioneering work which estimated the end of the last ice age. In a similar way to the way we count

Elizabeth clearly and accurately cites her sources to show where she obtained a set of specific details.

In each section, Elizabeth explores a different aspect of the ice ages. Here she is explaining scientific discovery.

tree rings to estimate a tree's age, De Geer used layers of sediment left by glacier's summer melts to calculate the history of the Ice Age. He did much of his work in Sweden, but he also visited areas that had been affected by glaciers in New England.

Thanks to scientists like De Geer and Agassiz, we know a great deal about that remote age when glaciers roamed the Earth. We can now estimate the history of ice ages and determine what features—valleys, inland seas, mountains, lakes, rocks—were caused, as you can see by the map displayed here of the Eastern United States. There is still a lot more to be discovered about the causes of ice ages, but one thing is clear: Glaciers had a powerful effect on the world as we know it today.

> The author restates the main idea that she presented in the introduction and supported in the body of the paper.

Bibliography

Department of Geosciences, University of Arizona. 10 Nov. 2000.
    <http://www.geoarizona.edu/Antevs/degeer.html>

History of the Universe. 11 Nov. 2000.
    <http://www.historyoftheuniverse.com/iceage.html>

Ice Age. Compton's Interactive Encyclopedia ©The Learning
    Company, Inc. [CD-Rom] (1998).

Roberts, David. "The Iceman." *National Geographic Magazine,* June
    1993: 37–49

University of California Museum of Paleontology. 11 Nov. 2000
    <http://www.ucmp.berkeley.edu/history/agassiz.html>

PBS Nova "The Big Chill." 10 Nov. 2000
    <http://www.pbs.org/wgbh/nova/ice/chill.html>

> In her bibliography, Elizabeth cites all the sources used to research her paper.

Editing and Proofreading

Review your report and correct errors in spelling and grammar.

Focus on Accuracy: Check the names of the authors that you quote, and the names of the books, articles, or other sources that you used. When in doubt, go back to the source materials to double-check the information.

Publishing and Presenting

Consider one of these ways to publish and present your report:
Create a bibliography or works-cited list. A works-cited page provides readers with full bibliographic information on each source you cite. Standards for documentation are set by several organizations, such as MLA and APA. Follow the format your teacher prefers and check that each entry is complete and properly punctuated. (For more information, see pages R25 and R26.)
Create a mini-lesson. Use your report as the basis for a short lesson on your topic. Plan a lesson that includes an activity related to the topic. Present your lesson to a group of classmates.

Reflecting on Your Writing

Writer's Journal Jot down a few notes on writing a research report. Begin by answering these questions:
- What was the most interesting thing that you learned about your topic?
- Which source provided you with the most useful information?

Rubric for Self-Assessment

To assess your research report, use the following rubric:

Criteria	Rating Scale not very → very
Focus: How clearly stated is your topic?	1 2 3 4 5
Organization: How clear is the method of organization?	1 2 3 4 5
Support/Elaboration: How well do you use a variety of media elements to provide support for the main ideas?	1 2 3 4 5
Style: How smooth are your transitions among media?	1 2 3 4 5
Conventions: How well have you corrected errors—including sentence fragments—in your material?	1 2 3 4 5

Delivering an Oral Response to Literature

After you have read a literary work, you may be asked to deliver an **oral response to literature.** An oral response includes many of the characteristics of a successful written response. (To review a response to literature, see the Writing Workshop, pp. 696-700.) The speaking strategies that follow will help you develop and deliver an organized response that your audience will appreciate. Use the checklist on this page to improve your performance.

Develop an Interpretation
The first step toward a successful oral response is to read carefully and thoughtfully to develop an interpretation.

Organize around clear ideas. Organize your response around a number of clear ideas, premises, or images. Your introduction should include your interpretation of the work. The body of the speech should have relevant examples and textual evidence to support your interpretation. Conclude by restating your interpretation and voicing your opinion.

Use examples and textual evidence. To give your oral response credibility, pull out quotations and examples from the literature to support your points. Keep yourself focused on what the text has to say.

Deliver With Confidence
To deliver an effective response to literature, use speaking techniques such as tone, volume, and pacing. Make eye contact to engage the audience and win them over to your interpretation of the literature.

Speak clearly and slowly. Use a strong, clear voice that can be heard in the back of the room. Speak slowly and enunciate every word. Do not be afraid to pause before reading a quotation or starting a new thought.

Activity ▶ *Videotape a Review* ▶ Select and listen to a book on tape from your library. After listening to the tape, develop your own interpretation of the piece of literature. Then, deliver a two- to three-minute review of the book to your class.

Tips for Engaging the Audience

Show the work
Hold up the novel or the collection in which you read the work.

Read from the work
When reading a quotation or passage, read directly from the work. Use sticky notes to mark pages before the presentation.

Use props
Hold up an object mentioned in your presentation.

The Call of the Wild

Jack London
Tor, 1986

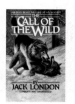

Novel *The Call of the Wild* is the story of a dog named Buck. Buck is kidnapped from his home in California and ends up in the Alaskan wilderness. He works as a sled dog and learns many hard lessons as he struggles for survival among the huskies and half-breed sled dogs in the northern wilderness. The greatest lesson he learns from his last owner is the power of love and loyalty. Yet even at the side of the human he loves, he still feels the urge to answer his wolf ancestors as they howl to him.

Charlie and the Chocolate Factory

Roald Dahl
Puffin, 1998

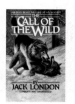

Novel Willy Wonka, the chocolate maker, is opening his doors to the public. Five lucky people who find a Golden Ticket in their Wonka chocolate bars will receive a private tour of the factory, given by Mr. Wonka himself. When Charlie Bucket finds a dollar bill in the street, he cannot help but buy two Wonka candy bars. As he unwraps the second chocolate bar, he sees the glimmer of gold! The very next day, Charlie and his fellow winners step through the factory gates to discover whether or not the rumors surrounding the Chocolate Factory and its mysterious owner are true.

The Iron Ring

Lloyd Alexander
Dutton, 1997

Novel In this stirring adventure, the author explores ideas about heroism and introduces students to the fantasy of ancient Indian mythology. The main character, Tamar, has to look inside himself to decide whether his *dharma*—the moral basis on which all actions are judged—is being fulfilled. He is an epic hero, much like a knight from the time of King Arthur, on a quest that requires him to practice (or show) commitment, courage, and love.

Boy of the Painted Cave

Justin Denzel
PaperStar Book, 1988

Novel This novel tells the story of a boy named Tao who longs to be a cave painter. He is forbidden from fulfilling his dream, however, because he is not a Chosen One. Instead, he is a tribal outcast with a crippled foot and no father to claim him. Forced into isolation by the superstitious leader of his tribe, Tao befriends a wolf dog, Ram, and the shaman, Greybeard, who teaches him to paint.

These titles are available in the Penguin/Prentice Hall Literature Library.

Think About It In the future there may no longer be such a place as a school, or so Isaac Asimov writes in "The Fun They Had." With technology on the rise, perhaps one day children will be taught and tested completely by computers. As you read, think about what would be lost or gained by such a dramatic change in schooling.

The Fun They Had
ISAAC ASIMOV

Margie even wrote about it that night in her diary. On the page headed May 17, 2155, she wrote, "Today Tommy found a real book."

It was a very old book. Margie's grandfather once said that when he was a little boy, his grandfather told him that there was a time when all stories were printed on paper.

They turned the pages, which were yellow and crinkly, and it was awfully funny to read words that stood still instead of moving the way they were supposed to—on a screen, you know. And then, when they turned back to the page before, it had the same words on it that it had had when they read it the first time.

"Gee," said Tommy, "what a waste. When you're through with the book, you just throw it away, I guess. Our television screen must have had a million books on it and it's good for plenty more. I wouldn't throw it away."

"Same with mine," said Margie. She was eleven and hadn't seen as many telebooks as Tommy had. He was thirteen.

She said, "Where did you find it?"

"In my house." He pointed without looking, because he was busy reading. "In the attic."

"What's it about?"

"School."

Margie was scornful. "School? What's there to write about school? I hate school." Margie always hated school, but now she hated it more than ever. The mechanical teacher had been giving her test after test in geography, and she had been doing worse and worse until her mother had shaken her head sorrowfully and sent for the county inspector.

He was a round little man with a red face and a whole box of tools with dials and wires. He smiled at her and gave her an apple, then took the teacher apart. Margie had hoped he wouldn't know how to put it together again, but he knew how all right, and after an hour or so, there it was again, large and ugly, with a big screen on which all the lessons were shown and the questions were asked. That wasn't so bad. The part she hated most was the slot where she had to put homework and test papers. She always had to write them out in a punch code they made her learn when she was six years old, and the mechanical teacher calculated the mark in no time.

The inspector had smiled after he was finished and patted her head. He said to her mother, "It's not the little girl's fault, Mrs. Jones. I think the geography sector was geared a little too quick. Those things happen sometimes. I've slowed it up to an average ten-year level. Actually, the overall pattern of her progress is quite satisfactory." And he patted Margie's head again.

Margie was disappointed. She had been hoping they would take the teacher away altogether. They had once taken Tommy's teacher away for nearly a month because the history sector had blanked out completely.

So she said to Tommy, "Why would anyone write about school?"

Tommy looked at her with very superior eyes. "Because it's not our kind of school, stupid. This is the old kind of school that they had hundreds and hundreds of year ago." He added loftily, pronouncing the word carefully, "*Centuries* ago."

Margie was hurt. "Well, I don't know what kind of school they had all that time ago." She read the book over his shoulder for a while, then said, "Anyway, they had a teacher."

"Sure they had a teacher, but it wasn't a *regular* teacher. It was a man."

"A man? How could a man be a teacher?"

"Well, he just told the boys and girls things and gave them homework and asked them questions."

"A man isn't smart enough."

"Sure he is. My father knows as much as my teacher."

"He can't. A man can't know as much as a teacher."

"He knows almost as much I betcha."

Margie wasn't prepared to dispute that. She said, "I wouldn't want a strange man in my house to teach me."

Tommy screamed with laughter. "You don't know much, Margie. The teachers didn't live in the house. They had a special building and all the kids went there."

"And all the kids learned the same thing?"

"Sure, if they were the same age."

"But my mother says a teacher has to be adjusted to fit the mind of each boy and girl it teaches and that each kid has to be taught differently."

"Just the same, they didn't do it that way then. If you don't like it, you don't have to read the book."

"I didn't say I didn't like it," Margie said quickly. She wanted to read about those funny schools.

They weren't even half finished when Margie's mother called, "Margie! School!"

Margie looked up. "Not yet, Mamma."

"Now," said Mrs. Jones. "And it's probably time for Tommy, too."

Margie said to Tommy, "Can I read the book some more with you after school?"

"Maybe," he said, nonchalantly. He walked away whistling, the dusty old book tucked beneath his arm.

Margie went into the schoolroom. It was right next to her bedroom, and the mechanical teacher was on and waiting for her. It was always on at the same time every day except Saturday and Sunday, because her mother said little girls learned better if they learned at regular hours.

The screen was lit up, and it said: "Today's arithmetic lesson is on the addition of proper fractions. Please insert yesterday's homework in the proper slot."

Margie did so with a sigh. She was thinking about the old schools they had when her grandfather's grandfather was a little boy. All the kids from the whole neighborhood came, laughing and shouting in the schoolyard, sitting together in the schoolroom, going home together at the end of the day. They learned the same things so they could help one another on the homework and talk about it.

And the teachers were people. . . .

The mechanical teacher was flashing on the screen: "When we add the fractions ½ and ¼ . . ."

Margie was thinking about how the kids must have loved it in the old days. She was thinking about the fun they had.

Check any section of a library and you will probably find a book by **Isaac Asimov** (1920–1992). He wrote fiction, medical books, humor, autobiography, essays, a guide to Shakespeare, and science books. Asimov was a professor of biochemistry and taught until his death at the age of seventy-two. He is best known for his science fiction.

Readings in Science Fiction
Talk About It

Use these questions to guide a discussion of the story:

1. **(a)** What does Margie write in her diary about the book Tommy found? **(b)** Why do you think she has such a strong reaction to the book?

2. **(a)** Why does Margie think that school in the past was fun? **(b)** Compare Margie's school to your school.

3. Is Asimov's school better or worse than today's classroom plan? In small groups, consider these questions:
   - Would you like to go to school the way Margie does?
   - What are the benefits of having a computer for a teacher?
   - What are the benefits of having a human teacher?

   Choose a point-person to share your group's ideas with the class.

RESOURCES

GLOSSARY

High-utility words and academic vocabulary appear in green.

A

abruptly (ə brupt´ lē) *adv.* suddenly, without warning

absentminded (ab´ sənt mīn´ did) *adj.* forgetful

accurate (ak´ yə rət) *adj.* exactly right; free from errors

achievement (ə chēv´ mənt) *n.* result of achieving or accomplishing

adapt (ə dapt´) *v.* adjust

admonishing (ad män´ ish iŋ) *adj.* disapproving

alley (al´ ē) *n.* narrow street between or behind buildings

ambition (am bish´ ən) *n.* important goal for the future

anecdotes (an´ ik dōts) *n.* short, entertaining tales

anxiously (aŋk´ shəs lē) *adv.* in a worried or uneasy way

apparently (ə per´ənt lē) *adv.* seemingly

applications (ap´ li kā´ shənz) *n.* forms filled out to make a request

aptitude (ap´ tə tōōd´) *n.* natural ability

awed (ôd) *v.* filled with feelings of fear and wonder

B

bellowed (bel´ ōd) *v.* cried out in a low, loud voice

beseech (bē sēch´) *v.* beg

billowing (bil´ ō iŋ) *v.* filling with wind

bound (bound) *v.* tied

brief (brēf) *adj.* short

C

cause (kôz) *n.* why something happens

ceased (sēsd) *v.* stopped

chaotic (kā ät´ ik) *adj.* completely confused

characteristic (kar´ək tər is´tik) *n.* quality or feature

chorus (kôr´ əs) *n.* the sound produced by many voices singing or speaking at the same time

claim (klām) *v.* to state as a fact

clatter (klat´ ər) *n.* rattling sound

coaxed (kōkst) *v.* persuaded by gentle urging

colossal (kə läs´ əl) *adj.* very large; huge

community (kə myōō´ nə tē) *n.* group of people living in the same area

compare (kəm per´) *v.* show how things are alike

composed (kəm pōzd´) *v.* made up

compulsion (kəm pul´ shən) *n.* driving force

conclude (kən klōōd´) *v.* to form an opinion

concludes (kən klōōdz´) *v.* comes to an end

confiscated (kän´ fis kāt´ ed) *v.* seized, usually by govenmental authority

consequently (kän´ si kwent´ lē) *adv.* as a result

consideration (kən sid´ ər ā´ shən) *n.* careful thought or attention

consoled (kän sōld´) *v.* comforted

consumption (kən sump´ shen) *n.* eating; drinking; using up

context (kän tekst´) *n.* situation in which a word is used

contrast (kən´trast´) *v.* show how things are different

convey (kən vā´) *v.* communicate; carry from place to place

cordial (kôr´ jəl) *adj.* warm and friendly

craned (krānd) *v.* stretched out for a better look

custody (kus´ tə dē) *n.* protection or supervision

D

decisively (dē sī´ siv lē´) *adv.* with determination

declined (dē klīnd´) *v.* refused

deem (dēm) *v.* judge

deficiency (di fish´ ən sē) *n.* shortage or lack

define (dē fīn´, di-) *v.* to state the meaning

dejectedly (dē jek´ tid lē) *adv.* sadly; with low spirits

demonstrate (dem´ ən strāt) *v.* show clearly; prove

describe (di skrīb´) *v.* tell or write about

detail (dē tāl´) *n.* a piece of information

determine (dē tur´mən, di-) *v.* decide or figure out

diagnosis (dī əg nō´sis) *n.* identification of a person's medical condition

dilution (di lōō´ shən) *n.* process of weakening by mixing with something else

direction (də rek´shən; *also* dī-) *n.* act of directing or supervising

dismal (diz´ məl) *adj.* causing gloom or misery

dispersed (di spʉrst´) *v.* distributed in many directions

dispute (di spyōōt´) *n.* argument; debate; quarrel

dissonance (dis´ ə nəns) *n.* harsh or unpleasant combination of sounds

distinguish (di stiŋ´gwish) *v.* to tell the difference between two things

distracted (di strakt´ id) *adj.* unable to concentrate

distress (di stres´) *n.* serious pain or sadness

diverse (də vʉrs´) *adj.* various; with differing characteristics

documentation (däk´ yōō mən tā´ shən) *n.* supporting evidence

drone (drōn) *n.* continuous humming sound

E

effect (e fekt´) *n.* the consequence of

element (el´ə mənt) *n.* part of the whole

eloquent (el´ ə kwənt) *adj.* persuasive and expressive

embedded (em bed´ əd) *adj.* firmly fixed in surrounding material

embraced (em brāsd´) *v.* clasped in the arms, usually as an expression of affection

emigrated (em´ i grāt´ id) *v.* left one country to settle in another

enable (en ā´bəl, in-) *v.* allow; assist

endured (en dʊord´) *v.* suffered through

engulfing (en gulf´ iŋ) *v.* flowing over and enclosing; swallowing up

envy (en´ vē) *n.* unhappy feeling of wanting what someone else has

escorting (es kort´ iŋ) *v.* going with as a companion

essential (ə sen´shəl, i-) *adj.* basic; necessary

establish (ə stab´lish, i-) *v.* set up; cause to be

etiquette (et´ i ket) *n.* acceptable social manners

evident (ev´ə dənt) *adj.* easy to see; very clear

evolved (ē välvd´) *v.* grew gradually; developed

examine (eg zam´ən, ig-) *v.* to look at carefully

exhaust (eg zôst´) *v.* use up

explain (ek splān´, ik-) *v.* make clear or understandable

exuded (eg zyōōd´ əd) *v.* gave off; oozed; radiated

F

fact (fakt) *n.* a statement that can be proved

famine (fam´ in) *n.* shortage of food

fellow (fel´ ō) *n.* man or boy

ferocious (fə rō´ shəs) *adj.* wild and dangerous

flaw (flô) *n.* break; crack

flee (flē) *v.* run; escape from danger

focus (fō´kəs) *n.* center of interest or attention

former (fôr´ mər) *adj.* existing in an earlier time; past

fostering (fôs´ tər iŋ) *n.* taking care of

fragrant (frā´ grənt) *adj.* pleasant-smelling

frenzied (fren´ zēd) *adj.* acting in a wild, uncontrolled way

fusing (fyōō´ ziŋ) *n.* joining permanently

G

glisten (glis´ ən) *v.* shine or sparkle

glumly (glum´ lē) *adv.* in a gloomy or sullen way

gnashes (nash´ iz) *v.* bites with grinding teeth

gnawing (nô´ iŋ) *v.* biting and cutting with the teeth

grant (grant) *v.* admit

greed (grēd) *n.* a selfish desire for more than one's share of something

grief (grēf) *n.* deep sadness

grudgingly (gruj´ iŋ lē) *adv.* in an unwilling or resentful way

H

hearing (hir´ iŋ) *n.* chance to give evidence and testimony

hesitated (hez´ i tāt´ id) *v.* stopped because of indecision

howl (houl) *v.* make a loud, sorrowful sound

I

identifiable (ī den´tə fī´ ə bəl) *adj.* able to be identified

identify (ī den´tə fī´) *v.* recognize or point out; connect with

ignorance (ig´ nə rəns) *n.* lack of knowledge, education, or experience

ignore (ig nôr´) *v.* pay no attention to

immense (i mens´) *adj.* huge

impractical (im prak´ ti kəl) *adj.* not workable or particularly useful

incessantly (in ses´ ənt lē) *adv.* constantly; continually

incidents (in´sə dənts´) *n.* events; occurrences

inedible (in ed´ ə bəl) *adj.* not fit to be eaten

inevitably (in ev´ i tə blē) *adv.* unavoidably

infer (in fʉr´) *v.* to assume something based on fact

influence (in´flōō əns, in flōō´əns) *n.* power to affect others

inhabited (in ha´ bit əd) *adj.* lived in; occupied

inscribed (in skrībd´) *v.* written on

instinctively (in stiŋk´ tiv lē) *adv.* done automatically, without thinking

integrate (in´ tə grāt´) *v.* remove all barriers and allow access to all

intent (in tent´) *n.* purpose; object; aim

intently (in tent´ lē) *adv.* with great attention or determination

intrigued (in trēgəd´) *v.* fascinated

invisible (in viz´ ə bəl) *adj.* not able to be seen

iridescent (ir´ ə des´ ənt) *adj.* showing different colors when seen from different angles

irrational (i rash´ ə nəl) *adj.* unreasonable

J

jubilation (jōō´ bə lā´ shən) *n.* great joy; triumph

K

key (kē) *n.* item used to unlock; *adj.* important

L

lair (ler) *n.* den or resting place of a wild animal

leisurely (lē´ zhər lē) *adv.* in an unhurried way

liable (lī´ ə bəl) *adj.* likely to do something or to happen

M

malicious (mə lish´ əs) *adj.* having or showing evil intentions

mauled (môld) *v.* badly injured by being attacked

melancholy (mel´ən käl´ ē) *adj.* sad; gloomy

menace (men´ əs) *n.* threat; danger

methods (meth´ ədz) *n.* ways of doing something

misapprehension (mis´ ap rē hen´ shən) *n.* misunderstanding

misery (miz´ ər ē) *n.* great sorrow

mode (mōd) *n.* way of doing something

monotonous (mə nät´n əs) *adj.* unchanging; tiresome because it does not vary

mortal (môr´ təl) *n.* referring to humans, who must eventually die

murmurs (mʉr´ mərz) *v.* makes a soft, continuous sound

N

naïve (nä ēv´) *adj.* innocent; not worldly

nigh (nī) *adv.* near

O

obscure (əb skyoor´) *adj.* not well known

obstinacy (äb´ stə nə sē) *n.* stubbornness

offense (ə fens´) *n.* harmful act

offensive (ə fen´ siv) *adj.* unpleasant

opinion (ə pin´yən, ō-) *n.* a statement that expresses a person's judgment or belief

orator (ôr´ ət ər) *n.* person who can speak well in public

P

paraphrase (par´ə frāz´) *n.* restate in your own words

passage (pas´ij) *n.* a body of text

perished (per´ ishd) *v.* died

perplexities (pər plek´ sə tēz) *n.* things that confuse or puzzle

petition (pə tish´ən) *n.* a document people sign to express demands

phrasings (frāz´ iŋs) *n.* ways of speaking

plagued (plāgd) *v.* tormented

pleaded (plēd´ id) *v.* begged

pleasant (plez´ ənt) *adj.* delightful

plight (plīt) *n.* awkward, sad, or dangerous situation

plunging (plunj´ iŋ) *v.* diving or falling suddenly

possible (päs´ə bəl) *adj.* able to be done

precautionary (pri kô´ shə ner´ ē) *adj.* done to prevent harm or danger

predict (prē dikt´, pri-) *v.* to make a logical guess about what will happen next, based on clues and knowledge

prelude (prā´lōōd´) *n.* introduction to a main event

preview (prē´vyōō´) *v.* view, or look at beforehand

prior (prī´ ər) *adj.* happening before the present time; established over time, during the past

proposition (präp´ ə zish´ ən) *n.* an offer

prove (prōōv) *v.* to show clear evidence that something is definitely true or false

provided (prə vīd´ id) *v.* supplied; furnished

prowled (prould) *v.* moved around quietly and secretly

purpose (pʉr´pəs) *n.* intention; plan

Q

quandaries (kwän´ də rēz) *n.* problems, uncertainties

quantities (kwänt´ ə tēz) *n.* great amounts

quarry (kwôr´ ē) *n.* prey; anything being hunted or pursued

R

rage (rāj) *n.* very strong anger

raggedy (rag´ i dē) *adj.* torn from wear

rancor (raŋ´ kər) *n.* bitter hate or ill will

rapidly (rap´ id lē) *adv.* quickly

ravaged (rav´ ijd) *v.* violently destroyed; ruined

ravenous (rav´ ə nəs) *adj.* greedily hungry

ravine (rə vēn´) *n.* a long, deep hollow in the earth's surface

reason (rē´zən) *n.* why something happens

recall (ri kôl´) *v.* remember

reckless (rek´ lis) *adj.* not careful; taking chances

recognize (rek´əg nīz´) *v.* know and remember

refer (ri fʉr´) *v.* to look back

reflecting (ri flekt´ iŋ) *v.* thinking seriously

reflection (ri flek´ shən) *n.* an image of one's self, as seen in a mirror

regally (rē´ gə lē) *adv.* in a stately manner, like a king or queen

regarded (ri gärd´ əd) *v.* thought of; considered

regret (ri gret´) *v.* be sorry for

regulation (reg´ yə lā´ shən) *n.* rule

relationship (ri lā´shən ship´) *n.* the connection between two things

reluctant (ri luk´ tənt) *adj.* showing doubt or unwillingness

remorse (re môrs´) *n.* guilt over a wrong one has done

represent (rep´ri zent´) *v.* stand for; speak and act for

repulse (ri puls´) *v.* drive back; repel an attack

resident (rez´ i dənt) *adj.* living in a place

resolutions (rez´ə loo´ shənz) *n.* intentions; things decided

restate (rē stāt´) *v.* state again

result (ri zult´) *n.* the consequence of

retaliated (ri tal´ē āt´id) *v.* punished in return for an injury or a wrong done

retreated (ri trēt´ id) *v.* moved away from something dangerous, difficult, or disagreeable

reunion (rē yoon´ yən) *n.* coming together after a separation

revelation (rev´ ə lā´ shən) *n.* sudden rush of understanding

review (ri vyoo´) *v.* look at again

revise (ri vīz´) *v.* to read or think about something again in order to look for places that might need changes or improvements

rudimentary (roo´ də men´ trē) *adj.* incompletely developed

rued (rood) *v.* regretted

S

satisfactorily (sat´ is fak´ tə rə lē) *adv.* in a way that fulfills a need or a goal

savoring (sā´ vər iŋ) *v.* enjoying; tasting with appreciation

seized (sēzd) *v.* grabbed; taken hold of

sensible (sen´ sə bil) *adj.* wise; intelligent

sheared (shird) *v.* cut off sharply

significant (sig nif´ ə kənt) *adj.* important

sinew (sin´ yoo) *adj.* muscular power, strength; any source of power or strength

skimming (skim´ iŋ) *adj.* gliding; moving swiftly and lightly over a surface

slanderous (slan´ dər əs) *adj.* including untrue and damaging statements

sleek (slēk) *adj.* smooth and shiny

slough (sluf) *v.* cast off; get rid of

smugly (smug´ lē) *adv.* in a way that shows satisfaction with oneself

sole (sōl) *adj.* single; one and only

sorting (sôrt´ iŋ) *v.* arranging materials into groups based on similar traits; classifying

spasm (spaz´ əm) *n.* a short sudden burst

speculate (spek´yə lāt´) *v.* to make a prediction

splendor (splen´ dər) *n.* great brightness

startled (stärt´ əld) *adj.* surprised

steeples (stē´ pəls) *n.* towers rising above churches or other structures

strategy (strat´ə jē) *n.* a plan for a specific outcome

summary (sum´ə rē) *n.* the main ideas in brief form

summit (sum´ it) *n.* highest part

support (sə port´) *v.* to show to be true

suspended (sə spen´ did) *v.* stopped for a time

sympathy (sim´pə thē) *n.* ability to share feelings

systematic (sis´ tə mat´ ik) *adj.* orderly

T

thicket (thik´ it) *n.* dense growth of shrubs or small trees

thrashing (thrash´ iŋ) *v.* moving wildly

thrives (thrīvz) *v.* grows well

timidly (tim´ id lē) *adv.* in a way that shows fear or shyness

trace (trās) *n.* mark left behind by something

traversed (trə vʉrst´) *v.* went across

treacherous (trech´ ər əs) *adj.* dangerous

trotted (trät´ təd) *v.* ran in a graceful, light way

U

unabridged (un´ ə brijd´) *adj.* complete; not shortened

unique (yo͞o nēk´) *adj.* one of a kind

unreasonable (un rē´ zən i bəl) *adj.* not fair; not sensible

V

verify (ver´ə fī´) *v.* to check something to make sure it is accurate; to prove to be true

vigilance (vij´ ə ləns) *n.* watchfulness

vow (vou) *n.* promise

W

wallowed (wäl´ ōd) *v.* rolled and tilted

wistfully (wist´ fə lē) *adv.* in a hopeful, yearning way

Using a Dictionary

Use a **dictionary** to find the meaning, the pronunciation, and the part of speech of a word. Consult a dictionary also to trace the word's *etymology*, or its origin. Etymology explains how words change, how they are borrowed from other languages, and how new words are invented, or "coined."

Here is an entry from a dictionary. Notice what it tells about the word *anthology*.

anthology (an thäl′ə jē) *n., pl.* **–gies** [Gr. *anthologia*, a garland, collection of short poems < *anthologos*, gathering flowers < *anthos*, flower + *legein*, to gather] a collection of poems, stories, songs, excerpts, etc., chosen by the compiler

Dictionaries provide the *denotation* of each word, or its objective meaning. The symbol < means "comes from" or "is derived from." In this case, the Greek words for "flower" and "gather" combined to form a Greek word that meant a garland, and then that word became an English word that means a collection of literary flowers—a collection of literature like the one you are reading now.

Activity: Use a dictionary to learn about the origins of these words. Then, write a sentence explaining how each word's origin contributes to its meaning.

1. literature
2. author
3. language

Using a Thesaurus

Use a **thesaurus** to increase your vocabulary. In a thesaurus, you will find synonyms, or words that have similar meanings, for most words. Follow these guidelines to use a thesaurus:

- Do not choose a word just because it sounds interesting or educated. Choose the word that expresses exactly the meaning you intend.
- To avoid errors, look up an unfamiliar word in a dictionary to check its precise meaning and to make sure you are using it properly.

Here is an entry from a thesaurus. Notice what it tells about the word *book*.

book *noun*

A printed and bound work: tome, volume. *See* **WORDS.**

book *verb* 1. To register in or as if in a book: catalog, enroll, inscribe, list, set down, write down. *See* **REMEMBER**. 2. To cause to be set aside, as for one's use, in advance: bespeak, engage, reserve. *See* **GET**.

If the word can be used as different parts of speech, as *book* can, the thesaurus entry provides synonyms for the word as each part of speech. Many words also have *connotations*, or emotional associations that the word calls to mind. A thesaurus entry gives specific synonyms for each connotation of the word.

Activity: Look up the word *story* in a thesaurus. Then, answer the questions.

1. What are two synonyms for this word?
2. In what way do the connotations of the synonyms differ?

The History of the English Language

Old English English began about the year 500 when Germanic tribes from the middle of Europe traveled west and settled in Britain. These peoples—the Angles, Saxons, and Jutes—spoke a Germanic language that combined with Danish and Norse when Vikings attacked Britain and added some Latin elements when Christian missionaries arrived. The result was Old English.

Middle English The biggest change in English took place after the Norman Conquest of Britain in 1066. The Normans spoke a dialect of Old French, and Old English changed dramatically when the Normans became the new aristocracy. From about 1100 to 1500, the people of Britain spoke what we now call Middle English.

Modern English During the Renaissance (1300-1600), with its emphasis on reviving classical culture, Greek and Latin languages exerted a strong influence on the English language. In addition, Shakespeare added about two thousand words to the language. Grammar, spelling, and pronunciation continued to change. Modern English was born.

Old Words, New Words

Modern English has a larger vocabulary than any other language in the world. Here are the main ways that new words enter the language:

• **War**—Conquerors introduce new terms and ideas—and new vocabulary, such as *anger* from Old Norse.

• **Immigration**—When large groups of people move from one country to another, they bring words with them, such as *boycott*, from Ireland.

• **Travel and Trade**—Those who travel to foreign lands and those who do business in faraway places bring new words back with them, such as *shampoo*, from Hindi.

• **Science and Technology**—In our time, the amazing growth of science and technology adds many new words to English, such as *Internet*.

• **Other Languages**—Sometimes borrowed words keep basically the same meanings they have in their original languages. Examples include *pajamas* (Hindi), *sauna* (Finnish), and *camouflage* (French). Sometimes borrowed words take on new meanings. *Sleuth*, for example, an Old Norse word for *trail*, has come to mean the person who follows a trail—a detective.

• **Mythology**—Some of the days of the week are named after Norse gods— Wednesday was Woden's Day, Thursday was Thor's Day. Greek and Roman myths have given us many words, such as *martial* (from Mars) and *herculean* (from Hercules).

Activity: Look up the following words in a dictionary. Describe the ways in which you think these words entered American English.

sabotage   burrito   moccasin   megabyte

TIPS FOR IMPROVING READING FLUENCY

When you were younger, you learned to read. Then, you read to expand your experiences or for pure enjoyment. Now, you are expected to read to learn. As you progress in school, you are given more and more material to read. The tips on these pages will help you improve your reading fluency, or your ability to read easily, smoothly, and expressively.

Keeping Your Concentration

One common problem that readers face is the loss of concentration. When you are reading an assignment, you might find yourself rereading the same sentence several times without really understanding it. The first step in changing this behavior is to notice that you do it. Becoming an active, aware reader will help you get the most from your assignments. Practice using these strategies:

- Cover what you have already read with a note card as you go along. Then, you will not be able to reread without noticing that you are doing it.

- Set a purpose for reading beyond just completing the assignment. Then, read actively by pausing to ask yourself questions about the material as you read.

- Use the Reading Skill instruction and notes that appear with each selection in this textbook.

- Stop reading after a specified period of time (for example, 5 minutes) and summarize what you have read. To help you with this strategy, use the Reading Check questions that appear with each selection in this textbook. Reread to find any answers you do not know.

Reading Phrases

Fluent readers read phrases rather than individual words. Reading this way will speed up your reading and improve your comprehension. Here are some useful ideas:

- Experts recommend rereading as a strategy to increase fluency. Choose a passage of text that is neither too hard nor too easy. Read the same passage aloud several times until you can read it smoothly. When you can read the passage fluently, pick another passage and keep practicing.

- Read aloud into a tape recorder. Then, listen to the recording, noting your accuracy, pacing, and expression. You can also read aloud and share feedback with a partner.

- Use the *Prentice Hall Listening to Literature* CDs to hear the selections read aloud. Read along silently in your textbook, noticing how the reader uses his or her voice and emphasizes certain words and phrases.

Understanding Key Vocabulary

If you do not understand some of the words in an assignment, you may miss out on important concepts. Therefore, it is helpful to keep a dictionary nearby when you are reading. Follow these steps:

- Before you begin reading, scan the text for unfamiliar words or terms. Find out what those words mean before you begin reading.
- Use context—the surrounding words, phrases, and sentences—to help you determine the meanings of unfamiliar words.
- If you are unable to understand the meaning through context, refer to the dictionary.

Paying Attention to Punctuation

When you read, pay attention to punctuation. Commas, periods, exclamation points, semicolons, and colons tell you when to pause or stop. They also indicate relationships between groups of words. When you recognize these relationships you will read with greater understanding and expression. Look at the chart below.

Punctuation Mark	Meaning
comma	brief pause
period	pause at the end of a thought
exclamation point	pause that indicates emphasis
semicolon	pause between related but distinct thoughts
colon	pause before giving explanation or examples

Using the Reading Fluency Checklist

Use the checklist below each time you read a selection in this textbook. In your Language Arts journal or notebook, note which skills you need to work on and chart your progress each week.

Reading Fluency Checklist
☐ Preview the text to check for difficult or unfamiliar words.
☐ Practice reading aloud.
☐ Read according to punctuation.
☐ Break down long sentences into the subject and its meaning.
☐ Read groups of words for meaning rather than reading single words.
☐ Read with expression (change your tone of voice to add meaning to the word).

Reading is a skill that can be improved with practice. The key to improving your fluency is to read. The more you read, the better your reading will become.

LITERARY TERMS

ALLITERATION *Alliteration* is the repetition of initial consonant sounds. Writers use alliteration to draw attention to certain words or ideas, to imitate sounds, and to create musical effects.

ALLUSION An *allusion* is a reference to a well-known person, event, place, literary work, or work of art. Understanding what a literary work is saying often depends on recognizing its allusions and the meanings they suggest.

ANALOGY An *analogy* makes a comparison between two or more things that are similar in some ways but otherwise unalike.

ANECDOTE An *anecdote* is a brief story about an interesting, amusing, or strange event. Writers tell anecdotes to entertain or to make a point.

ANTAGONIST An *antagonist* is a character or a force in conflict with a main character, or protagonist.

See *Conflict* and *Protagonist*.

ATMOSPHERE *Atmosphere*, or *mood*, is the feeling created in the reader by a literary work or passage.

AUTHOR'S INFLUENCES An *author's influences* are things that affect his or her writing. These factors include the author's time and place of birth and cultural background, or world events that took place during the author's lifetime.

AUTHOR'S STYLE *Style* is an author's typical way of writing. Many factors determine an author's style, including diction; tone; use of characteristic elements such as figurative language, dialect, rhyme, meter, or rhythmic devices; typical grammatical structures and patterns, typical sentence length, and typical methods of organization.

AUTOBIOGRAPHY An *autobiography* is the story of the writer's own life, told by the writer. Autobiographical writing may tell about the person's whole life or only a part of it.

Because autobiographies are about real people and events, they are a form of nonfiction. Most autobiographies are written in the first person.

See *Biography, Nonfiction,* and *Point of View*.

BIOGRAPHY A *biography* is a form of nonfiction in which a writer tells the life story of another person. Most biographies are written about famous or admirable people. Although biographies are nonfiction, the most effective ones share the qualities of good narrative writing.

See *Autobiography* and *Nonfiction*.

CHARACTER A *character* is a person or an animal that takes part in the action of a literary work. The main, or *major*, character is the most important character in a story, poem, or play. A *minor* character is one who takes part in the action but is not the focus of attention.

Characters are sometimes classified as flat or round. A *flat character* is one-sided and often stereotypical. A *round character*, on the other hand, is fully developed and exhibits many traits—often both faults and virtues. Characters can also be classified as dynamic or static. A *dynamic character* is one who changes or grows during the course of the work. A *static character* is one who does not change.

See *Characterization, Hero/Heroine,* and *Motive*.

CHARACTERIZATION *Characterization* is the act of creating and developing a character. Authors use two major methods of characterization—*direct* and *indirect*. When using *direct* characterization, a writer states the *character's traits,* or characteristics.

When describing a character *indirectly*, a writer depends on the reader to draw conclusions about the character's traits. Sometimes the writer tells what other participants in the story say and think about the character.

See *Character* and *Motive*.

CHARACTER TRAITS *Character traits* are the qualities, attitudes, and values that a character has or displays—for example, dependability, intelligence, selfishness, or stubbornness.

CLIMAX The climax, also called the turning point, is the high point in the action of the plot. It is the moment of greatest tension, when the outcome of the plot hangs in the balance.

See *Plot*.

COMEDY A *comedy* is a literary work, especially a play, which is light, often humorous or satirical, and ends happily. Comedies frequently depict ordinary characters faced with temporary difficulties and conflicts. Types of comedy include *romantic comedy*, which involves problems between lovers, and the *comedy of manners*, which satirically challenges social customs of a society.

CONCRETE POEM A *concrete poem* is one with a shape that suggests its subject. The poet arranges the letters, punctuation, and lines to create an image, or picture, on the page.

CONFLICT A *conflict* is a struggle between opposing forces. Conflict is one of the most important elements of stories, novels, and plays because it causes the action. There are two kinds of conflict: external and internal. An *external conflict* is one in which a character struggles against some outside force, such as another person. Another kind of external conflict may occur between a character and some force in nature.

An *internal conflict* takes place within the mind of a character. The character struggles to make a decision, take an action, or overcome a feeling.

See *Plot.*

CONNOTATIONS The *connotation* of a word is the set of ideas associated with it in addition to its explicit meaning. The connotation of a word can be personal, based on individual experiences. More often, cultural connotations—those recognizable by most people in a group—determine a writer's word choices.

See also *Denotation.*

DENOTATION The *denotation* of a word is its dictionary meaning, independent of other associations that the word may have. The denotation of the word *lake*, for example, is "an inland body of water." "Vacation spot" and "place where the fishing is good" are connotations of the word *lake*.

See also *Connotation.*

DESCRIPTION A *description* is a portrait, in words, of a person, place, or object. Descriptive writing uses images that appeal to the five senses—sight, hearing, touch, taste, and smell.

See *Image.*

DEVELOPMENT See *Plot.*

DIALECT *Dialect* is the form of a language spoken by people in a particular region or group. Dialects differ in pronunciation, grammar, and word choice. The English language is divided into many dialects. British English differs from American English.

DIALOGUE A *dialogue* is a conversation between characters. In poems, novels, and short stories, dialogue is usually set off by quotation marks to indicate a speaker's exact words.

In a play, dialogue follows the names of the characters, and no quotation marks are used.

DRAMA A *drama* is a story written to be performed by actors. Although a drama is meant to be performed, one can also read the script, or written version, and imagine the action. The *script* of a drama is made up of dialogue and stage directions. The *dialogue* is the words spoken by the actors. The *stage directions*, usually printed in italics, tell how the actors should look, move, and speak. They also describe the setting, sound effects, and lighting.

Dramas are often divided into parts called *acts*. The acts are often divided into smaller parts called *scenes*.

DYNAMIC CHARACTER See *Character.*

ESSAY An *essay* is a short nonfiction work about a particular subject. Most essays have a single major focus and a clear introduction, body, and conclusion.

There are many types of essays. An *informal essay* uses casual, conversational language. A *historical essay* gives facts, explanations, and insights about historical events. An *expository essay* explains an idea by breaking it down. A *narrative essay* tells a story about a real-life experience. An *informational essay* explains a process. A *persuasive essay* offers an opinion and supports it.

See *Exposition, Narration,* and *Persuasion.*

EXPOSITION In the plot of a story or a drama, the *exposition*, or introduction, is the part of the work that introduces the characters, setting, and basic situation.

See *Plot.*

EXPOSITORY WRITING *Expository writing* is writing that explains or informs.

EXTENDED METAPHOR In an *extended metaphor*, as in a regular metaphor, a subject is spoken or written of as though it were something else. However, extended metaphor differs from regular metaphor in that several connected comparisons are made.

See *Metaphor.*

EXTERNAL CONFLICT See *Conflict.*

FABLE A *fable* is a brief story or poem, usually with animal characters, that teaches a lesson, or moral. The moral is usually stated at the end of the fable.

See *Irony* and *Moral.*

FANTASY A *fantasy* is highly imaginative writing that contains elements not found in real life. Examples of fantasy include stories that involve supernatural elements, stories that resemble fairy tales, stories that deal with imaginary places and creatures, and science-fiction stories.

See *Science Fiction.*

FICTION *Fiction* is prose writing that tells about imaginary characters and events. Short stories and novels are works of fiction. Some writers base their fiction on actual events and people, adding invented characters, dialogue, settings, and plots. Other writers rely on imagination alone.

See *Narration, Nonfiction,* and *Prose.*

FIGURATIVE LANGUAGE *Figurative language* is writing or speech that is not meant to be taken literally. The many types of figurative language are known as *figures of speech.* Common figures of speech include metaphor, personification, and simile. Writers use figurative language to state ideas in vivid and imaginative ways.

See *Metaphor, Personification, Simile,* and *Symbol.*

FIGURE OF SPEECH See *Figurative Language.*

FLASHBACK A *flashback* is a scene within a story that interrupts the sequence of events to relate events that occurred in the past.

FLAT CHARACTER See *Character.*

FOLK TALE A *folk tale* is a story composed orally and then passed from person to person by word of mouth. Folk tales originated among people who could neither read nor write. These people entertained one another by telling stories aloud—often dealing with heroes, adventure, magic, or romance. Eventually, modern scholars collected these stories and wrote them down.

Folk tales reflect the cultural beliefs and environments from which they come.

See *Fable, Legend, Myth,* and *Oral Tradition.*

FOOT See *Meter.*

FORESHADOWING *Foreshadowing* is the author's use of clues to hint at what might happen later in the story. Writers use foreshadowing to build their readers' expectations and to create suspense.

FREE VERSE *Free verse* is poetry not written in a regular, rhythmical pattern, or meter. The poet is free to write lines of any length or with any number of stresses, or beats. Free verse is therefore less constraining than *metrical verse*, in which every line must have a certain length and a certain number of stresses.

See *Meter.*

GENRE A *genre* is a division or type of literature. Literature is commonly divided into three major genres: poetry, prose, and drama. Each major genre is, in turn, divided into lesser genres, as follows:

1. *Poetry:* lyric poetry, concrete poetry, dramatic poetry, narrative poetry, epic poetry

2. *Prose:* fiction (novels and short stories) and nonfiction (biography, autobiography, letters, essays, and reports)

3. *Drama:* serious drama and tragedy, comic drama, melodrama, and farce

See *Drama, Poetry,* and *Prose.*

HAIKU The *haiku* is a three-line Japanese verse form. The first and third lines of a haiku each have five syllables. The second line has seven syllables. A writer of haiku uses images to create a single, vivid picture, generally of a scene from nature.

HERO/HEROINE A *hero* or *heroine* is a character whose actions are inspiring, or noble. Often heroes and heroines struggle to overcome the obstacles and problems that stand in their way. Note that the term *hero* was originally used only for male characters, while heroic female characters were always called *heroines*. However, it is now acceptable to use hero to refer to females as well as to males.

HISTORICAL FICTION In *historical fiction,* real events, places, or people are incorporated into a fictional or made-up story.

IMAGES *Images* are words or phrases that appeal to one or more of the five senses. Writers use images to describe how their subjects look, sound, feel, taste, and smell. Poets often paint images, or word pictures, that appeal to your senses. These pictures help you experience the poem fully.

IMAGERY See *Images*.

INTERNAL CONFLICT See *Conflict*.

IRONY *Irony* is a contradiction between what happens and what is expected. The three main types of irony are *situational irony, verbal irony*, and *dramatic irony.*

JOURNAL A *journal* is a daily, or periodic, account of events and the writer's thoughts and feelings about those events. Personal journals are not normally written for publication, but sometimes they do get published later with permission from the author or the author's family.

LEGEND A *legend* is a widely told story about the past—one that may or may not have a foundation in fact. Every culture has its own legends—its familiar, traditional stories.

See *Folk Tale, Myth,* and *Oral Tradition.*

LETTERS A *letter* is a written communication from one person to another. In personal letters, the writer shares information and his or her thoughts and feelings with one other person or group.

Although letters are not normally written for publication, they sometimes do get published later with the permission of the author or the author's family.

LIMERICK A *limerick* is a humorous, rhyming, five-line poem with a specific meter and rhyme scheme. Most limericks have three strong stresses in lines 1, 2, and 5 and two strong stresses in lines 3 and 4. Most follow the rhyme scheme *aabba*.

LYRIC POEM A *lyric poem* is a highly musical verse that expresses the observations and feelings of a single speaker. It creates a single, unified impression.

MAIN CHARACTER See *Character*.

MEDIA ACCOUNTS *Media accounts* are reports, explanations, opinions, or descriptions written for television, radio, newspapers, and magazines. While some media accounts report only facts, others include the writer's thoughts and reflections.

METAPHOR A *metaphor* is a figure of speech in which something is described as though it were something else. A metaphor, like a simile, works by pointing out a similarity between two unlike things. See *Extended Metaphor* and *Simile*.

METER The *meter* of a poem is its rhythmical pattern. This pattern is determined by the number of *stresses*, or beats, in each line. To describe the meter of a poem, read it emphasizing the beats in each line. Then, mark the stressed and unstressed syllables, as follows:

Mў faíth | eˇr wás | theˇ firśt | toˇ heár |

As you can see, each strong stress is marked with a slanted line (´) and each unstressed syllable with a horseshoe symbol (˘). The weak and strong stresses are then divided by vertical lines (||) into groups called *feet*.

MINOR CHARACTER See *Character*.

MOOD See *Atmosphere*.

MORAL A *moral* is a lesson taught by a literary work. A fable usually ends with a moral that is directly stated. A poem, novel, short story, or essay often suggests a moral that is not directly stated.

The moral must be drawn by the reader, based on other elements in the work.

See *Fable*.

MOTIVATION See *Motive*.

MOTIVE A *motive* is a reason that explains or partially explains a character's thoughts, feelings, actions, or speech. Writers try to make their characters' motives, or motivations, as clear as possible. If the motives of a main character are not clear, then the character will not be believable.

Characters are often motivated by needs, such as food and shelter. They are also motivated by feelings, such as fear, love, and pride. Motives may be obvious or hidden.

MYTH A *myth* is a fictional tale that explains the actions of gods or heroes or the origins of elements of nature. Myths are part of the oral tradition. They are composed orally and then passed from generation to generation by word of mouth. Every ancient culture has its own mythology, or collection of myths. Greek and Roman myths are known collectively as *classical mythology*.

See *Oral Tradition*.

NARRATION *Narration* is writing that tells a story. The act of telling a story is also called narration. Each piece is a *narrative*. A story told in fiction, nonfiction, poetry, or even in drama is called a narrative.

See *Narrative, Narrative Poem,* and *Narrator*.

NARRATIVE A *narrative* is a story. A narrative can be either fiction or nonfiction. Novels and short stories are types of fictional narratives. Biographies and autobiographies are nonfiction narratives. Poems that tell stories are also narratives.

See *Narration* and *Narrative Poem*.

NARRATIVE POEM A *narrative poem* is a story told in verse. Narrative poems often have all the elements of short stories, including characters, conflict, and plot.

NARRATOR A *narrator* is a speaker or a character who tells a story. The narrator's perspective is the way he or she sees things. A *third-person narrator* is one who stands outside the action and speaks about it. A *first-person narrator* is one who tells a story and participates in its action.

See *Point of View*.

NONFICTION *Nonfiction* is prose writing that presents and explains ideas or that tells about real people, places, objects, or events. Autobiographies, biographies, essays, reports, letters, memos, and newspaper articles are all types of nonfiction.

See *Fiction*.

NOVEL A *novel* is a long work of fiction. Novels contain such elements as characters, plot, conflict, and setting. The writer of novels, or novelist, develops these elements. In addition to its main plot, a novel may contain one or more subplots, or independent, related stories. A novel may also have several themes.

See *Fiction* and *Short Story*.

NOVELLA A fiction work that is longer than a short story but shorter than a novel.

ONOMATOPOEIA *Onomatopoeia* is the use of words that imitate sounds. *Crash, buzz, screech, hiss, neigh, jingle,* and *cluck* are examples of onomatopoeia. *Chickadee, towhee,* and *whippoorwill* are onomatopoeic names of birds.

Onomatopoeia can help put the reader in the activity of a poem.

ORAL TRADITION *Oral tradition* is the passing of songs, stories, and poems from generation to generation by word of mouth. Folk songs, folk tales, legends, and myths all come from the oral tradition. No one knows who first created these stories and poems.

See *Folk Tale, Legend,* and *Myth*.

OXYMORON An *oxymoron* (pl. *oxymora*) is a figure of speech that links two opposite or contradictory words, to point out an idea or situation that seems contradictory or inconsistent but on closer inspection turns out to be somehow true.

PERSONIFICATION *Personification* is a type of figurative language in which a nonhuman subject is given human characteristics.

PERSPECTIVE See *Narrator* and *Point of View.*

PERSUASION *Persuasion* is used in writing or speech that attempts to convince the reader or listener to adopt a particular opinion or course of action. Newspaper editorials and letters to the editor use persuasion. So do advertisements and campaign speeches given by political candidates.

See *Essay.*

PLAYWRIGHT A *playwright* is a person who writes plays. William Shakespeare is regarded as the greatest playwright in English literature.

PLOT *Plot* is the sequence of events in which each event results from a previous one and causes the next. In most novels, dramas, short stories, and narrative poems, the plot involves both characters and a central conflict. The plot usually begins with an exposition that introduces the setting, the characters, and the basic situation. This is followed by the *inciting incident*, which introduces the central conflict. The conflict then increases during the *development* until it reaches a high point of interest or suspense, the *climax*. The climax is followed by the *falling action*, or end, of the central conflict. Any events that occur during the *falling action* make up the *resolution,* or *denouement*.

Some plots do not have all of these parts. Some stories begin with the inciting incident and end with the resolution.

See *Conflict.*

POETRY *Poetry* is one of the three major types of literature, the others being prose and drama. Most poems make use of highly concise, musical, and emotionally charged language. Many also make use of imagery, figurative language, and special devices of sound such as rhyme. Major types of poetry include *lyric poetry, narrative poetry,* and *concrete poetry.*

See *Concrete Poem, Genre, Lyric Poem,* and *Narrative Poem.*

POINT OF VIEW Point of view is the perspective, or vantage point, from which a story is told. It is either a narrator outside the story or a character in the story. *First-person point of view* is told by a character who uses the first-person pronoun "I."

The two kinds of *third-person point of view*, limited and omniscient, are called "third person" because the narrator uses third-person pronouns such as "he" and "she" to refer to the characters. There is no "I" telling the story.

In stories told from the *omniscient third-person point of view,* the narrator knows and tells about what each character feels and thinks.

In stories told from the *limited third-person point of view,* the narrator relates the inner thoughts and feelings of only one character, and everything is viewed from this character's perspective.

See *Narrator.*

PROBLEM See *Conflict.*

PROSE *Prose* is the ordinary form of written language. Most writing that is not poetry, drama, or song is considered prose. Prose is one of the major genres of literature and occurs in two forms—fiction and nonfiction.

See *Fiction, Genre,* and *Nonfiction.*

PROTAGONIST The *protagonist* is the main character in a literary work. Often, the protagonist is a person, but sometimes it can be an animal.

See *Antagonist* and *Character.*

REFRAIN A *refrain* is a regularly repeated line or group of lines in a poem or a song.

REPETITION *Repetition* is the use, more than once, of any element of language—a sound, word, phrase, clause, or sentence. Repetition is used in both prose and poetry.

See *Alliteration, Meter, Plot, Rhyme,* and *Rhyme Scheme.*

RESOLUTION The *resolution* is the outcome of the conflict in a plot.

See *Plot*.

RHYME *Rhyme* is the repetition of sounds at the ends of words. Poets use rhyme to lend a songlike quality to their verses and to emphasize certain words and ideas. Many traditional poems contain *end rhymes*, or rhyming words at the ends of lines.

Another common device is the use of *internal rhymes*, or rhyming words within lines. Internal rhyme also emphasizes the flowing nature of a poem.

See *Rhyme Scheme*.

RHYME SCHEME A *rhyme scheme* is a regular pattern of rhyming words in a poem. To indicate the rhyme scheme of a poem, one uses lowercase letters. Each rhyme is assigned a different letter, as follows in the first stanza of "Dust of Snow" by Robert Frost:

The way a crow	*a*
Shook down on me	*b*
The dust of snow	*a*
From a hemlock tree	*b*

Thus, the stanza has the rhyme scheme *abab*.

RHYTHM *Rhythm* is the pattern of stressed and unstressed syllables in spoken or written language.

See *Meter*.

ROUND CHARACTER See *Character*.

SCENE A *scene* is a section of uninterrupted action in the act of a drama.

See *Drama*.

SCIENCE FICTION *Science fiction* combines elements of fiction and fantasy with scientific fact. Many science-fiction stories are set in the future.

SENSORY LANGUAGE *Sensory language* is writing or speech that appeals to one or more of the five senses.

See *Images*.

SETTING The *setting* of a literary work is the time and place of the action. The setting includes all the details of a place and time—the year, the time of day, even the weather. The place may be a specific country, state, region, community, neighborhood, building, institution, or home. Details such as dialects, clothing, customs, and modes of transportation are often used to establish setting. In most stories, the setting serves as a backdrop—a context in which the characters interact. Setting can also help create a feeling, or atmosphere.

See *Atmosphere*.

SHORT STORY A *short story* is a brief work of fiction. Like a novel, a short story presents a sequence of events, or plot. The plot usually deals with a central conflict faced by a main character, or protagonist. The events in a short story usually communicate a message about life or human nature. This message, or central idea, is the story's theme.

See *Conflict, Plot,* and *Theme*.

SIMILE A *simile* is a figure of speech that uses *like* or *as* to make a direct comparison between two unlike ideas. Everyday speech often contains similes, such as "pale as a ghost," "good as gold," "spread like wildfire," and "clever as a fox."

SPEAKER The *speaker* is the imaginary voice a poet uses when writing a poem. The speaker is the character who tells the poem. This character, or voice, often is not identified by name. There can be important differences between the poet and the poem's speaker.

See *Narrator*.

STAGE DIRECTIONS *Stage directions* are notes included in a drama to describe how the work is to be performed or staged. Stage directions are usually printed in italics and enclosed within parentheses or brackets. Some stage directions describe the movements, costumes, emotional states, and ways of speaking of the characters.

STAGING *Staging* includes the setting, the lighting, the costumes, special effects, music, dance, and so on that go into putting on a stage performance of a drama.

See *Drama*.

STANZA A *stanza* is a group of lines of poetry that are usually similar in length and pattern and are separated by spaces. A stanza is like a paragraph of poetry—it states and develops a single main idea.

STATIC CHARACTER See *Character.*

SURPRISE ENDING A *surprise ending* is a conclusion that is unexpected. The reader has certain expectations about the ending based on details in the story. Often, a surprise ending is *foreshadowed*, or subtly hinted at, in the course of the work.

See *Foreshadowing* and *Plot.*

SUSPENSE *Suspense* is a feeling of anxious uncertainty about the outcome of events in a literary work. Writers create suspense by raising questions in the minds of their readers.

SYMBOL A *symbol* is anything that stands for or represents something else. Symbols are common in everyday life. A dove with an olive branch in its beak is a symbol of peace. A blindfolded woman holding a balanced scale is a symbol of justice. A crown is a symbol of a king's status and authority.

SYMBOLISM *Symbolism* is the use of symbols. Symbolism plays an important role in many different types of literature. It can highlight certain elements the author wishes to emphasize and also add levels of meaning.

THEME The *theme* is a central message, concern, or purpose in a literary work. A theme can usually be expressed as a generalization, or a general statement, about human beings or about life. The theme of a work is not a summary of its plot. The theme is the writer's central idea.

Although a theme may be stated directly in the text, it is more often presented indirectly. When the theme is stated indirectly, or implied, the reader must figure out what the theme is by looking carefully at what the work reveals about people or about life.

TONE The *tone* of a literary work is the writer's attitude toward his or her audience and subject. The tone can often be described by a single adjective, such as *formal* or *informal, serious* or *playful,* *bitter,* or *ironic.* Factors that contribute to the tone are word choice, sentence structure, line length, rhyme, rhythm, and repetition.

TRAGEDY A *tragedy* is a work of literature, especially a play, that results in a catastrophe for the main character. In ancient Greek drama, the main character is always a significant person—a king or a hero—and the cause of the tragedy is a tragic flaw, or weakness, in his or her character. In modern drama, the main character can be an ordinary person, and the cause of the tragedy can be some evil in society itself. The purpose of tragedy is not only to arouse fear and pity in the audience but also, in some cases, to convey a sense of the grandeur and nobility of the human spirit.

TURNING POINT See *Climax.*

UNIVERSAL THEME A *universal theme* is a message about life that is expressed regularly in many different cultures and time periods. Folk tales, epics, and romances often address universal themes like the importance of courage, the power of love, or the danger of greed.

TIPS FOR DISCUSSING LITERATURE

As you read and study literature, discussions with other readers can help you understand and enjoy what you have read. Use the following tips.

- ## Understand the purpose of your discussion.

  Your purpose when you discuss literature is to broaden your understanding of a work by testing your own ideas and hearing the ideas of others. Keep your comments focused on the literature you are discussing. Starting with one focus question will help keep your discussion on track.

- ## Communicate effectively.

  Effective communication requires thinking before speaking. Plan the points that you want to make and decide how you will express them. Organize these points in logical order and use details from the work to support your ideas. Jot down informal notes to help keep your ideas focused.

  Remember to speak clearly, pronouncing words slowly and carefully. Also, listen attentively when others are speaking, and avoid interrupting.

- ## Consider other ideas and interpretations.

  A work of literature can generate a wide variety of responses in different readers. Be open to the idea that many interpretations can be valid. To support your own ideas, point to the events, descriptions, characters, or other literary elements in the work that led to your interpretation. To consider someone else's ideas, decide whether details in the work support the interpretation he or she presents. Be sure to convey your criticism of the ideas of others in a respectful and supportive manner.

- ## Ask questions.

  Ask questions to clarify your understanding of another reader's ideas. You can also use questions to call attention to possible areas of confusion, to points that are open to debate, or to errors in the speaker's points. To move a discussion forward, summarize and evaluate conclusions reached by the group members.

When you meet with a group to discuss literature, use a chart like the one shown to analyze the discussion.

Work Being Discussed:	
Focus Question:	
Your Response:	Another Student's Response:
Supporting Evidence:	Supporting Evidence:
One New Idea That You Considered About the Work During the Discussion:	

TYPES OF WRITING

Narration

Whenever writers tell any type of story, they are using **narration**. While there are many kinds of narration, most narratives share certain elements, such as characters, a setting, a sequence of events, and, often, a theme.

Autobiographical writing tells the story of an event or person in the writer's life.

Biographical writing is a writer's account of another person's life.

Short story A short story is a brief, creative narrative—a retelling of events arranged to hold a reader's attention. A few types of short stories are realistic stories, fantasy, science-fiction stories, and adventure stories.

Description

Descriptive writing is writing that creates a vivid picture of a person, place, thing, or event. Descriptive writing includes descriptions of people or places, remembrances, observations, vignettes, and character profiles.

Persuasion

Persuasion is writing or speaking that attempts to convince people to accept a position or take a desired action. Forms of persuasive writing include persuasive essays, advertisements, persuasive letters, editorials, persuasive speeches, and public-service announcements. Problem-and-solution essays may also contain elements of persuasion.

Expository Writing

Expository writing is writing that informs or explains. The information you include in expository writing is factual. Effective expository writing reflects a well-thought-out organization—one that includes a clear introduction, body, and conclusion. Here are some types of exposition.

Comparison-and-Contrast essay A comparison-and-contrast essay analyzes the similarities and differences between two or more things.

Cause-and-Effect essay A cause-and-effect essay explains the reasons why something happened or the results an event or situation will probably produce. You may examine several causes of a single effect or several effects of a single cause.

Problem-and-Solution essay The purpose of a problem-and-solution essay is to describe a problem and offer one or more solutions to it. An effective problem-and-solution essay describes a clear set of steps to achieve a result and explains and defends the proposed solution. Elements of problem-and-solution writing may be found in advice columns, memos, and proposals.

How-to essay A how-to essay explains how to do or make something. You break the process down into steps and explain the steps in order.

Summary A summary is a brief statement that includes *only* the main ideas and significant supporting details presented in a piece of writing. A summary should be written in your own words.

Research Writing

Writers often use outside research to gather information and explore subjects of interest. The product of that research is called **research writing.** Good research writing does not simply repeat information. It guides readers through a topic, showing them why each fact matters and creating an overall picture of the subject. Here are some types of research writing.

Research report A research report presents information gathered from reference books, observations, interviews, or other sources.

Biographical report A biographical report examines the high points and achievements in the life of a notable person. It includes dates, details, and main events in the person's life as well as background on the period in which the person lived.

Multimedia report A multimedia report presents information through a variety of media, including text, slides, photographs, prerecorded music and sound effects, and digital imaging.

Response to Literature

A **response to literature** discusses and interprets what is of value in a book, short story, essay, article, or poem. You take a careful, critical look at various important elements in the work.

In addition to the standard literary essay, here are some other types of responses to literature.

Literary criticism Literary criticism is the result of literary analysis—the examination of a literary work or a body of literature. In literary criticism, you make a judgment or evaluation by looking carefully and critically at various important elements in the work. You then attempt to explain how the author has used those elements and how effectively they work together to convey the author's message.

Book or movie reviews A book review gives readers an impression of a book, encouraging them either to read it or to avoid reading it. A movie review begins with a basic response to whether or not you enjoyed the movie, and then explains the reasons why or why not.

Letter to an author People sometimes respond to a work of literature by writing a letter to the writer. It lets the writer know what a reader found enjoyable or disappointing in a work. You can praise the work, ask questions, or offer constructive criticism.

Comparisons of works A comparison of works highlights specific features of two or more works by comparing them.

Creative Writing

Creative writing blends imagination, ideas, and emotions, and allows you to present your own unique view of the world. Poems, plays, short stories, dramas, and even some cartoons are examples of creative writing. Here are some types of creative writing.

Lyric poem A lyric poem uses sensory images, figurative language, and sound devices to express deep thoughts and feelings about a subject. Writers give lyric poems a musical quality by employing sound devices, such as rhyme, rhythm, alliteration, and onomatopoeia.

Narrative poem A narrative poem is similar to a short story in that it has a plot, characters, and a theme. However, a writer divides a narrative poem into stanzas, usually composed of rhyming lines that have a definite rhythm, or beat.

Song lyrics Song lyrics contain many elements of poetry—rhyme, rhythm, repetition, and imagery. In addition, song lyrics convey emotions, as well as interesting ideas.

Drama A drama or a dramatic scene is a story that is intended to be performed. The story is told mostly through what the actors say (dialogue) and what they do (action).

Practical and Technical Documents

Practical writing is fact-based writing that people do in the workplace or in their day-to-day lives. A business letter, memorandum, school form, job application, and a letter of inquiry are a few examples of practical writing.

Technical documents are fact-based documents that identify the sequence of activities needed to design a system, operate a tool, follow a procedure, or explain the bylaws of an organization. You encounter technical writing every time you read a manual or a set of instructions. Here are some types of practical and technical writing.

Business letter A formal letter that follows one of several specific formats. (See page R23.)

News release A news release, also called a press release, announces factual information about upcoming events. A writer might send a news release to a local newspaper, local radio station, TV station, or other media that will publicize the information.

Guidelines Guidelines give information about how people should act or provide tips on how to do something.

Process explanation A process explanation is a step-by-step explanation of how to do something. The explanation should be clear and specific and might include diagrams or other illustrations to further clarify the process.

WRITING LETTERS

Writing Friendly Letters

A friendly letter is much less formal than a business letter. It is a letter to a friend, a family member, or anyone with whom the writer wants to communicate in a personal, friendly way. Most friendly letters are made up of five parts:

- the heading
- the salutation, or greeting
- the body
- the closing
- the signature

The purpose of a friendly letter is often one of the following:

- to share personal news and feelings
- to send or to answer an invitation
- to express thanks

Model Friendly Letter

In this friendly letter, Betsy thanks her grandparents for a birthday present and gives them some news about her life.

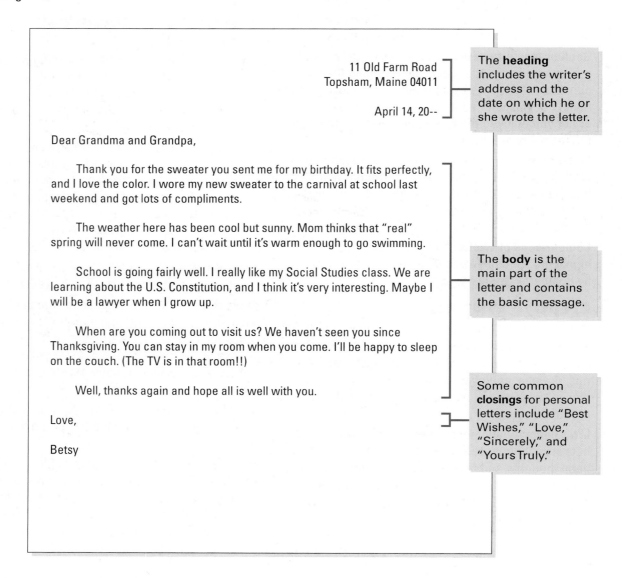

11 Old Farm Road
Topsham, Maine 04011

April 14, 20--

The **heading** includes the writer's address and the date on which he or she wrote the letter.

Dear Grandma and Grandpa,

Thank you for the sweater you sent me for my birthday. It fits perfectly, and I love the color. I wore my new sweater to the carnival at school last weekend and got lots of compliments.

The weather here has been cool but sunny. Mom thinks that "real" spring will never come. I can't wait until it's warm enough to go swimming.

School is going fairly well. I really like my Social Studies class. We are learning about the U.S. Constitution, and I think it's very interesting. Maybe I will be a lawyer when I grow up.

When are you coming out to visit us? We haven't seen you since Thanksgiving. You can stay in my room when you come. I'll be happy to sleep on the couch. (The TV is in that room!!)

Well, thanks again and hope all is well with you.

Love,

Betsy

The **body** is the main part of the letter and contains the basic message.

Some common **closings** for personal letters include "Best Wishes," "Love," "Sincerely," and "Yours Truly."

Formatting Business Letters

Business letters follow one of several acceptable formats. In **block format,** each part of the letter begins at the left margin. A double space is used between paragraphs. In **modified block format,** some parts of the letter are indented to the center of the page. No matter which format is used, all letters in business format have a heading, an inside address, a salutation or greeting, a body, a closing, and a signature. These parts are shown and annotated on the model business letter below, formatted in modified block style.

Model Business Letter

In this letter, Yolanda Dodson uses modified block format to request information.

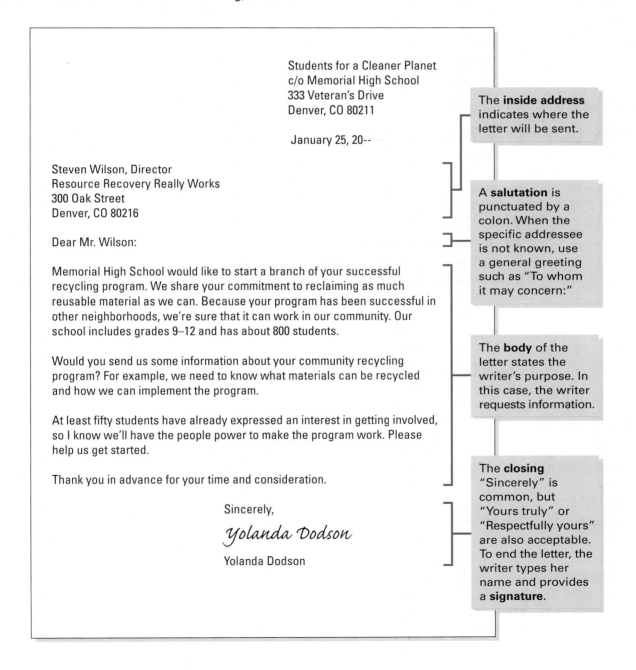

Students for a Cleaner Planet
c/o Memorial High School
333 Veteran's Drive
Denver, CO 80211

January 25, 20--

Steven Wilson, Director
Resource Recovery Really Works
300 Oak Street
Denver, CO 80216

Dear Mr. Wilson:

Memorial High School would like to start a branch of your successful recycling program. We share your commitment to reclaiming as much reusable material as we can. Because your program has been successful in other neighborhoods, we're sure that it can work in our community. Our school includes grades 9–12 and has about 800 students.

Would you send us some information about your community recycling program? For example, we need to know what materials can be recycled and how we can implement the program.

At least fifty students have already expressed an interest in getting involved, so I know we'll have the people power to make the program work. Please help us get started.

Thank you in advance for your time and consideration.

Sincerely,

Yolanda Dodson

Yolanda Dodson

The **inside address** indicates where the letter will be sent.

A **salutation** is punctuated by a colon. When the specific addressee is not known, use a general greeting such as "To whom it may concern:"

The **body** of the letter states the writer's purpose. In this case, the writer requests information.

The **closing** "Sincerely" is common, but "Yours truly" or "Respectfully yours" are also acceptable. To end the letter, the writer types her name and provides a **signature**.

USING THE INTERNET

Key Word Search

Before you begin a search, narrow your subject to a key word or a group of **key words.** These are your search terms, and they should be as specific as possible. For example, if you are looking for information about your favorite musical group, you might use the band's name as a key word. You might locate such information as band member biographies, the group's history, fan reviews of concerts, and hundreds of sites with related names containing information that is irrelevant to your search. Depending on your research needs you might need to narrow your search.

How to Narrow Your Search

If you have a large group of key words and still don't know which ones to use, write out a list of all the words you are considering. Then, delete the words that are least important to your search, and highlight those that are most important.

Use **search connectors** to fine-tune your search:

AND: narrows a search by retrieving documents that include both terms. For example: *baseball AND playoffs*

OR: broadens a search by retrieving documents including any of the terms. For example: *playoffs OR championships*

NOT: narrows a search by excluding documents containing certain words. For example: *baseball NOT history*

Tips for an Effective Search

1. Search engines can be case-sensitive. If your first attempt at searching fails, check your search terms for misspellings and try again.

2. Present key words in order, from the most important to the least important.

3. Avoid opening the link to every single page in your results list. Search engines present pages in descending order of relevancy. The most useful pages will be located at the top of the list.

4. Some search engines provide helpful tips for specializing your search.

Tips for Evaluating Internet Sources

Consider who constructed and who now maintains the Web page. Determine whether this author is a reputable source. Often, the URL endings indicate a source.

- Sites ending in *.edu* are maintained by educational institutions.
- Sites ending in *.gov* are maintained by government agencies (federal, state, or local).
- Sites ending in *.org* are normally maintained by nonprofit organizations and agencies.
- Sites with a *.com* ending are commercially or personally maintained.

Other Ways to Search

How you search should be tailored to what you are hoping to find. If you are looking for data and facts, use reference sites before you jump onto a simple search engine. For example, you can find reference sites to provide definitions of words, statistics about almost any subject, biographies, maps, and concise information on many topics. Useful online reference sites include online libraries, online periodicals, almanacs, and encyclopedias.

You can also use other electronic sources such as CD-ROMs. Ask a reference librarian to help you locate and use the full range of electronic resources.

Respecting Copyrighted Material

Because the Internet is a growing medium, issues of copyright and ownership arise almost daily. Laws that govern the use and reuse of material are posted online, and may change the way that people can access or reprint material. Text, photographs, music, and fine art printed online may not be reproduced without acknowledged permission of the copyright owner.

CITING SOURCES AND PREPARING MANUSCRIPT

Proofreading and Preparing Manuscript

Before preparing a final copy, proofread your manuscript. The chart shows the standard symbols for marking corrections to be made.

Proofreading Symbols	
insert	∧
delete	℘
close space	◠
new paragraph	¶
add comma	⌃
add period	⊙
transpose (switch)	∩
change to cap	a̲
change to lowercase	A̸

- Choose a standard, easy-to-read font.
- Type or print on one side of unlined 8 1/2" x 11" paper.
- Set the margins for the side, top, and bottom of your paper at approximately one inch. Most word-processing programs have a default setting that is appropriate.
- Double-space the document.
- Indent the first line of each paragraph.
- Number the pages in the upper right corner.

Follow your teacher's directions for formatting formal research papers. Most papers will have the following features:

- Title page
- Table of Contents or Outline
- Works-Cited List

Avoiding Plagiarism

Whether you are presenting a formal research paper or an opinion paper on a current event, you must be careful to give credit for any ideas or opinions that are not your own. Presenting someone else's ideas, research, or opinion as your own—even if you have phrased it in different words—is *plagiarism,* the equivalent of academic stealing, or fraud.

Do not use the ideas or research of others in place of your own. Read from several sources to draw your own conclusions and form your own opinions. Incorporate the ideas and research of others to support your points. Credit the source of the following types of support:

- Statistics
- Direct quotations
- Indirectly quoted statements of opinions
- Conclusions presented by an expert
- Facts available in only one or two sources

Crediting Sources

When you credit a source, you acknowledge where you found your information and you give your readers the details necessary for locating the source themselves. Within the body of the paper, you provide a short citation, a footnote number linked to a footnote, or an endnote number linked to an endnote reference. These brief references show the page numbers on which you found the information. Prepare a reference list at the end of the paper to provide full bibliographic information on your sources. These are two common types of reference lists:

- A **bibliography** provides a listing of all the resources you consulted during your research.
- A **works-cited list** indicates the works you have referenced in your paper.

The chart on the next page shows the Modern Language Association format for crediting sources. This is the most common format for papers written in the content areas in middle school and high school. Unless instructed otherwise by your teacher, use this format for crediting sources.

MLA Style for Listing Sources

Book with one author	Pyles, Thomas. *The Origins and Development of the English Language.* 2nd ed. New York: Harcourt Brace Jovanovich, Inc., 1971.
Book with two or three authors	McCrum, Robert, William Cran, and Robert MacNeil. *The Story of English.* New York: Penguin Books, 1987.
Book with an editor	Truth, Sojourner. *Narrative of Sojourner Truth.* Ed. Margaret Washington. New York: Vintage Books, 1993.
Book with more than three authors or editors	Donald, Robert B., et al. *Writing Clear Essays.* Upper Saddle River, NJ: Prentice Hall, Inc., 1996.
Single work from an anthology	Hawthorne, Nathaniel. "Young Goodman Brown." *Literature: An Introduction to Reading and Writing.* Ed. Edgar V. Roberts and Henry E. Jacobs. Upper Saddle River, NJ: Prentice Hall, Inc., 1998. 376–385. [Indicate pages for the entire selection.]
Introduction in a published edition	Washington, Margaret. Introduction. *Narrative of Sojourner Truth.* By Sojourner Truth. New York: Vintage Books, 1993, pp. v–xi.
Signed article in a weekly magazine	Wallace, Charles. "A Vodacious Deal." *Time* 14 Feb. 2000: 63.
Signed article in a monthly magazine	Gustaitis, Joseph. "The Sticky History of Chewing Gum." *American History* Oct. 1998: 30–38.
Unsigned editorial or story	"Selective Silence." Editorial. *Wall Street Journal* 11 Feb. 2000: A14. [If the editorial or story is signed, begin with the author's name.]
Signed pamphlet or brochure	[Treat the pamphlet as though it were a book.]
Pamphlet with no author, publisher, or date	*Are You at Risk of Heart Attack?* n.p. n.d. [n.p. n.d. indicates that there is no known publisher or date.]
Filmstrips, slide programs, videocassettes, DVDs, and other audiovisual media	*The Diary of Anne Frank.* Dir. George Stevens. Perf. Millie Perkins, Shelly Winters, Joseph Schildkraut, Lou Jacobi, and Richard Beymer. Twentieth Century Fox, 1959.
Radio or television program transcript	"Nobel for Literature." Narr. Rick Karr. *All Things Considered.* National Public Radio. WNYC, New York. 10 Oct. 2002. Transcript.
Internet	NACGM site. *National Association of Chewing Gum Manufacturers.* 19 Dec. 1999 <http://www.nacgm.org/consumer/funfacts.html> [Indicate the date you accessed the information. Content and addresses at Web sites change frequently.]
Newspaper	Thurow, Roger. "South Africans Who Fought for Sanctions Now Scrap for Investors." *Wall Street Journal* 11 Feb. 2000: A1+ [For a multipage article, write only the first page number on which it appears, followed by a plus sign.]
Personal interview	Smith, Jane. Personal interview. 10 Feb. 2000.
CD (with multiple publishers)	Simms, James, ed. *Romeo and Juliet.* By William Shakespeare. CD-ROM. Oxford: Attica Cybernetics Ltd.; London: BBC Education; London: HarperCollins Publishers, 1995.
Signed article from an encyclopedia	Askeland, Donald R. "Welding." *World Book Encyclopedia.* 1991 ed.

GUIDE TO RUBRICS

What is a rubric?

A rubric is a tool, often in the form of a chart or a grid, that helps you assess your work. Rubrics are particularly helpful for writing and speaking assignments.

To help you or others assess, or evaluate, your work, a rubric offers several specific criteria to be applied to your work. Then the rubric helps you or an evaluator indicate your range of success or failure according to those specific criteria. Rubrics are often used to evaluate writing for standardized tests.

Using a rubric will save you time, focus your learning, and improve the work you do. When you know what the rubric will be before you begin writing a persuasive essay, for example, as you write you will be aware of specific criteria that are important in that kind of an essay. As you evaluate the essay before giving it to your teacher, you will focus on the specific areas that your teacher wants you to master—or on areas that you know present challenges for you. Instead of searching through your work randomly for any way to improve it or correct its errors, you will have a clear and helpful focus on specific criteria.

How are rubrics constructed?

Rubrics can be constructed in several different ways.

- Your teacher may assign a rubric for a specific assignment.
- Your teacher may direct you to a rubric in your textbook.
- Your teacher and your class may construct a rubric for a particular assignment together.
- You and your classmates may construct a rubric together.
- You may create your own rubric with criteria you want to evaluate in your work.

How will a rubric help me?

A rubric will help you assess your work on a scale. Scales vary from rubric to rubric but usually range from 6 to 1, 5 to 1, or 4 to 1, with 6, 5, or 4 being the highest score and 1 being the lowest. If someone else is using the rubric to assess your work, the rubric will give your evaluator a clear range within which to place your work. If you are using the rubric yourself, it will help you make improvements to your work.

What are the types of rubrics?

- A **holistic rubric** has general criteria that can apply to a variety of assignments. See p. R29 for an example of a holistic rubric.
- An **analytic rubric** is specific to a particular assignment. The criteria for evaluation address the specific issues important in that assignment. See p. R28 for examples of analytic rubrics.

Sample Analytic Rubrics

Rubric With a 4-point Scale

The following analytic rubric is an example of a rubric to assess a persuasive essay. It will help you evaluate focus, organization, support, elaboration, and style conventions.

	Focus	Organization	Support/Elaboration	Style Conventions
4	Demonstrates highly effective word choice; clearly focused on task.	Uses clear, consistent organizational strategy.	Provides convincing, well-elaborated reasons to support the position.	Incorporates transitions; includes very few mechanical errors.
3	Demonstrates good word choice; stays focused on persuasive task.	Uses clear organizational strategy with occasional inconsistencies.	Provides two or more moderately elaborated reasons to support the position.	Incorporates some transitions; includes few mechanical errors.
2	Shows some good word choices; minimally stays focused on persuasive task.	Uses inconsistent organizational strategy; presentation is not logical.	Provides several reasons, but few are elaborated; only one elaborated reason.	Incorporates few transitions; includes many mechanical errors.
1	Shows lack of attention to persuasive task.	Demonstrates lack of organizational strategy.	Provides no specific reasons or does not elaborate.	Does not connect ideas; includes many mechanical errors.

Rubric With a 6-point Scale

The following analytic rubric is an example of a rubric to assess a persuasive essay. It will help you evaluate presentation, position, evidence, and arguments.

	Presentation	Position	Evidence	Arguments
6	Essay clearly and effectively addresses an issue with more than one side.	Essay clearly states a supportable position on the issue.	All evidence is logically organized, well presented, and supports the position.	All reader concerns and counterarguments are effectively addressed.
5	Most of essay addresses an issue that has more than one side.	Essay clearly states a position on the issue.	Most evidence is logically organized, well presented, and supports the position.	Most reader concerns and counterarguments are effectively addressed.
4	Essay adequately addresses issue that has more than one side.	Essay adequately states a position on the issue.	Many parts of evidence support the position; some evidence is out of order.	Many reader concerns and counterarguments are adequately addressed.
3	Essay addresses issue with two sides but does not present second side clearly.	Essay states a position on the issue, but the position is difficult to support.	Some evidence supports the position, but some evidence is out of order.	Some reader concerns and counterarguments are addressed.
2	Essay addresses issue with two sides but does not present second side.	Essay states a position on the issue, but the position is not supportable.	Not much evidence supports the position, and what is included is out of order.	A few reader concerns and counterarguments are addressed.
1	Essay does not address issue with more than one side.	Essay does not state a position on the issue.	No evidence supports the position.	No reader concerns or counterarguments are addressed.

Sample Holistic Rubric

Holistic rubrics such as this one are sometimes used to assess writing assignments on standardized tests. Notice that the criteria for evaluation are focus, organization, support, and use of conventions.

Points	Criteria
6 Points	• The writing is strongly focused and shows fresh insight into the writing task. • The writing is marked by a sense of completeness and coherence and is organized with a logical progression of ideas. • A main idea is fully developed, and support is specific and substantial. • A mature command of the language is evident, and the writing may employ characteristic creative writing strategies. • Sentence structure is varied, and writing is free of all but purposefully used fragments. • Virtually no errors in writing conventions appear.
5 Points	• The writing is clearly focused on the task. • The writing is well organized and has a logical progression of ideas, though there may be occasional lapses. • A main idea is well developed and supported with relevant detail. • Sentence structure is varied, and the writing is free of fragments, except when used purposefully. • Writing conventions are followed correctly.
4 Points	• The writing is clearly focused on the task, but extraneous material may intrude at times. • Clear organizational pattern is present, though lapses may occur. • A main idea is adequately supported, but development may be uneven. • Sentence structure is generally fragment free but shows little variation. • Writing conventions are generally followed correctly.
3 Points	• Writing is generally focused on the task, but extraneous material may intrude at times. • An organizational pattern is evident, but writing may lack a logical progression of ideas. • Support for the main idea is generally present but is sometimes illogical. • Sentence structure is generally free of fragments, but there is almost no variation. • The work generally demonstrates a knowledge of writing conventions, with occasional misspellings.
2 Points	• The writing is related to the task but generally lacks focus. • There is little evidence of organizational pattern, and there is little sense of cohesion. • Support for the main idea is generally inadequate, illogical, or absent. • Sentence structure is unvaried, and serious errors may occur. • Errors in writing conventions and spellings are frequent.
1 Point	• The writing may have little connection to the task and is generally unfocused. • There has been little attempt at organization or development. • The paper seems fragmented, with no clear main idea. • Sentence structure is unvaried, and serious errors appear. • Poor word choice and poor command of the language obscure meaning. • Errors in writing conventions and spelling are frequent.
Unscorable	The paper is considered unscorable if: • The response is unrelated to the task or is simply a rewording of the prompt. • The response has been copied from a published work. • The student did not write a response. • The response is illegible. • The words in the response are arranged with no meaning. • There is an insufficient amount of writing to score.

Student Model

Persuasive Writing

This persuasive essay, which would receive a top score according to a persuasive rubric, is a response to the following writing prompt, or assignment:

Most young people today spend more than 5 hours a day watching television. Many adults worry about the effects on youth of seeing too much television violence. Write a persuasive piece in which you argue against or defend the effects of television watching on young people. Be sure to include examples to support your views.

Until the television was invented, families spent their time doing different activities. Now most families stay home and watch TV. Watching TV risks the family's health, reduces the children's study time, and is a bad influence on young minds. Watching television can be harmful.

> The writer clearly states a position in the first paragraph.

The most important reason why watching TV is bad is that the viewers get less exercise. For example, instead of watching their favorite show, people could get exercise for 30 minutes. If people spent less time watching TV and more time exercising, then they could have healthier bodies. My mother told me a story about a man who died of a heart attack because he was out of shape from watching television all the time. Obviously, watching TV put a person's health in danger.

> Each paragraph provides details that support the writer's main point.

Furthermore, watching television reduces childern's study time. For example, children would spend more time studying if they didn't watch television. If students spent more time studying at home, then they would make better grades at school. Last week I had a major test in science, but I didn't study because I started watching a movie. I was not prepared for the test and my grade reflected my lack of studying. Indeed, watching television is bad because it can hurt a student's grades.

Finally, watching TV can be a bad influence on children. For example, some TV shows have inappropriate language and too much violence. If children watch programs that use bad language and show violence, then they may start repeating these actions because they think the behavior is "cool." In fact, it has been proven that children copy what they see on TV. Clearly, watching TV is bad for children and it affects children's behavior.

In conclusion, watching television is a bad influence for these reasons: It reduces people's exercise time and students' study time and it shows children inappropriate behavior. Therefore, people should take control of their lives and stop allowing television to harm them.

> The conclusion restates the writer's position.

GRAMMAR, USAGE, AND MECHANICS

Parts of Speech

Nouns

A **noun** is the name of a person, place, or thing. A **common noun** names any one of a class of people, places, or things. A **proper noun** names a specific person, place, or thing.

Common Nouns	Proper Nouns
writer	Francisco Jiménez
city	Los Angeles

Pronouns

A **pronoun** is a word that stands for a noun or for a word that takes the place of a noun.

A **personal pronoun** refers to (1) the person speaking, (2) the person spoken to, or (3) the person, place, or thing spoken about.

	Singular	Plural
First Person	I, me, my, mine	we, us, our, ours
Second Person	you, your, yours	you, your, yours
Third Person	he, him, his, she, her, hers, it, its	they, them, their, theirs

A **demonstrative** pronoun directs attention to a specific person, place, or thing.

These are the juiciest pears I have ever tasted.

An **interrogative pronoun** is used to begin a question.

Who is the author of "Jeremiah's Song"?

An **indefinite pronoun** refers to a person, place, or thing, often without specifying which one.

Many of the players were tired.

Everyone bought something.

Exercise A **Classifying Nouns and Pronouns** Identify the nouns and pronouns in the following sentences. Label each noun *compound, common,* or *proper,* and *singular* or *plural.* Label each pronoun *personal* or *demonstrative.*

1. One element of the weather is temperature.
2. Every day is warmest during the middle of the afternoon.
3. It is usually warmer in the Tropics.
4. The North Pole and the South Pole have the lowest temperatures.
5. Temperature varies with latitude, elevation, and season.
6. This means temperature can change suddenly.
7. These are the scales used for measuring temperature.
8. Scientists use Kelvin, or they use Celsius.
9. That is used in many countries.
10. The United States continues to use Fahrenheit.

Verbs

A **verb** is a word that expresses time while showing an action, a condition, or the fact that something exists.

An **action verb** indicates the action of someone or something.

A **linking verb** connects the subject of a sentence with a noun or a pronoun that renames or describes the subject.

A **helping verb** can be added to another verb to make a single verb phrase.

Exercise B **Classifying Verbs** Write the verbs in the following sentences, and label each one *action* or *linking.* Include and underline all helping verbs.

1. Wind moves horizontally through the atmosphere.
2. Some winds are called "prevailing."
3. The trade winds are included in the prevailing winds category.

4. The doldrums lie within 10 degrees of the equator.

5. The horse latitudes, 30 degrees from the equator, consist of calm, light winds.

6. Surface air travels from the horse latitudes to the equator.

7. Those are the trade winds.

8. Seasonal winds are determined by air temperature.

9. The air over the continents is warmer in the summer than the air over the oceans.

10. Then, winds from the colder ocean blow inland.

Adjectives

An **adjective** describes a noun or a pronoun or gives a noun or a pronoun a more specific meaning. Adjectives answer the questions *what kind, which one, how many,* or *how much.*

The articles *the, a,* and *an* are adjectives. *An* is used before a word beginning with a vowel sound.

A noun may sometimes be used as an adjective.

    family home   *science* fiction

Adverbs

An **adverb** modifies a verb, an adjective, or another adverb. Adverbs answer the questions *where, when, in what way,* or *to what extent.*

Exercise C Recognizing Adjectives and Adverbs
Label each underlined word in the following sentences as *adjective* or *adverb.* Then, write the word each one modifies.

1. Clouds are composed of small water droplets or <u>tiny</u> ice crystals.

2. They are <u>usually</u> divided into four families.

3. Cirrus clouds rise <u>higher</u> above the Earth.

4. They consist <u>mainly</u> of ice particles.

5. These feathery clouds are <u>commonly</u> arranged in bands.

6. <u>Thick</u> altostratus clouds may obscure the sun or moon.

7. Light <u>barely</u> filters through the bluish veil.

8. Altocumulus clouds resemble <u>dense</u> puffs.

9. Low clouds are <u>generally</u> less than one mile high.

10. Like <u>middle</u> clouds, they are composed of water droplets.

Prepositions

A **preposition** relates a noun or a pronoun following it to another word in the sentence.

Conjunctions

A **conjunction** connects other words or groups of words.

A **coordinating conjunction** connects similar kinds or groups of words.

Correlative conjunctions are used in pairs to connect similar words or groups of words.

    both Grandpa *and* Dad   *neither* they *nor* I

Interjections

An **interjection** is a word that expresses feeling or emotion and functions independently of a sentence.

    "Ah!" says he—

Exercise D Recognizing Prepositions, Conjunctions, and Interjections Identify the underlined words in the following sentences as *prepositions, conjunctions,* or *interjections.* Write the object of each preposition. Label the conjunctions *coordinating* or *correlative.*

1. <u>Wow</u>! Did you see the hail falling <u>to</u> the ground?

2. It looks like a combination of <u>both</u> ice <u>and</u> snow.

3. Raindrops <u>or</u> snow pellets become hailstones as they collide with each other.

4. <u>Gee</u>, that requires the wind characteristic of thunderstorms.

5. They travel through the clouds <u>but</u> become too heavy.

Exercise E **Supplying Interjections** In the following sentences, write an interjection that expresses the feeling shown in parentheses.

1. (surprise) Did you see that meteor shower last night?
2. (hesitation) I was not sure what that was.
3. (disappointment) did that happen while I was sleeping?
4. (amazement) I could not believe my eyes.
5. (agreement) it is a natural event.

Cumulative Review: Parts of Speech

Exercise F **Identifying All the Parts of Speech** Write the part of speech of each underlined word in the following paragraph. Be as specific as possible.

<u>Hey</u>, those <u>rainbows</u> are an interesting sight. <u>They</u> can be seen after a shower <u>or</u> <u>near</u> a waterfall. The <u>brightest</u> rainbows <u>show</u> the spectrum <u>colors</u> <u>with</u> red on the outside. When the sun is low <u>in</u> the sky, rainbows appear <u>relatively</u> high.

Exercise G **Supplying the Correct Part of Speech** In the following sentences, supply the part of speech indicated in parentheses.

1. Thunderstorms can be very (adjective).
2. Not only is there a lot of noise, (correlative conjunction) the lightning can be dangerous.
3. You should not stand under a (noun) during a thunderstorm.
4. The best place to be is (preposition) your house away from the windows.
5. (verb) not talk on the telephone during a storm.
6. Some thunderstorms also have (adverb) high winds.

7. Wind, rain, thunder, (conjunction) lightning are all elements of a storm.
8. Most thunderstorms (verb) in the spring and summer months.
9. (Adjective) tornadoes can accompany these storms.
10. (Interjection) It seems that every season has its (adjective) weather.

Exercise H **Revising With Adjectives and Adverbs** Revise the following passage by adding adjectives and adverbs to modify nouns, verbs, and adjectives.

Some people enjoy winter. They like snow and cold winds. Snow covers everything and makes it look clean. There are a lot of outdoor activities that people enjoy in the winter: skiing, ice skating, and sledding. Some people just like to sit by a fire and watch through the window as the snow falls.

Exercise I **Writing Application** Write a short narrative about a weather event that you have witnessed or learned about. Underline at least one noun, pronoun, verb, adjective, adverb, preposition, conjunction, and interjection. Then, label each word's part of speech as specifically as possible.

Phrases, Clauses, and Sentences

Sentences

A **sentence** is a group of words with two main parts: a complete subject and a complete predicate. Together, these parts express a complete thought.

We read that story last year.

A **fragment** is a group of words that does not express a complete thought.

"Not right away."

Subject

The **subject** of a sentence is the word or group of words that tells whom or what the sentence is about. The **simple subject** is the essential noun, pronoun, or group of words acting as a noun that cannot be left out of the complete subject. A **complete subject** is the simple subject plus any modifiers. In the following example, the complete subject is underlined. The simple subject is italicized.

> <u>Pony express *riders*</u> carried packages more than 2,000 miles.

A **compound subject** is two or more subjects that have the same verb and are joined by a conjunction.

> Neither the *horse nor the driver* looked tired.

Predicate

The **predicate** of a sentence is the verb or verb phrase that tells what the complete subject of the sentence does or is. The **simple predicate** is the essential verb or verb phrase that cannot be left out of the complete predicate. A **complete predicate** is the simple predicate plus any modifiers or complements. In the following example, the complete predicate is underlined. The simple predicate is italicized.

> Pony express riders <u>*carried* packages more than 2,000 miles</u>.

A **compound predicate** is two or more verbs that have the same subject and are joined by a conjunction.

> She *sneezed and coughed* throughout the trip.

Complement

A **complement** is a word or group of words that completes the meaning of the predicate of a sentence. Five different kinds of complements can be found in English sentences: *direct objects, indirect objects, objective complements, predicate nominatives*, and *predicate adjectives.*

A **direct object** is a noun, pronoun, or group of words acting as a noun that receives the action of a transitive verb.

> We watched the *liftoff.*

An **indirect object** is a noun, pronoun, or group of words that appears with a direct object and names the person or thing that something is given to or done for.

> He sold the *family* a mirror.

An **objective complement** is an adjective or noun that appears with a direct object and describes or renames it.

> I called Meg my *friend.*

A **subject complement** is a noun, pronoun, or adjective that appears with a linking verb and tells something about the subject. A subject complement may be a *predicate nominative* or a *predicate adjective.*

A **predicate nominative** is a noun or pronoun that appears with a linking verb and renames, identifies, or explains the subject.

> Kiglo was the *leader.*

A **predicate adjective** is an adjective that appears with a linking verb and describes the subject of a sentence.

> Roko became *tired.*

Exercise A **Using Basic Sentence Parts** Rewrite the following sentences according to the directions in parentheses. In your new sentences, underline each simple subject once and each simple predicate twice. Circle each complement.

1. Ice hockey is a winter sport. It is a rough game. (Combine by creating a compound predicate nominative.)
2. Hockey-playing countries include Canada. Hockey is a big sport in Russia. (Combine by creating a compound direct object.)
3. Defense is an important part of the game, and so is offense. (Rewrite by creating a compound subject.)
4. The players use hockey sticks. They wear protective pads. (Rewrite by creating a compound predicate.)

5. Goaltenders wear face masks. They wear other protective equipment. (Combine by creating a compound direct object.)

6. One area on the ice is the neutral zone. Another is the attacking zone. (Combine by creating a compound predicate nominative.)

7. Substitution of players is frequent. It occurs during the game. (Combine by creating a compound predicate.)

8. Hockey skate blades are thin. They are also short. (Combine by creating a compound predicate adjective.)

9. Teams pass the puck, shooting it with their sticks. (Rewrite by creating a compound predicate.)

10. Ancient Egyptians played games similar to hockey, and so did the Persians. (Rewrite by creating a compound subject.)

Simple Sentence

A **simple sentence** consists of a single independent clause.

Compound Sentence

A **compound sentence** consists of two or more independent clauses joined by a comma and a coordinating conjunction or by a semicolon.

Complex Sentence

A **complex sentence** consists of one independent clause and one or more subordinate clauses.

Compound-Complex Sentence

A **compound-complex sentence** consists of two or more independent clauses and one or more subordinate clauses.

Declarative Sentence

A **declarative sentence** states an idea and ends with a period.

Interrogative Sentence

An **interrogative sentence** asks a question and ends with a question mark.

Imperative Sentence

An **imperative sentence** gives an order or a direction and ends with either a period or an exclamation mark.

Exclamatory Sentence

An **exclamatory sentence** conveys a strong emotion and ends with an exclamation mark.

Exercise B **Recognizing Basic Sentence Parts**
Copy the following sentences, underlining each simple subject once and each simple predicate twice. Circle the complements, and label each one *direct object, indirect object, predicate nominative,* or *predicate adjective.* Then, identify each sentence as declarative, imperative, interrogative, or exclamatory.

1. Does Matt or Jeremy enjoy figure skating or speed skating?

2. Speed skating is good exercise.

3. There are races against the clock and against other skaters.

4. Speed skaters use skates with long straight edges.

5. Wow! The blades are so long and look so sharp!

6. Try that pair of skates.

7. I gave Danielle figure-skating lessons.

8. She and Hannah were eager and attentive.

9. We practiced cross-overs and snowplow stops.

10. Can you do any jumps?

Phrases

A **phrase** is a group of words, without a subject and a verb, that functions in a sentence as one part of speech.

A **prepositional phrase** is a group of words that includes a preposition and a noun or a pronoun that is the object of the preposition.

near the town   with them

An **adjective phrase** is a prepositional phrase that modifies a noun or a pronoun by telling *what kind* or *which one.*

Mr. Sanderson brushed his hands over the shoes *in the window.*

An **adverb phrase** is a prepositional phrase that modifies a verb, an adjective, or an adverb by pointing out *where, when, in what manner,* or *to what extent.*

The trees were black *where the bark was wet.*

An **appositive phrase** is a noun or a pronoun with modifiers, placed next to a noun or a pronoun to add information and details.

The story, *a tale of adventure,* takes place in the Yukon.

A **participial phrase** is a participle modified by an adjective or an adverb phrase or accompanied by a complement. The entire phrase acts as an adjective.

Running at top speed, he soon caught up with them.

An **infinitive phrase** is an infinitive with modifiers, complements, or a subject, all acting together as a single part of speech.

At first I was too busy enjoying my food *to notice how the guests were doing.*

Gerunds

A **gerund** is a noun formed from the present participle of a verb ending in *–ing.* Like other nouns, gerunds can be used as subjects, direct objects, predicate nouns, and objects of prepositions.

Exercise C Identifying Gerunds Write the gerund(s) from the sentences below, and label each one *subject, direct object, predicate noun,* or *object of a preposition.*

1. Tourists in New Mexico may enjoy horseback riding at a dude ranch.
2. Hiking and camping are year-round activities in New Mexico.
3. Visitors may also find excitement in visiting the ancient ruins of the Native Americans who have lived here for thousands of years.
4. Native American dancing and festivals drqw many visitors to New Mexico.
5. Above all, touring New Mexico is a pleasant vacation.

Gerund Phrases

A **gerund phrase** is a gerund with modifiers or a complement, all acting together as a noun.

Exercise D Identifying Gerund Phrases Write the gerund phrase(s) in the sentences below. Label each one *subject, direct object, predicate noun,* or *object of a preposition.*

1. Setting turquoise stones in silver is a common jewelry-making practice.
2. The Pueblo also earn money by shaping pottery.
3. The next step after baking a piece of pottery is painting it.
4. Some Pueblo groups teach pottery making to tourists.
5. The San Ildefonso Pueblo is famous for its black-on-black pottery making.

Clauses

A **clause** is a group of words with its own subject and verb.

An **independent clause** can stand by itself as a complete sentence.

"I think it belongs to Rachel."

A **subordinate clause** has a subject and a verb but cannot stand by itself as a complete sentence; it can only be part of a sentence.

"Although it was late"

Exercise E **Identifying Phrases and Clauses** Label each phrase in the following sentences as an *adjective prepositional phrase,* an *adverb prepositional phrase,* or an *appositive phrase.* Identify and label each clause.

1. Skiing is a popular winter sport in many countries.
2. Boots, flexible or rigid, are important pieces of equipment.
3. Ski poles that vary in length are used for balance.
4. There are three kinds of skiing that have been developed.
5. One type, Alpine skiing, involves racing down steep, snow-covered slopes.
6. Skiers descend in the fastest time possible.
7. A course is defined by a series of gates, which are made of poles and flag markers.
8. The racer passes through these gates.
9. This downhill racing includes the slalom, in which the course is made of many turns.
10. The super giant slalom, a combination of downhill and slalom, is decided after one run.

Exercise F **Using Phrases and Clauses** Rewrite the following sentences according to the instructions in parentheses.

1. Cross-country skiing is called Nordic skiing and is practiced in many parts of the world. (Rewrite by creating an appositive phrase.)
2. It is performed on longer courses. These courses are also flatter than downhill courses. (Combine by creating a clause.)
3. Nordic skiing emphasizes two things. Those are endurance and strength. (Combine by creating a clause.)
4. A side-to-side motion is the way cross-country skiers move. (Rewrite by creating an adverb prepositional phrase.)
5. Cross-country skiing developed to fill a need. That need was for transportation. (Combine by creating an adjective prepositional phrase.)

Cumulative Review: Phrases, Clauses, Sentences

Exercise G **Revising Sentences to Eliminate Errors and Create Variety** Rewrite the following sentences according to the instructions in parentheses.

1. Bobsledding was first developed in Saint Moritz, Switzerland, the first competition was held there. (Correct the run-on sentence.)
2. Teams of two or four people descend an icy run in bobsledding. (Vary the sentence by beginning with a prepositional phrase.)
3. The part of a bobsled run most critical is its start. (Correct the misplaced modifier.)
4. The captain occupies the front position in the sled. This person is also called the driver. (Combine the sentences by creating a phrase.)
5. The crew members lean backward and forward in unison and accelerate the speed of the sled. (Vary the sentence by beginning with a participial phrase.)
6. Bobsledding is different than the luge. (Correct the common usage problem.)
7. Lie on their backs with their feet at the front of the luge sled. (Correct the sentence fragment.)
8. Luge courses are not constructed for nothing other than this sport. (Correct the double negative.)
9. These courses feature turns. Courses also feature straight stretches. (Combine by creating a compound direct object.)
10. The reason it looks dangerous is because luges travel at high speeds. (Correct the common usage problem.)

Exercise H Revision Practice: Sentence **Combining** Rewrite the following passage, combining sentences where appropriate.

Most children are delighted when it snows. They wake up early. They listen for school cancellations on the radio. If school is cancelled, the children are excited. The parents say "Oh, no!" It means the schedule is off. The day has to be rearranged. They get out the boots and warm clothes. They get out the sleds. An unexpected vacation day.

Exercise I Writing Application Write a description of a winter activity that you enjoy. Vary the lengths and beginnings of your sentences. Underline each simple subject once and each simple verb twice. Then, circle at least three phrases and three clauses. Avoid fragments, run-ons, double negatives, misplaced modifiers, and common usage problems.

Using Verbs, Pronouns, and Modifiers

Principal Parts

A **verb** has four **principal parts**: the *present,* the *present participle,* the *past,* and the *past participle.*

Regular verbs form the past and past participle by adding *-ed* to the present form.

Present: walk

Present Participle: (am) walking

Past: walked

Past Participle: (have) walked

Irregular verbs form the past and past participle by changing form rather than by adding *-ed.*

Present: go

Present Participle: (am) going

Past: went

Past Participle: (have) gone

Verb Tense

A **verb tense** tells whether the time of an action or condition is in the past, the present, or the future. Every verb has six tenses: *present, past, future, present perfect, past perfect,* and *future perfect.*

The **present tense** shows actions that happen in the present.

The **past tense** shows actions that have already happened.

The **future tense** shows actions that will happen.

The **present perfect tense** shows actions that begin in the past and continue to the present.

The **past perfect tense** shows a past action or condition that ended before another past action.

The **future perfect tense** shows a future action or condition that will have ended before another begins.

Exercise A Using Verbs Choose the correct verb or verb phrase in parentheses to complete each sentence below. Identify its principal part and tense.

1. Several Native American groups (brung, brought) their culture to what is now Texas.
2. The foundations of early dwellings were found where they were (lain, laid).
3. The Karankawa (did, done) a great deal of fishing in the Gulf of Mexico.
4. The Apache and the Comanche (caught, catched) and (eat, ate) the buffalo.
5. Alonzo Álvarez de Piñeda (set, sat) foot in Texas in 1519.
6. He was (leading, led) a group around the mouth of the Rio Grande.
7. Cabeza de Vaca (began, begun) to explore more of inland Texas.
8. In 1682, the Spanish (built, builded) the first mission in Texas.
9. That was near the site where present-day El Paso (is, was).
10. Spain (knew, known) that France was claiming the area.

Pronoun Case

The **case** of a pronoun is the form it takes to show its use in a sentence. There are three pronoun cases: *nominative, objective,* and *possessive.*

The **nominative case** is used to name or rename the subject of the sentence. The nominative case pronouns are *I, you, he, she, it, we, you, they.*

> **As the subject:** *She* is brave.

> **Renaming the subject:** The leader is *she.*

The **objective case** is used as the direct object, indirect object, or object of a preposition. The objective case pronouns are *me, you, him, her, it, us, you, them.*

> **As a direct object:** Tom called *me.*

> **As an indirect object:** My friend gave *me* advice.

> **As an object of a preposition:** The coach gave pointers to *me.*

The **possessive case** is used to show ownership. The possessive pronouns are *my, your, his, her, its, our, their, mine, yours, his, hers, its, ours, theirs.*

Exercise B **Identifying the Case of Pronouns** Identify the case of each pronoun in the following sentences as *nominative, objective,* or *possessive.*

1. One French explorer was La Salle. He built a fort near Matagorda Bay.
2. La Salle named it Fort Saint Louis.
3. France claimed the Mississippi River and its tributaries.
4. In 1716, the Spanish established missions, founding them throughout the territory.
5. They include the city of San Antonio.
6. However, the Spanish found that their hold on the province of Texas was weak.
7. Expeditions of adventurers from the United States had been traveling through it.
8. Philip Nolan led one invasion, but the Spanish captured him.
9. In 1820, Moses Austin, a United States citizen, made his request to settle in Texas.
10. His son, Stephen F. Austin, carried out the plan.

Subject-Verb Agreement

To make a subject and a verb agree, make sure that both are singular or both are plural. Two or more singular subjects joined by *or* or *nor* must have a singular verb. When singular and plural subjects are joined by *or* or *nor,* the verb must agree with the closest subject.

> *He is* at the door.

> *They drive* home every day.

> Both *pets are* hungry.

> Either the *chairs or* the *table is* on sale.

Exercise C **Using Verb Agreement** Write the form of the verb in parentheses that agrees with the subject of each sentence below.

1. All of our reports (be) about the settling of the West.
2. Many students (want) to write about California.
3. No one (know) more about the early days in California than Rudy.
4. Everybody in our class (love) to look at the maps of the trails heading west.
5. Each of the students (have) to pick a trail to report on.
6. Julie and Thomas (ask) to read about the Oregon Trail.
7. Neither Sam nor Randy (have) picked a topic yet.
8. Tanya and I (hope) to do our report on the Santa Fe Trail.

9. Either the Santa Fe Trail or the Oregon Trail (be) interesting.

10. According to the map, each of the trails (appear) to begin in Independence, Missouri.

Pronoun-Antecedent Agreement

Pronouns must agree with their antecedents in number and gender. Use singular pronouns with singular antecedents and plural pronouns with plural antecedents. Many errors in pronoun-antecedent agreement occur when a plural pronoun is used to refer to a singular antecedent for which the gender is not specified.

Incorrect: Everyone did their best.

Correct: Everyone did his or her best.

The following indefinite pronouns are singular: *anybody, anyone, each, either, everybody, everyone, neither, nobody, no one, one, somebody, someone.*

The following indefinite pronouns are plural: *both, few, many, several.*

The following indefinite pronouns may be either singular or plural: *all, any, most, none, some.*

Exercise D **Using Agreement** Fill in each blank below with a pronoun that agrees with its antecedent.

1. In our social studies class, ___?___ are studying Texas and ___?___ fight for independence.

2. Texans decided that they wanted to make ___?___ own laws.

3. The Mexican government wanted settlers in Texas to obey ___?___ laws.

4. General Santa Anna gathered ___?___ troops together to crush the rebellious Texans.

5. Texans declared ___?___ independence from Mexico on March 2, 1836, in the town of Washington-on-the-Brazos.

6. Either Oleg or Sam will give ___?___ report on the Alamo today.

7. Fewer than 200 Texans tried to defend ___?___ territory against Santa Anna's army there.

8. Jim Bowie, Davey Crockett, and William B. Travis lost ___?___ lives at the Alamo.

9. I hope that I will do well on ___?___ test about the Alamo.

10. Texans captured Santa Anna and forced ___?___ to sign a treaty.

Modifiers

The **comparative** and **superlative** degrees of most adjectives and adverbs of one or two syllables can be formed in either of two ways: Use *–er* or *more* to form a comparative degree and *–est* or *most* to form the superlative degree of most one- and two-syllable modifiers.

More and *most* can also be used to form the comparative and superlative degrees of most one- and two- syllable modifiers. These words should not be used when the result sounds awkward, as in "A greyhound *is more* fast than a beagle."

Exercise E **Using Modifiers** In the sentences below, write the form of the adjective or adverb indicated in parentheses.

1. A Texan army gathered (quickly—comparative) than expected.

2. After taking San Antonio, (many—superlative) soldiers left the city.

3. They believed that Santa Anna, the Mexican dictator, would wait until (late—positive) spring.

4. Santa Anna's army was (large—comparative) than that of the settlers.

5. The (small—superlative) of all Texan forces withdrew to the Alamo.

6. (Brave—comparative) than expected, the Texans fought for thirteen days.

7. (Many—superlative) of the Texan forces were defeated in other battles.

8. Then, a group of Texans declared independence (cautiously—comparative) than they had earlier.

9. They attacked, (probably—superlative) surprising the Mexican Army.

10. Santa Anna (soon—positive) recognized Texas's independence.

Glossary of Common Usage

accept, except

Accept is a verb that means "to receive" or "to agree to." *Except* is a preposition that means "other than" or "leaving out." Do not confuse these two words.

> Aaron sadly *accepted* his father's decision to sell Zlateh.

> Everyone *except* the fisherman and his wife had children.

affect, effect

Affect is normally a verb meaning "to influence" or "to bring about a change in." *Effect* is usually a noun, meaning "result."

among, between

Among is usually used with three or more items. *Between* is generally used with only two items.

bad, badly

Use the predicate adjective *bad* after linking verbs such as *feel, look,* and *seem.* Use *badly* whenever an adverb is required.

> Mouse does not feel *bad* about tricking Coyote.

> In the myth, Athene treats Arachne *badly.*

beside, besides

Beside means "at the side of" or "close to." *Besides* means "in addition to."

can, may

The verb *can* generally refers to the ability to do something. The verb *may* generally refers to permission to do something.

different from, different than

Different from is generally preferred over *different than.*

farther, further

Use *farther* when you refer to distance. Use *further* when you mean "to a greater degree or extent" or "additional."

fewer, less

Use *fewer* for things that can be counted. Use *less* for amounts or quantities that cannot be counted.

good, well

Use the predicate adjective *good* after linking verbs such as *feel, look, smell, taste,* and *seem.* Use *well* whenever you need an adverb.

hopefully

You should not loosely attach this adverb to a sentence, as in *"Hopefully, the rain will stop by noon."* Rewrite the sentence so *hopefully* modifies a specific verb. Other possible ways of revising such sentences include using the adjective *hopeful* or a phrase like "everyone *hopes* that."

its, it's

The word *its* with no apostrophe is a possessive pronoun. The word *it's* is a contraction for *it is.* Do not confuse the possessive pronoun *its* with the contraction *it's,* standing for "it is" or "it has."

lay, lie

Do not confuse these verbs. *Lay* is a transitive verb meaning "to set or put something down." Its principal parts are *lay, laying, laid, laid. Lie* is an intransitive verb meaning "to recline." Its principal parts are *lie, lying, lay, lain.*

leave, let

Be careful not to confuse these verbs. *Leave* means "to go away" or "to allow to remain." *Let* means "to permit."

like, as

Like is a preposition that usually means "similar to" or "in the same way as." *Like* should always be followed by an object. Do not use *like* before a subject and a verb. Use *as* or *that* instead.

loose, lose

Loose can be either an adjective (meaning "unattached") or a verb (meaning "to untie"). *Lose* is always a verb (meaning "to fail to keep, have, or win").

many, much

Use *many* to refer to a specific quantity. Use *much* for an indefinite amount or for an abstract concept.

of, have

Do not use *of* in place of *have* after auxiliary verbs like *would, could, should, may, might,* or *must.*

raise, rise

Raise is a transitive verb that usually takes a direct object. *Rise* is intransitive and never takes a direct object.

set, sit

Set is a transitive verb meaning "to put (something) in a certain place." Its principal parts are *set, setting, set, set. Sit* is an intransitive verb meaning "to be seated." Its principal parts are *sit, sitting, sat, sat.*

than, then

The conjunction *than* is used to connect the two parts of a comparison. Do not confuse *than* with the adverb *then,* which usually refers to time.

that, which, who

Use the relative pronoun *that* to refer to things or people. Use *which* only for things and *who* only for people.

their, there, they're

Their is a possessive adjective and always modifies a noun. *There* is usually used either at the beginning of a sentence or as an adverb. *They're* is a contraction for "they are."

to, too, two

To is a preposition that begins a prepositional phrase or an infinitive. *Too,* with two o's, is an adverb and modifies adjectives and other adverbs. *Two* is a number.

when, where, why

Do not use *when, where,* or *why* directly after a linking verb such as *is.* Reword the sentence.

Faulty:	Suspense is *when* an author increases the reader's tension.
Revised:	An author uses suspense to increase the reader's tension.
Faulty:	A biography is *where* a writer tells the life story of another person.
Revised:	In a biography, a writer tells the life story of another person.

who, whom

In formal writing, remember to use *who* only as a subject in clauses and sentences and *whom* only as an object.

Exercise F **Correcting Usage Mistakes** Rewrite the following sentences, correcting any errors in usage.

1. The Republic of Texas continued their existence for almost ten years.
2. The more prominent of all Texas's problems was finances.
3. There was disputes about the new country's boundaries.

4. More immigrants came to Texas, and the troubles did not prevent they from settling.

5. Sam Houston will be one who wanted the United States to annex the republic.

6. After Sam Houston wins in the battle of San Jacinto, Texas had become independent.

7. These two groups, the Cherokee and the Mexicans, brought its concerns into battle.

8. However, the Cherokee and them were arrested by the Texas army.

9. A new president of Texas, Mirabeau Lamar, were elected in 1838.

10. The Cherokee resist his orders, but they were defeated and moved to what is now Oklahoma.

Exercise G **Writing Application** Write a short description of the state in which you live or one that you have visited. Be sure that the words in your sentences follow the rules of agreement and that your modifiers are used correctly. Then, list the verbs and verb phrases, identifying their tenses. Make a list of pronouns, and identify their case.

Capitalization and Punctuation Rules

Capitalization

1. Capitalize the first word of a sentence.
   Young Roko glances down the valley.

2. Capitalize all proper nouns and adjectives.
   Mark Twain   Amazon River   Thanksgiving Day
   Montana   October   Italian

3. Capitalize a person's title when it is followed by the person's name or when it is used in direct address.
   Doctor   General Khokhotov   Mrs. Price

4. Capitalize titles showing family relationships when they refer to a specific person, unless

they are preceded by a possessive noun or pronoun.
   Granny-Liz   Margie's mother

5. Capitalize the first word and all other key words in the titles of books, periodicals, poems, stories, plays, paintings, and other works of art.
   from *Tom Sawyer*   "Grandpa and the Statue"
   "Breaker's Bridge"   "The Spring and the Fall"

6. Capitalize the first word and all nouns in letter salutations and the first word in letter closings.
   Dear Willis,   Yours truly,

Exercise A **Using All the Rules of Capitalization**
Copy the following sentences, inserting the appropriate capital letters.

1. people throughout north america, south america, and europe ride bicycles.

2. around 1790, count divrac of france invented a wooden scooter.

3. a german inventor, baron drais, improved upon that model.

4. his version had a steering bar attached to the front wheel.

5. then, a scottish blacksmith, kirkpatrick macmillan, added foot pedals.

6. in 1866, pierre lallement, a french carriage maker, took out the first u.s. patent on a pedal bicycle.

7. mr. j. k. starley of england produced the first commercially successful bicycle.

8. by 1897, more than four million americans were riding bikes.

9. there are many road races like the tour de france.

10. other races, called bmx, are held on bumpy dirt tracks.

Punctuation

End Marks

1. Use a **period** to end a declarative sentence, an imperative sentence, and most abbreviations.
2. Use a **question mark** to end a direct question or an incomplete question in which the rest of the question is understood.
3. Use an **exclamation mark** after a statement showing strong emotion, an urgent imperative sentence, or an interjection expressing strong emotion.

Exercise B **Using End Marks** Copy the following sentences, inserting the appropriate end marks.

1. What was your favorite toy when you were young
2. My little brother has a rattle and a teething ring
3. Hey, I *really* miss my baby toys
4. Do you still sleep with a favorite stuffed animal
5. Maybe they will be collectible items one day

Commas

1. Use a comma before the conjunction to separate two independent clauses in a compound sentence.
2. Use commas to separate three or more words, phrases, or clauses in a series.
3. Use commas to separate adjectives of equal rank. Do not use commas to separate adjectives that must stay in a specific order.
4. Use a comma after an introductory word, phrase, or clause.
5. Use commas to set off parenthetical and nonessential expressions.
6. Use commas with places and dates made up of two or more parts.
7. Use commas after items in addresses, after the salutation in a personal letter, after the closing in all letters, and in numbers of more than three digits.

Semicolons

1. Use a semicolon to join independent clauses that are not already joined by a conjunction.
2. Use a semicolon to join independent clauses or items in a series that already contain commas.

   The Pengelly family had no say in the choosing of Lob; he came to them in the second way. . . .

Colons

1. Use a colon before a list of items following an independent clause.
2. Use a colon in numbers giving the time, in salutations in business letters, and in labels used to signal important ideas.

Exercise C **Using Commas, Semicolons, and Colons** Copy the following sentences, inserting the appropriate commas, semicolons, and colons.

1. Every summer at the beach we make sand castles using sand seashells and water.
2. I play catch with my cousins who visit us for several weeks each year.
3. Last summer I learned a new sport volleyball.
4. When we first started playing the net seemed so high.
5. Then I learned how to hit the ball it was not very difficult.
6. I enjoyed volleyball in fact we played from noon until about 530 p.m.
7. Some people do not play sports at the beach They read listen to music or just lie in the sun.
8. After a full enjoyable day we like to have a barbecue.
9. We cook many of my favorite foods hamburgers hot dogs and corn on the cob.
10. When the sun sets the temperature drops but we still stay outside.

Quotation Marks

1. A **direct quotation** represents a person's exact speech or thoughts and is enclosed in quotation marks.
2. An **indirect quotation** reports only the general meaning of what a person said or thought and does not require quotation marks.
3. Always place a comma or a period inside the final quotation mark of a direct quotation.
4. Place a question mark or an exclamation mark inside the final quotation mark if the end mark is part of the quotation; if it is not part of the quotation, place it outside the final quotation mark.

Titles

1. Underline or italicize the titles of long written works, movies, television and radio shows, lengthy works of music, paintings, and sculptures.
2. Use quotation marks around the titles of short written works, episodes in a series, songs, and titles of works mentioned as parts of collections.

Hyphens

1. Use a **hyphen** with certain numbers, after certain prefixes, with two or more words used as one word, and with a compound modifier that comes before a noun.

Apostrophes

1. Add an **apostrophe** and s to show the possessive case of most singular nouns.
2. Add an apostrophe to show the possessive case of plural nouns ending in s and es.

3. Add an apostrophe and s to show the possessive case of plural nouns that do not end in s or es.
4. Use an apostrophe in a contraction to indicate the position of the missing letter or letters.

Exercise D **Using All the Rules of Punctuation**

Copy the following sentences, inserting the appropriate end marks, commas, semicolons, colons, quotation marks, underlining, hyphens, and apostrophes.

1. Did you know that there are three types of kites
2. The most well known type is the diamond shaped kite
3. There are also box kites delta kites and bowed kites
4. Paper or cloth is used for the kite however the frame can be wood or metal
5. During the 1800s kites served an important purpose weather forecasting
6. When Benjamin Franklin flew a kite he proved his theory about electricity
7. Alexander Graham Bell the inventor of the telephone also created kites
8. Let's Go Fly a Kite is a great song
9. Remember the line Lets go fly a kite up to the highest height
10. It is from a famous movie Mary Poppins

Cumulative Review: Mechanics

Exercise E **Proofreading Dialogue for Punctuation and Capitalization** Copy the following dialogue, adding the proper punctuation and capitalization.

1. is that a new yo-yo asked pam i have never seen it before
2. no i have had it awhile replied joe i found it underneath my bed
3. i bet you do not know how yo-yos were invented
4. joe answered sure i do they are toys for children
5. no pam said they originated in the philippines
6. right as toys joe insisted
7. they were weapons and toys pam corrected
8. ok well i know what the word yo-yo means
9. pam said so do i tell me and i will see if you are correct
10. well joe said i am pretty sure it means come back
11. that is right pam said
12. it is a toy that has been around for more than 3,000 years joe continued
13. it was not until the 1920s pam added that they were developed in the united states
14. who was donald duncan asked joe
15. he was the man who improved upon the design of the yo-yo and made it a popular toy in the united states

Exercise F **Writing Sentences With Correct Punctuation and Capitalization** Write five sentences following the instructions given below. Be sure to punctuate and capitalize correctly.

1. Write a sentence about your favorite board game or video game.
2. Describe what you like about it.
3. Write a sentence about a favorite outdoor game.
4. Tell what time of year you play it, and name some of the friends who join in.
5. Write an exclamatory sentence about a great play in a game.

Exercise G **Proofreading Paragraphs for Punctuation and Capitalization** Proofread the following paragraphs, copying them into your notebook and adding punctuation and capitalization as needed.

Do children still play board games I wonder. perhaps tv and video games have begun to replace checkers and chess.

There was a time you know when i excitedly hoped for board games as gifts on certain special occasions birthdays and holidays. one birthday when my twin sister, lily, and i received our first checkers set we were thrilled we could not wait to begin playing i think we played for hours. when aunt dotti and uncle larry came over with our cousins joanie and mark we all took turns playing. wow what a great time we had.

Exercise H **Writing Application** Write a brief dialogue between you and a friend about your favorite toy from childhood. Be sure to include proper punctuation, capitalization, and indentation.

INDEX OF SKILLS

Boldfaced numbers indicate pages where terms are defined.

Reading Skills and Strategies

Vocabulary

Academic Vocabulary

Listening and Speaking

Research and Technology

INDEX OF FEATURES

Boldfaced numbers indicate pages where terms are defined.

Literature in Context

On Your Own

Reading Informational Materials

Spelling Workshop

Unit Introductions

Writing Workshop

INDEX OF AUTHORS AND TITLES

Nonfiction selections and informational text appears in red. Page numbers in italic text refer to biographical information.

ACKNOWLEDGMENTS (continued)

Boyds Mills Press From *The Case of The Monkeys That Fell from the Trees* by Susan E. Quinlan. Text and illustrations copright © 2003 by Susan E. Quinlan. Published by Boyds Mills Press, Inc. Reprinted by permission.

Brandt & Hochman Literary Agents, Inc. "Lob's Girl," from *A Whisper in the Night* by Joan Aiken. Delacorte Press. Copyright © 1984 by Joan Aiken Enterprises, Ltd. "Wilbur Wright and Orville Wright" by Stephen Vincent Benet, from *A Book of Americans* by Rosemary and Stephen Vincent Benet. Copyright © 1933 by Rosemary and Stephen Vincent. Copyright renewed © 1961 by Rosemary Carr Benet. Reprinted by permission of Brandt & Hochman Literary Agents, Inc.

John Brewton, George, M. Blackburn & Lorraine A. Blackburn "Limerick (Accidents – More or Less Fatal)" by Anonymous from *Laughable Limericks*. Used with permission of George M. Blackburn, et al.

Brooks Permissions "Cynthia in the Snow" from *Bronzeville Boys and Girls* by Gwendolyn Brooks. Copyright © 1956 by Gwendolyn Brooks. Copyright renewed © 1984 Gwendolyn Brooks Blakely. Reprinted by consent of Brooks Permissions.

The Caxton Printers, Ltd. "Business at Eleven" by Toshio Mori from *America Street: A Multicultural Anthology of Stories*. Copyright Toshio Mori. Reproduced by permission of The Caxton Printers, Ltd. Copyright © 1993 by Anne Mazer. All rights reserved.

Chronicle Books From *Oranges* by Gary Soto. Copyright © 1995 by Gary Soto. Used with permission of Chronicle Books, LLC, San Francisco, CA. Visit *www.chroniclebooks.com*.

Clarion Books/Houghton Mifflin Company "A Backwoods Boy" from *Lincoln: A Photobiography*. Copyright © 1987 by Russell Freedman. Reprinted by permission of Clarion Books/Houghton Mifflin Company. All rights reserved.

Ruth Cohen Literary Agency, Inc. "The All-American Slurp" by Lensey Namioka, copyright © 1987, from *Visions*, ed. by Donald R. Gallo. Reprinted by permission of Lensey Namioka. All rights reserved by the author.

Don Congdon Associates, Inc. "Hard As Nails" from *The Good Times* by Russell Baker. Copyright © 1989 by Russell Baker. "The Sound of Summer Running" (originally titled "Summer in the Air") by Ray Bradbury from *The Saturday Evening Post*, 2/8/56. Copyright © 1956 by Curtis Publishing Co., renewed 1984 by Ray Bradbury. Reprinted by permission of Don Congdon Associates, Inc.

Curtis Brown, Ltd. From *"Adventure of Isabel"* by Ogden Nash. Copyright © 1936 by Ogden Nash. Copyright © renewed 1951. Reprinted by permission of Curtis Brown, Ltd. From *"Greyling: A Picture Story from the Islands"* by Jane Yolen. Copyright 1968, 1996 by Jane Yolen. First published by Penguin Putnam. From *The Pigman and Me* by Paul Zindel. Copyright © 1992 by Paul Zindel. First published by HarperCollins. Reprinted by permission of Curtis Brown, Ltd.

Dell Publishing, a division of Random House, Inc. "Jeremiah's Song" by Walter Dean Myers, from *Visions* by Donald R. Gallo, editor, copyright © 1987 by Donald R. Gallo. "The Tail" from *Funny You Should Ask* by Joyce Hansen. Copyright © 1992 by Joyce Hansen. Used by permission of Dell Publishing, a division of Random House, Inc.

Dial Books for Young Readers, a member of Penguin Young Readers Group, a member of Penguin Group (USA) "Gluskabe and Old Man Winter: Abenaki" by Joseph Bruchac from *Pushing Up the Sky*. Copyright © 2000 by Joseph Bruchac, text. Used by permission of Dial Books for Young Readers, a division of Penguin Young Readers Group, a member of Penguin Group (USA) Inc.

Doubleday, a division of Random House, Inc. "Child on Top of a Greenhouse" by Theodore Roethke from *The Collected Poems Of Theodore Roethke*, copyright © 1946 by Editorial Publications, Inc. "The Fun They Had" from *Isaac Asimov: The Complete Stories Of Vol. I*, by Isaac Asimov, copyright © 1957 by Isaac Asimov. Used by permission of Doubleday, a division of Random House, Inc.

Paul S. Eriksson "My Papa Mark Twain" by Susy Clemens from *Small Voices* by Josef and Dorothy Berger. © Copyright 1966 by Josef and Dorothy Berger. Reproduced by permission of Paul S. Eriksson, Publisher.

Jean Grasso Fitzpatrick "The Ant and the Dove" by Leo Tolstoy from *Fables and Folktales Adapted from Tolstoy*, adapted by Maristella Maggi, translation by Jean Grasso Fitzpatrick. Published in 1986. Copyright © 1985 by Barrons.

Free Spirit Publishing "Social Interactions 101. The Rituals of Relating" by Alex J. Packer. Excerpted from *How Rude!™ The Teenager's Guide To Good Manners, Proper Behavior, and Not Grossing People Out* by Alex J. Packer, Ph.D. © 1997. Used with permission from Free Spirit Publishing, Inc., Minneapolis, MN; 1-866-703-7322; www.freespirit.com. All rights reserved.

Samuel French, Inc. "The Phantom Tollbooth" from *The Phantom Tollbooth: A Children's Play in Two Acts* by Susan Nanus and Norton Juster. Copyright © 1977 by Susan Nanus and Norton Juster. Reprinted by permission of Samuel French, Inc. All rights reserved. CAUTION: Professionals and amateurs are hereby warned that "The Phantom Tollbooth," being fully protected under the copyright laws of the United States of America, the British Commonwealth countries, including Canada, and the other countries of the Copyright Union, is subject to royalty. All rights, including professional, amateur, motion picture, recitation, lecturing, public reading, radio, television and cable broadcasting, and the rights of translation into foreign languages, are strictly reserved. In its present form the play is dedicated to the reading public only. The amateur live performance rights are controlled exclusively by Samuel French, Inc. Any inquiry regarding the availability of performance rights, or the purchase of individual copies of the authorized acting edition, must be directed to Samuel French, Inc., 45 West 25th Street, NY NY 10010 with other locations in Hollywood and Toronto, Canada.

Harcourt Education Limited "Why the Tortoise's Shell Is Not Smooth" from *Things Fall Apart* by Chinua Achebe. Copyright © 1959 by Chinua Achebe. Reprinted with permission of Harcourt Education Limited.

Harcourt, Inc. "Ode to Family Photographs" by Gary Soto from *Neighborhood Odes*. Text copyright © 1992 by Gary Soto. Reprinted by permission of Harcourt, Inc.

Harper & Row Publishers, Inc. "Limerick (Accidents -- More or Less Fatal)" by Anonymous from *Laughable Limericks*. Copyright © 1965 by Sara and John E. Brewton. Reprinted by permission of Harper & Row Publishers, Inc.

HarperCollins Publishers, Inc. "Ankylosaurus" from *Tyrannosaurus Was a Beast* by Jack Prelutsky. Text copyright © 1988 by Jack Prelutsky. "Zlateh the Goat" by Isaac Bashevis Singer from *Zlateh the Goat and Other Stories*. Text copyright © 1966 by Isaac Bashevis Singer, copyright renewed 1994 by Alma Singer. "Aaron's Gift" from *The Witch of Fourth Street and Other Stories* by Myron Levoy. Text copyright © 1972 by Myron Levoy. From *"The Wounded Wolf"* by Jean Craighead George. Text copyright © 1978 by Jean Craighead George. "The Homecoming" by Laurence Yep from *The Rainbow People*. Copyright © 1989 by Laurence Yep. "No Thank You" by Shel Silverstein from *Falling Up*. Copyright © 1996 by Shel Silverstein. All rights reserved. "Langston Terrace" by Eloise Greenfield, from *Childtimes: A Three-Generation Memoir*, copyright © 1979 by Eloise Greenfield and Lessie Jones Little. "The World is Not a Pleasant Place to Be" from *My House* by Nikki Giovanni. Copyright © 1972 by Nikki Giovanni. From "Bad Boy: A Memoir" by Walter Dean Myers from *Bad Boy: A Memoir*. Used by permission of HarperCollins Publishers.

Harper's Magazine "Preserving the Great American Symbol," (originally titled "Desecrating America") by Richard Durbin from *Harper's Magazine*, October 1989, p. 32. Copyright © 1989 by Harper's Magazine. All rights reserved. Reproduced by special permission of Harper's Magazine.

Harvard University Press "Fame Is a bee" (#1763) is reprinted by permission of the publishers and the Trustees of Amherst College from *The Poems of Emily Dickinson*, Thomas H. Johnson, editor, Cambridge, Mass.: The Belknap Press of Harvard University Press, Copyright © 1951, 1955, 1979 by the President and Fellows of Harvard College.

Diana Chang Herrmann From "Saying Yes" by Diana Chang. Copyright by Diana Chang. Reprinted by permission of the author.

The Barbara Hogenson Agency, Inc. "The Tiger Who Would Be King" by James Thurber, from *Further Fables for Our Time*. Copyright © 1956 James Thurber. Copyright © renewed 1984 by Rosemary A. Thurber. Reprinted by arrangement with Rosemary A. Thurber and The Barbara Hogenson Agency, Inc.

Henry Holt and Company, Inc. "Dust of Snow" by Robert Frost from *The Poetry of Robert Frost* edited by Edward Connery Lathem. Copyright 1923, © 1969 by Henry Holt & Co., copyright © 1951 by Robert Frost. "The Stone" from *The Foundling and Other Tales of Prydain* by Lloyd Alexander. Copyright, © 1973 by Lloyd Alexander. Reprinted by permission of Henry Holt and Company, LLC.

Houghton Mifflin Company "Arachne" from *Greek Myths* by Ollivia E. Coolidge. Copyright © 1949 by Olivia E. Coolidge; copyright renewed © 1977 by Olivia E. Coolidge. Reprinted by permission of Houghton Mifflin Company. All rights reserved.

Dr. Francisco Jiménez "The Circuit" by Francisco Jiménez from *America Street: A Mulicultural Anthology of Stories*. Copyright © 1993 by Anne Mazer. Reprinted with permission of the author.

Rachel Katz "Origami with Rachel Katz: Apatosauras" by Rachel Katz from *www.geocities.com/rachel_katz*. Copyright © 2001-2004 Rachel Katz. Used with permission of Rachel Katz.

Alfred A. Knopf Children's Books, a division of Random House, Inc. "He Lion, Bruh Bear, and Bruh Rabbit" from *The People Could Fly: American Black Folktales* by Virginia Hamilton, illustrated by Leo and Diane Dillon, copyright © 1985 by Virginia Hamilton. Illustrations copyright © 1985 by Leo and Diane Dillon. From "James and the Giant Peach" by Roald Dahl. Text copyright © 1961 by Roald Dahl, renewed 1989. Illustrations copyright © 1996 by Lane Smith. "Jackie Robinson: Justice at Last" from *25 Great Moments* by Geoffrey C. Ward and Ken Burns with S.A. Kramer, copyright © 1994 by Baseball Licensing International, Inc. From "*Stargirl*" by Jerry Spinelli. Copyright © 2000 by Jerry Spinelli. "Milo" from *The Phantom Tollbooth* by Norton Juster. Text copyright © 1961 by Norton Juster. Text copyright renewed 1989 by Norton Juster. Used by permission of Alfred A. Knopf, an Imprint of Random House Children's Books, a division of Random House, Inc.

Alfred A. Knopf, Inc., a division of Random House, Inc. "April Rain Song" from *The Collected Poems of Langston Hughes* by Langston Hughes, copyright © 1994 by The Estate of Langston Hughes. Used by permission of Alfred A. Knopf, a division of Random House, Inc.

The Lazear Agency "Turkeys" by Bailey White from *Mama Makes Up Her Mind*, copyright © 1993. Reprinted by permission of The Lazear Agency and author, Bailey White.

Lescher & Lescher, Ltd. "The Southpaw" by Judith Viorst. Copyright © 1974 by Judith Viorst. From *Free To Be...You And Me*. This usage granted by permission of Lescher & Lescher, Ltd. All rights reserved.

Liveright Publishing Corporation, an imprint of W.W. Norton & Company "who knows if the moon's" by E. E. Cummings. Copyright 1923, 1925, 1951, 1953, © 1991 by the Trustees for the E. E. Cummings Trust. Copyright © 1976 by George James Firmage, from *Complete Poems: 1904-1962* by E. E. Cummings, edited by George J. Firmage. Used by permission of Liveright Publishing Corporation.

Madison County Public Library (Kentucky) "Madison County Public Library Card Application Form" by Staff from Madison County Public Library. Used with permission of the Library.

National Geographic Society From "Race to the End of the Earth" by William G. Scheller from *National Geographic World, Number 294, February 2000*. Copyright © 2000 by National Geographic Society. "Where Do Turkeys Go After Being Pardoned by the President?" by Bijal P. Trivedi from *www.nationalgeographic.com*. Copyright © 2004 National Geographic Society. Used by permission. Used with permission of National Geographic Society.

New Directions Publishing Corporation "Wind and Water and Stone" by Octavio Paz, translated by Mark Strand, from *A Draft of Shadows*. Copyright © 1979 by The New Yorker Magazine, Inc. Reprinted by permission of New Directions Publishing Corp.

North Carolina Poetry Society "North Carolina Poetry Society Student Poetry Contest" by Staff from *www.sleepycreek.net/poetry/submissionsstudent.htm*.

Orchard Books, an imprint of Scholastic, Inc. "Becky and the Wheels-and-Brake Boys" by James Berry. *From A Thief in the Village and Other Stories* by James Berry. Published by Orchard Books, an imprint of Scholastic, Inc. Copyright © 1987 by James Berry. Reprinted by permission.

Pearson Education Inc., publishing as Pearson Prentice Hall "Poland: Tradition and Change" from *Prentice Hall World Explorer: Europe and Russia*. Copyright © 2003 by Pearson Education, Inc., publishing as Pearson Prentice Hall, Upper Saddle River, New Jersey 07458. Used by permission.

Penguin Putnam Books for Young Readers "Black Cowboy Wild Horses" by Julius Lester & Jerry Pinkney from *Black Cowboy Wild Horses*.

Random House, Inc. From *You're a Good Man, Charlie Brown* by Clark Gesner. Copyright © 1967 by Clark Gesner. Copyright © 1965, 1966, 1967 by Jeremy Music, Inc. "Life Doesn't Frighten Me" copyright © 1978 by Maya Angelou, from *And Still I Rise* by Maya Angelou. "At First, It Is True, I Thought There Were Only Peaches & Wild Grapes" by Alice Walker from *Absolute Trust in the Goodness of the Earth*. Copyright © 2002 by Alice Walker. Used by permission of Random House, Inc.

RAW Junior, LLC "The Princess and the Pea" by Barbara McClintock from *Little Lit: Folklore & Fairy Tale Funnies*. Copyright © 2000 by RAW Junior, LLC, 27 Greene Street, New York, NY 10013. Used by permission.

Reed Publishing (NZ) Ltd. From *The Whale Rider* by Witi Ihimaera. Copyright © 1987 Witi Ihimaera. Reprinted with permission of Reed Publishing (NZ) Ltd. All rights reserved.

Sherri Regalbuto "Boredom blues begone" by Sherri Regalbuto from *www.k9magazinefree.com*. Copyright © 2001-2003 Paperclip Publishing. Reprinted with permission of the author.

Marian Reiner for Eve Merriam "Simile: Willow and Gingko" by Eve Merriam, from *A Sky Full of Poems*. Copyright © 1964, 1970, 1973 by Eve Merriam; © renewed 1992 Eve Merriam. Reprinted by permission of Marian Reiner for the author. All rights reserved.

Marian Reiner for Lillian Morrison "The Sidewalk Racer or On the Skateboard" by Lillian Morrison, from *The Sidewalk Racer and Other Poems of Sports and Motion* by Lillian Morrison. Copyright © 1965, 1967, 1968, 1977 by Lillian Morrison. Reprinted by permission of Marian Reiner for the author.

Marian Reiner, Literary Agent "Haiku ("An old silent pond...")" by Matsuo Basho from *Cricket Songs: Japanese Haiku*, translated by Harry Behn, © 1964 by Harry Behn; © Renewed 1992 Prescott Behn, Pamela Behn Adam and Peter Behn. "Haiku ("Over the wintry")" by Muso Soseki translated by Harry Behn from *Cricket Songs; Japanese Haiku*. Copyright © 1964 by Harry Behn. Copyright renewed 1992 by Prescott Behn. Reprinted by permission of Marian Reiner.

Scholastic, Inc. "The Shutout" from *Black Diamond: The Story of the Negro Baseball Leagues* by Patricia C. McKissack and Fredrick McKissack, Jr. Copyright © 1994 by Patricia C. McKissack and Fredrick McKissack, Jr. "Why Monkeys Live in Trees" from *How Many Spots Does A Leopard Have? And Other Tales* by Julius Lester. Copyright © 1989 by Julius Lester. Reprinted by permission of Scholastic, Inc.

Scovil Chichak Galen Literary Agency, Inc., for Arthur C. Clarke "Feathered Friend" from *The Other Side of the Sky* by Arthur C. Clarke. Copyright © 1958 by Arthur C. Clarke. Used by permission of the author and the author's agents, Scovil Chichak Galen Literary Agency, Inc.

Scribner, an imprint of Simon & Schuster Adult Publishing Group "Letter to Scottie" by F. Scott Fitzgerald, from *F. Scott Fitzgerald: A Life In Letters*, edited by Matthey J. Bruccoli. Reprinted with permission of Scribner, an imprint of Simon & Schuster Adult Publishing Group. Copyright © 1994 by The Trustees under Agreement dated July 3, 1975. Created by Frances Scott Fitzgerald Smith.

Seacoast Newspapers "Traip music students' effort is commendable" by Staff from *www.seacoastonline.com*. Copyright © 2004 Seacost Online. All rights reserved. Seacoast Online is owned and operated by Seacoast Newspapers. Parent company is Ottaway Newspapers.

Simon & Schuster Books for Young Readers "Parade" reprinted with the permission of Simon & Schuster Books for Young Readers, an imprint of Simon & Schuster Children's Publishing Division from *Branches Green* by Rachel Field. Copyright © 1934 Macmillan Publishing Company; copyright renewed © 1962 by Arthur S. Pederson.

St. Martin's Press "The Market Square Dog" from James Herriot's Treasury for Children by James Herriot. Copyright © 1989 James Herriot. Reprinted by permission of St. Martin's Press, LLC. All rights reserved.

Third Woman Press "Abuelito Who" from *My Wicked Wicked Ways* by Sandra Cisneros. Copyright 1987 by Sandra Cisneros, published by Third Woman Press, Berkeley, California.

Dr. My-Van Tran "A Crippled Boy" from *Folk Tales from Indochina* by Tran My-Van. First published in 1987. Copyright © Vietnamese Language and Culture Publications and Tran My-Van. Used with permission of Dr. My-Van Tran.

University of Nebraska Press "The Old Woman Who Lived with the Wolves" from *Stories of the Sioux* by Luther Standing Bear Copyright © 1934 by Luther Standing Bear. Copyright © renewed 1961 by May M. Jones. Reprinted with permission of the University of Nebraska Press.

University Press of New England "The Drive-In Movies" by Gary Soto, from *A Summer Life* © 1990 by University Press of New England.

Valeo Intellectual Property for The Associated Press "36 Beached Whales Die in St. Martin" by Marvin Hokstam. Valeo License Number: 3.5648.3173362-129178. Used with permission of Valeo Intellectual Property, Inc.

Viking Penguin, Inc., a division of Penguin Group (USA) Inc. Retitled "La lena buena," from *Places Left Unfinished at the Time of Creation* by John Phillip Santos, copyright © 1999 by John Phillip Santos. "Zlata's Diary" by Zlata Filipovic. Copyright © 1994 Editions Robert Laffont/Fixot. Used by permission of Viking Penguin, a division of Penguin Group (USA) Inc.

Jane Yolen *From My Heart Is in the Highlands* by Jane Yolen. Copyright © Jane Yolen.

Note: Every effort has been made to locate the copyright owner of material reproduced in this component. Omissions brought to our attention will be corrected in subsequent editions.

MAP AND ART CREDITS

All graphic organizers: In-House Pros; All maps by Mapping Specialist, except where noted; Illustrative "Literature in Context": Keithley and Associates;

"More About the Author" illustration: Joseph Adolphe; "Writing Workshop" illustration: Marc Clamens

PHOTO CREDITS

Cover *Hand with Flowers*, Pablo Picasso, Art Resource, NY, © 2005 Estate of Pablo Picasso/Artists Rights Society (ARS), New York; **i** *Hand with Flowers*, Pablo Picasso, Art Resource, NY, © 2005 Estate of Pablo Picasso/Artists Rights Society (ARS), New York; **vii** Getty Images; **viii-ix** Private Collection/ The Bridgeman Art Library, London/New York; **ix** © Didier Dorval/Masterfile; **x-xi** *Girl Skipping*, 1995, (detail), Andrew Macara, Private Collection/The Bridgeman Art Library, London/New York; **xi** Tom and Pat Leeson/Photo Researchers, Inc.; **xii-xiii** Images.com/CORBIS; **xiii** © Doug Sokell/Visuals Unlimited; **xiv-xv** Catherine Hazard/SuperStock; **xv** Getty Images; **xvi-xvii** Images.com/CORBIS; **xviii-xix** Getty Images; **xix** Corel Professional Photos CD-ROM™; **xx-xxi** Evelyn Macduff/Getty Images; **xxviii** Jeff Greenberg/ PhotoEdit; **xxix** Animals Animals/© Michael Habicht; **1** Private Collection/ The Bridgeman Art Library, London/New York; **2 t.** Prentice Hall; **2 b.** © Images.com/CORBIS; **3 t.** The Art Archive/Marc Charmet; **4** www.CartoonStock.com; **5** Silver Burdett Ginn; **7** Jeremy Walker/Tony Stone Images; **8** Corel Professional Photos CD-ROM™; **10-11** Evelyn Macduff/Getty Images; **12** Corel Professional Photos CD-ROM™; **15** Silver Burdett Ginn; **19** Private Collection/The Bridgeman Art Library, London/ New York; **23** Courtesy of Cynthia Rylant; **24** Animals Animals/© Zig Leszczynski; **26** Tony Anderson/Getty Images; **27** Animals Animals/© Margot Conte; **29** Animals Animals/© Margot Conte; **30** Prentice Hall; **31** Christie's Images/CORBIS; **32** The Art Archive/Free Library of Philadelphia/Album/ Joseph Martin; **35** The Granger Collection, New York; **36** Christie's Images/ CORBIS; **39** The Granger Collection, New York; **43** Courtesy of the Author; **44** Bettmann/CORBIS; **46** Randy Faris/CORBIS; **50** Julian Calder/CORBIS; **51-59** Copyright © 1992 by James Herriot and Ruth Brown. From *James Herriot's Treasury for Children* by James Herriot, illustrated by Ruth Brown and Peter Barrett. Reprinted by permission of St. Martin's Press, LLC; **67 t.** Prentice Hall; **67 b.** Courtesy Susan Quinlan; **68** Wolfgang Kaehler/Liaison Agency; **70** Philip van den Berg/HPH Photography; **72** Gregory G. Dimijian/Photo Researchers, Inc.; **73** Gregory G. Dimijian/ Photo Researchers, Inc.; **75** © Frans Lanting/Minden Pictures, Inc.; **76 r.** Peter Anderson/© Dorling Kindersley; **76 l(1).** Cyril Laubscher/ © Dorling Kindersley; **76 l(2).** Geoff Dann/© Dorling Kindersley; **76 l(3).** Colin Keates © Dorling Kindersley, Courtesy of the Natural History Museum, London; **76 l(5).** Frank Greenway/© Dorling Kindersley; **76 l(4).** © Dorling Kindersley; **76 l(6).** © Geoff Dann/ Dorling Kindersley; **87** Private Collection/The Bridgeman Art Library, London/New York; **91** Bettmann/CORBIS; **92** Hulton-Deutsch Collection/CORBIS; **95** The Granger Collection, New York; **96** The Mark Twain House, Hartford, CT; **97** The Mark Twain House, Hartford, CT; **98-99** The Mark Twain House, Hartford, CT; **100** The Granger Collection, New York; **103** The Mark Twain House, Hartford, CT; **107** © Jenny Bornstein; **108** Joe McDonald/CORBIS; **109** © Didier Dorval/Masterfile; **110 l.** John McNally/PhotoLibrary.com; **110 r.** Geroge McCarthy/CORBIS; **113** © Didier Dorval/Masterfile; **114** Photo: © Daniel Cima; **115** © Pete Seaward/Stone; **117** *Collage* (detail), 1992, Juan Sanchez, Courtesy of Juan Sanchez and Guarighen, Inc., NYC; **119** Getty Images; **121** © Pete Seaward/Stone; **125** © Dorling Kindersley; **126 m.** © Dorling Kindersley; **129 b.** AP/Wide World Photos; **129 t.** AP/Wide World Photos; **130** Getty Images; **132** *New Shoes for H*, 1973-1974, Don Eddy, The Cleveland Museum of Art, Acrylic on canvas, 111.7 x 121.9 cm. © The Cleveland Museum of Art, 1998, Purchase with a grant from the National Endowment for the Arts and matched by gifts from members of The Cleveland Society for Contemporary Art, 1974.53;

134 Ralph A. Clevenger/CORBIS; **137** *Orange Sweater*, 1955, Elmer Bischoff, San Francisco Museum of Modern Art, Gift of Mr. and Mrs. Mark Schorer; **138** *Portrait*, From the Estate of Eloy Blanco, Collection of El Museo del Barrio, New York, NY; **146** istockphoto.com; **149** Prentice Hall; **156** Time Life Pictures/Getty Image; **158** Time Life Pictures/Getty Images; **159** Miriam Berkley/Authorpix; **160-161** *Girl Skipping*, 1995, Andrew Macara, Private Collection/The Bridgeman Art Library, London/New York; **162 t.** Pearson Education/PH School Division; **162 b.** © Andy Giarnella/ Stock Illustration Source, Inc.; **163** SuperStock; **164** PEANUTS reprinted by permission of United Feature Syndicate, Inc. ; **165** Lee Foster/Getty Images; **167** © Stephen J. Krasemann/Peter Arnold, Inc.; **168** © Still Picture/Peter Arnold, Inc.; **170** Tom and Pat Leeson/Photo Researchers, Inc.; **173** *Girl Skipping*, 1995, (detail), Andrew Macara, Private Collection/The Bridgeman Art Library, London/New York; **177** Photo by Austin V. Hansen, Jr. Courtesy of the author; **178** Stephen Simpson/Getty Images; **181** David Young-Wolff/ PhotoEdit; **183** Richard Hutchings/PhotoEdit; **184** Michael Dick/Animals Animals; **189** Michael Dick/Animals Animals; **190** © Joel Gardner; **191** Historical Picture Archive/CORBIS; **192** Mary Evans Picture Library; **195** Historical Picture Archive/CORBIS; **197** Dick Whittington on his way to London from "My Nursery Story Book," published by Blackie and Son (book illustration) by Frank Adams, Private Collection/ The Bridgeman Art Library, London; **199** Mary Evans/Edwin Wallace; **201** Mary Evans Picture Library; **205** Robert Maass/CORBIS; **207-211** from "Zlateh the Goat and Other Stories" by Isaac Bashevis Singer, illustrations by Maurice Sendak © 1966, HarperCollins Publishers, Inc.; **216** Bettmann/CORBIS; **217** Hulton Archive/Getty Images Inc.; **218 t.** The Granger Collection, New York; **218 b.** Bettmann/CORBIS; **220** Time to Hunt, John Newcomb/SuperStock; **223** Time to Hunt, John Newcomb/SuperStock; **227** SKJOLD PHOTOGRAPHS; **228** © Dorling Kindersley; **231 b.** Didi Cutler; **231 t.** gezette.de Buro fur Fotografie; **232** *Daddy's Girl*, 1992, Carlton Murrell, Courtesy of the artist, photo by John Lei/Omni-Photo Communications, Inc.; **235** *Mother, I Love to Ride*, 1992, Carlton Murrell, Courtesy of the artist, photo by John Lei/Omni-Photo Communications, Inc.; **237** Biking for Fun, 1992, Carlton Murrell, Courtesy of the artist, photo by John Lei/Omni-Photo Communications, Inc.; **240** Lou Jones/Getty Images; **241** Lou Jones/Getty Images; **251** *Girl Skipping*, 1995, (detail), Andrew Macara, Private Collection/ The Bridgeman Art Library, London/New York; **255** Courtesy of the author. Photo by Don Perkins; **256** Corel Professional Photos CD-ROM™; **258** Getty Images; **260** Getty Images; **262** David Young-Wolff/Tony Stone Images; **267** Getty Images; **268** Photo by Charles Barry. Copyright Santa Clara University; **269 r.** *My Brother*, 1942, Guayasamin (Oswaldo Guayasamin Calero), Oil on wood, 15 7/8 x 12 3/4", Digital Image © The Museum of Modern Art/Licensed by SCALA/Art Resource, NY; **269 r.** © Dorling Kindersley/Tim Ridley; **272** Mark Richards/PhotoEdit; **275** © Dorling Kindersley/Tim Ridley; **277** © Dorling Kindersley/Tim Ridley; **281** CORBIS-Bettmann; **282** The Granger Collection, New York; **285** Corel Professional Photos CD-ROM™; **288-289** *After Dinner Music*, 1988, Scott Kennedy, © 2002 Scott Kennedy, licensed by The Greenwich Workshop, Inc.; **290** Getty Image;s **293** Corel Professional Photos CD-ROM™; **294** Prentice Hall; **295** Jane Burton/Bruce Coleman, Inc.; **296** © 2004 Jupiter Images and its Licensors. All Rights Reserved; **298** *Pigeons*, John Sloan, Oil on canvas, 26 x 32", Courtesy, Museum of Fine Arts, Boston. Reproduced with permission. © 2002 Museum of Fine Arts, Boston. All Rights Reserved. The Hayden Collection, 35.52; **300** Underwood & Underwood/CORBIS;

STAFF CREDITS

PH Literature ©2007

Ernie Albanese, Diane Alimena, **Rosalyn Arcilla,** Jasjit Arneja, Penny Baker, **Nancy Barker, Amy Baron,** Rachel Beckman, Betsy Bostwick, **Ellen Bowler,** Jennifer Brady, Nikki Bruno, Evonne Burgess, Pradeep Byram, Rui Camarinha, **Pam Carey,** Lisa Carrillo, Anathea Chartrand, Jaime Cohen, Allison Cook, **Irene Ehrmann,** Leanne Esterly, Libby Forsyth, Steve Frankel, Philip Fried, **Maggie Fritz,** Michael Ginsberg, **Elaine Goldman,** Patricia Hade, **Monduane Harris, Martha Heller,** Beth Hyslip, Vicki A. Kane, Kimon Kirk, **Kate Krimsky,** Mary Sue Langan, Monica Lehmann, **Mary Luthi, George Lychock,** Gregory Lynch, John McClure, Jim McDonough, Kathleen Mercandetti, Kerrie Miller, Karyl Murray, Ken Myett, Michael O'Donnell, Kim Ortell, Carolyn Pallof, Sal Pisano, Jackie Regan, Erin Rehill-Seker, Bruce Rolff, **Laura Ross,** Carolyn Sapontzis, Donna Schindler, Mildred Schulte, **Melissa Shustyk, Robert Siek, Rita Sullivan, Cynthia Summers,** Patrice Titterington, **Elizabeth Torjussen,** Jane S. Traulsen, Daniela Velez

ADDITIONAL CREDITS

Susan C. Ball, William Bingham, Andrea Brescia, Donna Chappelle, Jennifer Ciccone, Jason Cuoco, Florrie Gadson, Judith Gaelick, Phillip Gagler, James Garratt, Allen Gold, Kristan Hoskins, Lisa Lozzia, Mohamed Kaptan, Barbara Kehr, Terry Kim, Stuart Kirschenbaum, Linda Latino, Julian Liby, Ginidir Marshall, Bill McAllister, Patrick J. McCarthy, Caroline McDonnell, Michael McLaughlin, Meg Montgomery, Gita Nadas, Karen Mancinelli Paige, Lesley Pierson, Maureen Raymond, Rachel Ross, Lloyd Sabin, James Savakis, Debi Taffet, Ryan Vaarsi, Alfred Voto, Gina M. Wangrycht, Lindsay White